LONDON
NETHERLANDS
HANNOVER
BERLIN
POLAND
BRUSSEL
GERMANY
LILLE
BELGIUM &
LUXEMBOURG
UKRAINE
CZECH
REPUBLIC
LUXEMBOURG
PARIS
STUTTGART
SLOVAKIA
TOURS
DIJON
MÜNCHEN
LINZ
WIEN
MOLDOVA
Bay
of
Biscay
ZÜRICH
AUSTRIA
BERN
INNSBRUCK
HUNGARY
FRANCE
GENÈVE
SWITZERLAND &
LIECHTENSTEIN
ROMANIA
MILANO
SLOVENIA
BORDEAUX
VENÉZIA
CROATIA
TORINO
LA CORUÑA
BILBAO
GÉNOVA
BOSNIA-
HERZEGOVINA
Black
Sea
TOULOUSE
MARSEILLE
PORTO
CORSICA
YUGOSLAVIA
ITALY
PORTUGAL
SPAIN
BARCELONA
AJACCIO
ROMA
MACEDON
LISBOA
MADRID
NÁPOLI
BARI
ALBANIA
VALENCIA
MENORCA
SARDINIA
PALMA
MALLORCA
IBIZA
LÁRISA
CÁGLIARI
SEVILLA
MÁLAGA
PALERMO
KEFALLONÍA
MEDITERRANEAN SEA
ZÁKYNTHOS
CATÁNIA
SICILY
0 kilometres 250
ALGERIA
0 miles 250
MOROCCO
TUNSIA

Waldhaus
Tannenhain
28

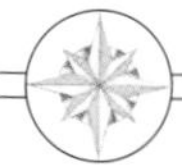

EYEWITNESS TRAVEL GUIDES

EUROPE'S BEST PLACES TO STAY

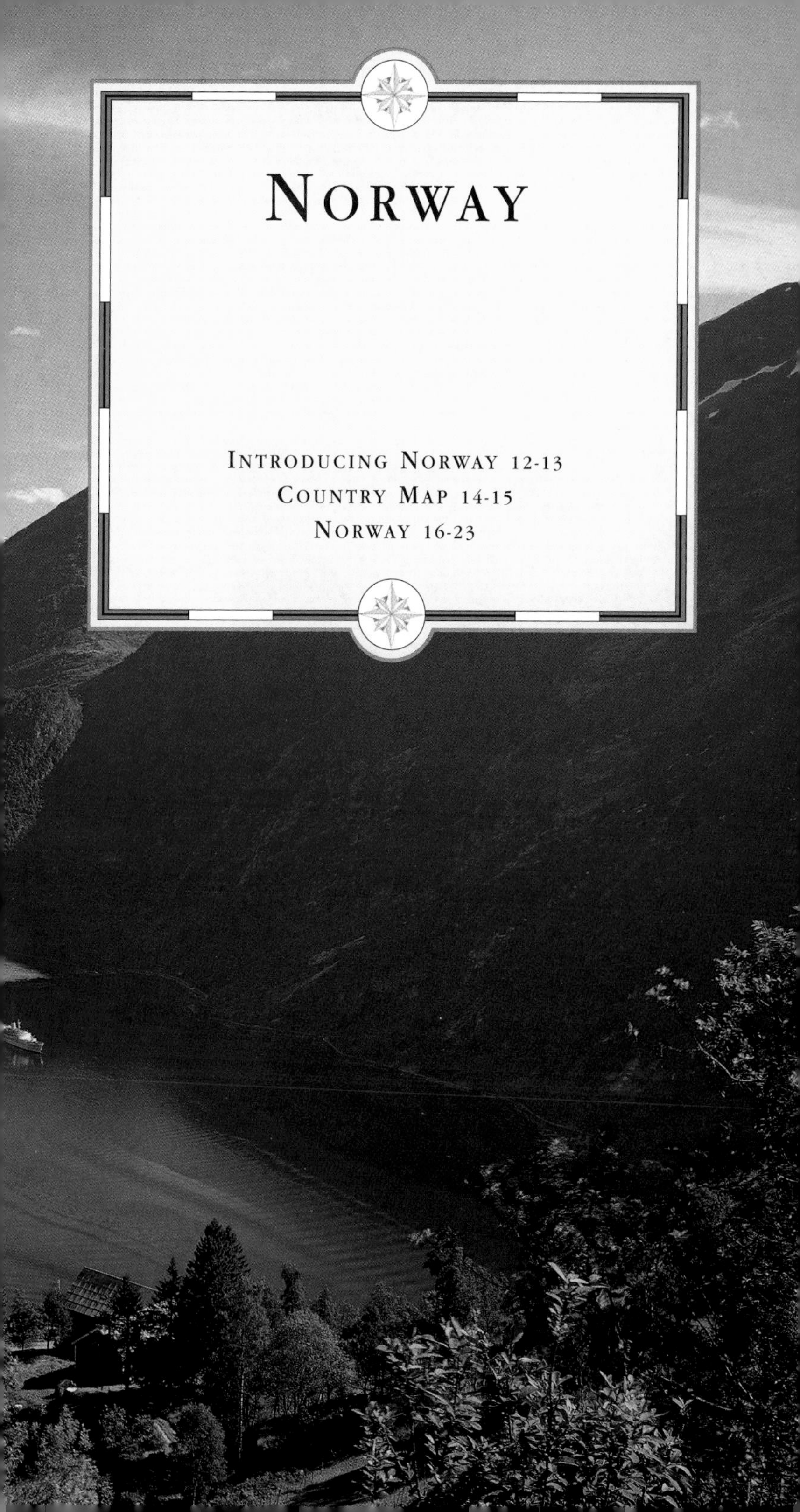

Norway

Norway

There's something about the pale Norwegian light that makes more southerly climes seem flat and slightly jaded. It gives the landscape a clean, gentle quality, and makes the locations of many of the hotels in this section particularly idyllic. The places themselves are often simple clapboard houses on, say, a harbour front or a spit of land next to a still fjord. Many are family run – some for as far back as three or four generations. Using our recommendations, you could construct an itinerary taking you from the islands of the south, via Oslo, through the western fjords to north of the Arctic circle, staying in unique places each night, without once having to resort to one of the many bland chain hotels.

Fairytale architecture at The Dalen at Dalen i Telemark, page 17

Norway Region by Region

Norway can be divided into Eastern Norway, Southern Norway, the Western fjords and Northern Norway.

Eastern Norway
Some of Europe's finest museums can be found in Oslo, the capital of Norway, but the city is also stirred by plenty of interesting street life and late night bars. Its 19th-century boulevards are also home to a number of handsome hotels.

Southern Norway
This is Norway's holidayland – an area of flat countryside, long beaches and small islands just off the coast. The town of Kristiansand's water-front is the closest Norway has to a beach resort. It also has a ferry link to Copenhagen, and many small family-run hotels.

The Western Fjords
At the southern end of the Western fjords is Stavanger, an old town with a maritime feel. In the narrow lanes are attractive tall, white wooden houses where seamen and merchants once lived.

Ferries chugging up the coast take thousands of visitors to the fjords in summer. Many head for Bergen, an old trading centre with restored wooden houses and a lively quayside. There's a wide choice of places to stay here, as well as in the surrounding countryside.

The rail route between Bergen and Oslo goes through great scenery. This is a fine journey at any time, but in winter it offers the bonus of viewing the mountains under snow and waterfalls frozen solid. A branch line – one of the steepest in the world – plunges down to Flåm, on the edge of the serene Sogne Fjord. In this area there are several of the remarkable Norwegian stave churches.

Northern Norway
Around Trondheim, north becomes far north. The landscape, driving conditions and weather all toughen up. You cross the Arctic circle between Mo-i-Rana and Bodø, before arriving at the biggest settlement in Northern Norway, the university city of Tromsø. By the time you get to the Northern Cape, and perhaps sail out to Spitsbergen, hotels tend to be functional and cosy, but not much more.

Highlights

Places illustrated on these introductory pages are by no means the only highlights. Among our other favourites are Hotel Mundal in Fjaerland (page 17), an imposing Victorian building in a great setting; Frogner House Hotel in Oslo (page 20), a smart town hotel with style and individuality; the Kongsvold Fjeldstue inn in Kongsvold (page 18), a 17th-century inn formerly used by pilgrims; and the Sygard Grytting near Hundorp (page 18), a beautiful hotel, open for only a couple of months in summer, with a simple wooden interior dating from the 17th century.

Food and Drink

Much Norwegian food is heavy and filling, perfect after a day's cross-country skiing. Some of the best traditional cooking is only available at Christmas, when special dishes like *pinnekjøtt* – smoked mutton steamed over

EYEWITNESS TRAVEL GUIDES

EUROPE'S BEST PLACES TO STAY

LONDON, NEW YORK,
MELBOURNE, MUNICH AND DELHI
www.dk.com

Edited and produced for Dorling Kindersley by Duncan Petersen Publishing Ltd, 31 Ceylon Road, London W14 OPY

PROJECT EDITORS Marion Moisy (1st edition), Chris Barstow (updates)
ASSISTANT EDITORS Nicola Davies, Zoe Ross
DESIGNERS Beverley Stewart, Chris Foley
EDITORIAL ASSISTANTS Catherine Iszard, Mark Adcock
EDITORIAL DIRECTOR Andrew Duncan
ART DIRECTOR Mel Petersen

Dorling Kindersley Ltd
Louise B Lang, Nick Inman, Nancy Jones, Kate Poole, Dave Pugh

MAIN CONTRIBUTORS
Fiona Duncan and Leonie Glass

CONTRIBUTORS
Philip Lee, Judith Hampson, David Sandhu, Jenny Rees, Dorine Scherpel, Celia Woolfrey, Sarah Toynbee, Kathy Arnold, Paul Wade, Robin Gauldie

MAPS
Colourmap Scanning Ltd

Reproduced by Colourscan (Singapore)
Printed and bound by South China Printing Co., Ltd, China

First published in Great Britain in 2000
by Dorling Kindersley Limited
80 Strand, London WC2R 0RL
Reprinted with revisions 2000, 2002, 2004

A CIP CATALOGUE RECORD IS AVAILABLE FROM THE BRITISH LIBRARY.

ISBN 0 7513 6885 7

The information in every DK Eyewitness Travel Guide is checked regularly.

Every effort has been made to ensure that this book is as up-to-date as possible at the time of going to press. Some details, however, such as telephone numbers, e-mail addresses and prices are liable to change. The publishers cannot accept responsibility for any consequences arising from the use of this book, nor for any material on third party websites, and cannot guarantee that any website address in this book will be a suitable source of travel information. We would be delighted to receive any corrections and suggestions for incorporation in the next edition; on page 432 you will find a reader's response form. Or write to: Publisher, DK Eyewitness Travel Guides, Dorling Kindersley, 80 Strand, London WC2R 0RL.

CONTENTS

Facing page 1 Hôtel Cléry, France; 2 The Manor House, Great Britain; 3 Castelo Bom Jesus, Portugal; 4 Cley Mill, Great Britain; 5 Hotel Real, Spain; 6 Verbano, Italy; 7 Wald & Schlosshotel Friedrichsruhe, Germany; 8 Château de Vault de Lugny, France.

◁ **Hotel Adler, Germany (large picture)**

1
2
3
4
5
VERBANO
ALBERGO RISTORANTE
6
7
8

How to Use this Guide

THIS GUIDE is designed to help you get the most from your travels in Europe. Each place to stay – whether a hotel, a bed-and-breakfast or a country inn – has been chosen because it is in some way special, an experience worth seeking out in its own right and more than just a bed for the night. There are 15 sections, each devoted to a single country. The sections run in loose geographical order, starting in Northern Europe and ending in Southern Europe.

Within each section there are always three parts: introductory pages, describing the accommodation scene overall; maps, showing where the hotels are located; and the hotel entries ('listings') themselves.

Our Eight Selection Criteria

- *Character - in the buildings, and the interior decoration.*
- *Atmosphere or ambience - often influenced by other guests.*
- *Style and taste not only in the interior decoration but in the details - the placing of furniture, the presentation of menus, and so on.*
- *An interesting, attractive location.*
- *A personal welcome - genuine, not forced - from staff or proprietor.*
- *Bedrooms like real bedrooms, not hotel rooms.*
- *Interesting food, prepared with care from fresh ingredients.*
- *Size: generally not very large, but some large hotels are included - see the qualifications below.*

A Question of Balance

As you would expect, our main entries – the ones illustrated with photographs – tend to score five, six, seven or even eight out of eight on the list described above. *But,* and you will find this clearly stated in the text where appropriate, a significant number of our main selections are especially strong on just one or two of the points, and weak on the others. It is very often the case for example that a lovely old building, in a magical setting, makes a truly special hotel, despite the fact that the bedrooms may be dull, possibly small, and the service not as some would wish. This is especially true of Venice hotels, but you'll find such places throughout the guide.

Generally speaking, our inspectors have rated setting, atmosphere and a personal welcome more important than service, food and sophisticated facilities. But, of course, they have rejected anywhere that doesn't reach their basic standards of comfort. We believe that this philosophy will give our readers more memorable experiences on their travels than a cushioning of standardized comfort and facilities.

Please do use the form on page 432 to let us know your views on the places where you have stayed, or to recommend others for the next edition.

Food

We don't underestimate its importance, and some entries would not have made it in to this guide, were it not for their food. However, it is increasingly true, especially in Britain, France and Italy, that good food is the norm. In these countries, hotels generally need to have more going for them than food alone to be featured in this guide.

Size

A few have less than 15 rooms; most have between 15 and 50; a few have many more than 50. As you might expect, our inspectors favoured the privately-owned, smaller hotels, guesthouses or inns because it's so much easier for them to offer a genuinely personal welcome and an atmosphere in which you feel like an individual, rather than one in a crowd.

Variety

Above all, our contributors have tried to provide variety. There are more than 2,000 entries in the guide, and among them there is every sort of lodging: bed-and-breakfasts in historic private houses; hotels in stately homes and châteaux; self-catering apartments in Venetian palaces; there is even a guest house in a windmill. And if you really need a retreat, try one of the monasteries in Spain that open their door to travellers. We've deliberately mixed the unusual with the more conventional restaurants-with-rooms, country inns, smart town houses and crumbling but beautiful farmhouses.

The Country Introductions

These pages provide an overview of the country's different types of accommodation, highlight some of the most interesting places to stay, and offer practical information on topics such as tipping and meal times.

Thumb tabs *Each country has a different-coloured thumb tab.*

Highlights *We use this section to single out a few of the outstanding places to stay in each country.*

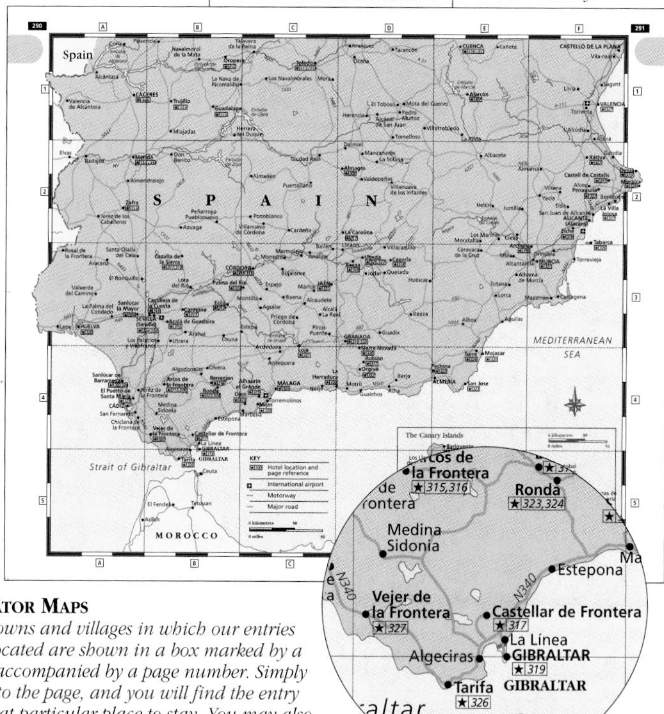

Locator Maps

The towns and villages in which our entries are located are shown in a box marked by a star, accompanied by a page number. Simply turn to the page, and you will find the entry for that particular place to stay. You may also find the maps useful for planning holiday routes linking places to stay.

Independently Inspected

This book has been created by a team of specialist hotel writers, most with many years' experience of inspecting hotels. None of the places featured in the book have paid to be in the guide. Those hotels which we did not already know were visited by inspectors. Most inspection visits were anonymous. For every hotel that appears in the guide, many were rejected.

How to Read the Entries

The Listings
These follow in alphabetical order by nearest town or city. Long entries follow their own alpha order, as do shorts.

Wales
Border Country • North Wales
South Wales
Abersoch
Cardiff

• Regional introduction
Britain, France, Italy, Germany and Spain have been divided into regional sub-sections, each with a short introduction. The other countries in the guide are not sub-divided.

• The description
Gives the essential character of the place.

• Entries with a photo
These are our favourite places. Each conforms to a large number of our selection criteria (see panel on page 6).

Don't expect them all to charge the same price or to conform to a rigid standard. In order to make the guide interesting, many different types of accommodation have been included, at every price level. Not just hotels, but guest houses, bed-and-breakfasts, inns and even a few self-catering places.

• Short entries without a photo
These are all great places to stay – each and every one of them a useful address – but for one reason or another our inspectors could not rate them as high as the entries with photos. Don't be surprised to find some well-known, luxurious places among these short entries. They may be top-class hotels, but our inspectors were briefed to look for places that offered the traveller something special, rather than places that follow a formula – however luxurious.

• The factual information
All you need to finalize your choice and book. For an explanation of the symbols, see page 9.

For Visitors from Outside Europe

First-time visitors are often surprised by the following features of European hotels and other places to stay:

Adaptors (adapters) The electricity points vary from country to country so you will find it useful to take a universal adaptor.

Tipping varies widely from country to country. See the advice given on the introductory pages for each country.

Face cloths and **Kleenex tissues** are not always provided.

Private bathrooms You'll mostly, but not always, get your own bathroom.

Floor numbers What Americans call the first floor is known as the ground floor (or "0") in Europe. In Britain, "elevators" are "lifts".

Breakfasts (especially in France and Italy) are often minimal compared with what's served in the US – often no more than bread rolls, butter, jam and possibly a choice of coffee or tea.

Passport as security Many of the places featured in this guide will ask for this when you check in. It will be returned when you leave.

Markings on hot and cold taps may be confusing. In France, for example, 'C' means hot (*chaud*).

How to Read the Entries

The Longer Entries with Photo

See opposite. The information is always given in the same sequence.

BROAD CAMPDEN — Village, town or city in which, or near which, the entry is located

Photo of hotel

Malt House In a tiny hamlet comprising little more than church and pub, is this delightful 17th-century Cotswold house. There are low, beamed ceilings and leaded windows overlooking a dream garden. The attractive bedrooms include a garden suite. The owners' son, Julian Brown, is the accomplished cook.
⊠ Broad Campden, Gloucestershire GL55 6UU.
Map p74 A2. (01386) 8402950. FAX (01386) 841334.
@ nick@the-malt-house.freeserve.co.uk b,d.
Rooms 8. Christmas. AE, DC, MC, V. ££

Description of hotel — Address — Telephone number — Map location — Fax number — E-mail address — Meals — Number of rooms — Garden — When closed — Credit cards — Price band

An Explanation of the Symbols

⊠ **Postal address**

Telephone number

FAX **Fax number**

@ **E-mail address**, if available when we went to press. Some hotels will have acquired e-mail after this edition of the guide was printed. Note, too, that many change their e-mail address from time to time. Many hotels with e-mail also have a website – you may find it worthwhile to search for this on the Internet – it is highly convenient to book through the Web.

Meals *generally* served in the establishment's own restaurant or eating area: **b** – breakfast, **l** – lunch, **d** – dinner. Some places serve a light lunch (or even provide a picnic) on request. Remember that restaurants may be closed on certain days of the week – enquire when booking.

We do not show whether room service is available or not.

Number of rooms. We give the total number, including singles, doubles and suites.

Garden, terrace or any outside area.

Air conditioning in most of the rooms, or throughout.

Pool – whether it is indoor, outdoor, heated or without heating.

Health facilities – whether exercise machines, fitness room, gymnasium, trainer, sauna, Jacuzzi or whirlpool.

Closed

Credit cards We note only whether American Express (AE), Diners Club (DC), Mastercard (MC) or Visa (V) are accepted. Other cards may be accepted too.

£££ **Price bands** in the local currency, referring to the price of a standard double room in high season. These prices were quoted to our contibutors and were correct at time of going to press – there is, however, no guarantee that you will be offered exactly the same prices. (Some hotels in tourist centres will raise their prices when demand looks as if it will exceed space.) The price band is therefore only an indication of the cost of staying in a hotel. Please note that our entries often offer a wide range of rooms, from cheap to expensive: enquire when booking. The price may or may not include breakfast. Depending on the country, breakfast is either included, or an extra, but the price of breakfast rarely makes a significant difference to the price band. The price bands differ for each country, and their actual values are given on the relevant introductory pages.

shredded birch bark and served with cabbage – appear on the menu, along with *ribbe, julepølse* and filling *medisterkake* – pork ribs, sausage and dumplings. Reindeer steaks are available throughout the year, either served with boiled potatoes and cranberry sauce, or as the main component of a rich stew. Venison, elk and seal meat – the latter marinaded until it is almost black and tasting slightly of the sea – are also occasionally offered.

A thick gravy (*brun saus*) seems to be served with anything meaty, but you can get away from this if you opt for fish such as pickled herring or salmon, which are particularly good. *Lutefisk* is preserved cod reconstituted to a jellylike consistency. It is good with potatoes and often served alongside herring dishes as part of a traditional feast. Dried cod fish – soaked to plump it up, but always slightly chewy – is also tasty when served in broth. Some of the simpler foods are the most memorable, and include different kinds of 'black' breads, fresh goat's cheese, and wild cloudberries – from north of the Arctic circle – served with cream.

Beers are classed as I, II or III, III being the strongest and available in bars and shops. Wine and spirits including the local 40 per cent proof *akevitt* can only be bought from the state-controlled Vinmonopol shops, or in bars. All alcoholic drink in Norway is surprisingly expensive.

Drinking is not a mainstream social activity during the week, but at weekends people kick over the traces and indulge in drinking sessions complete with drinking songs and other 'Viking' behaviour. Drinking in Oslo is more urbane, with a fickle bar scene and some 'microbreweries' serving real ale.

Bedrooms and Bathrooms

If you want twin beds, ask for them specifically when booking. Doubles are standard size – it's not usual to

Oslo's Nobel House Hotel, page 21

come across king size or extra king size beds. Bathrooms are en-suite and many hotels have shared saunas (mixed-sex).

Other Practical Information

Breakfast is substantial and typically comprises a help-yourself buffet of different kinds of bread, ham, cheese, pickled fish, sausages, fruit juices and coffee.

Smoking has been banned in all public places (including restaurants and the public areas of hotels) since 1988.

If you are deterred by the price of evening meals, try the lunchtime *koldtbord* that many restaurants offer (the Norwegian rendition of *smörgåsbord*) – all you can eat for a set price. Another good deal is the *dagens rett* – a daily special menu.

During the summer, businesses shut down from July onwards, and hotel prices drop considerably. Between October and June, too, luxury hotels suddenly become much more affordable at the weekends, when substantial discounts (often 40–50 per cent on the usual room rate) come into effect.

It is always worth asking what the 'special prices' are.

Language Norwegians have two mother tongues, *Bokmål* (book language) and *Landsmål* or *Nyorsk* (based on Old Norse dialects). *Bokmål* is the commonest, but it's not something you have to master to get around. English is widely spoken – and, moreover, spoken well.

Currency The Norwegian *krone*, written NKR.

Shops Open 9am–5pm Mon–Wed & Fri; 9am–6pm or 7pm Thu; 9am–2pm or 3pm Sat.

Tipping No extra charge is made for service on the bill, but it's normal to leave a tip of around 10 per cent in restaurants, and 5 to 10 per cent in bars.

Telephoning Inside Norway, dial all 8 digits of a number, wherever you are calling from.

If you wish to call Norway from the UK, dial 00 47 followed by the number, leaving out the initial 0 from the area code; from the US, dial 011 47.

Public holidays 1 January, Maundy Thursday and Good Friday, Easter Monday, 1 May, 17 May (Constitution Day), Ascension Day, Whit Monday and Tuesday, 15 August, 25 and 26 December.

Useful Words

Breakfast	*Frokost*
Lunch	*Lunsj*
Dinner	*Middag*
Free room?	*Ledig rom?*
How much?	*Hvor mye?*
Single room	*Enkeltrom*
Double room	*Dobbeltrom*

Norway Price Bands

There is no star (or any other symbol) system to classify the comfort level of Norwegian hotels, so if you are booking a room from a long list of hotels without descriptions, the only thing to go on is price.

Our price bands as usual refer to the price of a standard double room in high season. Prices quoted by hotels usually include breakfast and all taxes.

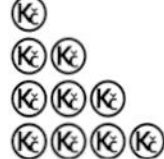

under 500NKR
500–1000NKR
1000–1,500NKR
over 1,500NKR

Norway

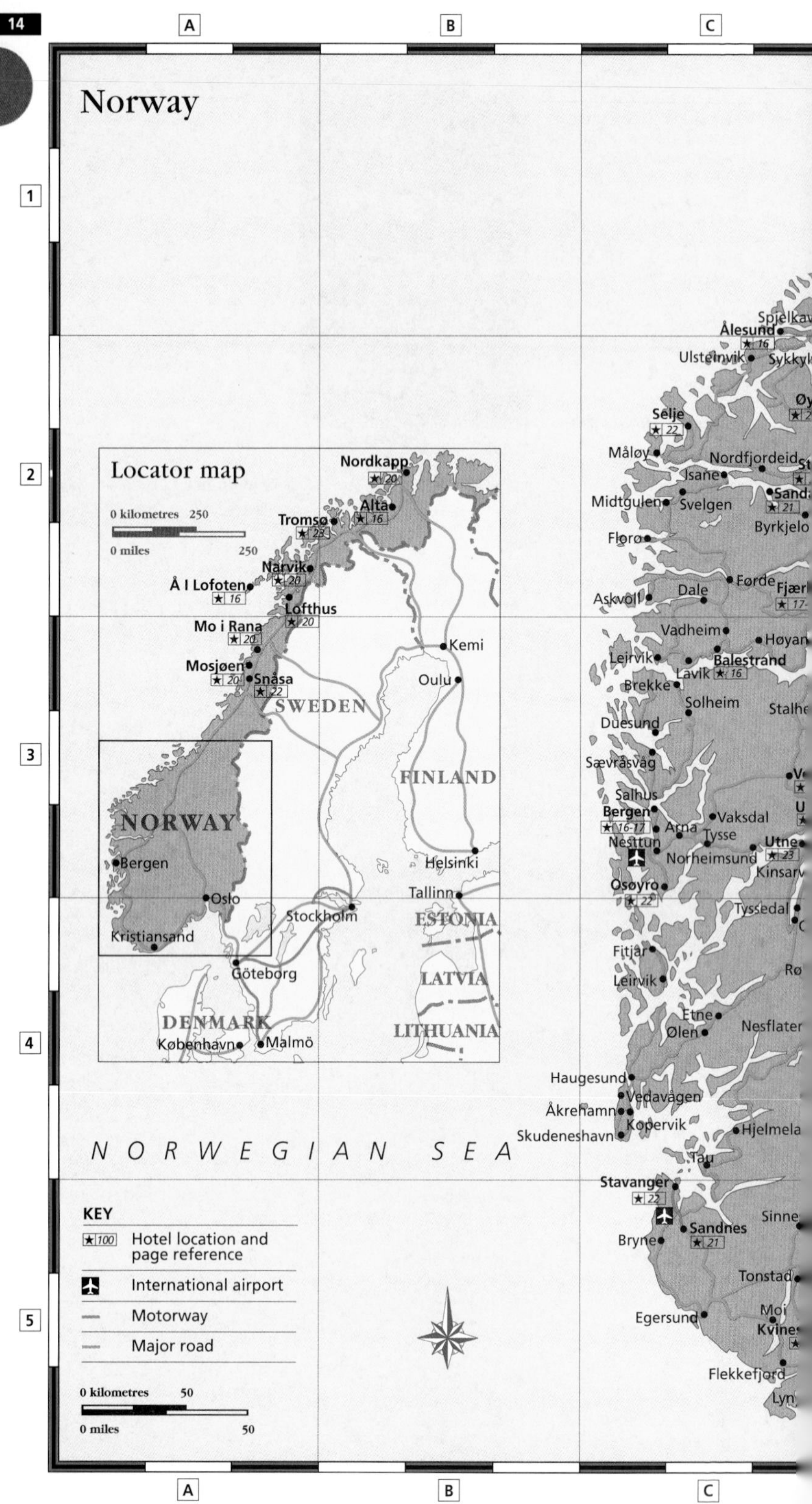
A
B
C
1
2
3
4
5
Locator map
0 kilometres 250
0 miles 250
Nordkapp 20
Alta 16
Tromsø 23
Narvik 20
Å I Lofoten 16
Lofthus 20
Mo i Rana 20
Mosjøen 20
Snåsa 22
SWEDEN
FINLAND
NORWAY
Kemi
Oulu
Bergen
Oslo
Kristiansand
Stockholm
Helsinki
Tallinn
ESTONIA
LATVIA
LITHUANIA
DENMARK
Göteborg
København
Malmö
Ålesund 16
Ulsteinvik
Selje 22
Måløy
Nordfjordeid
Isane
Midtgulen
Svelgen
Florø
Førde
Askvoll
Dale
Vadheim
Leirvik
Lavik
Balestrand 16
Brekke
Solheim
Duesund
Sævråsvåg
Salhus
Bergen 16-17
Arna
Vaksdal
Tysse
Nesttun
Norheimsund
Osøyro 22
Tyssedal
Fitjar
Leirvik
Etne
Ølen
Nesflaten
Haugesund
Vedavågen
Åkrehamn
Kopervik
Skudeneshavn
Hjelmeland
Tau
Stavanger 22
Sandnes 21
Bryne
Tonstad
Egersund
Moi
Flekkefjord
NORWEGIAN SEA
KEY
100 Hotel location and page reference
International airport
Motorway
Major road
0 kilometres 50
0 miles 50

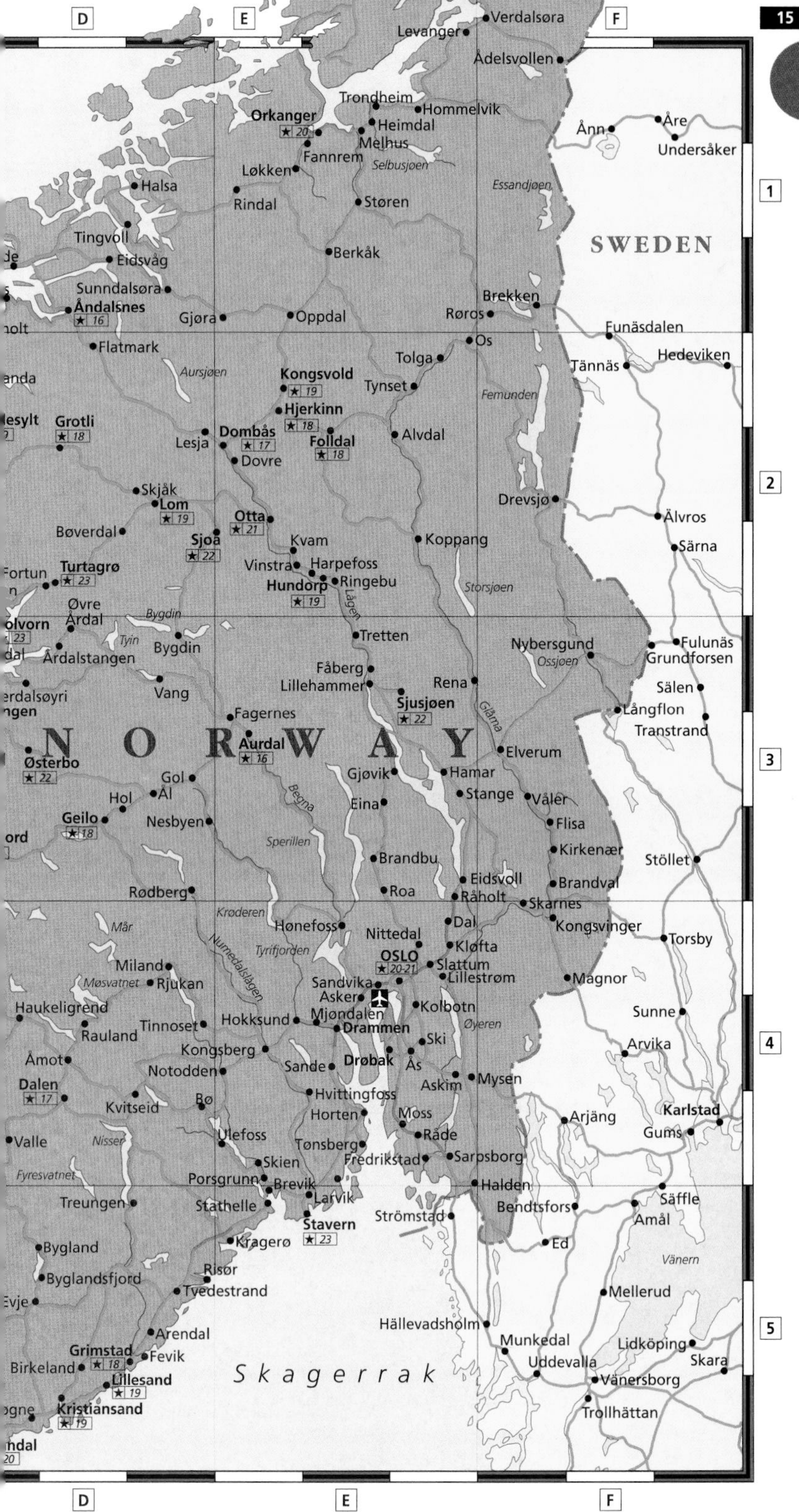

D
E
F
1
2
3
4
5
SWEDEN
NORWAY
Skagerrak
Verdalsøra
Levanger
Ådelsvollen
Trondheim
Hommelvik
Orkanger
★ 20
Heimdal
Melhus
Fannrem
Selbusjøen
Løkken
Halsa
Rindal
Støren
Essandjøen
Åre
Ånn
Undersåker
Tingvoll
Eidsvåg
Berkåk
Sunndalsøra
Åndalsnes
★ 16
Gjøra
Oppdal
Brekken
Røros
Os
Funäsdalen
Flatmark
Tolga
Tännäs
Hedeviken
Aursjøen
Kongsvold
★ 19
Tynset
Femunden
Hjerkinn
★ 18
Grotli
★ 18
Lesja
Dombås
★ 17
Folldal
★ 18
Alvdal
Dovre
Skjåk
Lom
★ 19
Drevsjø
Otta
★ 21
Älvros
Bøverdal
Sjoa
★ 22
Kvam
Koppang
Särna
Vinstra
Harpefoss
Turtagrø
★ 23
Hundorp
★ 19
Ringebu
Storsjøen
Fortun
Øvre Årdal
Bygdin
Lågen
Tretten
Tyin
Bygdin
Nybersgund
Fulunäs
Grundforsen
Årdalstangen
Ossjøen
Fåberg
Vang
Lillehammer
Rena
Sälen
Sjusjøen
★ 22
Långflon
Transtrand
Fagernes
Glåma
Aurdal
★ 16
Elverum
Østerbo
★ 22
Gjøvik
Hamar
Gol
Stange
Hol
Ål
Våler
Begna
Eina
Geilo
★ 18
Nesbyen
Flisa
Sperillen
Kirkenær
Stöllet
Brandbu
Eidsvoll
Brandval
Rødberg
Roa
Råholt
Skarnes
Krøderen
Dal
Mår
Hønefoss
Kongsvinger
Nittedal
Torsby
Numedalslågen
Tyrifjorden
Kløfta
OSLO
★ 20-21
Slattum
Miland
Lillestrøm
Magnor
Møsvatnet
Rjukan
Sandvika
Asker
Haukeligrend
Kolbotn
Sunne
Mjøndalen
Rauland
Tinnoset
Hokksund
Drammen
Øyeren
Kongsberg
Ski
Arvika
Åmot
Drøbak
Ås
Notodden
Sande
Askim
Mysen
Dalen
★ 17
Hvittingfoss
Kvitseid
Bø
Horten
Moss
Arjäng
Karlstad
Råde
Gums
Valle
Nisser
Ulefoss
Tønsberg
Skien
Fredrikstad
Sarpsborg
Fyresvatnet
Porsgrunn
Brevik
Halden
Treungen
Larvik
Säffle
Stathelle
Bendtsfors
Strömstad
Stavern
★ 23
Åmål
Bygland
Kragerø
Ed
Vänern
Risør
Byglandsfjord
Tvedestrand
Mellerud
Evje
Hällevadsholm
Arendal
Munkedal
Lidköping
Grimstad
★ 18
Fevik
Uddevalla
Skara
Birkeland
Lillesand
★ 19
Vänersborg
Kristiansand
★ 19
Trollhättan

Ålesund

Brosundet Gjestehus One of the most popular places to stay in the Art Nouveau town of Ålesund is this charming hotel-cum-guesthouse, which occupies an old wharfside warehouse down by the main harbour. The rooms boast beamed ceilings, white drapes and pine floors, all part of a bright and cheerful house style.
☒ Apotekergata 5, N-6004 Ålesund. **Map** p14 C1. ☎ 70 12 10 00. FAX 70 12 12 95. @ post@brosundet.no b. **Rooms** 44. ● Easter, Christmas, New Year. AE, DC, MC, V. ⓚⓚ

Åndalsnes

Grand Hotel Bellevue Despite its austere modern exterior, this long-established hotel, surrounded by mountains and almost on the bank of the Romdalsfjord, has a well-justified reputation as one of the premier places to stay in fjord Norway. The best rooms are on the upper floors and offer spectacular views.
☒ N-6301 Åndalsnes. **Map** p15 D1. ☎ 71 22 75 00. FAX 71 22 60 38. @ booking@grandhotel.no b,l (groups only),d. **Rooms** 84. ● Christmas, Easter. AE, DC, MC, V. ⓚⓚ

Alta

Quality Vica Hotell This cosy hotel has been decorated in the style of a mountain lodge, with acres of pine panelling, animal heads on the walls and a scattering of pretty curios. In the restaurant, the waiters wear national costume and serve up a tempting range of Lapland delicacies including cloudberries and caribou, as well as what is probably the best apple pie in town.
☒ Bossekop, N-9500 Alta. **Map** p14 B2. ☎ 78 43 47 11. FAX 78 43 42 99. @ booking@vica.no b,l,d. **Rooms** 24. ● Christmas and Easter AE, DC, MC, V. ⓚⓚⓚ

Balestrand

Midtnes Pensjonat Blessed with a lovely location, on the brow of a hill overlooking the Sognefjord, this friendly *pension* is an agreeable base for exploring the fjords. Breakfast, the best meal of the day here, is a sumptuous affair with everything from pickled herring, gherkins and fresh fish through to cornflakes and orange juice. A very popular place for summer weddings.
☒ N-6898 Balestrand. **Map** p14 C3. ☎ 57 69 11 33. FAX 57 69 15 84. @ booking@midtnes.no b,d. **Rooms** 31. ● mid-Dec to 3 Jan. Not accepted. ⓚⓚ

Å i Lofoten

Å Rorbu At the southern tip of the Lofoten Islands, the beautiful village of Å boasts this group of old and new fishing huts with stupendous sea views. Prior booking essential.
☒ Å i Lofoten, N-8392 Sørvågen. **Map** p14 A2. ☎ 76 09 11 21. FAX 76 09 12 82. b,l,d. **Rooms** 27. ⓚⓚ

Alta

Altafjord Hotell This sprawling modern complex incorporates traditional turf-roofed buildings and seashore cottages.
☒ Bossekopveien, Postboks 1424, N-9506 Alta. **Map** p14 B2. ☎ 78 43 70 11. FAX 78 43 70 13. b,l,d. **Rooms** 30. ⓚⓚ

Aurdal

Danebu Kongsgård & Hytter Deep in the countryside, this is a great place to unwind, with rooms in the lodge and in 14 surrounding cabins.
☒ N-2910 Aurdal. **Map** p15 E3. ☎ 61 35 76 00. FAX 61 35 76 01. @ post@danebu.no b,l,d. **Rooms** 32. ⓚⓚ

Balestrand

Kvikne's Hotel This long-established hotel, by the fjord in the resort of Balestrand, is a plush affair distinguished by an ornate woodcarved lounge in the Viking style.
☒ Postbox 24, N-6898 Balestrand. **Map** p14 C3. ☎ 57 69 11 01. FAX 57 69 42 01. b,l,d. **Rooms** 210. ⓚⓚⓚ

Bergen

Hotel Park Pension Long-established small hotel in two buildings on the edge of Bergen's town centre, and especially handy for the university. Everything is well-considered, from the attractive façade with its high-pitched gables and iron balconies, through to the pastel colours of the plush interior. A popular place, so book ahead.
⊠ Harald Hårfagresgate 35, N-5007 Bergen. **Map** p14 C3. ☎ 55 54 44 00. FAX 55 54 44 44. @ booking@parkhotel.no 🍴 b. **Rooms** 33. ● Christmas, Easter. 💳 AE, DC, MC, V. Ⓚⓚⓚ

Fjærland

Fjærland Fjordstue Hotell Tiny, unspoilt Fjærland was one of the last of the fjord villages to be connected to the road system. The public rooms and bedrooms of this attractive guesthouse are smart and cheerful. The loggia doubles as a sun-lounge and fjord vantage point. Breakfast features the best of Norwegian ingredients.
⊠ N-6848 Fjærland. **Map** p14 C2. ☎ 57 69 32 00. FAX 57 69 31 61. @ post@fjaerland.no 🍴 b,l,d. **Rooms** 16. ● Oct to mid-May. 💳 AE, DC, MC, V. ⓚⓚ

Dalen i Telemark

Hotel Dalen The fairytale-like Dalen, one of southern Norway's finest country hotels, was built in 1894 in the so-called 'dragon-style' inspired by Norway's medieval stave churches. Outside are gables and galleries, dragon heads and gargoyles; the period interior, with its leather upholstery and stained glass, is splendid too.
⊠ Box 123, N-3880, Dalen, Telemark. **Map** p15 D4. ☎ 35 07 70 00. FAX 35 07 70 11. @ dalenhaa@online.no 🍴 b,l,d. **Rooms** 38. ● Dec to mid-April. 💳 AE, DC, MC, V. ⓚⓚⓚ

Fjærland

Hotel Mundal Few hotels can match the instant appeal of the Mundal, whose Victorian façade nestles beside the fjord with the mountains rising steeply behind. Inside are nooks and crannies dripping with antiques and fishing memorabilia. Tasty meals are served in a spacious dining room that appears to have changed little in decades.
⊠ N-6848 Fjærland. **Map** p14 C2. ☎ 57 69 31 01. FAX 57 69 31 79. @ hotelmundal@fjordinfo.no 🍴 b,l,d. **Rooms** 35. ● mid-Sept to mid-May. 💳 AE, DC, MC, V. ⓚⓚ

Bergen

Crowded House The liveliest of Bergen's guesthouses, close to the city centre. Guests have access to self-catering facilities.
⊠ Håkonsgaten 27, N-5015 Bergen. **Map** p14 C3. ☎ 55 23 13 10. FAX 55 90 72 01. @ info@crowded-house.com 🍴 self-catering. **Rooms** 34. ⓚⓚ

Bergen

Grand Hotel Terminus Charming 1920s hotel by the train station, complete with period furnishings and acres of wood panelling.
⊠ Zander Kaaesgate 6, PO Box 1100, N-5809 Bergen. **Map** p14 C3. ☎ 55 21 25 01. FAX 55 31 85 76. 🍴 b,l,d (groups only, in July). **Rooms** 131. ⓚⓚⓚ

Bergen

Skansen Pensjonat A pretty *pension* in an old townhouse just above the funicular, providing simple accommodation at reasonable rates.
⊠ Vetrlidsallmenningen 29, N-5014 Bergen. **Map** p14 C3. ☎ 55 31 90 80. FAX 55 31 15 27. @ mail@skansen-pensjonat.no 🍴 b. **Rooms** 11. ⓚⓚ

Dombås

Dombås Hotell This long-established hotel has gracious public rooms, attentive service and a first-rate restaurant.
⊠ N-2660 Dombås. **Map** p15 E2. ☎ 61 24 10 01. FAX 61 24 14 61. @ dombas.hotel@online.nl 🍴 b,l,d. **Rooms** 78. ⓚⓚⓚ

Flåm

Heimly Pensjonat Twisting its way down the Flåm valley, the narrow-gauge Flåm railway drops 900m (3,000ft) in 20km (14 miles). It's one of Europe's most exhilarating train journeys and, at the bottom in the hamlet of Flåm, is the Heimly Pensjonat. This unassuming and well-maintained pension overlooks the fjord and has an informal, low-key public area.

N-5742 Flåm. **Map** p15 D3. 57 63 23 00. FAX 57 63 23 40. @ post@heimly.no b,l (groups only),d. **Rooms** 23. Never. AE, DC, MC, V. Kr Kr

Hundorp

Sygard Grytting One would not guess this antique farmstead nestling among orchards just north of Hundorp is a guesthouse. The 18th-century farm buildings have survived almost intact and have been carefully modified to accommodate visitors during the summer months. The main house has the best bedrooms.

Harpefoss, N-2647 Sør-Fron. **Map** p15 E2. 61 29 85 88. FAX 61 29 85 10. @ post@grytting.com b,l (groups only),d (by arrangement). **Rooms** 7. mid-June to mid-Aug. V. Kr Kr Kr

Hjerkinn

Hjerkinn Fjellstue In the remote windswept moors of central Norway is this homely lodge, a comforting place of open fires and cheerfully modern pine furniture. The restaurant serves delicious reindeer steak, culled from local herds, and the seafood is equally tasty. Guides are provided for elk and musk-ox safaris and there's horse-riding too.

N-2661 Hjerkinn. **Map** p15 E2. 61 24 29 27. FAX 61 24 29 49. @ anne.ekre@hjerkinn.no b,l,d. **Rooms** 26. Christmas. AE, DC, MC, V. Kr Kr

Kongsvold

Kongsvold Fjeldstue The inn at Kongsvold has been sheltering travellers and pilgrims on the great north road between Oslo and Trondheim since the closing years of the 17th century. The present incarnation has discretely and very tastefully adapted the old wooden buildings that comprise the complex, even down to the tinkers' hut beyond the picket fence.

Kongsvold, N-7340 Oppdal. **Map** p15 E2. 72 40 43 40. FAX 72 40 43 41. @ post@kongsvold.no b,l,d. **Rooms** 32. Nov to Jan. DC, MC, V. Kr Kr

Eidfjord

Eidfjord Hotel No frills, no fuss, in this smart, modern hotel on a hill in the heart of the fjords. The mountain views are spectacular.

N-5783 Eidfjord. **Map** p15 D3. 53 66 52 64. FAX 53 66 52 12. @ eidfjordhotel@produktnett.no b,l,d. **Rooms** 28. Kr Kr

Flåm

Fretheim Hotell The Flåm railway provides a superb introduction to the fjords; this comfortable hotel is just across from the station.

N-5742 Flåm. **Map** p15 D3. 57 63 22 00. FAX 57 63 64 00. @ mail@fretheim-hotel.no b,l,d. **Rooms** 118. Kr Kr Kr

Geilo

Solli Hotel Geilo is Norway's winter sports capital and this neat, modern hotel is a very convenient place to stay – it is sited just 100m from the nearest ski piste.

Skurdalsvegen 25, N-3580 Geilo. **Map** p15 D3. 32 09 11 11. FAX 32 09 15 60. b,l,d. **Rooms** 36. Kr-Kr Kr

Grimstad

Grimstad Hotell A clever conversion of several old timber buildings makes this a distinctive hotel. Ibsen worked at the Grimstad chemists'.

Kirkegaten 3, N-4878 Grimstad. **Map** p15 D5. 37 25 25 25. FAX 37 25 25 35. b,l,d. **Rooms** 49. Kr Kr-Kr Kr Kr

Kristiansand

Villa Frobusdal Hotel Hidden away beside the town's ring road, this extraordinary hotel occupies an appealing shipowner's mansion built in 1917. The interior boasts a wonderful assortment of antiques and some rare wood panelling alive with dragons and snakes. The light-filled bedrooms are charming.
Frobusdalen 2, N-4613 Kristiansand. **Map** p15 D5. 38 07 05 15. FAX 38 07 01 15. @ frobus@online.no b. **Rooms** 7. Dec, Easter. MC, V. Kr Kr

Lofthus

Ullensvang Gjesteheim Rarely does a hotel blend into its surroundings as delightfully as this one, sheltering in a little dell beside a gurgling stream. The whitewashed wooden lodge is surrounded by attractive farm buildings. Inside, the public rooms are strewn with antiques. Bedrooms are plainer, but entirely satisfactory.
N-5781 Lofthus, Hardanger. **Map** p14 A2. 53 66 12 36. FAX 53 66 15 19. @ ullensvang.gjesteheim@czi.net b,l,d. AE, DC, MC, V. Christmas Day. **Rooms** 13. Kr Kr

Lillesand

Hotel Norge This glamorous hotel is one of the most celebrated on Norway's peaceful south coast. Decorative highlights include the stained glass, the elegant banqueting hall and the suite where the Spanish King Alfonso XIII stayed in 1931. The restaurant serves the freshest of seafood and breakfasts are lavish banquets.
Strandgaten 3, N-4790 Lillesand. **Map** p15 D5. 37 27 01 44. FAX 37 27 30 70. @ lillesand@hotelnorge.no b,l,d. **Rooms** 25. Christmas. AE, DC, MC, V. Kr Kr

Mandal

Kjøbmandsgaarden Hotel Norway has not got many long sandy beaches; Mandal, a seaside resort on the south coast, has the country's longest. Cosy and intimate, this friendly family-run hotel is squeezed into the narrow streets at the heart of the little town. Rooms are bright and modern, and there is a very good restaurant offering traditional cuisine.
St Elvegate 57, N-4517 Mandal. **Map** p15 D5. 38 26 12 76. FAX 38 26 33 02. b,l,d. **Rooms** 12. Never. AE, DC, MC, V. Kr Kr

Grotli

Grotli Høyfjellshotel A mountain lodge with a warm and welcoming pine interior. At 900m (3,000ft) above sea level, there are opportunities for summer skiing, hiking and whitewater rafting.
N-2695 Grotli. **Map** p15 D2. 61 21 74 74. FAX 61 21 74 75. @ mail@grotli.no b,l,d. **Rooms** 53. Kr Kr

Gudvangen

Gudvangen Fjordtell Unusual modern hotel built in traditional Norwegian style. Huddle of circular log buildings roofed with turf.
N-5717 Gudvangen. **Map** p15 D3. 57 63 39 29. FAX 57 63 39 80. @ fjordtel@online.no b,l,d. **Rooms** 27. Kr Kr

Hellesylt

Grand Hotel Built in 1871, the Grand is a well-established favourite of visitors to fjord country. Recently refurbished.
P.O. Box 73, N-6218 Hellesylt. **Map** p15 D2. 70 26 51 00. FAX 70 26 52 22. @ grandhotel.hellesylt@czi.net b,l,d. **Rooms** 29. Kr Kr

Kvinesdal

Rafoss Hotel There has been an inn on this spot since the 1800s. The old house is now attached to a modern annexe, where rooms have river views.
N-4480 Kvinesdal. **Map** p14 C5. 38 35 03 88. FAX 38 35 09 66. b, d (by arrangement). **Rooms** 18. Kr Kr

Nordkapp

Repvåg Fjord Hotell og Rorbusenter The long road to the northern tip of Norway, Nordkapp, is known to thousands of tourists. Few turn down the country road leading to this remote fishing and trading station, where ancient wooden shacks have been turned into an atmospheric hotel. Rooms are in the main building or in cabins.
N-9768 Repvåg, Nordkapp. **Map** p14 B2.
78 47 54 40. FAX 78 47 27 51.
@ post@repvag-fjordhotel.no b,l,d. **Rooms** 77.
Nov to Mar. AE, DC, MC, V. Kr Kr

Oslo

Hotel Continental One of Oslo's most prestigious hotels, the Continental boasts sumptuous public rooms furnished in grand style with elegant chandeliers and acres of parquet flooring. Ideally located, footsteps from Oslo's main street. Of its several bars and restaurants, the Theatercaféen is the most popular.
Stortingsgaten 24/26, N-0117 Oslo. **Map** p15 E4.
22 82 40 00. FAX 22 42 96 89. @ booking@hotel-continental.no b,l,d. **Rooms** 154. Christmas to New Year. AE, DC, MC, V. Kr Kr Kr Kr

Orkanger

Bårdshaug Herregård In the old copper-mining town of Orkanger, the erstwhile manor house of Christian Thams, one of Norway's most successful entrepreneurs, has been turned into this plush hotel. A string of Scandinavian monarchs have spent the night in the all-timber 'Royal Room', which dates back to Thams.
N-7300 Orkanger. **Map** p15 E1. 72 47 99 00.
FAX 72 48 19 23. @ post@baardshaug.no b,l,d.
Rooms 65. Christmas, Easter. AE, DC, MC, V.
Kr Kr Kr

Oslo

Frogner House Hotel This handsome Victorian building is located in one of Oslo's smartest areas, 2km (1 miles) from the town centre. Stripped wood and thick carpets are the order of the day, but each of the bedrooms is different. The best have balconies overlooking the street; the large attic room is a honeymooners' favourite.
Skovveien 8, N-0257 Oslo. **Map** p15 E4.
22 56 00 56. FAX 22 56 05 00.
@ mail@ frognerhouse.com b, d. **Rooms** 60.
Christmas, Easter. AE, DC, MC, V. Kr Kr Kr

Loen

Hotel Alexandra Within easy striking distance of the Jostedalsbreen glacier, this large, ritzy hotel offers fine dining and ultra-modern rooms.
N-6789 Loen. **Map** p15 D2. 57 87 50 50.
FAX 57 87 50 51 @ alex@alexandra.no b,l,d.
Rooms 191. Kr Kr Kr Kr

Lom

Fossheim Turisthotell In the small town of Lom is a wonderful stave church. This excellent hotel has rooms in the main lodge and in cabins.
N-2686 Lom. **Map** p15 D2. 61 21 95 00.
FAX 61 21 95 01. @ resepjon@fossheimhotel.no b,l,d.
Rooms 50. Kr Kr Kr

Mo-i-Rana

Meyergården Hotell One of northern Norway's most enjoyable hotels: an imaginative mix of old and new, plus fjord views from the upper floors.
Fr. Nansensgt. 28, N-8601 Mo-i-Rana. **Map** p14 A3.
75 13 40 00. FAX 75 13 40 01. @ meyergarden@meyergarden.no b,l,d. **Rooms** 150. Kr Kr

Mosjøen

Fru Haugans Hotel Break the journey on the long road to northern Norway at this spacious hotel, parts of which date back to the 1790s.
N-8651 Mosjøen. **Map** p14 A3. 75 11 41 00.
FAX 75 11 41 01. @ res@fruhaugans.no b,l,d.
Rooms 87. Kr Kr

Oslo

Gabelshus Hotell Owned by the same family since it was opened in 1912, this is a firm favourite with many regular visitors to Oslo. The hotel's immaculately maintained interior – a major expansion is under way – is graced by an eclectic collection of antiques, such as monks' seats, candelabra and ornate fireplaces.
☒ Gabels gate 16, N-0272 Oslo. **Map** p15 E4.
☎ 23 27 65 00. FAX 23 27 65 60. @ reception@gabelshus.no 🍴 b. **Rooms** 110. ● Christmas, Easter. AE, DC, MC, V. ⓀⓀⓀ

Osøyro

Solstrand Fjord Hotel The Schau-Larsen family run this refined and elegant hotel with an eye to detail. The furnishings are smart and modern, the colours warm and inviting, and the grounds neatly manicured. There's a spa and a choice of bathing here too, either in the swimming pool or in the blue-grey waters of the Bjørnefjorden.
☒ Postbox 54, N-5201 Os per Bergen. **Map** p14 C3. ☎ 56 57 11 00. FAX 56 57 11 20. @ hotel@solstrand.com 🍴 b,l,d. **Rooms** 135. ● Christmas, New Year, Easter. AE, DC, MC, V. ⓀⓀⓀⓀ

Oslo

Nobel House Hotell It is close to several of the city's best restaurants and museums, and the decor is superb too – a smooth and eye-catching blend of tradition and modernity. Imaginative touches include the magnificent fireplace in the lounge area and the angel painted on the inside of the lift. Lovely roof terrace.
☒ Kongens Gate 5, N-0153 Oslo. **Map** p15 E4.
☎ 23 10 72 00. FAX 23 10 72 10. @ nobelhouse@firsthotels.no 🍴 b,l,d. **Rooms** 69. ● Christmas, Easter. AE, DC, MC, V. ⓀⓀⓀⓀ

Østerbo

Østerbo Fjellstove This smart, well-maintained mountain lodge lies at the start of the celebrated Aurlandsdal valley walk and is a favourite with hikers. Most of the rooms are in the main lodge; there is additional accommodation in cabins on the grounds, and in an old medieval storehouse. The last is a charming affair of warm wood and narrow bunkbeds.
☒ Østerbo, N-5745 Aurland. **Map** p15 D3.
☎ 57 63 11 77. FAX 57 63 11 52. @ oesterbo@c2i.net 🍴 b,l,d. **Rooms** 42. ● Nov to Apr. V. Ⓚ

Narvik

Breidablikk Gjestehus Narvik is short of good accommodation; this modest but well-tended guesthouse offers great views over the harbour.
☒ Tore Hundsgt 41, N-8514 Narvik. **Map** p14 A2.
☎ 76 94 14 18. FAX 76 94 57 86. @ post@breidablikk.no 🍴 b,l. **Rooms** 22. ⓀⓀ

Oslo

City Hotel This modest but endearing hotel is located above shops and offices in a traditional Oslo apartment block near the train station. Friendly, informal atmosphere; helpful staff.
☒ Skippergaten 19, N-0106 Oslo. **Map** p15 E4.
☎ 22 41 36 10. FAX 22 42 24 29. 🍴 b. **Rooms** 52. ⓀⓀ

Oslo

Rica Hotel Bygdøy Alle With its forest of spires and towers, the High Victorian façade is splendid.
☒ Bygdøy Allé 53, N-0265 Oslo. **Map** p15 E4.
☎ 23 08 58 00. FAX 22 08 58 08.
@ rica.hotel.bygdoy.alle@rica.no 🍴 b,l,d. **Rooms** 57. ⓀⓀⓀ

Otta

Rondane Høyfjellshotell Hotel-spa-leisure complex in the hills around Otta, and near the treeless steppes of Rondane National Park.
☒ N-2675 Otta. **Map** p15 E2. ☎ 61 23 39 33.
FAX 61 23 39 52. @ hotel@rondane.no 🍴 b,l,d. **Rooms** 50. ⓀⓀ-ⓀⓀⓀ

For key to symbols see backflap. For price categories *see p13*

Øye

Hotel Union In the late 19th century, European aristocrats gathered at the Hotel Union to fish for salmon and hike the hills. These halcyon days are recalled by the hotel's interior, in which every room is crammed with carefully chosen antiques. Fans of novelist Karen Blick, will enjoy seeing a pair of her lover's boots.
Øye, N-6196 Norangsfjorden. **Map** p14 C2. 70 06 21 00. FAX 70 06 21 16. @ post@unionoye.no b,l,d. **Rooms** 27. Oct to Apr. AE, DC, MC, V. (Kr)(Kr)(Kr)

Preikestolen

Preikestolen Vandrerhjem Simple lodgings in a magnificent setting. Built in traditional Norwegian style, these timber chalets, with their turf roofs, occupy a superb location on a steep hill overlooking a deep-blue lake. A good base for hiking, the famous Pulpit Rock, which features sheer 600m drops on three sides, is just two hours' walk away.
N-4001 Stavanger. **Map** p14 C5. 94 53 11 11. FAX 51 74 91 11. @ hilde.troeen@roe.skolepost.nls.no b,d. **Rooms** 15. Sept to May. AE, DC, MC, V. (Kr)

Sjoa

Sjoa Gjestehus Whitewater rafters keen to brave the River Sjoa flock to this guesthouse every summer weekend. Some fill the dormitories at the bottom of the hill, others prefer the spacious en suite chalet rooms and apartments above. They all meet in the 18th-century farmhouse, where the dining room has an open fire and log walls.
N-2670 Sjoa. **Map** p15 D2. 61 23 62 00. FAX 61 23 60 14. b, d (by arrangement). **Rooms** 6, plus 6 dormitories sleeping 6–10 people. Oct to mid-May MC, V. (Kr)

Solvorn

Walaker Hotel Facing the exquisite Urnes stave church across the narrow Lusterfjord is the little Walaker, owned and operated by the same family since 1690. In summer, the hotel gallery features exhibitions of contemporary art and the delightful garden is awash with roses. Most of the rooms overlook the fjord and the garden.
N-6879 Solvorn, Sognefjord. **Map** p15 D3. 57 68 20 80. FAX 57 68 20 81. @ hotel@walaker.com b,d. **Rooms** 23. end Sept to end Apr. DC, MC, V. (Kr)(Kr)(Kr)

Sandane

Gloppen Hotell Many visitors return to the Gloppen year after year. The 1860s hotel is one of the most attractive in the fjord region.
N-6823 Sandane. **Map** p14 C2. 57 86 53 33. FAX 57 86 60 02. @ post@gloppenhotell.no b,l,d. **Rooms** 40. (Kr)(Kr)

Sandnes

Kronen Gaard Hotell This venerable hotel prides itself on its scenic fjord country surroundings and intimate atmosphere.
Vatne, N-4309 Sandnes. **Map** p14 C5. 51 62 14 00. FAX 51 62 20 23. @ galt@kronen-gaard.no b,l,d. **Rooms** 34. (Kr)(Kr)

Selje

Selje Hotel If it's a remote location you're after, look no further than Selje, a tiny west coast fishing village. This attractive wood and stone hotel is at the heart of the village. Health facilities.
N-6740 Selje. **Map** p14 D2. 57 85 88 80. FAX 57 85 88 81. @ post@seljehotel.no b,l,d. **Rooms** 49. (Kr)(Kr)(Kr)

Sjusjøen

Sjusjøen Høyfjellshotell Located in the rolling, forest uplands, this dapper hotel has its own indoor pool. Smashing food too.
N-2612, Lillehammer, Sjusjøen. **Map** p15 E3. 62 34 76 70. FAX 62 34 76 71. @ post@sjusjoen-hotel.no b,l,d. **Rooms** 70. (Kr)(Kr)

Stavanger

Skagen Brygge Hotel This first-rate, modern hotel, perched on the water's edge in the oil-rich town of Stavanger, is built in the style of a wharfside warehouse. The rooms are smart and neat and most provide views over the harbour. Breakfasts are superb and in the early evening a tasty range of free snacks is available at the bar.
Skagen 30, N-4006 Stavanger. **Map** p14 C5. 51 85 00 00. FAX 51 85 00 01. @ booking@skagenbryggehotel.no b. **Rooms** 110. Never. AE, DC, MC, V. Kr Kr Kr

Ulvik

Ulvik Fjord Pensjonat There's nothing grand or pretentious about this welcoming family-run guesthouse. The rooms are decorated in simple modern style (the most appealing overlook the Hardangerfjord) and breakfast is served in an open-plan dining room. The best time to visit is the spring when the orchards on the surrounding hills are engulfed by pinky-white apple blossom.
Postboks 33, N-5731 Ulvik. **Map** p14 C3. 56 52 61 70. FAX 56 52 61 60. @ ulvikfjordpensjonat@ulvik.org b,l,d. **Rooms** 19. Nov MC, V. Kr Kr

Turtagrø

Turtagrø The modest exterior belies its handsome interior. Solid pine walls, decorated with photos dating from 1900, and furnished in Scandinavian style. The restaurant is a favourite haunt of mountaineers, who rest up here after climbing the majestic peaks of the Jotunheimen National Park. Prior booking essential.
N-6877 Fortun. **Map** p15 D2. 57 68 08 00. FAX 57 68 08 01. @ hotel@turtagro.no b,l (by arrangement),d. **Rooms** 30. late Oct to Easter. AE, DC, MC, V. Kr Kr Kr

Voss

Fleischer's Hotel One of Norway's premier hotels and an ideal base for exploring the fjords, Fleischer's is a real delight. The lakeside setting is charming and the restaurant outstanding. The modern rooms are extremely comfortable and cheerfully decorated. Supremely helpful and efficient staff make the place even more special.
Evangervegen 13, N-5700 Voss. **Map** p14 C3. 56 52 05 00. FAX 56 52 05 01. @ hotel@fleischers.no b,l,d. **Rooms** 90. Christmas. AE, DC, MC, V. Kr Kr Kr

Snåsa

Snåsa Hotell Rural, agricultural Norway is seen to good advantage at the Snåsa, a modern establishment in a fertile valley at the end of a lovely lake. Bedrooms are spacious.
N-7760 Snåsa. **Map** p14 A3. 74 15 10 57. FAX 74 15 16 15. @ snasa.hotell@c2i.net b,l,d. **Rooms** 37. Kr Kr

Stryn

Stryn Hotel Stryn is a place of extraordinary natural beauty. Take a helicopter flight over Nordfjord or go on a guided glacier walk.
Visnesvegen 1, N-6783 Stryn. **Map** p14 C2. 57 87 07 00. FAX 57 87 07 01. @ post@strynhotel.no b,l,d. **Rooms** 69. Kr Kr Kr

Tromsø

Rica Ishavshotel This stylish, ultra-modern establishment sits on the harbour's edge in Tromsø centre. Magnificent views.
Fr Langesgate 2, N-9252 Tromsø. **Map** p14 B2. 77 66 64 00. FAX 77 66 64 44. @ rica.ishavshotel@rica.no b,l,d. **Rooms** 180. Kr Kr Kr Kr

Utne

Utne Hotel Sitting prettily by the jetty in the Hardangerfjord, this is one of Norway's oldest and quaintest hotels, dating back to 1722. Next door is an excellent folk museum.
N-5779 Utne. **Map** p14 C3. 53 66 64 00. FAX 53 66 10 89. @ utnehot@online.no b,l,d. **Rooms** 25. Kr Kr

Sweden

SWEDEN

SWEDEN IS traditionally regarded as an expensive country to visit, but recent changes in exchange rates means it is presently more affordable than usual. For many tourists visiting for the first time, it may come as a surprise that the country has so many beautiful hotels. Often these have been converted from historic buildings such as castles, mountain lodges, medieval inns and 18th-century manor houses. They can provide excellent accommodation in beautiful surroundings. Many of the best places are members of two hotel marketing organisations: the Countryside Hotels and the Historiska Hotell groups. In Stockholm – which was European City of Culture in 1999 – we also have some exceptional entries.

Gripsholms Värdshus, page 33, Mariefred's delightful old inn

SWEDEN REGION BY REGION

SWEDEN CAN be divided into five regions: south, southwest, central, north and far north.

South and Southwest

These regions are relatively flat. Apart from the capital, the main towns are Gothenburg, Malmö and Helsingborg. Gothenburg has an elegant city hotel, a useful first stop before heading for the region's attractive beach resorts, often based around old, fortified towns. The Baltic islands of Öland and Gotland are both popular, relaxed beach holiday places – relatively uncrowded, with attractive seaside hotels.

Stockholm, Sweden's capital, makes a welcome urban interlude. It mixes brutalist modern design with medieval and Beaux-Arts architecture, and its reputation for open-mindedness is well founded. There are woods and water on its doorstep and an archipelago of islands a ferry ride away.

Central and North

The forest and fjords don't begin until you get some way farther north of the capital, and here there are many excellent places to stay – many in beautifully remote settings – served by the main highways or the 'Inland Railroad'. The choice ranges from an inn built on the site of a Carthusian monastery to manor houses dating from the 16th century and country house hotels in peaceful lake-side settings. These last are flourishing concerns, with tremendous atmosphere and very good food. Many have a dual personality: in summer they offer walking, windsurfing, fishing and boating; in winter, cross-country skiing. The winter months, especially around Christmas, are a sensible time for breaks if you can put up with the short days, as are May and September, because there are fewer mosquitoes than in July and August.

Far North

The tundra and forest of the far north, above the Arctic Circle, is the home of the nomadic Sami people. In June and July it never properly gets dark. Here hotels are few and far between; among them is the ultimate one-off hotel, the Ice Hotel near Kiruna, which operates in winter, carved each year out of ice. In fact, it's more comfortable than you might imagine and is popular for weddings and christenings. Its phone number is (0980) 668 00.

HIGHLIGHTS

HOTELS ILLUSTRATED on these introductory pages are by no means the only highlights. Other favourites include Stockholm's Mälardrottningen, converted from heiress Barbara Hutton's former yacht (page 35); and Tällberg's Åkerblads (page 36), a much-loved family property run, amazingly, by more than 20 generations of Åkerblads.

Food and Drink

Boar and berries are the traditional staples of Swedish food, the former roasted or made into sausages, the latter, *hjortron (*cloud-berry), served with fresh cream or ice cream. Meatballs with gravy and cranberry sauce, and *gravad lax* – raw salmon marinated with dill and served with mustard dressing – are also delicious.

The standard of food in the hotels listed here is generally very high, and will include game in season, along with international dishes.

The only drawback is the expense. You may find that after a few days of hotel dining that stocking up for a picnic lunch becomes a necessity. Lunch at a restaurant is usually not as expensive as dinner, especially if you go for the set menu (*dagens rätt*).

Another economical option is the *smörgåsbord* served at lunchtime in restaurants or hotels – a mouthwatering all-you-can-eat collation of herring, cooked meats, hard-boiled eggs, potato, salads, desserts and fruit.

Alcohol is also notoriously expensive in Sweden. The beer served in bars is classed according to strength. Class III or *starköl* is the strongest, weaker is class II or *folköl*, and the class 1 beer, *lättöl*, is virtually alcohol-free – and great for drivers. There is zero tolerance of drink-driving in this country and a few glasses of wine with dinner followed by a brandy could take you over the limit to drive, even the *following morning*. Outside bars and restaurants, class III beers can only be bought from government liquor stores – whose Swedish name is Systembolaget.

Akvavit, a herb-flavoured spirit, is traditionally served ice-cold with beer chasers – a potent combination.

Swedes eat lunch from 11am onwards (generally finishing by 2pm). Dinner starts from around 6pm and restaurants close from around 11pm to midnight.

Bedrooms and Bathrooms

If you want twin beds, ask for them specifically when booking. The Swedish have a tradition of being health and environment conscious so some hotels, including larger chains, are switching to anti-allergenic bedding and biodegradeable cleaning products. As well as sparkling bathrooms, many places will have a sauna (usually open to both sexes).

The Grand Hotell, Marstrand, page 33

Other Practical Information

Breakfast at most hotels is lavish – a buffet with cheeses, including the sweet, brown *mesost*, hams, yogurt, muesli, an array of rye and 'black' breads, crispbreads and fruit. The standard of housekeeping is outstanding: everything is immaculately clean, and it works. During the summer business shut-down hotel prices drop considerably. Year-round, luxury hotels become much more affordable at the weekend, when substantial discounts (often 40–50 per cent on the usual room rate) come into effect. Ask what the 'special prices' are.

Language Swedes are true polyglots and often sound like native speakers of whichever language they are using – including English.

Currency The Swedish *krona*, written 'SEK'.

Shops Open 9am–6pm Mon–Fri, and 9am–1pm Sat (department stores till 4pm). Large shops in the cities are sometimes open until 8 or 10pm and on Sunday.

Tipping Hotel room rates and restaurant menu prices are inclusive of service charges. Tipping isn't expected, but if bills come to an odd amount they are often rounded up to the nearest 10Kr, or you can leave a tip of around 10 per cent if you want to.

Telephoning As well as the usual call boxes there are Turist Telefon payphones in summer in the major cities, offering half-price calls. To make a phone call within Sweden, dial the full number. To phone Sweden from the UK, dial the international code 00 46, then the phone number, omitting the initial zero; from the US, dial 011 46.

Public holidays 1 January; 6 January; Good Friday and Easter Monday; 1 May; Ascension Day; Whit Monday; Midsummer's Day; 1 November; 24, 25 and 26 December.

Useful Words

Breakfast	*Frukost*
Lunch	*Lunch*
Dinner/supper	*Middag/ supé*
Free room?	*Ledigt rum?*
How much?	*Vad kostar?*
Single room	*Enkelrum*
Double room	*Dubbelrum*

Sweden Price Bands

Swedish hotels are classified by stars, from one to five, but don't be too swayed by this. Our price bands are simpler, and as elsewhere in the guide refer to the price of a standard double room in high season (but don't forget to ask about discounts, which can be substantial). Breakfast is usually included in the room rate; prices include all taxes.

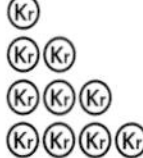

under 900Kr
900Kr–1,200Kr
1,200Kr–1,600Kr
over 1,600Kr

Sweden

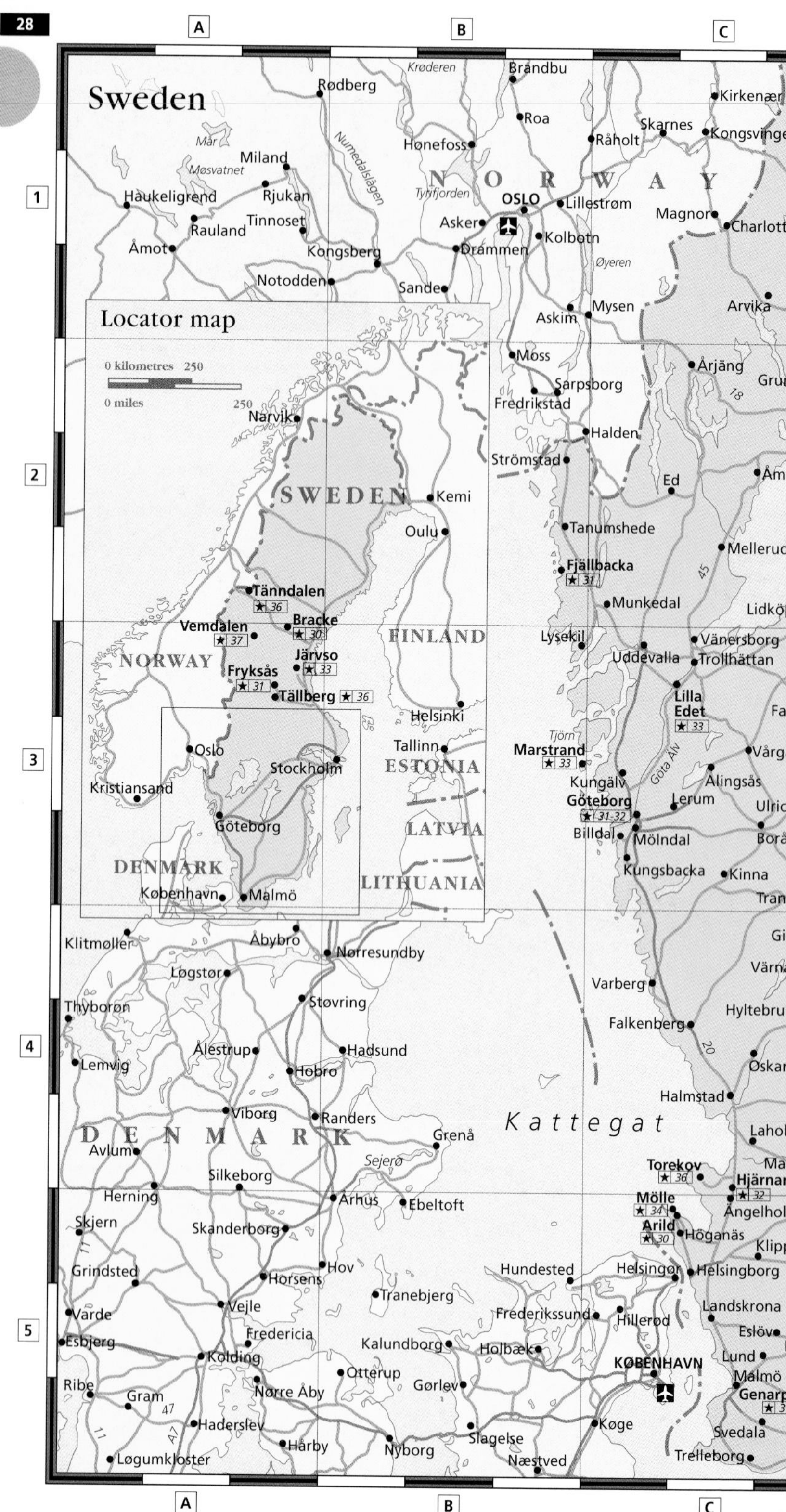

A
B
C
1
2
3
4
5
Locator map
0 kilometres 250
0 miles 250
NORWAY
SWEDEN
FINLAND
ESTONIA
LATVIA
LITHUANIA
DENMARK
Narvik
Kemi
Oulu
Tänndalen 36
Vemdalen 37
Bracke 30
Järvso 33
Fryksås 31
Tällberg 36
Helsinki
Tallinn
Oslo
Stockholm
Kristiansand
Göteborg
København
Malmö
Rødberg
Krøderen
Brandbu
Roa
Hønefoss
Råholt
Skarnes
Kirkenær
Kongsvinger
Mår
Miland
Møsvatnet
Numedalslågen
Tyrifjorden
Haukeligrend
Rjukan
Rauland
Tinnoset
Åmot
Kongsberg
Notodden
Sande
Asker
OSLO
Lillestrøm
Kolbotn
Drammen
Øyeren
Magnor
Charlott
Askim
Mysen
Arvika
Moss
Sarpsborg
Fredrikstad
Årjäng
Halden
Strömstad
Ed
Åm
Tanumshede
Mellerud
Fjällbacka 31
Munkedal
Lidkö
Lysekil
Uddevalla
Vänersborg
Trollhättan
Lilla Edet 33
Tjörn
Marstrand 33
Kungälv
Göta Älv
Alingsås
Vårgå
Göteborg 31-32
Lerum
Billdal
Mölndal
Kungsbacka
Kinna
Varberg
Falkenberg
Hyltebru
Halmstad
Kattegat
Torekov 36
Hjärnar 32
Mölle 34
Arild 30
Höganäs
Ängelhol
Helsingør
Helsingborg
Hundested
Frederikssund
Hillerød
Landskrona
KØBENHAVN
Lund
Malmö
Genarp
Køge
Svedala
Trelleborg
Klitmøller
Åbybro
Nørresundby
Løgstør
Thyborøn
Støvring
Ålestrup
Hadsund
Lemvig
Hobro
Viborg
Randers
DENMARK
Avlum
Grenå
Sejerø
Silkeborg
Herning
Århus
Ebeltoft
Skjern
Skanderborg
Grindsted
Hov
Horsens
Tranebjerg
Varde
Vejle
Fredericia
Esbjerg
Kolding
Kalundborg
Holbæk
Otterup
Ribe
Gram
Nørre Åby
Gørlev
Haderslev
Slagelse
Hårby
Nyborg
Løgumkloster
Næstved

Ålands hav
SWEDEN
BALTIC SEA
Vansbro
Dala-Floda 31
Borlänge
Hofors
Dalälven
Ulfshyttan 37
Säter
Hedemora
Tierp
Östhammar
Fredriksberg
Gimo 32
Grisslehamn 32
Tärnsjö
Hagfors
Ludvika
Smedjebacken
Avesta
Fagersta
Heby
Sala
Uppsala
Hällefors
Ramnäs
Rimbo
Norrtälje
Kapellskär
Grythyttan 32
Västerås
Enköping
Lindesberg
Bålsta 30
Täby
Åkersberga
Nora
Köping
Mälaren
Sollentuna
Vaxholm
Karlskoga
Arboga
Strängnäs 36
Värmdö 37
Örebro
Eskilstuna 30
STOCKHOLM 34-36
Degerfors
Hjälmaren
Mariefred 33
Tumba
Saltsjöbaden 34
Södertälje
Svartå 35
Hallsberg
Flen 31
Gnesta 31
Västerhaninge
Skagern
Laxå
Katrineholm
Askersund
Nynäshamn
Trosa 37
Töreboda
Jönåker 33
Nyköping
Aspa Bruk 30
Finspång
Oxelösund
Norrköping
Karlsborg
Motala
Mauritzberg 37
Tibro
Roxen
Vadstena 37
Söderköping 34
Hjo
Linköping
Vättern
Mjölby
Tidaholm
Ödeshög
Åtvidaberg
Valdemarsvik
Gränna
Tranås
Sommen
Kisa
Hestra 32
Gamleby
Fårö
Fårösund
Lekeryd 33
Slite
Eksjö 30
Västervik
Visby 37
Nässjö
Vimmerby
Hok 32
Gotland
Hultsfred
Vetlanda
Klintehamn
Ljugarn
Kristdala
Virserum
Byxelkrok
Smålandsstenar
Oskarshamn
Hemse
Lammhult
Högsby
Mönsterås
Lenhovda
Burgsvik
Alvesta
Växjö
Borgholm 30
Gemla
Lessebo
Nybro
Kalmar 33
Öland
Emmaboda
Älmhult
Mörbylånga
Tingsryd
Osby
Söderåkra 34
Olofström
Karlshamn
Karlskrona
Ronneby
Sölvesborg
Kristianstad
Åhus 30
Simrishamn
Tommarp 36
KEY
100 Hotel location and page reference
International airport
Motorway
Major road
0 kilometres 50
0 miles 50

Arild

Rusthållargården This 17th-century inn, set in a little fishing hamlet, enjoys stunning sea views. Inside is a tasteful mixture of modern and old-style elegance; rooms are luxurious, and some have balconies. Recent awards include Best Countryside Hotel, and a place in Sweden's Best Table. Gorgeous sauna suite, jet-stream Jacuzzi.
SE-260 43 Arild. **Map** p28 C5. (042) 34 65 30. FAX (042) 34 67 93. receptionen@rusthallargarden.se b,l,d. **Rooms** 63. Christmas and New Year. AE, DC, MC, V. ⓀⓀⓀ

Bålsta

Krägga Herrgård Beauty is the keynote of this stylish manor house, filled to the brim with fresh flowers and lovely antiques. In the dining room, seasonal dishes echo the surroundings – each plate is a little masterpiece. Total seclusion, deep in the forest at the lake's edge, yet only 40 minutes' drive from Stockholm and the airport.
SE-746 93 Bålsta. **Map** p29 F2. (0171) 532 80. FAX (0171) 532 65. info@kragga.se b,l,d. **Rooms** 50. Never. AE, DC, MC, V. ⓀⓀⓀⓀ

Aspa Bruk

Aspa Herrgård A casual elegance pervades this unique and exquisitely lovely little manor, which stands in tranquil parkland by Lake Vättern. In the wings of the house, rooms open off cosy lounges. Superb cuisine and fine wines are Aspa's pride, as is attention to every detail for the comfort of its guests.
SE-696 93 Aspa Bruk. **Map** p29 D2. (0583) 502 10. FAX (0583) 501 50. aspa@edbergs.com. b,l,d. **Rooms** 39. Never. AE, DC, MC, V. ⓀⓀⓀⓀ

Borgholm, Öland

Halltorps Gästgiveri A unique country inn. Each bedroom is designed and decorated by craftsmen from the province it represents and has exquisite hand-made furniture. Enjoy walks by the sea or in the nature reserve. Return to cosy lounges, open fires and local speciality dishes in one of Sweden's finest restaurants.
SE-387 92 Borgholm, Öland. **Map** p29 E4. (0485) 85 000. FAX (0485) 85 001. info@halltorpsgastgiveri.se b,l,d. **Rooms** 41. Never. AE, DC, V. ⓀⓀⓀ

Åhus

Åhus Gestgivaregård The fine food served at this rustic canalside inn goes a long way towards making up for the slight tattiness.
Gamla Skeppsbron 1, SE-296 21 Åhus. **Map** p29 D5. (044) 28 9050. FAX (044) 28 9250. lasse@ahusgastis.com b,l,d. **Rooms** 17. ⓀⓀⓀ

Bräcke

Björknäsgårdens Quaint hotel in northerly region, rich in history of the old timber trade, 5km (3 miles) from the little town of Bräcke.
Box 188, SE-840 60 Bräcke. **Map** p28 A3. (0693) 160 20. FAX (0693) 160 80. bjorknasgardens@telia.com b,l,d. **Rooms** 27. Ⓚ

Eksjö

Romantik Hotel Ullinge Traditional style and pretty, with a main building surrounded by cabins. In a forest, on a lake with its own jetty.
SE-575 96, Eksjö. **Map** p29 D3. (0381) 810 60. FAX (0381) 810 50. info@ ullinge.se b,l,d. **Rooms** 34. ⓀⓀ

Eskilstuna

Sundbyholms Slott Old castle with view over the marina. Baronial dining room, picnics by the lake, barbecues; sauna on an island.
SE-635 08 Eskilstuna. **Map** p29 E2. (016) 965 00. FAX (016) 965 78. hotel.conference@sundbyholms-slott.se b,l,d. **Rooms** 99. ⓀⓀⓀ

Dala-Floda

Värdshuset i Dala-Floda This wonderful inn has the air of a Provence farmhouse. It boasts its own painting and dance studios while its corners are stuffed full of traditional arts and crafts, and English literature. The owners, who've travelled the world, prepare traditional ethnic dishes with organic local produce – try Cuban elk.
Badvägen 6, SE-780 44 Dala-Floda. **Map** p29 D1.
(0241) 220 50. FAX (0241) 220 38.
@ info@dala-floda.net b,l,d. **Rooms** 17.
Jan to Mar. DC, MC, V. Kr.Kr

Flen

Yxtaholm This sumptuous manor stands on a strip of land between two lakes. Patrick Arneke has built his reputation on the quality and simplicity of his restaurant. Relax in one of the two elegant salons with a vintage Calvados from his extensive collection, or a refreshing cider, another of the Yxtaholm's specialities.
SE-6642 91 Flen. **Map** p29 E2. (0157) 244 40.
FAX (0157) 244 41. @ info@yxtaholmsslott.se b,l,d.
Rooms 43. Christmas and New Year.
AE, DC, MC, V. KrKrKr

Fjällbacka

Stora Hotellet Recently renovated, Stora Hotellet pays homage to the seafarers of the past – particularly Captain Klassen, the hotel's patron saint. This idyllic setting was a favourite of Swedish actress Ingrid Bergman. The bedrooms, with names such as Mombasa, Sheba and Columbus, have an international flavour.
Galärbacken SE-450 71 Fjällbacka **Map** p28 B2.
(0525) 31003. FAX (0525) 31093.
@ rec@storahotellet-fjallbacka.se b,l,d. **Rooms** 23.
Never. AE, DC, MC, V. KrKrKr

Fryksås

Fryksås Hotell och Gestgifveri This unspoilt mountain inn sits near the small town of Orsa, on the edge of true wilderness with commanding views over forest and sea. Brown bear, wolves, lynx and elk may all be spotted on arranged treks. Seasonal game, fish and berries feature heavily on the fine menu. Outdoor hot tub.
Fryksås Fäbod, SE-794 98 Orsa. **Map** p28 A3.
(0250) 460 00. FAX (0250) 460 90.
@ fryksas.hotell@orsa.mail.utfors.se b,l,d.
Rooms 12. Never. AE, DC, MC, V. KrKr

Filipstad

Hennickehammars Herrgård Manor house jointly owned by two families, with beautiful grounds and excellent food.
Box 52, SE-682 22 Filipstad. **Map** p29 D1.
(0590) 60 85 00. FAX (0590) 60 85 05.
@ hotel@hennickehammar.se b,l,d. **Rooms** 54. KrKr

Genarp

Häckeberga Slott An historic castle with a stupendous setting. Packages include a gourmet dinner.
SE-240 13 Genarp. **Map** p28 C5. (040) 48 04 40.
FAX (040) 48 04 02. @ info@hackebergaslott.se
b,l (in winter),d. **Rooms** 19. KrKrKrKr

Gnesta

Södertuna Slott Eighteenth-century castle in idyllic lakeside setting. Gorgeous public rooms, afternoon teas and country pursuits.
SE-646 91 Gnesta. **Map** p29 F2. (0158) 705 00.
FAX (0158) 705 40. @ info@sodertuna.se b,l,d.
Rooms 70. KrKrKrKr

Göteborg

Rederiaktiebolaget Göta Kanal Sail right across Sweden on one of three charming old steamships. The oldest boat, *MS Juno*, dates from 1874.
Tusterviksgatam 13, Box 272, SE-401 24 Göteborg.
Map p28 C3. (031) 80 63 15. FAX (031) 15 83 11.
@ bookings@ gotakanal.se b,l,d. **Rooms** 28. KrKrKrKr

Gimo

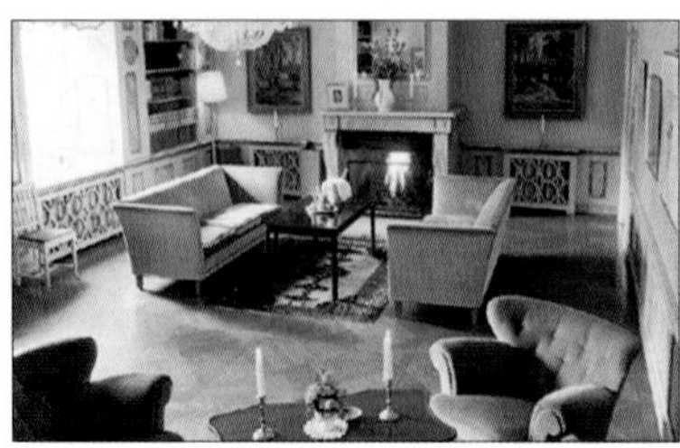

Gimo Herrgård A grand hotel occupying an 18th-century manor house set in the forests of Northern Roslagen, north of Stockholm. On or close to the premises, enjoy golf, clay-pigeon shooting, wine-tastings, sauna, rowing, canoeing, cycling and walking – and after all that activity, just luxuriate in the first-class restaurant.
SE 747 02 Gimo. **Map** p29 F1. (0173) 889 00. FAX (0173) 408 38. @ info@gimoherrgard.se. b,l,d. **Rooms** 67. 24 to 27 Dec. AE, DC, MC, V. ⓀⓀⓀ

Grisslehamn

Havsbaden This old spa hotel in a fishing village, lovingly restored, offers a very warm welcome. Seasonal local food, such as smoked eel, is a speciality. The sea views, space, and tasteful rooms are a delight. Explore nature, take a ferry to the islands, or enjoy a fishing trip.
SE-760 45 Grisslehamn. **Map** p29 F1. (0175) 309 30. FAX (0175) 330 14. @ info@hotell-havsbaden.se. b,l,d. **Rooms** 50. Christmas; some Suns Nov-Jan. AE, DC, MC, V. ⓀⓀ

Göteborg

Eggers One of Sweden's oldest hotels, the Eggers still evokes a bygone elegance and remains the stylish place to stay in Göteborg. Superb old double glazing maintains peace in the spacious rooms, just a stone's throw from the train, tram and bus stations.
Drottningtorget, Box 323, SE-401 25 Göteborg. **Map** p28 C3. (031) 80 60 70. FAX (031) 15 42 43. @ hotel.eggers@telia.com b,l,d. **Rooms** 67. Christmas. AE, DC, MC, V. ⓀⓀⓀⓀ

Grythyttan

Grythyttans Gästgivaregård It's one of the most atmospheric old inns in all of Sweden – almost like a little village all by itself, with rooms in several separate buildings and many old salons and cosy parlours. The former dungeon now houses more than 450 fine wines to complement the international gourmet menu.
Prästgatan 2, SE-712 81 Grythyttan. **Map** p29 D1. (0591) 147 00. FAX (0591) 141 24. @ info@grythyttan.com. b,l,d. **Rooms** 69. Never. AE, DC, MC, V. ⓀⓀⓀⓀ

Grythyttan

Loka Brunn This luxurious 18th-century royal spa is like a little village in the forest, offering total pampering. Museum on spa history.
SE-712 94 Grythyttan. **Map** p29 D1. (0591) 631 00. FAX (0591) 300 00. @ loka.brunn@swipnet.se b,l,d. **Rooms** 167. ⓀⓀⓀⓀ

Hestra

Hestravikens Wärdshus Country lodge with excellent food. Some rooms have river views and verandas. Pool.
Vik, SE-330 27 Hestra. **Map** p29 D3. (0370) 33 68 00. FAX (0370) 33 62 90. @ info@hestraviken.se b,l,d. **Rooms** 40. ⓀⓀⓀ

Hjärnarp

Margretetorps Gästgifvaregård Smart, stylish inn with tasteful rooms off tranquil courtyard with water garden. Noted for its Smörgåsbord.
SE-266 98 Hjärnarp. **Map** p28 C4. (0431) 45 44 50. FAX (0431) 45 48 77. @ info@margretetorp.se b,l,d. **Rooms** 60. ⓀⓀⓀⓀ

Hok

Hooks Herrgård Elegant golf and leisure hotel in a manor house where the salons all look out onto the lake. Excellent food.
SE-560 13 Hok. **Map** p29 D3. (0393) 210 80. FAX (0393) 215 67. @ hook.herrgard @edberg.com b,l,d. **Rooms** 103. ⓀⓀⓀⓀ

Jönåker

Wreta Gestgifveri Cancel all other plans in order to visit this delightful little pearl, in a hamlet near Nyköping. You are welcomed into the home of someone who understands the meaning of beauty and comfort. No detail is neglected. Delight in Vivaldi on the CD in your room before drinks and a dinner that lives up to the surroundings.
⊠ Wreta Gård H, SE-610 50 Jönåker. **Map** p29 E2.
(0155) 720 22. FAX (0155) 720 32.
@ wreta@wreta.com b,l,d. **Rooms** 21.
Never. AE, MC, V. Ⓚ Ⓚ Ⓚ Ⓚ

Mariefred

Gripsholms Värdshus and Hotel In the tranquil old town of Mariefred, enjoy unashamed luxury and informal hospitality at this divine old inn. Exquisite food, and wine tastings in the old monastery below. In summer, old steam trains and boats from Stockholm stop here; at Christmas there are log fires and skating on the lake.
⊠ Kyrkogatan 1, Box 114, SE-647 23 Mariefred. **Map** p29 E2. (0159) 347 50. FAX (0159) 347 77.
@ info@gripsholms-vardshus.se b,l,d. **Rooms** 45.
part of Jan. AE, DC, MC, V. Ⓚ Ⓚ Ⓚ Ⓚ

Lilla Edet

Thorskogs Slott This gorgeous old castle offers a totally homely welcome. Numerous heads of state have enjoyed its exquisite Gustavian salons and dishes from its famous kitchen. After drinks in the flower room, step out onto the terrace for a barbecue, then enjoy boules on the lawn. One of the best breakfasts in Sweden is served here.
⊠ SE-463 93, Västerlanda. **Map** p28 C3.
(0520) 66 10 00. FAX (0520) 66 09 18.
@ info@thorskogsslott.se b,l,d. **Rooms** 36.
July. AE, DC, MC, V. Ⓚ Ⓚ Ⓚ

Marstrand

Grand Hotell Marstrand Less than an hour from Göteborg, leave your car behind and take the ferry to this timeless island. The porter collects you on the quay. Sumptuous rooms, some with balconies looking onto the bandstand and harbour beyond. Eat delicious seafood in the popular veranda restaurant. Enchanting.
⊠ Rådhusgatan 2, SE-440 30 Marstrand. **Map** p28 B3.
(0303) 603 22. FAX (0303) 600 53.
@ info@grandmarstrand.se b,d. **Rooms** 22.
Christmas and New Year. AE, DC, MC, V. Ⓚ Ⓚ Ⓚ Ⓚ

Järvsö

Järvsöbaden A very personal welcome in a charming family-run hotel with lovely gardens. Good, traditional food; nine-hole golf course.
⊠ Box 43, SE-820 40 Järvsö. **Map** p28 A3.
(0651) 404 00. FAX (0651) 414 37.
@ infor@jarvsobaden.se b,l,d. **Rooms** 44. Ⓚ Ⓚ

Kalmar

Slottshotellet A 19th-century seaman's house offering old world charm in historic town with castle. Personal service and good food.
⊠ Slottsvägen 7, SE-392 33 Kalmar. **Map** p29 E4.
(0480) 882 60. FAX (0480) 882 66. @ info@slottshotellet.se b,d (in summer). **Rooms** 44. Ⓚ Ⓚ Ⓚ

Lagan

Toftaholm Herrgård A warm welcome awaits in this pretty, 600-year-old family-run manor house with lake views, sauna and Jacuzzi.
⊠ Toftaholm, SE-340 14 Lagan. **Map** p29 D4.
(0370) 440 55. FAX (0370) 440 45. @ frontoffice@toftaholmherrgard.com b,l,d. **Rooms** 45. Ⓚ Ⓚ Ⓚ

Lekeryd

Sunds Herrgård An idyllic country retreat in the heart of the beautiful lakeland scenery of Småland, with its own wildlife park.
⊠ SE 560 28 Lekeryd. **Map** p29 D3. (036) 820 06. FAX (036) 821 40. @ info@sundsherrgard.se b,l,d. **Rooms** 60. Ⓚ Ⓚ Ⓚ

For key to symbols see backflap. For price categories *see p27*

Mölle

Kullaberg This Neo-Renaissance early 1900s building offers a sojourn in a gracious era long gone. The exquisite dining room affords panoramic views of the harbour. Some rooms have balconies with similar views. There has been a recent change of management at the hotel.
Gyllenstiernas allé 16. Box 43, SE-260 42 Mölle. **Map** p28 C5. (042) 34 70 00. FAX (042) 34 71 00. @ info@hotelkullaberg.se b,l,d. **Rooms** 32. Never. AE, DC, MC, V. (Kr)(Kr)(Kr)(Kr)

Simrishamn

Karlaby Kro A haven of calm, close to fishing villages and sandy beaches. Artists flock here for the special light. At this tastefully renovated farmhouse, hunters, mushroom pickers and fishermen come knocking on the door, ensuring that the six-course, award-winning gourmet dinner is never the same twice.
SE-272 93 Simrishamn. **Map** p29 D5. (0414) 203 00. FAX (0414) 204 73. @ receptionen@karlabykro.se b,l,d. **Rooms** 22. Christmas. AE, DC, MC, V. (Kr)(Kr)(Kr)

Saltsjöbaden, Stockholm

Grand Hotel Saltsjöbaden This stylish hotel on the edge of the Baltic Sea bathes in 19th-century tranquillity. Original bathing houses still stand on the private island, and a little train built to serve the hotel still does. The piano bar and elegant French dining room have views of the sunset over the marina.
SE-133 83 Saltsjöbaden, Stockholm. **Map** p29 F2. (08) 506 170 00. FAX (08) 506 170 25. @ reservations@grandsaltsjobaden.se b,l,d. **Rooms** 104. Never. AE, DC, MC, V. (Kr)(Kr)(Kr)

Söderåkra

Stufvenäs Gästgifveri Food and drink are specialities at this family-run inn, beautifully furnished with a homely mix of antique and modern design. Superb dishes are complemented by wines from the extensive, award-winning collection. For a special treat, ask to have your coffee in the lounge-like wine cellar.
PL 7488, SE-385 97 Söderåkra. **Map** p29 E5. (0486) 219 00. FAX (0486) 218 68. @ info@stufvenas.se b,l,d. **Rooms** 55. Never. AE, MC, V. (Kr)(Kr)(Kr)

Söderköping

Söderköpings Brunn Old spa hotel, with all mod-cons; outdoor pool.
Skönbergagatan 35, Box 44 SE-614 21, Söderköping. **Map** p29 E3. (0121) 109 00. FAX (0121) 139 41. @ soderkopingsbrunn@ameca.se b,l,d. **Rooms** 103. (Kr)(Kr)(Kr)(Kr)

Stockholm

Clas På Hörnet Old-world style in the heart of the city. Busy dining room, quiet terrace. Recent new management.
Surbrunnsgatan 20, SE-113 48 Stockholm. **Map** p29 F2. (08) 16 51 30. FAX (08) 612 53 15. @ clas.pa.hornet@ telia.com b,l,d. **Rooms** 10. (Kr)(Kr)(Kr)(Kr)

Stockholm

Esplanade Faithfully preserved, this Art Nouveau haven of peace is set back off the main street in a quiet courtyard.
Strandvägen 7A, SE-114 56 Stockholm. **Map** p29 F2. (08) 663 07 40. FAX (08) 662 59 92. @ hotel@hotelesplanade.se b. **Rooms** 34. (Kr)(Kr)(Kr)(Kr)

Stockholm

Lady Hamilton Just a few steps from the royal palace in Stockholm's old town, a friendly atmosphere, and many fine antiques.
Storkyrkobrinken 5, SE-111 28 Stockholm. **Map** p29 F2. (08) 506 401 00. FAX (08) 506 401 10. @ info@lady-hamilton.se b,l,d. **Rooms**, 34. (Kr)(Kr)(Kr)(Kr)

STOCKHOLM

Hotel Diplomat This long-established family-run hotel sits on Stockholm's most fashionable street, Strandvägen, overlooking an inlet of the Baltic Sea. Inside is all old-style elegance, with tasteful bedrooms and a pleasant streetfront restaurant. International cruise ships dock here and boat trips are available.
⊠ Strandvägen 7C, SE-104 40, Stockholm. **Map** p29 F2. (08) 459 68 00. FAX (08) 459 68 21. @ reservations.sto @diplomathotel.se b,l,d. **Rooms** 128. Christmas. AE, DC, MC, V. ⓀⓀⓀⓀ

STOCKHOLM

Villa Källhagen It's a delight to discover this exceptionally tasteful modern hotel, only a few minutes' drive from the city centre in a quiet waterside setting. Its large rooms are very light and airy, and the dining terrace is a pleasant place to enjoy the delicious food, prepared by one of Sweden's top chefs.
⊠ Djurgårdsbrunnsvägen 10, SE-11527 Stockholm. **Map** p29 F2. (08) 665 03 00. FAX (08) 665 03 99. @ villa@kallhagen.se b,l,d. **Rooms** 20. Never. AE, DC, MC, V. ⓀⓀⓀⓀ

STOCKHOLM

Victory Hotel It's almost like a nautical museum: each sumptuous room is named after a Swedish captain and contains his portrait and model ship. This old-town townhouse is the jewel in the crown of a trio of hotels (with the Lady Hamilton and Lord Nelson, see below). Its Leijontornet Restaurant is one of Stockholm's finest.
⊠ Lilla Nygatan 5, Gamla Stan, SE-111 28 Stockholm. **Map** p29 F2. (08) 506 400 00. FAX (08) 506 400 10. @ info@victory-hotel.se b,l,d. **Rooms** 45. Christmas and New Year. AE, DC, MC, V. ⓀⓀⓀⓀ

SUNNE

Länsmansgården You'll feel at home in minutes in this exceptionally pretty country house, home to the same family since 1914. The comfy parlours are full of family heirlooms, and stories of the house's history abound. It has its own little beach with boats, and is close to both cross-country and downhill skiing. Wonderful regional cooking.
⊠ SE-686 93 Sunne. **Map** p28 C1. (0565) 140 10. FAX (0565) 71 18 05. @ info@lansman.com b,l,d. **Rooms** 30. Never. AE, DC, MC, V. ⓀⓀ

STOCKHOLM

Långholmen On an island, close to the city, enjoy a cell in this delightfully converted prison. A museum explains its history.
⊠ Långholmsmuren 20, Box 9116, SE-102 72 Stockholm. **Map** p29 F2. (08) 720 85 00. FAX (08) 720 85 75. @ hotell@langholmen.com b,l,d. **Rooms** 112. ⓀⓀⓀ

STOCKHOLM

Lord Nelson In Stockholm's old town, a narrow, nautical theme hotel, built like a ship. Small 'cabins' on the upper decks.
⊠ Västerlånggatan 22, SE-111 29 Stockholm. **Map** p29 F2. (08) 506 401 20. FAX (08) 506 401 30. @ hotel@lord-nelson.se b. **Rooms** 31. ⓀⓀⓀⓀ

STOCKHOLM

Lydmar This hotel is also a popular music and arts venue. Stylish bedrooms, lively bars.
⊠ Sturegatan 10, SE-114 36 Stockholm. **Map** p29 F2. (08) 566 113 00. FAX (08) 566 113 01. @ info@lydmar.se b,l,d. **Rooms** 62. ⓀⓀⓀⓀ

STOCKHOLM

Mälardrottningen Anchored in the heart of the city, Barbara Hutton's large yacht offers affordable luxury. Book well ahead.
⊠ Riddarholmen SE-111 28 Stockholm. **Map** p29 F2. (08) 545 187 80. FAX (08) 24 36 76. @ reception@ malardrottningen.se b,l,d. **Rooms** 60. ⓀⓀⓀ

For key to symbols see backflap. For price categories *see p27*

Svartå

Svartå Herrgård This little manor house, run by the same family since 1946, is midway between Stockholm and Göteborg, right on a lake. In summer, the gardens are filled with fragrance and birdsong, and lake pursuits, picnics and country sports are arranged; log fires and skating in winter. Exquisite rooms, many with lake views.
SE-693 93 Svartå. **Map** p29 D2. (0585) 500 03. FAX (0585) 503 03. @ svarta.herrgard@swipnet.se
b,l,d. **Rooms** 37. early Jan; Sun eves. AE, DC, MC, V. Kr

Tällberg

Klockargården A unique experience of local culture and tradition are offered here. A handicraft shop in 1937, it has now grown into a little village of crafts studios, and 'living museums' where you can try your hand at baking local breads or smithying. Pretty rooms are dotted throughout the buildings. Music and theatre.
Siljansvägen 6, SE-793 70 Tällberg. **Map** p28 A3. (0247) 502 60. FAX (0247) 502 16.
@ hotell@klockargarden.com b,l,d. **Rooms** 40.
Never. AE, MC, V. KrKrKr

Tällberg

Åkerblads Romantik Hotell More than 20 generations of Åkerblads have run this much-loved property. Quality and an excellent restaurant combine here with real family hospitality. There is a log cabin in the grounds, and freshly baked bread is always served. The uniquely gorgeous pool is enclosed by hand-painted family 'cottages'.
Sjögattu 2, SE-793 70 Tällberg. **Map** p28 A3. (0247) 508 00. FAX (0247) 506 52.
@ info@akerblads-tallberg.se b,l,d. **Rooms** 67.
Never. DC, MC, V. KrKrKr.

Torekov

Kattegatt Gastronomi & Logi The reputation of this 100-year-old restaurant with rooms could not get much higher – it was voted one of Sweden's best in 1998. Watch chefs at work in the open-plan kitchen behind the bar. Rooms are modern, with bright Italian colours. Walk by the sea, play golf, or visit the old spa Bathhouse close by.
Storgatan 46, SE-260 93 Torekov. **Map** p28 C4. (0431) 36 30 02. FAX (0431) 36 30 03.
@ kattegat@rikardnilsson.com b,l,d. **Rooms** 11.
Sept to May. AE, DC. MC, V. KrKrKrKr

Stockholm

Tre Små Rum A tiny hotel in an arty suburb, very sociable, ecologically conscious and excellent value for money. A home-from-home.
Högbergsgatan 81, SE-118 54 Stockholm. **Map** p29 F2. (08) 641 2371. FAX (08) 642 8808.
@ info@tresmarum.se **Rooms** 7. b. Kr

Strängnäs

Ulvhälls Herrgård Gourmet food in a 17th-century manor looking out onto Lake Mälaren, run by the same family since 1947.
Ulvhälls Herrgård SE-645 40 Strängnäs. **Map** p29 E2. (0152) 186 80. FAX (0152) 177 97. @ info@ulvhall.se
Rooms 42. b,l,d. KrKr

Tällberg

Tällbergsgården The only hotel here with panoramic views over Siljan Lake. Steeped in family history, cosy and friendly.
Holgattu 1, SE-793 70 Tällberg. **Map** p28 A3. (0247) 508 50. FAX (0247) 502 00.
@ info@tallbergsgarden.se b,d. **Rooms** 38. Kr

Tänndalen

Hotell Tänndalen This family-run alpine hotel is popular winter and summer alike. Ideal for nature treks, cross-country and alpine skiing.
SE-840 98 Tänndalen. **Map** p28 A2. (0684) 220 20. FAX (0684) 224 24. @ hotel.tanndalen@tanndalen.se
Rooms 65. b,d. KrKrKr

TROSA

Bomans Absolutely no detail is overlooked in this picture-perfect old house right by the River Trosa. The product of years of care lavished by the Bomans, it is filled with family antiques, mementoes, hand-made furniture and flowers. The small rooms are exquisite, each decorated by the family. Glorious home cooking.
Östra Hamnplan, SE-61930 Trosa. **Map** p29 F2.
(0156) 525 00. FAX (0156) 525 10. @ info@bomans.se
b,l,d. **Rooms** 33. 21 Dec–8 Jan.
AE, DC, MC, V. ⓀⓀⓀ

VEMDALEN

Storhogna Högfjällshotell In the heart of the mountains, Storhogna is unique, combining the action of a winter ski resort with the luxury of a top-class spa. There is ice fishing, climbing and dog sledging in winter; bear and elk safaris in summer. Relax with sauna and massage treatments. The restaurant uses the best local ingredients.
Box 43, SE-840 92 Vemdalen. **Map** p28 A3.
(0682) 23060. FAX (0682) 413042.
@ info@storhogna.com b,l,d. **Rooms** 55.
Never. AE, DC, MC, V. ⓀⓀⓀⓀ

VADSTENA

Vadstena Klosterhotell Recordings of monks singing plainchant welcome you into this atmospheric former monastery, now a protected building. The thick walls shelter cool, quiet rooms. Breakfast is served in an old workroom, under gothic arches. In summer, plays by Shakespeare are performed in the courtyard.
Klosterområdet, SE-592 24 Vadstena. **Map** p29 D3.
(0143) 315 30. FAX (0143) 136 48.
@ hotell@klosterhotel.se b,l,d. **Rooms** 29.
Christmas. AE, DC, MC, V. ⓀⓀⓀ

VISBY, GOTLAND

Toftagården A four-and-a-half-hour ferry trip from Oskarshamn brings you to the enchanting Baltic island of Gotland, a paradise for nature lovers. Toftagården stands in its own wooded park, near a sandy beach. The superb restaurant is famous for the island's lamb and salmon. Very cosy, friendly service and relaxed atmosphere.
Tofta, SE-621 98 Visby. **Map** p29 F3.
(0498) 29 70 00. FAX (0498) 26 56 66.
@ info@toftagarden.se b,l,d. **Rooms** 70.
Christmas. AE, DC, MC, V. ⓀⓀⓀ

TROSA

Romantik Trosa Stadshotell This lovely old inn is run by a Swiss owner, who has a talent for making guests welcome. Exellent cooking.
Västra Långgatan 19, Box 18, SE-619 00 Trosa. **Map** p29 F2. (0156) 170 70. FAX (0156) 166 96.
@ info@trosastadshotell.se b,l,d. **Rooms** 44. ⓀⓀⓀ

ULFSHYTTAN

Ulfshyttans Herrgård A tiny road leads to this lakeside country house (Borlänge 25km/19 miles). Old-style comfort, home cooking.
SE-781 96 Borlänge. **Map** p29 D1. (0243) 25 13 00. FAX (0243) 25 11 11. @ info@ulfshyttan.se b,l,d. **Rooms** 20. ⓀⓀ

VÄRMDÖ

FågelbroHus Country club style in the Stockholm archipelago 30 minutes' drive from the city, with parkland, golf course and tennis.
FågelbroHus AB, SE-139 60 Värmdö. **Map** p29 F2.
(08) 571 419 00. FAX (08) 571 419 99.
@ info@fagelbrohus.se b,l,d. **Rooms** 72. ⓀⓀⓀ

VIKBOLANDET

Mauritzbergs Slott Most rooms have sea views at this clifftop 16th-century castle. Norrköping international airport 25km (20 miles) away.
SE-610 31 Vikbolandet. **Map** p29 E3. (0125) 501 00. FAX (0125) 501 04. @ service@mauritzberg.se
b,l,d. **Rooms** 16. ⓀⓀⓀⓀ

DENMARK

DENMARK

ACCOMMODATION IN Denmark, like most things Danish, is usually high quality, spotlessly clean and well run, albeit at a price. Perhaps Denmark's most characterful form of accommodation is the *kro*, the historic stage-coach inn. Located on main roads (don't worry – Danish traffic is light), the *kro* is ideal for touring the country and it offers value for money. Leaving aside the lights of Copenhagen and other large cities, Denmark remains essentially a rural country. Farmhouse holidays are enduringly popular, and economical. Staying on a farm for a few days as well as in a hotel or inn could make a happy combination.

The elegant retreat of Steensgaard Herregård, Millinge, page 48

DENMARK REGION BY REGION

WE DIVIDE Denmark into three main areas:

Jutland (Jylland)
The bridge between Scandinavia and Europe, this unhurried rural peninsula makes up Denmark's biggest land mass. It is the most attractive part of the country, dotted with lakes, and with a coast lined by windswept dunes. East Jutland is home to Aarhus, Denmark's second largest city and cultural capital, while southeast Jutland has Legoland. The former has a useful choice of hotel accommodation while Legoland offers a clutch of child-friendly hotels.

Farm accommodation is very popular throughout Jutland, and country cottages and summer houses for rent are particularly common in West Jutland.

Funen (Fyn)
The island-peninsula immediately east of Jutland is known as The Garden of Denmark because of its natural beauty, fruit and vegetable farms and its many flowery gardens. The seaside resorts in the south of Funen feature family holiday centres with a wide range of indoor and outdoor activities and high-quality accommodation. The main cultural draw is the attractive town of Odense, birthplace of the writer Hans Christian Andersen, which has a wide choice of hotels. Elsewhere in this area, accommodation is both simple and relatively cheap.

Many B&Bs have sprung up in recent years, and these are prominently sign-posted along the main roads and elsewhere.

Zealand (Sjaelland)
The larger island east of Funen and nudging Sweden, Zealand is dominated by the bustling city of Copenhagen and has a wide selection of accommodation; from tourist-board-approved private rooms and cheap hostels, to five-star hotels.

Out of town there is the Karen Blixen Museum, Helsingør (Hamlet's Elsinore) and the historic town of Roskilde – all worth a visit.

The island of Bornholm, the 'Jewel of the Baltic', a seven-hour ferry journey from Copenhagen, is a traditional fishing-and-farming settlement, popular for walking and cycling holidays. See our recommendations here on pages 44 and 50.

HIGHLIGHTS

THE PLACES to stay illustrated on these introductory pages are by no means Denmark's only highlights. In Copenhagen, the Admiral (page 48) stands out for having the best location in town, right on the harbour, and for the way it reflects its nautical past. Henne Kirkeby Kro at Henne (page 46) can rightly claim to have among the best food in Scandinavia. Store Kro at Fredensborg (page 45) is another favourite – it lives up to its grand setting next to the Danish Royal Family's summer residence. And we especially like the Hotel Dagmar at Ribe (page 49) for retaining, despite great popularity, its historic atmosphere.

Food and Drink

Traditional Danish fare comprises hearty helpings of meat (mostly pork, beef and veal) and fish from the Baltic Sea, North Sea and lakes. The quality is consistently high and so, often, are prices. One home-grown food which you probably will not see is Danish bacon – it is reserved for export.

In Copenhagen there are all manner of ethnic restaurants, many operating on the traditional Danish 'open table' policy: the whole party eats all it can for a fixed price.

At lunchtime, around midday to 2:30pm, look out for the *dagen's ret* (dish of the day). If you are on a tight budget this is the time to eat, as prices at dinner time for similar food in similar establishments are significantly higher.

The local fast food is hot sausages (*pølser*) dispensed by street vendors. The ubiquitous Danish pastry, called *wienerbrød,* (literally, Vienna bread) is standard café fare.

Unlike its Scandinavian neighbours, Denmark is very relaxed in its attitude to alcohol. The Danes are a nation of beer drinkers – Denmark is famous as the home of Carlsberg lager. Tuborg is the alternative. The Danish version of schnapps is *akvavit*. It comes in several forms, most often flavoured with dill or caraway, and is drunk as a chaser or (to the consternation of foreigners) to accompany a meal.

Denmark's best known culinary institution is *smørrebrød,* a selection of open rye sandwiches *(rugbrød)* and trimmings. This term is sometimes also extended to a complete buffet (*det store kolde bord*), including traditional fare such as salmon, crayfish, prawns, herring, hot and cold meats, cheeses and dessert.

Other Practical Information

Book well in advance if you are planning to visit Copenhagen or the popular seaside resorts in Funen during July and August. Note also that many hotels are taken over at weekends all year for local celebrations such as weddings.

Breakfast is usually a buffet of breads, cheeses, cold meats, fruit and cereals.

Petrol is very expensive by western European standards. Expect high charges for bridge tolls and ferries.

Language English and German are widely understood and most menus are also translated into these two languages.

Currency The Danish *krone,* written Kr, usually before the amount, and divided into 100 *øre*.

Shops Generally open from 9am–5:30pm Mon–Thu, 9am–7 or 8pm Fri, 9am–1 or 2pm Sat (9am–5pm first Sat of the month). Many supermarkets in larger towns open until 7 or 8pm Mon–Fri and some shops also open until 4 or 5pm on Saturdays. Some also open on Sundays.

Tipping This is not required or expected – restaurant bills always include a service charge.

Telephoning To telephone inside Denmark, dial the number, including the first zero of the area code. To call Denmark from the UK, dial 00 45, then the number, dropping the first zero of the area code; from the US, dial 011 45 and drop the first 0 of the area code.

Public holidays 1 January; Maundy Thursday; Good Friday; Easter Sunday; Easter Monday; Great Prayer Day (fourth Friday after Good Friday); Ascension Day (mid-May); Constitution Day (5 Jun); Whit Sunday; Whit Monday (late May); 24–26 December.

Useful Words

Breakfast	*Morgenmad*
Lunch	*Frokost*
Dinner	*Aftensmad*
Free room?	*Værelser?*
How much?	*Hvad koster det?*
Single room	*Enkelt værelse*
Double	*Dobbelt værelse*

Denmark Price Bands

Danish hotels are officially classified by stars, from one to five. A hotel without a restaurant, but with one to three stars, is called a *hotel garni*. Our price bands are simpler and refer, as usual, to the price of a standard double room in high season. Prices quoted usually include breakfast and sales tax. You may, however, encounter a small 'green tax' on your hotel bill in some places.

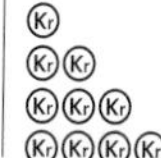

below 600Kr
600–900Kr
900–1400Kr
above 1400Kr

Bromølle Kro, Jyderup, page 46

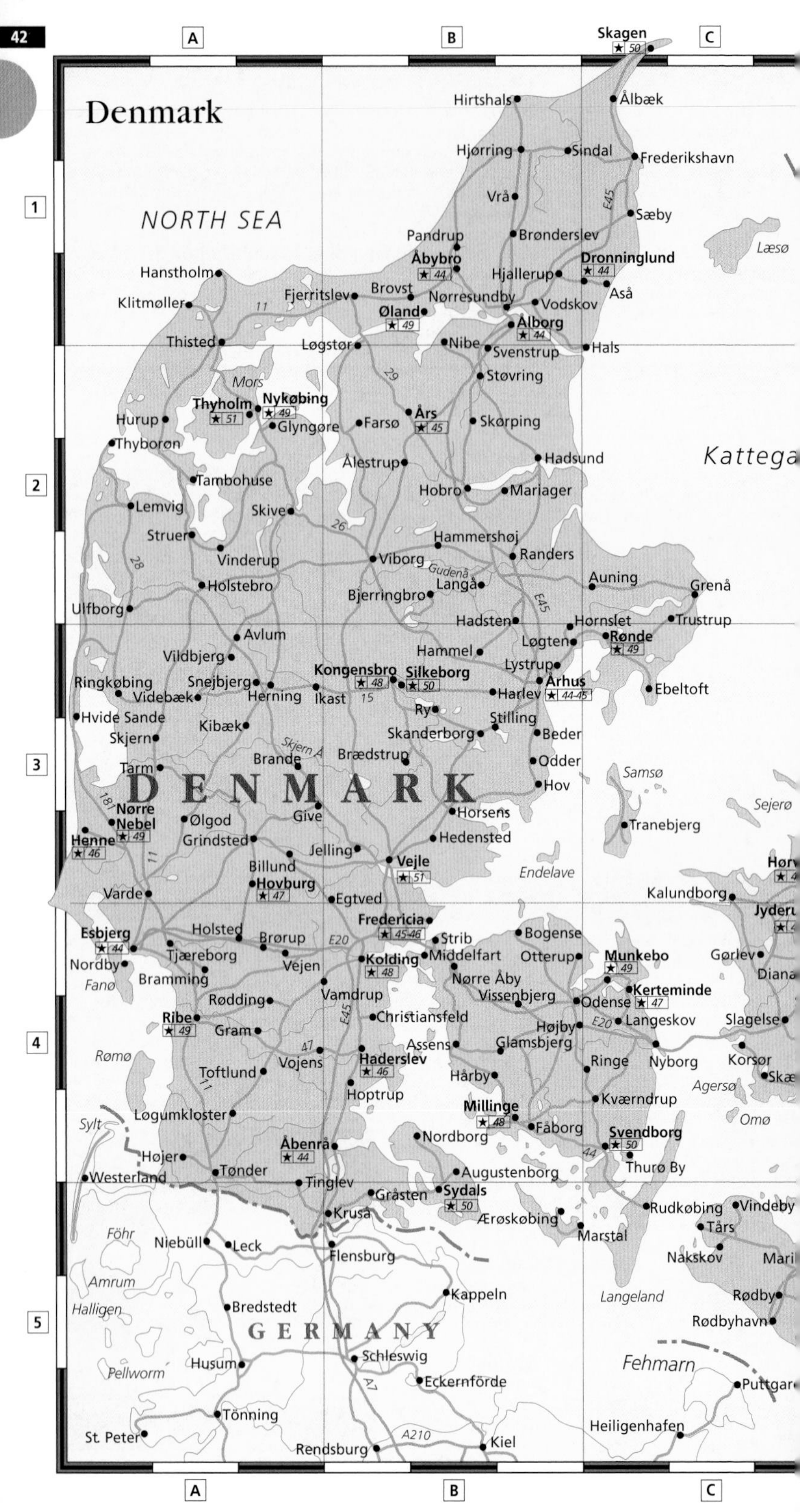
Denmark
A
B
C
1
2
3
4
5
Skagen
★ 50
Hirtshals
Ålbæk
Hjørring
Sindal
Frederikshavn
Vrå
E45
Sæby
NORTH SEA
Pandrup
Brønderslev
Læsø
Åbybro
★ 44
Dronninglund
★ 44
Hanstholm
Hjallerup
Aså
Brovst
Klitmøller
11
Fjerritslev
Nørresundby
Vodskov
Øland
★ 49
Ålborg
★ 44
Thisted
Løgstør
Nibe
Svenstrup
Hals
Mors
29
Støvring
Thyholm
★ 51
Nykøbing
★ 49
Hurup
Glyngøre
Farsø
Års
★ 45
Skørping
Thyborøn
Ålestrup
Hadsund
Kattega
Tambohuse
Hobro
Mariager
Lemvig
Skive
26
Struer
Hammershøj
Vinderup
Viborg
Randers
28
Gudenå
Holstebro
Langå
Auning
Grenå
Bjerringbro
E45
Ulfborg
Hadsten
Hornslet
Trustrup
Avlum
Rønde
★ 49
Hammel
Løgten
Vildbjerg
Lystrup
Kongensbro
★ 48
Silkeborg
★ 50
Ringkøbing
Snejbjerg
Århus
★ 44-45
Videbæk
Herning
Ikast
15
Harlev
Ebeltoft
Hvide Sande
Ry
Stilling
Kibæk
Skanderborg
Beder
Skjern
Skjern Å
Brande
Brædstrup
Odder
Tarm
Samsø
Hov
DENMARK
181
Nørre Nebel
★ 49
Give
Horsens
Sejerø
Ølgod
Tranebjerg
Henne
★ 46
Grindsted
Hedensted
11
Jelling
Billund
Vejle
★ 51
Endelave
Hørv
Hovburg
★ 47
Varde
Egtved
Kalundborg
Fredericia
★ 45-46
Jyderu
Holsted
Esbjerg
★ 44
Brørup
E20
Strib
Bogense
Tjæreborg
Middelfart
Otterup
Munkebo
★ 49
Gørlev
Nordby
Vejen
Kolding
★ 48
Diana
Fanø
Bramming
Nørre Åby
Vamdrup
Vissenbjerg
Kerteminde
★ 47
Rødding
Odense
Ribe
★ 49
E45
Christiansfeld
E20
Langeskov
Slagelse
Gram
Højby
Assens
Glamsbjerg
A7
Rømø
Vojens
Haderslev
★ 46
Nyborg
Korsør
Ringe
Toftlund
Hårby
Agersø
Skæ
11
Hoptrup
Kværndrup
Millinge
★ 48
Omø
Løgumkloster
Sylt
Fåborg
Nordborg
Svendborg
★ 50
Åbenrå
★ 44
Højer
44
Thurø By
Tønder
Augustenborg
Westerland
Tinglev
Gråsten
Sydals
★ 50
Rudkøbing
Vindeby
Ærøskøbing
Kruså
Tårs
Marstal
Föhr
Niebüll
Leck
Flensburg
Nakskov
Mari
Amrum
Kappeln
Langeland
Rødby
Halligen
Bredstedt
Rødbyhavn
GERMANY
Schleswig
Fehmarn
Husum
Pellworm
A7
Eckernförde
Puttgar
Tönning
Heiligenhafen
St. Peter
A210
Kiel
Rendsburg
A
B
C

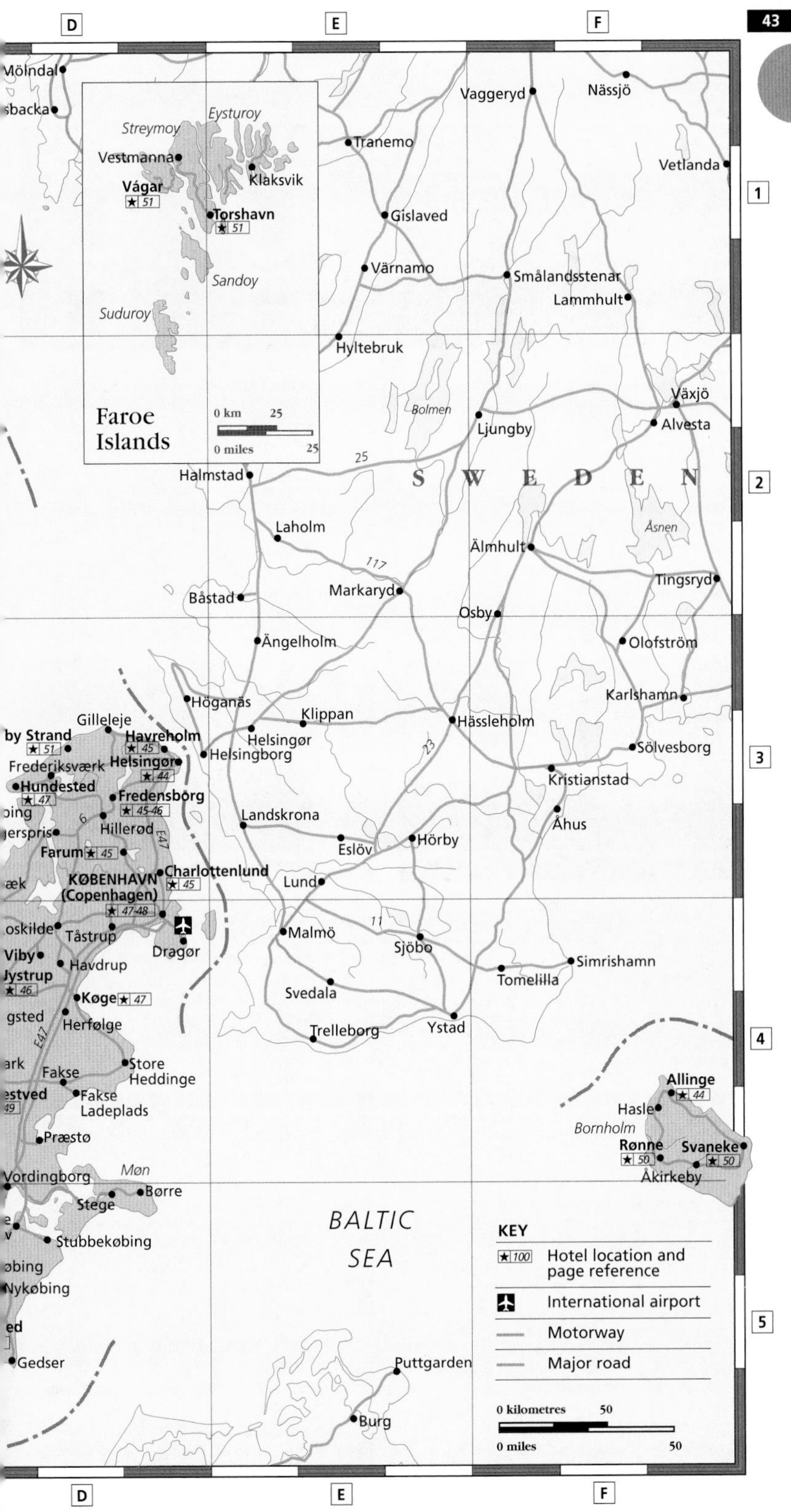
D
E
F
1
2
3
4
5
Mölndal
Vaggeryd
Nässjö
Tranemo
Vetlanda
Gislaved
Värnamo
Smålandsstenar
Lammhult
Hyltebruk
Växjö
Bolmen
Ljungby
Alvesta
25
Halmstad
SWEDEN
Åsnen
Laholm
Älmhult
117
Tingsryd
Båstad
Markaryd
Osby
Ängelholm
Olofström
Karlshamn
Höganäs
Klippan
Hässleholm
Gilleleje
Havreholm
★ 45
Helsingør
Helsingborg
23
Sölvesborg
Frederiksværk
Helsingør
★ 44
Kristianstad
Hundested
★ 47
Fredensborg
★ 45-46
Landskrona
Åhus
Hillerød
E47
Hörby
Farum
★ 45
Eslöv
Charlottenlund
★ 45
KØBENHAVN (Copenhagen)
★ 47-48
Lund
11
Tåstrup
Malmö
Sjöbo
Simrishamn
Viby
Dragør
Havdrup
Tomelilla
★ 46
Svedala
Køge
★ 47
Herfølge
Trelleborg
Ystad
E47
Store Heddinge
Allinge
★ 44
Fakse
Fakse Ladeplads
Hasle
Bornholm
Præstø
Rønne
★ 50
Svaneke
★ 50
Åkirkeby
Vordingborg
Møn
Børre
Stege
Stubbekøbing
Nykøbing
Gedser
Puttgarden
Burg
BALTIC SEA
Faroe Islands
Eysturoy
Streymoy
Vestmanna
Klaksvik
Vágar
★ 51
Torshavn
★ 51
Sandoy
Suduroy
0 km 25
0 miles 25
KEY
★ 100 Hotel location and page reference
International airport
Motorway
Major road
0 kilometres 50
0 miles 50

Ålborg

Helnan Phønix Since 1853 when Brigadier William von Haling's vast 18th-century residence was converted into a hotel, this has been the smart choice of accommodation in Ålborg, Denmark's fourth city. The heritage of this protected building is reflected within its grand dining halls and plush lounges.
☒ Vesterbro 77, 9000 Ålborg. **Map** p42 B1.
☎ 98 12 00 11. FAX 98 10 10 20.
@ hotel@helnan.dk b,l,d. **Rooms** 219.
● Never. AE, DC, MC, V. ⓀⓀⓀ

Dronninglund

Dronninglund Slot Dronninglund Palace has played an important role in Danish history over the past 800 years. Today, within the pristine whitewashed walls is a luxurious hotel and restaurant in harmony with its heritage. Rooms are exquisite, and are excellent value. The original palace gardens are open to hotel guests.
☒ Slotsgade 8, 9330 Dronninglund. **Map** p42 C1.
☎ 98 84 33 00. FAX 98 84 34 13. @ slot@dronninglund-slot.dk b,l,d. **Rooms** 23.
● Never. AE, DC, MC, V. ⓀⓀ

Århus

Hotel Royal The striking stained glass windows, huge tapestries, and modern art provide an uplifting introduction, and the stunning aquarium is an additional attraction at this sophisticated, busy city hotel. The individually appointed rooms are done out in soft hues and sport original artwork on the walls. One of Scandinavia's top casinos is located here.
☒ Store Torv 4, 8000 Århus. **Map** p42 B3. ☎ 86 12 00 11. FAX 86 76 04 04. @ royal@hotelroyal.dk b,l,d. **Rooms** 102. ● Never. AE, DC, MC, V. ⓀⓀⓀ

Esbjerg

Hotel Hjerting Located opposite one of Denmark's most popular beaches at Ho Bugt, this old seaside hotel operates to a particularly high standard. Rooms are modern and stylish, and the restaurant offers both excellent views and good-quality modern Danish cuisine. The hotel's English-style pub gets lively at weekends and throughout the summer.
☒ Strandpromenaden 1, 6710 Esbjerg. **Map** p42 A4.
☎ 75 11 70 00. FAX 75 11 76 77. @ hh@hotelhjerting.dk
b,l,d. **Rooms** 48. ● Never. AE, DC, MC, V. ⓀⓀⓀ

Åbenrå

Christie's Sdr Hostrup Kro Super-stylish stopover in the heart of rural South Jutland. Renowned cooking.
☒ Sdr Hostrup Østergade 21, 6200 Åbenrå. **Map** p42 B4.
☎ 74 61 34 46. FAX 74 61 30 67. @ christiessdrhostrupkro@get2net.dk b,l,d. **Rooms** 28. ⓀⓀⓀ

Åbenrå

Knapp Unusual and rather formal restaurant-hotel. A grand piano takes pride of place in the ballroom. Rooms are individually furnished.
☒ Stennevej 79, Stollig, 6200 Åbenrå.
Map p42 B4. ☎ 74 62 00 92. FAX 74 62 10 92.
@ knapp@stollej.dk b,l,d. **Rooms** 10. ⓀⓀ

Åbybro

Hotel Søparken Modern hotel. Luxurious indoor swimming pool. Smart restaurant. Good place for children. Well located for the Fårup Aquapark.
☒ Søparken 1, 9440 Åbybro. **Map** p42 B1.
☎ 98 24 45 77. FAX 98 24 46 76. @ info@soparken.dk
b,l,d. **Rooms** 50. ⓀⓀ

Allinge, Bornholm

Strandhotellet Cosy, good-value inn with modern rooms. Beachside recreation area with indoor swimming pool and tennis courts.
☒ Sandvig, 3770 Allinge, Bornholm. **Map** p43 F4.
☎ 56 48 03 14. FAX 56 48 02 09. @ bornholm@hotel-romantik.dk b,l,d. **Rooms** 49. ⓀⓀ

Farum

Bregnerød Kro A roadside inn has stood in this hamlet, surrounded by deer-filled forests, for centuries. The original was destroyed by Swedish troops in 1700 but was rebuilt five years later, and it has continued to thrive ever since. The extensive use of light and dark woods throughout the thatched building creates a pleasing aesthetic that adds to the sense of comfort.
Bregnorød Byvej 2, 3520 Farum. **Map** p43 D3.
44 95 00 57. FAX 44 95 06 55. b,l,d. **Rooms** 9.
Never. DC, V. Kr Kr Kr

Fredensborg

Store Kro The palatial establishment was built in 1723 for king Frederick IV. Adjacent to Fredensborg Castle, the Danish royal summer residence, Store Kro's classical architecture is reflected in its regal bedrooms. This is a confident, assured hotel with helpful staff and great attention to detail.
Slotgade 6, 3480 Fredensborg. **Map** p43 D3.
48 40 01 11. FAX 48 48 45 61.
info@storekro.dk b,l,d. **Rooms** 49.
Christmas and New Year. AE, DC, MC, V. Kr Kr Kr

Fredericia

Kryb-I-ly Kro This royal-appointed inn manages to combine informality with opulence under its huge thatched roof. Facilities include a mahogany-panelled library with log fire and a luxury sauna/solarium. Rooms are spacious and staff cheery and helpful. The extensive restaurant menu specializes in fresh fish and game.
Taulov, 7000 Fredericia. **Map** p42 B4.
75 56 25 55. FAX 75 56 45 14. krybily@krybily.dk
b,l,d. **Rooms** 77. Never.
AE, DC, MC, V. Kr Kr Kr

Havreholm

Havreholm Slot This lakeside manor house near the stylish resort of Hornbæk gives a rather forbidding first impression. This is soon dissolved by the graceful white and pale green lobby, and the clean lines of Scandinavian design in the rooms. Guests can explore the parkland, which includes a splendid rose garden, or play golf.
Kloterrisvej 4, 3100 Havreholm. **Map** p43 D3.
49 75 86 00. FAX 49 75 80 23. havreholm@havreholm.dk b,l,d. **Rooms** 32.
Christmas. AE, DC, MC, V. Kr Kr Kr Kr

Års

Aars Hotel Built in 1897 as a railway inn, now a modern hotel, with sauna. Impressive Danish/French menu.
Himmerlandsgade 111, 9600 Års. **Map** p42 B2.
98 6216 00. FAX 98 62 11 87. aars@aarshotel.dk
b,d. **Rooms** 27. Kr Kr

Århus

Best Western Hotel Ritz Luxury hotel in the city centre. Excellent restaurant with French/Danish cuisine; extensive wine cellar.
Banegårdspladsen 12, 8000 Århus. **Map** p42 B3.
86 13 44 44. FAX 86 13 45 87. hotel.ritz@image.dk
b,l,d. **Rooms** 67. Kr Kr Kr

Broby

Brobyværk Kro This historic inn, dating back to 1645 and set alongside the Odense River in rural Funen, specializes in traditional fish cuisine.
Marsk-Billesvej 15, 5672 Broby. **Map** p42 B4.
62 63 11 22. FAX 62 63 21 22.
brobyvaerk.kro@Qmail.dk b,l,d. **Rooms** 19. Kr Kr

Charlottenlund

Shovshoved A few minutes' drive from chic Charlottenlund, and 20 minutes to Copenhagen. Modern interior; Mediterranean food.
Strandvejen 267, 2920 Charlottenlund. **Map** p43 D3.
39 64 00 28. FAX 39 64 06 72. b,l,d.
Rooms 22. Kr Kr Kr-Kr Kr Kr Kr

For key to symbols see backflap. For price categories *see p41*

HENNE

Henne Kirkeby Kro Gourmets from the whole of Denmark come here to sample the inventive modern cooking. The former Royal Palace chef Hans Beck Thomsen is regarded as among the nation's best. The homely rooms feature paintings by Danish artist Johannes Larsen, who stayed here to paint the nearby lake.
Strandvejen 234, 6854 Henne. **Map** p42 A3.
75 25 54 00. FAX 75 25 54 99.
@ hennekirkebykro@mail.dk b,l,d. **Rooms** 6.
Oct-Apr. AE, DC, MC, V. (Kr)(Kr)(Kr)

HØRVE

Dragsholm Slot From bishop's castle to royal palace and baron's estate, Denmark's oldest secular building is awash with 800 years of history. Situated by Nekselø Bay and several sheltered beaches, the whitewashed building is surrounded by woodland. The cellar restaurant serves Danish specialities.
Dragsholm Alle, 4534 Hørve. **Map** p42 C3.
59 653 300. FAX 59 653 033.
@ dragsholm@dragsholm-slot.dk b,l,d. **Rooms** 29.
Never. AE, DC, MC, V. (Kr)(Kr)(Kr)

JYDERUP

Bromølle Kro This thatched highway inn proudly claims to be the oldest in Denmark (dating back to 1198). Pheasant and venison are among the specialities of an excellent kitchen. Compared to the pleasant, subdued tone of the public rooms, the vivid pinks, oranges, lime greens in the bedrooms might seem incongruous.
Slagelsevej 78, 4450 Jyderup. **Map** p42 C3.
58 25 00 90. FAX 58 25 02 38. @ mail@bromoelle-kro.dk b,l,d. **Rooms** 20. Christmas Eve, New Year's Eve. AE, DC, MC, V. (Kr)(Kr)

JYSTRUP

Skjoldenæsholm Hotel Built in 1766, this elegant neo-Classical building is surrounded by beautiful countryside and woodland. The hotel's luxury suites feature marble bathrooms for sybaritic relaxation, while more active guests can choose from angling, walking, golf, or a trip to the nearby tram museum. The area was recently featured in the acclaimed Danish film, ***Festen***.
Skjoldenæsvej 106, 4174 Jystrup. **Map** p43 D4.
57 528 104. FAX 57 528 855. @ hotel@skj.dk b,l,d.
Rooms 38. Dec 21 to Jan 3. AE, DC, MC, V. (Kr)(Kr)(Kr)

FREDENSBORG

Pension Bondehuset A 180-year-old thatched farmhouse with panoramic views over Lake Esrum and Grib Forest. Salmon fishing, golf.
Sørupvej 14, 3480 Fredensborg. **Map** p43 D3. 48 48 01 12. FAX 48 48 03 01. @ contact@bondehuset.dk
b,d (included in room rate). **Rooms** 15. (Kr)(Kr)(Kr)

FREDERICIA

Hotel Kronprinds Frederik Comfortable, well-equipped modern hotel close to an area of outstanding natural beauty – and Legoland.
Vestre Ringvej 96, 7000 Fredericia. **Map** p42 B4. 75 91 00 00. FAX 75 91 19 19. @ info@hotel-kronprinds-frederik.dk b,l,d. **Rooms** 78. (Kr)(Kr)(Kr)

HADERSLEV

Hotel Harmonien A deceptively modern, smart city hotel: King Frederick VII danced in the banqueting hall in 1863. Friendly staff.
Gåskærgade 19, 6100 Haderslev. **Map** p42 B4.
74 52 37 20. FAX 74 52 44 51. @ hotel@harmonien.dk
b,d. **Rooms** 34. Christmas and New Year. (Kr)(Kr)

HELSINGØR

Marienlyst Offering an impressive view of Kronborg Castle, this contemporary hotel includes an aquapark, casino and beach bar.
Nordre Strandvej 2, 3000 Helsingør. **Map** p43 D3.
49 21 40 00. FAX 49 21 49 00. @ gw@marienlyst.dk.
b,l,d. **Rooms** 204. (Kr)(Kr)(Kr)(Kr)

KØBENHAVN (COPENHAGEN)

Ascot This former public bathhouse for Copenhagen's high society was redesigned by architect Martin Nyrop in 1902, utilizing the same Italian Renaissance aesthetic he employed on the city's town hall. The result is a light and airy city retreat. Etchings and a blue-and-white colour scheme evoke the building's bathing history.
⊠ Studiestræde 61, 1554 København. **Map** p43 D4.
33 12 60 00. FAX 33 14 60 40. @ hotel@ascot-hotel.dk
b. **Rooms** 165. Never.
AE, DC, MC, V. (Kr)(Kr)(Kr)

KØBENHAVN (COPENHAGEN)

Triton A poorly maintained exterior does little justice to a fashionable hotel located in the heart of town. Marble floors, light wood panelling and steel pillars are incorporated into a contemporary aesthetic. Rooms feature huge windows and are informally stylish. Breakfast is served in the hotel's chic café-bar.
⊠ Helgolandsgade 7-11, 1653 København.
Map p43 D4. 33 31 32 66. FAX 33 31 69 70.
@ triton@accorhotel.dk b. **Rooms** 123. Never.
AE, DC, MC, V. (Kr)(Kr)(Kr)

KØBENHAVN (COPENHAGEN)

Ibsens A quirky use of antique furnishings makes Ibsens an individualistic choice. Room styles range from the romantic through the bohemian to Scandinavian simplicity. Located in the elegant 'Latin Quarter' area, in central Copenhagen, with plenty of Italian and Spanish restaurants to choose from nearby.
⊠ Vendersgade 23, 1363 København.
Map p43 D4. 33 13 19 13. FAX 33 13 19 16.
@ hotel@ibsenshotel.dk b. **Rooms** 103.
Never. AE, DC, MC, V. (Kr)(Kr)(Kr)

KØGE

Vallø Slot Expectations inevitably rise on the long drive up the tree-lined path to the brooding Vallø Castle, and the surroundings within landscaped grounds are certainly regal in this unsurpassable location. But despite the very romantic setting, much of the accommodation here is rather plain and unimaginative; two suites include spa-pools and luxurious four-poster beds.
⊠ Slotsgade 1, Vallø, 4600 Køge. **Map** p43 D4. 56 26 70 20. FAX 56 26 70 71. @ hotel@valloslotkao.dk b,l,d. **Rooms** 11. Never. AE, DC, MC, V. (Kr)(Kr)(Kr)

HOVBORG

Hovborg Kro A small river runs through the inn's garden; angling opportunities. Traditional cooking. Adventure playground for kids.
⊠ Holmeavej 2, 6682 Hovborg. **Map** p42 A3.
75 39 60 33. FAX 75 39 60 13. @ hovborg-kro@post.tele.dk b,l,d. **Rooms** 55. (Kr)(Kr)

HUNDESTED

Hundested Kro A lively harbourside hotel in the industrial port of Hundested, renowned for delicious locally caught fish specialities.
⊠ Nørregade 10, 3390 Hundested. **Map** p43 D3.
47 93 75 38. FAX 47 93 78 61.
@ hundested.kro@ adr.dk. b,l,d. **Rooms** 66. (Kr)(Kr)

KERTEMINDE

Tornøes Hotel Popular harbourside hotel. Rooms are quite basic but the Danish cuisine is of a high standard. The café gets lively at weekends.
⊠ Strandgade 2, 5300 Kerteminde. **Map** p42 C2.
65 32 16 05. FAX 65 32 48 40.
@ tornoes@tornoeshotel.dk b,l,d.**Rooms** 27. (Kr)(Kr)

KØBENHAVN (COPENHAGEN)

71 Nyhavn Watch cruise ships dock from this converted 19th-century spice warehouse. Rooms make good use of the original wooden beams.
⊠ Nyhavn 71, 1051 København. **Map** p43 D4.
33 43 62 00. FAX 33 43 62 01. @ 71nyhavnhotel@arp-hansen.dk b,d. **Rooms** 150. (Kr)(Kr)(Kr)(Kr)

Kolding

Radisson SAS Kolding-Fjord Hotel A stylish modern hotel, set in a forest that slopes down to the fjord. Rooms are fashionably neutral and overlook the surrounding countryside. A handy location for nearby Legoland, Trapholt Museum of Modern Art, and the Hans Christian Andersen museum. Several golf courses nearby.
Fjordvej 154, 6000 Kolding. **Map** p42 B4. 75 51 00 00. FAX 75 51 00 51. @ koldingfjord@radissonsas.com b,l,d. **Rooms** 134. Christmas and New Year. AE, DC, MC, V. Ⓚⓚⓚⓚ

Millinge

Steensgaard Herregård This grand manor house dates back to the 14th century. The tone is set by touches such as the Louis XIV desk in the sitting room and the Italian rococo furnishings in the 'Yellow Room'. Surprisingly contemporary restaurant menu. The queen of Denmark often stays here during the autumn hunting season.
Steensgaard, 5642 Millinge. **Map** p42 B4. 62 61 94 90. FAX 63 61 78 61. @ steensgaard@herregaardspension.dk b,l,d. Christmas Eve, New Year's Eve. AE, DC, MC, V. Ⓚⓚⓚⓚ

Millinge

Falsled Kro It's no wonder that most visitors to this upmarket retreat (originally a 16th-century smuggler's inn) are loyal regulars. The culinary reputation of owner Jean-Louis Lieffroy reaches far beyond Danish borders. Here, the fresh produce of South Funen (the 'Garden of Denmark') is given a classical French twist.
Assensvej 513, 5642 Millinge. **Map** p42 B4. 62 68 11 11. FAX 62 68 11 62. @ falsled@relaischateaux.com b,l,d. **Rooms** 19. Christmas. AE, DC, MC, V. Ⓚⓚⓚⓚ

Næstved

Menstrup Kro A vivacious place, especially at weekends when the large bars and lounges play host to live music and dancing. Other facilities include an indoor pool, a sauna and tennis courts. Rooms feature all mod-cons and the staff always have a smile. There is an interesting memorial to the Danish Hussar Regiment.
Menstrup Bygade 29, 4700 Næstved. **Map** p43 D4. 55 44 30 03. FAX 55 44 33 63. @ menstrup@menstrupkro.dk b,l,d. **Rooms** 79. Never. AE, DC, MC, V. ⓚⓚ-ⓚⓚⓚ

København (Copenhagen)

Admiral Lots of timbered joists and views of ships gliding into harbour from this converted granary. Staff wear naval uniform.
Toldbodgade 24-28, 1253 København. **Map** p43 D4. 33 74 14 14. FAX 33 74 14 15. @ booking@admiral-hotel.dk b,l,d. **Rooms** 366. ⓚⓚⓚⓚ

København (Copenhagen)

Mayfair An ornate, stately hotel furnished in classic English style. Friendly staff reduce the air of formality. Close to Tivoli Gardens.
Helgolandsgade 3, 1653 København. **Map** p43 D4. 33 31 48 01. FAX 33 23 96 86. @ info@themayfairhotel.dk b. **Rooms** 105. ⓚⓚⓚ

København (Copenhagen)

Sophie Amalie Hotel Modern harbourside hotel decorated in bold hues. Suites feature floor-to-ceiling windows. Inventive international menu.
Sankt Annæ Plads 21, 1022 København K. **Map** p43 D4. 33 37 06 56. FAX 33 32 65 70. @ booking.hsa@remmen.dk b,l,d. **Rooms** 134. ⓚⓚⓚ

Kongensbro

Kongensbro Kro Friendly family-run inn. All the rooms have great views across the biggest river in Denmark, the Gudenåen.
Kongensbro 46, 4424 Kongensbro. **Map** p42 B3. 86 87 01 77. FAX 86 87 92 17. @ kongensbro@kongensbro-kro.dk b,l,d.**Rooms** 15. ⓚⓚ

Næstved

Hotel Vinhuset Located in the old town, on the site of a former monastery, this 18th-century inn now makes a characterful yet smart hotel with stylishly modern rooms. Dinner is served in the 'Vinhuset' restaurant in the cellar, and there is a vaulted bar where Black Friar monks lived in the 15th century.
☒ Sct. Peders Kirkeplads 4, 4700 Næstved. **Map** p43 D4. ☎ 55 72 08 07. FAX 55 72 03 35. @ vinhuset@hotelvinhuset.dk 🍴 b,d. **Rooms** 57. ● Never. 💳 AE, DC, MC, V. Ⓚ Ⓚ

Nysted, Lolland

The Cottage The chic retreat on the quiet island of Lolland is situated close to a pretty beach and to Nysted, Denmark's oldest harbour. Its English influence stems from the hotel's original owners, two English teachers from a nearby music school, who created a home-from-home in 1920. The food is excellent – fish dishes are a speciality.
☒ Skansevej 19, 4880 Nysted, Lolland. **Map** p43 D5. ☎ 54 87 16 00. FAX 54 87 18 78. @ cottage@cottage.dk 🍴 b,d. **Rooms** 16. ● Never. 💳 DC, MC, V. Ⓚ Ⓚ

Nørre Nebel

Nymindegab Kro With superb views across Jutland's wild western landscape, its position makes it popular with deer hunters in autumn, bird watchers during the summer (bird sanctuary open April to August). Fish only is served in the restaurant, and there is a daily three-course menu. Good choice for families: pool, friendly staff.
☒ Nymindegab 1, 6830 Nørre Nebel. **Map** p42 A3. ☎ 75 28 92 11. FAX 75 28 94 25. @ admin@nymindegabkro.dk 🍴 b,l,d. **Rooms** 42. ≋ 🍸 ● mid-Dec to end Jan. 💳 AE, DC, MC, V. Ⓚ Ⓚ

Ribe

Hotel Dagmar Ribe is Denmark's oldest town, and the tremendously popular Dagmar its oldest hotel (built 1581). The small, unprepossessing house became a protected building in 1963 and there is a genuine respect for its history. The two restaurants are majestic – it almost feels like eating within a grand museum.
☒ Torvet 1, 6760 Ribe. **Map** p42 A4. ☎ 75 42 00 33. FAX 75 42 36 52. @ dagmar@hoteldagmar.dk 🍴 b,l,d. **Rooms** 50. ● Christmas and New Year. 💳 AE, DC, MC, V. Ⓚ Ⓚ Ⓚ

Munkebo

Munkebo Kro Highway inn with a restrained décor under its vast thatched roof and tudor timbering. A good stop-off.
☒ Fjordvej 56-58, 5330 Munkebo. **Map** p42 C4. ☎ 65 97 40 30. FAX 65 97 55 64. @ munkebo@munkebo-kro.dk 🍴 b,l,d. **Rooms** 20. Ⓚ Ⓚ Ⓚ

Nykøbing Mors

Sallingsund Færgekro On the enchanting island of Mors, individualistic interiors created by celebrated decorator/florist Jan Munch Lassen.
☒ Sallingsundvej 104, 7900 Nykøbing Mors. **Map** p42 A2. ☎ 97 72 00 88. FAX 97 72 25 40. @ info@sallingsund-faergekro.dk 🍴 b,l,d. **Rooms** 42. Ⓚ Ⓚ

Øland

Øland Kroen An unusual mix of the old and new in this converted bakery. Small cottages in the nearby beech wood are also available.
☒ Hammershøj 29-31, 9460 Øland. **Map** p42 B1. ☎ 98 23 61 00. FAX 98 23 61 20. @ info@oelandkroen.dk 🍴 b,l,d. **Rooms** 30. Ⓚ Ⓚ

Rønde

Hubertus Kroen Intimate half-timbered inn built in 1710 within a pheasant-hunting area. There is a piano and log fire in the restaurant.
☒ Møllerup Gods, 8410 Rønde. **Map** p42 C3. ☎ 86 37 10 03. FAX 86 37 30 29. @ info@hubertuskroen.dk 🍴 b,l,d. **Rooms** 7. Ⓚ Ⓚ

Skagen

Brøndums Hotel Skagen's luminous heath and dune landscape has been inspiring writers and artists since the 1800s, and Brøndums has become *the* place to stay. Hans Christian Andersen was just one of its illustrious guests. The hotel's special atmosphere makes up for its small rooms. The Skagen Museum next door has a fine collection of landscape paintings.
Anchersvej 3, 9990 Skagen. **Map** p42 C1. 98 44 15 55. FAX 98 45 15 20. @ info@brondums.dk b,l,d. **Rooms** 48. Christmas. AE, DC, MC, V. ⓀⓀⓀ

Svendborg

Valdemars Slot This 17th-century treasure, one of Denmark's largest privately owned palaces, enjoys a commanding position within a beachside forest. At night, it's eerily quiet, with only the Baltic wind for company – there is no reception or on-call staff. Each room is furnished with antiques and few modern conveniences (no TV).
Slotsalleen 100, 5700 Svendborg. **Map** p42 C4. 62 22 59 00. FAX 62 22 53 87. @ restaurant@valdemarsslot.dk b,l,d. **Rooms** 8. Jan to Mar. not accepted. ⓀⓀ

Svaneke, Bornholm

Hotel Østersøen Apartment-style comfort in the idyllic island town of Svaneke. Each apartment features a kitchenette, reception room with phone and television, and one, two or three bedrooms. Rooms overlook either the cheerful harbour or the hotel's sheltered back garden and swimming pool. Beach and tennis courts 5 minutes' walk.
Havnebryggen 5, 3740 Svaneke, Bornholm. **Map** p43 F4. 56 49 60 20. FAX 56 49 72 79. @ hotel@ostersoen.dk b,l,d (groups only). **Rooms** 21 apartments. Never. AE, DC, MC, V. ⓀⓀ

Sydals

Hotel Baltic Understated elegance underpins the Baltic's modish sophistication, and the hotel continually delights the eye. Rooms are individually designed with antique furnishings from across Europe, and most have sea views. A gourmet restaurant, and vintage wine-tasting evenings are another classy touch. A real gem.
Havbo 29, 6470 Sydals. **Map** p42 B5. 74 41 52 00. FAX 74 41 53 33. @ info@hotel-baltic.dk b,l,d. **Rooms** 11. Christmas and New Year. AE, DC, MC, V. ⓀⓀ

Rønne, Bornholm

Hotel Fredensborg Ideally located near woods and a small beach, and highly regarded Danish cuisine. Smart rooms, some with balconies.
Strandvejen 116, 3700 Rønne, Bornholm. **Map** p43 F4. 56 95 44 44. FAX 56 95 03 14. @ info@hotelfredensborg.dk b,l,d. **Rooms** 72. ⓀⓀⓀ

Silkeborg

Svostrup Kro Cosy inn by the Gudenå lake with fine views of the Gjern hills. Relaxed company, hearty Danish cuisine. Paddle steamer trips.
Svostrupvej 58-60, 8600 Silkeborg. **Map** p42 B3. 86 87 70 04. FAX 86 87 70 47. @ svostrup@svostrup-kro.dk b,l,d. **Rooms** 15. Ⓚ

Skagen

Aalbæk gl. Kro Modern hotel on the site of a 19th-century inn, with a dose of country spirit with a healthy dinner menu. Eco-friendly policies.
Skagensvej 42, 9982 Aalbæk. **Map** p42 C1. 98 48 90 22. FAX 98 48 83 65. @ aalbak@aalbak-gl-kro.dk b,l,d. **Rooms** 51. ⓀⓀ

Svaneke, Bornholm

Siemsens Gaard Beautifully restored 17th-century merchant's house with stunning views across the harbour. Fine seafood restaurant.
Havnebryggen 9, 3740 Svaneke, Bornholm. **Map** p43 F4. 56 49 61 49. FAX 56 49 61 03. @ hotel@siemsens.dk b,l,d. **Rooms** 51. ⓀⓀ-ⓀⓀⓀ

Thyholm

Tambohus Kro This harbourside inn, directly opposite the island of Jegindø, is located on the site of a Viking base. Today, this traditional fishing area is popular with nature-lovers and seafood connoisseurs. Rooms are functional; several have views across the fjord. The restaurant is famous for its speciality, fried eel.
☒ Tambohuse, 7790 Thyholm. **Map** p42 A2.
☎ 97 87 53 00. FAX 97 87 51 55. @ tambohus@tambohus.dk 🍴 b,l,d. **Rooms** 29. ● Christmas and New Year. 💳 AE, DC, MC, V. ⓀⓀ

Vejby Strand

Havgården The emphasis is on relaxation and tranquillity at this old-fashioned farmhouse: rooms have no phones and there is no television. Appreciate the silence and the secluded beaches nearby, or sample an excellent Danish/French menu utilizing fresh ingredients from the inn's vegetable gardens. The rococo-style rooms are at ground level, by the gardens.
☒ Strandlyvej 1, 3210 Vejby Strand. **Map** p43 D3.
☎ 48 70 57 30. FAX 48 70 57 72. 🍴 b,l,d. **Rooms** 18.
● Sept-June. 💳 AE, DC, MC, V. ⓀⓀ

Tórshavn, Streymoy

Hotel Hafnia In the heart of one of the largest towns of the Faroes, this traditional hotel commands a fine view over the harbour and the old town. Excellent Danish/French menu as well as Faroese fish specialities in the restaurant. Good access to both the airport and ferries. The international dialling code for Streymoy is 298.
☒ Áarvegur 4-10, FO-110 Tórshavn, Streymoy. **Map** p43 E1. ☎ 31 32 33. FAX 31 52 50. @ hafnia@hafnia.fo
🍴 b,l,d. **Rooms** 57. ● Christmas, New Year. 💳 AE, DC, MC, V. ⓀⓀⓀ

Vejle

Munkebjerg Hotel High in the hills of the Munkebjerg Forest, this top-class hotel offers everything from a professional golf course and museum to a casino, nightclub, bakery and butcher. Rooms combine clean Danish design with modern comforts. Panorama restaurant with breathtaking views across the fjord.
☒ Munkebjerg 125, 7100 Vejle. **Map** p42 B3.
☎ 76 42 85 00. FAX 75 72 08 86. @ reception@munkebjerg.dk 🍴 b,l,d. **Rooms** 149.
● Christmas. 💳 AE, DC, MC, V. ⓀⓀⓀⓀ

Tórshavn, Streymoy

Hotel Föroyar Arguably the pick of hotels in the Faroes, and the best view. Bright, airy rooms. See Hotel Hafnia above for dialling code to Streymoy.
☒ Vió Oyggjavegin, FO-110 Tórshavn, Streymoy.
Map p43 E1. ☎ 31 75 00. FAX 31 75 01.
@ hf@hotelforoyar.com 🍴 b,l,d. **Rooms** 108. ⓀⓀⓀ

Tórshavn, Streymoy

Skansin Guesthouse Friendly and clean, but rather basic. Convenient for ferries. See Hotel Hafnia above for dialling code to Streymoy.
☒ Jekaragøta, FO-110 Tórshavn, Streymoy.
Map p43 E1. ☎ 31 22 42. FAX 31 06 57.
🍴 b. **Rooms** 11. Ⓚ

Vágar

Hotel Vágar Modern facilities among the natural beauty of the region. Hiking, fishing and sailing trips around the cliffs can be arranged. The international dialling code to Vágar is 298.
☒ FO-380 Sørvágur. **Map** p43 D1. ☎ 33 29 55.
FAX 33 23 10. @ hotel@ff.fo 🍴 b,l,d. **Rooms** 25. ⓀⓀ

Viby

Viby Kro Located next to the railway station, this traditional town inn comes complete with smoky bar and hearty Scandinavian fare. Rooms are quite basic but homely.
☒ Skolvej 1, 4130 Viby. **Map** p43 D4. ☎ 46 19 30 21.
FAX 46 30 49 21. 🍴 b,d. **Rooms** 23. ⓀⓀ

Ireland

Ireland

Visiting Ireland is not just about historic sights, dramatic scenery, immersing yourself in great literary and musical traditions, or indulging in a pint or two of the Black Stuff (see under Food and Drink). It's also about meeting the Irish people on their own turf. Their friendly welcome and easy-going way of life may be a well-worn cliché, but as anyone who has visited the Emerald Isle will tell you, it is very much the point of Ireland. An informal atmosphere and personal attention prevail in the plentiful guest-houses, farmhouses and small hotels dotted around Ireland, from traditional cottages in the West, to Georgian townhouses in Dublin.

Ashford Castle and Country Estate, page 60, has a stunning location

Ireland Region by Region

Ireland divides approximately into six regions.

Northern Ireland

In recent years 'The Troubles' have all but extinguished the Northern Irish overseas tourist economy. In reality, however, you are far safer here than in many other destinations.

The countryside is striking: the lunar landscape of the legendary Giant's Causeway, the nine green Glens of Antrim and the romantic Mountains of Mourne are the area's three highlights.

Northern Ireland's three principal cities, Belfast, Londonderry and Armagh ('the spiritual capital of Ireland'), pack in a wealth of ancient and recent history.

The Northwest and West

The classic West of Ireland verdant valleys and hillscapes are to be found here, particularly in Counties Sligo, Mayo and Galway and the Connemara region. The lively city of Galway is a delight, as are the timeless Aran Islands. County Clare boasts the awesome Cliffs of Moher and the extraordinary limestone landscape of the Burren. Part of 'the South' in name only, dramatic windswept County Donegal is in fact Ireland's northernmost point.

The Midlands

The least-known and visited part of the country comprises large tracts of farmland and bogland, small county towns and a number of historic sites. Perhaps chief of these is Clonmacnoise, which can claim to be Ireland's most important monastic remains.

Dublin

Booming and bustling on a tide of high technology and tourism, the capital city has some top-notch hotels; from U2's post-modern Clarence Hotel to the splendidly old-world Shelbourne (both page 61) and some beautiful Georgian townhouses with every facility and comfort. You'll pay a premium for the privilege of staying here, but it's worthwhile.

The Southeast

Nestled amid the beautiful Wicklow Mountains are two of Ireland's most memorable sights: the atmospheric ruined monastic settlement of Glendalough, and the gardens of Powerscourt. Counties Wexford and Kilkenny are also known for their medieval monastic settlements and the attractive historic towns of Waterford (world-famous for its glass) and Kilkenny.

The Southwest

The Dingle Peninsula is the greenest part of the Emerald Isle and is rich in ancient sites. Nearby, the equally breathtaking landscapes of the Ring of Kerry attract coach parties by the score. County Cork is the home of the Blarney Stone and the enjoyable little town of Cork.

Highlights

Hotels illustrated on these introductory pages are by no means the only highlights. Other favourites include the idyllically secluded St Ernan's House Hotel in Donegal Bay (page 60); the charming, waterfront Narrows in Portaferry (page 64); and Dublin's sleek Fitzwilliam Hotel (page 61).

Food and Drink

The traditional food of Ireland – simple fish and meat dishes with potatoes and root vegetables – has improved beyond recognition in recent years. The cooking has become lighter, healthier and more cosmopolitan – in fact, 'New Irish'.

Old favourites include the ubiquitous Irish stew, a casserole of mutton or lamb and vegetables, and coddle, a mix of pork sausages, bacon, potato and onion. Champ is buttery mashed potatoes with scallions (spring onions). The Irish are also justifiably proud of their fish and shellfish.

The full Irish breakfast is a national institution. Typically it comprises egg, sausage, bacon, black pudding (made from dried blood), tomatoes and toast. The Irish also eat heartily at lunch and dinner.

The best genuine Irish food can be found in pubs. These are also often the most congenial and the cheapest places to eat, but quality can vary enormously.

Few visitors leave Ireland without sampling a drop of smooth, creamy Black Stuff, which is invariably Guinness, a stout or porter-style of beer which derives its distinct flavour and colour from roasted malt and barley and a high hop content. Guinness is always drunk chilled and is allowed to settle for a few minutes. The other national drink is Irish whiskey. This is smoother than Scotch (Scottish whisky) and lacks its smoky flavour. In the pub, asking for a beer by name will get you a pint. If you want a half-pint, ask for a 'glass' of your chosen beer.

Other Practical Information

Book well in advance for hotels in Dublin year-round and in other heavily visited spots.

The rules of the road follow those of Great Britain: drive on the left, give way to the right. Road signs are often in both English and Gaelic, and it may be useful to

Longueville House, page 63

remember that *An Lár* means town centre. Note too that old signs in miles and new signs in kilometers may (confusingly) both be in use.

Language Although Ireland is officially bilingual, English is the principal language. However, in the parts of Ireland known as the Gaeltacht (principally along the west coast), Gaelic is still the main language. In the remotest parts of the Gaeltacht, English may not be spoken at all.

Currency Republic of Ireland: from 1 January 2002, the European *euro* ('**EUR**'), made up of 100 *cents*. Northern Ireland: the British pound.

Shops Generally open 9am–5:30 or 6pm, Mon–Sat. Smaller towns may have an early closing day, many towns have late shopping on Thursday and/or Friday. In towns and cities, supermarkets may open from noon to 6pm on Sundays.

Tipping Ireland is not a tip-conscious society. Where restaurants add a service charge there is no need to tip. Otherwise, round up the bill to around 10 per cent. A helpful taxi-driver will expect 10 per cent, and porters, tour guides and chambermaids are also usually tipped.

If you want to show the bartender your appreciation, offer him or her a drink.

Telephoning To make calls inside the Republic of Ireland, dial the whole number, including the initial zero. To call the Irish Republic from the UK, dial 00 353 and omit the first zero; from the US, 011 353.

To call Northern Ireland from the UK, dial the number, including the first zero of the area code; from the US, dial 011 44, omitting the zero of the area code.

Public Holidays Republic of Ireland: 1 January; 17 March (St Patrick's Day); Easter Monday; first Monday in May (May Holiday); first Monday in June (June Holiday); first Monday in August (August Holiday); last Monday in October; 25 and 26 December.

Northern Ireland: *See Great Britain, page 71.*

Ireland Price Bands

Our price bands refer, as usual, to the price of a standard double room in high season. The bands below are for the Republic of Ireland; for Northern Ireland, *see Britain Price Bands, page 71.*

Breakfast is often, but not always, quoted within the room rate. Prices quoted for rooms include all taxes and often the service charge.

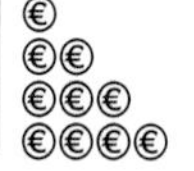

€	under 75 EUR
€€	75–150 EUR
€€€	150–225 EUR
€€€€	over 225 EUR

The K Club, page 65

A
B
C
Ireland
1
2
3
4
5
ATLANTIC
OCEAN
Belmullet
Bangor Erris
Easky
N59
Ballina
Lough
Conn
N26
Mulrany
Newport
★ 64
Ballaghaderre
Westport
N5
Castlebar
Ballyhaunis
N84
Claremorris
Renvyle
★ 64
Lough
Mask
Ballinrobe
Clifden
★ 59-60
Letterfrack
★ 63
N59
N17
Tuam
Cong
★ 60
Lough
Corrib
Ballynahinch
★ 58
Cashel
★ 59
Oughterard
★ 64
N63
Galway
★ 62
Ballyvaughan
★ 58
Kinvarra
★ 64
Gort
Ennistimon
Milltown
Malbay
Ennis
Newmarket-
on-Fergus
★ 64
Kilkee
Kilrush
Shannon
Listowel
Rathkeale
Adare
★ 58
Newcastle
West
N69
Abbeyfeale
Tralee
N21
Castleisland
Dingle
★ 60
Kanturk
★ 62
Killorglin
★ 63
Killarney
N72
Mallow
★ 63
Caherciveen
N22
Kenmare
★ 63
Macroom
Cork
★ 60
Sneem
★ 65
Dunmanway
Inishannon
★ 62
Ballylickey
★ 58
Bantry
Bandon
Clonakilty
Ballydehob
Skull
Skibbereen
★ 65

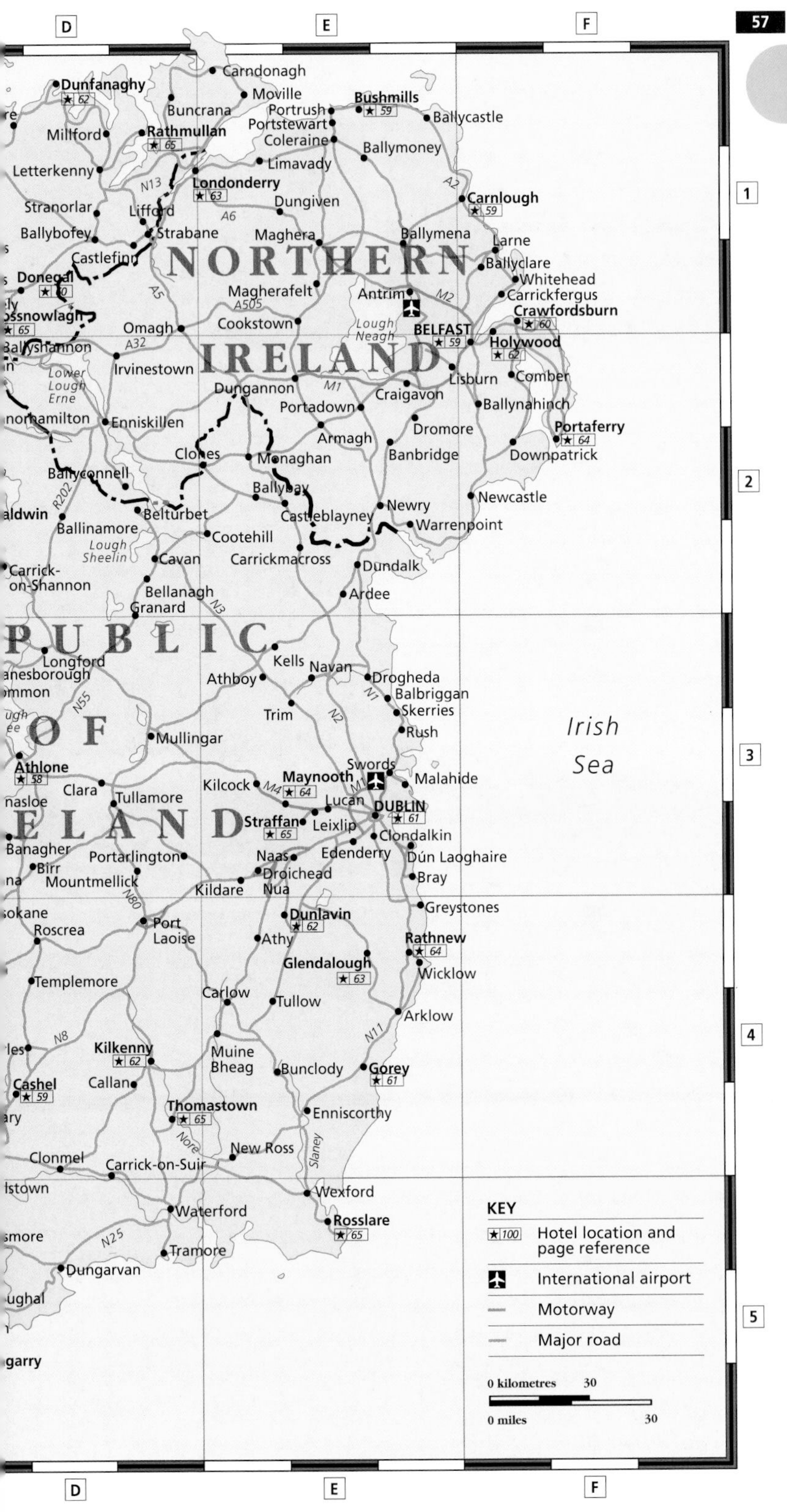
D
E
F
1
2
3
4
5
NORTHERN IRELAND
REPUBLIC OF IRELAND
Irish Sea
Dunfanaghy 62
Carndonagh
Moville
Buncrana
Bushmills 59
Ballycastle
Portrush
Portstewart
Coleraine
Rathmullan 65
Millford
Ballymoney
Limavady
Letterkenny
Londonderry 63
Carnlough 59
Stranorlar
Lifford
Dungiven
Ballybofey
Strabane
Maghera
Ballymena
Larne
Castlefinn
Ballyclare
Whitehead
Donegal
Magherafelt
Antrim
Carrickfergus
Crawfordsburn 60
Omagh
Cookstown
Lough Neagh
BELFAST 59
Holywood 62
Irvinestown
Dungannon
Lisburn
Comber
Lower Lough Erne
Craigavon
Portadown
Ballynahinch
Enniskillen
Armagh
Dromore
Portaferry 64
Clones
Monaghan
Banbridge
Downpatrick
Ballyconnell
Ballybay
Newcastle
Belturbet
Castleblayney
Newry
Warrenpoint
Ballinamore
Cootehill
Lough Sheelin
Cavan
Carrickmacross
Dundalk
Carrick-on-Shannon
Bellanagh
Ardee
Granard
Longford
Kells
Navan
Athboy
Drogheda
Balbriggan
Trim
Skerries
Rush
Mullingar
Athlone 58
Swords
Maynooth 64
Malahide
Clara
Kilcock
Tullamore
Lucan
DUBLIN 61
Straffan 65
Leixlip
Clondalkin
Banagher
Portarlington
Naas
Edenderry
Dún Laoghaire
Birr
Mountmellick
Droichead Nua
Kildare
Bray
Greystones
Dunlavin 62
Roscrea
Port Laoise
Athy
Rathnew 64
Glendalough 63
Wicklow
Templemore
Carlow
Tullow
Arklow
Kilkenny 62
Muine Bheag
Bunclody
Gorey 61
Cashel 59
Callan
Thomastown 65
Enniscorthy
Nore
Slaney
New Ross
Clonmel
Carrick-on-Suir
Wexford
Waterford
Rosslare 65
Tramore
Dungarvan
N13
A6
A5
A505
A32
M1
M2
A2
R202
N3
N55
N1
N2
M4
M1
N80
N8
N11
N25
KEY
★100 Hotel location and page reference
International airport
Motorway
Major road
0 kilometres 30
0 miles 30

Adare

Dunraven Arms Hotel Adare is described as the prettiest tourist village in Ireland; this long, low, yellow-fronted inn is in the main street, among thatched cottages and prize-winning gardens. It is smoothly run along traditional lines, but there is nothing old-fashioned about the extensive facilities, including a health and leisure centre. ☒ Adare, Co Limerick. **Map** p56 C4. (061) 396633. FAX (061) 396541. @ reservations@dunravenhotel.com b,l,d. **Rooms** 74. Never. AE, DC, MC, V. €€€€

Athlone

Hodson Bay Hotel The large white hotel stands by the shores of Lough Ree, in open countryside and next to the golf course, with views of islands in the lake from the bar and dining room. Rooms are smartly co-ordinated; dinner is eaten by candlelight. Superb facilities and reasonable prices make this excellent value. Private marina. ☒ Roscommon Rd, Athlone, Co Westmeath. **Map** p57 D3. (0906) 442000. FAX (0906) 480520. @ info@hodsonbayhotel.com b,l,d. **Rooms** 133. Never. AE, DC, MC, V. €€

Ardfert

Barrow House This 18th-century house on the water's edge at Barrow Harbour and next to Arnold Palmer-designed Tralee golf course has been extensively refurbished, providing comfort, style, warm hospitality and dramatic views. One room has a spa bath and there is a house helicopter for guests. ☒ West Barrow, Ardfert, Tralee, Co Kerry. **Map** p56 B4. (066) 7136437. FAX (066) 7136402. @ info@barrowhouse.com b. **Rooms** 16. Never. AE, MC, V. €

Ballylickey

Ballylickey Manor House Ireland's veteran Relais and Chateaux establishment is perfectly placed at the head of Bantry Bay, with views of the sea from the front rooms. In the main house are pretty suites; wooden cottages by the pool house tidy rooms. Poolside restaurant and charming gardens. ☒ Ballylickey, Bantry Bay, Co Cork. **Map** p56 B5. (027) 50071. FAX (027) 50124. @ ballymh@eircom.net b,d. **Rooms** 12. early Nov to late March. AE, DC, MC, V. €€€€

Adare

Adare Manor Hotel Massive Victorian pile with Gothic façade, formal gardens and vast estate. Style is grand; indoor pool; golf course; riding. ☒ Adare, Co Limerick. **Map** p56 C4. (061) 396566. FAX (061) 396124. @ reservations@adaremanor.com b,l,d. **Rooms** 63. €€€€

Ballylickey

Sea View House Hotel Owner-run Victorian house with garden and sea views. Legendary hospitality; accomplished country-house cooking. ☒ Ballylickey, Bantry, Co Cork. **Map** p56 B5. (027) 50073. FAX (027) 51555. @ info@seaviewhousehotel.com b,d. **Rooms** 25. €€€

Ballynahinch

Ballynahinch Castle A Connemara castle with its own salmon and trout fishery and 13,000-acre shoot. Dine on local produce. ☒ Recess, Connemara, Co Galway. **Map** p56 B3. (095) 31006. FAX (095) 31085. @ bhinch@iol.ie b,l,d. **Rooms** 40. €€€

Ballyvaughan

Hyland's Hotel In a small seaside village, among the strange limestone landscape of The Burren, this snug old coaching inn offers good value. ☒ Ballyvaughan, Co Clare. **Map** p56 C3. (065) 7077037. FAX (065) 7077131. @ hylandsburren@eircom.net b,l,d. **Rooms** 29. €€

Ballyvaughan

Gregans Castle High standards of service and an excellent table are assured at this country house hotel, set in a green valley in the limestone Burren area. The dining room has views of Galway Bay; lunch is served in the bar, with turf fires and beams. The largest bedrooms are in the west wing. Good walking country, within easy driving distance of Shannon.
Ballyvaughan, Co Clare. **Map** p56 C3. (065) 7077005. FAX (065) 7077111. @ res@gregans.ie b,l,d. **Rooms** 22. Nov to early Mar. MC, V. €€€

Bushmills

The Bushmills Inn This restored coaching inn is the perfect place to enjoy an evening in front of a turf fire, and a Black Bush from the nearby Bushmills whiskey distillery. The Victorian-style bar (gas lighting) adjoins the original kitchen. Bedrooms in the Coaching Inn are smallish; those in the riverside Mill House are much larger.
9 Dunluce Rd, Bushmills, Co Antrim BT57 8QG. **Map** p57 E1. (028) 2073 3000. FAX (028) 2073 2048. @ mail@bushmillsinn.co.uk b,l,d. **Rooms** 32. Never. MC, V. ££

Belfast

McCausland Hotel In the city's commercial heart, two former seed warehouses opened as a stylish luxury hotel in 1998. Individually designed bedrooms, including three for disabled guests, provide state-of-the-art technology. Fine dining in the Merchants Restaurant, or enjoy the continental atmosphere of Café Marco Polo.
34-38 Victoria St, Belfast BT1 3GH. **Map** p57 F2. (028) 9022 0200. FAX (028) 9022 0220. @ info@mccauslandhotel.com b,l,d. **Rooms** 60. Christmas. AE, DC, MC, V. £££

Cashel (Co Tipperary)

Cashel Palace Hotel At the foot of the Rock of Cashel (dramatically lit at night), a lovingly restored and intriguing 18th-century townhouse in delightful walled gardens. Public rooms are panelled in pine; bedrooms have canopied beds and good-sized bathrooms. New rooms in former stables opened in 1999. Historic town.
Main Street, Cashel, Co Tipperary. **Map** p57 D4. (062) 62707. FAX (062) 61521. @ reception@cashel-palace.ie b,l,d. **Rooms** 23. Christmas. AE, DC, MC, V. €€€€

Carnlough

Londonderry Arms Hotel Georgian coaching inn, once bequeathed to Winston Churchill, in an historic fishing village; rooms with harbour views.
Carnlough, Co Antrim, BT44 0EU. **Map** p57 F1. (028) 2888 5255. FAX (028) 2888 5263. @ info@glensofantrim.com b,l,d. **Rooms** 35. ££

Cashel (Co Galway)

Cashel House The relaxed country house has winding paths through exotic gardens to its own beach. Antiques, turf fires; tennis, riding.
Cashel Bay, Connemara, Co Galway. **Map** p56 B3. (095) 31001. FAX (095) 31077. @ info@cashel-house-hotel.com b,l,d. **Rooms** 32. €€€€

Cashel (Co Galway)

Zetland Country House Hotel The 19th-century manor house is garlanded in awards for its food and care. Pretty gardens; sea views; tennis court.
Cashel Bay, Connemara, Co Galway. **Map** p56 B3. (095) 31111. FAX (095) 31117. @ zetland@iol.ie b,l,d. **Rooms** 20. €€€

Clifden

Ardagh Hotel Purpose-built, family-run hotel, as close to the seashore as could be managed; wonderful sunset views from the dining room.
Ballyconneely Rd, Clifden, Co Galway. **Map** p56 B3. (095) 21384. FAX (095) 21314 @ ardaghhotel@eircom.net b,l,d. **Rooms** 20. €€€

Castlebaldwin

Cromleach Lodge Country House The small, beautifully appointed hotel is set among hills with views over Lough Arrow. All rooms have lake views. The hotel and its restaurant scoop up awards for their impressive attention to detail and friendly service. The area has peacefulness in abundance and is a walker's paradise.
Castlebaldwin, Boyle, Co Sligo. **Map** p57 D2. (071) 9165155. FAX (071) 9165455. @ info@cromleach.com b,d. **Rooms** 10. early Nov to end Jan. AE, MC, V. €€€

Clifden

Rock Glen Country House Hotel The 18th-century shooting lodge, refurbished in 2002, is renowed as one of the most romantic hotels in Ireland. In the extensive grounds, grassy paths lead through a meadow down to the seashore. Inside, sitting rooms are cosy, with turf fires; a large conservatory has views towards the bay. Tennis court.
Clifden, Co Galway. **Map** p56 B3. (095) 21035. FAX (095) 21737. @ rockglen@iol.ie b,d. **Rooms** 26. end Oct to mid-Mar. AE, DC, MC, V. €€€

Cong

Ashford Castle and Country Estate The massive mock-Gothic pile, built for the Guinness family in the late 1800s, is now American-owned and one of Ireland's most luxurious castle hotels. It has a stunning location on the shores of Lough Corrib, with views of the lake's many islands, and is surrounded by formal gardens. Egon Ronay Best Hotel in Ireland for seven years running.
Cong, Co Mayo. **Map** p56 C3. (092) 46003. FAX (092) 46260. @ ashford@ashford.ie b,l,d. **Rooms** 83. Never. AE, DC, MC, V. €€€€

Donegal

St Ernan's House Hotel The hotel achieves its aim of providing a bolt-hole from the pressures of modern life: it is set on a secluded tidal island in Donegal Bay, joined to the mainland by a causeway. The house was built in 1826 by a nephew of the Duke of Wellington; original features remain. Sea views from all rooms.
St Ernan's Island, Donegal, Co Donegal. **Map** p57 D1. (074) 9721065. FAX (074) 9722098. @ info@sainternans.com b,d. **Rooms** 10. end Oct to mid-April. MC, V. €€€€

Collooney

Markree Castle In Yeats country and home of the Cooper family for 350 years, one of the finest castles of its age; magnificent gilded dining room.
Collooney, Co Sligo. **Map** p56 C2. (071) 9167800. FAX (071) 9167840. @ markreecastle@iol.ie b,l,d. **Rooms** 30. €€€

Cork

Maryborough House Hotel A mix of old and new gives charm and character to fine Georgian house. Garden; library; heated indoor pool.
Maryborough Hill, Douglas, Cork, Co Cork. **Map** p56 C5. (021) 365555. FAX (021) 365662. @ maryboro@indigo.ie b,l,d. **Rooms** 79. €€€

Crawfordsburn

The Old Inn One of Ireland's oldest inns, with history going back to 1614; panelling, log fires, canopied beds and modern comfort.
Crawfordsburn, Co Down BT19 1JH. **Map** p57 F1. (028) 9185 3255. FAX (028) 9185 2775. @ info@theoldinn.com b,l,d. **Rooms** 32. ££

Dingle

Dingle Skellig Hotel Lively, modern hotel with sea views and pleasant decor. Irish entertainment; heated pool; gardens; local seafood.
Dingle, Co Kerry. **Map** p56 B5. (066) 9150200. FAX (066) 9151501. @ dsk@iol.ie b,d. **Rooms** 110. €€€

Dublin

The Clarence The 1850s building on the Liffey's 'Left Bank', now owned by the rock band U2, has become one of the most fashionable places to stay and be seen. A makeover in 1996 retained and enhanced the original Arts and Crafts features. Bedrooms have a classy minimalist simplicity; the penthouse has a rooftop hot tub.
6-8 Wellington Quay, Dublin 2. **Map** p57 E3.
(01) 407 0800. FAX (01) 407 0818.
@ reservations@theclarence.ie b,l,d. **Rooms** 50.
Christmas. AE, DC, MC, V. €€€€

Dublin

Number 31 City-centre, award-winning guesthouse in a leafy mews (once home of one of Ireland's leading architects, Sam Stephenson) that has spread to an adjacent Georgian house. Californian-style 1970s design extends to the sunken sitting area and the garden. Breakfast is served in the plant-filled conservatory. Good value. New owners took over in 1999.
31 Leeson Close, Dublin 2. **Map** p57 E3. (01) 676 5011. FAX (01) 676 2929. @ number31@iol.ie b.
Rooms 19. Never. AE, MC, V. €€€

Dublin

The Fitzwilliam Hotel Opened in 1998, the Fitzwilliam is a sleek essay in designer chic by the Conran Group: frosted glass, leather sofas, moody lighting, and everywhere grey. The roof garden, Thornton's Michelin 2-star restaurant and the hotel's position on St Stephen's Green make this one of the city's most fashionable venues.
St Stephen's Green, Dublin 2. **Map** p57 E3.
(01) 478 7000. FAX (01) 478 7878.
@ enq@fitzwilliamhotel.com b,l,d. **Rooms** 129.
Never. AE, DC, MC, V. €€€€

Gorey

Marlfield House Hotel The magnificent and romantic 1830s country house – once the home of the Earls of Courtown – has received many accolades. Rooms and bathrooms are suitably luxurious; there are six sumptuous 'state' rooms and a helipad. The vast and beautiful gardens include a lake and wildlife preserve.
Gorey, Co Wexford. **Map** p57 E4. (055) 21124.
FAX (055) 21572. @ info@marlfieldhouse.ie b,l,d.
Rooms 20. mid-Dec to early Feb. AE, DC, MC, V. €€€€

Donegal

Harvey's Point Country Hotel Luxury lakeside hotel provides quiet seclusion, attentive staff and a fine table. Prior booking essential.
Lough Eske, Donegal, Co Donegal. **Map** p57 D1.
(07497) 22208. FAX (07497) 22352. @ bookings@harveyspoint.com b,l,d. **Rooms** 20. €€

Dublin

Hibernian Hotel Ornately Victorian and once a nurses' home, this luxury townhouse hotel feels like a private club; well-equipped bedrooms.
Eastmoreland Pl, Ballsbridge, Dublin 4. **Map** p57 E3.
(01) 668 7666. FAX (01) 660 2655. @ info@hibernianhotel.com b,l,d. **Rooms** 40. €€€

Dublin

Merrion Hotel Classical elegance and superb interiors in four restored listed Georgian houses with formal gardens. Modern extension; pool.
Upper Merrion St, Dublin 2. **Map** p57 E3.
(01) 603 0600. FAX (01) 603 0700. @ info@merrionhotel.com b,l,d. **Rooms** 145. €€€€

Dublin

Le Meridien Shelbourne Legendary charm and style. It's *the* place for afternoon tea. Health and fitness club including pool; parking.
27 St Stephen's Green, Dublin 2. **Map** p57 E3.
(01) 663 4500. FAX (01) 661 6006. @ shelbourneinfo@lemeridien.com b,l,d. **Rooms** 190. €€€€

Holywood

Culloden Hotel Once a palace of the Bishops of Down and set in the Holywood Hills overlooking Belfast Lough and the County Antrim coast, the Culloden is now a five-star hotel. Facilities include a health spa with pool and steam room. Ten suites were refurbished in 1998. Golf nearby. Courtesy car service.
Bangor Rd, Holywood, Co Down BT18 0EX. **Map** p57 F20. (028) 9042 1066. FAX (028) 9042 6777. res@cull.hastingshotels.com. b,l,d. **Rooms** 79. Never. AE, DC, MC, V. £££

Kanturk

Assolas Country House The family-owned, 17th-century greystone house has gained a reputation for good food and warm hospitality. The North Cork countryside is extremely peaceful, and the house stands on the banks of a small river, in award-winning gardens. The kitchen makes much use of local cheeses and the house's own organic vegetables and fruits.
Kanturk, Co Cork. **Map** p56 C5. (029) 50015. FAX (029) 50795. assolas@eircom.net b,d. **Rooms** 9. early Nov to mid Mar. MC, V. €€€

Innishannon

Innishannon House Hotel The River Brandon borders the gardens of the country house (built 1720), and there are many walks; boating and fishing in the grounds. Rooms are imaginatively furnished, with modern art on the walls and a growing collection of 'historic' baths. Seafood is a speciality in the award-winning restaurant.
Innishannon, Co Cork. **Map** p56 C5. (021) 4775121. FAX (021) 4775609. info@innishannon-hotel.ie b,l,d. **Rooms** 12. Christmas. AE, DC, MC, V. €€€

Kilkenny

Butler House The large Georgian townhouse was once the dower house to Kilkenny Castle, the family seat of the earls of Ormond. The stylish 1970s interior is simple and modern, with airy, uncluttered rooms and lots of black, cream and white. Walk through the formal garden to the castle. Cellar restaurant.
16 Patrick St, Kilkenny, Co Kilkenny. **Map** p57 D4. (056) 65707. FAX (056) 65626. res@butler.ie b. **Rooms** 13. early Nov to mid-March. AE, DC, MC, V. €€€

Dunfanaghy

Arnold's Hotel This friendly, family-run waterside hotel makes a perfect touring base. Good food; helpful staff; striking bay views.
Dunfanaghy, Co Donegal. **Map** p57 D1. (074) 9136208. FAX (074) 9136352. arnoldshotel@eircom.net b,l,d. **Rooms** 30. €

Dunlavin

Rathsallagh House Converted Queen Anne stables with golf course. Luxurious bedrooms and country house cooking at its best.
Dunlavin, Co Wicklow. **Map** p57 E4. (045) 403112. FAX (045) 403343. info@rathsallagh.com b,l,d. **Rooms** 29. €€€

Galway

Ardilaun House Hotel Open fires and award-winning restaurant await at the end of the tree-lined avenue to this 19th-century house. Sauna.
Taylor's Hill, Salthill, Galway, Co Galway. **Map** p56 C3. (091) 521433. FAX (091) 521546. info@ardilaunhousehotel.ie b,l,d. **Rooms** 90. €€€€

Galway

Norman Villa An inspiring mixture of brass beds, modern art and polished pine floors. Helpful hosts provide tea, maps and parking.
86 Lower Salthill, Galway, Co Galway. **Map** p56 C3. FAX (091) 521131. normanvilla@oceanfree.net b. **Rooms** 6. €€

KINSALE

Blue Haven Hotel This cosy, busy hotel is much loved by Irish and American media folk. Brightly painted in blue and yellow, it features lots of nautical brass and plants; log fires in cold weather. Acclaimed seafood restaurant. The largest bedrooms are in the next-door annexe. New owners took over in 1999.
3 Pearse St, Kinsale, Co Cork. **Map** p56 C5.
(021) 4772209. FAX (021) 4774268.
@ bluhaven@iol.ie b,l,d. **Rooms** 17.
one week in Jan. AE, DC, MC, V. €€€

MALLOW

Longueville House The O'Callaghan family is back at Longueville after a 300-year absence; from their imposing Georgian manor, the ruins of their former castle can be seen. History blends well with the culinary brilliance of chef William O'Callaghan, who uses produce from the estate's farm, gardens and nearby Blackwater River.
Mallow, Co Cork. **Map** p56 C5. (022) 47156.
FAX (022) 47459. @ info@longuevillehouse.ie b,d.
Rooms 20. mid-Feb to mid-Mar.
AE, DC, MC, V. €€€€

LONDONDERRY

Beech Hill Country House Hotel In a quiet suburb of Londonderry, within woodland with streams and a small lake, is this gracious late 18th-century house. Food – 'Modern Irish with global overtones' – is taken seriously; formal, elegant restaurant. A leisure centre with sauna, steam room and fitness room opened in 1999.
32 Ardmore Rd, Londonderry, Co Londonderry BT47 3QP. **Map** p57 E2. (028) 7134 9279. FAX (028) 7134 5366. @ info@beech-hill.com b,l,d. **Rooms** 27.
Christmas. AE, MC, V. ££

MAYNOOTH

Moyglare Manor Half a mile of avenue leads to this Georgian country house, set in extensive parkland near the historic town and within easy driving distance of Dublin airport. The interior is opulent yet unusual and comfortable, with furniture and fittings of many periods; antiques in the bedrooms. The cosy, intimate bar and dining room are candlelit and have open fires.
Maynooth, Co Kildare. **Map** p57 E3. (01) 6286351.
FAX (01) 6285405. @ moyglare@ iol.ie b,l,d. **Rooms** 17. Christmas. AE, DC, MC, V. €€€€

GLENDALOUGH

Glendalough Hotel Family-run hotel in the Wicklow Mountains. Good traditional cooking and remarkable dining-room views.
Glendalough, Co Wicklow. **Map** p57 E4. (0404) 45135. FAX (0404) 45142. @ info@glendaloughhotel.ie b,l,d. **Rooms** 40. €€€

KENMARE

Park Hotel Kenmare Gracious living, world-class cuisine, friendly staff; newly opened luxury spa. Good base on the Ring of Kerry.
Kenmare, Co Kerry. **Map** p56 B5. (064) 41200.
FAX (064) 41402. @ info@parkkenmare.com b,l,d.
Rooms 46. €€€€

KENMARE

Sheen Falls Lodge Manor house in a splendid setting, in semi-tropical gardens, within sight and sound of the River Sheen. Heated indoor pool.
Kenmare, Co Kerry. **Map** p56 B5. (064) 41600.
FAX (064) 41386. @ info@sheenfallslodge.ie b,l,d.
Rooms 66. €€€€

KILLORGLIN

Ard-na-Sidhe The 'Hill of the Fairies' is a suitably romantic Edwardian house in lakeside gardens.
Caragh Lake, Killorglin, Co Kerry. **Map** p56 B5.
(066) 9769105. FAX (066) 9769282. @ reception.ardnasidhe@kih.liebherr.com b,l,d.
Rooms 20. €€€€

Newmarket-on-Fergus

Dromoland Castle The ancestral home of the O'Briens, descendants of Brian Boru, 11th-century king of Ireland, is a fairy-tale castle. It was made over in Gothic style with turrets and ramparts in the 1800s, and stands beside a lake. Today's luxury hotel has lavish amenities and oak panelling. Jackets and ties to be worn after 7pm. Newmarket-on-Fergus, Co Clare. **Map** p56 C4. (061) 368144. FAX (061) 363355. @ sales@dromoland.ie b,l,d. **Rooms** 100. Never. AE, MC, V. €€€€€

Portaferry

The Narrows Once through the 18th-century entrance archway, guests might never want to leave this inspiring waterfront courtyard restoration. All rooms have views of Strangford Lough; local artists' work are dotted about the walls; the restaurant looks out on boats and sunsets. Yachtspeople welcome; berths available. 8 Shore Rd, Portaferry, Co Down BT22 1JY. **Map** p57 F2. (028) 4272 8148. FAX (028) 4272 8105. @ info@narrows.co.uk b,l,d. **Rooms** 13. Never. AE, MC, V. ££

Newport

Newport House Fisherfolk heaven: the owners of the traditionally-run country house have fishing rights on a stretch of the River Newport, which borders the parkland, and the nearby lough. Fish is always on the menu; the house has its own superb whiskey-cured salmon. Lunchtime picnic hampers provided; anglers' tales in the bar in the evening. Four-poster beds in some rooms. Newport, Co Mayo. **Map** p56 C2. (098) 41222. FAX (098) 41613. @ info@newporthouse.ie b,d. **Rooms** 19. Oct to mid-March. AE, DC, MC, V. ££££

Rathmullan

Rathmullan House Inside or out, there are glorious views of Lough Swilly and mountains from this large, rambling, informal country house. Its gardens slope down to long, sandy beaches, and the area is ideal for walking. There are three attractive sitting-rooms, with log fires. Excellent facilities include an indoor pool and steam room. Rathmullan, Co Donegal. **Map** p57 D1. (074) 9158188. FAX (074) 9158200. @ info@rathmullanhouse.com b,d. **Rooms** 24. Jan to mid-Feb. AE, MC, V. €€€€

Kinvara

Merriman Hotel The fishing village hotel has one of the largest thatched roof in Ireland. There are regular sessions of Irish music in the bar. Main St, Kinvara, Co Galway. **Map** p56 C3. (091) 638222. FAX (091) 637686. @ merrimanhotel@eircom.net b,l,d. **Rooms** 32. €€

Oughterard

Currarevagh House Country house hotel in woodland beside Lough Corrib sets a relaxed tone; fishing, tennis. Superb breakfasts. Oughterard, Connemara, Co Galway. **Map** p64 C3. (091) 552312. FAX (091) 552731. @ currarevagh@ireland.com b,d. **Rooms** 15. €€€

Rathnew

Tinakilly Country House Victorian house with views of the Irish Sea and a celebrated kitchen. Bedrooms have four-poster beds. Rathnew, Wicklow, Co Wicklow. **Map** p57 E4. (0404) 69274. FAX (0404) 67806. @ reservations@tinakilly.ie b,l,d. **Rooms** 51. €€€

Renvyle

Renvyle House Hotel The grounds of this house with a fascinating history jut out into the Atlantic, with the Connemara countryside all around. Pool. Renvyle, Connemara, Co Galway. **Map** p56 B3. (095) 43511. FAX (095) 43515. @ info@renvyle.com b,l,d. **Rooms** 65. €€€

RATHNEW

Hunter's Hotel In the same family for five generations, this former coaching inn with delightful, riverside garden oozes old-fashioned charm. Popular with Dubliners seeking rusticity: open fires; polished brass; fresh flowers; simple, pretty bedrooms with antiques. Good food; summer teas on the lawn a tradition of the house. Newrath Bridge, Rathnew, Co Wicklow. **Map** p57 E4. (0404) 40106. FAX (0404) 40338. @ reception@hunters.ie b,l,d. **Rooms** 16. Christmas. AE, MC, V. €€€

STRAFFAN

The K Club The chateau-style building, complete with a mansard roof, looks like it was transplanted from France, yet it was built in the 1870s as a private home. It is now an unashamedly smart hotel, with views over to the renowned K Club golf course. Some bedrooms overlook the River Liffey. A French restaurant completes the luxury package. Straffan, Co Kildare. **Map** p57 E3. (01) 6017200. FAX (01) 6017297. @ hotel@kclub.ie b,l,d. **Rooms** 45. Never. AE, DC, MC, V. €€€€

SHANAGARRY

Ballymaloe House First rustled up for guests in the Allens' farmhouse kitchen in the 1960s, Ballymaloe cooking has become the cornerstone of modern Irish country house cuisine. Now there's a cookery school of international repute and an organic farm. But this is still a welcoming family home, with excellent breakfasts. No TV. Shanagarry, Midleton, Co Cork. **Map** p57 D5. (021) 4652531. FAX (021) 4652021. @res@ballymaloe.com b,d. **Rooms** 32. Christmas. AE, DC, MC, V. €€€€

THOMASTOWN

Mount Juliet Conrad A world of its own. The splendid greystone Georgian house sits in a private estate on the River Nore, surrounded by converted outbuildings and cottages. Features include stuccoed ceilings and marble mantelpieces. Riding on trails on the estate; Jack Nicklaus-designed golf course. Super king-sized beds. Thomastown, Co Kilkenny. **Map** p57 D4. (056) 73000. FAX (056) 73019. @ mountjulietinfo@conradhotels.com b,l,d. **Rooms** 58 Never. AE, DC, MC, V. €€€€

ROSSLARE

Kelly's Resort Hotel Almost an Irish institution. Bill Kelly's cellar and art collection are among his many gifts as an hotelier. Leisure facilities; beach. Rosslare, Co Wexford. **Map** p57 E5. (053) 32114. FAX (053) 32222. @ kellyhot@iol.ie b,l,d. **Rooms** 99. €€

ROSSNOWLAGH

Sand House Hotel Pink castellated hotel on a popular sandy beach in Donegal Bay. Many rooms have sea views. Award-winning restaurant. Rossnowlagh, Co Donegal. **Map** p57 D1. (072) 9151777. FAX (072) 9152100. @ info@sandhouse-hotel.ie b,l,d. **Rooms** 64. €€

SKIBBEREEN

West Cork Hotel This busy family-run establishment was once a railway hotel; it is still a focal point of West Cork life. Courtesy, relaxed hospitality; excellent crab cakes and steaks. Ilen St, Skibbereen, Co Cork. **Map** p56 C5. (028) 21277. FAX (028) 22333. b,l,d. **Rooms** 30. €€

SNEEM

Great Southern Hotel Parknasilla A spacious Victorian hotel known for welcoming service; subtropical gardens lead down to the shore. Pool. Sneem, Co Kerry. **Map** p56 B5. (064) 45122. FAX (064) 45323. @ res@parknasilla-gsh.ie b,d. **Rooms** 83. €€€€

For key to symbols see backflap. For price categories *see p55*

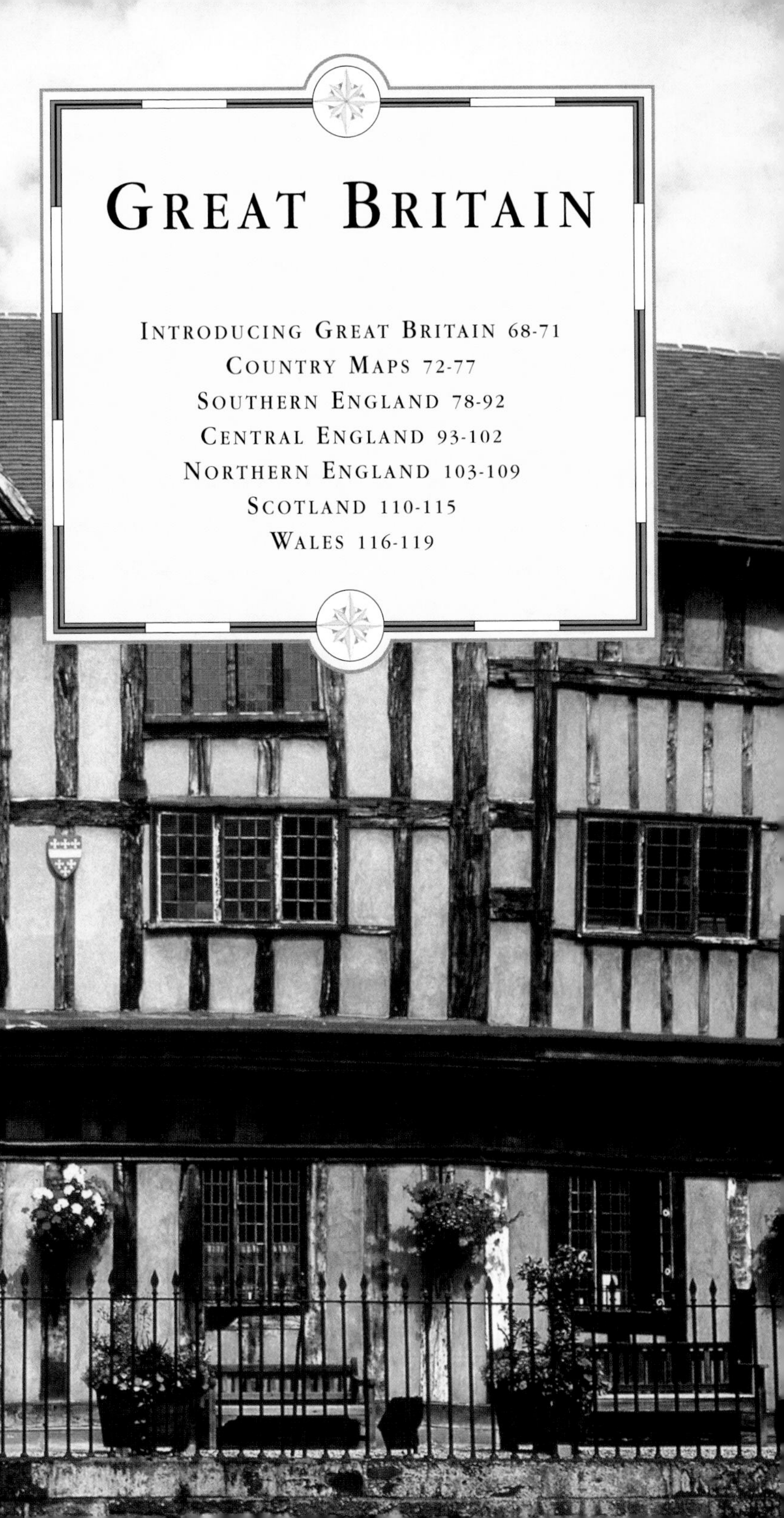

GREAT BRITAIN

Great Britain

Britain's hotels tend to fall into one of two camps: town or country. The metropolitan 'boutique' hotels of London and Glasgow draw a style-conscious and demanding clientele, while the national pastime of the weekend break means that escapees from the city have a wide selection of country hotels to choose from – many of them offering excellent food in beautiful surroundings. As with the other countries in this guide, we include a selection of places to stay across the board, from the best B&Bs (bed & breakfasts) to classic hotels such as Gleneagles, page 110. Many of our listings are in unusual locations, for example, a Norfolk windmill, or a croft on a Scottish island. There's as much variety and character in this small country as anywhere.

Inverlochy Castle Hotel, page 113, in magnificent Highland scenery at the foot of Ben Nevis

Great Britain Region by Region

In this guide, Britain is divided into five sections: Southern England, Central England, Northern England, Scotland and Wales.

Southern England

In London, recommendations include great places to stay that are also well-placed for shopping, theatres, museums and restaurants. Within easy reach of the capital are the B&Bs of the Weald and downland of Kent and Sussex, luxurious spa hotels such as Chewton Glen in the New Forest (page 87), and fun places like the traditional beach huts that can be booked at the Hotel Continental, in Whitstable, Kent (page 92). Two hotels in the neighbourhood of Bath – the stylish Royal Crescent in Bath itself (page 79), and Babington House in nearby Frome (page 82) – show how British hotel styles are on the move. The Georgian Royal Crescent is one of the new breed of polished townhouse hotel. Babington House is the country offshoot of a Soho club; where the knowing informality is typical of the developing style of the British country-house hotel.

Lobby, the Dorchester, page 85

Further west, Devon and Cornwall offer some of the most beautiful stretches of coastline in Britain, plenty of B&Bs, and understated luxury in hotels such as Tresco's Island Hotel (page 90).

Central England

The sandstone villages of the Cotswolds are a plentiful source of guesthouses, coaching inns and manor house hotels. Many offer first-rate service, provide picnic hampers, or transport you to and from great walking country. The old counties of Hereford and Worcester, the university town of Oxford, and the East Anglian counties

West Usk Lighthouse, page 119

of Suffolk and Norfolk also offer some special places to stay, the latter including a B&B in a windmill at Cley-next-the-Sea (page 95).

Northern England

Newcastle is home to one of the Malmaison chain (page 107) – the only hotel chain included in this section – which is noted for its somewhat unconventional ambience and affordable prices. In the northwest, the Lake District is packed out with tourists in summer, but it is easy enough to escape the crowds if you like hill walking or if you visit in autumn when the weather can be clear and warm. There are many B&Bs which don't mind muddy walking boots, and some special country house hotels too, including Old Church at Watermillock on the edge of Ullswater (page 108). Other famous areas of outstanding beauty in the north include the Yorkshire Dales and the Peak District. Nearby are country hotels such as Amerdale House at Arncliffe (page 103), and small hotels with character, among them a former cotton mill.

Scotland

Country hotels in Scotland are memorable for location, character and food: many occupy imposing positions on peaceful lochs, and employ chefs who make full use of the local specialities such as seafood and game, and have a loyal clientele who rearrange their itinerary to be sure of getting a room. Glasgow and Edinburgh are obvious centres for their art galleries and architecture (and assured townhouse hotels), as well as the annual Edinburgh Festival (and associated Fringe) in August. The Highlands and Islands offer some of the most remote and peaceful places to stay in Britain, one such being Scarista House on the Isle of Harris (page 115), whose solitary, windswept exterior does not prepare you for the warm welcome and relaxed atmosphere within.

Wales

The walking is superb in the Brecon Beacons, Snowdonia and along Offa's Dyke. The Pembrokeshire coastline, with its crumbling medieval castles, and seaside resorts such as Tenby and St David's is well worth a detour. Potential overnight stops include many family-run hotels offering good food – often with fresh local produce on the menu.

Some hotels in this chapter are Wolsey Lodges – neither hotels, nor just guesthouses. A stay at a Wolsey Lodge is like being at a private house party – except that the host presents you with a bill at the end of your stay.

Highlights

Hotels illustrated on these introductory pages are by no means our only highlights. Others include: Tresanton at St Mawes in Cornwall (page 90) for marrying sophistication with sea-side fun; The Old Rectory at Cricket Malherbie (page 82) for its calm atmosphere and charming setting; and Hambleton Hall (page 96), for offering stylish pampering in a secluded location on Rutland Water, near Oakham in the Midlands. In London,

Wykeham Arms at Winchester, page 92, the archetypal pub-with-character

Upper Court at Kemerton, page 96, a favourite venue for house parties

London, the Covent Garden (page 84) gets many people's vote for its panache and superb service. And in the north, Amerdale House, in Arncliffe, North Yorkshire (page 103), is extra special because of its stunning setting and good food.

Food and Drink

Eating has become a form of entertainment for many Londoners, with a hardcore of 'foodie' enthusiasts making – or ruining – the fortunes of restaurants and affording many chefs celebrity status. Sometimes you have to book weeks in advance if you want to dine somewhere in vogue.

However, some of the best British food is served outside the capital, and the 1990s produced some excellent new establishments. As well as the country hotels where food takes pride of place, there are 'restaurants with rooms', which illustrate the 1980s' and 1990s' renaissance in British food; with inventive cooking that often uses locally-grown, seasonal produce. The quality of fish, game, lamb, and the controversial beef on the bone is high, and at many hotels chefs have access to a kitchen garden or buy the freshest local produce. Many hotels are at the forefront of the campaign against genetically modified crops, and organically produced food on the menu is now increasingly commonplace.

Modern British cookery is actually an amalgam of many influences and styles, among them provincial Italian and Pacific Rim, with an imaginative use of fresh herbs and spices borrowed from foreign cuisines. Britain is one of the few countries where you can be vegetarian and eat well. Classy pub food continues to be excellent value for money, and so is traditional fish and chips, eaten straight from the paper wrapping.

Tea at the Priory Steps, page 80

Lunch is generally served from 1–3pm and dinner from 7:30–10:30pm; many pubs stop serving lunch at 2:30pm and dinner at 9 or 9:30pm. Afternoon tea at about 4pm is an old-fashioned institution that city hotels do particularly well. Even better is the West Country (typically Devon and Cornwall) speciality of cream tea – scones eaten with clotted cream and jam – served, of course, with strong traditional English tea.

Britain produces little wine, still less any of note. Beer from the tap is the ubiquitous national drink of the pub or hotel bar, reaching its highest quality in the 'real' ales of independent specialist brewers. It is served by the pint or the half-pint.

Scottish whisky is, of course, renowned. Everyday 'Scotch' is blended. 'Single malts', from one distilling, achieve gourmet status and are accordingly expensive. There are many from which you can choose, and some hotels make a feature of offering a wide range, each with its distinctive style.

Bedrooms and Bathrooms

If you want twin beds, ask for them specifically when booking. Even the humblest B&B can have a four-poster bed, a great view or some other interesting feature – it's worth asking beforehand. Some hotels in historic buildings will have a new wing – generally with more spacious rooms and better bathrooms, but less character. You will usually be given the choice when you book, but it is worth making sure that you state which you prefer.

Bathrooms generally mean just a bath – specify if you want a shower.

Other Practical Information

British hoteliers seem very sensitive about 'no-shows' (people who book a room but don't turn up), and you may be asked for your credit card number or a cheque to secure the booking. Under English law, by making a booking you are entering into a contract. Hotels are within their rights to charge you for the room if you cancel at the last minute, although they must try to re-let the room and are not supposed to profit from your cancellation.

The English cooked breakfast, high in cholesterol, is often a major feature, worth trying at least once.

Language English, and, in Wales, Welsh, tend to be the only languages spoken.

Currency The pound sterling, written '£'.

Shops Generally open from 9:30am–5:30pm Mon–Sat in the country, and until 6 or 7pm in central London. Banks are open Mon–Fri; most closing at 3:30pm, but some staying open until 4:30 or 5:30pm. Supermarkets and shops in tourist areas often open between about noon and 4pm on Sundays.

Tipping A tip of around 15 per cent is the norm for waiters, hairdressers and taxi drivers. A service charge of 10–15 per cent is often added to restaurant bills, in addition to the tip, but the extra rarely goes to the waiting staff. You can negotiate not to pay the service charge (if you have ordered expensive wines, for example, which are already subject to a high mark-up) but be ready for consternation from the management.

In metropolitan bars and cafés the staff may give you your change on a tray, hinting that donations are welcome. In pubs, the terminology of tipping is to say, 'and a drink for yourself' in which case the price of a drink will be added into the total for the round.

Telephoning Hotels are shameless at racking up the phone charges, defending themselves by saying that they publicize their price per unit charges. Some will even charge you for using your own charge card for calls. Public call boxes are plentiful, accepting coins, phonecards or credit cards (minimum call charge for the latter is 50p). For calls within Britain, dial the zero before the area code. To call Britain from the US, dial 011 44, then the number, dropping the initial zero.

Public holidays England and Wales: 1 January; Good Friday; Easter Monday; first Monday after 1 May; last Monday in May; last Monday in August; 25 and 26 December.

Scotland: 1 and 2 January; 25 December; plus assorted local public holidays.

Britain Price Bands

Don't be distracted by the array of stars, crowns or other symbols of the many hotel awards in Britain. Our price bands are much simpler, referring to the price of a standard double room in high season. Prices usually include breakfast and all taxes.

£	below £60
££	£60–£120
£££	£120–£180
££££	above £180

Lavenham Priory, page 97, in the charming town of Lavenham, Suffolk

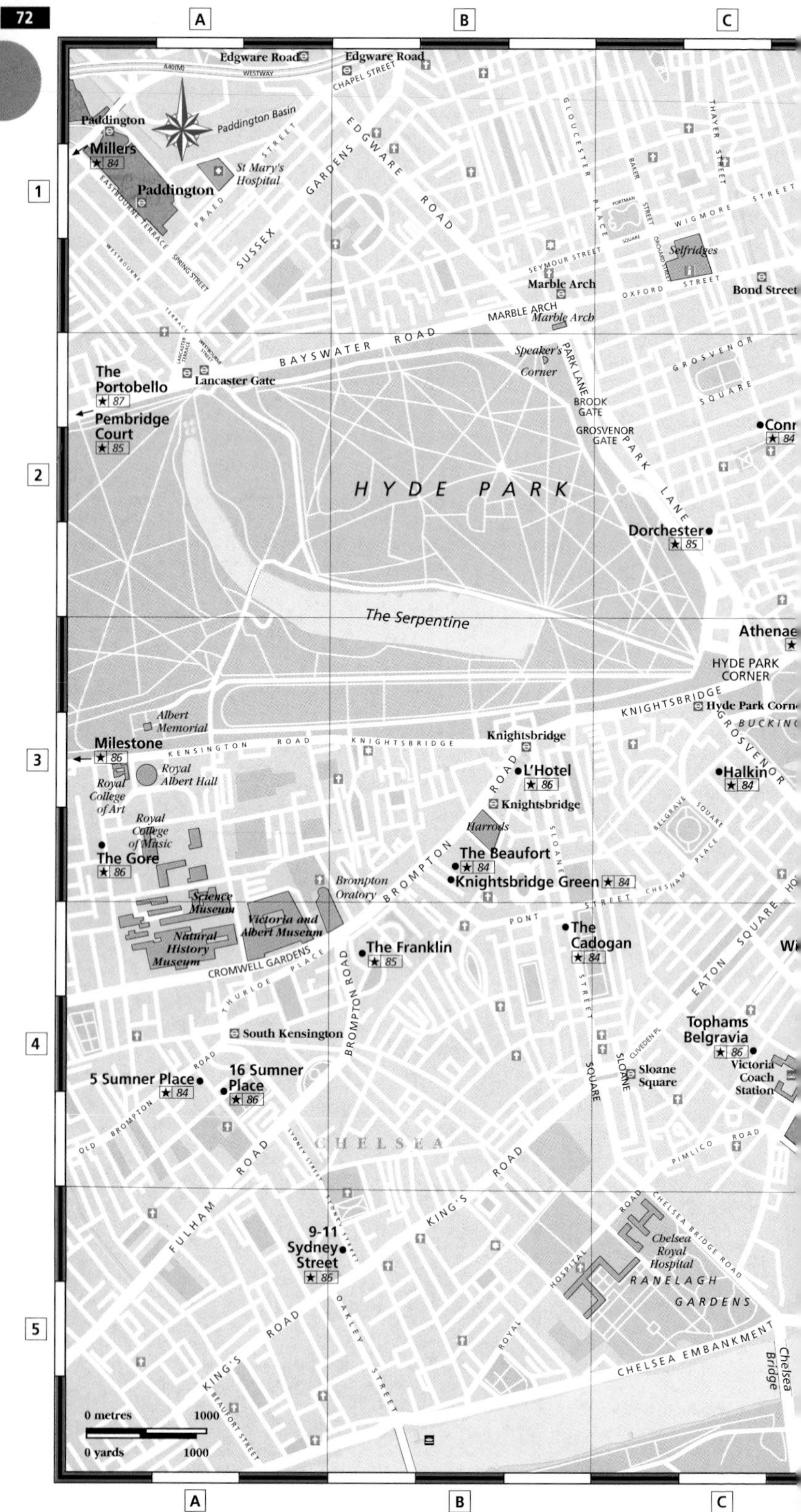
A
B
C
1
2
3
4
5
Edgware Road
Paddington
Millers ★ 84
Paddington
St Mary's Hospital
Paddington Basin
Marble Arch
Bond Street
Selfridges
MARBLE ARCH
Speaker's Corner
BROOK GATE
GROSVENOR GATE
The Portobello ★ 87
Pembridge Court ★ 85
Lancaster Gate
HYDE PARK
Dorchester ★ 85
The Serpentine
HYDE PARK CORNER
Hyde Park Corner
Albert Memorial
Milestone ★ 86
Royal Albert Hall
Royal College of Art
Royal College of Music
The Gore ★ 86
Knightsbridge
L'Hotel ★ 86
Knightsbridge
Harrods
The Beaufort ★ 84
Knightsbridge Green ★ 84
Halkin ★ 84
Brompton Oratory
Science Museum
Victoria and Albert Museum
Natural History Museum
The Franklin ★ 85
The Cadogan ★ 84
South Kensington
Tophams Belgravia ★ 86
Victoria Coach Station
5 Sumner Place ★ 84
16 Sumner Place ★ 86
Sloane Square
CHELSEA
9-11 Sydney Street ★ 85
Chelsea Royal Hospital
RANELAGH GARDENS
CHELSEA EMBANKMENT
Chelsea Bridge
0 metres 1000
0 yards 1000

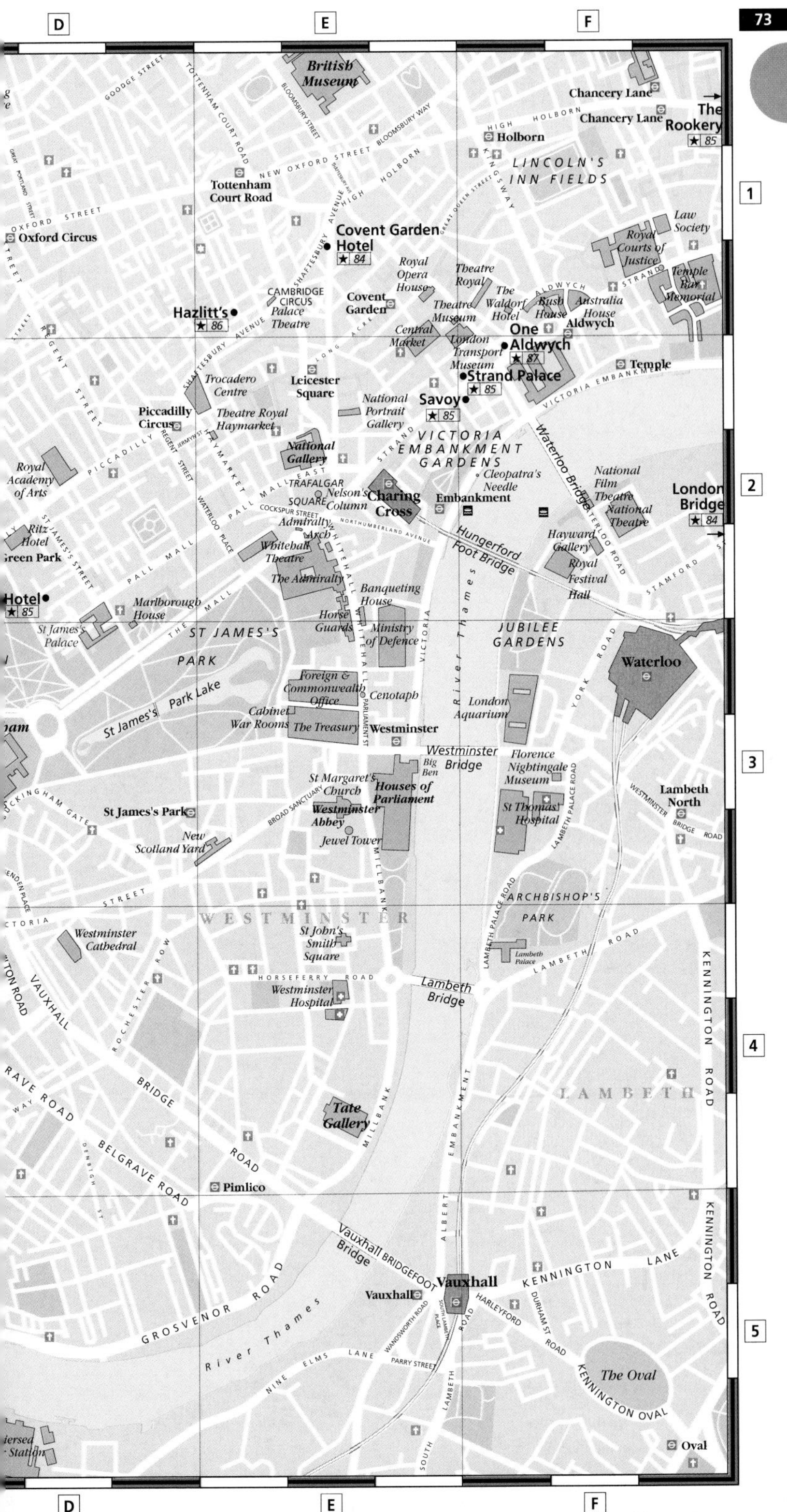

D
E
F
1
2
3
4
5
British Museum
Chancery Lane
The Rookery ★ 85
Holborn
LINCOLN'S INN FIELDS
Tottenham Court Road
Oxford Circus
Covent Garden Hotel ★ 84
Law Society
Royal Courts of Justice
Royal Opera House
Theatre Royal
Temple Bar Memorial
Hazlitt's ★ 86
Cambridge Circus
Palace Theatre
Covent Garden
Theatre Museum
The Waldorf Hotel
Bush House
Australia House
Aldwych
Central Market
London Transport Museum
One Aldwych ★ 87
Strand Palace ★ 85
Temple
Trocadero Centre
Leicester Square
Savoy ★ 85
National Portrait Gallery
Piccadilly Circus
Theatre Royal Haymarket
VICTORIA EMBANKMENT GARDENS
National Gallery
Cleopatra's Needle
National Film Theatre
National Theatre
Royal Academy of Arts
Trafalgar Square
Nelson's Column
Charing Cross
Embankment
Waterloo Bridge
London Bridge ★ 84
Ritz Hotel
Green Park
Admiralty Arch
Whitehall Theatre
The Admiralty
Hungerford Foot Bridge
Hayward Gallery
Royal Festival Hall
Hotel ★ 85
Marlborough House
Banqueting House
St James's Palace
ST JAMES'S PARK
Horse Guards
Ministry of Defence
JUBILEE GARDENS
Waterloo
Park Lake
Foreign & Commonwealth Office
Cenotaph
London Aquarium
Cabinet War Rooms
The Treasury
Westminster
River Thames
Westminster Bridge
Big Ben
Florence Nightingale Museum
St Margaret's Church
Houses of Parliament
St James's Park
Westminster Abbey
St Thomas' Hospital
Lambeth North
New Scotland Yard
Jewel Tower
ARCHBISHOP'S PARK
WESTMINSTER
Westminster Cathedral
St John's Smith Square
Lambeth Palace
Westminster Hospital
Lambeth Bridge
LAMBETH
Tate Gallery
Pimlico
Vauxhall Bridge
Vauxhall
The Oval
Oval
GOODGE STREET
TOTTENHAM COURT ROAD
BLOOMSBURY STREET
BLOOMSBURY WAY
NEW OXFORD STREET
HIGH HOLBORN
KINGSWAY
GREAT QUEEN STREET
OXFORD STREET
SHAFTESBURY AVENUE
ALDWYCH
STRAND
LONG ACRE
REGENT STREET
PICCADILLY
JERMYN ST
HAYMARKET
PALL MALL
PALL MALL EAST
COCKSPUR STREET
NORTHUMBERLAND AVENUE
WATERLOO PLACE
ST JAMES'S STREET
THE MALL
VICTORIA EMBANKMENT
WATERLOO ROAD
STAMFORD
YORK ROAD
WHITEHALL
PARLIAMENT ST
BUCKINGHAM GATE
BROAD SANCTUARY
WESTMINSTER BRIDGE ROAD
LAMBETH PALACE ROAD
MILLBANK
VICTORIA STREET
HORSEFERRY ROAD
LAMBETH ROAD
ROCHESTER ROW
VAUXHALL BRIDGE ROAD
BELGRAVE ROAD
DENBIGH ST
KENNINGTON ROAD
ALBERT EMBANKMENT
GROSVENOR ROAD
BRIDGEFOOT
KENNINGTON LANE
HARLEYFORD ROAD
DURHAM ST
WANDSWORTH ROAD
SOUTH LAMBETH PLACE
PARRY STREET
NINE ELMS LANE
KENNINGTON OVAL
SOUTH LAMBETH ROAD

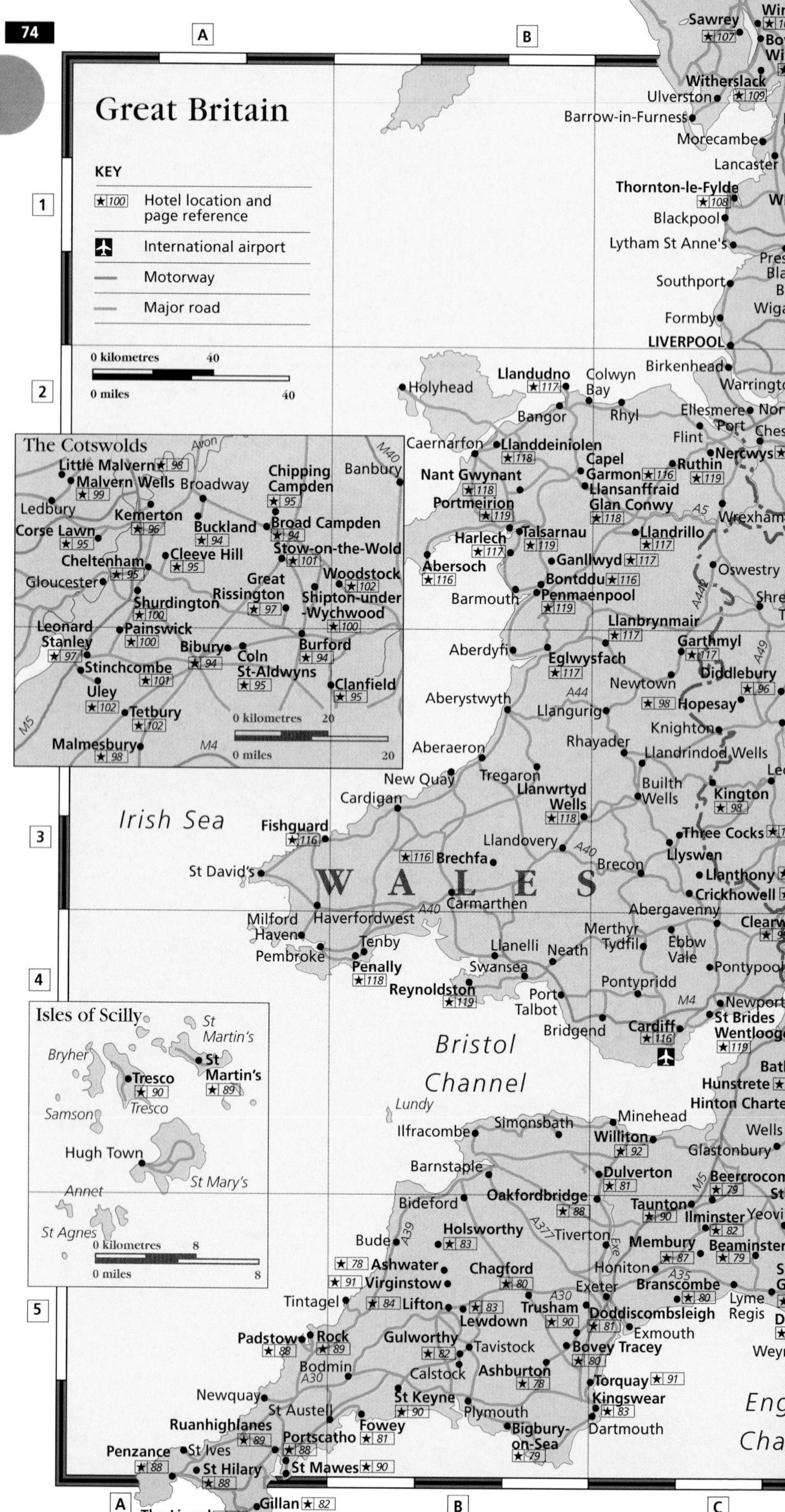

Great Britain
KEY
Hotel location and page reference
International airport
Motorway
Major road
0 kilometres 40
0 miles 40
The Cotswolds
Isles of Scilly
Irish Sea
WALES
Bristol Channel
Holyhead
Llandudno 117
Colwyn Bay
Bangor
Rhyl
Caernarfon
Llanddeiniolen 118
Nant Gwynant 118
Portmeirion 119
Capel Garmon 116
Llansanffraid Glan Conwy 118
Ruthin 119
Harlech 117
Talsarnau 119
Llandrillo 117
Abersoch 116
Ganllwyd 117
Bontddu 116
Penmaenpool 119
Barmouth
Llanbrynmair 117
Garthmyl 117
Aberdyfi
Eglwysfach 117
Newtown
Diddlebury 96
Hopesay 98
Aberystwyth
Llangurig
Knighton
Rhayader
Llandrindod Wells
Aberaeron
Tregaron
Builth Wells
Kington 98
New Quay
Llanwrtyd Wells 118
Cardigan
Fishguard 116
Llandovery
Three Cocks
Llyswen
Brechfa 116
Brecon
Llanthony
Crickhowell
St David's
Carmarthen
Abergavenny
Haverfordwest
Milford Haven
Tenby
Pembroke
Penally 118
Llanelli
Neath
Merthyr Tydfil
Ebbw Vale
Pontypool
Swansea
Pontypridd
Reynoldston 119
Port Talbot
Newport
St Brides Wentlooge 119
Bridgend
Cardiff 116
Sawrey 107
Witherslack 109
Ulverston
Barrow-in-Furness
Morecambe
Lancaster
Thornton-le-Fylde 108
Blackpool
Lytham St Anne's
Southport
Formby
LIVERPOOL
Birkenhead
Ellesmere Port
Flint
Nercwys
Wrexham
Oswestry
A5
A44
A40
A49
A483
M4
Lundy
Ilfracombe
Simonsbath
Minehead
Williton 92
Wells
Glastonbury
Barnstaple
Dulverton 81
Beercrocombe 79
Bideford
Oakfordbridge 88
Taunton 90
Ilminster 82
Bude
Holsworthy 83
Tiverton
Membury 87
Beaminster 79
Ashwater 78
Virginstow 91
Chagford 80
Honiton
Branscombe 80
Exeter
Tintagel
Lifton 84
Lewdown 83
Trusham 90
Doddiscombsleigh 81
Lyme Regis
Padstow 88
Rock 89
Gulworthy 82
Tavistock
Exmouth
Bovey Tracey 80
Bodmin
Calstock
Ashburton 78
Torquay 91
Newquay
St Keyne 90
Kingswear 83
St Austell
Plymouth
Dartmouth
Ruanhighlanes 89
Fowey 81
Bigbury-on-Sea 79
Penzance 88
St Ives
Portscatho 88
St Hilary 88
St Mawes 90
Gillan 82
The Lizard 83
A30
A39
A377
A35
M5
Little Malvern 98
Malvern Wells 99
Broadway
Chipping Campden 95
Banbury
Ledbury
Kemerton 96
Buckland 94
Broad Campden 94
Corse Lawn 95
Cleeve Hill 95
Stow-on-the-Wold 101
Cheltenham 95
Woodstock 102
Gloucester
Great Rissington 97
Shipton-under-Wychwood 100
Shurdington 100
Leonard Stanley 97
Painswick 100
Bibury 94
Coln St-Aldwyns 95
Burford 94
Stinchcombe 101
Clanfield 95
Uley 102
Tetbury 102
Malmesbury 98
0 kilometres 20
0 miles 20
Avon
M40
St Martin's
Bryher
Tresco 90
St Martin's 89
Samson
Tresco
Hugh Town
St Mary's
Annet
St Agnes
0 kilometres 8
0 miles 8
1
2
3
4
5
A
B
C

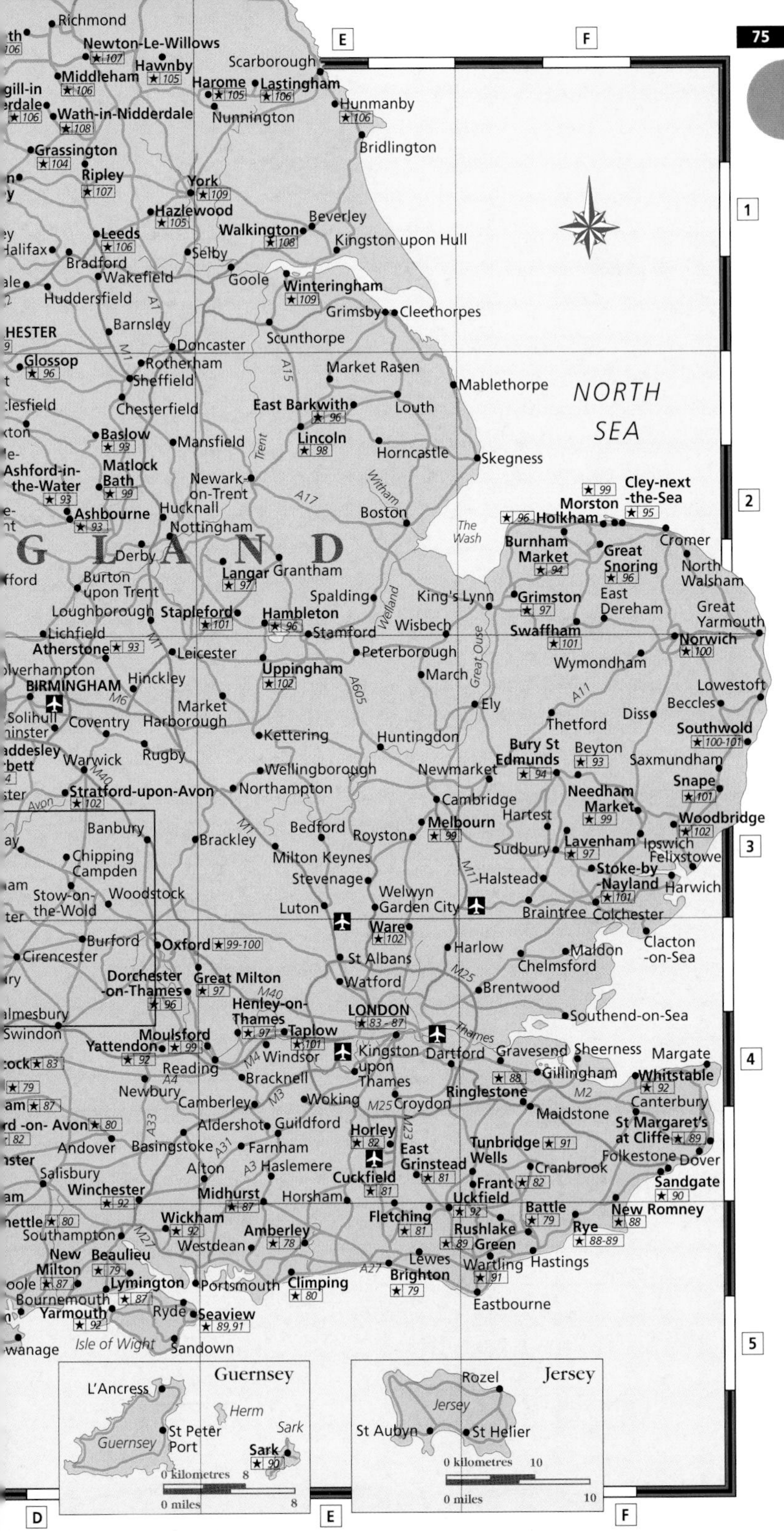

NORTH SEA
ENGLAND
Richmond
Newton-Le-Willows
Hawnby
Scarborough
Middleham
Harome
Lastingham
Hunmanby
Nunnington
Wath-in-Nidderdale
Bridlington
Grassington
Ripley
York
Hazlewood
Beverley
Leeds
Walkington
Kingston upon Hull
Halifax
Selby
Bradford
Wakefield
Goole
Winteringham
Huddersfield
Grimsby
Cleethorpes
Barnsley
Scunthorpe
Doncaster
Glossop
Rotherham
Market Rasen
Sheffield
Mablethorpe
Chesterfield
East Barkwith
Louth
Baslow
Mansfield
Lincoln
Horncastle
Matlock Bath
Skegness
Ashford-in-the-Water
Newark-on-Trent
Cley-next-the-Sea
Morston
Hucknall
Boston
Holkham
Ashbourne
Nottingham
The Wash
Burnham Market
Great Snoring
Cromer
Derby
North Walsham
Langar
Grantham
Burton upon Trent
Spalding
King's Lynn
Grimston
East Dereham
Loughborough
Stapleford
Hambleton
Great Yarmouth
Lichfield
Stamford
Wisbech
Swaffham
Norwich
Atherstone
Leicester
Peterborough
Wymondham
Uppingham
March
BIRMINGHAM
Hinckley
Lowestoft
Solihull
Coventry
Market Harborough
Ely
Beccles
Thetford
Diss
Southwold
Kettering
Huntingdon
Bury St Edmunds
Beyton
Warwick
Rugby
Saxmundham
Wellingborough
Newmarket
Snape
Stratford-upon-Avon
Northampton
Needham Market
Cambridge
Hartest
Woodbridge
Banbury
Bedford
Royston
Melbourn
Brackley
Lavenham
Ipswich
Chipping Campden
Sudbury
Felixstowe
Milton Keynes
Stoke-by-Nayland
Halstead
Stow-on-the-Wold
Woodstock
Stevenage
Harwich
Welwyn Garden City
Luton
Braintree
Colchester
Ware
Burford
Oxford
Harlow
Clacton-on-Sea
Cirencester
St Albans
Maldon
Chelmsford
Dorchester-on-Thames
Great Milton
Watford
Brentwood
Henley-on-Thames
LONDON
Southend-on-Sea
Swindon
Moulsford
Taplow
Yattendon
Kingston upon Thames
Dartford
Gravesend
Sheerness
Margate
Windsor
Reading
Gillingham
Whitstable
Bracknell
Newbury
Ringlestone
Camberley
Woking
Croydon
Canterbury
Maidstone
Aldershot
Guildford
St Margaret's at Cliffe
Horley
Andover
Basingstoke
Farnham
Tunbridge Wells
East Grinstead
Dover
Folkestone
Salisbury
Alton
Haslemere
Cranbrook
Cuckfield
Sandgate
Winchester
Midhurst
Frant
Horsham
Uckfield
Battle
New Romney
Wickham
Fletching
Rye
Southampton
Amberley
Rushlake Green
Westdean
New Milton
Beaulieu
Lewes
Hastings
Wartling
Lymington
Portsmouth
Climping
Brighton
Bournemouth
Eastbourne
Yarmouth
Ryde
Seaview
Isle of Wight
Sandown
Guernsey
L'Ancress
Herm
Sark
St Peter Port
Jersey
Rozel
St Aubyn
St Helier
0 kilometres 8
0 miles 8
0 kilometres 10
0 miles 10

A
B
C
1
2
3
4
5
Lewis
Stornoway
A859
Outer
Hebrides
Tarbert
Scarista
115
North
Uist
A865
Achiltibule
110
Ullapool
115
A832
Loch
Shin
Uig
115
Colbost
111
Dunvegan
Portree
114
Skye
South
Uist
Kyle of Lochalsh
A850
A896
113
Muir of Ord
110
Drumnadrochit
111
Dingwa
Inver
ATLANTIC
OCEAN
Isle Ornsay
112
A87
Sleat
115
Mallaig
Arisaig
Fort
Augustus
Loch
Lochy
Loch Morar
A830
Inner
Hebrides
Loch
Shiel
Spean Bridg
115
Fort William
111, 113
Strontian
115
Tobermory
Port Appin
114
Kentallen
112
A82
112
Eriska
Mull
Oban
A85
Loch
Awe
Kilchrenan
113
Inveraray
Balquhidder
110
Colonsay
110
Jura
A83
Strachur
115
Loch
Lomond
Greenock
Dumb
Tarbert
115
Largs
GLASGOW
Islay
East Kilb
A78
Arran
Irvine
Kilm
Troon
Prestw
Ayr
Campbeltown
Maybole
114
Carndonagh
Dunfanaghy
Buncrana
Portrush
Girvan
North
Channel
Coleraine
Ballymoney
A77
Letterkenny
Londonderry
A2
A6
Stranraer
A75
Ballybofey
Strabane
Maghera
Larne
Portpatrick
114
Ballymena
Kirkcudb
Donegal
M22
M2
NORTHERN
IRELAND
Antrim
Carrickfergus
Omagh
A505
Cookstown
Lough
Neagh
Bangor
Ballyshannon
A32
BELFAST
Lisburn
Newtownards
Lower
Lough
Erne
Dungannon
M1
Portadown
Isle of Man
Enniskillen
Armagh
Banbridge
Clones
Monaghan
Newry
Newcastle
Douglas
A
B
C

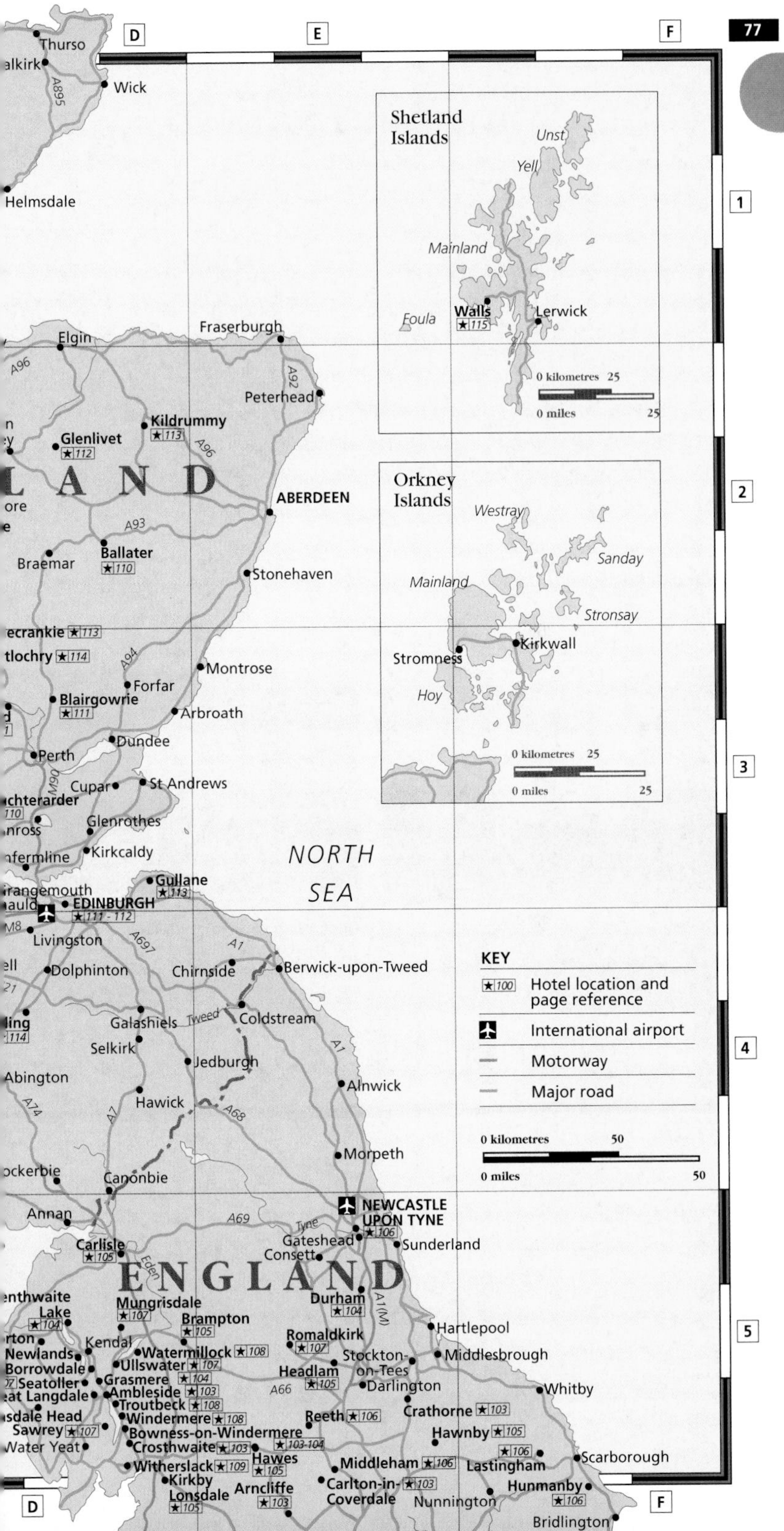
D
E
F
1
2
3
4
5
Thurso
Wick
Helmsdale
Shetland Islands
Unst
Yell
Mainland
Foula
Walls
★115
Lerwick
0 kilometres 25
0 miles 25
Elgin
Fraserburgh
Peterhead
Kildrummy
★113
Glenlivet
★112
LAND
ABERDEEN
Orkney Islands
Westray
Sanday
Mainland
Stronsay
Kirkwall
Stromness
Hoy
0 kilometres 25
0 miles 25
Braemar
Ballater
★110
Stonehaven
Montrose
Forfar
Blairgowrie
★111
Arbroath
Dundee
Perth
Cupar
St Andrews
Glenrothes
Kirkcaldy
NORTH SEA
Gullane
★113
EDINBURGH
★111 - 112
Livingston
Dolphinton
Chirnside
Berwick-upon-Tweed
Galashiels
Coldstream
Selkirk
Jedburgh
Abington
Hawick
Alnwick
Morpeth
Canonbie
Annan
Carlisle
★105
NEWCASTLE UPON TYNE
★106
Gateshead
Consett
Sunderland
ENGLAND
Mungrisdale
★107
Brampton
★105
Durham
★104
Hartlepool
Romaldkirk
★107
Kendal
Watermillock ★108
Ullswater ★107
Grasmere ★104
Ambleside ★103
Troutbeck ★108
Windermere ★108
Bowness-on-Windermere
★103-104
Crosthwaite ★103
Witherslack ★109
Kirkby Lonsdale
★105
Hawes
★105
Arncliffe
★103
Headlam
★105
Stockton-on-Tees
Middlesbrough
Darlington
Crathorne ★103
Reeth ★106
Hawnby ★105
Middleham ★106
Carlton-in-Coverdale
★103
Lastingham
★106
Whitby
Scarborough
Hunmanby
★106
Nunnington
Bridlington
KEY
★100 Hotel location and page reference
International airport
Motorway
Major road
0 kilometres 50
0 miles 50

Southern England

London • Southeast • Southwest
Isle of Wight • Isles of Scilly • Channel Islands

The deep lanes, hidden valleys and sheltered creeks and coves of Cornwall and Devon make magical settings for a range of charming places to stay, from sophisticated seaside hotels to simple farmhouse B&Bs. In Dorset, Somerset and Avon there are a wealth of gracious mansions and manor houses which have been turned into hotels, perfect choices for a weekend treat. In the southeast, Sussex and Kent are favoured with a crop of delightful traditional buildings, some of them medieval, in which to stay. London had spent many years in the doldrums, but the city and its environs now have an impressive range of beautifully run, highly individual hotels. Note, however, that they are expensive and there are as yet few which stand out in the budget category.

Bath

Bath Priory This is a perfect choice for a weekend treat, combining the seclusion of a country house hotel with the attractions of Bath a stroll away. The bedrooms are luxurious yet homely; the sophisticated drawing room is done out in deep reds and ochre yellow. Smooth service and excellent food (Michelin star).
Weston Rd, Bath, Somerset BA1 2XT. **Map** p74 C4. (01225) 331922. FAX (01225) 448276. @ mail@thebathpriory.co.uk b,l,d. **Rooms** 32. Never. AE, DC, MC V. ££££

Bath

Queensberry Discreet, quiet and beautifully decorated central Bath haven, with a lift to all levels. Along the characterful maze of corridors are spacious bedrooms with lovely cotton sheets on the (mainly) king-size beds and lavish bathrooms. Two attractive drawing rooms and a popular basement restaurant, the Olive Tree.
Russel St, Bath, Somerset BA1 2QF. **Map** p74 C4. (01225) 447928. FAX (01225) 446065. @ enquiries@bathqueensberry.com b,l,d. **Rooms** 29. Never. AE, DC, MC, V. £££

Amberley

Amberley Castle The real thing, complete with battlements and portcullis in a charming village. Baronial luxury, plus Jacuzzis.
Amberley, Arundel, West Sussex BN18 9ND. **Map** p75 E5. (01798) 831992. FAX (01798) 831998. @ info@amberleycastle.co.uk b,l,d. **Rooms** 19. ££££

Ashburton

Holne Chase Quiet, restful former hunting lodge inside Dartmoor National Park. Perfect for sporting enthusiasts: fishing and shooting on tap.
Ashburton, Devon TQ13 7NS. **Map** p74 B5. (01364) 631471. FAX (01364) 631453. @ info@holne-chase.co.uk b,l,d. **Rooms** 17. £££

Ashwater

Blagdon Manor Small country house hotel, lost in lovely countryside, run on personal yet professional lines. Pretty bedrooms; good food.
Ashwater, Devon EX21 5DF. **Map** p74 B5. (01409) 211224. FAX (01409) 211634. @ stay@blagdon.com b,l,d. **Rooms** 7. ££

Bath

Sydney Gardens This large Italianate house overlooking a small park on the edge of town makes a light, attractive and spacious B&B.
Sydney Rd, Bath, Somerset BA2 6NT. **Map** p74 C4. (01225) 464818. FAX (01225) 484347. @ book@sydneygardens.co.uk b. **Rooms** 6. ££

Bath

Royal Crescent Occupying the central section of Bath's immaculate Georgian Royal Crescent, the hotel operates to the highest standards and is now one of the country's grandest and most gracious townhouse hotels. It comes complete with secluded garden, pampering health spa, hot air balloon for flights over Bath and river launch. ☒ 16 Royal Crescent, Bath, Somerset BA1 2LS. **Map** p74 C4. (01225) 823333. FAX (01225) 339401. @ reservations@royalcrescent.co.uk b,l,d. **Rooms** 45. Never. AE, DC, MC, V. ££££

Battle

Little Hemingfold This rural haven is hidden away amid farm and woodland yet close to many historic places, including the site of the Battle of Hastings. The rambling house is surrounded by gardens and overlooks a trout lake (fishing, rowing). Inside is cosy (log fires) and full of interesting corners, with plain but individual bedrooms; traditional, satisfying cooking. ☒ Battle, East Sussex TN33 0TT. **Map** p75 F5. (01424) 774338. FAX (01424) 775351. b,d. **Rooms** 12. 1 Jan to 12 Feb. AE, DC, MC, V. ££

Bathford

Eagle House In a fine village near Bath, this gracious Georgian mansion is run as a guesthouse by its professional yet informal owners, the Napiers. The house is decorated without pomp, using an eclectic mix of furniture, and has an elegant drawing room overlooking landscaped gardens and beyond. Children stay free. ☒ Church St, Bathford, Somerset BA1 7RS. **Map** p75 D4. (01225) 859946. FAX (01225) 859430. @ jonap@eagleho.demon.co.uk b. **Rooms** 8. 12 Dec to 8 Jan. MC, V. ££

Bigbury-on-Sea

Burgh Island Board a wheezing sea tractor to the small island that houses this genuine Art Deco hotel. It has been lovingly restored and is still acting out the Roaring Twenties, when it played host to a string of famous people including Agatha Christie. There is a feast of Art Deco furniture and fittings in every room. Great views. ☒ Bigbury-on-Sea, Devon TQ7 4BG. **Map** p74 B5. (01548) 810514. FAX (01548) 810243. @ reception @burghisland.com b,l,d. **Rooms** 21. 2 to 23 Jan. AE, MC, V. ££££

Beaminster

Bridge House Originally a 13th-century clergy house, deep in Hardy country with pretty bedrooms and more than adequate food. ☒ Beaminster, Dorset DT8 3AY. **Map** p74 C5. (01308) 862200. FAX (01308) 863700. @ enquiries@ bridge-house.co.uk b,l,d. **Rooms** 14. £££

Beaulieu

Montagu Arms In a charming New Forest village, a pleasant, smart, sedate hotel. ☒ Palace Lane, Beaulieu, Hampshire SO42 7ZL. **Map** p75 D5. (01590) 612324. FAX (01590) 612188. @ reservations@montaguarmshotel.co.uk b,l,d. **Rooms** 23. £££

Beercrocombe

Frog Street Farm Hidden, flower-bedecked Somerset longhouse run by friendly farmers and racehorse breeders Veronica and Henry Cole. Log fires, fine Jacobean panelling. ☒ Beercrocombe, Taunton, Somerset TA3 6AF. **Map** p74 C4. FAX (01823) 480430. b,d. **Rooms** 3. £

Brighton

Hotel du Vin The newest hotel in this stylish micro-chain. Sleekly modern yet warm and intimate. ☒ Ship Street, Brighton, West Sussex BN1 1AD. **Map** p75 E5. (01273) 718588. FAX (01273) 718599. @ info@ brighton.hotelduvin.com b,l,d. **Rooms** 37. £££

Bradford-on-Avon

Priory Steps A row of 17th-century weavers' cottages has been sympathetically restored by Carey and Diana Chapman to become both their home and a welcoming small hotel. The bedrooms, carefully decorated with antiques, are surprisingly spacious and light, with sweeping views. Dinner is served at the communal table.
Newtown, Bradford-on-Avon, Wiltshire BA15 1NQ. **Map** p75 D4. (01225) 862230. FAX (01225) 866248. @ priorysteps@clara.co.uk b,d. **Rooms** 5. Never. MC, V. ££

Chagford

Gidleigh Park This luxurious Dartmoor hotel has been run by the Hendersons for the past 25 years, and is still as polished and relaxing as ever. In the oak-panelled sitting room and the bedrooms a feeling of good living and serenity abounds. The superb food (two Michelin stars) is a highlight, as is the wine. Golf, fishing, tennis, croquet.
Chagford, Devon TQ13 8HH. **Map** p74 B5. (01647) 432367. FAX (01647) 432574. @ gidleighpark@gidleigh.co.uk b,l,d. **Rooms** 14, plus 1 cottage. Never. MC, V. ££££

Branscombe

Mason's Arms Branscombe is a picturesque Devon seaside village surrounded by steep, wooded hills. It's a hive of activity for walkers in winter and beachcombers in summer, and the Mason's Arms makes a perfect base for both camps. The bedrooms are cottagey, with (mainly) ensuite bathrooms.
Branscombe, Devon EX12 3DJ. **Map** p74 C5. (01297) 680300. FAX (01297) 680500. @ reception@masonsarms.co.uk b,l,d. **Rooms** 22. Never. MC,V. ££

Chettle

Castleman Chettle is special: the estate village is still owned by one family, the Bourkes, who live in its fine Queen Anne manor house. The former dower house is now a hotel and restaurant, run by Teddy Bourke and Barbara Garnsworthy along informal lines: no frills, but period features and spacious rooms attractively decorated.
Chettle, Blandford Forum, Dorset DT11 8DB. **Map** p75 D5. (01258) 830096. FAX (01258) 830051. @ chettle@globalnet.co.uk b,d. **Rooms** 8. Christmas, Feb. MC,V. ££

Bovey Tracey

Bel Alp House On Dartmoor's edge, a sedate Edwardian house with glorious seaward views from the terrace across a patchwork of fields.
Haytor, Bovey Tracey, Devon TQ13 9XX. **Map** p74 C5. (01364) 661217. FAX (01364) 661292. b,d. **Rooms** 8. £££

Bradford-on-Avon

Bradford Old Windmill Simple, romantic bedrooms, ethnic curiosities and exotic cooking.
Masons Lane, Bradford-on-Avon, Wiltshire BA15 1QN. **Map** p75 D4. (01225) 866842. FAX (01225) 866648. @ gtpleurope@bradfordoldwindmill.co.uk b,d. **Rooms** 3. ££

Climping

Bailiffscourt An astonishingly realistic 1930s' re-creation of a medieval manor houses a slightly corporate luxury hotel, handy for Gatwick.
Climping, West Sussex BN17 5RW. **Map** p75 E5. (01903) 723511. FAX (01903) 723107. @ bailiffscourt@hshotels.co.uk b,l,d. **Rooms** 39. £££

Colerne

Lucknam Park Stately hotel with aristocratic interior, formal dining and a leisure complex.
Colerne, Chippenham, Wiltshire SN14 8AZ. **Map** p75 D4. (01225) 742777. FAX (01225) 743536. @ reservations@lucknampark.co.uk b,l,d. **Rooms** 41. ££££

CUCKFIELD

Ockenden Manor Superb views of the South Downs can be had from the grounds of this fine 16th-century manor. The hotel is elegantly furnished; creative English food is served in the atmospheric wood-panelled dining room with painted ceiling and stained-glass windows. Rooms are individual and spacious, service is friendly.
Ockenden Lane, Cuckfield, West Sussex RH17 5LD. **Map** p75 E5. (01444) 416111. FAX (01444) 415549. ockenden@hshotels.co.uk b,l,d. **Rooms** 22. Never. AE, DC, MC, V. £££

EVERSHOT

Summer Lodge The many devotees of this former dower house in the heart of Dorset love its assets: French windows leading onto flowery gardens; airy bedrooms; good food served in a formal but pretty dining room. Peace, comfort, and a touch of extravagance without intimidation. For exercise there is tennis and croquet.
Summer Lane, Evershot, Dorset DT2 0JR. **Map** p74 C5. (01935) 83424. FAX (01935) 83005. reservations@summerlodgehotel.com b,l,d. **Rooms** 18. Never. AE, DC, MC, V. £££

EAST GRINSTEAD

Gravetye Manor For more than 40 years this serene Elizabethan house has exuded understated luxury – at a price. It is close to London, yet surrounded by natural English gardens and woodland. Standards are unfailingly high, with award-winning cooking and attentive yet unobtrusive service.
Vowels Lane, East Grinstead, West Sussex RH19 4LJ. **Map** p75 E4. (01342) 810567. FAX (01342) 810080. info@gravetyemanor.co.uk b,l,d. **Rooms** 18. Never. MC, V. ££££

FOWEY

Fowey Hall The grandest of a group of hotels designed specifically for families. The facilities for children are endless, yet there is plenty of sophistication for grown-ups too. The setting, overlooking the Fowey estuary and the sea, is an extravagant late 19th-century mansion; modern comforts and leisure activities.
Hanson Drive, Fowey, Cornwall PL23 1ET. **Map** p74 B5. (01726) 833866. FAX (01726) 834100. info@foweyhall.com b,l,d. **Rooms** 25. Never. AE, MC, V. £££

DODDISCOMBSLEIGH

Nobody Inn Quintessential West Country inn with satisfying food and wines; the large rooms are a stroll away in an old house, Town Barton.
Doddiscombsleigh, Exeter, Devon EX6 7PS. **Map** p74 C5. (01647) 252394. FAX (01647) 252978. info@nobodyinn.co.uk b,l,d. **Rooms** 7. ££

DORCHESTER

Casterbridge Georgian town-centre hotel with bright rooms (some small); generous breakfasts served in pretty conservatory. Good value.
49 High East St, Dorchester, Dorset DT1 1HU. **Map** p74 C5. (01305) 264043. FAX (01305) 260884. reception@casterbridgehotel.co.uk b. **Rooms** 15. ££

DULVERTON

Ashwick House Edwardian house on Exmoor. Galleried hall, traditional dining room, thoughtfully equipped bedrooms.
Dulverton, Somerset TA22 9QD. **Map** p74 C4. FAX (01398) 323868. ashwickhouse@talk21.com b,d. **Rooms** 6. ££

FLETCHING

Griffin Inn Popular pub and local restaurant with above-average food. Mostly four-posters. Rooms in the Coach House are sought after.
Fletching, Uckfield, East Sussex TN22 3NE. **Map** p 75 E5. (01825) 722890. FAX (01825) 722810. b,l,d. **Rooms** 8. ££

Frant

Old Parsonage In a charming village, a gracious Georgian country house run as a B&B by Tony and Mary Dakin. Tall, spacious reception rooms are impressively decorated without being overpowering: antiques, Persian rugs, chandeliers, photographs and lithographs on the walls. There is an airy conservatory, and the fresh bedrooms have large bathrooms. Excellent breakfasts.
Church Lane, Frant, Tunbridge Wells, Kent TN3 9DX. **Map** p75 F4. FAX (01892) 750773. @ oldparson@aol.com b. **Rooms** 4. Never. MC, V. ££

Horley

Langshott Manor Gatwick is only a couple of miles away, and urban sprawl is close at hand, but this brick-and-timber Elizabethan manor remains at peace in its own landscaped grounds. The expense-account luxury includes swish, well-equipped bedrooms and an intimate dining room; the price includes a week's free airport parking.
Langshott, Horley, Surrey RH6 9LN. **Map** p75 E4. (01293) 786680. FAX (01293) 783905. @ admin@langshott.co.uk b,l,d. **Rooms** 22. Never. AE, DC, MC, V. ££££

Frome

Babington House This contemporary country house hotel offers child-friendly metropolitan chic and unpretentious luxury: cinema, computers, health centre, crêche, tennis, snooker, relaxed but efficient 24-hour service and wonderful bedrooms. In the bathrooms are huge bottles of complimentary lotions – no mean sachets here.
Babington, Frome, Somerset BA11 3RW. **Map** p75 D4. (01373) 812266. FAX (01373) 812112. @ enquiries@babingtonhouse.co.uk b,l,d. **Rooms** 28. Never. AE, DC, MC, V. ££££

Ilminster

Old Rectory Down a winding road in the Somerset countryside, the Old Rectory – a 16th-century building sensitively preserved and enhanced with modern comforts – is the perfect place to unwind. Dinner, on request, is served at a communal table, from a menu of all-local produce.
Cricket Malherbie, Ilminster, Somerset TA19 0PW. **Map** p74 C5. (01460) 54364. FAX (01460) 51374. @ theoldrectory@malherbie.freeserve.co.uk b,d (by appointment). **Rooms** 5. Christmas. MC, V. ££

Gillan

Tregildry In a magical setting overlooking a romantic Cornish creek, a vividly decorated hotel with breezy Far Eastern feel.
Gillan, Manaccan, Helston, Cornwall TR12 6HG. **Map** p74 A5. (01326) 231378. FAX (01326) 231561. @ trgildry@globalnet.co.uk b,d. **Rooms** 10. £££

Gillingham

Stock Hill House Victorian manor, set in wooded grounds and decorated in the grandly personal style of its owners. Formal dining.
Gillingham, Dorset SP8 5NR. **Map** p75 D4. (01747) 823626. FAX (01747) 825628. @ reception@stockhillhouse.co.uk b,l,d. **Rooms** 8. ££££

Gulworthy

Horn of Plenty Secluded, creeper-covered house in a splendid location overlooking the Tamar Valley. Notable restaurant.
Gulworthy, Tavistock, Devon PL19 8JD. **Map** p74 B5. (01822) 832528. FAX (01822) 832528. @ enquiries@thehornofplenty. co.uk b,l,d. **Rooms** 10. £££

Hinton Charterhouse

Homewood Park Georgian building in award-winning gardens.
Hinton Charterhouse, Bath, Somerset BA2 7TB. **Map** p74 C4. (01225) 723731. FAX (01225) 723820. @ res@homewoodpark.com b,l,d. **Rooms** 19. £££

Lacock

At The Sign of the Angel The epitome of the medieval English inn – half-timbered, with great log fires in cold weather, beamed ceilings, oak panelling, venerable old beds and gleaming antique furniture. The village is owned and cared for by the National Trust. The pleasures are simple, the setting memorable.
6 Church St, Lacock, Chippenham, Wiltshire SN15 2LB. **Map** p75 D4. (01249) 730230. FAX (01249) 730527. @ angel@lacock.co.uk b,l,d. **Rooms** 10. Christmas. AE, DC, MC, V. ££

London

The Athenaeum Hotel and Apartments The Athenaeum has a caring reputation, but lone women are made to feel particularly welcome. Most rooms are comfortable rather than luxurious, with standard bathrooms, but each has a CD and video player and a proper bar. There is also a range of serviced apartments, some sumptuous.
116 Piccadilly, London W1J 7BJ. **Map** p72 C3. (020) 7499 3464. FAX (020) 7493 1860. @ info@athenaeumhotel.com b,l,d. **Rooms** 157, plus 34 apts. Never. AE, DC, MC, V. ££££

The Lizard

Landewednack House This lovely old rectory in a thatched hamlet has a superb headland position. The views across the garden and the church to the sea are heavenly, and the three bedrooms are supremely elegant and luxurious. Guests dine *en famille*; local seafood dishes, perhaps lobster or crab, are a highlight.
Church Cove, The Lizard, Helston, Cornwall TR12 7PQ. **Map** p74 A5. (01326) 290909. FAX (01326) 290192. @ landewednack.house@amserve.com b,d. **Rooms** 3. Never. MC, V. ££

London

Beaufort Consistently praised and with a high percentage of faithful regulars, this is an exceptional townhouse hotel. It is noted for the friendly attitude of its mainly female staff, the smart, tasteful decor, and the wealth of extras included in the rates (airport limo, cream teas, champagne). In a quiet street near Harrods.
33 Beaufort Gardens, London SW3 1PP. **Map** p72 B3. (020) 7584 5252. FAX (020) 7589 2834. @ reservations@thebeaufort.co.uk b. **Rooms** 27. Never. AE, DC, MC, V. ££££

Holsworthy

Court Barn Easy-going warmth is the keynote in this reassuringly homely old house. Elegant dining room; park-like grounds.
Clawton, Holsworthy, Devon EX22 6PS. **Map** p74 B5. (01409) 271219. FAX (01409) 271309. @ courtbarnhotel@talk21.com b,l,d. **Rooms** 8. ££

Hunstrete

Hunstrete House A refined atmosphere fills this mellow, Georgian townhouse. Classy cooking.
Hunstrete, Pensford, Bath, Somerset BS39 4NS. **Map** p74 C4. (01761) 490490. FAX (01761) 490732. @ info@hunstretehouse.co.uk b,l,d. **Rooms** 25. £££

Kingswear

Nonsuch House Fabulous views across the River Dart. Bedrooms named after local sea areas.
Church Hill, Kingswear, Dartmouth, Devon TQ6 0BX. **Map** p74 C5. (01803) 752829. FAX (01803) 752357. @ enquiries@nonsuch-house.co.uk b,d. **Rooms** 3. ££

Lewdown

Lewtrenchard Manor Stunning 400-year-old house with a splendid antique-filled interior. New restaurant added recently; reports, please.
Lewdown, Okehampton, Devon EX20 4PN. **Map** p74 B5. (01566) 783256. FAX (01566) 783332. @ stay@lewtrenchard.co.uk b,l,d. **Rooms** 9. £££

For key to symbols see backflap. For price categories *see p71*

London

Cadogan This quietly old-fashioned hotel on the borders of Chelsea and Knightsbridge is where Oscar Wilde was arrested (room 118). You can stay here, surrounded by photographs of the playwright. (In Paris, at l'Hotel, you can stay in the room in which he died.) Lilly Langtry's home was also here. Dignified, warm and comforting.
75 Sloane St, London SW1X 9SG. **Map** p72 B4.
(020) 7235 7141. FAX (020) 7245 0994.
@ info@cadogan.com b,l,d. **Rooms** 65.
Never. MC, V. ££££

London

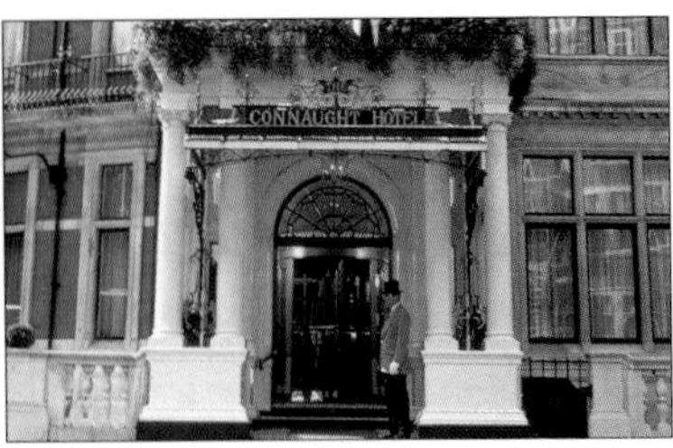

Connaught For service – the type of impeccable, deferential service perfected by Jeeves – look no further. Now almost a living time-warp, this bastion of Britishness continues to turn a haughtily blind eye to the modern world; there are few newfangled frills. Restaurant is managed by top chef Gordon Ramsay.
Carlos Place, London W1K 2AL. **Map** p72 C2.
(020) 7499 7070. FAX (020) 7495 3262.
@ info@the-connaught.co.uk b,l,d. **Rooms** 92.
Never. AE, DC, MC, V. ££££

London

Colonnade Set amongst the canals and bridges of Little Venice, the Colonnade occupies a pair of Victorian townhouses that once did duty as a maternity hospital (Alan Turing was born here). Sigmund Freud stayed here; you can too, in eclectic but comfortable surroundings. Eat contemporary Mediterranean in the Enigma bar and restaurant.
2 Warrington Crescent, Little Venice, London W9 1ER. **Map** p75 E4. (020) 7286 1052. FAX (020) 7286 1057.
@ res_colonnade@etontownhouse.com b,l,d.
Rooms 43. Christmas. AE, DC, MC, V. £££

London

Covent Garden If you are at home in a trendy location and starry company, you will delight in this exceptional hotel, smack in the bustling heart of London. The former hospital combines inspired design and the latest technology with panache. Stunning drawing room with honesty bar; smiling young staff. Screening room.
10 Monmouth St, London WC2H 9HB.
Map p73 E1. (020) 7806 1000. FAX (020) 7806 1100.
@ covent@firmdale.com b,l,d. **Rooms** 58.
Never. AE, MC, V. ££££

Lifton

Arundell Arms Traditional, characterful sporting inn with 20 miles of fishing on the Tamar river and its four tributaries. Log fires, modish food.
Lifton, Devon PL16 0AA. **Map** p74 B5. (01566) 784666. FAX (01566) 784494. @ reservations@arundellarms.com b,l,d. **Rooms** 27. £££

London

Five Sumner Place Award-winning, recently renovated, fairly priced South Kensington B&B.
5 Sumner Place, London SW7 3EE. **Map** p72 A4.
(020) 7584 7586. FAX (020) 7823 9962.
@ reservations@sumnerplace.com b.
Rooms 13. £££

London

Halkin Armani-dressed staff deliver seriously good service at this sleek, minimalist yet friendly hotel. Michelin-starred Thai restaurant.
5 Halkin St, London SW1X 7DJ. **Map** p72 C3.
(020) 7333 1000. FAX (020) 7333 1100.
@ res@halkin.co.uk b,l,d. **Rooms** 41. ££££

London

Knightsbridge Green Comfortable, friendly, no-frills hotel midway between Harrods and Harvey Nics. Excellent full English breakfast.
159 Knightsbridge. **Map** p72 B3. (020) 7584 6274.
FAX (020) 7225 1635. @ thekghotel@aol.com b.
Rooms 28. £££

London

Dorchester Of London's great hotels, this has the edge, sweeping into the lead after its 1990 refurbishment. The 1930s building, looming over Park Lane like an ocean liner, was designed as the perfect grand hotel, and it is. It encompasses corporate events, film star guests, traditional atmosphere, and sumptuous modern luxury.
Park Lane, London W1A 2HJ. **Map** p72 C2. (020) 7629 8888. FAX (020) 7409 0114. @ reservations@dorchesterhotel.com b,l,d. **Rooms** 250. Never. AE, DC, MC, V. ££££

London

Franklin This is a top-notch townhouse hotel by any standards, protective and relaxing, but what sets the Franklin apart is the bedrooms. Some are enormous, or look onto beautifully kept communal gardens, full of white roses in summer. Inside are florals and stripes, flounces and swags and huge beds, some canopied.
28 Egerton Gardens, London SW3 2DB. **Map** p72 B4. (020) 7584 5533. FAX (020) 7584 5449. @ bookings@franklinhotel.co.uk b,l,d. **Rooms** 47. Never. AE, DC, MC, V. ££££

London

Dukes Hotel Discreetly set back in its own gas-lit courtyard, this civilized Edwardian hideaway contrives to be both intimate and animated. This is particularly true of the clubby bar, renowned for its dry Martinis. English country house decoration without excess; charming, helpful staff. Health club and spa.
St James's Place, London SW1A 1NY. **Map** p73 D2. (020) 7491 4840. FAX (020) 7493 1264. @ enquiries@dukeshotel.co.uk b,l,d. **Rooms** 89. Never. AE, DC, MC, V. ££££

London

Gore With loads of character, including an animated public bar and bistro but a contrastingly quiet sitting room, this makes a delightfully congenial place to stay. Walls are covered in paintings and prints; bedrooms are crammed with antiques and idiosyncracies – ornate beds, a throne loo here, a gallery there.
190 Queen's Gate, London SW7 5EX. **Map** p72 A3. (020) 7584 6601. FAX (020) 7589 8127. @ reservations@gorehotel.co.uk b,l,d. **Rooms** 53. Never. AE, DC, MC, V. £££

London

London Bridge Glossy, elegant business and leisure hotel in regenerated area near City.
8-18 London Bridge St, London SE1 9SG. **Map** p73 F2. (020) 7855 2210. FAX (020) 7855 2233. @ reservations@london-bridge-hotel.co.uk b,l,d. **Rooms** 138, plus 3 apts. ££££

London

Millers Literally crammed with antiques and collectables, a theatrical, well-run hideaway owned by antiques expert Martin Miller.
111a Westbourne Grove, London W2 4UW. **Map** p72 A1 (020) 7243 1024. FAX (020) 7243 1064. @ enquiries@millersuk.com b. **Rooms** 8. ££££

London

Pembridge Court Two ginger cats, a friendly manager and a mass of framed fans are some of the distinguishing features of this cosy hotel.
34 Pembridge Gardens, London W2 4DX. **Map** p72 A2. (020) 7229 9977. FAX (020) 7727 4982. @ reservations@pemct.co.uk b,d. **Rooms** 20. ££££

London

Rookery Created from 18th-century brick buildings and full of clubby period charm.
12 Peter's Lane, Cowcross St, London EC1M 6DS. **Map** p73 F1. (020) 7336 0931. FAX (020) 7336 0932. @ reservations@rookery.co.uk b. **Rooms** 33. ££££

For key to symbols see backflap. For price categories *see p71*

LONDON

Hazlitt's Visiting authors leave signed copies for literary folk who like their comforts authentic yet stylish. A good Soho base, the three unspoilt Georgian townhouses have retained their sloping floorboards (it can be an uphill walk to bed). They have been decorated with suitable antiques, busts and prints, and Victorian bathroom fittings.
6 Frith Street, London W1D 3JA. **Map** p73 E1.
(020) 7434 1771. FAX (020) 7439 1524.
@ reservations@hazlitts.co.uk b. **Rooms** 23.
Never. AE, DC, MC, V. ££££

LONDON

Milestone Hotel and Apartments At once opulent and refreshingly low-key, the Milestone occupies a spectacular position opposite Kensington Palace. An exclusive townhouse hotel with individually themed rooms and suites, it has won several top awards.
1/2 Kensington Court, London W8 5DL. **Map** p72 A3.
(020) 7958 7727. FAX (020) 7958 7725.
@ reservations@milestone.redcarnationhotels.com
b,l,d. **Rooms** 57, plus 6 apartments. Never.
AE, DC, MC, V. ££££

LONDON

L'Hotel Baby sister of, and adjacent to, the suave Capital Hotel, this is an upmarket B&B, well situated for shopping sprees at Harrods. Breakfast is taken in the basement restaurant, Le Metro; there is no sitting room or room service. Bedrooms are mostly quite small, but sophisticated and well-equipped.
28 Basil Street, London SW3 1AS. **Map** p72 B3.
(020) 7589 6286. FAX (020) 7823 7826.
@ reservations@lhotel.co.uk b,l,d. **Rooms** 12.
Never. AE, MC, V. £££

LONDON

Number Sixteen The elegant South Kensington B&B encompasses four smart terraced houses, and exudes a familial atmosphere of home: richly traditional, harmonious decor, with the bonus of a conservatory and patio garden. Bedrooms are well-proportioned; four have their own terrace.
16 Sumner Place, London SW7 3EG. **Map** p72 A4.
(020) 7589 5232, US toll free:1 800 553 6674.
FAX (020) 7584 8615. @ sixteen@firmdale.com b.
Rooms 40. Never. AE, MC, V. ££££

LONDON

Savoy Still charismatic, and a byword for luxury and Art Deco elegance. The Savoy Grill has a strong draw for the country's elite.
The Strand, London WC2R 0EU. **Map** p73 F2.
(020) 7950 5492. FAX (020) 7950 5482. @ info@the-savoy.co.uk b,l,d. **Rooms** 263. ££££

LONDON

Strand Palace Opposite the Savoy, and very different; but fresh, pleasant rooms represent very good value. Perfect for theatre visits.
Strand, London WC2R 0JJ. **Map** p73 F2. (020) 7379 4737. FAX (020) 7257 9402. @ reservations@strandpalacehotel.co.uk b,l,d. **Rooms** 785. £££

LONDON

Sydney Spread across a terrace of mid-19th-century townhouses, a luxury B&B with an international feel. 24-hour room service.
9-11 Sydney St, London SW3 6PU. **Map** p72 B5.
(020) 7376 7711. FAX (020) 7376 4233.
@ sh@zoohotels.com b. **Rooms** 21. ££££

LONDON

Tophams Belgravia Cosy family-owned hotel with plenty of personality. Small rooms.
24-32 Ebury St, London SW1W 0LU. **Map** p72 C4.
(020) 7730 8147. FAX (020) 7823 5966.
@ tophams_belgravia@compuserve.com b,d.
Rooms 37. £££

LONDON

One Aldwych High-profile contemporary hotel whose dramatic lobby has a bar rather than reception desk centre-stage. The best of the soothing bedrooms is the circular suite overlooking Waterloo Bridge. All are filled with state-of-the-art equipment – and flowers – though the vacuum plumbing can be anything but restful.
1 Aldwych, London WC2B 4RH. **Map** p73 F2.
(020) 7300 1000. FAX (020) 7300 1001.
reservations@onealdwych.co.uk b,l,d. **Rooms** 105.
Never. AE, DC, MC, V. ££££

MELKSHAM

Shurnhold House This beautifully proportioned stone-built Jacobean house sits close to a main road on the outskirts of the unremarkable town of Melksham, but is well screened by trees. Inside you will find flagstones, beams, floral fabrics, a room full of books, and spacious bedrooms. Licensed bar. Well placed for touring in several directions.
Shurnhold, Melksham, Wiltshire SN12 8DG.
Map p75 D4. (01225) 790555. FAX (01225) 793143.
b. **Rooms** 6. Never. AE, MC, V. ££

LONDON

Portobello The stylish Notting Hill base appeals to people who appreciate its laid-back approach, eclectic Victoriana furnishings, and airy, 24-hour restaurant/bar. Rooms vary from tiny 'cabins' to sybaritic suites (bath in bedroom, mirrors above bed). The best have antique beds and baths – others have showers only.
22 Stanley Gardens, London W11 2NG. **Map** p72 A2.
(020) 7727 2777. FAX (020) 7792 9641.
info@portobello-hotel.co.uk b,l,d. **Rooms** 24.
28 Dec to 2 Jan. AE, DC, MC, V. £££

NEW MILTON

Chewton Glen Once inside this superbly run hotel you are enveloped in an exceptional degree of luxury (with a price tag to match). Rooms and suites are correspondingly faultless, and both service and cuisine are of the highest quality. Many guests come for the golf and the superb, sybaritic health club.
Christchurch Road, New Milton, Hampshire BH25 6QS.
Map p75 D5. (01425) 282212. FAX (01425) 272310.
reservations@chewtonglen.com b,l,d. **Rooms** 59.
Never. AE, DC, MC, V. ££££

LONDON

Winchester Hotel Stands out among budget options for its neat rooms, excellent housekeeping and en suite facilities (shower only).
17 Belgrave Road, London SW1 1RB.
Map p72 C4. (020) 7828 2972.
FAX (020) 7828 5191. b. **Rooms** 22. ££

LYMINGTON

Stanwell House Decorated with great flair. Attractive bistro and courtyard.
14-15 High St, Lymington, Hampshire SO41 9AA.
Map p75 D5. (01590) 677123. FAX (01590) 677756.
sales@stanwellhousehotel. co.uk b,l,d.
Rooms 29. ££

MEMBURY

Lea Hill This superior B&B hotel consists of a dreamy thatched Devon longhouse in an isolated position amidst rolling countryside.
Membury, Axminster, Devon EX13 7AQ. **Map** p74 C5.
(01404) 881881. FAX (01404) 881890.
b,d. **Rooms** 4. ££

MIDHURST

Angel Coaching inn with Georgian façade and plush, warmly decorated Tudor interior. Many rooms have beams.
North Street, Midhurst, West Sussex GU29 9DN.
Map p75 E5. (01730) 812421. FAX (01730) 815928.
info@theangelmidhurst.co.uk b,l,d. **Rooms** 28. ££

New Romney

Romney Bay House This remarkable house was designed by Sir Clough Williams-Ellis, creator of Portmeirion (see page 119). It stands on the edge of Romney Marsh, with wonderful sea views (telescope in the first-floor lookout). The rooms are fresh and individually decorated. Tennis, croquet, golf. Under new management.
Coast Road, Littlestone, New Romney, Kent, TN28 8QY. **Map** p75 F5. (01797) 364747. FAX (01797) 367156. b,d. **Rooms** 10. Christmas. DC MC V. ££

Penzance

Abbey This characterful, rather imposing hotel overlooking Penzance harbour and St Michael's Mount continues to exert its many charms. Set in a building dating back to 1660, the Abbey contains antiques and curios in abundance, yet retains the intimate feel of a private home. Lovely walled garden. Under new management.
Abbey St, Penzance, Cornwall TR18 4AR. **Map** p74 A5. (01736) 366906. FAX (01736) 351163. @ bookings@abbey-hotel.co.uk b,d. **Rooms** 8. 3 weeks in Jan. MC, V. ££

Padstow

The Seafood Restaurant/St Petroc's Hotel/ Rick Stein's Café Choose from one of three places, all friendly and stylish, and all owned by chef Rick Stein. The best rooms (Nos 5 and 6 have estuary views) are above his famous fish restaurant; St Petroc's is a proper hotel; rooms above the café are the least expensive.
Padstow, Cornwall PL28 8BY. **Map** p74 A5. (01841) 532700. FAX (01841) 532942. @ reservations@rickstein.com b,l,d. **Rooms** 32. 1 May, Christmas, New Year. MC, V. ££–££££

Ringlestone

Ringlestone Inn An 'ale house' since 1615, Ringlestone Inn is today affably run by Mike Millington Buck and his daughter. They offer comfortable rooms in the converted farmhouse opposite. Hearty pies and English country wines are the specialities of the restaurant, which comprises several intimate dining areas.
Ringlestone, Maidstone, Kent ME17 1NX. **Map** p75 F4. (01622) 859900. FAX (01622) 859966. @ bookings@ringlestone.com b,l,d. **Rooms** 3. Christmas Day. AE, DC, MC, V. £££

Oakfordbridge

Bark House Interesting newcomer in lovely Exe Valley, simple yet intimate, with innovative food served in the candlelit dining room.
Oakfordbridge, nr Bampton, Devon EX16 9HZ. **Map** p74 B5. (01398) 351236. b,d. **Rooms** 5. ££

Portscatho

Driftwood Hotel Stylish yet comfortable haven in whitewashed, refurbished family house. Good restaurant with spectacular views of Cornish coast.
Rosevine, nr Portscatho, Cornwall TR2 5EW. **Map** p74 A5. (01872) 580644. FAX (01872) 580801. @ info@driftwoodhotel.co.uk b,l,d. **Rooms** 10. £££

Rye

Old Vicarage Central but peaceful Tudor-Georgian family-run B&B. Breakfast is a highlight: home-made scones and jams.
66 Church Square, Rye, East Sussex TN31 7HF. **Map** p75 F5. (01797) 222119. FAX (01797) 227466. @ oldvicarageye@tesco.net b. **Rooms** 4. ££

St Hilary

Ennys Beautiful 17thC manor house with grounds that lead to the River Hayle, where you can walk and picnic. Exemplary B&B.
Trewhella Lane, St Hilary, Penzance, Cornwall TR20 9BZ. **Map** p74 A5. (01736) 740262. FAX (01736) 740055. @ ennys@ennys.co.uk b. **Rooms** 5. ££

Rock

St Enodoc This child-friendly seaside holiday hotel, with slate roof and pebbledash walls, is typical of the area, and has splendid views across the Camel estuary. Its breezy interior suits the location perfectly: bright colours, painted furniture, modern art. Golf, surfing, sailing, fishing.
Rock, Wadebridge, Cornwall PL27 6LA. **Map** p74 B5. (01208) 863394. FAX (01208) 863970. @ enodochotel@aol.com b,l,d. **Rooms** 20. 8 to 27 Dec, Jan to mid-Feb. AE, MC, V. £££

Rushlake Green

Stone House Peter and Jane Dunn's ancestral home is a fine 16th-century manor with graceful interior. Of the seven sumptuous bedrooms, two have antique four-posters and huge bathrooms. Jane cooks elegant dinners, and produces picnics for Glyndebourne. Other attractions: log fires, shooting, billiards, woodland walks, croquet.
Rushlake Green, Heathfield, East Sussex TN21 9QJ. **Map** p75 F5. (01435) 830553. FAX (01435) 830726. b,d. **Rooms** 7. Christmas to New Year. MC, V. £££

Ruanhighlanes

Crugsillick Manor Elegant Queen Anne manor in a sheltered hollow on the lovely Roseland Peninsula. Owners the Barstows treat you as their house guests (communal candlelit dinners) but know when privacy is required. The drawing room has a ceiling moulded by Napoleonic prisoners. Picnic hampers available for lunch.
Ruanhighlanes, nr St Mawes, Truro, Cornwall TR2 5LJ. **Map** p74 A5. (01872) 501214. FAX (01872) 501228. @ barstow@adtel.co.uk b,d. **Rooms** 3, plus 3 self-catering cottages. Never. MC, V. ££

Rye

Jeake's House The 17th-century building makes a fitting B&B in picture-perfect Rye: beamed bedrooms, furnished with brass or mahogany bedsteads, lace bedspreads and antiques, look out over rooftops or over Romney Marsh. There is a comfortable book-lined sitting room and bar; breakfast is taken in a galleried former chapel.
Mermaid Street, Rye, East Sussex TN31 7ET. **Map** p75 F5. (01797) 222828. FAX (01797) 222623. @ jeakeshouse@btinternet.com b. **Rooms** 11. Never. MC, V. ££

St Margaret's At Cliffe

Walletts Court Handsome old manor. Smart period or more modern bedrooms; pool, spa.
Westcliffe, St Margaret's at Cliffe, Dover, Kent CT15 6EW. **Map** p75 F4. (01304) 852424. FAX (01304) 853430. @ wc@wallettscourt.com b,l,d. **Rooms** 16. ££

St Martin's, Isles of Scilly

St Martin's Welcoming holiday hotel in a superb, remote location. Modern, built of local stone, with comfortable bedrooms.
St Martin's, Isles of Scilly TR25 0QW. **Map** p74 A4. (01720) 422090. FAX (01720) 422298. b,l,d. **Rooms** 30. £££

Seaview, Isle of Wight

Seaview Popular seaside hotel and local watering hole, run with care and bonhomie.
High St, Seaview, Isle of Wight PO34 5EX. **Map** p75 E5. (01983) 612711. FAX (01983) 613729. @ reception@seaviewhotel.co.uk b,l,d. **Rooms** 16, plus 1 suite and 1 cottage. £££

Shipton Gorge

Innsacre Peaceful farmhouse set amongst hills and orchards. French country-style bedrooms; secluded terrace; imaginative set dinners.
Shipton Gorge, Bridport, Dorset DT6 4LJ. **Map** p74 C5. (01308) 456137. @ innsacre.farmhouse@btinternet.com b,d. **Rooms** 4. ££

For key to symbols see backflap. For price categories *see p71*

St Keyne

Well House Victorian hilltop house built by a tea-planter in 1894, obviously with no expense spared. The mood is calm and stylish, although a few more personal touches – such as books and current magazines – would be welcome. What stands out is the food and the impressive wine list. Convenient for the Eden Project.
St Keyne, Liskeard, Cornwall PL14 4RN.
Map p 74 B5. (01579) 342001. FAX (01579) 343891.
enquiries@ wellhouse.co.uk b,l,d. **Rooms** 9
2 weeks Jan. MC, V. ££££

St Mawes

Tresanton Owned by Olga Polizzi, daughter of hotelier Lord Forte, this much-vaunted hotel marries cool city sophistication with Cornish character. The cluster of cottages, built on different levels, overlooks the unspoilt town and the sea. Yacht, watersports available. Excellent food and service, but very expensive.
27 Lower Castle Rd, St Mawes, Cornwall TR2 5DR.
Map p74 A5. (01326) 270055. FAX (01326) 270053.
info@ tresanton.com b,l,d. **Rooms** 26.
Never. AE, MC, V. ££££

Sandgate

Sandgate This hotel/restaurant stands on land that is as close to France as it is possible to be without actually being there. Ten minutes' drive from the Channel Tunnel, overlooking the sea, the Sandgate has traditionally been staffed by a charming, mainly French team. Try to get a room with sea view, and book dinner. Under new management.
The Esplanade, Sandgate, Folkestone, Kent CT20 3DY.
Map p75 F4. (01303) 220444. FAX (01303) 220496.
b,l,d. **Rooms** 16. Never. AE, DC, MC, V. ££

Sark, Channel Islands

La Sablonnerie A long, low, 16th-century farmhouse at the southern tip of traffic-free Sark, this is the Channel Islands' sweetest hotel, and the one serving the best food. Guests return year after year for utter peace and lovely scenery. There are no phones or TVs in the rooms; instead, each has a vase of flowers and bowl of fruit, and crisp linen on the comfy beds.
Little Sark, Sark, Channel Islands GY9 OSD. **Map** p75 E5. (01481) 832061. FAX (01481) 832408. b,l,d.
Rooms 22. Oct to Easter. AE, MC, V. ££

Sturminster Newton

Plumber Manor A relaxed restaurant with cosy rooms, in a handsome Jacobean manor. The fish is superb, and the desserts tempting.
Sturminster Newton, Dorset DT10 2AF. **Map** p74 C5.
(01258) 472507. FAX (01258) 473370. book@ plumbermanor.com b,d. **Rooms** 16. ££

Taunton

Castle Castellated, wisteria-clad site of Judge Jeffreys' Bloody Assize. Pricey, acclaimed British cooking. Best rooms overlook garden.
Castle Green, Taunton, Somerset TA1 1NF. **Map** p74 C5.
(01823) 272671. FAX (01823) 336066. reception @the-castle-hotel.com b,l,d. **Rooms** 44. £££

Tresco, Isles of Scilly

Island Smoothly run hotel on this charming privately owned island. Public rooms have huge picture windows onto the sea.
Tresco, Isles of Scilly TR24 0PU. **Map** p74 A4.
(01720) 422883. FAX (01720) 423008. islandhotel@ tresco.co.uk b,l,d. **Rooms** 48. ££££

Trusham

Cridford Inn Admire a Saxon mosaic in the oldest house in Devon, a cosy thatched inn run by a friendly young pair.
Trusham, Teign Valley, Newton Abbot, Devon TQ13 0NR. **Map** p74 B5. FAX (01626) 853694.
cridford@ eclipse.co.uk b,l,d. **Rooms** 4. ££

Seaview, Isle of Wight

Priory Bay Stylish decor and contemporary cuisine are successfully married with a relaxed ambience to suit both families and romantic couples. The eclectic house embraces many periods, including a Georgian muralled dining room and a French Gothic porch. A highlight is the private beach, with beach bar in summer.
⊠ Priory Drive, Seaview, Isle of Wight PO34 5BU. **Map** p75 D5. (01983) 613146. FAX (01983) 616539. @ reservations@priorybay.co.uk b,l,d. **Rooms** 18, plus 10 chalets. Never. AE, MC, V. £££

Torquay

Orestone Manor Rudyard Kipling lived just up the road from this grand, colonial-style manor house on the English Riviera, high above Lyme Bay. Outside, large conservatory and palm trees on the lawn; inside, Indian fabrics and Oriental prints. New proprietors Rose and Mark Ashton welcome you like old friends. Excellent food.
⊠ Rockhouse Lane, Maidencombe, Torquay, Devon TQ1 4SX. **Map** p74 C5. (01803) 328098. FAX (01803) 328336. @ enquiries@orestone.co.uk b,l,d. **Rooms** 12. Never. AE, MC, V. ££

Shepton Mallet

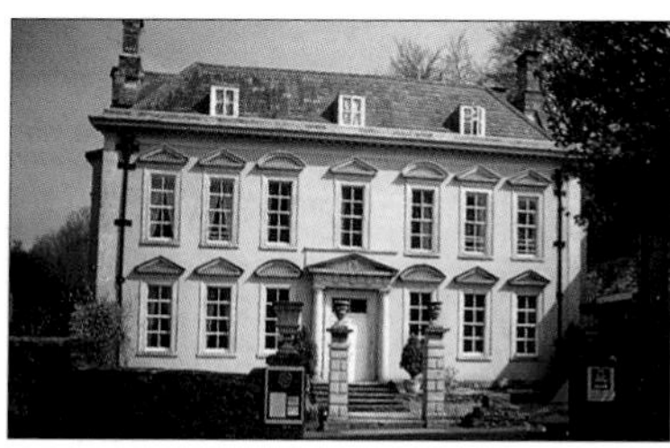

Bowlish House Recently taken over by Darren Carter and Jason Goy, and currently undergoing major restoration work, Bowlish House feels relaxed and homelike, despite the fine Georgian mansion's august air. The dining room makes a popular local restaurant. The unobtrusive bedrooms have large bathrooms.
⊠ Wells Road, Shepton Mallet, Somerset BA4 5JD. **Map** p74 C4. (01749) 342022. FAX (01749) 345311. @ enquiries@bowlishhouse.com b,l,d. **Rooms** 3. Never. AE, MC, V. ££

Tunbridge Wells

Hotel du Vin A faded but grand hotel became the second Hotel du Vin (see page 92). This one has more space and period features than the first but similarly stylish bedooms and bathrooms. It also has the same friendly, efficient service and buzzing bistro, down to the hop garlands, the sunny food and the world-class sommelier.
⊠ Crescent Road, Tunbridge Wells, Kent TN1 2LY. **Map** p75 F4. (01892) 526455. FAX (01892) 512044. @ reception@tunbridgewells.hotelduvin.co.uk b,l,d. **Rooms** 36. Never. AE, DC, MC, V. ££

Virginstow

Percy's Elegant country hotel occupying a Devon longhouse. Every comfort is provided, in rural surroundings.
⊠ Coombeshead Estate, Virginstow, Okehampton, Devon EX21 5EA. **Map** p 74 B5. (01409) 211236. FAX (01409) 411460. @ relax@percys.co.uk b,l,d. **Rooms** 8. ££

Wareham

Priory Former priory on River Frome. Some bedrooms are in the old boathouse.
⊠ Church Green, Wareham, Dorset BH20 4ND. **Map** p75 D5. (01929) 551666. FAX (01929) 554519. @ reservations@theprioryhotel.co.uk b,l,d. **Rooms** 18. £££

Warminster

Bishopstrow House Swish Georgian mansion with state-of-the-art health spa and much more. Six fantastic suites, but other rooms are small.
⊠ Warminster, Wilts BA12 9HH. **Map** p75 D4. (01985) 212312. FAX (01985) 216769. @ enquiries@bishopstrow.co.uk b,l,d. **Rooms** 32. ££££

Wartling

Wartling Place Georgian house in 2 acres of gardens, run as a sophisticated guest-house.
⊠ Wartling, Herstmonceux, East Sussex BN27 1RY. **Map** p75 F5. (01323) 832590. FAX (01323) 831558 @ accom@wartlingplace.prestel.co.uk b,d. **Rooms** 4. ££

Uckfield

Hooke Hall In the centre of Uckfield, this elegant Queen Anne townhouse makes a smart, yet informal hotel. Public rooms and bedrooms (some named after famous lovers) are decorated with designer fabrics by owner Juliet Percy. Despite the homely atmosphere, there are such unexpected accoutrements as trouser presses.
250 High Street, Uckfield, East Sussex TN22 1EN. **Map** p75 E4. (01825) 761578. FAX (01825) 768025. @ a.percy@virgin.net b. **Rooms** 10. 23 Dec to 6 Jan. MC, V. ££

Winchester

Wykeham Arms Plain outside, but convivial within. Guests tuck into top-notch pub food, washed down by real ales and an impressive selection of wines. Cosy, low-ceilinged bedrooms upstairs; less characterful but smarter ones in the annexe across the road.
75 Kingsgate Street, Winchester, Hampshire SO23 9PE. **Map** p75 D4. (01962) 853834. FAX (01962) 854411. @ wykehamarms@accommodation-inns.co.uk b,l,d. **Rooms** 14. Christmas Day. AE, MC, V. ££

Winchester

Hotel du Vin The owners of this extremely popular modern-day hostelry wrought a miracle when they took over a dowdy town centre hotel. Stylish but unpretentious, its heart is the bustling Bistro (be sure to book), serving zesty food and excellent but affordable wines. The elegant bedrooms are sponsored by wine companies.
Southgate Street, Winchester, Hampshire SO23 9EF. **Map** p75 D4. (01962) 841414. FAX (01962) 842458. @ reservations@winchester.hotelduvin.com b,l,d. **Rooms** 23. Never. AE, DC, MC, V. £££

Yarmouth, Isle of Wight

George Hotel The carefully restored former 17th-century governor's residence sits in the centre of this breezy and historic little harbour town. It has much to recommend it, including a panelled sitting room and elegant bedrooms. The amiable brasserie, where lunch is served all week, is preferable to the sombre dining room.
Yarmouth, Isle of Wight PO41 0PE. **Map** p75 D5. (01983) 760331. FAX (01983) 760425. @ res@thegeorge.co.uk b,l,d. **Rooms** 17. Never. MC, V. £££

Whitstable

Continental Breezy, youthful, Deco-style hotel, plus six simple, gaily decorated fisherman's huts for a bit of seaside fun.
29 Beach Walk, Whitstable, Kent CT5 2BP. **Map** p75 F4. (01227) 280280. FAX (01227) 280257. b,l,d. **Rooms** 24, plus 7 fisherman's huts. ££

Williton

White House Comfortable house with pretty courtyard garden run for 30 years by the affable Smiths. They have a passion for good food and wine: their list has won awards.
11 Long St, Williton, Somerset TA4 4QW. **Map** p74 C4. (01984) 632306. b,d. **Rooms** 10. ££

Wickham

Old House A Georgian house in an ancient market square. Contemporary comfort with award-winning restaurant.
The Square, Wickham, Hampshire PO17 5JG. **Map** p75 D5. (01329) 833049. FAX (01329) 833672. @ enq@theoldhousehotel.co.uk b,l,d. **Rooms** 8. ££

Yattendon

Royal Oak Village pub transformed into a suave, sophisticated and pricey restaurant and buzzing brasserie; attractive bedrooms upstairs.
The Square, Yattendon, Tatcham, Berkshire RG18 0UG. **Map** p75 D4. (01635) 201325. FAX (01635) 201926. b,l,d. **Rooms** 5. £££

Central England

Cotswolds • Thames Valley
Midlands • East Anglia

Stretching between the Thames Valley in the south and a line drawn east-west from the mouth of the Humber river, Central England encompasses idyllic rural landscapes and great cathedral and university cities such as Lincoln, Manchester and Oxford. In the quintessentially English Cotswolds you will find fine places to stay in every category, from meltingly beautiful manor houses to enchanting vine-clad inns; the East Anglian counties of Norfolk and Suffolk also have a wide choice. Elsewhere there are smart townhouse hotels, a smattering of stately homes-turned-hotels and a tempting selection of country houses, located in widely differing yet easily accessible settings, and perfect for a restful few days.

Baslow

Fischer's Baslow Hall A 1907 mock-Elizabethan house has become a Michelin-starred restaurant with rooms under the aegis of chef Max Fischer and his wife Susan, an excellent hostess. The food is the point of the place (you can eat more simply in Café Max) but the smart bedrooms make a perfectly good overnight base.
⊠ Calver Rd, Baslow, Derbyshire DE45 1RR. **Map** p75 D2. ☎ (01246) 583259. FAX (01246) 583818. 🍴 b,l,d. **Rooms** 11. ● Christmas. 💳 AE, DC, MC, V. £££

Beyton

Manorhouse This spacious B&B in a beautiful 15th-century Suffolk longhouse overlooks the village green. It's an elegant, but down-to-earth place – the half-timbered, colourwashed rooms are filled with antiques, but outside, chickens have the run of the gravelled yard, and provide most of the eggs served at breakfast. Dinner on request; or it's a short stroll to the village pubs.
⊠ Beyton, Bury St Edmunds, Suffolk IP30 9AF **Map** p75 F3. ☎ (01359) 270960. @ manorhouse@ beyton.com 🍴 b. **Rooms** 4. ● Christmas. 💳 not accepted. £

Ashbourne

Callow Hall Above the Dove valley, a Victorian country house and grounds, lovingly restored. Comfortable and well-run, with good food.
⊠ Mappleton, Ashbourne, Derbyshire DE6 2AA. **Map** p75 D2. ☎ (01335) 300900. FAX (01335) 300512. @ reservations@callowhall.co.uk 🍴 b,d. **Rooms** 16. £££

Ashford-in-the-Water

Riverside This stone-built, creeper-clad country house has secluded grounds bordering the River Wye. Accommodation is luxurious.
⊠ Ashford-in-the-Water, Bakewell, Derbyshire DE45 1QF. **Map** p75 D2. ☎ (01629) 814275. FAX (01629) 812873. @ riversidehouse@enta.net 🍴 b,l,d. **Rooms** 15. ££££

Atherstone

Chapel House A quiet address (church bells excepted) in an old market town. Walled garden, light bedrooms, enjoyable food.
⊠ Friar's Gate, Atherstone, Warwickshire CV9 1EY. **Map** p75 D3. ☎ (01827) 718949. FAX (01827) 717702. 🍴 b,d. **Rooms** 14. ££

Baslow

Cavendish Owned by the Duke and Duchess of Devonshire, and overlooking their estate, Chatsworth. Homely rather than grand.
⊠ Baslow, Derbyshire DE45 1SP. Map p75 D2. ☎ (01246) 582311. FAX (01246) 582312. @ info@ cavendish-hotel.net 🍴 b,l,d. **Rooms** 24 £££

For key to symbols *see* backflap. For price categories *see p71*

Broad Campden

Malt House In a tiny Cotswold hamlet, comprising little more than church and pub, is this delightful 17th-century stone house. There are low, beamed ceilings and leaded windows overlooking a dream garden. The attractive bedrooms include a garden suite. Under new management.
☒ Broad Campden, Chipping Campden, Gloucestershire GL55 6UU. **Map** p74 A2. ☎ (01386) 8402950. FAX (01386) 841334. @ info@the-malt-house.freeserve.co.uk 🍴 b,d. **Rooms** 8. ● Christmas. 💳 AE, MC, V. ££

Burford

Lamb Most guests agree that the Lamb gets it just right, combining the convivial atmosphere of a cosy traditional pub with the comforts of a hotel. The beamed bedrooms are surprisingly spacious, decorated with floral fabrics and antiques. The daily-changing menus are served in a dining room overlooking a geranium-filled patio. Elsewhere are comfy sofas and log fires.
☒ Sheep St, Burford, Oxfordshire OX18 4LR. **Map** p74 A3. ☎ (01993) 823155. FAX (01993) 822228. 🍴 b,l,d. **Rooms** 15. ● Never. 💳 MC, V. ££

Burford

Burford House This 15th-century Cotswold stone and timbered building positively gleams with care and attention. The smart bedrooms (some with four-posters) are awash with polished furniture, glossy magazines, flowers, teddies, lotions, sachets and the like. Light lunches and teas are served in the adjacent restaurant.
☒ 99 High St, Burford, Oxfordshire OX18 4QA. **Map** p74 A3. ☎ (01993) 823151. FAX (01993) 823240. @ stay@burfordhouse.co.uk 🍴 b,l. **Rooms** 8. ● Never. 💳 AE, MC, V. ££

Chaddesley Corbett

Brockencote Hall Close to the M5/M42 motorways, this lakeside mansion has a fair proportion of business guests, but Anglo-French owners Alison and Joseph Petitjean ensure a discreetly privileged ambience. This is amply reflected in the decoration, which has distinctly French flourishes. Excellent for disabled guests.
☒ Chaddesley Corbett, Kidderminster, Worcestershire DY10 4PY. **Map** p75 D3. ☎ (01562) 777876. FAX (01562) 777872. @ info@brockencotehall.com 🍴 b,l,d. **Rooms** 17. ● First week Jan. 💳 AE, DC, MC, V. £££

Bibury

Bibury Court Beautiful, affordable Jacobean mansion in idyllic riverside setting (fishing rods available). Atmospheric, if simple, rooms.
☒ Bibury, Gloucestershire GL7 5NT. **Map** p74 A3. ☎ (01285) 740337. FAX (01285) 740660. @ info@biburycourt.co.uk 🍴 b,l,d. **Rooms** 18. £££

Buckland

Buckland Manor One of the Cotswolds' most exclusive hotels; lavish bedrooms.
☒ Buckland, nr Broadway, Worcestershire WR12 7LY. **Map** p74 A2. ☎ (01386) 852626. FAX (01386) 853557. @ enquiries@bucklandmanor.com 🍴 b,l,d. **Rooms** 14. ££££

Burnham Market

Hoste Arms Buzzing, characterful local inn, sometimes very busy, with attractive bedrooms.
☒ The Green, Burnham Market, Norfolk PE31 8HD. **Map** p75 F2. ☎ (01328) 738777. FAX (01328) 730103. @ reception@hostearms.co.uk 🍴 b,l,d. **Rooms** 36. ££££

Bury St Edmunds

Ounce House Meals are taken round a long table in this elegant Victorian house. It's in the town centre, with a large garden and private parking.
☒ Northgate St, Bury St Edmunds, Suffolk IP33 1HP. **Map** p75 F3. ☎ (01284) 761779. FAX (01284) 768315. @ pott@globalnet.co.uk 🍴 b. **Rooms** 3. ££

Cheltenham

Hotel on the Park Despite some twee touches (two teddies centre stage in the dining room, plastic ducks artfully placed in bathrooms), this is a stylish establishment. The spacious bedrooms are embellished by sumptuous fabrics and antiques, although, at the front, traffic noise can destroy the calm so carefully engendered within. ☒ 38 Evesham Rd, Cheltenham, Gloucestershire GL52 2AH. **Map** p74 A2. (01242) 518898. FAX (01242) 511526. @ stay@hotelonthepark.com b,l,d. **Rooms** 12. Never. AE, DC, MC, V. £££

Cley-next-the-Sea

Cley Mill Memories of your favourite childrens' adventure stories crowd in as you climb ever higher in this 'real' windmill, finally mounting the ladder to the look-out room. The views over Cley Marshes, a bird-watchers' paradise, are superb. In the pretty, rustic bedrooms, bathrooms are fitted into the most challenging spaces. Dishes include fresh fish and samphire in season. ☒ Cley-next-the-Sea, Holt, Norfolk NR25 7RP. **Map** p75 F2. FAX (01263) 740209. b,d. **Rooms** 8. Never. MC, V. ££

Chipping Campden

Cotswold House Each of the scrupulously detailed bedrooms has a different theme, such as regimental souvenirs in 'Military' or lace in 'Aunt Lizzy'. All have impeccable bathrooms. There is a magnificent spiral staircase, a walled garden and two snazzy dining rooms, one a brasserie. ☒ The Square, Chipping Campden, Gloucestershire GL55 6AN. **Map** p74 A2. (01386) 840330. FAX (01386) 840310. @ reception@cotswoldhouse.com b,l,d. **Rooms** 15. Never AE, MC, V. ££££

Corse Lawn

Corse Lawn House Should you arrive in a coach and four, you could still drive it down the slipway of this old coaching inn to water the horses and wash the carriage. Instead you will probably be content to enjoy the advantages of this relaxed, long-favourite, recently refurbished country hotel. Bedrooms are large. ☒ Corse Lawn, Gloucestershire GL19 4LZ. **Map** p74 A2. (01452)780771. FAX (01452) 780840. @ enquiries@corselawn.com b,l,d. **Rooms** 19. Christmas. AE, DC, MC, V. £££

Clanfield

Plough A mellow Elizabethan inn with a glossy interior. Bedrooms (two with four-poster beds) vary in size. Sophisticated cooking. ☒ Bourton Rd, Clanfield, Bampton, Oxfordshire OX18 2RB. **Map** p74 B3. (01367) 810222. FAX (01367) 810596. b,l,d. **Rooms** 12. ££

Clearwell

Tudor Farmhouse Cosy, neat and simple, with fine oak spiral staircase; breakfast a minor feast. ☒ Clearwell, Coleford, Gloucestershire GL16 8JS. **Map** p74 C4. (01594) 833046. FAX (01594) 837093. @ reservations@tudorfarmhse.u-net.com b,d. **Rooms** 21. ££

Cleeve Hill

Cleeve Hill Bob and Georgie Tracy's well-kept Edwardian-style B&B has superb views from the spacious bedrooms. Notable breakfasts. ☒ Cleeve Hill, Cheltenham, Gloucestershire GL52 3PR. **Map** p74 A2. (01242) 672052. FAX (01242) 679969. @ gbtoncleevehill@aol.com b. **Rooms** 10. ££

Coln St-Aldwyns

New Inn at Coln The epitome of a creeper-clad 16th-century Cotswold inn, now smart, glossy, sophisticated and highly successful. ☒ Coln St-Aldwyns, Cirencester, Gloucestershire GL7 5AN. **Map** p74 A3. (01285) 750651. FAX (01285) 750657. @ stay@new-inn.co.uk b,l,d. **Rooms** 14. ££

For key to symbols see backflap. For price categories *see p71*

Great Snoring

The Manor House The sleepy village lives up to its name, and this low-key hotel, hidden behind high stone walls beside the church, is easy to miss. It's a quiet, restrained, relaxing sort of place, of mixed vintage, with a hotch-potch of squashy armchairs in the sitting room, comfortable bedrooms and a traditional English menu.

☒ Barsham Rd, Great Snoring, Norfolk NR21 0HP. **Map** p75 F2. (01328) 820597. FAX (01328) 820048. @ gtsnoringmanorho@aol.com b,d. **Rooms** 6. Christmas. AE, DC, MC, V. ££

Holkham

Victoria at Holkham Named after the Empress of India, the Victoria is an eclectic but stylish blend of the colonial and the local. Many of the furnishings have been flown in from Rajasthan, so there's a strong sense of the exotic. Seriously comfy beds, big, warm duvets and deep baths for a serious soak. Good food, long wine list.

☒ Park Road, Holkham, Norfolk NR23 1RG. **Map** p75 F2. (01328) 711008. FAX (01328) 711009. @ victoria@holkham.co.uk b,l,d. **Rooms** 11. Never. MC, V. £££

Hambleton

Hambleton Hall For a sybaritic break in the grandest sort of country hotel, this is a prime contender. A former Victorian shooting lodge, it stands isolated on Rutland Water. It is decorated in glamorous, yet intimate fashion, with stylish bedrooms and a formal dining room serving excellent food. Terrace with views of the lake.

☒ Hambleton, Oakham, Rutland LE15 8TH. **Map** p75 E2. (01572) 756991. FAX (01572) 724721. @ hotel@hambletonhall.com b,l,d. **Rooms** 17. Never. MC, V. ££££

Kemerton

Upper Court The lovely grounds of this well-loved family home (open to the public under the National Garden Scheme) include a ruined watermill, a lake and a tennis court. The Georgian manor, furnished in country house style, is popular for self-catering house parties; single bookings no longer accepted.

☒ Kemerton, Tewkesbury, Gloucestershire GL20 7HY. **Map** p74 A2. (01386) 725351. FAX (01386) 725472. @ diana@uppercourt.co.uk b,d. **Rooms** 6. Christmas. MC, V. ££

Diddlebury

Delbury Hall In lovely countryside and grounds, this gracious Georgian mansion overlooking a lake is also a friendly family home.

☒ Diddlebury, Shropshire SY7 9DH. **Map** p74 C3. (01584) 841267. FAX (01584) 841441. @ wrigley@delbury.com b,d. **Rooms** 4. ££

Dorchester-on-Thames

George A spruce 15th-century coaching inn (old beams, open fires), one of the country's oldest, opposite the abbey in a delightful village.

☒ Dorchester-on-Thames, Oxfordshire OX10 7HH. **Map** p75 D4. (01865) 340404. FAX (01865) 341620. @ thegeorgehotel@fsmail.net b,l,d. **Rooms** 18. ££

East Barkwith

Bodkin Lodge Walk the wildlife trails on the owners' conservation farm; stay in their light, airy home, with views to Lincoln Cathedral.

☒ Grange Farm, Torrington Lane, East Barkwith, Market Rasen, Lincolnshire LN8 5RY. **Map** p75 E2. (01673) 858249. FAX (01673) 868249. b,d. **Rooms** 2. £

Glossop

Wind in the Willows Welcoming, family-run establishment. Thoughtful touches in the bedrooms. Peace, quiet and total relaxation.

☒ Derbyshire Level, Glossop, Derbyshire SK13 7PT. **Map** p75 D2. (01457) 868001. FAX (01457) 853354. @ info@windinthewillows.co.uk b,d. **Rooms** 12. £££

Langar

Langar Hall The owner of this idiosyncratic family-home-turned-hotel, Imogen Skirving, has an eye for beautiful things and a taste for fun. Her apricot-coloured house in the Vale of Belvoir has a homely yet uplifting atmosphere. The rather grand restaurant is adorned with classsical statues; the bedrooms are highly individual.
Langar, Nottinghamshire NG13 9HG. **Map** p75 E2. (01949) 860559. FAX (01949) 861045. langarhall-hotel@ndirect.co.uk b,l,d. **Rooms** 11. Never. MC, V. £££

Lavenham

Great House This very English building (15th-century, with a Georgian façade) has a French accent, brought to it by its owners, Régis and Martine Crépy, and their largely French staff. The *raison d'être* is the often very busy restaurant, but the rooms are restful and smart, with surprisingly luxurious marble bathrooms.
Market Place, Lavenham, Suffolk CO10 9QZ. **Map** p75 F3. (01787) 247431. FAX (01787) 248007. info@greathouse.co.uk b,l,d. **Rooms** 5. Jan. AE, MC, V. ££

Lavenham

Lavenham Priory The Grade I listed building is one of the finest in this charming half-timbered town. Owners Tim and Gilli Pitt can offer three delightful bedrooms to guests (dinner by arrangement). Choose between a *lit bateau*, a four-poster and a Polonaise bed. Downstairs, the sitting room boasts a huge inglenook fireplace.
Water St, Lavenham, Suffolk CO10 9RW. **Map** p75 F3. (01787) 247404. FAX (01787) 248472. mail@lavenhampriory.co.uk b. **Rooms** 6. Christmas, New Year. MC, V. ££

Leonard Stanley

Grey Cottage The 175-year-old stone cottage with a 100ft sequoia in the garden stands out for the attention to detail paid by its owner, Rosemary Reeves. From the carefully prepared dinners to the firm beds, reliable hot water, heated towel rails and fresh fruit in the bedrooms, everything reflects her friendly, helpful attitude.
Bath Road, Leonard Stanley, Stonehouse, Gloucestershire GL10 3LU. **Map** p74 A3. (01453) 822515. FAX (01453) 822515. b,d. **Rooms** 3. Occasionally. Not accepted. ££

Great Milton

Le Manoir aux Quat' Saisons Raymond Blanc's temple of gastronomy, a Cotswold manor with appropriately swish accommodation.
Church Rd, Great Milton, Oxfordshire OX44 7PD. **Map** p75 E4. (01844) 278881. FAX (01844) 278847. lemanoir@blanc.co.uk b,l,d. **Rooms** 32. ££££

Great Rissington

Lamb Inn A lovely 300-year-old inn built of Cotswold stone. Recent change of ownership; new bar.
Great Rissington, Bourton-on-the-Water, Gloucestershire GL54 2LP. **Map** p74 A2. (01451) 820388. FAX (01451) 820724. b,l,d. **Rooms** 14. ££

Grimston

Congham Hall Elegant Georgian manor house set in parkland.
Grimston, King's Lynn, Norfolk PE32 1AH. **Map** 75 F2. (01485) 600250. FAX (01485) 601191. info@conghamhallhotel.demon.co.uk b,l,d. **Rooms** 14. £££

Henley-on-Thames

Red Lion Long-established town-centre coaching inn fronting the Thames at the busy road bridge.
Hart St, Henley-on-Thames, Oxfordshire RG9 2AR. **Map** p75 E4. (01491) 572161. FAX (01491) 410039. reservations@redlionhenley.co.uk b,l,d. **Rooms** 26. £££

For key to symbols see backflap. For price categories *see p71*

Lincoln

D'Isney Place This spruce Georgian house is on a busy street close to Lincoln Cathedral. Though it has a garden, which incorporates a 700-year-old tower, it has no public rooms. Breakfast is delivered to guests in their bedrooms. Rooms vary; the best have carefully co-ordinated fabrics and whirlpool baths.
Eastgate, Lincoln LN2 4AA. **Map** p75 E2. (01522) 538881. FAX (01522) 511321. info@disneyplacehotel.co.uk b. **Rooms** 17. Never. AE, DC, MC, V. ££

Manchester

Malmaison This growing chain of city hotels offers notable value for money. The well-equipped rooms are cool and fresh in a modern, rather masculine style. Public facilities include a mini-spa and hi-tech gym, a jazzy bar and a French brasserie. A major new extension is now complete.
Piccadilly, Manchester M1 3AQ. **Map** p75 D1. (0161) 278 1000. FAX (0161) 278 1002. manchester@malmaison.com b,l,d. **Rooms** 187. Never. AE, DC, MC, V. £££

Malmesbury

Old Bell Reputed to be the oldest inn in England, the Old Bell was set up in the 13th century to serve refreshments to visitors to the nearby abbey. It now offers a variety of places to eat, period bedrooms and comfortable lounges – all decorated with antique furniture and specially commissioned paintings. Children very welcome.
Abbey Row, Malmesbury, Wiltshire SN16 0AG. **Map** p74 A3. (01666) 822344. FAX (01666) 825145. info@oldbellhotel.com b,l,d. **Rooms** 31. Never. AE, DC, MC, V. £££

Melbourn

Melbourn Bury Lush parkland surrounds this whitewashed and crenellated manor house. Inside are an elegant drawing room and splendid Victorian billiard room, book-lined library and sunny conservatory. Of the three bedrooms, the 'pink room' is particularly delightful, with a large bathroom. Communal dining, dinner-party style.
Melbourn, Cambridgeshire SG8 6DE. **Map** p75 E3. (01763) 261151. FAX (01763) 262375. melbournbury@biztobiz.co.uk b,d (by arrangement). **Rooms** 3. Christmas, New Year, Easter. AE, MC, V. ££

Hopesay

Old Rectory The elegant home of Roma Villar, an excellent cook. Beautiful wooded valleys to explore nearby.
Hopesay, Craven Arms, Shropshire SY7 8HD. **Map** p74 C3. (01588) 660245. FAX (01588) 660502. villar.oldrectory@virgin.net b. **Rooms** 3. ££

Kington

Penhros Court A 700-year-old manor farm incorporating a superb medieval cruck hall. Charming bedrooms and inspired organic food.
Kington, Herefordshire HR5 3LH. **Map** p74 C3. (01544) 230720. FAX (01544) 230754. jean@penhros.co.uk b,d. **Rooms** 17. ££

Little Malvern

Holdfast Cottage A Victorian farmhouse with the cosy intimacy of a cottage. Lovely garden.
Marlbank Rd, Little Malvern, Worcestershire WR13 6NA. **Map** p74 A2. (01684) 310288. FAX (01684) 311117. enquiries@holdfast.cottage.co.uk b,d. **Rooms** 8. ££

Ludlow

Number 28 Bedrooms are distributed across three separate period houses at this excellent B&B. A useful base for visiting historic Ludlow.
28 Lower Broad St, Ludlow, Shropshire SY8 1PQ. **Map** p74 C3. (01584) 875 466. FAX (01584) 875 517. ludlowno28@aol.com b. **Rooms** 5. ££

MORSTON

Morston Hall Dominating the ground floor of this brick and flint Norfolk house is the strikingly decorated restaurant, the establishment's main attraction and holder of a Michelin star. Enjoy a seasonal dinner (included in price of room) before retiring to one of the (mostly) spacious bedrooms; one is small.
✉ Morston, Holt, Norfolk NR25 7AA. **Map** p75 F2. ☎ (01263) 741041. FAX (01263) 740419. @ reception@morstonhall.com 🍴 b,d. **Rooms** 7. ● Jan. AE, DC, MC, V. ££££

OXFORD

Old Bank Metropolitan chic has arrived amongst the dreaming spires in the guise of this classy new hotel done out in cool creams and caramels. Bathrooms are luxurious. The hotel's centrepiece is the former banking hall – now a buzzing bar and brasserie, The Quod. Sitting room, bar, terrace and private parking.
✉ 92-94 High Street, Oxford OX1 4BN. **Map** p75 D4. ☎ (01865) 799599. FAX (01865) 799598. @ info@oldbank-hotel.co.uk 🍴 b,l,d. **Rooms** 42. ● Christmas. AE, DC, MC, V. ££££

MOULSFORD

Beetle and Wedge A delight in summer when the Thames-side setting comes into its own – Jerome K. Jerome wrote *Three Men in a Boat* here. To eat, choose from the brasserie-style Boathouse or the more formal Dining Room; in fine weather the Watergarden is open. Bedrooms are spacious, interesting, and individually furnished.
✉ Ferry Lane, Moulsford, Wallingford, Oxfordshire OX10 9JF. **Map** p75 D4. ☎ (01491) 651381. FAX (01491) 651376. @ kate@beetleandwedge.co.uk 🍴 b,l,d. **Rooms** 11. ● Never. AE, DC, MC, V. £££

OXFORD

Old Parsonage No themed 'olde worlde' charm here, despite the great age of the building. The rather small bedrooms are prettily decorated with pale panelling and unfussy chintz, with marble bathrooms (with telephone). The bar/restaurant has a clubby, cosmopolitan feel. A welcoming, laid-back, well-run hotel.
✉ 1 Banbury Rd, Oxford OX2 6NN. **Map** p75 D4. ☎ (01865) 310210. FAX (01865) 311262. @ info@oldparsonage-hotel.co.uk 🍴 b,l,d. **Rooms** 30. ● Christmas. AE, DC,MC,V. £££

MALVERN WELLS

Cottage in the Wood Three buildings, at whose heart is a Georgian dower house. Setting is all.
✉ Holywell Rd, Malvern Wells, Worcestershire WR14 4LG. **Map** p74 A2. ☎ (01684) 575859. FAX (01684) 560662. @ reception@cottageinthewood.co.uk 🍴 b,l,d. **Rooms** 31. ££

MANCHESTER

11 Didsbury Park Luxurious city chic 15 minutes from the centre of Manchester.
✉ 11 Didsbury Park, Didsbury Village, Manchester M20 5LH. **Map** p75 D1. ☎ (0161) 448 7711. FAX (0161) 448 8282. @ elevendidsburypark.com 🍴 b,d. **Rooms** 14. £££

MATLOCK BATH

Hodgkinson's The dull exterior belies a kitsch, amusing interior, filled with eye-catching objects.
✉ 150 South Parade, Matlock Bath, Matlock, Derbyshire DE4 3NR. **Map** p75 D2. ☎ (01629) 582170. FAX (01629) 584891. @ enquiries@hodgkinsons-hotel.co.uk 🍴 b,d. **Rooms** 7. ££

NEEDHAM MARKET

Pipps Ford Country guesthouse at its best: home produced bread, honey, vegetables and more in a lovely Tudor house with flowery gardens.
✉ Needham Market, Ipswich, Suffolk IP6 8LJ. **Map** p75 F3. ☎ (01449) 760208. FAX (01449) 760561. @ b+b@pippsford.co.uk 🍴 b,d. **Rooms** 9. ££

For key to symbols see backflap. For price categories *see p71*

Painswick

Cardynham House Californian artist Carol Keyes has endowed a fine 15th-century Cotswold town house with panache. The bedrooms are beautiful (some have efficient showers, not baths) and are superb value. One has a swimming pool in it! Breakfasts include American specialities. Dinner can be taken in her adjoining Thai restaurant.
☒ The Cross, Painswick, Stroud, Gloucestershire GL6 6XX. **Map** p74 A3. ☎ (01452) 814006. FAX (01452) 812321. @ info@cardynham.co.uk 🍴 b,d. **Rooms** 9. ● Never. 💳 AE, MC, V. ££

Shurdington

Greenway This smart, traditional hotel is impeccably run and set in extensive gardens and parkland, with the Cotswold Hills in the background. The conservatory dining room, in which elaborate dishes are served, opens onto a sunken garden and lily pond, where drinks can be taken in summer.
☒ Shurdington, Cheltenham, Gloucestershire GL51 4UG. **Map** p74 A2. ☎ (01242) 862352. FAX (01242) 862780. @ greenway@btconnect.com 🍴 b,l,d. **Rooms** 21. ● Never. 💳 AE, DC, MC, V. £££

Shipton-under-Wychwood

Lamb Inn A characterful inn in a charming village – perfection. There are stripped floors and old settles, log fires and a cosy sitting room. Bedrooms are in keeping; two have four-posters. For dinner, choose between pub food in the bar, or more sophisticated dishes in the dining room.
☒ Upper High St, Shipton-under-Wychwood, Chipping Norton, Oxfordshire OX7 6DQ. **Map** p74 B2. ☎ (01993) 830465. FAX (01993) 832025. @ lamb@ suwychwood. fsbusiness.co.uk 🍴 b,l,d. **Rooms** 5. ● Never. 💳 AE, MC, V. ££

Southwold

Crown Good advice: eat at the Crown but stay at the Swan (see page 101), both owned by Adnam's Brewery. If you can't, fear not: the rooms here, though simple, are pleasing, with well-fitted bathrooms (not all en suite). Downstairs, the brasserie-style bar and popular restaurant add to the informal atmosphere.
☒ 90 High St, Southwold, Suffolk, IP18 6DP. **Map** p75 F3. ☎ (01502) 722275. FAX (01502) 727263. @ crownreception@adnams.co.uk 🍴 b,l,d. **Rooms** 14. ● Never. 💳 DC, MC, V. ££

Norton

Hundred House Georgian house with offbeat decoration – patchwork quilts, gold-painted ceilings and swings in some bedrooms.
☒ Norton, nr Shifnal, Shropshire TF11 9EE. **Map** p74 C3. ☎ (01952) 730353. FAX (01952) 730355. @ hundredhouse@ lineone.net 🍴 b,l,d. **Rooms** 10. £££

Norwich

Catton Old Hall Impressive 17th-century gentleman's residence, with mullioned windows, beamed ceilings and inglenook fireplaces.
☒ Lodge Lane, Old Catton, Norwich, Norfolk NR6 7HG. **Map** p75 F3. ☎ (01603) 419379. FAX (01603) 400339. @ enquiries@catton-hall.co.uk 🍴 b,d. **Rooms** 7. ££

Norwich

By Appointment A flamboyant, colourful restaurant-with-rooms, filled with Victoriana and other *objets trouvés*. Wonderful breakfasts.
☒ 25-29 St George's St, Norwich, Norfolk NR3 1AB. **Map** p75 F3. ☎ FAX (01603) 630730. 🍴 b,d. **Rooms** 4. ££

Oxford

Cotswold House High standards and attention to detail distinguish this Cotswold stone family home B&B in residential north Oxford.
☒ 363 Banbury Rd, Oxford OX2 7PL. **Map** p75 D4. ☎ (01865) 310558. FAX (01865) 310558. @ d.r.walker@talk21.com 🍴 b. **Rooms** 7. ££

SOUTHWOLD

Swan The finest of breezy Southwold's medieval inns has a thoroughly comfortable interior, with checks and chintzes and open fires creating the country house look. The main building is complemented by newer garden rooms. The atmosphere is slightly formal, but staff are friendly and helpful.
Market Place, Southwold, Suffolk IP18 6EG. **Map** p75 F3. (01502) 722186. FAX (01502) 724800. swan.hotel@adnams.co.uk b,l,d. **Rooms** 43. Never. AE, DC, MC, V. £££

SWAFFHAM

Strattons The Scotts are natural hosts, and have created a very individual hotel from an elegant listed villa, recently adding two smart suites. Their taste is far from minimalist: there are possessions everywhere: cushions, objects, books, pictures. Vanessa's award-winning cooking is cheerfully served by Les in the cosy basement restaurant.
4 Ash Close, Swaffham, Norfolk PE37 7NH. **Map** p75 F2. (01760) 723845. FAX (01760) 720458. strattonshotel@btinternet.com b,d. **Rooms** 8. Christmas. MC, V. £££

STAPLEFORD

Stapleford Park The stately home experience is taken to extremes here: the finest wines, the most expensive cigars, and bedrooms designed by upmarket companies such as Crabtree & Evelyn and David Hicks. On the sporting front, you can fish, ride, clay pigeon shoot, play golf or practise falconry and archery.
Stapleford, Melton Mowbray, Leicestershire LE14 2EF. **Map** p75 D2. (01572) 787522. FAX (01572) 787651. reservations@stapleford.co.uk b,l,d. **Rooms** 52. Never. AE, DC, MC, V. ££££

TAPLOW

Cliveden This stately home was the former residence of the Astor family (and became associated in the public mind with the 1960s Profumo scandal). It still exudes a subtle combination of privileged grandeur and faintly louche luxury. The accommodation includes a cottage hideaway perfect for honeymooners.
Taplow, Berkshire SL6 0JF. **Map** p75 E4. (01628) 668561. FAX (01628) 661837. reservations@clivedenhouse.co.uk b,l,d. **Rooms** 39. Never. AE, DC, MC, V. ££££

SNAPE

Crown Inn An excellent base for visits to Snape Maltings concert hall, this is a cosy, characterful pub with good food; pretty, beamed bedrooms (one with four-poster), simple bathrooms.
Snape, Suffolk IP17 1SL. **Map** p75 F3. (01728) 688324. b,l,d. **Rooms** 3. ££

STINCHCOMBE

Drakestone House For a taste of bygone elegance, try the splendid Edwardian family home of Hugh and Crystal St John-Mildmay.
Stinchcombe, Dursley, Gloucestershire GL11 6AS. **Map** p74 A3. (01453) 542140. FAX (01453) 542140. b. **Rooms** 3. ££

STOKE-BY-NAYLAND

Angel In the heart of the village, a welcoming inn with well-regarded food and bars buzzing with activity. Bedrooms are homely.
Polstead Street, Stoke-by-Nayland, Colchester, Essex CO6 4SA **Map** p75 F3. (01206) 263245. FAX (01206) 263373. b,l,d. **Rooms** 6. ££

STOW-ON-THE-WOLD

Wyck Hill House Manor house with superb views over Windrush Valley. Formal restaurant.
Burford Rd, Stow-on-the-Wold, Gloucestershire GL54 1HY. **Map** p74 A2. (01451) 831936. FAX (01451) 832243. wyckhill@wrensgroup.com b,l,d. **Rooms** 32. £££

For key to symbols see backflap. For price categories *see p71*

Tetbury

Calcot Manor Various outbuildings surround this old Cotswold manor. The renovated stables house the superb family rooms, with video, fridge, bunks and baby-listening. Children are especially welcome (there is a playroom supervised by a nanny). Adults enjoy the excellent cooking in the cool Conservatory or the Gumstool Inn.
Tetbury, Gloucestershire GL8 8YJ. **Map** p74 A3. (01666) 890391. FAX (01666) 890394. reception@calcotmanor.co.uk b,l,d. **Rooms** 28. Never. AE, DC, MC, V. £££

Uppingham

Lake Isle It's a surprise to find something so rustic and countrified in the middle of a busy High Street, even a pretty one like Uppingham's. The restaurant-with-rooms is entered through a flowery courtyard. Bedrooms are cosy, and the bar has a log fire on chilly evenings. Fully refurbished by new management.
16 High St East, Uppingham, Rutland LE15 9PZ. **Map** p75 E3. (01572) 822951. FAX (01572) 824400. info@lakeislehotel.com b,l,d. **Rooms** 11. Never. AE, DC, MC, V. ££

Uley

Owlpen Manor Only superlatives are used to describe Owlpen Manor, hidden in its own little valley. Once seen, the magical Tudor house is never forgotten. This is luxurious 'serviced' self-catering: stay in a delightful cottage, barn or mill. Eat (Saturdays only) in the atmospheric restaurant, the Cyder House.
Owlpen, nr Uley, Gloucestershire GL11 5BZ. **Map** p74 A3. (01453) 860261. FAX (01453) 860819. sales@owlpen.com b Oct–Mar; l Apr–Sept. **Rooms** 9 cottages. Never. AE, DC, MC, V. £££

Woodstock

Feathers This exceptionally civilized hotel is fashioned from four tall 17th-century townhouses. The place is hard to fault: relaxing upstairs drawing room (with library and open fire); beautifully decorated bedrooms; friendly, unobtrusive service; and excellent food in the lively wood-panelled dining room.
Market St, Woodstock, Oxfordshire OX20 1SX. **Map** p74 B2. (01993) 812291. FAX (01993) 813158. enquiries@feathers.co.uk b,l,d. **Rooms** 20. Never. AE, DC, MC, V. £££

Stratford-upon-Avon

Caterham House This centrally located B&B, set in two Georgian houses, is very attractive both inside and out. Stylish and well run.
58 Rother St, Stratford-upon-Avon, Warwickshire CV37 6LT. **Map** p75 D3. (01789) 267309. FAX (01789) 414836. b. **Rooms** 10. ££

Ware

Marriott Hanbury Manor Hotel & Country Club This five-star hotel incorporates modern amenities (health spa, golf) in a grandiose setting.
Ware, Hertfordshire SG12 0SD. **Map** p75 E4. (01920) 487722. FAX (01920) 487682. b,l,d. **Rooms** 161. £££

Woodbridge

Ramsholt Arms Right by the water, this pub makes a perfect base for sailing, birdwatching or riverside treks.
Dock Road, Ramsholt, Woodbridge, Suffolk IP12 3AB. **Map** p75 F3. (01394) 411229. FAX (01394) 411818. b,l,d. **Rooms** 2. ££

Worfield

Old Vicarage Immaculately kept small hotel, with mostly large bedrooms and a sunny conservatory.
Worfield, Bridgnorth, Shropshire WV15 5JZ. **Map** p74 C3. (01746) 716497. FAX (01746) 716552. admin@ the-old-vicarage.demon.co.uk b,l,d. **Rooms** 14 £££

NORTHERN ENGLAND

YORKSHIRE • LANCASHIRE
NORTHUMBERLAND • LAKE DISTRICT

THE LAKE DISTRICT and the Yorkshire Dales are the areas of Northern England which have the largest number of visitors and the greatest concentration of places to stay. Windermere, in particular, offers a bewildering choice; we recommend the best and most secluded. But don't overlook the rest of this region, which stretches north from the mouth of the River Humber to the Scottish borders: not least Northumberland and the North Yorkshire Moors for their rugged beauty, nor the cathedral cities of Durham and York. Wherever our entries are situated, they range from luxurious hideaways to plain, no-nonsense inns and are often in dramatic settings, perfect for walkers and lovers of the great outdoors.

AMBLESIDE

Wateredge Of the many places to stay around tourist-ridden Lake Windermere, this is a long-standing favourite. Family-run, with courteous, willing staff, it's a quiet, traditional holiday inn situated right on the shores of the lake, its core being two fishermen's cottages. Suites in the annexe. Private jetty. Recently refurbished.
☒ Waterhead Bay, Ambleside, Cumbria LA22 0EP. **Map** p77 D5. ☎ (015394) 32332. FAX (015394) 31878. @ stay@wateredgeinn.co.uk 🍴 b,l,d. **Rooms** 21. ● mid-Dec to early Jan. 💳 AE, MC, V. ££

ARNCLIFFE

Amerdale House The setting is one of the most seductive in all the Dales: on the fringe of a pretty village, wide meadows in front, high hills behind. This admirable hotel is distinguished by its warm welcome and exceptional cooking (dinner included in price of room). Best bedroom is the top-floor room with four-poster bed.
☒ Arncliffe, Littondale, Skipton, North Yorkshire BD23 5QE. **Map** p75 D1, p77 E5. ☎ (01756) 770250. FAX (01756) 770266. 🍴 b,d. **Rooms** 11. ● Nov to mid-March. 💳 MC, V. £££

BOWNESS-ON-WINDERMERE

Linthwaite House Glorious lake views and fine grounds. A consummate, pampering hotel.
☒ Crook Rd, Bowness-on-Windermere, Cumbria LA23 3JA. **Map** p74 C1, p77 E5. ☎ (015394) 88600. FAX (015394) 88601. @ admin@linthwaite.com 🍴 b,l,d. **Rooms** 26. £££

CARLTON-IN-COVERDALE

Foresters Arms Atmospheric pub in a stone-built Dales village. Noted for its good food.
☒ Carlton-in-Coverdale, Leyburn, North Yorkshire DL8 4BB. **Map** p77 E5. ☎ (01969) 640272. FAX (01969) 640272. @ theforestersarms@aol.com 🍴 b,l,d. **Rooms** 3. ££

CRATHORNE

Crathorne Hall Edwardian stately home, now part of the Hand Picked Hotels group, set in wooded grounds overlooking River Leven.
☒ Crathorne, Yarm, North. Yorkshire TS15 0AR. **Map** p77 E5. ☎ (01642) 700398. FAX (01642) 700814. @ enquiries@ cranthornehall.com 🍴 b,l,d. **Rooms** 37. £££

CROSTHWAITE

Crosthwaite House Handsome Georgian house; kind hosts; honest food served in an attractive dining room. Simple accommodation.
☒ Crosthwaite, Kendal, Cumbria LA8 8BP. **Map** p77 D5. ☎ (015395) 68264. @ bookings@ crosthwaitehouse.co.uk 🍴 b,d. **Rooms** 6. £

For key to symbols see backflap. For price categories *see p71*

Bassenthwaite Lake

Pheasant The old oak bar, full of dark nooks and crannies, is a gem, little changed from its earliest days. Beyond that are several lounges with generous sitting space. Bedrooms are modern and light, without TV or telephone. The food makes few concessions to fashion – a simple characterful inn, recently refurbished.
⊠ Bassenthwaite Lake, Cockermouth, Cumbria CA13 9YE. **Map** p77 D5. (017687) 76234. FAX (017687) 76002. @ info@the-peasant.co.uk b,l,d. **Rooms** 16. Christmas Day. MC, V. ££

Borrowdale

Leathes Head Previous owners Patricia Brady and Mark Payne breathed new life into this Edwardian house, refurbishing it in traditional style with bold touches. It has splendid views across the fells. Dinner is a four-course affair with plenty of choice and delicious puddings. Now under the ownership of Roy and Janice Smith.
⊠ Borrowdale, Keswick, Cumbria CA12 5UY. **Map** p77 D5. (017687) 77247. FAX (017687) 77363. @ enq@leatheshead.co.uk b,d. **Rooms** 11. Nov to Feb, except Christmas and New Year. MC, V. £

Bolton Abbey

Devonshire Arms This glossy, go-ahead country hotel is owned by the Duke and Duchess of Devonshire, and furnished largely with objects from Chatsworth House. There are two dining rooms, the formal Burlington Restaurant and the designer Brasserie. Best of the bedrooms are the themed four-poster rooms in the Old Wing.
⊠ Bolton Abbey, Skipton, North Yorkshire BD23 6AJ. **Map** p75 D1. (01756) 710441. FAX (01756) 710564. @ reservations@thedevonshirearms.co.uk b,l,d. **Rooms** 41. Never. AE, DC, MC, V. ££££

Bowness-on-Windermere

Lindeth Fell Large mature gardens glowing with azaleas and rhododendrons in spring, tremendous views, and a warm, courteous welcome from Pat and Diana Kennedy at this comfortable country house. Wood-panelled hall, two sitting rooms, and pleasingly decorated bedrooms. Drinks and tea can be taken on the terrace.
⊠ Bowness-on-Windermere, Cumbria LA23 3JP . **Map** p77 D5. (015394) 43286. FAX (015394) 47455. @ kennedy@lindethfell.co.uk b,l,d. **Rooms** 14. Jan. MC, V. £££

Durham

Georgian Town House Town-centre Georgian house decorated with flair (and a profusion of stencils). Breakfasts are taken in the conservatory.
⊠ 10-11 Crossgate, Durham, Co. Durham DH1 4PS. **Map** p77 E5. FAX (0191) 386 8070. @ enquiries@georgian-townhouse.fsnet.co.uk b. **Rooms** 6. ££

Grasmere

White Moss House Renowned for its cuisine, with pretty bedrooms (two in a secluded cottage). In the Wordsworth family until the 1930s.
⊠ Rydal Water, Grasmere, Cumbria LA22 9SE. **Map** p77 D5. (015394) 35295. FAX (015394) 35516. @ sue@whitemoss.com b,d. **Rooms** 7. ££

Grassington

Ashfield House Simple guesthouse tucked behind main village square; large walled garden.
⊠ 3 Summers Fold, Grassington, Skipton, North Yorkshire BD23 5AE. **Map** p75 D1. (01756) 752584. FAX (01756) 752584. @ info@ashfieldhouse.co.uk b,d. **Rooms** 7. ££

Great Langdale

Old Dungeon Ghyll At the heart of the Lake District, a slate-and-stone walkers' hostelry: simple, somewhat worn, with hearty food.
⊠ Great Langdale, Ambleside, Cumbria LA22 9JY. **Map** p77 D5 FAX (015394) 37272. @ neil.odg@lineone.net b,l,d. **Rooms** 14. ££

BRAMPTON

Farlam Hall Though mainly Victorian, the roots of this elegant Borders house are Elizabethan. Set in rolling countryside, it is beautifully furnished and imbued with a traditional, discreet atmosphere. In the dining room, superb dinners (included in price of room) range from plain country dishes to mild extravagances.
Brampton, Cumbria CA8 2NG. **Map** p77 D5. (016977) 46234. FAX (016977) 46683. @ farlamhall@dial.pipex.com b,d. **Rooms** 12. Christmas. MC, V. ££££

HAWES

Simonstone Hall A former hunting lodge (the American owner still takes it over for private shooting parties) with a welcoming, traditional interior. Slump in the elegant drawing room, fraternize in the Game Tavern, or withdraw to your room. The superior and deluxe ones are magnificent: huge and splendidly furnished.
Hawes, North Yorkshire DL8 3LY. **Map** p77 E5. (01969) 667255. FAX (01969) 667741. @ mail@simonstonehall.demon.co.uk b,l,d. **Rooms** 20. Never. AE, DC, MC, V. £££

CARLISLE

Number Thirty One A winning combination of imagination and hands-on professionalism. There are just three rooms: Green (Oriental style), Blue, the largest, with walk-in wardrobe, and Yellow, with half-tester. Philip Parker's dinners are based on what's freshest that day. As much as possible – breads, preserves and so on – is home-made.
31 Howard Place, Carlisle, Cumbria CA1 1HR. **Map** p77 D5. (01228) 597080. FAX (01228) 597080. @ bestpep@aol.com b,d. **Rooms** 3. Nov to Mar. AE, DC, MC, V. ££

KIRKBY LONSDALE

Hipping Hall Guests can eat communally in the splendid beamed Great Hall with minstrels' gallery. After a day on the fells, sink into sofas around a wood-burning stove at the other end of the Hall. Bedrooms are spacious. Child-friendly. Pets allowed in the cottages.
Cowan Bridge, Kirkby Lonsdale, Cumbria LA6 2JJ. **Map** p74 C1, p77 D5. (015242) 71187. FAX (015242) 72452. @ hippinghall@aol.com b,d. **Rooms** 5, plus 2 cottages. 21 Dec to Easter AE, MC, V. ££

HAROME

Star Inn Michelin-starred restaurant with accommodation across the road in Cross House Lodge and Black Eagle Cottages. Outstanding.
Harome, nr Helmsley, North Yorkshire YO62 5JE. **Map** p75 E1. (01439) 770397. FAX (01439) 771833. b,l,d. **Rooms** 8, plus 3 suites. €€€

HAWNBY

Hawnby Hotel 'Village pub' façade hides an exquisite small hotel, with six bedrooms and an elegant sitting room. Popular with walkers.
Hilltop Hawnby, North Yorkshire YO62 5QS. **Map** p77 E5, p75 D1. (01439) 798202. FAX (01439) 798344. b,l,d. **Rooms** 9. ££

HAZLEWOOD

Hazlewood Castle Once a castle, now a luxury hotel with the latest accoutrements.
Paradise Lane, Hazlewood, Tadcaster, North Yorkshire LS24 9NJ. **Map** p75 D1. (01937) 535353. FAX (01937) 530630. @ info@hazlewood-castle.co.uk b,l,d. **Rooms** 21. £££

HEADLAM

Headlam Hall Creeper-covered Jacobean house in formal gardens; popular for functions.
Headlam, Gainford, Darlington, Co. Durham DL2 3HA. **Map** p77 E5. (01325) 730238. FAX (01325) 730790. @ admin@headlamhall.co.uk b,l,d. **Rooms** 36. ££

For key to symbols see backflap. For price categories *see p71*

Leeds

42 The Calls The converted riverside corn mill is *the* place to stay in Leeds. Stylishly contemporary, amusingly different, it retains original features such as beams, girders, bare brick walls and the odd hoist. Bedrooms and bathrooms are well-equipped. At weekends, some meals available by means of room service only.
42 The Calls, Leeds, West Yorkshire LS2 7EW. **Map** p75 D1. (0113) 244 0099. FAX (0113) 234 4100. @ hotel@42thecalls.co.uk b,l,d. **Rooms** 41. Christmas. AE,DC, MC, V. ££££

Ramsgill-in-Nidderdale

Yorke Arms This creeper-clad former shooting lodge stands on the green in a little Dales hamlet close to Gouthwaite Reservoire – a birdwatchers' paradise. It is now run by chef Frances Atkins and her husband Gerald. Roaring log fires, snug bedrooms, good food in the candlelit, beamed dining room (dinner included in price of room).
Ramsgill-in-Nidderdale, Harrogate, North Yorkshire HG3 5RL. **Map** p75 D1. (01423) 755243. FAX (01423) 755330. @ enquiries@yorke-arms.co.uk b,l,d. **Rooms** 14. Never. AE, DC, MC, V. ££££

Newlands

Swinside Lodge Immaculately decorated and maintained, with attentive service and agreeable personal touches, this typical Victorian lakeland house makes an excellent country hotel. There is exhilarating walking right from the door. On your return, dinner is a no-choice, four-course, mildly adventurous delight.
Newlands Valley, Keswick, Cumbria CA12 5UE. **Map** p77 D5. (017687) 74948. @ info@swinsidelodge-hotel.co.uk b,l,d. **Rooms** 6. Christmas Day. AE, DC, MC, V. ££

Reeth

Burgoyne This outwardly severe stone-walled house makes an excellent base for touring or walking the region. The hotel is smoothly run by owners Derek Hickson and Peter Carwardine, with public rooms that are welcoming yet elegant. The smart bedrooms are peppered with thoughtful extras
On the Green, Reeth, Richmond, North Yorkshire DL11 6SN. **Map** p77 E5. FAX (01748) 884292. @ enquiries@theburgoyne.co.uk b,d. **Rooms** 8. Jan to mid-Feb. MC, V. ££

Hunmanby

Wrangham House Former Georgian vicarage. Comfortable sitting room, cosy bar and elegant dining room.
Stonegate, Hunmanby, North Yorkshire YO14 0NS. **Map** p75 E1, p77 F5. (01723) 891333. FAX (01723) 892973. @ info@wranghamhouse.co.uk b,d. **Rooms** 12. ££

Lastingham

Lastingham Grange Family-run, child-friendly hotel in delightful village with lovely gardens.
Lastingham, York, North Yorkshire YO62 6TH. **Map** p75 E1, p77 F1. (01751) 417345. FAX (01751) 417358. @ reservations@lastinghamgrange.com b,l, d. **Rooms** 12. £££

Low Lorton

Winder Hall Beautiful manor house with a 17th-century façade and many period features. Fine bedrooms; good food.
Low Lorton, Cockermouth, Cumbria CA13 9UP. **Map** p77 D5. (01900) 85107. FAX (01900) 85479. @ stay@winderhall.co.uk b,d. **Rooms** 7. ££

Middleham

Middleham Grange Impressive bedrooms at this elegant Georgian house, formerly Miller's House Hotel. Bed and breakfast only.
Market Place, Middleham, Wensleydale, North Yorkshire DL8 4NR. **Map** p75 D1, p77 E5. (01969) 622630. b. **Rooms** 4. £££

Ripley

Boar's Head Opened in the late 1980s by the present residents of Ripley Castle, Sir Thomas and Lady Ingilby, this former inn has elegant, even sumptuous, interiors, augmented by ancestral portraits and ornaments. The candlelit dining room is romantic, and the cooking is taken very seriously.
Ripley Castle Estate, Harrogate HG3 3AY.
Map p75 D1. (01423) 771888. FAX (01423) 771509.
reservations@boarsheadripley.co.uk b,l,d. **Rooms** 25. Never. AE, DC, MC, V. ££

Seatoller

Seatoller House This is not a run-of-the-mill hotel, but, if you are convivial, it is a delight. Guests eat communally at set times, and, to get the best out of the place, should take part in its social life. A guesthouse for more than 100 years, it has simple bedrooms, a low-ceilinged sitting room, plain country dining room and good food.
Seatoller, Borrowdale, Keswick, Cumbria CA12 5XN.
Map p77 D5. (017687) 77218. FAX (017687) 77189.
seatollerhouse@ btconnect.com b,d. **Rooms** 9. end Nov to mid-March. MC, V. ££

Romaldkirk

Rose and Crown This thriving former coaching inn, set on the village inn, is noted for the modish English food. Eat in the wood-panelled, candlelit dining room, then withdraw to the rustic bar, with log fires, old photographs and much brass. Courtyard rooms are modern; those in the main building more characterful.
Romaldkirk, Barnard Castle, Co. Durham DL12 9EB.
Map p77 E5. (01833) 650213. FAX (01833) 650828.
hotel@rose-and-crown.co.uk b,l,d. **Rooms** 12. Christmas. MC, V. ££

Ullswater

Sharrow Bay For more than 50 years, Sharrow Bay has been famed for its food, service, luxury and lakeside setting. It claims to have been the world's first country house hotel, and to have the finest views in the Lake District. Nigel Lightburn, involved with the hotel for more than 30 years, is now in charge. New garden wing recently added.
Ullswater, Penrith, Cumbria CA10 2LZ. **Map** p77 D5.
(017684) 86301. FAX (017684) 86349.
enquiries@sharrow-bay.com b,l,d. **Rooms** 26. Dec to end Feb. AE, MC, V. ££££

Mungrisdale

Mill A 17th-century former mill cottage in lovely setting, with simple, airy bedrooms and a chintzy sitting room. Vegetarians are well catered for.
Mungrisdale, Penrith, Cumbria CA11 0XR.
Map p77 D5. (017687) 79659. FAX (017687) 79155.
themill@quinlan.evesham.net b,d. **Rooms** 9. ££

Newcastle upon Tyne

Malmaison The converted warehouse is one in a chain of hotels representing excellent value. Slick rooms are equipped with all the latest requisites.
104 Quayside, Newcastle upon Tyne, Tyne & Wear NE1 3DX. **Map** p77 E5. (0191) 245 5000.
FAX (0191) 245 4545. b,l,d. **Rooms** 116. £££

Newton-le-Willows

Hall The Georgian country house, gracious both inside and out, is made extra-special by the vivacious, sympathetic character of its owner.
Newton-le-Willows, Bedale, North Yorkshire DL8 1SW.
Map p75 D1. (01677) 450210. b,d.
Rooms 3. ££

Sawrey

Ees Wyke In a glorious spot above Esthwaite Water; grand views. Old-fashioned in the best sense, and lovingly cared for. Welcoming owners.
Near Sawrey, Hawkshead, Ambleside, Cumbria LA22 0JZ. **Map** p74 C1, p77 D5. FAX (015394) 36393. eeswyke@aol.com b,d. **Rooms** 8. £££

For key to symbols see backflap. For price categories *see p71*

Wasdale Head

Wasdale Head Inn In a site unrivalled even in the Lake District, this robust old inn stands above deep, dramatic Wastwater. There are convivial bars, a comfortable lounge, a panelled dining room decorated with china and pewter. Mixture of simple bedrooms, all with bathrooms, and self-catering apartments. ✉ Wasdale Head, Gosforth, Cumbria CA20 1EX. **Map** p77 D5. ☎ (019467) 26229. FAX (019467) 26334. @ wasdaleheadinn@msn.com 🍴 b,d. **Rooms** 14. ● Never. 💳 AE, MC, V. ££

Whitewell

Inn at Whitewell Just the right note is struck at this mellow Forest of Bowland inn. The owners ensure a relaxed, unstuffy atmosphere, extending an equally warm welcome to adults, children and pets. The decoration is full of good taste, particularly in the bedrooms – some of which have peat fires. Most have videos, CD players and impressive bathrooms. Fly fishing. ✉ Whitewell, Clitheroe, Lancashire BB7 3AT. **Map** p74 C1. ☎ (01200) 448222. FAX (01200) 448298. 🍴 b,l,d. **Rooms** 17. ● Never. 💳 MC, V. ££

Watermillock

Old Church The whitewashed 18th-century house on the shores of Ullswater has been in the care of Kevin Whitemore and his family since the late 1970s. They have created bold interiors, with a confident but harmonious use of colour in the bedrooms, most with lake views. Kevin is the cook, producing satisfying menus. Boating. ✉ Watermillock, Penrith, Cumbria CA11 0JN. **Map** p77 D5. ☎ (017684) 86204. FAX (017684) 86368. @ info@oldchurch.co.uk 🍴 b,d. **Rooms** 10. ● Nov to March. 💳 AE, MC, V. £££

Windermere

Gilpin Lodge Notable for its high standards and attention to detail, Victorian Gilpin Lodge presents a fresh, white, flower-bedecked exterior. Its immaculate, cosy yet smart interior is embellished with many ornaments and flower arrangements. Some bedrooms have four-posters. Dinner included in price of room. ✉ Crook Rd, Windermere, Cumbria LA23 3NE. **Map** pp74 C1, p77 D5. ☎ (015394) 88818. FAX (015394) 88058. @ hotel@gilpinlodge.com 🍴 b,l,d. **Rooms** 14. ● Never. 💳 AE, DC, MC, V. ££££

Thornton-le-Fylde

River House Characterful hotel, set beside a tidal estuary. Two hooded 19th-century baths. ✉ Skippool Creek, Thornton-le-Fylde, nr Blackpool, Lancashire FY5 5LF. **Map** p74 C1. ☎ (01253) 883497. FAX (01253) 892083. @ enquiries@theriverhouse.org.uk 🍴 b,d. **Rooms** 4. ££

Troutbeck

Mortal Man Glorious views of Windermere from this friendly Lakeland inn. The bedrooms are functional; traditional bars, hearty food. ✉ Troutbeck, Windermere, Cumbria LA23 1PL. **Map** p77 D5. ☎ (015394) 33193. FAX (015394) 31261. @ themortalman@btinternet.com 🍴 b,l,d. **Rooms** 12. ££

Walkington

Manor House Late-Victorian house in tranquil position. Elaborate food; long wine list. ✉ Northlands, Walkington, East Yorkshire HU17 8RT. **Map** p75 E1. ☎ (01482) 881645. FAX (01482) 866501. @ derek@the-manor-house.co.uk 🍴 b,d. **Rooms** 7. ££

Wath-in-Nidderdale

Sportsman's Arms Modest, clean accommodation at this popular Dales village inn. Lively menu in the busy restaurant. ✉ Wath-in-Nidderdale, Pately Bridge, North Yorkshire HG3 5PP. **Map** p75 D1. ☎ (01423) 711306. FAX (01423) 712524. 🍴 b,l,d. **Rooms** 13. ££

Windermere

Holbeck Ghyll The set-back position of this classic Victorian lakeland hotel provides welcome privacy from the bustle of Windermere, as well as grand lake views from the immaculate gardens. Traditional and rather formal in style, with a professional, friendly staff, it has mostly very spacious bedrooms and bathrooms.

☒ Holbeck Lane, Windermere, Cumbria LA23 1LU. **Map** pp74 C1, p77 D5. (015394) 32375. FAX (015394) 34743. @ stay@holbeckghyll.com b,l,d. **Rooms** 21. 3 weeks in Jan. AE, DC, MC, V. ££££

Witherslack

Old Vicarage This Georgian country house is hidden in a large wooded garden, and the owners have invested it with an easy-going atmosphere. The straightforward decoration combines new with old; five of the bedrooms have private terraces. Dinner is a highlight, using local ingredients in fresh and thoughtful ways,

☒ Witherslack, nr Grange-over-Sands, Cumbria LA11 6RS. **Map** p74 C1, p77 D5. (015395) 52381. FAX (015395) 52373. @ hotel@oldvicarage.com b,d. **Rooms** 14. Never. MC, V. £££

Windermere

Storrs Hall A change of ownership a while back gave a new and opulent lease of life to this spectacularly positioned Georgian pile, built to look like an Italian villa. Beautifully proportioned rooms are filled with antiques, paintings, rare books and model ships.

☒ Storrs Park, Bowness-on-Windermere, Cumbria LA23 3LG. **Map** p74 C1, p77 D5. (015394) 47111. FAX (015394) 47555. @ reception@storrshall.co.uk b,l,d. **Rooms** 30. Never. AE, DC, MC, V. £££

York

Middlethorpe Hall The magnificent William III house, once home of diarist Lady Mary Wortley Montagu, is now part of Historic House Hotels, which transforms important buildings into places to stay. One feels special just walking in, yet the atmosphere is not intimidating. Set in large garden and parkland not far from centre of York.

☒ Bishopthorpe Rd, York YO23 2GB. **Map** p75 E1. (01904) 641241. FAX (01904) 620176. @ info@middlethorpe.com b,l,d. **Rooms** 30. Never. MC, V. ££££

Windermere

Samling Luxurious country house hotel with wonderful views over Lake Windermere.

☒ Ambleside Road, Windermere, Cumbria LA23 1LR. **Map** p74 C1, p77 D5. (015394) 31922. FAX (015394) 30400. @ info@thesamling.com b,l (Sun only),d. **Rooms** 10. ££££

Winteringham

Winteringham Fields A 16th-century manor house, whose owners have created an alluring formula: highly praised food, lovely bedrooms.

☒ Winteringham, North Lincolnshire DN15 9PF. **Map** p75 E1. (01724) 733096. FAX (01724) 733898. @ wintfields@aol.com b,l,d. **Rooms** 10. £££

York

Grange Handsome Regency townhouse with richly decorated interior and tranquil ambience. Elegant dining room; helpful service

☒ 1 Clifton, York, North Yorkshire YO30 6AA. **Map** p75 E1. (01904) 644744. FAX (01904) 612453. @ info@grangehotel.co.uk b,l,d. **Rooms** 30. £££

York

Holmwood House Very comfortable B&B about 15 minutes' walk from the centre of the city.

☒ 114 Holgate Rd, York, North Yorkshire YO24 4BB. **Map** p75 E1. (01904) 626183. FAX (01904) 670899. @ holmwood.house@dial.pipex.com b. **Rooms** 14. ££

For key to symbols see backflap. For price categories *see p71*

SCOTLAND

BORDERS • LOWLANDS • SOUTHWESTERN SCOTLAND HIGHLANDS AND ISLANDS

FROM PASTORAL border country to the raw, majestic scenery of the Highlands and Islands, Scotland's landscape never ceases to amaze, and presents endless opportunities for outdoor pursuits – notwithstanding the rain and the summer midges. On the following pages you will find some of the most remote hotels in Europe, as well as ones fashioned from buildings as diverse as castles and crofts. The vast majority are in superb locations and are wonderfully secluded, perhaps overlooking a quiet loch with a view of distant mountains, or with lawns running down to a deserted swathe of golden beach. Of Scotland's cities, Edinburgh is well served with fine hotels, and we include several useful addresses in Glasgow.

ACHILTIBUIE

Summer Isles The very remote, cottage-like hotel has a Michelin star for its impressive cookery, which makes much use of fresh local fish; the cheeseboard is justly famous. Only seven of the rooms have a TV. If possible, go for the suite: it has a spiral staircase, huge bathroom and breathtaking views.
✉ Achiltibuie, Ullapool, Ross-shire IV26 2YG. **Map** p76 C1. ☎ (01854) 622282. FAX (01854) 622251. @ info@summerisleshotel.co.uk 🍴 b,l,d. **Rooms** 13. ● mid-Oct to 1 April. 💳 MC, V. ££

AUCHTERARDER

Gleneagles This spectacular Art Deco hotel was built in the 1920s as the 'playground of the gods'. Intimate it is not; occupied you will certainly be, with a raft of activities, both leisure and sporting, now on offer (including, of course, the world-class golf which made the hotel's name). Suites and 'Estate Rooms' are nicest, but very expensive.
✉ Auchterarder, Perthshire PH3 1NF. **Map** p77 D3. ☎ (01764) 662231. FAX (01764) 662134. @ resort.sales@gleneagles.com 🍴 b,l,d. **Rooms** 275. ● Never. 💳 AE, DC, MC, V. ££££

BALLATER

Darroch Learg An imposing Victorian country house hotel, splendidly situated and easy-going. Noted for its inventive food and excellent wines.
✉ Braemar Rd, Ballater, Aberdeenshire AB35 5UX. **Map** p77 D2. ☎ (013397) 55443. FAX (013397) 55252. @ info@darrochlearg.co.uk 🍴 b,d. **Rooms** 17. £££

BALQUHIDDER

Monachyle Mhor 17th-century farmhouse by Loch Voil, run with verve by the Lewis family.
✉ Balquhidder, Lochearnhead, Perthshire FK19 8PQ. **Map** p76 C3. ☎ (01877) 384622. FAX (01877) 384305. @ info@monachylemhor.com 🍴 b,l,d. **Rooms** 10. ££

BUNCHREW

Bunchrew House A pink sandstone turreted mansion with large, comfortable bedrooms and a rather formal dining room.
✉ Bunchrew, Inverness-shire IV3 8TA. **Map** p76 C2. ☎ (01463) 234917. FAX (01463) 710620. @ welcome@bunchrew-inverness.co.uk 🍴 b,l,d. **Rooms** 14. ££

COLONSAY, ISLE OF

Isle of Colonsay Hotel Perfect island life: away from it all in a warmly civilized house serving good fresh food. Cycling, fishing, golf, sailing.
✉ Isle of Colonsay, Argyll PA61 7YP. **Map** p76 B3. ☎ (01951) 200316. FAX (01951) 200353. @ colonsay.hotel@pipemedia.co.uk 🍴 b,l,d. **Rooms** 11. £££

Blairgowrie

Kinloch House The early Victorian country house, adorned with a neatly trimmed creeper on the outside and pincushion-neat inside, is set in wooded parkland and has a fine walled garden. The atmosphere is quiet, the staff traditionally dressed, the rooms furnished with antiques. Bar for cocktails or a wee dram; conservatory.
Blairgowrie, Perthshire PH10 6SG. **Map** p77 D3.
(01250) 884237. FAX (01250) 884333.
info@kinlochhouse.com b,l,d. **Rooms** 20.
Christmas. MC, V. ££££

Comrie

Royal Hotel In an endearing village, well placed for touring, this 18th-century former coaching inn became 'royal' when Queen Victoria stayed. Today it is a beautifully presented, traditional hotel with an eye for modern tastes and a cool yet homely ambience: heavy iron bedsteads are offset by pale walls and gleaming wooden floors.
Melville Square, Comrie, Perthshire PH6 2DN.
Map p77 D3. (01764) 679200. FAX (01764) 679219.
reception@royalhotel.co.uk b,l,d. **Rooms** 11.
Never. AE, MC, V. ££

Colbost, Isle of Skye

Three Chimneys Long-established as one of Skye's best restaurants – with the emphasis on fish – Three Chimneys can now count itself the island's most interesting hotel. A new annexe, called the House Over-By, houses six contemporary suites, designed to blend with the magical views across water and mountains.
Colbost, Dunvegan, Isle of Skye, IV55 8ZT.
Map p76 B2. (01470) 511258. FAX (01470) 511358.
eatandstay@threechimneys.co.uk b,l,d. **Rooms** 6.
3 weeks Jan. AE, MC, V. ££££

Dunkeld

Kinnaird This Edwardian mansion harks back to a more gracious age, with modern requirements subtly blended in: the dining room is decorated with frescoes, bedrooms are spacious and luxurious. The River Tay (fishing possible) flows through the estate. Also self-catering cottages.
Kinnaird Estate, Dunkeld, Perthshire PH8 0LB.
Map p77 D3. (01796) 482440. FAX (01796) 482289.
enquiry@kinnairdestate.com b,l,d.
Rooms 9, plus 8 cottages. Never. AE, MC, V.
££££

Drumnadrochit

Polmaily House Secluded hotel near Loch Ness; both adults and children are well taken care of. Horse riding; sailing yachts on Loch Ness.
Drumnadrochit, Inverness-shire IV63 6TL. **Map** p76 C2.
(01456) 450343. FAX (01456) 450813.
polmaily@btinternet.com b,l,d. **Rooms** 14. ££

Edinburgh

Albany Peaceful Georgian terrace close to Princes Street. Pleasant bedrooms, sparkling bathrooms.
39 Albany St, Edinburgh EH1 3QY. **Map** p77 D3.
(0131) 556 0397. FAX (0131) 557 6633.
info@albanyhotel-edinburgh.co.uk b,d.
Rooms 21. ££££

Edinburgh

Balmoral In the heart of the city, baronial grandeur, modern luxury and fine dining.
1 Princes St, Edinburgh EH2 2EQ. **Map** p77 D3.
(0870) 4407040. FAX (0131) 557 8740
reservations@thebalmoralhotel.com b,l,d.
Rooms 188. ££££

Fort William

Grange Jessica Lange stayed in this B&B while filming *Rob Roy*. Maybe she had the Turret Room, but all are charming with lovely loch views.
Grange Rd, Fort William, Inverness-shire PH33 6JF.
Map p76 C2. (01397) 705516. FAX (01397) 701595.
jcampbell@grangefortwilliam.com b. **Rooms** 4. ££

For key to symbols see backflap. For price categories *see p71*

EDINBURGH

Bonham In the same ownership as the Howard, the townhouse hotel is situated in a leafy side street close to the city centre. It has been equipped for the 21st century, with communications technology installed in the calm, contemporary bedrooms; these also feature original paintings by young Scottish artists.
35 Drumsheugh Gardens, Edinburgh EH3 7RN. **Map** p77 D3. (0131) 226 6050. FAX (0131) 226 6080. reserve@thebonham.com b,l,d. **Rooms** 48. Never. AE, DC, MC, V. ££££

EDINBURGH

Witchery by the Castle Vivienne Westwood, Jack Nicholson, Michael Douglas and Catherine Zeta-Jones have stayed here – so it's good enough for you. Why the Witchery? – because hundreds of 'witches' were burned at the stake nearby. The only thing to burn now will be a hole in your pocket. Award-winning restaurant.
Castlehill, The Royal Mile, Edinburgh EH1 2NF. **Map** p77 D3. (0131) 225 5613. FAX (0131) 220 4392. mail@thewitchery.com b,l,d. **Rooms** 6. Never. AE, DC, MC, V. ££££

EDINBURGH

Howard The most luxurious of three Edinburgh hotels in the same stable (see also The Bonham, below left), The Howard is a made up of three richly decorated terraced townhouses. Original features include romantic Italianate frescoes in the breakfast room. All guests are assigned their own personal butler.
34 Great King St, Edinburgh EH3 6QH. **Map** p77 D3. (0131) 557 3500. FAX (0131) 557 6515. reserve@thehoward.com b,l,d. **Rooms** 18. Christmas. AE, DC, MC, V. ££££

ERISKA

Isle of Eriska Close to Oban and connected to the mainland by a road bridge, Eriska feels a world away, and the family-run baronial house is a pleasant echo of the Victorian age. High tea is served at 6pm in old-fashioned public rooms. The bedrooms are light and mainly spacious. Families can expect a warm welcome. Private golf course.
Eriska, Ledaig, Oban, Argyll PA37 1SD. **Map** p76 A2. (01631) 720371. FAX (01631) 720531. office@eriska-hotel.co.uk b,l,d. **Rooms** 19. 6 Jan to 6 Feb. AE, DC, MC, V. ££££

GLASGOW

Malmaison Cosmopolitan chic and value for money are the hallmarks of the Malmaison chain; this one created a very useful address.
278 West George Street, Glasgow G2 4LL. **Map** p76 C4. (0141) 572 1000. FAX (0141) 572 1002. glasgow@mailmaison.com b,l,d. **Rooms** 72. £££

GLENLIVET

Minmore House Friendly and comfortable small hotel close to the famous whiskey distillery.
Glenlivet, Moray AB37 9DB. **Map** p77 D2. (01807) 590378. FAX (01807) 590472. minmorehouse@ukonline.co.uk b,l,d. Rooms 10. £££

ISLE ORNSAY

Eilean Iarmain Traditional 19th-century seaside inn with a Gaelic feel. Wonderful views from the comfy bedrooms and public rooms.
Sleat, Isle of Skye, Highland IV43 8QR. **Map** p76 B2. (01471) 833332. FAX (01471) 833275. hotel@eilean-iarmain.co.uk b,l,d. **Rooms** 16. £££

KENTALLEN

Ardsheal House Set above Loch Linnhe, with stunning views. Hospitable, slightly old-fashioned; guest rooms are decorated with family antiques.
Kentallen of Appin, Argyll PA38 4BX. **Map** p76 C3. (01631) 740227. FAX (01631) 740342. info@ardsheal.co.uk b. **Rooms** 3. ££

Fort William

Inverlochy Castle Set in the foothills of Ben Nevis, Britain's highest mountain, Inverlochy prompted Queen Victoria to write: 'I never saw a lovelier or more romantic spot.' A hotel for 35 years, the Scottish Baronial pile is neither intimidating nor stuffy, but deeply, elegantly luxurious. Superb food; tennis, billiards, fishing.
Torlundy, Fort William, Inverness-shire PH33 6SN. **Map** p76 C2. (01397) 702177. FAX (01397) 702953. @ info@inverlochycastlehotel.com b,l,d. **Rooms** 17. early Jan to mid-Feb. AE, MC, V. ££££

Gullane

Greywalls An obvious choice for golfers, since it overlooks the 10th green of the Muirfield course, this immaculate honey-stoned, crescent-shaped building was designed by Sir Edwin Lutyens. The feel is still one of an elegant private house; the panelled library is particularly appealing. Refined dinners and hearty breakfasts.
Muirfield, Gullane, East Lothian EH31 2EG. **Map** p77 D3. (01620) 842144. FAX (01620) 842241. @ hotel@greywalls.co.uk b,d. **Rooms** 23. Nov to Apr. AE, DC, MC, V. ££££

Glasgow

One Devonshire Gardens Even among London's myriad town house hotels, One Devonshire Gardens would stand out. It comprises four handsome houses on a busy road close to the city centre. Step inside, and the effect is one of richly coloured opulence. Gordon Ramsay recently took over the hotel restaurant.
One Devonshire Gardens, Glasgow G12 0UX. **Map** p76 C4. (0141) 339 2001. FAX (0141) 337 1663. @ reservations@onedevonshiregardens.com b,l,d. **Rooms** 35. Never. AE, DC, MC, V. £££

Kilchrenan

Taychreggan A sophisticated hideaway in a sensational setting on the banks of Loch Awe. Peace and quiet are assured: it's approached by a seven-mile single-track road. The hotel's core is an old stone drovers' inn, with buildings arranged around a central courtyard. Smart decor with rather loud modern art on the walls.
Kilchrenan, by Tainuilt, Argyll PA35 1HQ. **Map** p76 C3. (01866) 833211. FAX (01866) 833244. @ info@taychregganhotel.co.uk b,l,d. Rooms 19. Jan. AE, V. £££

Kildrummy

Kildrummy Castle Large Victorian building, set in lovely gardens overlooking a castle ruin.
Kildrummy, Alford, Aberdeenshire AB33 8RA. **Map** p77 D2. (019755) 71288. FAX (019755) 71345. @ bookings@kildrummy.castlehotel.co.uk b,l,d. **Rooms** 16. £££

Killiecrankie

Killiecrankie House A modest Scottish country hotel, perfectly placed for watching out for wildlife, including red squirrels and roe deer.
Killiecrankie, by Pitlochry, Perthshire PH16 5LG. **Map** p77 D3. (01796) 473220. FAX (01796) 472451. @ enquiries@killiecrankiehotel.co.uk b,l,d. **Rooms** 10. £££

Kirkudbright

Gladstone House Excellent B&B in an appealing town. It is decorated with taste and makes a civilized place to stay, with bountiful breakfasts.
48 High St, Kirkcudbright, Dumfries and Galloway DG6 4JX. **Map** p76 C5. FAX (01557) 331734. @ hilarygladstone@aol.com b. **Rooms** 3. £

Muir of Ord

Dower House An elegant private home noted for its attentive owners and good food.
Highfield, Muir of Ord, Ross-shire IV6 7XN. **Map** p76 C2. (01463) 870090. FAX (01463) 870090. @ tostay@thedowerhouse.co.uk b,d. **Rooms** 6. £££

Maybole

Culzean Castle On a windswept clifftop, Robert Adam's last masterpiece (c.1785). The top floor was given by Scotland to the late ex-US President Eisenhower for his lifetime, and is now a small hotel. It includes a wonderful circular sitting room with views to Arran and Mull of Kintyre. Or you can rent the entire apartment for a private party.
Culzean Castle, Maybole, Ayrshire KA19 8LE. **Map** p76 C4. (01655) 884455. FAX (01655) 884503
@ culzean@nts.org.uk b,d. **Rooms** 6.
Christmas, Feb. MC, V. ££££

Port Appin

Airds Hotel Airds is an old ferry inn in a pretty waterfront village, with spectacular views across Loch Linnhe to the hills beyond. It's a sophisticated place, with a flower-filled conservatory and a Michelin-starred kitchen. Dinner included in price. Afternoon tea is served. Under new management.
Port Appin, Appin, Argyll PA38 4DF. **Map** p76 C3.
(01631) 730236. FAX (01631) 730535.
@ airds@airds-hotel.com b,d. **Rooms** 16.
3 weeks in Jan. MC, V. ££££

Nairn

Clifton House Though it's not unusual to find hotels with a theatrical touch, this hotel *is* a theatre, staging concerts and recitals in the dining room during winter. The Victorian house is richly furnished, the bedrooms with a mix of antiques and painted pieces. Dinner, bed and breakfast (all included) is the only available package.
Viewfield St, Nairn, Nairnshire IV12 4HW.
Map p77 D2. (01667) 453119. FAX (01667) 452836.
@ macintyre@clifton-hotel.co.uk b,l,d. **Rooms** 7.
Dec, Jan. AE, DC, MC, V. ££££

Portpatrick

Knockinaam Lodge This is a most comfortable place to get away from the hurly burly, or perhaps take a break en route to the Stranraer ferry. Set in a remote wooded glen, its lawned garden runs down to a sandy cove. Peace reigns, both in the smart public rooms and the large, dignified bedrooms. Michelin-starred cuisine.
Portpatrick, Wigtownshire, Dumfries and Galloway DG9 9AD. **Map** p76 C5. (01776) 810471.
FAX (01776) 810435. b,l,d. **Rooms** 10.
Never. AE, DC, MC, V. ££

Pitlochry

Knockendarroch House A château-style house run by gracious and welcoming hosts. Set on a plateau above the town, the views are spectacular.
Higher Oakfield, Pitlochry, Perthshire PH16 5HT.
Map p77 D3. (01796) 473473. FAX (01796) 474068.
@ info@knockendarroch.co.uk b,d. **Rooms** 12. £££

Portree, Isle of Skye

Viewfield House Distinctive guesthouse, home of the Macdonalds, run on house-party lines and full of colonial memorabilia.
Portree, Isle of Skye IV51 9EU. **Map** p76 B2.
(01478) 612217. FAX (01478) 613517.
@ info@viewfieldhouse.com b,d. **Rooms** 12. ££

Skirling

Skirling House A fascinating Arts and Crafts house surrounded by lovely gardens. Superb dinner-party-style food; sympathetic hosts.
Skirling, Biggar, Lanarkshire ML12 6HD. **Map** p77 D4.
(01899) 860274. FAX (01899) 860255.
@ enquiry@skirlinghouse.com b,d. **Rooms** 5. ££

Sleat, Isle of Skye

Kinloch Lodge Home of Lord and Lady Macdonald; guests stay either in the Lodge or the New House, which is every bit as gracious.
Sleat, Isle of Skye IV43 8QY. **Map** p76 B2.
(01471) 833214. FAX (01471) 833277.
@ kinloch@dial.pipex.com b,d. **Rooms** 14. £££

SCARISTA, ISLE OF HARRIS

Scarista House The manse stands alone on a windswept slope overlooking the Atlantic. The decoration is quite formal, but the atmosphere is relaxed and conversation replaces television. Two of the bedrooms are in a separate single-storey building. A great attraction, as well as the solitude, is the mostly organic food.
Scarista, Isle of Harris, Western Isles HS3 3HX. **Map** p76 B1. (01859) 550238. FAX (01859) 550277. @ timandpatricia@scaristahouse.com b,d. **Rooms** 5. Never. MC, V. £££

TARBERT

Skipness Castle The 'castle' is a fine 13th-century Scottish Norman keep adjoining the beautifully furnished home of Libby and Nick James, which rose, phoenix-like, from the ashes of the original Victorian mansion, severely damaged by fire in 1969. Magical views across Kilbrannan Sound. Excellent seafood in the James's Seafood Cabin.
Skipness by Tarbert, Argyll. **Map** p76 C4. (01880) 760207. FAX (01880) 760208. @ james@skipness.freeserve.co.uk b,d. **Rooms** 2. Nov to Apr. Not accepted. ££

STRACHUR

Creggans Inn On the opposite side of Loch Fyne from the whisky town of Inverary, this historic country hotel is distinguished by its award-winning food and stylishly refurbished rooms, as well as its enthusiast's wine list and exceptional range of whiskies. Breathtaking scenery, a warm welcome and charming decor.
Strachur, Argyll PA27 8BX. **Map** p76 C3. (01369) 860279. FAX (01369) 860637. @ info@creggans-inn.co.uk b,l,d. **Rooms** 14. Christmas Day. MC, V. £££

WALLS, SHETLAND ISLANDS

Burrastow House A long, single-track road through Burrastow's spacious grounds ends at a remote spot by a rocky shore. In this isolated setting, the calm, solid stone house exudes a genuinely friendly and welcoming ambience. After a day in the open, everyone appreciates Bo Simmons's comforting food.
Walls, Shetland ZE2 9PD. **Map** p77 F1. (01595) 809307. FAX (01595) 809213. @ burr.hs@zetnet.co.uk d. **Rooms** 5. 23 Dec to mid-Mar, 1 week Oct. AE, MC, V. ££

SPEAN BRIDGE

Corriegour Lodge Anglers, walkers, climbers, pony trekkers and sailors will love this former hunting lodge with spectacular views over the Loch.
Loch Lochy, by Spean Bridge, Inverness-shire PH34 4EB. **Map** p76 C2. (01397) 712685. FAX (01397) 712696. @ info@corriegour-lodge-hotel.com b,l,d. **Rooms** 9. ££

STRONTIAN

Kilcamb Lodge Pleasant country house hotel on the shores of Loch Sunart. A welcoming bar and updated dining area sets the tone.
Strontian, Argyll PH36 4HY. **Map** p76 B3. (01967) 402257. FAX (01967) 402041. @ kilcamblodge@aol.com b,l,d. **Rooms** 11. ££

UIG, ISLE OF LEWIS

Baile-na-Cille The relaxed, beautifully set 18th-century manse makes a special guesthouse.
Timsgarry, Uig, Isle of Lewis, Outer Hebrides HS2 9JD. **Map** p76 B2. (01851) 672242. FAX (01851) 672241. @ RandJGollin@compuserve.com b,l,d. **Rooms** 11. ££

ULLAPOOL

Ceilidh Place Happy centre of music, song, theatre, food, and more. Beds and bunks.
West Argyle St, Ullapool, Ross-shire IV26 2TY. **Map** p76 C1. (01854) 612103. FAX (01854) 612886. @ reservations@ceilidh.demon.co.uk. b,l,d. **Rooms** 13. £££

Wales

Border Country • North Wales South Wales

Although Wales now has its first cutting edge five-star hotel, on Cardiff's waterfront, this is a land best suited to the traditional country house establishment: warm, welcoming and above all, restful. Many places take advantage of the superb landscape of Wales, with views across tidal estuaries or of distant mountains. Some of the hotels we list – including a smattering of fine historic mansions – are in rolling border country. Others are along the beautiful coastline; others by the peaks of Snowdonia. Accommodation in Wales ranges from private ancestral homes, with a mere handful of rooms set aside for guests, to sophisticated retreats. Hearty Welsh breakfasts and good local cooking (with Welsh cheese a speciality) are often a feature.

Abersoch

Porth Tocyn For 50 years, the Fletcher-Brewer family have run this excellent family-orientated hotel with magnificent views across Cardigan Bay and Snowdonia. The plain building was fashioned from a group of lead-miners' cottages. Inside is a series of homely sitting rooms, and simple bedrooms, some interconnecting.
Abersoch, Gwynedd LL53 7BU. **Map** p74 B2. (01758) 713303. FAX (01758) 713538. porthtocyn.hotel@virgin.net b,l,d. **Rooms** 17. mid-Nov to mid-Mar. MC, V. £££

Cardiff

St David's Spa This swish waterfront establishment, which features a hydrotherapy centre and spa, is a five-star oasis, particularly for businessmen. The imposing structure is topped by an extraordinary flying tail fin; the interior is suitably nautical, cool and curvacious. Every room has a private bay-view deck.
Havannah St, Cardiff CF10 5SD. **Map** p74 C4. (029) 2045 4045. FAX (029) 2031 3075. reservations@thestdavidshotel.com b,l,d. **Rooms** 136. Never. AE, DC, MC, V. ££££

Brechfa

Ty Mawr Smart farmhouse hotel. Bedrooms overlook garden. Under new management.
Brechfa, Carmarthen, Carmarthenshire SA32 7RA. **Map** p74 B3. (01267) 202332/202330. FAX (01267) 202437. tymawr@tymawrcountryhotel.co.uk b,l,d. **Rooms** 5. ££

Capel Garmon

Tan-y-Foel Beautiful and original country house in the heart of Snowdonia. Award-winning food.
Capel Garmon, nr Betws-y-Coed, Llanrwst, Conwy LL26 0RE. **Map** p74 B2. (01690) 710507. FAX (01690) 710681. enquiries@tyfhotel.co.uk b,d. **Rooms** 6. ££

Crickhowell

Bear Hotel Bustling traditional inn situated in the centre of town. Well-run, with good food, comfortable bedrooms and warm atmosphere.
High Street, Crickhowell, Powys NP8 1BW. **Map** p 74 C3. (01873) 810408. FAX (01873) 811696. bearhotel@aol.com b,l,d. **Rooms** 34. ££

Fishguard

Three Main Street Excellent, easy-going restaurant which serves light lunches and teas during the day. Three good bedrooms.
3 Main Street, Fishguard, Pembrokeshire SA65 9HG. **Map** p74 A3. (01348) 874275. FAX (01348) 874017. b,d. **Rooms** 3. ££

Eglwysfach

Ynyshir Hall The house stands in glorious gardens next to the Ynyshir Bird Reserve and Dovey estuary. Its boldly coloured interior is the creation of owner Rob Reen, as are the striking paintings. The zesty Michelin-starred cooking is similarly adventurous. Bedrooms are named and furnished after famous artists.
Eglwysfach, Machynlleth, Powys SY20 8TA. **Map** p74 B3. (01654) 781209. FAX (01654) 781366 info@ynshir-hall.co.uk b,l,d. **Rooms** 9. January. AE, DC, MC, V. ££££

Llandrillo

Tyddyn Llan The warm and welcoming ambience is the mark of a country house hotel which gets it just right. Spacious sitting rooms furnished with style; and elegant dining room where imaginative dishes are served. The well-equipped bedrooms are enhanced by original pieces of furniture. Under new management.
Llandrillo, Corwen, Denbighshire LL21 0ST. **Map** p74 C2. (01490) 440264. FAX (01490) 440414. tyddynllan@compuserve.com b,l,d. **Rooms** 12. 2 weeks Jan. DC, MC, V. ££££

Garthmyl

Garthmyl Hall Designers Tim and Nancy Morrow have brought youthful, affordable flair to this handsome red-brick Georgian house. The velvety drawing room retains its ornate ceiling; there is a cosy library, and the bedrooms are cool, contemporary and perfectly judged. The food is simple but good, the ambience informal.
Garthmyl, Montgomery, Powys SY15 6RS. **Map** p74 C3. (01686) 640550. FAX (01686) 640609. b,d. **Rooms** 9. Never. AE, MC, V. ££

Llandudno

Bodysgallen Hall At the core of this 17th-century Grade I listed house is a 13th-century tower, which should be climbed for the view. There are impressive formal gardens, including a walled rose garden and a knot garden. Inside, the atmosphere is one of traditional and rather formal elegance, with corresponding – pricey – cuisine.
Llandudno, Conwy LL30 1RS. **Map** p74 B2. (01492) 584466. FAX (01492) 582519. info@ bodysgallen.com b,l,d. **Rooms** 35. Never. MC, V. £££

Fishguard

Tregynon Cosy self-catering retreat with 16th-century farmhouse restaurant.
Gwaun Valley, Fishguard, Pembrokeshire SA65 9TU. **Map** p74 A3. (01239) 820531. FAX (01239) 820808. tregynon@online-holidays.net b,d. **Rooms** 3 cottages. ££

Ganllwyd

Plas Dolmelynllyn Excellent, easy-going restaurant which serves light lunches and teas during the day. Three good bedrooms.
Ganllwyd, Dolgellau, Gwynedd LL40 2HP. **Map** p74 B2. (01341) 440273. FAX (01341) 440640. info@dolly-hotel.co.uk b,d. **Rooms** 10. ££

Harlech

Castle Cottage The plain exterior belies the traditional beamed interior of this friendly little hotel in the shadow of Harlech's mighty castle.
Yllech, Harlech, Gwynedd LL46 2YL. **Map** p74 B2. (01766) 780479. FAX (01766) 781251. glyn@castlecottageharlech.co.uk b,d. **Rooms** 9. £

Llanbrynmair

Barlings Barn One large self-catering barn and health complex. Homemade supper dishes available; fabulous enclosed swimming pool.
Llanbrynmair, Powys SY19 7DY **Map** p74 C2. (01650) 521479. barlbarn@zetnet.co.uk d. **Rooms** 7. £

For key to symbols see backflap. For price categories *see p71*

LLANDUDNO

St Tudno With 31 years at the helm, the Blands are meticulous in attending to every detail of this Victorian seafront hotel. Period charm is balanced with modern facilities, plus a long list of thoughtful extras which add to the sense of comfort. The food is right on target in the inviting dining room; the staff are young and attentive.
Promenade, Llandudno, Conwy LL30 2LP. **Map** p74 B2. (01492) 874411. FAX (01492) 860407. sttudnohotel@btinternet.com b,l,d. **Rooms** 19. Never. AE, DC, MC, V. ££

NANTGWYNANT

Pen-y-Gwryd This charming old coach inn, set high in the heart of Snowdonia, is where Edmund Hillary and his team set up their training base before their attempt on Everest in 1953 – and it's still run by the same family. Simple, warm and welcoming, with good, plain home cooking. Soak your muscles in the natural pool in the garden after a hard day on the hill, or relax in the sauna.
Nant Gwynant, Gwynedd LL55 4NT. **Map** p74 B2. (01286) 870211. b,l,d. **Rooms** 15. Nov to Dec. Not accepted. £

LLANSANFFRAID GLAN CONWY

Old Rectory This pretty Georgian rectory has two memorable assets: the glorious sweeping view across the Conwy estuary and the delicious cooking of Wendy Vaughan, supported by her husband's intelligent wine list. Relax in the elegant wood-panelled sitting room. Old-fashioned bedrooms with grandiose beds.
Llansanffraid Glan Conwy, Colwyn Bay, Conwy LL28 5LF. **Map** p74 C2. (01492) 580611. FAX (01492) 584555. info@oldrectorycountryhouse.co.uk b,d. **Rooms** 6. Dec, Jan. MC, V. £££

PENALLY

Penally Abbey Smart yet informal hotel in a Gothic-style country house next to a ruined medieval chapel. Commanding views of the Pembrokeshire coast. There's a comfortable, well-furnished drawing room, a tall, candlelit dining room and a welcoming bar. Some bedrooms are grand; all are freshly decorated.
Penally, Tenby, Pembrokeshire SA70 7PY. **Map** p74 B4. (01834) 843033. FAX (01834) 844714 penally.abbey@btinternet.com b,d. **Rooms** 12. Never. AE,MC, V. £££

LLANDDEINIOLEN

Ty'n Rhos A quiet, traditional, well-run country hotel. New conference centre.
Seion, Llanddeiniolen, Caernarfon, Gwynedd LL55 3AE. **Map** p74 B2. (01248) 670489. FAX (01248) 670079. enquiries@ty'nrhos.co.uk b,d. **Rooms** 11. ££

LLANGAMMARCH WELLS

Lake A grand country house hotel, with polished service and plenty of activities.
Llangammarch Wells, Powys LD4 4BS. **Map** p74 C3. (01591) 620202. FAX (01591) 620457. info@lakecountryhouse.co.uk b,l,d. **Rooms** 19. £££

LLANTHONY

Abbey Hotel A chance to sleep in a unique piece of history at these ancient Prior's quarters. Sixty spiral steps lead to the highest bedroom.
Llanthony, Abergavenny, Gwent NP7 7NN. **Map** p74 C3. (01873) 890487. FAX (01873) 890844. b,l,d. **Rooms** 5. £

LLYSWEN

Llangoed Hall Luxury hotel in Clough Williams-Ellis mansion created by Laura Ashley's husband.
Llyswen, Brecon, Powys LD3 0YP. **Map** p74 C3. (01874) 754525. FAX (01874) 754545. b,l,d. llangoed_hall_co_wales_uk@compuserve.com. **Rooms** 23. £££

Penmaenpool

Penmaenuchaf Hall A sturdy grey stone Victorian manor set in 21 acres of grounds on the south bank of the Mawddach estuary, with wonderful views across Snowdonia. Rose and water gardens add yet more charm. The interior continues to be imposing yet welcoming and standards are exceptionally high.
Penmaenpool, Dolgellau, Gwynedd LL40 1YB. **Map** p74 B2. (01341) 422129. FAX (01341) 422787. @ relax@penhall.co.uk b,l,d. **Rooms** 14. Never. DC, MC, V. £££

Reynoldston

Fairyhill A quiet and civilized retreat in the heart of the Gower Peninsula. Set in vast grounds – much of them still semi-wild – it features a walled garden, orchard, trout stream and lake. A series of spacious public rooms lead to the dining room, where fine food might include Penclawdd cockles, Welsh lamb and laverbread.
Reynoldston, Swansea SA3 1BS. **Map** p74 B4. (01792) 390139. FAX (01792) 391358. @ postbox@fairyhill.net b,l,d. **Rooms** 8. 1 to 16 Jan. AE, MC, V. £££

Portmeirion

Portmeirion 'Magical' is the most apposite word to describe the hotel at the centre of Clough Williams-Ellis's enchanting fantasy village. The heady ensemble mixes Wales (bilingual staff and menus, harpist), Capri (Italianate gardens, statues, columns) and Rajasthan (Indian fabrics, paintings, objects). Improving reports of the food.
Portmeirion, Gwynedd LL48 6ET. **Map** p74 B2. (01766) 770000. FAX (01766) 771331. @ hotel@portmeirion-village.com b,l,d. **Rooms** 51. Never. AE, DC, MC, V. ££££

St Brides Wentlooge

West Usk Lighthouse A B&B to visit for novelty value, and for very good breakfasts. You will have spent the night in a wedge-shaped portion of an unusual 1821 lighthouse. You may also have slept in a waterbed, showered in a red telephone box, had an aromatherapy massage and soaked away your cares in a flotation tank.
St Brides Wentlooge, Newport NP1 9SF. **Map** p74 C4. (01633) 810126. @ lighthouse1@tesco.net b. **Rooms** 4. Never. AE, DC, MC, V. ££

Nercwys

Tower B&B in historic castellated border house, the ancestral home of the owners. Baronial rooms, and a dining room hook from which the Mayor of Chester was hung in 1465.
Mold, Flintshire CH7 4EW. **Map** p74 C2. FAX (01352) 700220. b. **Rooms** 3. ££

Ruthin

Eyarth Station A former railway station transformed into a cheerful B&B. Fine views across the valley, and outdoor pool.
Llanfair D C, Ruthin, Denbighshire LL15 2EE. **Map** p74 C2. (01824) 703643. FAX (01824) 707464 @ stay@eyarthstation.com b. **Rooms** 6. £

Talsarnau

Maes-y-Neuadd 600-year-old granite manor house with panelled walls, comfortable public rooms and luxurious bedrooms.
Talsarnau, Gwynedd LL47 6YA. **Map** p74 B2. (01766) 780200. FAX (01766) 780211. @ maes@neuadd.com b,l,d. **Rooms** 16. £££

Three Cocks

Three Cocks Characterful inn with a palpable Belgian influence supplied by its Belgian-born owner and her chef husband.
Three Cocks, Brecon, Powys LD3 0SL. **Map** p74 C3. (01497) 847215. FAX (01497) 847339. b,l,d. **Rooms** 7. ££

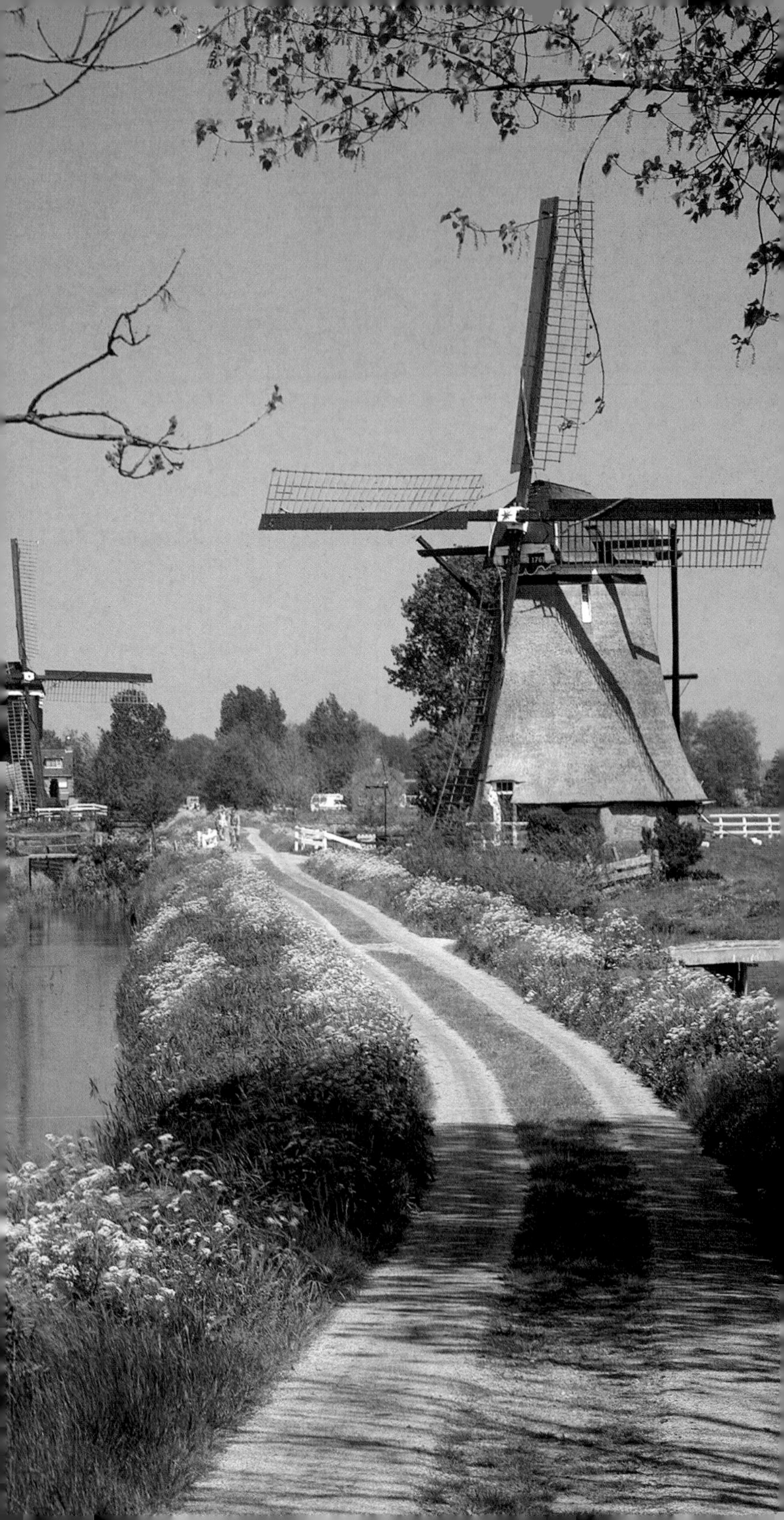

The Netherlands

THE NETHERLANDS

DUTCH HOTELS offer some interesting contrasts. In Amsterdam you'll find rows of canalhouses knocked through to make one hotel. Decorated with great panache, these places mix antiques with contemporary urban style. Away from the big cities, you'll find smart rusticity: old box beds, or flagged floors and candlelight, and great cooking. The level of hospitality is high, with some hotels prepared to set up the Jacuzzi or light a log fire for your arrival. If your taste is for gritty realism, head instead for the bustling port of Rotterdam, where the 'left bank' has been revitalized with bars and cafés, presided over by the Hotel New York (page 131), a stylish hotel in a landmark port building.

The graceful Château St Gerlach, at Valkenburg, page 131

THE NETHERLANDS, REGION BY REGION

THE NETHERLANDS is not a big country, but it divides conveniently into west, north, east and south.

The West

This region includes the cities of Amsterdam, The Hague, Utrecht and Rotterdam – known as *De Randstad* or 'rim towns'. Each offers distinctive townhouse hotels. Amsterdam's attractions include its canals and three big museums (namely the Rijksmuseum, the Van Gogh and the Stedelijk). The palace city of The Hague is the seat of government.

Smaller cities with equally attractive places to stay include Maastricht, home to a flamboyant carnival in February and a gourmet food festival in August; and Delft, known as the Prinsenstad (city of princes). Three other attractive towns worth a visit include Utrecht, with its pretty canals, alleyways, and specialist shops in the streets around the old centre; Leiden, an historic university town; and Gouda, famous for its cheese.

The North

Friesland is an intriguing area of farms, lakes and black-and-white cows, with its own language and cultural identity. There's a grand hotel in Leeuwarden, a town of small canals and shopping streets. In the otherwise rural province of Groningen you can stay in an old guardhouse on the former toll bridge in the university city capital (also called Groningen).

The East

The provinces of Flevoland, Gelderland and Overijssel were created from reclaimed land. This is the site of the Hoge Veluwe National Park, the principal national park of the Netherlands and one in which you can stay, in a 'cottage' hotel at Otterlo (page 129). In this area of canals and fertile farmland, there are many other relaxing country hotels offering excellent food.

The South

The region encompasses Limburg, Noord-Brabant and Zeeland, the delta province. This is a pleasure-loving area and the food here is said to be the best in the Netherlands. Limburg's Geul Valley is really special, overlooked by a beautiful hotel at Valkenburg (see above).

HIGHLIGHTS

HOTELS ILLUSTRATED on these introductory pages are only a few of our favourites. Others include the Jachtslot de Mookerheide castle hotel in Molenhoek, with its Art Nouveau interior (page 129);

and the half-timbered Winselerhof, a 17th-century farmhouse serving good food at Landgraaf (page 128).

FOOD AND DRINK

CLASSIC DUTCH cooking is generally brasserie-style food in generous portions, with especially good grilled meat and fish. There are plentiful fresh supplies of mussels (*mosselen*), eel (*paling*), served smoked, and herring (*haring*). Traditional standbys include a pea soup thick enough to stand your spoon up in (*erwtensoep*) and mashed vegetable dishes (*stamppotten*), many of them incorporating lard.

Perhaps more enticing are the pancakes, sweet mini pancakes (*poffertjes*) and hard waffles (*stroopwafel*) of traditional Dutch cooking.

International cuisine is the order of the day in city restaurants, and many hotels offer a Dutch-French hybrid. Vegetarians won't do too badly, especially if they don't mind fish. Holland's colonial past means there's a wide choice of Indonesian and Chinese restaurants, where the *rijsttafel* ('rice table') is a feast of many dishes.

Amsterdam is home to the atmospheric *bruine kroeg* ('brown cafés'), warm bolt-holes (named due to colour of decoration) that are sometimes literary cafés, and sometimes simply a venue for enjoying a cup of coffee, a glass of wine or a beer. There are also modernist white cafés which tend to be more popular with a younger crowd. You'll also find the occasional *proeflokalen* (tasting house) bar which traditionally used to serve only spirits such as the national drink *jenever* (gin) made from juniper berries.

Lunch is often just a snack or a cold collation known as *koffietafel* which can be had from 11am to 2:30 or 3pm.

Many restaurants do not open for lunch, but open for dinner from about 5:30pm; most shut at about 10pm in the provinces, 11pm or later in cities. The traditional day of closure for restaurants is Monday, and sometimes Tuesday as well. Restaurants with rooms may be shut on one or both of these days, too.

BEDROOMS AND BATHROOMS

ROOMS IN canalhouse hotels are often at the top of narrow rickety wooden stairs and it's the exception rather than the rule for these small hotels to have lifts – so while there will be someone to help you with your bags when you arrive, they might not suit those who have restricted mobility. Rooms in these historic hotels are often small, or narrow, but of course what they lack in space they make up for in character.

OTHER PRACTICAL INFORMATION

BREAKFAST IS usually an extensive buffet of different kinds of bread, cheese, cold meats, hard-boiled eggs, yoghurt, muesli and stewed fruit.

Language English is widely spoken and understood, so too is German and, in some places, French.

Currency From 1 January 2002, the European *euro* (written 'EUR'), made up of 100 *cents*.

Shops Generally open 8:30 or 9am–5:30 or 6pm Mon–Sat; many close on Monday mornings, and from 4 or 5pm on Saturdays. Late-night shopping is on Thursday and Friday evenings. In Amsterdam many shops stay open until 10pm. Banks are open 9am–4 or 5pm Mon–Fri; in some places they are open until 9pm on Thursday evenings and open on Saturday mornings.

Tipping Generally, you'll find a 15 per cent service charge added to restaurant bills. Otherwise, it's normal practice to round up the total, the tip being left in cash, not added to the total on the cheque or card.

Telephoning Public call boxes take mainly phonecards and credit cards, though a few still take coins. Post offices have booths where you can pay the amount due after your call. Inside the country, dial the full area code. To call the Netherlands from the UK or US, dial 00 31, then the number, omitting the initial zero; from the US, 011 31.

Public holidays 1 January; Good Friday and Easter Sunday and Monday; 30 April (Queen's Day); 5 May (Liberation Day); Ascension Day; Whit Sunday (Pentecost) and Monday; 15 August; 25 and 26 December.

USEFUL WORDS

Breakfast	*Ontbijt*
Lunch	*Lunch*
Dinner	*Diner*
Free room?	*Kamer vrij?*
How much?	*Wat kost?*
Single	*Een eenpersoons kamer*
Double	*Een tweepersoons kamer*

NETHERLANDS PRICE BANDS

OUR PRICE bands refer to the price of a standard room in high season, and usually include breakfast. Most prices quoted include all taxes, but you may encounter local taxes in some places.

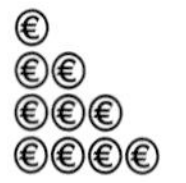

€	up to 90 EUR
€€	90–225 EUR
€€€	225–455 EUR
€€€€	over 455 EUR

The Canal House, Amsterdam, page 126

The Netherlands
NORTH SEA
KEY
★100 Hotel location and page reference
International airport
Motorway
Major road
0 kilometres 20
0 miles 20
A
B
C
1
2
3
4
5
Vlieland
De Koog
Marsdiep
Den Helder
Julianadorp
Schagen
Warmenhuizen
Schoorl
★131
Heerhugowaard
Alkmaar
Heiloo
Oosthuizen
Purmerend
★130
Heemskerk
Beverwijk
Zaanstad
Haarlem
AMSTE
Ouderkerk aan de Amstel
★130
Hillegom
Katwijk aan Zee
DEN HAAG (The Hague)
★128
Leiden
Alphen aan den Rijn
Leidschendam
Voorburg
Rijswijk
Zoetermeer
Woerden
Gouda
's-Gravenzande
Hoek van Holland
Delft
★126
Capelle aan den IJssel
Maassluis
Schiedam
Vlaardingen
ROTTERDAM
★131
Lek
Ridderkerk
A15
Hellevoetsluis
Spijkenisse
Zwijndrecht
Dordrecht
Haringvliet
A29
NETHER
Grevelingen
Hollands Diep
Zierikzee
A58
Oosterhout
Serooskerke
Veere
★130
Oosterschelde
Bergen op Zoom
A17
Roosendaal
Breda
Middelburg
Goes
A58
Vlissingen
Oost-Souburg
Kapelle
Zundert
Kruiningen-Yerseke
★128
A58
Essen
Westerschelde
Wuustwezel
Zeebrugge
Terneuzen
Stabroek
Oostburg
Merksem
Oostende
Brugge (Bruges)
Hulst
ANTWERPEN (Antwerp)
A21
Turnho
Middelkerke
Maldegem
Zelzate
Sint-Niklaas
Wilrijk
A13
Herent
BELGIUM
Torhout
A10
Aalter
A14
Gent
Lokeren
Willebroek
Tielt
Lebbeke
Merelbeke
Roeselare
Aalst
Zemst
Aarsch
Asse
Ieper
Lille
Leuven
Oudenaarde
Menen
Dilbeek
BRUSSEL (Brussels)
A
B
C

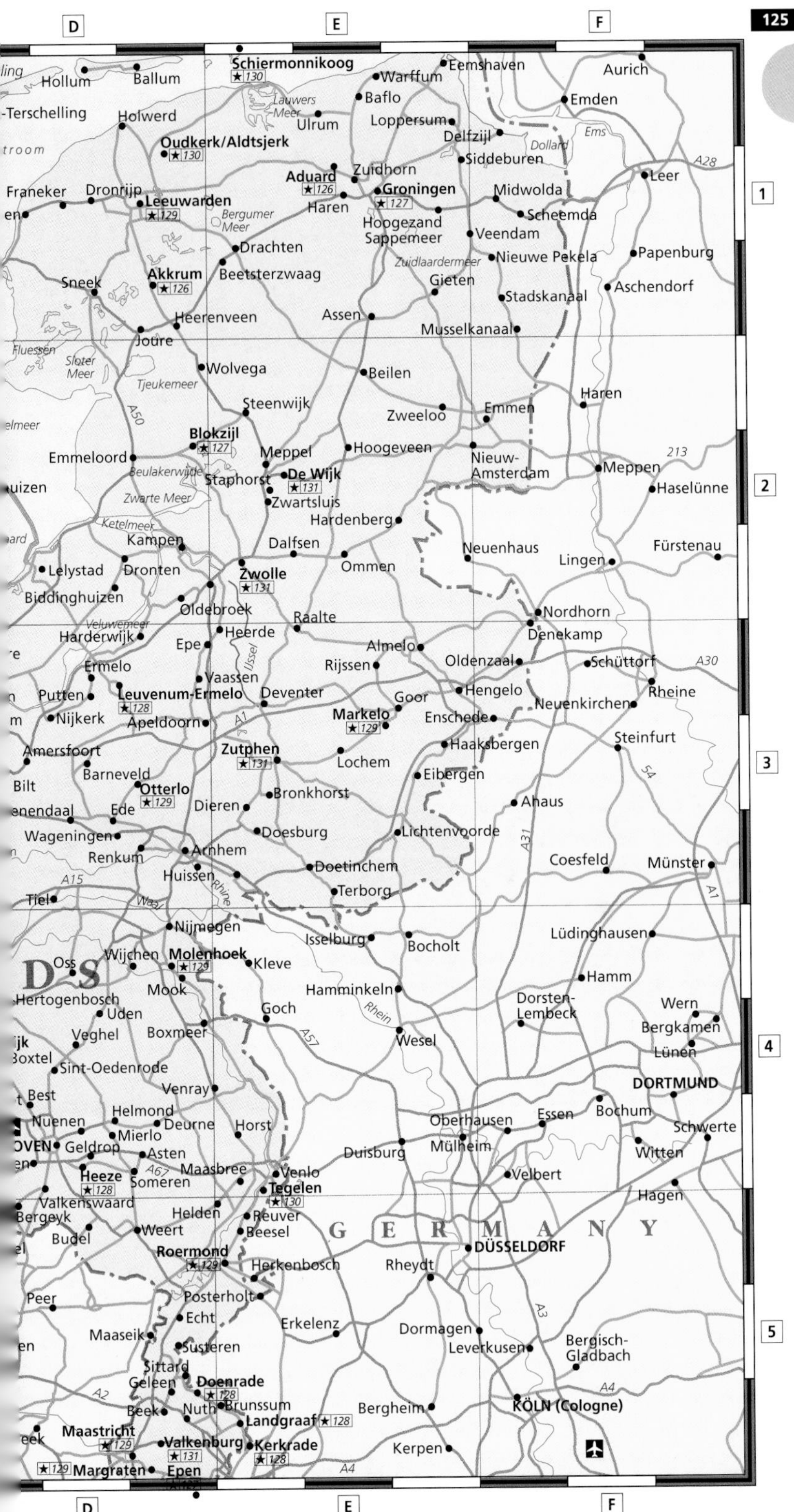
D
E
F
Schiermonnikoog
Eemshaven
Aurich
Hollum
Ballum
Warffum
Baflo
Emden
Terschelling
Holwerd
Lauwers Meer
Ulrum
Loppersum
Delfzijl
Ems
Dollard
Oudkerk/Aldtsjerk
Siddeburen
Leer
Aduard
Zuidhorn
A28
Franeker
Dronrijp
Leeuwarden
Groningen
Midwolda
Haren
Scheemda
Bergumer Meer
Hoogezand Sappemeer
Veendam
Drachten
Papenburg
Nieuwe Pekela
Zuidlaardermeer
Akkrum
Beetsterzwaag
Sneek
Gieten
Aschendorf
Stadskanaal
Heerenveen
Assen
Musselkanaal
Joure
Fluessen
Sloter Meer
Wolvega
Beilen
Tjeukemeer
Haren
A50
Steenwijk
Zweeloo
Emmen
Blokzijl
213
Emmeloord
Meppel
Hoogeveen
Nieuw-Amsterdam
Meppen
Beulakerwijde
Staphorst
De Wijk
Haselünne
Zwarte Meer
Zwartsluis
Hardenberg
Ketelmeer
Kampen
Dalfsen
Neuenhaus
Fürstenau
Lingen
Lelystad
Dronten
Ommen
Zwolle
Biddinghuizen
Oldebroek
Nordhorn
Veluwemeer
Raalte
Denekamp
Harderwijk
Heerde
Epe
Almelo
IJssel
Ermelo
Rijssen
Oldenzaal
Schüttorf
A30
Vaassen
Putten
Leuvenum-Ermelo
Deventer
Hengelo
Rheine
Goor
Neuenkirchen
Nijkerk
Markelo
Enschede
Apeldoorn
A1
Steinfurt
Amersfoort
Zutphen
Haaksbergen
Lochem
Barneveld
54
Eibergen
Bilt
Otterlo
Bronkhorst
Ahaus
Ede
Dieren
Wageningen
Doesburg
Lichtenvoorde
A31
Renkum
Arnhem
Coesfeld
Münster
Huissen
Doetinchem
A15
Rhine
Terborg
Tiel
Waal
A1
Nijmegen
Lüdinghausen
Isselburg
Bocholt
Wijchen
Molenhoek
Oss
Kleve
Hamm
Mook
Hamminkeln
's-Hertogenbosch
Dorsten-Lembeck
Wern
Uden
Goch
Rhein
Bergkamen
Veghel
Boxmeer
A57
Wesel
Lünen
Boxtel
Sint-Oedenrode
DORTMUND
Venray
Best
Helmond
Bochum
Nuenen
Oberhausen
Essen
Schwerte
Deurne
Horst
Mierlo
Geldrop
Mülheim
Asten
Duisburg
Witten
A67
Maasbree
Venlo
Heeze
Someren
Velbert
Tegelen
Valkenswaard
Hagen
Bergeyk
Helden
Reuver
Budel
Weert
Beesel
GERMANY
Roermond
DÜSSELDORF
Herkenbosch
Rheydt
Peer
Posterholt
Echt
A3
Erkelenz
Maaseik
Dormagen
Susteren
Leverkusen
Bergisch-Gladbach
Sittard
Geleen
Doenrade
A2
A4
Beek
Nuth
Brunssum
Bergheim
KÖLN (Cologne)
Landgraaf
Maastricht
Valkenburg
Kerkrade
Kerpen
Margraten
Epen
A4
1
2
3
4
5

Aduard

Herberg Onder de Linden In an inn dating back to 1735 is this Michelin-starred restaurant with rooms, serving enticing French and Dutch specialities. The old building is well maintained and free of historic tweeness; rooms are decorated in restful, contemporary style.
Burg. van Barneveldweg 3, 9831 RD Aduard. **Map** p125 E1. (050) 403 1406. FAX (050) 403 1814. herberg@slaanamar.nl b,l,d. **Rooms** 5. Sun, Mon; 1 week July; New Year. AE, DC, MC, V. €

Amsterdam

Blakes Overlooking the prestigious Keizersgracht canal, Blakes is arguably the city's *chic*est hotel. Anouska Hempel has created a stylish retreat in a discreet location. Rooms are decorated in luxury fabrics and individually themed on Dutch history. The restaurant's cuisine is equally distinctive, inspired by 16th-century merchant adventurers.
Keizersgracht 384, 1016 GB Amsterdam. **Map** p124 C3. (20) 530 2010. FAX (20) 530 2030. hotel@blakes.nl b,l,d (restaurant closed Sat lunch, Sun). **Rooms** 41. Never. AE, DC, MC, V. €€€

Amsterdam

Ambassade The atmosphere is quiet, and service solicitous in this hotel occupying a series of elegant canalside houses. Books by many of the writers who have stayed here adorn the Louis XVI lounge. Bedrooms are decorated in French classical or English country style. The hotel has its own massage centre and internet room.
Herengracht 341, 1016 AZ Amsterdam. **Map** p124 C3. (020) 555 0222. FAX (020) 555 0277. info@ ambassade-hotel.nl b. **Rooms** 59. Never. AE, DC, MC, V. €€

Amsterdam

Canal House 17th-century house with narrow winding stairs, beautifully executed period decoration, and an old-fashioned bar where guests meet to chat. Breakfast is served in the salon, where guests are welcome to play the grand piano. Ask for a room facing the canal or the garden.
Keizersgracht 148, 1015 CX Amsterdam. **Map** p124 C3. (020) 622 5182. FAX (020) 624 1317. info@canalhouse.nl b. **Rooms** 26. Never. DC, MC, V. €€

Akkrum

De Oude Schouw A hotel-restaurant in a rural waterfront setting, with pool and a boat for hire. The restaurant specializes in game.
Oude Schouw 6, 8491 MP Akkrum. **Map** p125 D1. (0566) 652125. FAX (0566) 652102. postbus@ oudeschouw.nl b,l,d. **Rooms** 15. €€

Amsterdam

Seven Bridges You can count seven bridges from this charming and immaculately decorated hotel. Wooden floors, Persian carpets and antique furniture. Breakfast served in your room.
Reguliersgracht 31, 1017 LK Amsterdam. **Map** p124 C3. (020) 623 1329. b. **Rooms** 8. €€

Bronkhorst

De Gouden Leeuw This 17th-century inn has an extensive seasonal menu, and simple rooms with wooden floors, fresh flowers and box beds.
Bovenstraat 2, 7226 LM Bronkhorst. **Map** p125 E3. (0575) 451231. FAX (0575) 450123. oechies@ worldonline.nl b,l,d. **Rooms** 11. €€

Delft

Museumhotel The name refers to the Delftware specially commissioned for this elegant canalside hotel, and the art displays. Bedrooms are modern.
Oude Delft 189, 2611 HD Delft. **Map** p125 C3. (015) 214 0930. FAX (015) 215 3079. info@museumhotel.nl b. **Rooms** 51. 

Amsterdam

The Grand This well-loved hotel lives up to its name. A former convent, it was turned into a hotel for royal guests in the 16th century, becoming the Town Hall in the early 1900s. The beautiful courtyard is used for outdoor dining from a mainly French menu. Locals pack out the hotel's Café Roux.
Oudezijds Voorburgwal 197, 1012 EX Amsterdam. **Map** p124 C3. (020) 555 3111. FAX (020) 555 3222. hotel@thegrand.nl b,l,d. **Rooms** 182. Never. AE, DC, MC, V. €€€

Amsterdam

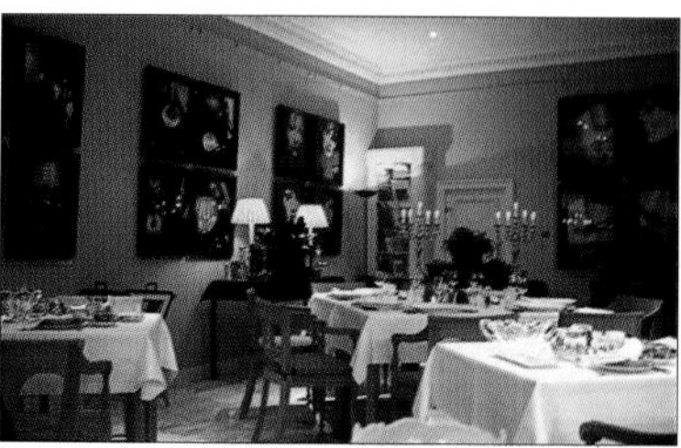

Seven One Seven Men's fashion stylist Kees van der Valk has created a glossy canalhouse hotel in the city centre. There are log fires, candles and art books in the lounge, and the breakfast room leads out to patios. Glasses of wine and afternoon tea are on the house. Each of the individual suites has CD player and VCR.
Prinsengracht 717, 1017 JW Amsterdam. **Map** p124 C3. (020) 427 0717. FAX (020) 423 0717. info@717hotel.nl b. **Rooms** 9. Never. AE, DC, MC, V. €€€

Amsterdam

Pulitzer Sunday opera brunches, a sculpture garden, and a restaurant in a former pharmacy are all part of this unusual city-centre hotel. It consists of 25 neighbouring canalside houses, each with their own character. A walkway linking the houses contains an art gallery. Bedrooms are furnished with classic fabrics and good furniture.
Prinsengracht 315–331, 1016 GZ Amsterdam. **Map** p124 C3. (020) 523 5235. FAX (020) 627 6753. b,l,d. **Rooms** 226. Never. AE, DC, MC, V. €€€

Amsterdam

Toro This patrician townhouse is a short taxi-ride from the city centre but is close to the Rijksmuseum, and its location in a residential area overlooking the Vondelpark ensures tranquillity. The terrace is a relaxing place to enjoy the view of the facing lake, and the birdsong that fills the garden. Inside are stained-glass windows, tasteful antiques and a wonderful Art Nouveau ceiling.
Koningslaan 64, 1075 AG Amsterdam. **Map** p124 C3. (020) 673 7223. FAX (020) 675 0031. toro@ams.nl b. **Rooms** 22. Never. AE, DC, MC, V. €€

Edam

De Fortuna A row of old step-gabled houses now makes a popular restaurant with rooms, decked in pine and patchwork quilts.
Spuistrat 3, 1135 AV Edam. **Map** p124 C2. (0299) 371671. FAX (0299) 371469. fortuna@fortuna-edam.nl b,d. **Rooms** 24. €

Epen

De Smidse Clapboard-clad guesthouse with simple rooms, good home cooking and quite old-fashioned atmosphere. Walkers welcome.
Molenweg 9, 6285 NJ Epen. **Map** p125 D5. (043) 455 1253. FAX (043) 455 2390. info@smidse.nl b,l,d. **Rooms** 10. €

Groningen

Corps de Garde Bedrooms are in military guards' former sleeping quarters in this relaxed hotel, which dates from 1634.
Oude Boteringestraat 74, 9712 GN Groningen. **Map** p125 E1. (050) 314 5437. FAX (050) 313 6320. info@corpsdegarde.nl b. **Rooms** 24. €€

Groningen

Hotel de Ville Oriental carpets and modern art are well mixed in this fine 19th-century building, as are the cocktails in the conservatory.
Oude Boteringestraat 43, 9712 GD Groningen. **Map** p125 E1. (050) 318 1222. FAX (050) 318 1777. hotel@deville.nl b,l (on request),d. **Rooms** 45. €€

Doenrade

Kasteel Doenrade This informal hotel in a turreted castle dating back to 1118 will appeal to collectors: armour and stained-glass windows decorate the former chapel, and a farmer's cart from 1780 graces the walls of the restaurant. Food is rich and well prepared, but you can cycle it off in the surrounding countryside.

Limpensweg 20, 6439 BE Doenrade. **Map** p125 D5. (046) 442 4141. FAX (046) 442 4030. info@kasteeldoenrade.nl b,l,d. **Rooms** 25. Never. AE, DC, MC, V. €€

Kruiningen-Yerseke

Inter Scaldes Exceptional food is produced by Iannis Brevet in this 'manoir restaurant'. Hostess Claudia Brevet maintains the cottage-style garden, a fine backdrop for summer dining. The rooms and suites – some split-level or with Jacuzzi and balcony – feature antiques and fresh colours.

Zandweg 2, 4416 NA Kruiningen-Yerseke. **Map** p124 B4. (0413) 381753. FAX (0413) 381763. info@interscaldes.nl b,l,d (not Mon, Tue). **Rooms** 12. 2 weeks Jan, 1week Oct. AE, DC, MC, V. €€

Den Haag (The Hague)

Golden Tulip Hotel Corona In the 1700s it was a coffee house. Today it's a city-centre hotel whose conservatory brasserie attracts guests and hungry shoppers alike. The foyer is all swirling marble and revolving doors. Veneered furniture reflects the Art Deco feel of the rooms. Suites are more Louis XVI in style.

Buitenhof 39–42, 2513 AH Den Haag. **Map** p124 B3. (070) 363 7930. FAX (070) 361 5785. hotelcorona@planet.nl b,l,d. **Rooms** 36. Never. AE, DC, MC, V. €€

Landgraaf

Winselerhof If you stay at this characterful, half-timbered 17th-century farmhouse, you should expect to eat well. Breakfast is served in the conservatory, and there's a vast vaulted cellar for pre-dinner drinks. The Pirandello restaurant, decorated with *trompe l'oeil* murals of Tuscany, serves imaginative Italian dishes.

Tunnelweg 99, 6372 XH Landgraaf. **Map** p125 E5. (045) 546 4343. FAX (045) 535 2711. info@winslerhof.com b,l,d. **Rooms** 49. Never. AE, MC, DC, V. €€

Den Haag (The Hague)

Carlton Ambassador Choose between Old Dutch (Hindeloopen) or Old English (Tudor) style bedrooms. Restaurant and bar-bistro.

Sophialaan 2, 2514 JP Den Haag. **Map** p124 B3. (070) 363 0363. FAX (070) 360 0535. info@ambassador.carlton.nl b,l,d. **Rooms** 78. €€€

Heeze

Van Gaalen Welcoming restaurant-with-rooms run by chef and Harley-Davidson rider Jules van Gaalen and his wife Josephine.

Kapelstraat 48, 5591 HE Heeze. **Map** p125 D4. (040) 226 3515. FAX (040) 226 3876. info@hostellerie.nl b,l,d. **Rooms** 14. €

Kerkrade

Brughof Stately 18th-century castle hotel with rooms in the farmhouse opposite. Romantics will enjoy the restaurant's candle-lit entrance.

Oud Erensteinerweg 6, 6468 PC Kerkrade. **Map** p125 E5. (045) 546 1333. FAX (045) 546 0748. info@erenstein.com b,l,d. **Rooms** 44. €€

Leuvenum-Ermelo

Het Rooder Koper An English-style Edwardian villa transplanted to the Gelderland countryside. Some bedrooms are in outbuildings.

Sandbergweg 82, 3852 PV Leuvenum-Ermelo. **Map** p125 D3. (0577) 407393. FAX (0577) 407561. info@rooderkoper.nl b,l,d. **Rooms** 35. €€

Leeuwarden

Het Stadhouderlijk Hof The services akin to a much larger hotel are on offer at this former royal palace in the old city: covers are turned down at night; newspapers are available in the morning. The atmosphere is relaxed, however, with a choice of à la carte dining in the courtyard garden or a splendid buffet in the 'Royal Living'.
Hofplein 29, 8911 HJ Leeuwarden. **Map** p125 D1.
(058) 216 2180. FAX (058) 216 3890.
@ info@stadhouderlijkhof.nl b,l,d. **Rooms** 21.
Never. AE, MC, V. €€

Margraten

Groot Welsden Set in tranquil countryside, Groot Welsden is done out in the style of an English country house. Many people stay on half-board basis, but the hotel is also wonderful for a shorter stay and for trips into the Ardennes. The deluxe rooms have their own whirlpool baths. Cosy restaurant, beautiful garden and friendly service.
Groot Welsden 27, 6269 Margraten. **Map** p125 D5.
(043) 458 1394. FAX (043) 458 2355.
@ info@hotelgrootwelsden.nl b,l,d.
Rooms 14. Carnival week. AE, MC, V. €€

Maastricht

Hotel Botticelli A passion for Renaissance art, bold colours and contemporary furniture sets the style for this townhouse hotel. Hosts Louis Hendriks and Pierre Janssens treat guests as if they were personal friends. The back bedrooms and the courtyard are very quiet, despite being a few steps from Vrijthof Square. Lavish breakfasts.
Papenstraat 11, 6211 LG Maastricht. **Map** p125 D5.
(043) 352 6300. FAX (043) 352 6336.
@ reception@botticellihotel.nl b. **Rooms** 18.
Christmas, New Year. AE, DC, MC, V. €€

Molenhoek

Jachtslot de Mookerheide The tall tower of this castle hotel – once a hunting lodge for the Baron of Luden – gives wide views of the wooded estate. Hennie and Anne van Hout have created dramatic bedrooms in the original Art Nouveau interior, and in the coach house. Game features on the menu of both restaurants.
Heumensebaan 2, 6584 CL Molenhoek.
Map p125 D4. (024) 358 3035. FAX (024) 358 4355.
@ info@mookerheide.nl b,l,d. **Rooms** 23.
Never. AE, DC, MC, V. €€-€€€

Maastricht

Hotel d'Orangerie Friendly city-centre hotel with mosaic floors and ornate friezes, owned and run by Jolanda Lutgens. Comfortable and relaxed.
Kleine Gracht 4, 6211 CB Maastricht. **Map** p125 D5.
(043) 326 1111. FAX (043) 326 1287. @ info@hotel-orangerie.nl b, (l,d, by arrangement). **Rooms** 22. €

Markelo

In de Kop'ren Smorre Rustic farmhouse restaurant with waitresses in regional costume. Small and medium-sized bedrooms next door.
Holterweg 20, 7475 AW Markelo. **Map** p125 E3.
(0547) 361344. FAX (0547) 362201.
@ markelo@koprensmorre.nl b,l,d. **Rooms** 4. €

Otterlo

Carnegie Cottage Hotel with conservatory restaurant in the heart of the De Hoge Veluwe national park. Smallish, colourful bedrooms.
Onderlands 35, 6731 BK Otterlo.
Map p125 D3. (0318) 591220. FAX (0318) 592 093.
@ info@carnegiecottage.nl b,l,d. **Rooms** 13. €

Roermond

Kasteel Hattem Castle hotel. Suites have Jacuzzis; some have waterbeds. Covered dining terrace (heated in cold weather).
Maastrichterweg 25, 6041 NZ Roermond.
Map p125 E5. (0475) 319222. FAX (0475) 319292.
b,l,d. **Rooms** 7. €€

For key to symbols see backflap. For price categories *see p123*

Oisterwijk

De Swaen A village inn which serves imaginative gourmet meals in a formal restaurant or in a younger, more relaxed bistro. Bedrooms are in a mix of styles; the most lavish, a suite, is in a new wing built in 1997. The suite contains a beautiful antique walnut bed, a large Jacuzzi and an open fire lit for guests' arrival.
De Lind 47, 5061 HT Oisterwijk. **Map** p125 D4. (013) 523 3233. FAX (013) 528 5860. @ swaen@swaen.nl b,l,d. **Rooms** 24. 2 weeks July. AE, DC, MC, V. €€

Oudkerk/Aldtsjerk

De Klinze The owner of this stucco-clad country hotel, Gert Snijders, has been known to give spur of the moment rides to guests in his horsedrawn carriage or Rolls-Royce. The house dates from the 17th century but the rooms are modern; Carol Dauvergne's management ensures a relaxed atmosphere. Classic Italian food in the restaurant.
Van Sminiaweg 32–36, 9064 KC Oudkerk/Aldtsjerk. **Map** p125 D1. (058) 256 1050. FAX (058) 256 1060. @ klinze@wxs.nl b,l,d. **Rooms** 27. Never. AE, DC, MC, V. €€

Ouderkerk aan de Amstel

't Jagershuis This well-known restaurant with rooms has a dozen bedrooms and suites, all with a view over the Amstel river. The food is traditional French with a modern Mediterranean touch. Activities revolve around the river: watching yachts, or skating on the Amstel when it freezes, then warming up by the open fire.
Amstelzijde 2–4, 1184 VA Ouderkerk aan de Amstel. **Map** p124 C3. (020) 496 2020. FAX (020) 496 4541. @ receptie@jagershuis.com b,l,d. **Rooms** 11. 31 Dec to 4 Jan. AE, DC, MC, V. €€

Purmerend

Hotel de Boerenkamer In the picturesque fen area of North Holland, the Hotel de Boerenkamer combines four-star luxury with country hospitality. Several spacious farmhouses spread within a 15km radius have been converted into homely hotel suites with wonderful views across the verdant meadows. The helpful staff can arrange fishing and boating trips.
Koemarkt 53–1, 1441DB Purmerend. **Map** p124 C2. (0299) 655726. FAX (0299) 656346. @ hoboeka@knoware.nl b. **Rooms** 22. Never. Not accepted. €

Schiermonnikoog

Van der Werff On a small island with few cars, this is a peaceful hotel with modest but comfortable rooms, friendly bar and pool room.
Reeweg 2, 9166 PX Schiermonnikoog. **Map** p125 E1. (0519) 531203. FAX (0519) 531748. @ hotelvanderwerff@cello.nl b,l,d. **Rooms** 49. €

Tegelen

Château Holtmühle Beautiful pitched-roof castle furnished in English style and guarded by enthusiastic geese. Spa centre and indoor pool.
Kasteellaan 10, 5932 AG Tegelen. **Map** p125 E4. (077) 373 8800. FAX (077) 374 0500. @ holtmuehle@bilderberg.nl b,l,d. **Rooms** 66. €€

Veere

De Campveerse Toren Ancient castle-like inn and hotel on the town fortifications, overlooking the harbour and the Veerse Meer. Bright rooms.
Kade 2, 4351 AA Veere. **Map** p124 B4. (0118) 501291. FAX (0118) 501695. @ info@campveersetoren.nl b,l,d. **Rooms** 14. €

Volendam

Spaander This lively hotel-café-restaurant is packed with paintings and knick-knacks in the Dutch equivalent of High Victorian style.
Haven 15-19, 1131 EP Volendam. **Map** p124 C2. (0299) 363595. FAX (0299) 369615. @ info@spaander.com b,l,d. **Rooms** 80. €

Rotterdam

Hotel New York This landmark hotel occupies a prime position in the rejuvenated port area. The former headquarters of the Holland America shipping line, it retains the feel of a busy port hotel. There are harbour views from most rooms. CD players and videos can be rented. The restaurant specializes in fish dishes; oyster bar.
☒ Koninginnenhoofd 1, 3072 AD Rotterdam. **Map** p124 C3. (010) 439 0539. FAX (010) 484 2701. @ info@hotelnewyork.nl b,l,d. **Rooms** 72. Never. AE, DC, MC, V. €–€€

Valkenburg

Château St Gerlach Accommodation is in a series of beamed outbuildings, decorated in rich fabrics and colours, on the estate of this grand château. Dining is in the formal restaurant with its crystal chandeliers or in the old kitchen, done out like a 19th-century Liège pub. The breakfast room overlooks the herb garden and the Geul valley.
☒ Joseph Corneli Allée 1, 6301 KK Valkenburg a/d Geul. **Map** p125 D5. (043) 608 8888. FAX (043) 604 2883. @ reservations@stgerlach.chateauhotels.nl b,l,d. **Rooms** 97. Never. AE, DC, MC, V. €€

Schoorl

Merlet The informal atmosphere of this family-run hotel is enhanced by the Mediterranean feel of its Michelin-starred restaurant, with red tiled floors and warm colours. In summer, dinner is served on the terrace overlooking the dunes. Bedrooms are stylish, and the swimming pool is a delight.
☒ Duinweg 15, 1871 AC Schoorl. **Map** p124 C2. (072) 509 3644. FAX (072) 509 1406. @ merlet@worldonline.nl b,l,d. **Rooms** 18. 2 weeks early Jan. AE, DC, MC, V. €

De Wijk

De Havixhorst Bedrooms are unusually spacious at this rural chateau hotel and restaurant, and those in the attic have beamed ceilings. The hotel's own kitchen garden supplies many of the ingredients for the elaborate cuisine. To work off the calories, bicycles can be hired for exploring the local lanes and nature reserves.
☒ Schiphorsterweg 34–36, 7966 NV De Schiphorst. **Map** p125 E2. (0522) 441487. FAX (0522) 441489. @ info@dehavixhorst.nl **Rooms** 8. b,l,d. end Dec. AE, DC, MC, V. €€

Vreeland aan de Vecht

De Nederlanden Country-house hotel on the River Vecht, with a terrace overlooking the waterway, busy with yachts.
☒ Duinkerken 3, 3633 EM Vreeland aan de Vecht. **Map** p124 C3. (0294) 232326. FAX (0294) 231407. @ denederlanden@hetnet.nl b,l,d. **Rooms** 7. €€

Zeist

Kasteel 't Kerkebosch Baronial 1904 mansion in the woods with a lively atmosphere, busy restaurant and informal garden.
☒ Arnhemse Bovenweg 31, 3708 AA Zeist. **Map** p125 D3. (030) 691 4734. FAX (030) 691 3114. @ info@bilderberg.nl b,l,d. **Rooms** 30. €€

Zwolle

Bilderberg Grand Hotel Wientjes Friendly, modern city hotel in a quiet district of Zwolle, 60km (38 miles) northeast of Amsterdam.
☒ Stationsweg 7, 8011 CZ Zwolle. **Map** p125 E2. (038) 425 4254. FAX (038) 425 4260. @ wientjes@bilderberg.nl b,l,d. **Rooms** 59. €€

Zutphen

Museumhotel A hotel of murals and sculpture. Bedrooms have designer furniture; suites in the wooden 'attic' are all decorated individually.
☒ 's-Gravenhof 6, 7201 DN Zutphen. **Map** p125 E3. (0575) 546111. FAX (0575) 545999. @ info@zutphen-museumhotel.nl b,d. **Rooms** 65. €€

For key to symbols see backflap. For price categories *see p123*

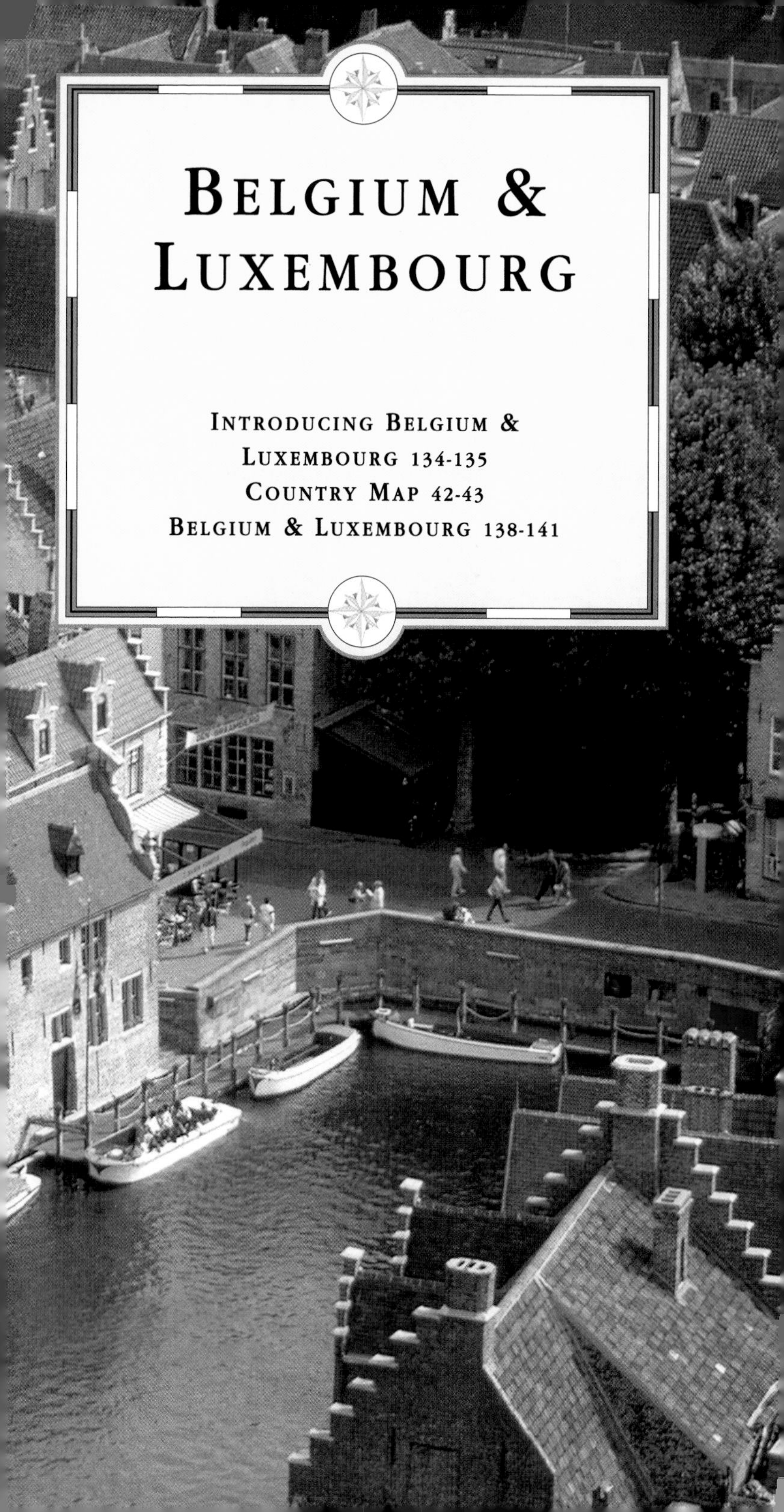

BELGIUM & LUXEMBOURG

BELGIUM AND LUXEMBOURG

BELGIUM AND ITS diminutive neighbour have much in common: they fall naturally into the same section. Many of their old castles and pretty half-timbered mansions have been converted into luxury hotels, and everywhere you will find an emphasis on food. Some hotels do two rounds of breakfast (the second starting at 11am). Expect generous portions. Simple soup can turn out to be a 'relay race' of several different flavours; a humble *espresso* may be elaborated with a side order of whipped cream and pralines. If the eating gets too much, you could try resting your liver at a 'thermal centre', such as one of those found in the Belgian town of Spa – parent of 'health farms' worldwide.

Shamrock, Maarkedal, page 141, great food and landscaped gardens

BELGIUM AND LUXEMBOURG REGION BY REGION

BELGIUM DIVIDES neatly into north and south, along the so-called 'language divide' (see below), formalised constitutionally in 1962. In the southeastern corner, on the border with Germany, is the 999-sq mile (2,600 sq km) Grand Duchy of Luxembourg.

The North

The Flemish north and the Walloon south of Belgium have different languages, communities and indeed administrations. The capital, Brussels, is on the dividing line separating the two. In the north are the provinces of West and East Flanders, Antwerp, Limburg and the upper reaches of Brabant. The region is flat and very similar to Holland. Antwerp mixes sleaze and wealth in equal measure, is Europe's second largest port and centre of the world diamond trade. Some wonderful places to stay here include a town-house hotel dating from the 16th century, and an Art Deco villa. In Flanders, to the southwest, there's the chance to stay in a couple of quay-side hotels in Bruges, and visit Ghent, with its artistic and architectural treasures.

The South

The Walloon south begins at the province of Hainaut. To the east are the Ardennes, an area of thickly forested hills which also spill over into Luxembourg and northeast-ern France. Whereas the French Ardennes are indust-rialised, the Belgian Ardennes are largely unspoilt, and some of the region's most beautiful hill-top castles have been converted into hotels. The Ardennes town of Spa was noted in Roman times by Pliny the Elder as a health resort, and there are some interesting places to stay in and around the town. If the treatments don't appeal, then make your way to Namur, the gastronomic capital of Belgium.

Luxembourg

Luxembourg has two aspects: the hilly Ardennes in the north and the farmland of the south – called the Bon Pays or Gutland (Good Land). The Grand Duchy (population about 400,000) has its own steel industry which is concentrated in the southwest. The rest of the country is covered in vineyards, particularly the slopes on either side of the Moselle river.

HIGHLIGHTS

THE PLACES to stay illustrated on these introductory pages are by no means the only highlights of this section. Other favourites include: Le Val d'Amblève at Stavelot (page 141), a half-timbered house in the Liège countryside, combining understated but smart decoration with great food; and De Witte Lelie in Antwerp (page 138), three 16th-century houses knocked together to make an unusual B&B hotel – grand and spac-ious, with high ceilings, but an informal atmosphere.

FOOD AND DRINK

BELGIANS ARE keen to point out that their country con-tains more Michelin-starred restaurants than France. Dishes are similar in style to French cuisine and specialities include *foie gras*, fine cheeses, snails served with herb butter, and fresh trout, pike, perch and crayfish from the rivers. Beef from Herve and lamb from Hainaut are particularly good. In Brussels, café snacks include mussels and chips, shrimp croquettes, chips and mayonnaise or *stoemp* (steak tartare). Vegetarians are not particularly well catered for: in fact, vegetarian restaurants are rare – the notable exception being Lombardia (03 233 6819) in Antwerp.

Sweets and pastries are on sale everywhere. As any chocoholic knows, Belgium and chocolate go together as readily as Plastic Bertrand and Europop. There is a Chocolat Jacques 'kingdom of chocolate' at Eupen, 30km (18 miles) from Liège, but if you don't make it there, look out for their chocolates on sale everywhere, or those of Galler Manufacture, Léonidas or Godiva, who are the other top chocolate producers.

There are more than 400 types of Belgian beer, including three strong beers brewed in the traditional way by the Trappist monks at Chimay, Rochefort and Orval. It's also worth trying the equally lively fruit beers. Brussels' famous beers are Faro, Gueuze, Lambic and Kriek.

Luxembourg's specialities include mussels, Ardennes ham, pastries and trout. Its Moselle wines are similar in style if not in quality to those over the border in Germany.

Bedrooms and Bathrooms

Rooms usually have double beds. If you would like twin or single beds, these must be requested when booking. It's very rare for any of the hotels listed here not to have en suite bathrooms, but a bathroom with a bath costs more than one with a shower.

Other Practical Information

In northern Belgium, breakfasts are like Dutch breakfasts; in the south, they are more like the French. Luxembourg breakfasts are a mixture of Dutch and French.

Many of the restaurants with rooms offer reductions for half board or *demi-pension* (a per person rate for the room, dinner and breakfast). These are often good value.

Language About 60 per cent of Belgians are Flemish speakers; the rest (the Walloons) speak French. There are also some German speakers in the eastern provinces.

In Luxembourg, the two official languages are French and Letzeburgesch. The latter is a Germanic language which most of the population speaks. Road signs are written in both.

Currency From 1 January 2002, the European *euro* (written 'EUR'), made up of 100 *cents*.

Shops 9am–5:30pm Mon–Fri. Some shops are closed on Monday mornings and for lunch. On Saturdays, shops open for half a day or all day and are closed on Sunday.

Tipping In hotels, service is included in the bill, and a 16 per cent service charge is usually added to restaurant bills. A further tip is only required for exceptional service. As in France, cinema usherettes are given a small tip (about 50 cents).

Telephones Public phones in Belgium take coins or telecards, which are on sale at post offices, newsstands and stations.

But with cheap, unlimited local calls, phoning from a hotel may, unusually for Europe, be a relatively economical option.

To make phone calls inside Belgium, dial the whole number including the initial 0. To telephone Belgium (or Luxembourg) from the UK, dial 00 32 (00 352), then the number omitting the initial 0 from the area code; from the US, dial 011 32 (00 352), also omitting the initial zero from the area code.

Public holidays Carnival time (the week around Shrove Tuesday) sees many businesses shut, and the grape harvest in Luxembourg's Moselle Valley is another occasion for holidays. The official holidays are: Belgium: January 1; Easter Sunday and Monday; 1 May; Ascension Day; Whit Sunday and Monday; 21 July; 15 August; 1 November; 11 November (Armistice Day); 15 November (King's Birthday); 25 and 26 December. Luxembourg: As above, but with the addition of Good Friday; 23 June (National Day).

Useful Words

See France, page 217; and Germany, page 147.

Price bands

Price bands refer to the price of a standard double room in high season, and usually include breakfast. Prices quoted for rooms include all taxes.

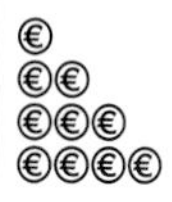

€	below 90 EUR
€€	90–240 EUR
€€€	240–470 EUR
€€€€	above 470 EUR

We give a single price band for hotels in Belgium and Luxembourg since the cost of living in the two countries is very similar; prior to currency convergence, the Belgian and Luxembourg francs usually had the same exchange value.

Oud-Huis Amsterdam in Brugge, page 138

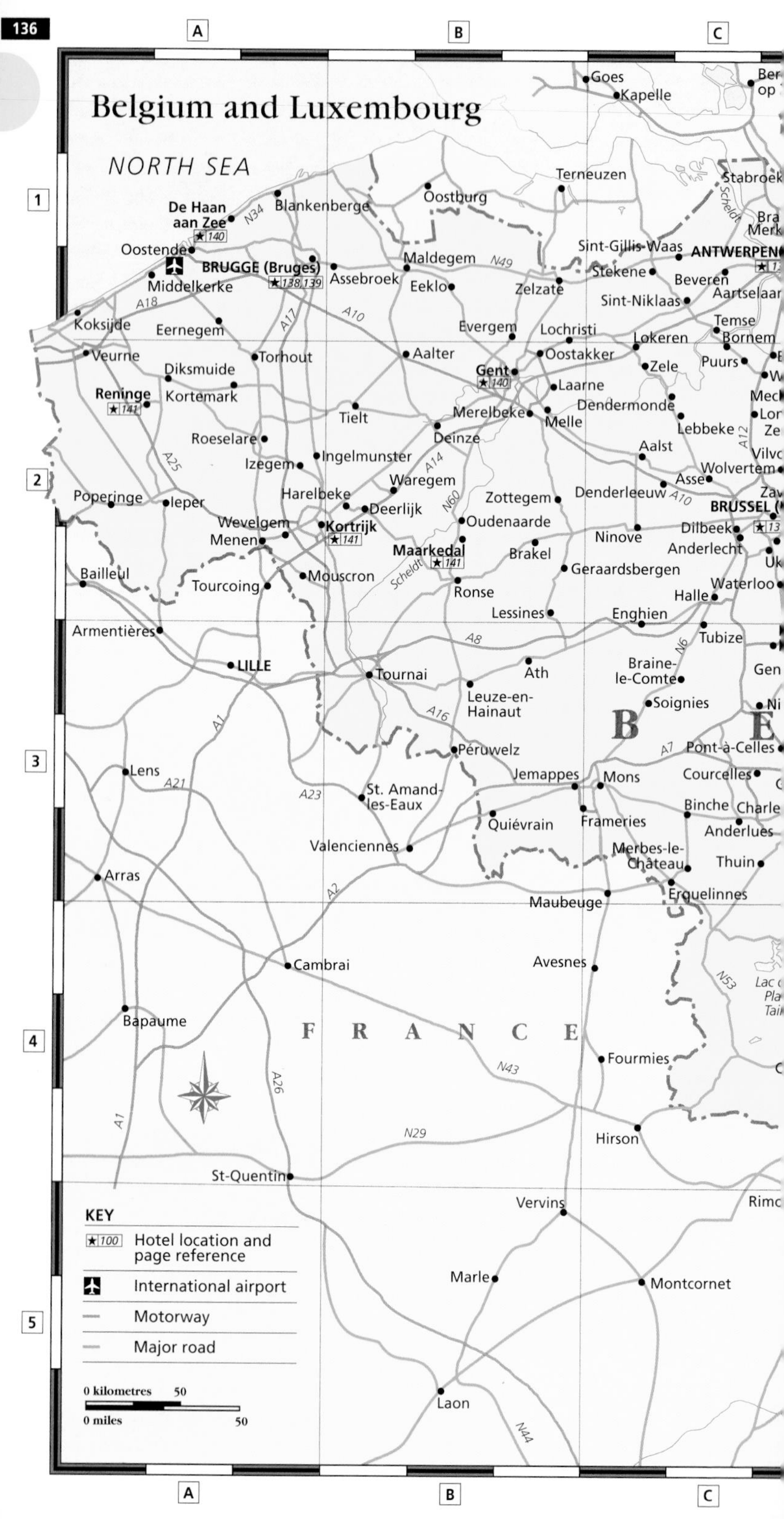

Belgium and Luxembourg
NORTH SEA
De Haan aan Zee 140
Blankenberge
Oostende
BRUGGE (Bruges) 138, 139
Middelkerke
Assebroek
Koksijde
Eernegem
Veurne
Torhout
Diksmuide
Reninge 141
Kortemark
Roeselare
Izegem
Ingelmunster
Poperinge
Ieper
Harelbeke
Wevelgem
Menen
Kortrijk 141
Deerlijk
Waregem
Bailleul
Tourcoing
Mouscron
Armentières
LILLE
Tournai
Oostburg
Maldegem
Eeklo
Aalter
Tielt
Deinze
Gent 140
Merelbeke
Melle
Evergem
Zelzate
Lochristi
Oostakker
Laarne
Zottegem
Oudenaarde
Maarkedal 141
Ronse
Brakel
Geraardsbergen
Lessines
Ath
Leuze-en-Hainaut
Péruwelz
St. Amand-les-Eaux
Valenciennes
Quiévrain
Jemappes
Mons
Frameries
Goes
Kapelle
Terneuzen
Sint-Gillis-Waas
Stekene
Sint-Niklaas
Lokeren
Zele
Dendermonde
Lebbeke
Aalst
Denderleeuw
Ninove
Enghien
Braine-le-Comte
Soignies
ANTWERPEN
Beveren
Aartselaar
Temse
Bornem
Puurs
Wolvertem
Asse
BRUSSEL
Dilbeek
Anderlecht
Waterloo
Halle
Tubize
Pont-à-Celles
Courcelles
Binche
Anderlues
Merbes-le-Château
Thuin
Erquelinnes
Maubeuge
Avesnes
Fourmies
Hirson
Vervins
Montcornet
Marle
Laon
St-Quentin
Cambrai
Bapaume
Arras
Lens
FRANCE
B
KEY
★100 Hotel location and page reference
International airport
Motorway
Major road
0 kilometres 50
0 miles 50

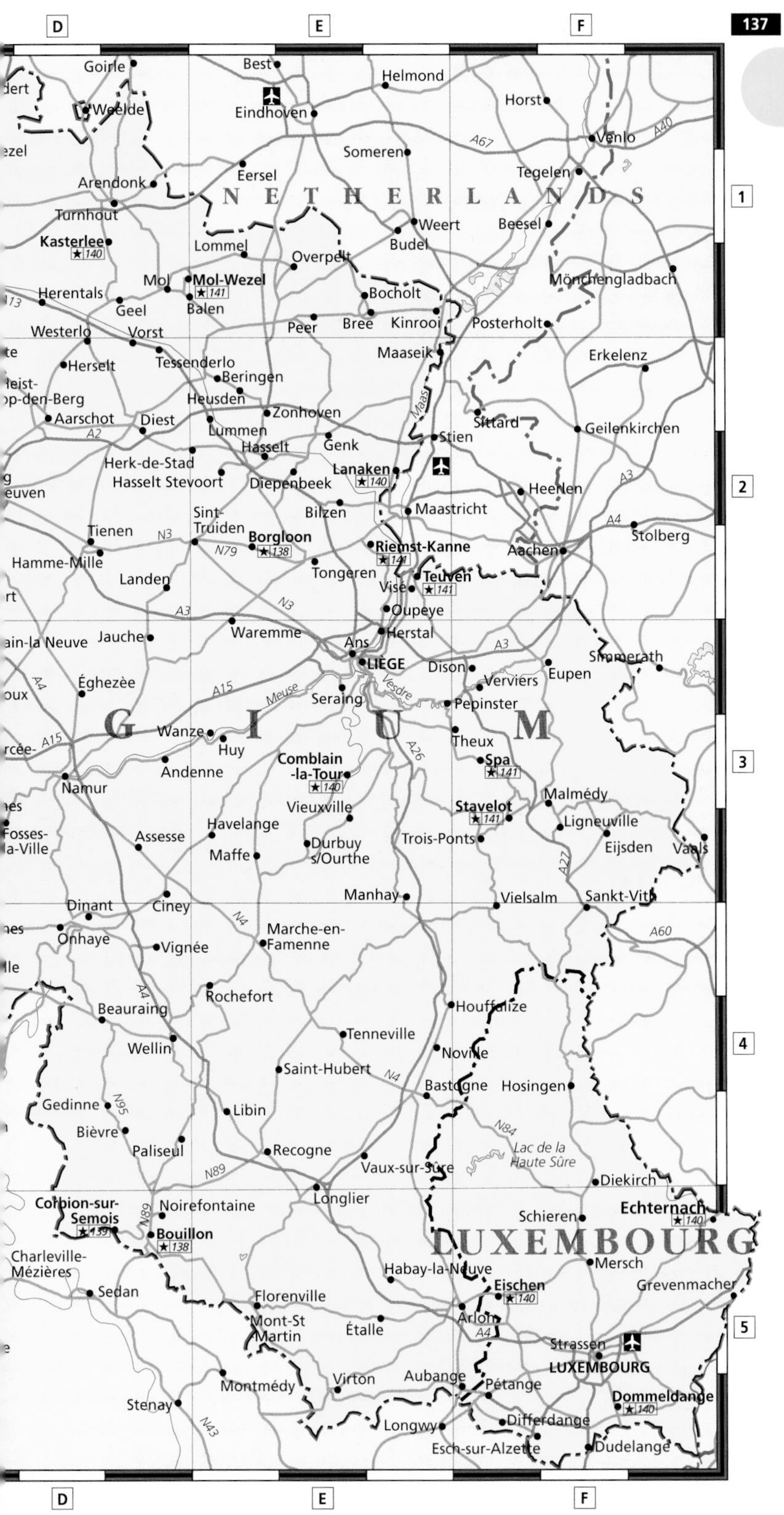

NETHERLANDS
LUXEMBOURG
Eindhoven
Helmond
Venlo
Maastricht
Aachen
LIÈGE
Namur
Kasterlee ★140
Mol-Wezel ★141
Lanaken ★140
Borgloon ★138
Riemst-Kanne ★141
Teuven ★141
Comblain-la-Tour ★140
Spa ★141
Stavelot ★141
Corbion-sur-Semois ★139
Bouillon ★138
Echternach ★140
Eischen ★140
Dommeldange ★140
LUXEMBOURG
Mönchengladbach
Bastogne
Sedan
Charleville-Mézières
Lac de la Haute Sûre

ANTWERPEN

De Witte Lelie This modish yet restfully decorated B&B hotel occupies three interlinked 16th-century houses in the oldest street in Antwerp, and is run by a mother and son. High ceilings emphasize the spaciousness of the bedrooms. In the morning, a filling breakfast is accompanied by the day's newspapers.
Keizerstraat 16-18, 2000 Antwerpen. **Map** p136 C1. (03) 226 1966. FAX (03) 234 0019. @ hotel@dewittelelie.be b. **Rooms** 10. Christmas and New Year. AE, MC, V. €€€

BRUGGE (BRUGES)

Oud-Huis Amsterdam This canalside hotel with a 400-year-old façade is packed with antique treasures. Córdoba leather covers some walls, and there are original 18th-century chimneypieces and staircases. Bedrooms are individually decorated and furnished. There's a bar in the old kitchen, a crackling fire in the breakfast room in winter, and a courtyard terrace for summer drinks.
Spiegelrei 3, 8000 Brugge. **Map** p136 A1. (050) 341 810. FAX (050) 338 891. @ info@oha.be b. **Rooms** 34. Never. AE, DC, MC, V. €€

BORGLOON

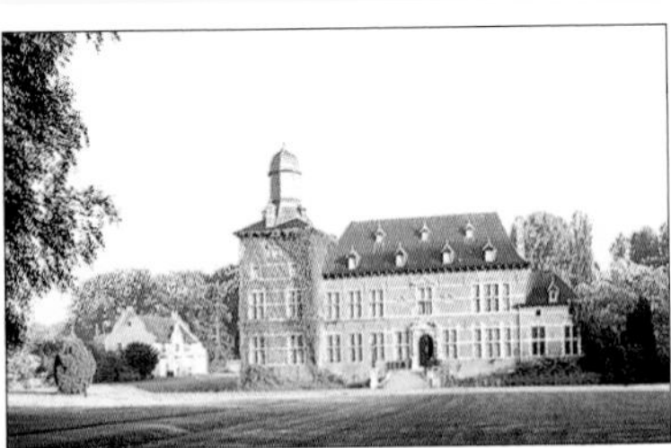

Kasteel van Rullingen The public rooms at this serene lakeside castle have grand chandeliers and pastoral wall paintings; bedrooms are decorated in a simpler style but with beautiful casement windows. On summer weekends the chapel is a popular place for weddings. Under new management.
Rullingen 1, 3840 Borgloon. **Map** p137 E2. (012) 743 146. FAX (012) 745 486. @ info@rullingen.com b,l,d. **Rooms** 16. Never. Not accepted. €€

BRUGGE (BRUGES)

Pandhotel The nine Ralph Lauren suites set the style for this hotel in the city centre. The designer's signature furnishings, plus four-poster beds, piles of leather-bound books and oil paintings make this a comforting bolt-hole. The calm drawing rooms are great places to relax and read a book after a day exploring the streets of the old town.
Pandreitje 16, 8000 Brugge. **Map** p136 A1. (050) 340 666. FAX (050) 340 556. @ info@pandhotel.com b. **Rooms** 24. Never. AE, DC, MC, V. €€

ANTWERPEN

Firean In a quiet suburb a ten-minute tram ride from the centre, Firean is in a 1920s' mansion decorated with warm colours and Persian rugs.
Karel Oomsstraat 6, 2018 Antwerpen. **Map** p136 C1. (03) 237 0260. FAX (03) 238 1168. @ info@hotelfirean.com b. **Rooms** 15. €€

ANTWERPEN

't Sandt A former spice merchant's house in the city centre, now Neo-Classical in style. One suite has a roof terrace with a view of the cathedral.
Zand 1719, 2000 Antwerpen. **Map** p136 C1. (03) 232 9390. FAX (03) 232 5613. @ reservations@hotel-sandt.be b. **Rooms** 17. €€€

BOUILLON

Hostellerie la Pommeraie At this grand hotel, dine on the terraces in sight of Bouillon's floodlit medieval castle in summer.
rue de la Poste 2, B6830 Bouillon. **Map** p137 D5. (061) 469 017. FAX (061) 469 083. b,l,d. **Rooms** 10. €€

BRUGGE (BRUGES)

De Orangerie Wrought-ironwork and leaded windows gives this canalside hotel a medieval feel. Leather sofas and open fires in the lounge.
Kartuizerinnenstraat 10, 8000 Brugge. **Map** p136 A1. (050) 341 649. FAX (050) 333 016. @ info@hotelorangerie.com b. **Rooms** 20. 

Brugge (Bruges)

Die Swaene Originally the chambers for the guild of tailors, Die Swaene has a drawing room which dates back to 1779, but the three canalhouses the hotel occupies are a few hundred years older still. Much remains of the original buildings. The large bedrooms are decorated in modern Baroque style. Service is good and the welcome friendly.
Steenhouwersdijk 1, 8000 Brugge. **Map** p136 A1.
(050) 342 798. FAX (050) 336 674.
@ info@dieswaene-hotel.com b,l,d. **Rooms** 32.
Never. AE, DC, MC, V. €€

Brussel (Brussels)

Manos Premier A spectacularly styled hotel of deep comfort and character, the Manos feels like a large and elegant private home where everything has been carefully thought out to charm and surprise. There are comfortable public rooms overlooking an extensive garden, and a fitness suite with Moroccan-style hammam.
Chaussée de Charleroi 100-106, 1060 Brussel. **Map** p136 C2. (02) 537 9682. FAX (02) 539 3655. @ manos @manoshotel.com b,l,d. **Rooms** 50 inc 13 apartments.
Never. AE, DC, MC, V. €€

Brussel (Brussels)

Hotel Amigo A stone's throw from the Grand Place and its superb Town Hall, the Amigo is a handsome hotel that has been totally refurbished. Each room is individually decorated and there is a choice of seven luxury suites, including one with its own terrace on the top floor. The French cuisine served at the hotel's restaurant is in keeping with its five-star status.
Rue de l'Amigo 1-3, 1000 Brussel. **Map** p136 C2.
(02) 547 4709. FAX (02) 502 2805. b,l,d.
Rooms 174. Never. AE, DC, V. €€€€

Brussel (Brussels)

Stanhope A Brighton Pavilion theme dominates at the Stanhope. A portrait of King George IV, builder of that fantasy Oriental palace, hangs in the restaurant – called Brighton – and Chinoiserie extends into the bedrooms and suites. The garden, with a magnolia tree strung with lights, is a lovely place to dine in summer.
rue du Commerce 9, 1000 Brussel. **Map** p136 C2.
(02) 506 9111. FAX (02) 512 1708. @ summithotel@ stanhope.be b;l,d (not Sat, Sun). **Rooms** 94.
Never. AE, DC, MC, V. €€€

Brugge (Bruges)

De Snippe Long renowned for its seafood, the elegant De Snippe also has a small number of similarly smart bedrooms.
Nieuwe Gentweg 53, 8000 Brugge. **Map** p136 A1.
(050) 337 070. FAX (050) 337 662.
@ desnippe@pandora.be b,l,d. **Rooms** 8. €€

Brugge (Bruges)

de Tuilerieën Choose between chintzy rooms overlooking the canal or quieter ones at the back. Swimming pool in the conservatory.
Dijver 7, 8000 Brugge. **Map** p136 A1. (050) 343 691. FAX (050) 340 400. @ patrick.verbaeys@ hoteltuilerieen.com b. **Rooms** 45. €€€

Brussel (Brussels)

Le Dixseptième A chic 18th-century residence decorated in hot colours, with 12 studios and 12 spacious suites, most with kitchenettes.
rue de la Madeleine 25, 1000 Brussel.
Map p136 C2. (02) 517 1717. FAX (02) 502 6424.
@ info@ledixseptieme.be b. **Rooms** 24. €€

Corbion-sur-Semois

Hotel des Ardennes This family-run hotel run in wooded countryside has two excellent restaurants, a pool table and games for children.
rue de la Hate 1, 6838 Corbion. **Map** p137 D5.
(061) 466 621. FAX (061) 467 730. @ contact@ hoteldesardennes.be b,l,d. **Rooms** 30. €€

For key to symbols see backflap. For price categories *see p135*

Comblain-la-Tour

L'Hostellerie St-Roch An old post house is now a solid, ivy-clad hotel on the edge of the Ardennes; its decking terrace overlooks the River Ourthe. Rooms are decorated with tapestry fabrics, some chintz, and warm subdued colours. The restaurant serves seasonal country cuisine.
Vallée de l'Ourthe, 4180 Comblain-la-Tour. **Map** p137 E3. (04) 369 1333. FAX (04) 369 3131. info@st-roch.be b,l,d. **Rooms** 15. early Jan to mid-March; Mon, Tue except July, Aug. AE, DC, MC, V. €€

Eischen, Luxembourg

Hotel de La Gaichel Behind the pink façade of this 19th-century building stretch vast grounds bordered by a little river. The bedrooms all face the park, and the restaurant is bordered by a large, tree-shaded dining terrace. Guests can choose between activities such as golf and tennis, or simply enjoying the peace of this rural spot.
8469 Eischen, Luxembourg. **Map** p137 F5. 39 01 29. FAX 39 00 37. Gaichel@relaischateaux.com b,l,d. **Rooms** 13. Sun night, Mon; 10 days end Aug, 1 month Jan to Feb. AE, MC, V. €€€

Echternach, Luxembourg

Hotel Bel-Air This smooth four-star hotel is set just outside the medieval town of Echternach, surrounded by a vast private park and forests, with splendid views to the Sûre valleys. The original mansion house is practically hidden by modern extensions, but inside all is deeply soothing. Fine dining in the elegant dining room.
route de Berdorf, 6409 Echternach, Luxembourg. **Map** p137 F5. 72 93 83. FAX 72 86 94. belair@pt.lu b,l,d. **Rooms** 39. 2 weeks Jan. AE, DC, MC, V. €€

Lanaken

La Butte Aux Bois De-stress in the Shiseido and Thalgo beauty centres, cycle through the woods, or simply unwind in this calm 1920s mansion complete with lawns and lake. There's a choice of 'castle' rooms in the main building, or romantic bedrooms in the house opposite. The second round of breakfasts begins at 11am.
Paalsteenlaan 90, 3620 Lanaken. **Map** p137 E2. (089) 739770. FAX (089) 721647. info@labutteauxbois.be b,l,d. **Rooms** 41. Never. AE, DC, MC, V. €€

Dommeldange, Luxembourg

Hostellerie du Grunewald Gently old-fashioned hotel done out with Oriental carpets and button-backed chairs. Gourmet restaurant.
10-16 route d'Echternach, 1453 Dommeldange, Luxembourg. **Map** p137 F5. 43 18 82. FAX 42 06 46. b. **Rooms** 28. €€

De Haan aan Zee

Manoir Carpe Diem This seaside hotel has recently been completely refurbished.
Prins Karellaan 12, 8420 De Haan aan zee. **Map** p136 A1. (059) 233220. FAX (059) 233396. manoircarpediem@hotmail.com b,l. **Rooms** 15. €€

Gent

St Jorishof This guesthouse claims to be in Europe's oldest building (1228). Flemish specialities on the menu; helpful service.
Botermarkt 2, 9000 Gent. **Map** p136 B2. (09) 224 2424. FAX (09) 224 2640. courstgeorges@skynet.be b. **Rooms** 32. €€

Kasterlee

De Watermolen A watermill turned hotel and restaurant serving traditional French cuisine. Bedrooms are modern and spacious.
Houtum 61, 2460 Kasterlee. **Map** p137 D1. (014) 852 374. FAX (014) 852 370. info@watermolen.be b,l,d. **Rooms** 18. €€

Maarkedal

Hostellerie Shamrock The half-timbered country house was built as a summer residence in 1928, and the gardens were landscaped by the internationally known designer Jacques Wirtz. It's now a gourmet *hostellerie* owned and run by Claude and Livine De Beyter, with an ambitious menu and florally decorated bedrooms.
Ommegangstraat 148, 9681 Maarkedal.
Map p136 B2. (055) 215 529. FAX (055) 215 683.
@ shamrock@edpnet.be b,l,d. **Rooms** 5.
2 weeks Jan, 2 weeks July. AE, DC, V. €€

Reninge

't Convent Chef Rudi De Volder is a truffle enthusiast; guests sometimes fly in by helicopter to savour the Périgordian speciality in his regional and French-based cuisine. The style of the bedrooms varies widely, from Venetian through rustic to modern. The stone and timber-built farm and manor house has its own vineyard.
Halve Reningestraat 1, 8647 Reninge. **Map** p136 A2.
(057) 400 771. FAX (057) 401 127.
@ convent@itinera.be b,l,d. **Rooms** 15.
Feb and March. AE, DC, MC, V. €€

Mol-Wezel

Manoir Hippocampus The food at this manor house is particularly good, with owner-chef Francis Scheyvaerts planning his menu around what's best at market that day. In summer, tables are set out next to the white house overlooking the lily pond. The bedrooms are named after puddings: *tarte tatin*, *sabayon* and *javanais*.
Sint Jozeflaan 79, 2400 Mol-Wezel. **Map** p137 E1.
(014) 810 808. FAX (014) 814 590.
@ chef@hippocampus.be b,l,d. **Rooms** 3.
2 weeks Aug. AE, DC, MC, V. €.

Stavelot

Le Val d'Amblève '*Carpe diem*' is the motto of the owners of this half-timbered hotel in the Liège countryside; you would be hard-pressed to find more elegant surroundings in which to enjoy the pleasures of the moment. The style is in details such as the cool 'garden room' restaurant. The garden has recently been renovated.
route de Malmedy 7, 4970 Stavelot.
Map p137 F3. (080) 281 440. FAX (080) 281 459.
@ info@levaldambleve.com b,l,d. **Rooms** 12.
Jan. AE, DC, MC, V. €€€

Kortrijk

Damier An old coaching inn now furnished in English country-house style, and popular with business people. Breakfast is in the orangery.
Grote Markt 41, 8500 Kortrijk. **Map** p136 B2.
(056) 221547. FAX (056) 228631.
@ info@hoteldamier.be b,d. **Rooms** 49. €€

Riemst-Kanne

Huize Poswick This relaxed hotel's bedrooms have wood floors, beamed ceilings, period furniture and bright walls.
Muizenberg 7, 3770 Riemst-Kanne.
Map p137 E2. (012) 457127. FAX (012) 458105.
b. **Rooms** 6. €€

Spa

Villa des Fleurs A town-centre mansion built in 1880, characterized by yards of draped and swagged curtains and crystal-drop chandeliers.
rue Albin Body 31, 4900 Spa. **Map** p137 F3.
(087) 795 050. FAX (087) 795 060.
@ info@villadesfleurs.be b. **Rooms** 12. €€

Teuven

Hof De Draeck A very popular hotel in what was once a feudal manor house, with creaking stairs and a park with deer. Dinner is good value.
Hoofdstraat 6, 3793 Teuven. **Map** p137 E2.
(04) 381 1017. FAX (04) 381 1188. b,l,d.
Rooms 11. €

GERMANY

GERMANY

GERMANY HAS plenty of family-run hotels of character and style, but the successful ones tend to grow in size. The really small hotel (say, five to ten rooms) is uncommon – as are hotel chains; some hotels group together for joint promotion, such as the Romantik chain, Silencehotels, renowned for their secluded settings, and Gast im Schloss, a group of converted castles, some still run by their ancestral owners. Our selection offers places to suit all tastes, from simple country inns, picturesque *Gasthöfe* (guesthouses) and town hotels to palatial mansions and *Kur-hotels* (located in spas or health resorts).

Schloss Hugenpoet at Essen-Kettwig, page 172, has style on a grand scale

GERMANY REGION BY REGION

IN THIS GUIDE, we have divided the country into three areas: Northern Germany, Central Germany and Southern Germany.

Northern Germany
This comprises the states of Lower Saxony, Schleswig-Holstein and Mecklenburg-West Pomerania. It also includes the two great Baltic seaports of Hamburg and Bremen (each is almost a semi-autonomous state on its own), and numerous historic towns and seaside resorts where the handsome and spacious mansions of wealthy merchants and seafarers now make magnificent hotels. In Mecklenburg-West Pomerania, a low-lying, rural region of lakes, meadows, forests and beaches, are hidden country guesthouses and small family-run hotels. Alternatively, log-cabin-style inns and hunting lodges in the picturesque Harz mountains make for a perfect year-round sporting getaway, with plenty of opportunities for skiing, cycling and hiking.

Central Germany
The region stretches from the sprawling cityscapes of Düsseldorf, Dortmund and Frankfurt in the west, to the new capital, Berlin, in the east. It includes the former capital, Bonn, many of Germany's best wine-growing regions, the states of Hesse, Thuringia, Brandenburg and Saxony, and the newly-fashionable, one-time eastern cities of Dresden and Leipzig.

Most hotels in the former German Democratic Republic (GDR, or East Germany) are now moving closer to standards of service, food and comfort found in the rest of Germany, although their prices tend to be marginally cheaper. The city hotels tend to be efficient but sometimes rather large and impersonal. Look out for the smaller, family-run hotels, called *Pensionen*, friendlier in character but usually lacking full hotel facilities. Alternatively, head to the vineyard *Gasthöfe* of the Rhine and its various tributaries, or splash out on one of several castle-hotels here. In the little-known Erzgebirge mountains by the Czech border, Sächsiche Schweiz (Saxony's 'Little Switzerland'), you will find reasonably-priced, quaint chalet-style accommodation.

Southern Germany
The southern part of the country boasts more than its fair share of sensational scenery, from the dreamy landscapes of the Black Forest and the Swabian Jura, to the chocolate-box villages and lakes of Bavaria, where country excursions frequently end with a warm welcome at a typically rustic country inn.

The region also includes some of the country's finest cities – Heidelberg, Konstanz, Nürnber, Regensburg and Ulm – with their magnificent half-timbered houses and accommodation to suit all pockets, not to mention the bustling metropolis of Munich, Germany's most popular city, which also has some of its finest hotels.

To the south, the snow-capped Alps, with their numerous mountain inns and sophisticated sports hotels, make a majestic backdrop to the entire region.

The garden restaurant at the Residence, Essen-Kettwig, page 172

Highlights

Hotels illustrated on these introductory pages are just a selection. Other favourites include the romantic Malerwinkel, a tiny lakeside hotel in Seebruck, at the foot of the Alps (page 166); Zum Krug in Eltville-Hattenheim, at the heart of the Rheingau wine region (page 172); the palatial castle-hotels Burg Colmberg (page 156), with its four-poster beds, log fires and private chapel, and Schlosshotel Kronberg (page 175), with its antique furnishings, golf course and rose gardens; Munich's Insel-Mühle (page 162), a fine converted watermill; and, in Konstanz, Seehotel Siber (page 160) with its renowned gourmet restaurant and magnificent rooms with views over Lake Constance to keep you entranced all day.

Parkhotel Wehrle at Triberg im Schwarzwald, page 167

Food and Drink

German cuisine is reputedly simple and solid, and it is an undeniable fact that heavy foods such as sausages, sauerkraut, potatoes, beer and huge cream cakes frequently feature on the menu.

However, from the lowland Dutch borders and Baltic seaboard in the north to the Alpine fringes of the south, German food and drink is as varied as its landscapes. Also, the country's restaurant scene has recently been transformed by *Neue Deutsche Küche*, the German answer to *nouvelle cuisine*, with an innovative new range of light, creative dishes based on traditional German ingredients.

Breakfast is something of a German speciality and, except in the smallest hotels, is generally served as a buffet of yoghurt and muesli, platters of cheese, cold cuts and bread. Germans can consume a truly staggering amount of bread, and the variety of breads in bakeries is

Berlin's Brandenburger Hof, page 169, a successful mix of new and old

astounding. Traditionally, lunch is the main meal of the day, and normally consists of meat in large portions, vegetables, potatoes and sauces and is usually accompanied by beer.

Regional specialities worth looking out for include Rhine salmon prepared with steamed plums; *Sauerbraten* (marinated beef in vinegar and herb gravy); snails in herb butter from Baden; Bavarian *Weisswürste* (white sausages, customarily eaten before midday); and *Leberkäs* ('livercheese'), a chunky meat-loaf which, despite its name, contains neither cheese nor liver. German desserts are usually fruit or cream-based; perhaps the best-known is the Black Forest gâteau.

Germany is also famous for its beer. It is found in a variety of forms, from Pils and Kölsch to the dark brown Düssel ale, popular in Düsseldorf, and Berlin's light, foamy Weisse, containing a sweet raspberry syrup.

German beers vary greatly in their alcohol content. While a normal brew contains around 5.5 per cent alcohol, *Starkbier* (especially popular in Southern Germany) can contain up to 16 per cent or more. Beer is usually ordered in one-litre mugs, and perhaps best enjoyed in the legendary and often atmospheric *Bierkeller* and *Biergarten*.

Wine is drunk less often than beer, but can be a welcome and refreshing addition to a solid German meal. The main wine-producing areas follow the valleys of the Rhine and its tributaries, the Mosel, Main, Nahe and Neckar, although there are also some lesser-known but equally notable vineyards, particularly around Naumburg and Dresden.

Most German wine is white, produced mainly from Riesling, Müller-Thurgau and Silvaner grapes. Only about one-eighth of the total production is red. All wines are divided into three qualities: *Tafelwein* (table wine), *Qualitätswein* (quality wine) and *Qualitätswein mit Prädikat* (quality wine with distinctive features). These are printed on the label. Some of the finest wines include the golden coloured and sweet whites from late-harvested grapes (labelled *Spätlese* or *Auslese*).

Bedrooms and Bathrooms

In most hotels, duvets (*Federbetten*) rather than sheets and blankets are the norm. Asking for a double room does not necessarily mean you will get a double bed: usually it is two single mattresses in a 'double' frame, topped with two single duvets. If you require twin beds, ask for them specifically when booking.

As a friendly gesture, many hotels will leave a chocolate or sweet on the pillow as a small goodnight gift.

Many hotels have showers rather than baths, so if you would prefer a room with a bath remember to request this when booking. Some of the hotels in the lower price bands have shared bathrooms. If you require an en suite bathroom, be sure to specify this when making your reservation.

The 300-year-old Hotel Adler in Eichstätt, page 156

Bülow Residenz, page 171, a Baroque house in the old part of Dresden

Other Practical Information

RESERVATIONS SHOULD be made as far ahead as possible, especially during holiday seasons, and in cities, which often get fully booked in advance for trade fairs and popular festivals. These include the Oktoberfest in Munich (late September–early October), the Cologne Carnival (late February–early March) and the Bayreuth opera festival (June–July).

There has recently been a move in Germany towards environmentally conscious 'eco-tourism' (*Ökotourismus*). Coincidentally, German hotels and restaurants have become more tolerant of smokers, and are now less prepared to prohibit smoking in certain rooms or areas. However, at the other extreme, some hotels offer special *Antiallergica* rooms, for those prone to such allergies as household dust.

Many hotels contain top-class restaurants where you can eat even if you are not a resident. Note that it is customary in some restaurants to share your table with other diners, especially if the table is marked *Stammtisch*. Note also that you will be charged for each piece of bread consumed.

Language *Hochdeutsch*, 'High German', is the official language, but regional dialects, often with strong local accents, are spoken in many areas.

Saxony, Bavaria and Swabia have particularly pronounced local dialects, while Berlin and Cologne retain their own 'city dialects' which even visitors from nearby areas may find hard to understand. In the north, *Plattdeutsch* is another regional variation.

Currency From 1 January 2002, the European *euro* (written '**EUR**'), made up of 100 *cents*.

Shops As a rule, shops open from 9am–6:30pm Mon–Fri (some remain open until 8:30pm on Thursdays), and 8:30am–2pm Sat – except for the first Saturday of each month, when they open until 4pm.

Tipping Prices in hotels and restaurants are always inclusive of service. You therefore need leave nothing extra for room service; in restaurants it is customary to add a little to the bill for service.

Telephoning For calls within Germany, dial the initial zero of the area code. To call Germany from the UK, dial 00 49, then the number, omitting the initial zero; from the US, 011 49, again without the initial zero.

Public holidays 1 January; Good Friday and Easter Monday; 1 May; Ascension Day; Whit Monday; Corpus Christi; 3 October (Unification Day); 25 and 26 December.

Useful Words

Breakfast	*Frühstück*
Lunch	*Mittagessen*
Dinner	*Abendessen*
Free room?	*Zimmer frei?*
How much?	*Wieviel?*
Single room	*Einzelzimmer*
Double room	*Doppelzimmer*

Germany Price Bands

GERMANY DOES NOT have a hotel classification system with star ratings. Instead, hotels and guesthouses are differentiated and described according to their type – *Hotel Garni*, *Kur-hotel*, *Hotel Pension*, and so on.

Our price bands, as elsewhere in the guide, refer to the price of a standard double room in high season. Breakfast is usually, but not always, included in the room price. VAT, *Mehrwertsteuer*, is always included in the prices quoted by hotels.

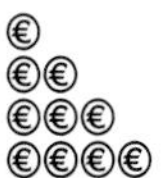

€	under 55 EUR
€€	55–105 EUR
€€€	105–160 EUR
€€€€	over 160 EUR

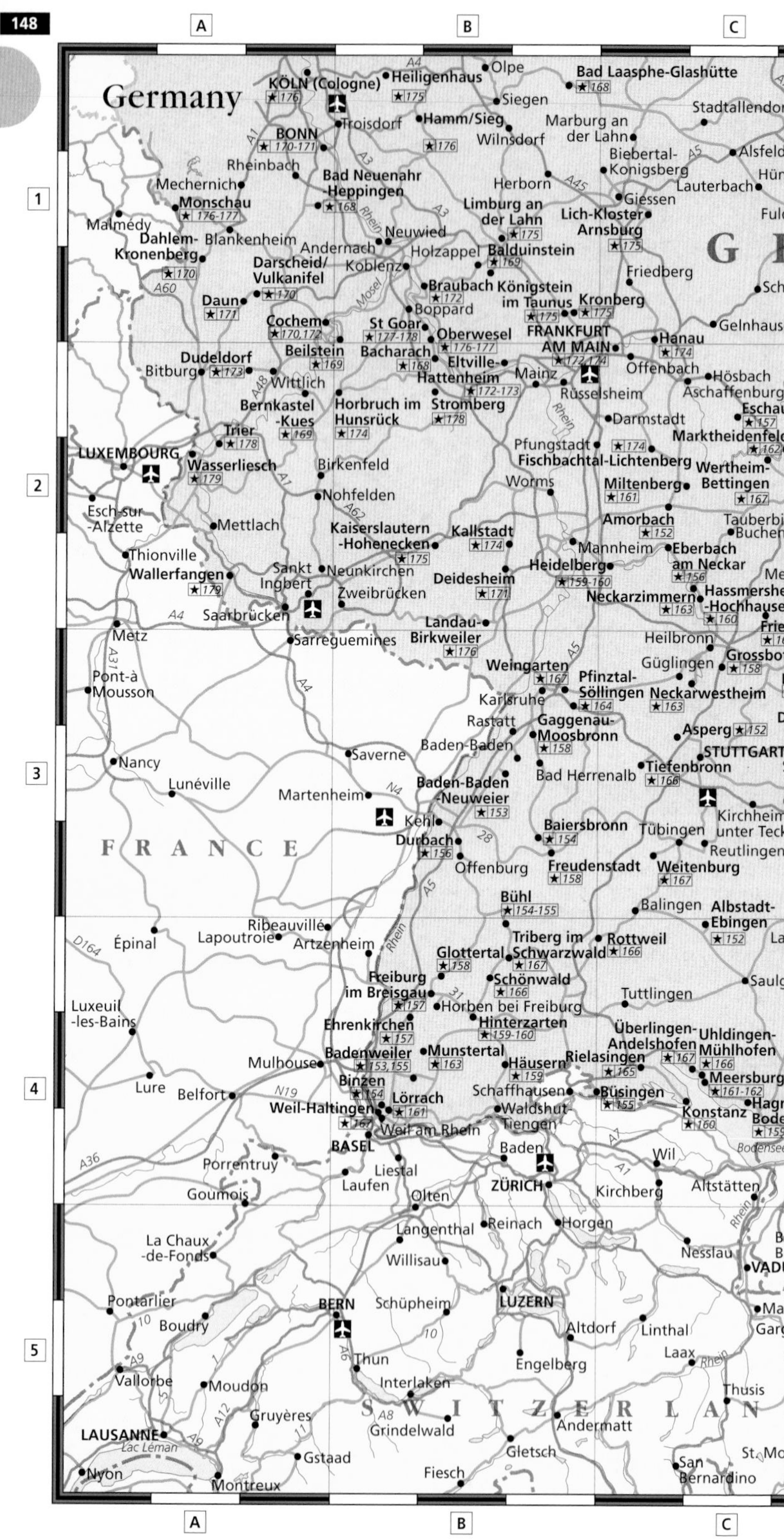
Germany
A
B
C
1
2
3
4
5
KÖLN (Cologne) ★176
Heiligenhaus ★175
Olpe
Bad Laasphe-Glashütte ★168
Siegen
Troisdorf
Hamm/Sieg ★176
Wilnsdorf
Marburg an der Lahn
Stadtallendorf
BONN ★170-171
Rheinbach
Biebertal-Konigsberg
Alsfeld
Mechernich
Bad Neuenahr-Heppingen ★168
Herborn
Lauterbach
Monschau ★176-177
Giessen
Malmédy
Limburg an der Lahn ★175
Lich-Kloster Arnsburg ★175
Dahlem-Kronenberg ★170
Blankenheim
Neuwied
Andernach
Holzappel
Balduinstein ★169
Darscheid/Vulkanifel ★170
Koblenz
Friedberg
G E
Braubach ★172
Königstein im Taunus ★175
Kronberg ★175
Daun ★171
Boppard
Cochem ★170,172
St Goar ★177-178
Oberwesel ★176-177
FRANKFURT AM MAIN ★172,174
Hanau ★174
Gelnhausen
Beilstein ★169
Bacharach ★168
Eltville-Hattenheim ★172-173
Mainz
Offenbach
Hösbach
Dudeldorf ★173
Bitburg
Wittlich
Rüsselsheim
Aschaffenburg
Bernkastel-Kues ★169
Horbruch im Hunsrück ★174
Stromberg ★178
Darmstadt
Eschau ★157
Trier ★178
Pfungstadt
★174
Marktheidenfeld ★162
LUXEMBOURG
Wasserliesch ★179
Birkenfeld
Fischbachtal-Lichtenberg
Wertheim-Bettingen ★167
Worms
Miltenberg ★161
Esch-sur-Alzette
Nohfelden
Mettlach
Kaiserslautern-Hohenecken ★175
Kallstadt ★174
Amorbach ★152
Tauberbischofsheim
Buchen
Thionville
Mannheim
Eberbach am Neckar ★156
Wallerfangen ★179
Sankt Ingbert
Neunkirchen
Deidesheim ★171
Heidelberg ★159-160
Zweibrücken
Neckarzimmern ★163
Hassmersheim-Hochhausen ★160
Saarbrücken
Landau-Birkweiler ★176
Metz
Sarreguemines
Heilbronn
Pont-à-Mousson
Weingarten ★167
Güglingen
Grossbottwar ★158
Pfinztal-Söllingen ★164
Neckarwestheim ★163
Karlsruhe
Rastatt
Gaggenau-Moosbronn ★158
Asperg ★152
Baden-Baden
STUTTGART
Saverne
Nancy
Tiefenbronn ★166
Bad Herrenalb
Lunéville
Martenheim
Baden-Baden-Neuweier ★153
Kehl
Kirchheim unter Teck
Baiersbronn ★154
Tübingen
F R A N C E
Durbach ★156
Reutlingen
Offenburg
Freudenstadt ★158
Weitenburg ★167
Bühl ★154-155
Balingen
Albstadt-Ebingen ★152
Ribeauvillé
Épinal
Lapoutroie
Artzenheim
Triberg im Schwarzwald ★167
Rottweil ★166
Glottertal ★158
Freiburg im Breisgau ★157
Schönwald ★166
Saulgau
Tuttlingen
Luxeuil-les-Bains
Horben bei Freiburg
Ehrenkirchen ★157
Hinterzarten ★159-160
Überlingen-Andelshofen ★167
Uhldingen-Mühlhofen ★166
Mulhouse
Badenweiler ★153,155
Munstertal ★163
Häusern ★159
Rielasingen ★165
Meersburg ★161-162
Lure
Belfort
Binzen ★154
Schaffhausen
Büsingen ★155
Weil-Haltingen ★167
Lörrach ★161
Waldshut-Tiengen
Konstanz ★160
Weil am Rhein
BASEL
Baden
Wil
Bodensee
Porrentruy
Liestal
Laufen
ZÜRICH
Kirchberg
Altstätten
Goumois
Olten
Langenthal
Reinach
Horgen
La Chaux-de-Fonds
Willisau
Nesslau
VADUZ
Pontarlier
BERN
Schüpheim
LUZERN
Boudry
Altdorf
Linthal
Engelberg
Laax
Thun
Vallorbe
Moudon
Interlaken
Thusis
S W I T Z E R L A N
Gruyères
Grindelwald
Andermatt
LAUSANNE
Lac Léman
Gstaad
Gletsch
San Bernardino
Nyon
Montreux
Fiesch
Rhein
Mosel
A1
A3
A4
A5
A7
A8
A9
A12
A31
A36
A45
A48
A60
A62
N4
N19
D164

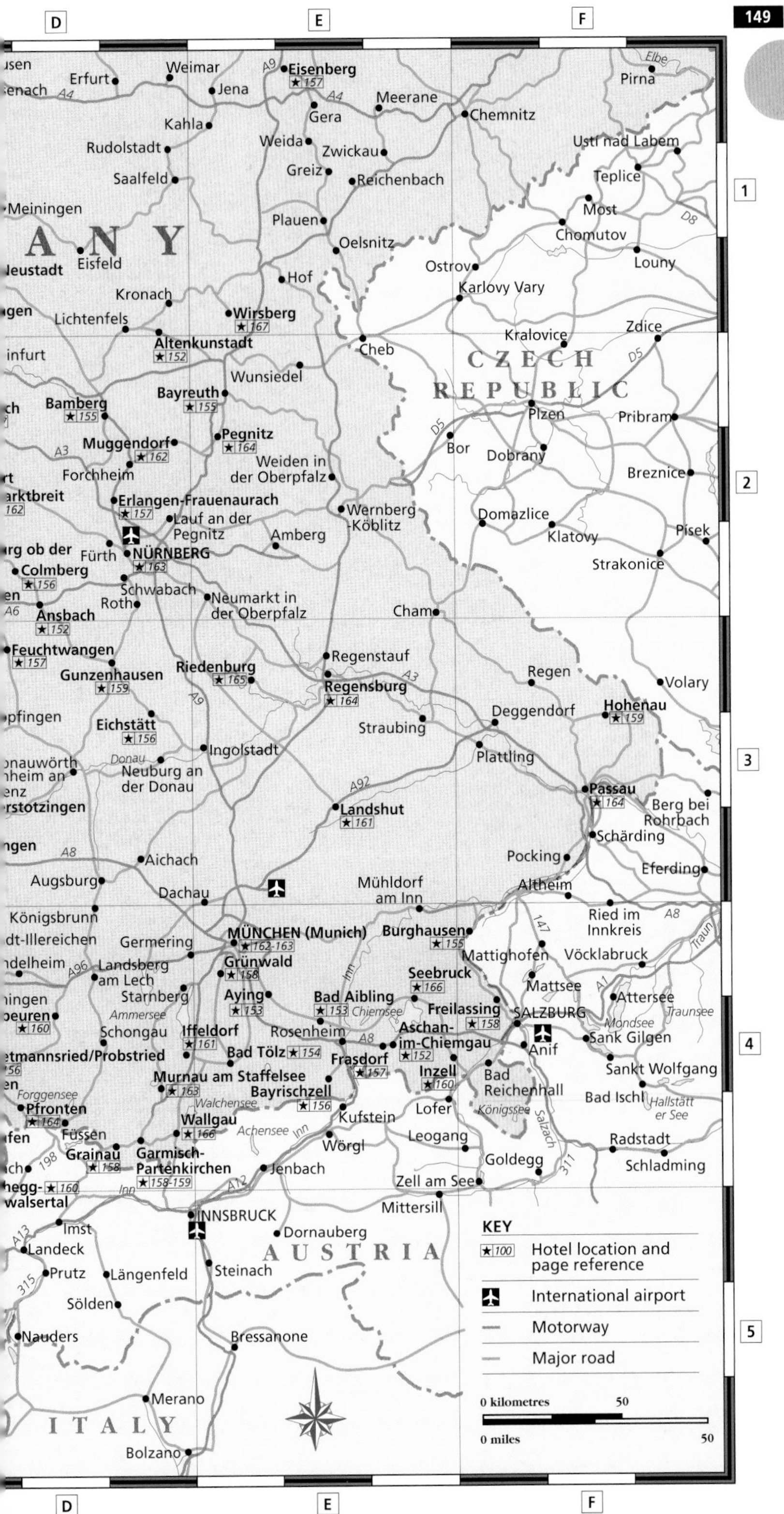
D
E
F
1
2
3
4
5
Erfurt
Weimar
Jena
Eisenberg ★157
Meerane
Gera
Chemnitz
Kahla
Pirna
Weida
Zwickau
Rudolstadt
Usti nad Labem
Greiz
Saalfeld
Reichenbach
Teplice
Meiningen
Most
Plauen
Chomutov
Oelsnitz
Eisfeld
Louny
Ostrov
Hof
Karlovy Vary
Kronach
Wirsberg ★167
Lichtenfels
Zdice
Altenkunstadt ★152
Kralovice
Cheb
CZECH REPUBLIC
Wunsiedel
Bayreuth ★155
Bamberg ★155
Plzen
Pribram
Pegnitz ★164
Muggendorf ★162
Bor
Dobrany
Weiden in der Oberpfalz
Forchheim
Breznice
Erlangen-Frauenaurach ★157
Wernberg -Köblitz
Domazlice
Lauf an der Pegnitz
Amberg
Klatovy
Pisek
Fürth
NÜRNBERG ★163
Strakonice
Colmberg ★156
Schwabach
Roth
Neumarkt in der Oberpfalz
Cham
Ansbach ★152
Feuchtwangen ★157
Regenstauf
Gunzenhausen ★159
Riedenburg ★165
Regen
Regensburg ★164
Volary
Hohenau ★159
Deggendorf
Straubing
Eichstätt ★156
Ingolstadt
Plattling
Donau
Neuburg an der Donau
Passau ★164
Berg bei Rohrbach
Landshut ★161
Schärding
Aichach
Pocking
Eferding
Augsburg
Mühldorf am Inn
Altheim
Dachau
Königsbrunn
Ried im Innkreis
MÜNCHEN (Munich) ★162-163
Burghausen ★155
Germering
Mattighofen
Vöcklabruck
Grünwald ★158
Landsberg am Lech
Seebruck ★166
Mattsee
Starnberg
Aying ★153
Bad Aibling ★153
Chiemsee
Attersee
Freilassing ★158
SALZBURG
Traunsee
Ammersee
Mondsee
Schongau
Iffeldorf ★161
Rosenheim
Aschan-im-Chiemgau ★152
Anif
Sank Gilgen
Bad Tölz ★154
Frasdorf ★157
Sankt Wolfgang
Inzell ★160
Bad Reichenhall
Murnau am Staffelsee ★163
Bayrischzell ★156
Bad Ischl
Forggensee
Hallstätter See
Pfronten ★164
Walchensee
Königssee
Kufstein
Lofer
Wallgau ★166
Füssen
Achensee
Wörgl
Leogang
Radstadt
Grainau ★158
Garmisch-Partenkirchen ★158-159
Goldegg
Schladming
Jenbach
Zell am See
Mittersill
INNSBRUCK
Imst
Dornauberg
Landeck
AUSTRIA
Prutz
Längenfeld
Steinach
Sölden
Nauders
Bressanone
Merano
ITALY
Bolzano
KEY
★100 Hotel location and page reference
International airport
Motorway
Major road
0 kilometres 50
0 miles 50

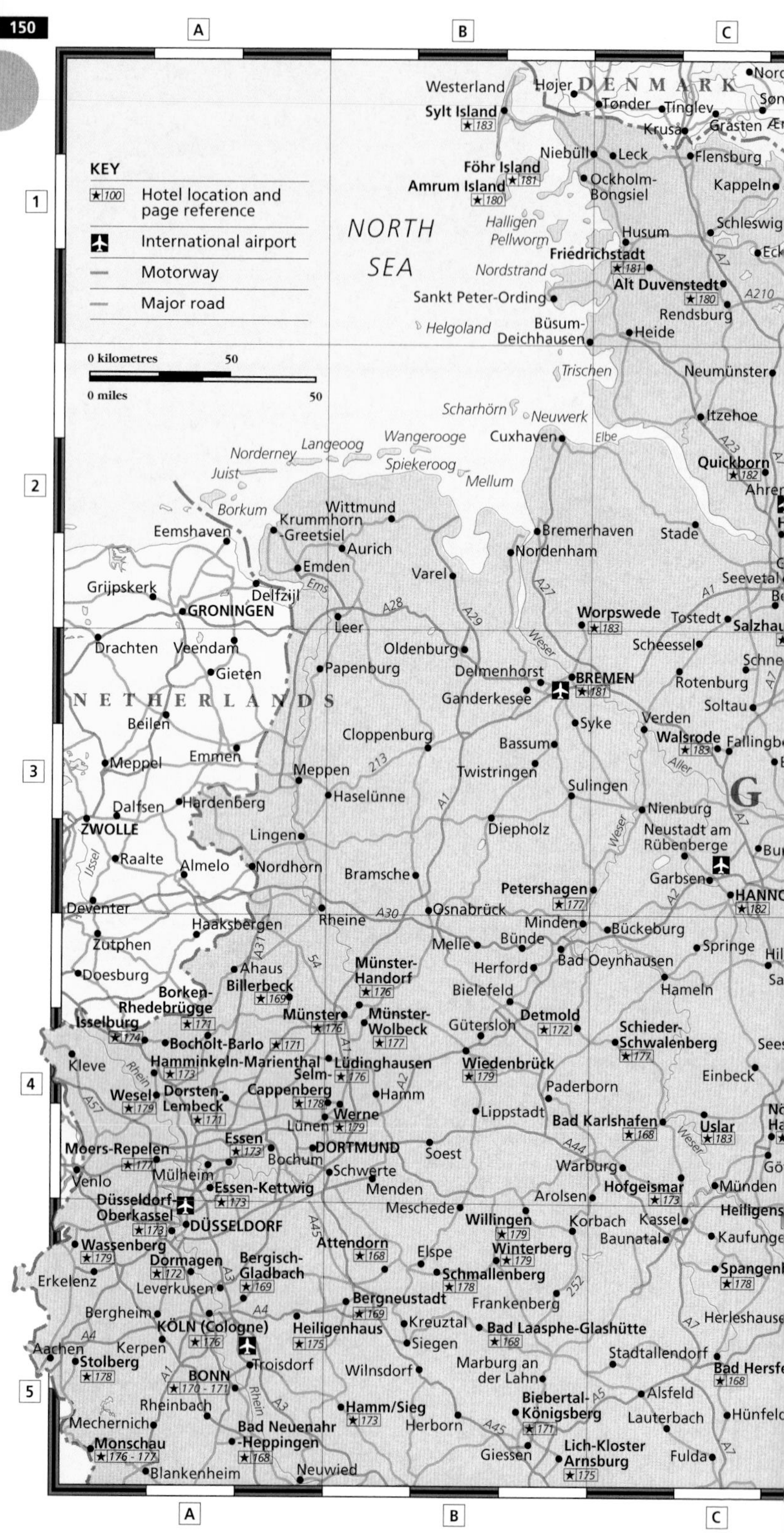
A
B
C
1
2
3
4
5
KEY
Hotel location and page reference
International airport
Motorway
Major road
0 kilometres 50
0 miles 50
NORTH SEA
DENMARK
NETHERLANDS
Westerland
Sylt Island 183
Føhr Island 181
Amrum Island 180
Friedrichstadt 181
Alt Duvenstedt 180
Quickborn 182
Worpswede 183
BREMEN 181
Walsrode 183
Petershagen 177
HANNOVER 182
Münster-Handorf 176
Billerbeck 169
Borken-Rhedebrügge 171
Isselburg 174
Bocholt-Barlo 171
Münster 176
Münster-Wolbeck 177
Detmold 172
Schieder-Schwalenberg 177
Hamminkeln-Marienthal 173
Selm-Lüdinghausen 176
Wiedenbrück 179
Wesel 179
Dorsten-Lembeck 171
Cappenberg 178
Werne 179
Bad Karlshafen 168
Uslar 183
Essen 173
DORTMUND
Moers-Repelen 177
Essen-Kettwig 173
Hofgeismar 173
Düsseldorf-Oberkassel 173
DÜSSELDORF
Willingen 179
Wassenberg 179
Dormagen 172
Bergisch-Gladbach 169
Attendorn 168
Winterberg 179
Schmallenberg 178
Spangenberg 178
Bergneustadt 169
KÖLN (Cologne)
Heiligenhaus 175
Bad Laasphe-Glashütte 168
Stolberg 178
BONN 170 - 171
Bad Hersfeld 168
Hamm/Sieg 173
Biebertal-Königsberg 171
Bad Neuenahr-Heppingen 168
Monschau 176 - 177
Lich-Kloster Arnsburg 175
Højer
Tønder
Tinglev
Kruså
Gråsten
Niebüll
Leck
Flensburg
Ockholm-Bongsiel
Kappeln
Halligen
Pellworm
Husum
Schleswig
Nordstrand
Sankt Peter-Ording
Rendsburg
Helgoland
Büsum-Deichhausen
Heide
Trischen
Neumünster
Scharhörn
Neuwerk
Itzehoe
Norderney
Langeoog
Wangerooge
Cuxhaven
Elbe
Juist
Spiekeroog
Mellum
Borkum
Wittmund
Eemshaven
Krummhorn-Greetsiel
Bremerhaven
Stade
Aurich
Nordenham
Emden
Varel
Seevetal
Grijpskerk
Delfzijl
Ems
GRONINGEN
Tostedt
Salzhausen
Leer
Drachten
Veendam
Oldenburg
Weser
Scheessel
Gieten
Papenburg
Delmenhorst
Rotenburg
Ganderkesee
Soltau
Beilen
Syke
Verden
Cloppenburg
Bassum
Meppel
Emmen
Meppen
Twistringen
Aller
Sulingen
G
Haselünne
Dalfsen
Hardenberg
Nienburg
ZWOLLE
Diepholz
Lingen
Neustadt am Rübenberge
IJssel
Raalte
Almelo
Nordhorn
Bramsche
Garbsen
Deventer
Rheine
Osnabrück
Minden
Haaksbergen
Bückeburg
Zutphen
Melle
Bünde
Springe
Ahaus
Herford
Bad Oeynhausen
Doesburg
Hameln
Bielefeld
Gütersloh
Kleve
Rhein
Einbeck
Hamm
Paderborn
Lippstadt
Lünen
Bochum
Soest
Warburg
Venlo
Mülheim
Schwerte
Menden
Arolsen
Münden
Meschede
Korbach
Kassel
Baunatal
Kaufungen
Erkelenz
Leverkusen
Elspe
Frankenberg
Bergheim
Herleshausen
Kreuztal
Aachen
Kerpen
Siegen
Stadtallendorf
Troisdorf
Wilnsdorf
Marburg an der Lahn
Alsfeld
Rheinbach
Mechernich
Herborn
Lauterbach
Hünfeld
Giessen
Fulda
Blankenheim
Neuwied
A1
A2
A3
A4
A5
A7
A23
A27
A28
A29
A30
A31
A44
A45
A57
A210
54
213
252

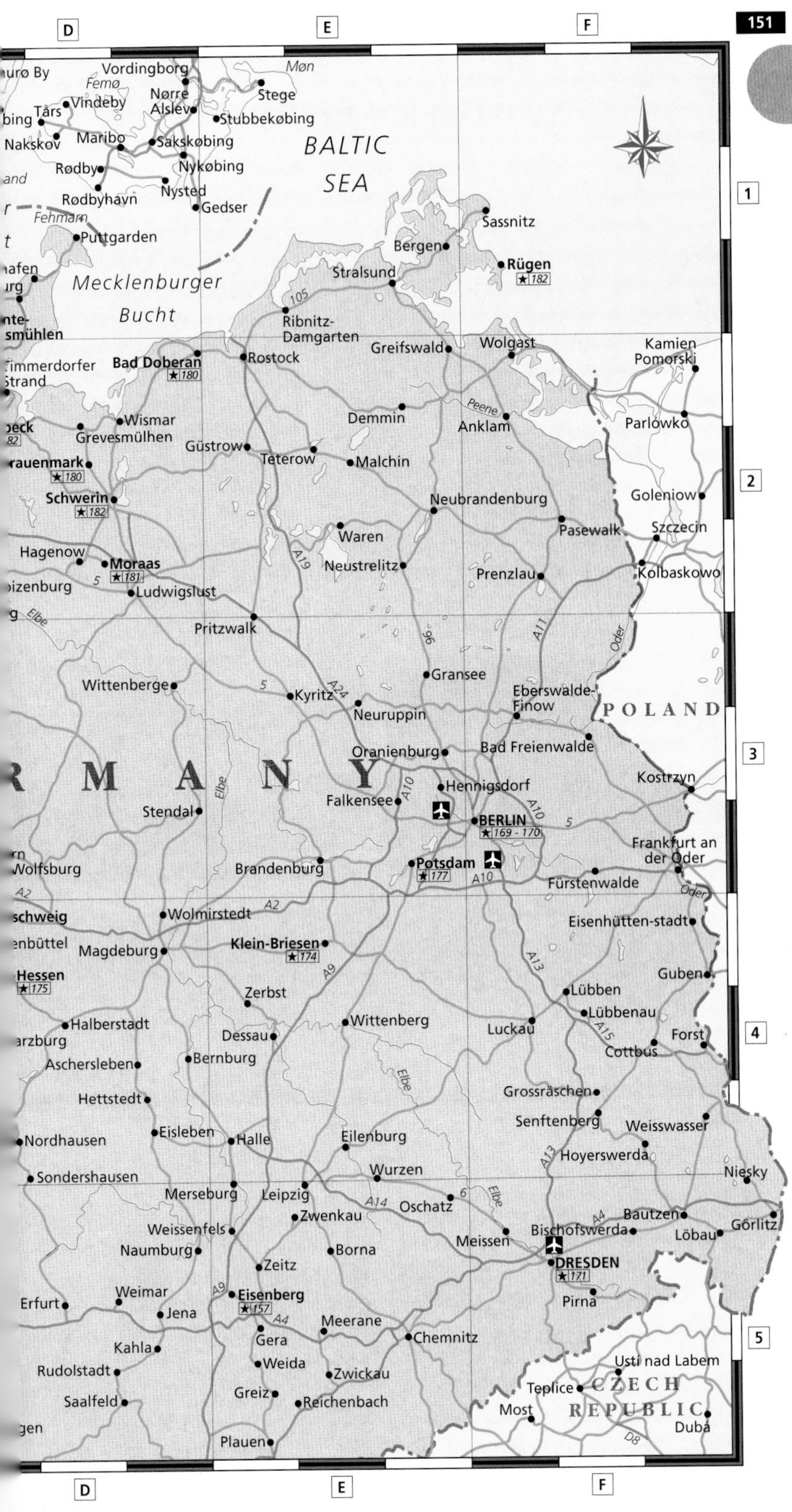
D
E
F
1
2
3
4
5
BALTIC
SEA
Møn
Vordingborg
Femø
Nørre
Alslev
Stege
Vindeby
Tårs
Stubbekøbing
Nakskov
Maribo
Sakskøbing
Nykøbing
Rødby
Rødbyhavn
Nysted
Gedser
Fehmarn
Puttgarden
Mecklenburger
Bucht
Sassnitz
Bergen
Rügen
★182
Stralsund
105
Ribnitz-
Damgarten
Greifswald
Wolgast
Kamien
Pomorski
Bad Doberan
★180
Rostock
Timmerdorfer
Strand
Demmin
Peene
Anklam
Parlowko
Wismar
Grevesmülhen
Güstrow
Teterow
Malchin
★180
Schwerin
★182
Neubrandenburg
Goleniow
Pasewalk
Szczecin
Waren
Hagenow
Moraas
★181
A19
Neustrelitz
Prenzlau
Kolbaskowo
5
Ludwigslust
Elbe
Pritzwalk
A11
Oder
96
Gransee
Wittenberge
5
Kyritz
A24
Neuruppin
Eberswalde-
Finow
POLAND
Oranienburg
Bad Freienwalde
M
A
N
Y
Kostrzyn
Hennigsdorf
Elbe
Falkensee
A10
A10
Stendal
BERLIN
★169 - 170
5
Frankfurt an
der Oder
Wolfsburg
Brandenburg
Potsdam
★177
A10
Fürstenwalde
A2
Oder
Wolmirstedt
A2
Eisenhütten-stadt
Klein-Briesen
★174
Magdeburg
Hessen
★175
A13
A9
Guben
Zerbst
Lübben
Lübbenau
Halberstadt
Wittenberg
Luckau
A15
Forst
Dessau
Cottbus
Aschersleben
Bernburg
Elbe
Hettstedt
Grossräschen
Senftenberg
Weisswasser
Eisleben
Nordhausen
Halle
Eilenburg
Hoyerswerda
A13
Sondershausen
Wurzen
Niesky
Merseburg
Leipzig
6
Elbe
A14
Oschatz
A4
Bautzen
Zwenkau
Weissenfels
Bischofswerda
Görlitz
Meissen
Löbau
Naumburg
Borna
Zeitz
DRESDEN
★171
Weimar
A9
Eisenberg
★157
Erfurt
Jena
Pirna
A4
Meerane
Gera
Chemnitz
Kahla
Usti nad Labem
Weida
Rudolstadt
Zwickau
Teplice
CZECH
Greiz
REPUBLIC
Saalfeld
Reichenbach
Most
Dubá
D8
Plauen

Southern Germany

Northern Bavaria • Southern Bavaria
Baden-Württemberg and the Black Forest

For many visitors, Southern Germany is a microcosm of the whole country, with its stereotypical brass bands, beer halls and locals clad in Lederhosen. *The whole region brims with good-quality hotels and represents Germany at its most picturesque. Choose between the wooded hills and tranquil valleys of the Black Forest to the west, with its smart spa hotels and* Gasthöfe *(guesthouses) that could have come straight from a picture postcard, and Bavaria's lush rolling countryside and snow-capped Alps, dotted with half-timbered inns, rustic* Landhäuser *(farmhouses) and chalet-style hostelries – not forgetting the converted castles and top-notch townhouse hotels of some of Germany's most majestic cities.*

Amorbach

Der Schafhof The red sandstone house, surrounded by meadows, is a perfect retreat. It feels virtually self-sufficient, with almost all the food coming from the estate or the local market. There are snug attic bedrooms and slightly grander ones on the first floor. Peaceful terraces, with views over the countryside.
☒ 63916 Amorbach, Schafhof 1. **Map** p148 C2. (09373) 97330. FAX (09373) 4120. @ info@schafhof.de b,l,d. **Rooms** 24. Never. AE, DC, V. €€€

Aschau-im-Chiemgau

Residenz Heinz Winkler This striking red-and-white shuttered 17th-century coaching inn in the picture-perfect village of Aschau is the luxurious domain of award-winning chef Heinz Winkler, who has two Michelin stars to his credit. After dinner, retire to the spacious and elegant bedrooms and ready yourself for breakfast.
☒ 3229 Aschau-im-Chiemgau, Kirchplatz 1. **Map** p149 E4. (08052) 17990. FAX (08052) 179966. @ info@residenz-heinz-winkler.de b,l,d. **Rooms** 32. Never. AE, DC, V. €€€€€

Albstadt-Ebingen

Linde Under new ownership and recently modernized, this 17th-century townhouse still takes its gastronomic reputation very seriously.
☒ 72458 Albstadt-Ebingen, Untere Vorstadt 1. **Map** p148 C4. (07431) 134140. FAX (07431) 13414300. @ info@hotel-linde-albstadt.de b, l, d. **Rooms** 39. €€€

Altenkunstadt

Gondel The Jahn family have run this cheerful white-and-timber village inn for some hundred years. Neat, unassuming bedrooms.
☒ 96264 Altenkunstadt, Markplatz 7. **Map** p148 D1. (09572) 3661. FAX (09572) 4596. b. **Rooms** 40. €€

Ansbach

Bürger Palais Lavishly renovated baroque townhouse hotel: chandeliers, silk furnishings, marble-tiled bathrooms. Garden and terrace.
☒ 91522 Ansbach, Neustadt 48. **Map** p149 D2. (0981) 95131. FAX (0981) 95600. @ info@hotel-buerger-palais.de b. **Rooms** 12. €€€

Asperg

Adler Town hotel with a clever mixture of old and new: the original half-timbered building is yoked to a glossy modern extension. Indoor pool.
☒ 71679 Asperg, Stuttgarter Str. 2. **Map** p148 C3. (07141) 26600. FAX (07141) 266060 @ info@adler-asperg.de b,l,d. **Rooms** 70. €€€

Aying

Brauereigasthof Hotel Aying The village is famous for its Bavarian beer, and this vine-smothered inn is right next door to the brewery. Its beer garden and halls are the perfect place to sample the local brew from the huge choice on offer. Inside are rooms large enough to host banquets, as well as intimate dining rooms. The bedrooms are spacious and well appointed.
☒ 85653 Aying, Zornedingerstr. 2. **Map** p149 E4.
(08095) 90650. FAX (08095) 906566. b,l,d.
Rooms 34. 23, 24 Dec. AE, DC, V. €€€

Bad Neustadt

Kur- & Schlosshotel Indulge yourself at modest cost at this little 18th-century baroque castle, set in a popular spa town. Public rooms include two glorious dining rooms, serving 'anti-stress' food, and a comfy bar. Bedrooms are large and bright, furnished with silks, and have gleaming, marble-lined bathrooms.
☒ 97616 Bad Neustadt an der Saale, Kurhausstr. 37.
Map p149 D1. (09771) 61610. FAX (09771) 2533.
b,l,d. **Rooms** 13. Never.
AE, MC, V. €€

Bad Aibling

Romantik Hotel Lindner A stylish exterior of yellow-washed walls and smart striped shutters hints at the building's thousand-year history. Inside, the association continues, with vaulted ceilings, crystal chandeliers and oil paintings. But the spacious bedrooms are up to date; some are across the courtyard in a modern annexe.
☒ 83043 Bad Aibling, Marienplatz 5. **Map** p149 E4.
(08061) 90630. FAX (08061) 30535.
@ lindner@romantikhotels.com b,l,d. **Rooms** 26.
Never. AE, DC, MC, V. €€€

Bad Neustadt

Schwan & Post This bustling hotel is set by Bad Neustadt's old town gate, an area of narrow cobbled streets and inviting little shops. Outside is a tiny, tree-shaded terrace; inside, a dining room and vaulted cellar bar. A grand staircase leads to the older bedrooms, others are in an annexe. Sauna, fitness room and whirlpool complex add to the attractions.
☒ 97616 Bad Neustadt, Hohnstr. 35. **Map** p149 D1.
(09771) 91070. FAX (09771) 910767. b,l,d.
Rooms 31. Never. AE, V. €€€

Bad Kissingen

Laudensacks Parkhotel Elegant townhouse spa hotel. First-rate food. Sophisticated modern design. Surrounded by beautiful gardens.
☒ 97688 Bad Kissingen, Kurhausstr. 28. **Map** p149 D1.
(0971) 72240. FAX (0971) 722444. @ laudensacks-parkhotel@t-online.de b,l,d. **Rooms** 21. €€€

Baden-Baden

Am Markt Simple hotel on cobbled square in the old town. Good sightseeing base.
☒ 76530 Baden-Baden, Marktplatz 18. **Map** p148 B3.
(07221) 27040. FAX (07221) 270444.
@ hotel.am.markt.bad@t-online.de b.
Rooms 25. €€

Badenweiler

Villa Schlössle A neat villa houses a guesthouse with a personal touch and cosy bedrooms. Pretty terrace, garden; swimming pool.
☒ 79410 Badenweiler, Kanderner Str. 4. **Map** p148 B4.
(07632) 240. FAX (07632) 828233.
@ villa.schloessle@web.de b. **Rooms** 14. €€

Badenweiler

Villa Hedwig Recently converted to apartments. Peaceful atmosphere in design-conscious setting.
☒ 79410 Badenweiler, Römerstr. 10. **Map** p148 B4.
(07632) 82000. FAX (07632) 820031.
@ info@villa-hedwig.de None.
Rooms 8 apartments. €€€

For key to symbols see backflap. For price categories *see p147*

Bad Tölz

Altes Fährhaus The old ferry boathouse on the river Isar, which separates the old town of Bad Tölz from the spa town, makes an attractive location for this smart restaurant with rooms. Breakfasts with parma ham and marinated salmon are a highlight. The bedrooms all have balconies over the river.

83646 Bad Tölz, An der Isarlust 1. **Map** p149 E4. (08041) 6030. FAX (08041) 72270. @ info@altes-faehrhaus-toelz.de b,l,d. **Rooms** 5. 1 week Feb, 1 week Nov. Not accepted. €€

Baden-Baden

Belle Epoque This grand hotel set in its own parkland is housed in the former mansion of Duke Ferdinand von Lotzbeck, a 19th-century entrepeneur with a taste for the high life. Lunch and dinner are served next door in the restaurant of Der Kleine Prinz (see below), the Belle Epoque's sister hotel.

76530 Baden-Baden, Maria-Viktoria-Str. 2c. **Map** p148 B3. (07221) 300660. FAX (07221) 300666. @ info@hotel-belle-epoque.de b,l,d. **Rooms** 16. Never. AE, MC, V. €€€€

Baden-Baden

Bad Hotel Zum Hirsch The cheerful Hirsch is in the pedestrianized centre of this busy spa town, offering plenty of opportunity for people-watching. The delightful bedrooms – some with balconies – are spacious and beautifully furnished with antiques. Taps in the bathrooms are connected to Baden-Baden's famous thermal water.

76530 Baden-Baden, Hirschstrasse 1. **Map** p148 B3. (07221) 9390. FAX (07221) 38148. @ zum-hirsch@steigenberger.de b,d. **Rooms** 58. Never. AE, DC, MC, V. €€€

Baden-Baden

Der Kleine Prinz An elegant, central hotel, close to the public gardens, the baths and the festival house. A solid, unremarkable exterior hides an extremely individual interior. Each of the stylish bedrooms has its own feature, be it a fireplace, a balcony or even a whirlpool. The restaurant serves French and regional cuisine.

76530 Baden-Baden, Lichtentaler Str. 36. **Map** p148 B3. (07221) 346600. FAX (07221) 38264. @ info@derkleineprinz.de b,l,d. **Rooms** 40. Never. AE, MC, V. €€€

Baiersbronn-Mitteltal

Lamm Traditional country hotel with massive wooden beams and arches aplenty. Bedrooms have beautiful views. Pets allowed.

72270 Baiersbronn-Mitteltal. **Map** p148 B3. (07442) 4980. FAX (07442) 49878. @ info@lamm.mitteltal.de b,l,d. **Rooms** 46. €€€

Binzen

Mühle Old mill done up with lush fabrics and pretty antiques; well-designed rooms, good food.

79589 Binzen, Mühlenstr. 26. **Map** p148 B4. (07621) 6072. FAX (07621) 65808. @ Hotel.Muehle.Binzen@t-online.de b,l,d. **Rooms** 20. €€

Blaufelden

Gasthof zum Hirschen Glossy country inn, relentlessly modernized throughout. Enjoy the hearty regional cooking.

74572 Blaufelden, Haupstr. 15. **Map** p149 D2. (07953) 1041. FAX (07953) 1043. @ info@hirschen-blaufelden.de b,l,d. **Rooms** 12. €€

Bühl

Grüne Bettlad In the centre of the Black Forest town, an ancient building housing a French-influenced restaurant with romantic rooms.

77815 Bühl, Blumenstr. 4. **Map** p148 B3. (07223) 93130. FAX (07223) 931310. @ gruene.bettlad@t-online.de b,l,d. **Rooms** 6. €€

Badenweiler

Sonne You are guaranteed a warm welcome at this pretty hotel in the centre of a small spa town. The new owners run this place with great thought for detail – there are fresh flowers everywhere and it is sparklingly clean. The bedrooms are comfortable; some have chic modern bathrooms.

☒ 79405 Badenweiler, Moltkestr. 4. **Map** p148 B4. (07632) 75080. FAX (07632) 750865. @ hotel@zur-sonne.de b,l,d. **Rooms** 41. Never. AE, DC, MC, V. €€€

Bamberg

Romantik Hotel Messerschmitt A wine-house began trading on this spot in the 15th century. It was transformed into a restaurant in 1832 and has remained in the same family ever since. Tiled floors and polished wood predominate. Eel and sage is one of the regional specialities served in the restaurant. The Gothic cathedral is close by.

☒ 96047 Bamberg, Lange Str. 41. **Map** p149 D2. (0951) 297800. FAX (0951) 2978029. @ hotel-messerschmitt@t-online.de b,l,d. **Rooms** 19. 12-19 Jan. AE, DC, MC, V. €€€

Bamberg

Barock Hotel am Dom An ornate Baroque façade envelops this tidy little hotel in the centre of the old town. Inside are unfussy, modern rooms, impeccably kept by a team of friendly staff. Sympathetic modernization has retained the ancient vaulted breakfast room. Breakfast is a hearty affair. The hotel has its own parking spaces outside – unusual in this busy town.

☒ 96049 Bamberg, Vorderer Bach 4. **Map** p149 D2. (0951) 54031. FAX (0951) 54021. b. **Rooms** 19. Christmas, Feb. AE, DC, V. €€

Bayreuth

Jagdschloss Thiergarten Despite its proximity to the motorway, this late-Baroque hunting lodge just 6km (4 miles) from Bayreuth is a wonderfully peaceful place. The impressive public rooms have huge oil paintings, sparkling chandeliers and stucco walls by Domenico Caddenazi. Most of the spacious bedrooms have rural views.

☒ 95448 Bayreuth, Oberthiergärtner Str. 36. **Map** p149 E2. (09209) 9840. FAX (09209) 98429. @ schlosshotel-thiergarten@t-online.de b,l,d. **Rooms** 8. Never. AE, MC, V. €€€

Bühl

Plättig Large, late-18th-century building in beautiful country, with elegant furnishings. Pretty terrace, garden and indoor swimming pool.

☒ 77815 Bühl/Baden. **Map** p148 B3. (07226) 530. FAX (07226) 53444. @ plaettig@t-online.de b,l,d. **Rooms** 57. €€€

Burghausen

Klostergasthof Raitenhaslach The extremely popular, large vaulted dining rooms ensure a lively atmosphere at this former monastery.

☒ 84489 Burghausen, Raitenhaslach 9. **Map** p149 F4. (08677) 91300. FAX (08677) 63126. b,l,d. **Rooms** 14. €€

Bühl

Springmann Badischer Hoff A waterside terrace draws diners to this attractive 17th-century house. Modern bedrooms.

☒ 77815 Buhl, Haupstr. 36. **Map** p148 B3. (07223) 93350. FAX (07223) 933550. @ springmannbadischerhof@t-online.de b,l,d. **Rooms** 24. €€

Büsingen

Alte Rheinmühle Set right on the banks of the Rhine, a beautifully converted old mill. Prior booking essential.

☒ 78266 Büsingen, Junkerstr. 93. **Map** p148 C4. (07734) 93190. FAX (07734) 931926. b,l,d. **Rooms** 14. €€

BAYRISCHZELL

Postgasthof Rote Wand This plain but welcoming village inn has a glorious location – a valley surrounded by Alps – and caring service. It has a large terrace, and is very popular with hikers and skiers who appreciate the hearty food. The kitchen closes at 10pm. There are no TVs in the rooms. Children and dogs welcome.
83735 Bayrischzell, Geitau 15.
Map p149 E4. (08023) 9050. FAX (08023) 656.
@ info@gasthofrotewand.de b,l,d. **Rooms** 30.
mid-Nov to mid-Dec. AE, DC, MC, V. €€

DURBACH

Ritter An extremely well-run hotel in the centre of the little wine town of Durbach. It has been carefully decorated to keep its country style, but with luxurious touches too. Bedrooms in the main house are traditional, but there are also some modern apartments with their own terraces. The restaurant is Michelin-starred.
77770 Durbach, Talstr. 1. **Map** p148 B3.
(0781) 93230. FAX (0781) 9323100.
@ ritter-durbach@t-online.de b,l,d. **Rooms** 40.
3 weeks in Jan. AE, V. €€

COLMBERG

Burg Colmberg The massive castle comes complete with stone staircases, a private chapel and huge beamed rooms with open fires. The bedrooms are magnificent, with vast carved wooden beds (some four-posters) and beautiful furniture. Some of the rooms have stunning views. Children are welcome. Golf course.
91598 Colmberg, Burg 1-3. **Map** p149 D2.
(09803) 91920. FAX (09803) 262. @ info@burg-colmberg.de b,l,d. **Rooms** 26. Feb.
AE, MC, V. €€

EICHSTÄTT

Adler A 300-year-old building with a wonderful baroque exterior, set right on the town marketplace. Inside it has been completely modernized to make a thoroughly pleasant and modern hotel. The bedrooms are large and plainly decorated. There are two dining rooms. Good buffet breakfast.
85072 Eichstätt, Marktplatz 22. **Map** p149 D3.
(08421) 6767. FAX (08421) 8283. b,l,d.
Rooms 38. first week Nov, mid-Dec to mid-Jan.
AE, DC, MC, V. €€

DIETMANNSRIED/PROBSTRIED

Landhaus Henze Chalet hotel and restaurant with large, well-designed bedrooms. Book ahead for the restaurants – one formal, one rustic.
87463 Dietmannsried/Probstried, Wohlmutser Weg 2.
Map p149 D4. (08374) 58320. FAX (08374) 583222.
@ pia@landhaus-henze.de b,l,d. **Rooms** 9. €€

DINKELSBÜHL

Deutsches Haus The welcoming ancient town inn is crammed full with wall paintings, painted ceilings and doors, and antique furniture.
91550 Dinkelsbühl, Weinmarkt 3. **Map** p148 C3.
(09851) 6058. FAX (09581) 7911. @ deutsches.haus@t-online.de b,l,d. **Rooms** 10. €€€

DINKELSBÜHL

Gasthof zum Goldenen Anker Family-run town inn, a peaceful haven away from the busy streets; traditional public rooms, spacious bedrooms.
91550 Dinkelsbühl, Untere Schmiedgasse 22.
Map p148 C3. (09851) 57800. FAX (09851) 578080.
@ goldener.anker@t-online.de b,l,d. **Rooms** 25. €€

EBERBACH AM NECKAR

Altes Badhaus Town hotel in which traditional beamed bedrooms have been successfully modernized with a touch of high-tech.
69412 Eberbach am Neckar, Am Lindenplatz 1.
Map p148 C2. (06271) 92300. FAX (06271) 923040.
@ info@altes.badhaus.de b,l,d. **Rooms** 7. €€

Eisenberg

Magnushof Not only is this delightful place in a beautiful rural location at the foot of the Alps, but there is also a pool and a fitness room. Inside, the mix of styles is charming. The bedrooms are equipped with books and games. Breakfasts are hearty. The restaurant offers regional food with an excellent wine list. Under new management.
87637 Eisenberg, Unterreuten 51. **Map** p149 E1, p151 E5. (08363) 91120. FAX (08363) 911250. @ magnushof@t-online.de b,l,d. **Rooms** 9. Nov. MC, V. €€

Feuchtwangen

Hotel Greifen-Post Great sensitivity has been shown in renovating this ancient marketplace inn. Look for the lovely frescoes in one of the four dining rooms. Each bedroom is different, some furnished in Laura Ashley, others in Biedermeier; some have four-poster beds. Superb swimming pool in the old stables.
91555 Feuchtwangen, Markplatz 8. **Map** p149 D3. (09852) 6800. FAX (09852) 68068. @ greifen@romantik.de b,l,d. **Rooms** 35. Never. AE, MC, V. €€

Erlangen-Frauenaurach

Schwarzer Adler The industrial town of Erlangen is close by yet this feels a million miles away. The old inn is truly rustic, but beautifully and unfussily decorated. Each delightful bedroom is named after a bird and has both lovely old furniture and all the modern conveniences.
91056 Erlangen-Frauenaurach, Herdegenpl 1. **Map** p149 D2. (09131) 992051. FAX (09131) 993195. @ schwarzeradler-frauenaurach@web.de b,d. **Rooms** 14. Easter, second half Aug, Christmas. AE, DC, MC, V. €€

Friedrichsruhe

Wald & Schlosshotel Friedrichsruhe This elegant and rather formal hotel is home to one of the best chefs in Germany, Lothar Eiermann. The lavishly furnished dining room does justice to the menu. The bedrooms, in four buildings set in 3 hectares of parkland, are appropriately luxurious and tranquil.
74639 Friedrichsruhe. **Map** p148 C2. (07941) 60870. FAX (07941) 61468. @ hotel@friedrichsruhe.de b,l,d. **Rooms** 43. Never. AE, DC, V. €€€€

Ehrenkirchen

Hotel Restaurant Krone Inspiring regional wine tastings and well-prepared food mark out this whitewashed country inn.
79238 Ehrenkirchen, Herrenstr. 5. **Map** p148 B4. (07633) 5213. FAX (07633) 83550. @ info@gasthaus-krone.de b,l,d. **Rooms** 8. €

Eschau-Hobbach

Gasthof Engel This 200-year-old country inn is tucked away on the edge of the Spessart nature reserve. Modern bedroom extension.
63863 Eschau-Hobbach, Bayernstrasse 47. **Map** p148 C2. (09374) 388. FAX (09374) 7831. @ 060927326@t-online.de b,l,d. **Rooms** 25. €€

Frasdorf

Landgasthof Karner Extremely popular and stylish country hotel, with a wonderful garden terrace. The restaurant is Michelin-starred.
83112 Frasdorf, Nussbaumstr. 6. **Map** p149 E4. (08052) 4071. FAX (08052) 4711. @ info@landgasthof-karner.de b,l,d. **Rooms** 26. €€€

Freiburg im Breisgau

Zum Roten Bären In the centre of the old town, this has been a hostellery since the early 12th century. Cleverly modernized inside.
79098 Freiburg im Breisgau, Oberlinden 12. **Map** p148 B4. (0761) 387870. FAX (0761) 3878717. @ info@roter-baeren.de b,l,d. **Rooms** 25. €€€

Glottertal

Gasthaus zum Adler Home-made black pudding is one of the highlights of the unusual menu offered at this guesthouse, set in a tranquil valley in the south of the Black Forest. There is also a menu for child gourmets. The decor is simple and unfussy, and the bedrooms full of colour and character. Home-made schnapps is also on offer.
79286 Glottertal, Talstr 11. **Map** p148 B4.
(07684) 90870. FAX (07684) 908766.
@ adler.glottertal@t-online.de b,l,d. **Rooms** 13.
24 Dec. AE, MC, V. €€

Grossbottwar

Stadtschänke Grossbottwar, in the Württenberg wine-growing area, is an old town of cobbled streets. This 15th-century building is in keeping with its half-timbered neighbours on the marketplace; timbered rooms with rustic furniture retain a medieval atmosphere. The five bedrooms are cosy and carefully decorated. The menu is strong on fish; wine tastings are encouraged.
71723 Grossbottwar, Hauptstr 36. **Map** p148 C3.
(07148) 8024. FAX (07148) 4877. b,l,d. **Rooms** 5.
first 2 weeks Sept. AE, DC, MC, V. €€

Grainau

Alpenhof This modern chalet hotel stands out for its restrained use of traditional styles, with muted fabrics and antique furnishings softening the large, white-painted rooms. The indoor pool looks out onto the lush garden, where theme evenings are held in summer. The mountain train to the Zugspitze peak passes through the village.
82491 Grainau, Alpspitzstr 34. **Map** p149 D4.
(08821) 9870. FAX (08821) 98777.
@ alpenhof-grainau@t-online.de b,l,d. **Rooms** 36.
Never. DC, MC, V. €€€

Grünwald

Alter Wirt This friendly and welcoming place is handily located just off the road into Munich, and offers larger, brighter rooms than many city-centre hotels. It has a particularly pretty terrace, canopied by trees, where snacks and drinks are served, and a pleasant garden. Some of the public rooms are wood-panelled.
82031 Grünwald, Marktpl 1. **Map** p149 E4.
(089) 641 9340. FAX (089) 641 93499.
@ info@alterwirt.de b,l,d. **Rooms** 52.
24 Dec. AE, MC, V. €€€

Freilassing

Gasthof Moosleitner Elegantly simple furnishings enhance the atmosphere of this country hotel, set in an 800-year-old building.
83395 Freilassing, Wasserburger Str. 52.
Map p149 F4. (08654) 63060. FAX (08654) 630699.
@ info@moosleitner.com b,l,d. **Rooms** 50. €€

Freudenstadt

Langenwaldsee A large pool, small lake and vast forest attract sporty types to this country hotel just outside of town. Bedrooms are modern.
72250 Freudenstadt, Strassburger Str. 99. **Map** p148 B3.
(07441) 88930. FAX (07441) 88936. @ langenwaldsee@t-online.de b,l,d. **Rooms** 35. €€

Gaggenau-Moosbronn

Mönchhof This 18th-century half-timbered house makes a smart yet cosy country hotel retaining beams, tiled floors and rustic furniture.
76571 Gaggenau-Moosbronn. **Map** p148 B3.
(07204) 619. FAX (07204) 1256. @ ice-line@t-online.de
b, d. **Rooms** 20. €€

Garmisch-Partenkirchen

Garmischer Hof A chic chalet hotel in the centre of town, with stunning views of the Alps from the delightful garden.
82467 Garmisch-Partenkirchen, Chamonixstr 10.
Map p149 D4. (08821) 9110. FAX (08821) 51440.
@ hotel@garmischer-hof.de b,l,d. **Rooms** 54. €€€

Häusern

Adler Modern, Michelin-starred cuisine is one of the highlights of this village hotel. The place has been beautifully spruced up, with mellow wood panelling and deeply coloured rugs on the tiled floors. The modern bedrooms have handsome furniture; many have balconies.
79838 Häusern, Fridolin Str 15. **Map** p148 B4. (07672) 4170. FAX (07672) 417150. hotel-adler-schwarzwald@t-online.de b,l,d. **Rooms** 47. mid-Nov to mid-Dec. DC, MC, V. €€€

Hinterzarten

Sassenhof This welcoming hotel on the green of the little Black Forest resort village of Hinterzarten is pleasantly furnished in a more sophisticated way than is usual in this rural area. Bedrooms differ in size – those in the attic can be small. The breakfasts are hearty and delicious. No restaurant. Swimming pool and whirlpool.
79856 Hinterzarten, Adlerweg 17. **Map** p148 B4. (07652) 1515. FAX (07652) 484. sassenhof@t-online.de b. **Rooms** 20. Nov. AE, MC, V. €€

Heidelberg

Hirschgasse This city hotel is a real gem. Mark Twain once stayed here. Each of the charming suites is different – the Chinoiserie suite has lacquered walls and Chinese lamps – and has a lavish bathroom to match. The cosy 'Le Gourmet' restaurant lives up to its name; if you want to get in, booking is essential.
69120 Heidelberg, Hirschgasse 3. **Map** p148 C2. (06221) 4540. FAX (06221) 454111. hirschgasse@compuserve.com b,d. **Rooms** 20 suites. Never. AE, DC, MC, V. €€€€

Hohenau

Parkhotel Bierhütte Both the hearty food and the rural seclusion (close to the Czech border) attract visitors to this informal village hotel. Terrace tables overlook the hotel pond; inside, the stylish *Stube* has a marvellous painted ceiling. Traditional rooms in the main building and a chalet annexe; ultra-modern in a third house.
94545 Hohenau, Bierhütte 10. **Map** p149 F3. (08558) 96120. FAX (08558) 961270. info@bierhuette.de b,l,d. **Rooms** 43. Never. AE, DC, V. €€

Garmisch-Partenkirchen

Posthotel Partenkirch A beautifully maintained 16th-century coaching inn, with rich wood panelling in some bedrooms. Five restaurants.
82467 Garmisch-Partenkirchen, Ludwigstrasse 49. **Map** p149 D4. (08821) 93630. FAX (08821) 93632222. info@privathotel.net b,l,d. **Rooms** 59. €€€

Gunzenhausen

Zur Post Modern hotel in an old post-house. Guests lounge in panelled public rooms. Well-presented, ambitious cooking.
91710 Gunzenhausen, Bahnhofstr. 7. **Map** p149 D3. (09831) 67470. FAX (09831) 6747222. info@ hotel zurpost-gunzenhausen.de b,l,d. **Rooms** 26. €€

Hagnau am Bodensee

Villa am See Tiny, immaculately clean hotel with a personal touch, right on the shores of Lake Constance. Verandas, garden, swimming.
88709 Hagnau am Bodensee. **Map** p148 C4. (07532) 43130. FAX (07532) 6997. erbguth@villa-am-see.de b. **Rooms** 9. €€€

Hagnau am Bodensee

Der Löwen This 17th-century house has a private lake foreshore a few minutes away. Bright rooms.
88709 Hagnau am Bodensee, Hansjakobstr. 2. **Map** p148 C4. (07532) 433980. FAX (07532) 43398300. loewen-hagnau@t-online.de b,d. **Rooms** 17. €€

For key to symbols see backflap. For price categories *see p147*

INZELL

Sport und Wellness Hotel 'Zur Post' This traditional Bavarian hotel is located in the middle of the village, by the church, and is a popular place. The public rooms are welcoming and elegant, the bedrooms spacious and rather luxurious. There are health and sporting activities on offer, and the swimming pool is terrific.
83334 Inzell, Reichenhaller Str. 2. **Map** p149 E4.
(08665) 985140. FAX (08665) 985100.
@ kontakt@post-inzell.de b,l,d. **Rooms** 60.
First 3 weeks Dec. V. €€€

KAUFBEUREN

Goldener Hirsch The 17th-century house is Kaufbeuren's main hotel, and has been sensitively modernized to retain some old features. It makes an ideal base for visiting the famous castles built by King Ludwig II – all under an hour's drive away. The public rooms are light and airy and the bedrooms plainly but comfortably furnished.
87600 Kaufbeuren, Kasier-Max Str. 39-41.
Map p149 D4. (08341) 43030. FAX (08341) 430375.
@ info@goldener-hirsch-kaufbeuren.de b,l,d.
Rooms 42. Never. V. €€

KAISERSBACH

Schassberger's Ebnisee This thriving complex of chalet-type buildings by the Ebnisee offers plenty of opportunities for leisure activities. Swimming, tennis, squash, lakeside and rural walks, fishing, boating and cycling are all available. What with two restaurants (creative-classic and regional), some visitors never leave the grounds.
73667 Kaisersbach, Ebnisee, Winnenderstr. 10. **Map** p148 C3. (07184) 2920. FAX (07184) 292204.
@ reservation@schassbergers.de b,l,d. **Rooms** 47.
Never. V. €€€

KONSTANZ

Seehotel Siber Chef Berthold Siber opened his 19th-century lakeside villa as a hotel and restaurant in 1984; both his gourmet cooking and the accommodation are highly regarded. The best of the restrained bedrooms have lake views, as does the dining room terrace. The casino is next door, central Konstanz a short walk away.
78464 Konstanz, Seestr 25. **Map** p148 C4.
(07531) 63044. FAX (07531) 99669933
@ seehotel.siber@t-online.de b,l,d. **Rooms** 12.
1 week Feb. AE, DC, MC, V. €€€€

HASSMERSHEIM-HOCHHAUSEN

Schloss Hochhausen Manor house hotel set within a deer park. Lots of open fires; spacious Biedemeier-furnished bedrooms. Meals feature meat and vegetables from the park and garden.
74855 Hassmersheim-Hochhausen. **Map** p148 C2.
(06261) 893142. b,l,d. **Rooms** 26. €€

HEIDELBERG

Perkeo A good base for sight-seeing, bang in the middle of Heidelberg's old town. Cheery atmosphere, helpful staff, competitively priced.
69117 Heidelberg, Hauptstrasse 75. **Map** p148 C2.
(06221) 14130. FAX (06221) 141337. @ perkeo@hotels-in-heidelberg.de b. **Rooms** 24. €€€

HINTERZARTEN

Reppert Family-run country hotel with lake, wood and meadow backdrop. Smart bedrooms. Health treatments. Thermal baths.
79856 Hinterzarten, Adlerweg 21-23.
Map p148 B4. (07652) 12080. FAX (07652) 120811.
@ hotel@reppert.de b,l,d. **Rooms** 43. €€€€

HIRSCHEGG-KLEINWALSERTAL

Walserhof Country hotel. Respectable sports facilities. Built on a hillside, with views across the beautiful Kleinwalsertal.
87568 Hirschegg, Walserstr. 11. **Map** p149 D4.
(08329) 5684. FAX (08329) 5938. @ walserhof@ron.rt
b,l,d. **Rooms** 35. €€€€

Landshut

Romantik Hotel Fürstenhof The care and attention lavished on this establishment more than makes up for its unremarkable location on the outskirts of Landshut. The owner's flair for decor is apparent, from the stylish dining rooms and sitting room to the tasteful bedrooms. Food in the three dining rooms is modern German.
84034 Landshut, Stethaimer Str. 3. **Map** p149 E3.
(0871) 92550. FAX (0871) 925544.
@ fuerstenhof@romantikhotels.com b,l,d. **Rooms** 24.
Never. AE, V. €€€

Miltenberg

Jagd Hotel Rose The exterior of this town inn is marvellously welcoming, with stripy red and white shutters and wisteria dripping over the entrance. It is attractive inside, too: plain but cosy bedrooms and unfussy public rooms, all with a light airy atmosphere, with natural woods and tiled floors. There is an attractive terrace.
63897 Miltenberg, Hauptstr 280. **Map** p148 C2.
(09371) 40060. FAX (09371) 400617.
@ jagd-hotel-rose@t-online.de b,l,d.
Rooms 23. 24 Dec. AE, V. €€

Meersburg

Zum Bären This is all you could want of an inn in a lakeside town like old Meersburg. It's on the marketplace, parts of the gabled building date back to 1250, and it's been run by the Gilowsky family for five generations. It's a homely place, with carefully furnished rooms; some are rather grand. Good, simple food.
88709 Meersburg, Marktplatz 11. **Map** p148 C4.
(07532) 43220. FAX (07532) 432244.
@ gasthofzumbaeren@t-online.de b,l,d. **Rooms** 20.
Not accepted. Nov to mid-Mar. €€

Miltenberg

Zum Riesen This small guesthouse – claimed to be the oldest in Germany – is right in the pedestrianized centre of Miltenberg. Proprietor Werner Jöst trained as an architect and has used his skills wisely. Each room has a different style; one has its own roof terrace. Hearty breakfasts are served in a room under the eaves. Separate *Stube* downstairs.
63897 Miltenberg, Haupstr. 97. **Map** p148 C2.
(09371) 3644. b. **Rooms** 14.
mid-Dec to mid-March. DC, MC. €€

Iffeldorf

Landgasthof Osterseen Grand views over the lake from the terraces of this popular chalet hotel, beautifully run by the Link family.
82393 Iffeldorf, Hofmark 9. **Map** p149 D4.
(08856) 92860. FAX (08856) 928645. b,l,d.
Rooms 24. €€

Lindau Island

Lindauer Hof Old building with a contemporary feel, perfectly located above the harbour of the island, with Lake Constance beyond.
88121 Lindau, An der Seepromenade. **Map** p148 C4. (08382) 4064. FAX (08382) 24203. @ info@lindauerhof.de b,l,d. **Rooms** 30. €€€

Lörrach

Villa Elben A tranquil Art Deco town hotel with its own grounds and a galleried reception area. Thoughtfully decorated bedrooms. No restaurant.
79539 Lörrach, Hünerbergweg 26. **Map** p148 B4.
(07621) 2066. FAX (07621) 43280. @ info@villa-elben.de b. **Rooms** 34. €€

Maierhöfen bei Isny

Gasthof zur Grenze Traditional chalet hotel: lots of flowers and murals. Most rooms have balcony views over the hills. Cheerful dining room.
88167 Maierhöfen bei Isny, Schanz 103.
Map p149 D4. (07562) 975510. FAX (07562) 9755129.
@ hotel.zur.grenze@t-online.de b,l,d. **Rooms** 13. €€

For key to symbols see backflap. For price categories *see p147*

Muggendorf

Feiler This solid village building houses spacious rooms above its fine restaurant, which no visitor should pass up. Horst Feiler, whose family have run the establishment for more than 100 years, is a mushroom expert; summer truffles are a highlight of the gourmet menu. The terrace is heavenly. Informal but beautifully run.
91346 Muggendorf, Oberer Markt 4. **Map** p149 D2. (09196) 92950. FAX (09196) 362. @ info@hotel-feiler.de b,l,d. **Rooms** 15. Weekdays from Jan to Easter, 24 Dec. AE, MC, V. €€€

München (Munich)

Insel-Mühle Perfectly situated by the river, this old watermill has been tastefully converted in an elegant Bavarian rustic style. The bedrooms are pretty, the best ones being under the eaves, and the bathrooms are modern. The riverside beer garden makes the most of the hotel's location, and is a popular local meeting place.
80999 München, Von-Kahr-Str 87. **Map** p149 E4. (089) 81010. FAX (089) 8120571. @ insel-muehle@t-online.de b,l,d. **Rooms** 38. Never. DC, MC, V. €€€

München (Munich)

Acanthus Choose your preferred style at this central city hotel: antique furniture and 'English-style' furnishings on the Alba-Rose floor, or a cleaner, more modern look (and cheaper prices) on the Rustikana floors. All are tastefully done out. There is a wide range of tempting buffet dishes for breakfast. 24-hour bar.
80331 München, An der Hauptfeuerwache 14. **Map** p149 E4. (089) 231880. FAX (089) 2607364. @ acanthus@t-online.de b. **Rooms** 36. Christmas. AE, MC, V. €€

München (Munich)

Mandarin Oriental Munich The roof terrace with pool, right in the city centre, gives a hint of what to expect at this large hotel. The place has been carefully furnished with a blend of modern and traditional elements, and cosy public areas include a piano bar. Bedrooms are large and sumptuous, with bathrooms to match.
80331 München, Neuturmstr. 1. **Map** p149 E4. (089) 290980. FAX (089) 222539. @ momuc-reservation@mohg.com b,l,d. **Rooms** 73. Never. AE, DC, MC, V. €€€€

Marktbreit

Loewen A magnificent 15th-century half-timbered building with a high-ceilinged dining room. Some of the bedrooms are fantastic too.
97340 Marktbreit, Marktstr. 8. **Map** p149 D2. (09332) 50540. FAX (09332) 9438. @ info@loewen-marktbreit.de b,l,d. **Rooms** 30. €€

Marktheidenfeld

Anker The modern town hotel is not strong on style but is hospitable, very effficiently run and comfortable. Excellent restaurant.
97828 Marktheidenfeld, Obertorstr. 6. **Map** p148 C2. (09391) 60040. FAX (09391) 60040. @ info@hotel-anker.de b,l,d. **Rooms** 39. €€€

Meersburg

Weinstube Löwen Cheerful old town inn on the marketplace. Snug dining rooms; simple, comfortable bedrooms.
88709 Meersburg, Marktpl. 2. **Map** p148 C4. (07532) 43040. FAX (07532) 430410. @ info@hotel-loewen-meersburg.de b,l,d. **Rooms** 21. €€

München (Munich)

Prinzregent Riverside hotel with marvellous panelling and interesting bedrooms. Sauna.
81675 München, Ismaninger Str. 42-44. **Map** p149 E4. (089) 416050. FAX (089) 41605466. @ rezeption2@prinzregent.de b. **Rooms** 65. €€€€

München (Munich)

Schrenkof This seemingly ordinary town chalet on the southern outskirts of Munich is unexpectedly lavish inside. A great deal of marquetry and paintwork is used throughout, and each room is furnished in a different historical style. The breakfast room is delightful, with a Renaissance tiled stove.

82008 München, Leonhardsweg 6, Unterhaching. **Map** p149 E4. (089) 6100910. FAX (089) 61009150. b,l,d. **Rooms** 25. 20 Dec to 8 Jan. AE, DC, MC, V. €€€

Neckarwestheim

Schlosshotel Liebenstein Impeccably renovated in the 1980s, this 16th-century hilltop castle provides a wonderfully historic atmosphere as well as great comfort. A highlight is the huge vaulted dining room. For snacks and drinks, there is a tavern with a terrace. The large bedrooms are decorated with taste. Golf course.

74382 Neckarwestheim. **Map** p148 C3. (07133) 98990. FAX (07133) 6045. @ info@liebenstein.com b,l,d. **Rooms** 24. 23 Dec to 6 Jan. AE, MC, V. €€€

Münstertal

Romantik Hotel Spielweg Country *gasthof* with a warm heart but no shortage of modern facilities. Low-ceilinged, traditional dining room; bedrooms, some small, some spacious, are in the main building and three adjacent ones. Impressive play areas for children; indoor and outdoor pools. In the same family for five generations.

79244 Münstertal, Spielweg 61. **Map** p148 B4. (07636) 70977. FAX (07636) 70966. @ fuch@spielweg.com b,l,d. **Rooms** 42. Never. AE, DC, MC, V. €€€

Niederstotzingen

Schlosshotel Oberstotzingen It's a manor house rather than a castle, but the 700-year-old building in the flat countryside near the Danube makes a stylish hotel. Food in the elegant vaulted dining room is imaginative, with a regional slant. Bedrooms make good use of bold colour schemes; some of the prettiest are in the tower.

89166 Niederstotzingen, Stettener Str. 35-37. **Map** p149 D3. (07325) 1030. FAX (07325) 10370. @ reserwearung@welawetaschlosshotel.com b,l,d. **Rooms** 17. Never. AE, DC, MC, V. €€€€

München (Munich)

Splendid Traditional, central hotel with large bedrooms. There is no dining room but snacks and drinks are served on the terrace.

80538 München 22, Maximilianstr. 54. **Map** p149 E4. (089) 238080. FAX (089) 23808365. @ splendid-muc@t-online.de b. **Rooms** 30. €€€

Murnau am Staffelsee

Alpenhof Murnau Smart chalet hotel with Alpine views. Extensive health facilities. New gourmet restaurant.

82418 Murnau am Staffelsee, Ramsachstr. 8. **Map** p149 D4. (08841) 4910. FAX (08841) 491100. @ info@alpenhof-murnau.com b,l,d. **Rooms** 77. €€€€

Neckarzimmern

Burg Hornberg This converted castle is also partly a museum, so is bustling with people. Beautiful position above the river Neckar.

74865 Neckarzimmern. **Map** p148 C2. (06261) 92460. FAX (06261) 924644. @ info@burg-hotel-hornberg.com b,l,d. **Rooms** 24. €€€

Nürnberg

Zirbelstube In an enchanting position on the Ludwig canal. Charming bedrooms, attractive terrace and smart dining room.

90455 Nürnberg, Friedrich-Overbeck-Str. 1. **Map** p149 D2. (0911) 998820. FAX (0911) 9988220. @ kunkel.zirbelstube@t-online.de b,l,d. **Rooms** 2. €€€

For key to symbols see backflap. For price categories *see p147*

Oberstaufen

Hotel Löwen This is a spa hotel, with fitness rooms and treatments, but you can ignore all that and enjoy yourself anyway – the food is delicious, the bedrooms vast and stylish, and the indoor pool is stunning. All the bedrooms have balconies with views onto the hills. Choice of two dining rooms, and a long wine list.
87534 Oberstaufen, Kirchplatz 8.
Map p149 D4. (08386) 4940. FAX (08386) 494222.
@ info@lowenoberstaufen.de b,l,d. **Rooms** 30.
Never. MC, V. €€€

Pegnitz

Pflaums Posthotel It looks like a typical inn, with a flower-bedecked exterior; inside it is anything but. Wagner is the theme here, with films of his operas shown in the foyer. The theme recurs in the quirky bedrooms. The taste for the dramatic extends to the ambitious food. Free shuttle bus service to the Bayreuth Festival.
91257 Pegnitz, Nürnbergerstrasse 12-16.
Map p149 E2. (09241) 7250. FAX (09241) 80404.
@ info@ppp.com b,l,d. **Rooms** 50.
Never. AE, DC, MC, V. €€€€

Passau

Wilder Mann This beautifully preserved rococo-style hotel occupies a prime position in the centre of Passau. Elegance and a faded grandeur characterize the interior, and the restaurant is Michelin-starred. Choice of the bedrooms are the quieter ones overlooking the garden. The building also houses a major collection of Bohemian glass.
94032 Passau, am Rathausplatz. **Map** p149 F3.
(0851) 35071. FAX (0851) 31712. b,l (Sun only), d.
Rooms 48. Never. AE, DC, MC, V. €€€

Pfinztal-Söllingen

Villa Hammerschmiede This 19th-century villa on the edge of the Black Forest is best described as a restaurant with rooms – chef Markus Nagy has won it a Michelin star. Five dining rooms: one in the conservatory. Chic, large bedrooms, plush bathrooms.
76327 Pfinztal-Söllingen, Hauptstrasse 162.
Map p148 B3. (07240) 6010. FAX (07240) 60160.
@ info@villa-hammerschmiede.de b,l,d.
Rooms 30. 24 Dec.
AE, DC, MC, V. €€€€

Ochsenfurt

Polisina A welcoming atmosphere in this sporty hotel, a stone-and-wood building with tennis courts and a first-rate indoor pool.
97199 Ochsenfurt, Markbreiter Str. 265.
Map p149 D2. (09331) 8440. FAX (09331) 7603.
@ info@polisina.de b,l,d. **Rooms** 93. €€€

Pfronten

Bavaria At the head of a tranquil valley is this lavishly comfortable hotel, with open fires, pool, solarium and sauna.
87459 Pfronten-Dorf, Kienbergstr. 62. **Map** p149 D4.
(08363) 9020. FAX (08363) 902222. @ bavaria-pfronten@t-online.de b,l,d. **Rooms** 45. €€€

Rammingen

Landgasthaus Adler Village guesthouse with a large informal garden. Charming bedrooms, generous and modern bathrooms. Hearty meals.
89192 Rammingen, Riegestr 15. **Map** p149 D3.
(07345) 96410. FAX (07345) 964110. @ adler@romantik.de b,l,d. **Rooms** 12. €€

Regensburg

Bischofshof am Dom An old bishops' palace makes a very attractive hotel with a charming courtyard. Lavish furnishings, fine cuisine.
93047 Regensburg, Krauterermarkt 3. **Map** p149 E3.
(0941) 58460. FAX (0941) 5846146. @ info@ hotel-bischofshof.de b,l,d. **Rooms** 55. €€€

Riedenburg

Schloss Eggersberg This solid 15th-century castle combines a warm welcome with stylish interiors and fabulous sporting opportunities: guests can boat, fish and bicycle on the vast estate, and there's even stabling for horses. There is good skiing too. Bedrooms do not disappoint. Accomplished international cooking. There is also a theatre in the granary.
9333 Riedenburg. **Map** p149 E3. (09442) 91870. FAX (09442) 918787. b,l,d. **Rooms** 15. Christmas, Jan, Feb. Not accepted. €€

Rothenburg ob der Tauber

Klosterstueble This 16th-century inn is tucked away from the crowds in a side street off the marketplace. It's a traditional place, peaceful and cool. The delightful dining room has French windows out onto the terrace. Bedrooms at the back have views of the wooded Tauber valley.
91541 Rothenburg ob der Tauber, Heringsbronnengasse 5. **Map** p149 D2. (09861) 6774. FAX (09861) 6474 @ hotel@klosterstueble.de b,l,d. **Rooms** 21. Never. MC, V. €€.

Rothenburg ob der Tauber

Burghotel The severe exterior of this little hotel, set in old monastery grounds on the edge of the medieval town, hides a stylish retreat with plush furnishings. The terrace is set into the city walls – views are stunning. Some of the bedrooms are really quite large: try to get one with views of the Tauber river.
91541 Rothenburg ob der Tauber, Klostergasse 1-3. **Map** p149 D2. (09861) 94890. FAX (09861) 948940. @ burghotel.rothenburg@t-online.de b. **Rooms** 15. Never. MC, V. €€€

Rothenburg ob der Tauber

Romantik Hotel Markusturm The core of this central hotel is a 13th-century building, once the town's customs house, and the place became an inn in 1488. New management have given the interiors a friendly modern feel while retaining the building's historical ambience. The wood-panelled restaurant serves regional specialities.
91541 Rothenburg ob der Tauber, Rödergasse 1. **Map** p149 D2. (09861) 94280. FAX (09861) 9428113. @ info@markusturm.de b,d. **Rooms** 25. Never. AE, DC, MC, V. €€€

Rielasingen

Zur Alten Mühle Pretty little rustic inn, formerly a mill. Imaginative food from the split-level bar/dining room; charming terrace for outside eating.
78239 Rielasingen, Singener Str 3. **Map** p148 C4. (07731) 911371. FAX (07731) 911472. @ info@alte-muehle.biz b,l,d. **Rooms** 6. €€

Rothenburg ob der Tauber

Eisenhut This charming hotel in the heart of the medieval town dates from the 15th century. Comfortable, with an historic atmosphere.
91541 Rothenburg ob der Tauber, Herrngasse 3-7. **Map** p149 D2. (09861) 7050. FAX (09861) 70545. @ hotel@eisenhut.com b,l,d. **Rooms** 79. €€€€

Rothenburg ob der Tauber

Meistertrunk Sensitively restored former 14th-century merchant's house. Good plain cooking.
91541 Rothenburg ob der Tauber, Heringsbronnengasse 26. **Map** p149 D2. (09861) 6077. FAX (09861) 1253. @ meistertrunk-hotel@t-online.de b,l,d. **Rooms** 16. €€

Rothenburg ob der Tauber

Reichs-Küchenmeister A 14th-century inn in the centre of the old town.
91541 Rothenburg ob der Tauber, Kirchpl. 8-10. **Map** p149 D2 (09861) 9700. FAX (09861) 86965. @ hotel@reichskuechenmeister.com b,l,d. **Rooms** 45. €€

ROTTWEIL

Romantik Hotel Haus zum Sternen Rottweil is one of Germany's oldest fortified towns; this 14th-century building is one of the town's oldest. The hotel has a marvellously historic atmosphere, with beamed ceilings and antique furniture beautifully set off by plain carpets and white walls. Choice of regional food or modern German.
78628 Rottweil, Hauptstr 60. **Map** p148 C4.
(0741) 53300. FAX (0741) 533030.
sternen@romantikhotels.com b,d. **Rooms** 11.
Restaurant: 1 week in August. AE, MC, V. €€€

SEEBRUCK

Malerwinkel A lakeside position overlooking the Chiemsee, with stunning views to the Alps beyond, and the warmth of the welcome, make the Malerwinkel a real gem. First-rate food is served from the dining room, which in summer opens out to the terrace and hotel jetty. Bedrooms are tastefully furnished.
83358 Seebruck, Lambach 23. **Map** p149 E4.
(08667) 88800. FAX (08667) 888044.
malerwinkel@info-seebruck.de b,l,d. **Rooms** 20.
Never. V. €€

SCHÖNWALD

Dorer This charming little place, deep in the Black Forest, is untypical of the rural inns of the area both in its restrained decor and its imaginative cuisine. All the uncluttered bedrooms have a balcony or shared terrace. Look out for the amazing ancient gramophone on the first floor. Solarium, indoor pool, tennis court.
78141 Schönwald, Schubertstr. 20.
Map p148 B4. (07722) 95050. FAX (07722) 950530.
hotel-dorer-schoenwald@t-online.de b,l,d.
Rooms 19. Never. AE, DC, MC, V. €€

TIEFENBRONN

Ochsen Post The village inn looks the image of a traditional establishment, with its half-timbered façade and lush flower-boxes; inside, there are two restaurants, one specializing in Swabian food, the other French. Some of the bedrooms feature timbered walls, some are plainer, but all have luxurious bathrooms.
75233 Tiefenbronn, Franz-Josef-Gall-Str. 13.
Map p148 C3. (07234) 95450.
FAX (07234) 9545145. info@ochsen-post.de b,l,d.
Rooms 19. Never. V. €€

SCHÖNWALD

Zum Ochsen Good food and comfortable bedrooms in the Black Forest country.
78141 Schönwald, Ludwig-Uhlandstr 18.
Map p148 B4. (07722) 866480. FAX (07722) 8664888.
ringhotel@ochsen.com b,l,d. **Rooms** 37.
€€€

UHLDINGEN-MÜHLHOFEN

Fischerhaus Picture-postcard hotel by Lake Constance, with its own private beach.
88690 Uhldingen-Mühlhofen 1, Seefelden am Bodensee. **Map** p148 C4. (07556) 8563. FAX (07556) 6063. fischerhaus.seefeldon@t-online.de b,l,d.
Rooms 27. €€€

WALLGAU

Parkhotel Wallgau Richly ornate public rooms, plainer bedrooms (some with balconies). Terrace, large garden, indoor pool.
82499 Wallgau, Barmseestr 1. **Map** p149 D4.
(08825) 290. FAX (08825) 366.
parkhotel@wallgau.de b,l,d.**Rooms** 35. €€

WANGEN IM ALLGÄU

Romantik Hotel Alte Post Stylishly furnished centrally located inn with countrified bedrooms.
88239 Wangen im Allgäu, Postpl 2.
Map p148 C4. (07522) 97560.
FAX (07522) 22604. altepost@t-online.de
b. **Rooms** 19. €€

Triberg im Schwarzwald

Parkhotel Wehrle This country resort hotel has been run by the same family for hundreds of years, and despite the renowned food and luxurious fittings it is a relaxed place. It is furnished in traditional style, with several further buildings dotted around the landscaped garden. Indoor and outdoor heated pools.
78098 Triberg im Schwarzwald, Gartenstr. 24. **Map** p148 B4. (07722) 86020. FAX (07722) 860290. info@parkhotel-wehrle.de b,l,d. **Rooms** 50. Never. AE, DC, MC, V. €€€

Volkach

Romantik Hotel Zur Schwane The courtyard restaurant makes a charming entrance to this family-run inn (founded in 1404). The area is one of vine-covered hills, and the Pfaff family produce award-winning wines from their own vineyards. The imaginative food has a regional slant. The bedrooms are well equipped.
97332 Volkach, Hauptstrasse 12. **Map** p149 D2. (09381) 80660. FAX (09381) 806666. schwane@romantikhotels.com b,l,d. **Rooms** 27. 21-28 Dec. AE, V. €€€

Überlingen-Andelshofen

Romantik Hotel Johanniter-Kreuz The building started as a village guest house in the early 1900s. Still in the same family, it has matured into a comfortable and attractive inn. It's a cosy place, with agreeably plain rooms, a large garden and a pretty terrace used for dining in the summer. Regional food, fish is the speciality.
88662 Überlingen-Andelshofen, Johanniterweg 11. **Map** p148 C4. (07551) 61091. FAX (07551) 67336. johanniter-kreuz@romantikhotels.com b,l,d. **Rooms** 25. Never. DC, MC, V. €€

Wertheim-Bettingen

Schweizer Stuben This country hotel in the Main valley was a single hotel-restaurant building in 1971; it's now a cluster of buildings set in a park. Facilities include pool and tennis courts; bicycles are available. Accommodation ranges from rooms and suites to apartments. Two fine restaurants: French and Swiss.
97877 Wertheim-Bettingen, Geiselbrunnweg 11. **Map** p148 C2. (09342) 3070. FAX (09342) 307155. stuben@relaischateaux.fr b,l,d. **Rooms** 33. Never. AE, DC, MC, V. €€

Weil-Haltingen

Zum Hirschen Good value for money: a simple, family-run village inn with understated stylish rooms; charming garden for summer eating.
79576 Weil-Haltingen, Grosse Gass 1. **Map** p148 B4. (07621) 9407860. FAX (07621) 9407880. b,l,d. **Rooms** 5. €€

Weingarten

Romantik Hotel Walk'sches Haus Rustic inn whose owner is a keen cook. The dining rooms are carved and panelled; plainer bedrooms.
76356 Weingarten, Marktplatz 7. **Map** p148 B3. (07244) 70370. FAX (07244) 703740. info@walksches-haus.de b,l,d. **Rooms** 26. €€€

Weitenburg

Schloss Weitenburg Historic castle with stunning location above the Neckar river. Sporting facilities include indoor pool and nearby golf course.
72181 Starzach. **Map** p148 C3. (07457) 9330. FAX (07457) 933100. info@schloss-weitenburg.de b,l,d. **Rooms** 33. €€€

Wirsberg

Herrmann's Romantik Posthotel Village hotel with a superb indoor pool and lovely gardens.
95339 Wirsberg, Marktplatz 11. **Map** p149 E1. (09227) 2080. FAX (09227) 5860. posthotel@romantikhotels.com b,l,d. **Rooms** 44. €€€€

For key to symbols see backflap. For price categories *see p147*

Central Germany

Rhine Valley • Hesse and Thuringia • Saxony Saxony-Anhalt • Berlin • Brandenburg

There's something to suit all tastes and budgets in Central Germany: from simple country inns and smart townhouse hostelries, to log cabin-style hunting lodges, mountain chalets, lakeside villas, converted water mills, monasteries and fanciful fairytale castles. What's more, the region's scenery is as diverse as its accommodation. This section covers the popular wine-growing Rhine Valley region in the west, through Hesse and Thuringia (often called the 'green heart' of Germany) to Berlin, the flat lake-lands of Brandenburg, and Saxony. The latter, the most densely populated region of eastern Germany, is divided from the Czech Republic by the delightful, little-known Erzgebirge mountains.

Attendorn

Burg Schnellenberg High on a hill, deep in the forest, is this dramatic castle dating from the 13th century, complete with its own chapel. It is lavishly done up without being intimidating, and has a cosy bar and a peaceful garden to lounge around in. Some of the bedrooms are huge, with stunning views over the woods.
✉ 57439 Attendorn. **Map** p150 B5. ☎ (02722) 6940. FAX (02722) 694169. 🍴 b,l,d. **Rooms** 42. Christmas. AE, DC, MC, V. €€€

Bad Neuenahr-Heppingen

Zur Alten Post The epitome of a restaurant with rooms – and this restaurant has two Michelin stars. Choose between Hans-Stefan Steinheuer's impressive new German cooking and a range of 400 wines, or more traditional regional dishes in an informal setting. Recently renovated.
✉ 53474 Bad Neuenahr-Heppingen, Landskronerstr 110. **Map** p148 A1, p150 A5. ☎ (02641) 94860. FAX (02641) 948610. @ steinheuers.restaurant@t-online.de 🍴 b,l,d. **Rooms** 11. Three weeks Jul/Aug (restaurant only). AE, DC, V. €€€

Bacharach

Altkölnischer Hof This family-run town inn dates from the 11th century, and has a large restaurant and cosy bar.
✉ 55422 Bacharach, Am Marktpl. **Map** p148 B2. ☎ (06743) 1339. FAX (06743) 2793. @ altkoelnischerhof@t-online.de 🍴 b,l,d. **Rooms** 19. €€

Bad Hersfeld

Romantik Hotel Zum Stern A delightful, flower-decked hotel and restaurant in the marketplace of this spa town. Swimming pool and sauna.
✉ 36251 Bad Hersfeld, Linggpl 11. **Map** p148 C1, p150 C5. ☎ (06621) 1890. FAX (06621) 189260. @ zum-stern@romantikhotels.com 🍴 b,l,d. **Rooms** 45. €€

Bad Karlshafen

Parkhotel Haus Schöneck Understated elegance at this late-19th-century villa, surrounded by tree-shaded terraces and rolling grounds. Indoor pool.
✉ 34381 Bad Karlshafen, C D Stunweg 10. **Map** p150 C4 ☎ (05672) 925010. FAX (05672) 925011. @ parkhotel-schoeneck@gmx.de 🍴 b,l,d. **Rooms** 20. €€

Bad Laasphe-Glashütte

Jaghof Glashütte A wonderfully comfortable, family-run former hunting lodge with an amazing swimming pool built into the rock.
✉ 57334 Bad Laasphe-Glashütte. **Map** p148 B1, p150 B5. ☎ (02754) 3990. FAX (02754) 399222. @ info@jaghof-glashutte.de 🍴 b,l,d. **Rooms** 29. €€€

Bergisch Gladbach

Schlosshotel Lerbach This is a place for spoiling yourself – a truly luxurious manor house hotel, set in its own beautiful park with a lake, tennis court and pool. Chef Dieter Muller's cooking is Michelin-starred, and the wine list is excellent. Bedrooms are richly furnished.
51465 Bergisch Gladbach, Lerbacher Weg. **Map** p150 A5. (02202) 2040. FAX (02202) 204940. @ info@schlosshotel-lerbach.com b,l,d. **Rooms** 54. 2 weeks in Jan. AE, DC, MC, V. €€€€

Bernkastel-Kues

Zur Post Cheerful, geranium-bedecked inn on the main riverside road of Bernkastel-Kues, one of the main tourist towns of the Mosel. The modest 19th-century building has a busy restaurant; the warm welcome makes up for the slighty plain bedrooms. There are some family apartment-style rooms in the annexe next door.
54470 Bernkastel-Kues, Gestade 17. **Map** p148 A2. (06531) 96700. FAX (06531) 967050. @ info@hotel-zur-post-bernkastel.de b,l,d. **Rooms** 43. Jan. DC, MC, V. €€

Berlin

Brandenburger Hof Wonderfully central yet tranquil, this historic hotel has been luxuriously decorated with a successful mix of old and modern styles. The lavish bedrooms are Bauhaus style. There is a large conservatory with a Japanese garden, and a courtyard. The restaurant is Michelin-starred. Beauty treatments.
10789 Berlin, Eislebener Str. 14. **Map** p151 F3. (030) 21405600. FAX (030) 21405100. @ info@brandenburger-hof.com. b,l,d. **Rooms** 82. Never. AE, MC, DC, V. €€€€

Billerbeck

Domschenke Hard by Billerbeck's cathedral, in the pedestrianized town centre, is this long-established inn – an expanded 17th-century building run by the Groll family for more than 130 years. Ancient beams in the bar and dining room, which specializes in Westphalian dishes. Bedrooms are neat, if not stylish.
48727 Billerbeck, Markt 6. **Map** p150 A4. (02543) 93200. FAX (02543) 932030. @ domschenke@t-online.de b,l,d. **Rooms** 30. 23 & 24 Dec. AE, DC, MC, V. €€

Balduinstein

Zum Bären Ambitious food in the two marvellous dining rooms, cooked by Walter Buggle whose family have been here since 1827.
65558 Balduinstein, Bahnhofstr. 24. **Map** p148 B1. (06432) 800780. FAX (06432) 8007820. @ info@landhotel-zum-baeren.de b,l,d. **Rooms** 10. €€

Beilstein

Haus Lipmann In a delightful village, a simple guesthouse owned by the same family since 1795. Charming dining room; terrace with great views.
56814 Beilstein, Marktplatz 3. **Map** p148 B1. (02673) 1573. FAX (02673) 1521. b,l,d. **Rooms** 5. €€

Bergish Gladbach

Romantik Waldhotel Mangold Peaceful, family-run country hotel only a short drive from Cologne.
51429 Bergisch Gladbach, Am Milchbornbach 39-43. **Map** p150 A5. (02204) 955555. FAX (02204) 955560. @ mangold@waldhotel.de b,l,d. **Rooms** 22. €€€€

Bergneustadt

Rengser Mühle Delightful little restored mill, tucked away in lovely countryside. Traditional food; waffles and cakes in the garden.
51702 Bergneustadt, Niederrengse 4. **Map** p150 B5. (02763) 91450. FAX (02763) 914520. @ info@rengser-muehle.de b,l,d. **Rooms** 4. €€

For key to symbols see backflap. For price categories *see p147*

Bonn

Schlosshotel Kommende Ramersdorf The castle this hotel is named after is now a museum; the hotel occupies the converted stable block. Downstairs are a snug bar and a stylish Italian restaurant, considered to be one of the best in the country. A collection of restored antiques furnishes the bedrooms; some are for sale.

53227 Bonn, Oberkasseler Str. 10. **Map** p148 A1, p150 A5. (0228) 440734. FAX (0228) 444400. b,l,d. **Rooms** 18. 4 weeks Jul-Aug; 2 weeks Dec-Jan. AE, DC, MC, V. €€

Dahlem-Kronenberg

Eifelhaus A pretty series of whitewashed grey slate-capped houses with thick peach-coloured window surrounds in the small medieval village of Kronenburg. The menu offers healthy food with an impressive number of vegetarian dishes. Good walking country all around. A nearby lake is good for bathing and fishing.

53949 Dahlem-Kronenburg, Burgbering 12. **Map** p148 A1. (06557) 295. FAX (06557) 1359. @ eifelhaus_kronenburg@web.de b,l,d. **Rooms** 19. 2 weeks in Nov and Feb. Not accepted. €€

Cochem

Alte Thorschenke Right in the centre of Cochem's old town, by the medieval city wall, is the 14th-century Alte Thorschenke. With its gables, towers and timbers, it has a truly historic ambiance. Bedrooms at the front have the most character – the Napoleon suite has a huge four-poster bed. Good regional fish and game dishes.

56812 Cochem, Brückenstr. 3. **Map** p148 A1. (02671) 7059. FAX (02671) 4202. @ altethorschenke@t-online.de b,l,d. **Rooms** 35. Never. AE, DC, MC, V. €€€

Darscheid/Vulkaneifel

Kucher's Landhotel Run with great enthusiasm by the young Heidi and Martin Kucher, this hotel has a gourmet restaurant and lovely gardens and terrace to sit out on. The bedrooms are charming and the bathrooms are bright and modern. All in all, Kucher's represents excellent value for money. A good place for walks on the Eifel hills.

54552 Darscheid/Vulkaneifel, Karl-Kaufmann Str. 2. **Map** p148 A1. (06592) 629. FAX (06592) 3677. @ kucherslandhotel@t-online.de b,l,d. **Rooms** 14. Jan. AE, V. €€

Berlin

Forsthaus Paulsborn A strange but rather enchanting 19th-century hunting lodge in wooded park, suitably decorated with hunting trophies.

14193 Berlin 33, Am Grunewaldsee, Huttenweg 90. **Map** p151 F3. (030) 8181910. FAX (030) 81819150. b,l,d. @ paulsborn@t-online.de **Rooms** 10. €€€

Berlin

Hecker's Choose classic or modern design for your room at this chic hotel in the centre of town. Noted regional food in the restaurant.

10623 Berlin, Grolmanstr. 35. **Map** p151 F3. (030) 88900. FAX (030) 8890260 @ info@heckers-hotel.de b,l,d. **Rooms** 69. €€€€

Berlin

Landhaus Schlachtensee A large, cool villa in an area of woods and lake, yet only a short underground train-ride from the centre.

14163 Berlin, Bogotastr. 9. **Map** p151 F3. (030) 8099470. FAX (030) 80994747. @ hotel-landhaus-schlachtensee@t-online.de b. **Rooms** 20. €€€

Berlin

Residenz A superb dining room and first-rate bedrooms mark out this attractive large hotel, set on a quiet but central street.

10719 Berlin, Meinekestr. 9. **Map** p151 F3. (030) 884430. FAX (030) 8824726. @ info@hotelresidenz.com b,l,d. **Rooms** 81. €€€

DAUN

Schlosshotel Kurfürstliches Amtshaus The hotel boasts a bed that was slept in by more than 50 visiting heads of state when it was in the government residence in Bonn. The terrace has superb views over the village. Inside, rooms have all modern comforts, with a scattering of antiques. Italian-influenced cooking; good wine list.
54550 Daun, Auf dem Burgberg. **Map** p148 A1. (06592) 9250. FAX (06592) 925255. @ kurfuerstliches.amtshaus@t-online.de b,d. **Rooms** 30. 3 weeks Jan. AE, DC, MC, V. €€€

DORSTEN-LEMBECK

Schlosshotel Lembeck A magical 17th-century castle, surrounded by a moat and with its own ravishing grounds. Meals can be eaten on the terrace, with its magnificent views, or in the huge cellar bar with its extraordinary domed ceiling. The bedrooms are vast and furnished with antique furniture; some have four-poster beds.
46286 Dorsten 12-Lembeck. **Map** p150 A4. (02369) 7213. FAX (02369) 77370. @ info@schlosshotel-lembeck.de b,l,d. **Rooms** 17. Jan. AE, DC, MC, V. €€

DEIDESHEIM

Deidesheimer Hof This luxurious inn located in the centre of the village was a favourite with Chancellor Kohl. Choose between a smart gourmet restaurant, a less formal flowery terrace, and *weinstube* with regional food. The spacious bedrooms are decorated in a traditional style.
67146 Deidesheim, Am Marktplatz 1. **Map** p148 B2. (06326) 96870. FAX (06326) 7685. @ info@deidesheimerhof.de b,l,d. **Rooms** 28. first week Jan. AE, DC, MC, V. €€€€

DRESDEN

Bülow Residenz In the old part of Dresden, this beautiful Baroque house offers large lavish rooms and bathrooms, and an elegant but intimate restaurant with an impressive wine list. The cosy bar downstairs is a popular rendezvous. There is a delightful courtyard for quiet drinks or quiet times. Conference facilities.
01097 Dresden, Rähnitzgasse 19. **Map** p151 F5. (0351) 80030. FAX (0351) 8003100. @ info@buelow-residenz.de b,l,d. **Rooms** 30. Never. AE, DC, MC, V. €€€€

BOCHOLT-BARLO

Schloss Diepenbrock Facilities are split between the twin-turreted castle (still a family home) and a modern house.
46397 Bocholt-Barlo, Schlossallee 5. **Map** p150 A4. (02871) 21740. FAX (02871) 217433. b,l,d. **Rooms** 16. €€

BONN

Domicil A slick, modern hotel with lots of glass and chrome and minimalist decoration.
53111 Bonn, Thomas-Mann-Str. 24 & 26. **Map** p148 A1, p150 A5. (0228) 729090. FAX (0228) 691207. @ info@domicil-bonn.bestwestern.de b,l,d. **Rooms** 44. €€€€

BONN

Kaiser Karl The smart town house hotel is conveniently situated for the airport. Bathrooms are opulent. Terrace; French bistro.
53119 Bonn, Vorgebirgsstrasse 56. **Map** p148 A1, p150 A5. (0228) 985570. FAX (0228) 9855777. @ info@kaiser-karl-hotel.de b,l,d. **Rooms** 42. €€€€

BORKEN-RHEDEBRUGGE

Grüneklee An attractive little village inn with nice food (served on the garden terrace in fine weather) and comfortable, rustic rooms.
46325 Borken, Rhedebrügger Str. 16. **Map** p150 A4. (02872) 1818. FAX (02872) 2716. b,d. **Rooms** 5. €€

ELTVILLE-HATTENHEIM

Zum Krug Eltville-Hattenheim is right in the middle of the wine-growing area of Rheingau, and this peaceful inn is ideal for serious wine drinkers. Rooms are comfy, but the real point of this place is the wine; the restaurant offers a four-course gourmet menu with a specially chosen glass of local wine to go with each.
✉ 65347 Eltville-Hattenheim, Hauptstr. 34.
Map p148 B2. ☎ (06723) 99680. FAX (06723) 996825.
🍴 b,l,d. **Rooms** 8. ● 20 Dec to 20 Jan.
💳 MC, V. €€

ESSEN-KETTWIG

Schloss Hugenpoet There's nothing gloomy or claustrophobic about the interior of this striking moated castle, now a smart and luxurious hotel. The reception rooms are marvellously done out with great style and panache. The large bedrooms are lavishly decorated and furnished with antiques.
✉ 45219 Essen-Kettwig 18, August-Thyssen-Str. 51.
Map p150 A4. ☎ (02054) 12040. FAX (02054) 120450.
@ reservierung@hugenpoet.de 🍴 b,l,d. **Rooms** 25.
● Never. 💳 DC, MC, V. €€€€

ESSEN-KETTWIG

Residence Guests are cossetted at this (extremely pricey) Michelin-starred restaurant with rooms. The efficiently run white villa, surrounded by its leafy landscaped garden, is hidden away in a quiet suburb. The bedrooms are small but chic. Book well ahead
✉ 45219 Essen-Kettwig, Auf der Forst 1.
Map p150 A4. ☎ (02054) 95590. FAX (02054) 82501.
@ info@hotel-residence.de 🍴 b,d. **Rooms** 18.
● 1 week Jan, mid-Aug to early Sep.
💳 AE, DC, MC, V. €€€

FRANKFURT AM MAIN

Westend The great bonus in this peaceful haven, close to the centre of Frankfurt, is its delightful walled garden. The 18th-century building is beautifully preserved, with some wonderful furniture and oil paintings, and retains the feel of a private house. Cosy bedrooms. Cold snacks are offered in the evening.
✉ 60325 Frankfurt 1, Westendstr. 15. **Map** p148 C2.
☎ (069) 78988180. FAX (069) 745396.
@ hotel_westend@t-online.de 🍴 b. **Rooms** 20. ●
Christmas to New Year. 💳 AE, DC, MC, V. €€€€

BRAUBACH

Zum Weissen Schwanen Half-timbered old inn right by the town walls, with lively public rooms. The best bedrooms are in the old watermill.
✉ 56338 Braubach, Brunnenstr. 4. **Map** p148 B1.
☎ (02627) 9820. FAX (02627) 8802. @ zum-weissen-schwanen@rz-online.de 🍴 b,l,d. **Rooms** 19. €€

COCHEM

Weissmühle Secluded chalet-style hotel near the busy Mosel and Rhine valleys. The Alpine exterior hides thouroughly modern rooms.
✉ 56812 Cochem, Enderttal. **Map** p148 A1.
☎ (02671) 8955. FAX (02671) 8207. @ info@hotel-weissmuehle.de 🍴 b,l,d. **Rooms** 36. €€

DETMOLD

Detmolder Hof Pleasant townhouse hotel on the main pedestrian street. Charming bar and bright bedrooms; attractive outdoor terrace.
✉ 32756 Detmold, Lange Strasse 19. **Map** p150 B4.
☎ (05231) 99120. FAX (05231) 991299. @ detmolderhof@t-online.de 🍴 b,l,d. **Rooms** 39. €€

DORMAGEN

Höttche The town hotel has a guesthouse feel and similarly warm welcome. Excellent cuisine is served in the panelled dining rooms.
✉ 41539 Dormagen 1, Krefelder Str. 14-18.
Map p150 A5. ☎ (02133) 2530. FAX (02133) 10616.
@ hoettche@gmhicks.net 🍴 b,l,d. **Rooms** 49. €€

HAMM/SIEG

Romantik Hotel Alte Vogtei An ancient half-timbered hotel set in the middle of a small village, surrounded by woods. Beautifully preserved old furniture makes the most of the simple decor. Markus Wortelkamp, the son of the proprietors, has spent several years in France and England, and his excellent cuisine reflects this. ✉ 57577 Hamm/Sieg, Lindenallee 3. **Map** p148 B1, p150 B5. ☎ (02682) 259. FAX (02682) 8956. @ alte-vogtei@romantikhotels.com. 🍴 b,l,d. **Rooms** 15. ● 3 weeks Jul/Aug, 24-26 Dec. 💳 AE, DC, MC, V. €€

HAMMINKELN-MARIENTHAL

Romantik Hotel Haus Elmer Efficiency and professionalism are the bywords at this hotel, situated in a village near the Dutch border. The best bedrooms are in the old buildings, with modern furniture and exposed beams. The popular restaurant serves hearty meals. Perfect cycling country – bikes are available for guests. ✉ 46499 Hamminkeln-Marienthal, An der Klosterkirche 12. **Map** p150 A4. ☎ (02856) 9110. FAX (02856) 91170. @ info@haus-elmer.de 🍴 b,l,d. **Rooms** 31. ● Never. 💳 AE, DC, MC, V. €€€

HERLESHAUSEN

Hohenhaus A quiet setting in wooded countryside, and proximity to the former East German border and E40 motorway, make this a very popular hotel. The building is not new, but the bright rooms have been thoughtfully designed in contemporary style; bedrooms retain a traditional feel. Imaginative food. ✉ 37293 Herleshausen 7, Holzhausen. **Map** p150 C5. ☎ (05654) 680. FAX (05654) 1303. @ hohenhaus@t-online.de 🍴 b,l,d. **Rooms** 26. ● Never. 💳 AE, DC, MC, V. €€€

HOFGEISMAR

Dornroschenschloss Sababurg It's nicknamed 'Sleeping Beauty Castle'; visitors are greeted by Sleeping Beauty herself and can buy themed gifts. But don't be put off. It's a very romantic place, with fantastic views, and the hotel part of the castle has been beautifully furnished. Peaceful evenings, excellent food. ✉ 34369 Hofgeismar, Hofgeismar-Sababurg. **Map** p150 C4. ☎ (05671) 8080. FAX (05671) 808200. @ reception@sababurg.de 🍴 b,l,d. **Rooms** 18. ● Never. 💳 AE, DC, MC, V. €€€

DUDELDORF

Flair Hotel 'Zum alten Brauhaus' Former brewery beautifully decorated with fine antiques. Delightful bedrooms; outdoor terrace and garden. ✉ 54647 Dudeldorf, Herrengasse 2. **Map** p148 A2. ☎ (06565) 92750. FAX (06565) 927555. @ rhdudel@t-online.de. 🍴 b,l,d. **Rooms** 16. €€

DÜSSELDORF-OBERKASSEL

Hanseat An elegantly furnished townhouse just across the Rhine from the city. Tasteful bedrooms; tranquil public rooms. ✉ 40545 Düsseldorf-Oberkassel, Belsenstr. 6. **Map** p150 A5. ☎ (0211) 575060. FAX (0211) 589662. @ info@hotel-hanseat.de 🍴 b. **Rooms** 37. €€€€

ELTVILLE-HATTENHEIM

Kronen Schlösschen In the cobbled town, with its own grounds. Bedrooms all differ and have plush bathrooms. Two popular restaurants. ✉ 65347 Eltville-Hattenheim, Rheinallee. **Map** p148 B2. ☎ (06723) 640. FAX (06723) 7663. @ info@kronenschloesschen.de 🍴 b,l,d. **Rooms** 18. €€€€

ESSEN

Parkhaus Hügel Handsome hotel, originally a casino. Grand terrace with wonderful views on to the lake and the surrounding countryside. ✉ 45133 Essen 1, Freiherr-vom-Stein Str 209. **Map** p150 A4. ☎ (0201) 471091. FAX (0201) 444207. 🍴 b,l,d. **Rooms** 13. €€

Horbruch im Hunsrück

Historiche Schlossmühle Thick walls, a water wheel and stream are evidence of the building's original purpose as a mill. It is now a smart yet extremely hospitable hotel. Walls covered in books and paintings give the reception rooms a homely feel, and bedrooms are tastefully furnished. Excellent French-influenced food.
55483 Horbruch im Hunsrück. **Map** p148 B2.
(06543) 4041. FAX (06543) 3178.
info@castle-mill.net b,l,d. **Rooms** 18. 1-15 Jan.
MC, V. €€€

Kallstadt

Weinkastell 'Zum Weissen Ross' Modern refurbishment has not spoiled the ancient atmosphere of this eye-catching village hotel. At its heart is the pine-panelled *Stube*, used for breakfast and evening drinking, and an ambitious restaurant. The bedrooms are relatively plain; the honeymoon room has a huge four-poster bed.
67169 Kallstadt, an der Weinstr. 80-82. **Map** p148 B2.
(06322) 5033. FAX (06322) 66091. b,l,d.
Rooms 14. 4 weeks Jan-Feb, 1 week July-Aug.
AE, MC, V. €€

Isselburg

Wasserburg Anholt One of central Germany's most impressive castles: the massive red-brick building seems to be floating on its lake. One part is open to the public; another has been converted into an attractive hotel. A highlight is the ground-floor café, with a terrace overlooking the water. The bedrooms are mainly unexceptional.
46419 Isselburg, Kleverstr 2. **Map** p150 A4.
(02874) 4590. FAX (02874) 4035.
wasserburg-anholt@t-online.de b,l,d. **Rooms** 33.
24 Dec. AE, DC, MC, V. €€€

Klein-Briesen

Parkhotel Juliushof This former hunting lodge deep in the pine woods is popular with outdoor types; hunting and fishing are available. But it's also an extremely civilized place to stay, with suites in the main building and double rooms in a separate cabin. Not the best place for vegetarians – the menu is strong on wild boar, venison and local trout.
14806 Klein-Briesen (Kreis Belzig). **Map** p151 E4.
(033846) 40056. FAX (033846) 40245. hotel juliushof@t-online.de b,l,d. **Rooms** 14. Never.
AE, MC. €€

Fischbachtal-Lichtenberg

Landhaus Baur Soon after the hotel opened, the restaurant was listed in Germany's top 100. You can even book a cookery course here.
64405 Fischbachtal-Lichtenberg, Lippmannweg 15.
Map p148 C2. (06166) 8313. FAX (06166) 8841.
info@landhausbaur.de b,l (Sun only),d. **Rooms** 7 €€€

Frankfurt am Main

Hessischer Hof Of Frankfurt's two grand hotels, this tends to be the choice for discerning visitors.
60325 Frankfurt am Main, Friedrich-Ebert Anlage 40.
Map p148 C2. (069) 75402911. FAX (069) 75402912.
reservations@hessischer-hof.de b,l,d. **Rooms** 117
€€€€

Frankfurt am Main

Palmenhof A perfect refuge from the city with lavish bedrooms and a good restaurant.
60325 Frankfurt am Main, Bockenheimer Landstr. 89-91. **Map** p148 C2. (069) 7530060. FAX (069) 75300666. info@palmenhof.com b,l,d. **Rooms** 46.
€€€€

Hanau

Birkenhof A pretty villa in landscaped gardens, the Birkenhof is close to a castle, a church and restaurants. Recently renovated and enlarged.
63456 Hanau-Steinheim, von Eiff Str. 37-41.
Map p148 C1. (06181) 64880. FAX (06181) 648839.
info@hotelbirkenhof.de b,d. **Rooms** 52. €€

Königstein im Taunus

Sonnenhof A former palace of the Rothschilds now makes a marvellously peaceful and quiet country house hotel, only 20 minutes' drive from Frankfurt. Inside are elegant public rooms and beautifully decorated bedrooms (some with balconies). Outside are a pretty terrace, vast grounds and some good walks. Fine food.
☒ 61462 Königstein im Taunus, Falkensteinerstr 9. **Map** p148 B1. ☎ (06174) 29080. FAX (06174) 290875. @ sonnenhof-koenigstein@t-online.de 🍴 b,l,d. **Rooms** 40. Never. AE, DC, MC, V. €€€

Lich-Kloster Arnsburg

Alte Klostermühle A mill, brewery and monastery once occupied the ancient buildings that make up this charming country hotel. Vast grounds and a welcoming beer garden ensure a mix between seclusion and sociability. The bedrooms are large and public rooms are inviting. Choice of several countrified dining rooms.
☒ 35423 Lich-Kloster Arnsburg. **Map** p148 C1, p150 B5. ☎ (06404) 91900. FAX (06404) 919091. @ alterklostermuhle@lich.de 🍴 b,l,d. **Rooms** 25. Never. AE, DC, MC, V. €€

Kronberg

Schlosshotel Kronberg This extraordinary place was built by a daughter of Queen Victoria. It is stuffed full of wonderful furniture and pictures and still has the atmosphere of a superb and friendly country house. Set in a splendid park it has a golf course and rose garden too. The food is excellent.
☒ 61476 Kronberg, Hainstr. 25. **Map** p148 B1. ☎ (06173) 70101. FAX (06173) 701267. @ reservations@schlosshotel-kronberg.de 🍴 b,l,d. **Rooms** 58. Never. AE, DC, MC, V. €€€€

Limburg an der Lahn

Zimmermann This unexpectedly opulent hotel is the smallest in town. The majority of its sumptuously decorated rooms are singles – so book ahead. There is plenty to explore in Limburg, most notably the beautiful cathedral, which towers over the town from its perch overlooking the River Lahn.
☒ 65549 Limburg an der Lahn, Blumenröder Str. 1. **Map** p148 B1. ☎ (06431) 4611. FAX (06431) 41314. @ zimmerman@romantik.de 🍴 b,d. **Rooms** 20. 1 week late Dec/early Jan. AE, MC, V. €€€

Heiligenhaus

Waldhotel This steep-roofed country hotel is furnished with taste and confidence in modern style. Attractive terrace looking out onto woods.
☒ 42579 Heiligenhaus, Parkstr. 38. **Map** p148 B1, p150 A5. ☎ (02056) 5970. FAX (02056) 597260. @ waldhotel-heiligenhaus@t-online.de 🍴 b,l,d. **Rooms** 78. €€€€

Heiligenstadt

Traube An inn with turrets and half-timbering, on the main road out of the town. Pristinely clean and good, plentiful food.
☒ 91332 Heiligenstadt/Eichsfeld, Bahnhofstr. 2. **Map** p150 C4. ☎ (03606) 612253. FAX (03606) 604509. 🍴 b,l,d. **Rooms** 10. €

Hessen

Schlosshotel Rettershof A sturdy Victorian building in the Taunaus mountains. Charming public rooms, bedrooms elegant.
☒ 65779 Kelkheim. **Map** p151 D4. ☎ (06174) 29090. FAX (06174) 25352. @ schlosshotel-rettershof@t-online.de 🍴 b,l,d. **Rooms** 35. €€€

Kaiserslautern-Hohenecken

Burgschänke An attractive inn with a cheerful beer garden and cosy bar. Bedrooms are simple but chic, with good furniture and ornaments.
☒ 67661 Kaiserslautern 32-Hohenecken, Schlossstr 1. **Map** p148 B2. ☎ (0631) 56041. FAX (0631) 56301. @ info@burgschaenke-kl.de 🍴 b,l,d. **Rooms** 42. €€

Monschau

Haus Vecqueray This tall, delicately timbered guesthouse with window boxes full of flowers, was built in 1716. The bedrooms, at the top of a spiral staircase, are delightful, with pretty rugs on the wood floors, antiques and views over the attractive old town. There is limited room to sit downstairs but you will get a substantial breakfast in cosy surroundings.
52156 Monschau, Kirchstr 5. **Map** p148 A1, p150 A5. (02472) 3179. FAX (02472) 4320. @ info@vecqueray.de b,l,d. **Rooms** 11. Never. None. €€

Münster-Handorf

Romantik Hotel Hof zur Linde The Lofken family have run turned this ancient farmhouse into a sophisticated rural retreat. Inside, trophies and paintings reflect Otto Lofken's passion for hunting. Bedrooms range from country style through Victorian to modern. Beautifully served food in the rustic restaurant.
48157 Münster-Handorf, Am Handorfer Werseufer 1. **Map** p150 B4. (0251) 32750. FAX (0251) 328209. @ hof-zur-linde@t-online.de b,l,d. **Rooms** 47. 23-25 Dec. AE, DC, MC, V. €€€

Münster

Schloss Wilkinghege A formal garden with a tiny private chapel is the introduction to this grand 18th-century moated mansion. Inside are a lofty hallway and spacious rooms with period furniture; those at the back have views of the moat and open countryside. Some bedrooms are in an annexe. Golf course nearby.
48159 Münster, Steinfurter Str. 374. **Map** p150 B4. (0251) 213045. FAX (0251) 212898. @ schloss_wilkinghege@t-online.de b,l,d. **Rooms** 35. 24-25 Dec. AE, DC, MC, V. €€€€

Oberwesel

Burghotel Auf Schönburg The walls of an ancient castle high on a ridge above the Rhine shelter this newer Gothic building. Each room in this quirky hotel is different – some round, some tiny, some with magnificent views – but all blend comfort with romance. Good regional food and friendly service from the Huttl family.
55430 Oberwesel. **Map** p148 B1. (06744) 93930. FAX (06744) 1613. @ huettl@hotel-schoenburg.com b,l,d. **Rooms** 22. Jan to Mar. MC, V. €€€

Köln (Cologne)

Atrium Rheinhotel A few miles from the city centre, this slick 'designer' hotel has a restrained colour scheme and elegant furniture.
50996 Köln, Karlstr. 2-12. **Map** p148 A1, p150 A5. (0221) 935720. FAX (0221) 93572222. @ reservation@atrium-rheinhotel.de b. **Rooms** 69. €€€€

Landau-Birkweiler

St Laurentius Hof A quaint little village inn with a charming vine-smothered courtyard and good country food, such as suckling pig.
768131 Landau-Birkweiler, Haupstr. 21. **Map** p148 B2. (06345) 942194. FAX (06345) 942195. @ st.laurentiushof@t-online.de b,l,d. **Rooms** 12. €€

Köln (Cologne)

Viktoria Chic villa hotel by the left bank of the Rhine (some of the rooms have views), with Art Nouveau decor. Great breakfasts.
50668 Köln, Worringer Str. 23. **Map** p148 A1, p150 A5. (0221) 9731720. FAX (0221) 727067. @ hotel@hotelviktoria.com b. **Rooms** 47. €€€

Lüdinghausen

Borgmann An attractive little townhouse, run with great care by the Borgmann family. Rooms vary. Pretty terrace and hearty food.
59348 Lüdinghausen, Munsterstr. 17. **Map** p150 B4. (02591) 91810. FAX (02591) 918130. @ bigborgmann@aol.com b,l,d. **Rooms** 14. €€

Oberwesel

Römerkrug This delightful 15th-century inn, right on the cobbled market square of this Rhine Valley village, has kept all its traditional charm. The interior has been very carefully renovated – in fact, much of it has been left well alone – and it is extremely cosy. Attractive little pavement terrace; heartily satisfying food. Nearby there are wine-tastings and boat trips.
55430 Oberwesel, Marktpl 1. **Map** p148 B1.
(06744) 7091. FAX (06744) 1677. @ roemerkrug@web.de b,l,d. **Rooms** 7. Jan. AE, MC, V. €€

Potsdam

Relexa Schloss Cecilienhof This castle was built as a retreat for the Crown Prince Wilhelm and his wife Cecilie in 1914, and now combines museum and public gardens with modern hotel. The interior retains its old elegance, with spacious rooms offering stunning views over the English gardens, known locally as Neuer Garten.
14469 Potsdam, Neuer Garten. **Map** p151 E3.
(0331) 37050. FAX (0331) 292498.
@ reservierung.potsdam@relexa-hotel.de b,l,d.
Rooms 41. Never. AE, DC, MC, V. €€€

Petershagen

Romantik Hotel Schloss Petershagen The riverside castle, built in the 14th century as a local stronghold, was transformed into an elegant hotel 35 years ago. Rooms are cool, peaceful and richly furnished, and the park invites relaxation. The restaurant has a view of the river and offers imaginative modern dishes.
32469 Petershagen 1, Schloss Str. 5-7. **Map** p150 C3.
(05707) 93130. FAX (05707) 931345.
@ info@schloss-petershagen.com b,l,d. **Rooms** 13.
3 weeks in Jan. DC, MC, V. €€€

Schieder-Schwalenberg

Burghotel Schwalenberg This 13th-century fortress, perched up on a wooded hill above the town, is the real thing. Towers and turrets outside; inside, creaky corridors, suits of armour, boars' heads on the walls and huge old sofas. Bedrooms are spacious. Regional cookery from a modern extension with panoramic windows.
32816 Schieder-Schwalenberg 2. **Map** p150 C4.
(05284) 98000. FAX (05284) 980027.
b,l,d. **Rooms** 15. Jan; Feb.
AE, MC, V. €€

Moers-Repelen

Welling Hotel zur Linde The old inn has a lively beer garden, several bars and dining rooms; a modern wing houses the large bedrooms.
47445 Moers-Repelen, An der Linde 2. **Map** p150 A4.
(02841) 9760. FAX (02841) 97666.
@ info@hotel-zur-linde.de b,l,d. **Rooms** 60. €€

Monschau

Burghotel Monschau Traditional townhouse in the centre of medieval Monschau, full of character and charm.
52156 Monschau. **Map** p148 A1, p150 A5.
FAX (02472) 2332. @ info@burg-hotel-monschau.de
b,l,d. **Rooms** 11. €€

Münster-Wolbeck

Thier-Hülsmann This converted farmhouse has been decorated with panache: old beams contrast with bright colours. Modern rooms in annexe.
48167 Münster-Wolbeck, Münsterstr. 33.
Map p150 B4. (02506) 83100. FAX (02506) 831035.
@ info@thier-huelsmann.de b,l,d. **Rooms** 37. €€

St Goar

Landsknecht Beautifully positioned on the banks of the Rhine with valley views and charming terrace. Food hearty, bedrooms plush.
56329 St Goar, Rheinuferstrasse. **Map** p148 B1.
(06741) 2011. FAX (06741) 7499. @ info@hotel-landsknecht.de b,l,d. **Rooms** 15. €€€

Spangenberg

Schloss Spangenberg Not only is this 13th-century converted castle wonderfully peaceful, but it also has stunning hilltop views, a moat and a drawbridge. The charming dining room looks out on to wooded hills; venison is one of the specialities. Of the characterful rooms, perhaps the best is the family apartment in the gatehouse. 34286 Spangenberg. **Map** p150 C5. (05663) 866. FAX (05663) 7567. hotelschloss.spangenberg@t-online.de b,l,d. **Rooms** 24. First 2 weeks in Jan. AE, DC, MC, V. €€€

Stromberg

Johann Lafer's Stromburg A castle was first built here, at the heart of what is now the Nahe wine region, in the 11th century, but the present building is a 19th-century reconstruction. It makes a suitable backdrop to the fine food served in its two restaurants, one modern, one traditional. Lavish bedrooms include a suite in the tower. 55442 Stromberg. **Map** p148 B2. (06724) 93100. FAX (06724) 931090. reservierung@johannlafer.de b,d. **Rooms** 14. Never. AE, DC, MC, V. €€€€

Stolberg

Altes Brauhaus Burgkeller A series of ancient riverside buildings, built around Stornber's oldest house (1594), make up this rambling inn. Despite modernization, many of the rooms retain great character; bedrooms are modern. The riverside terrace is a delight. Now under new management and recently renovated. 52222 Stolberg, Klatterstr. 8-12. **Map** p150 A5. (02402) 27272. FAX (02402) 27270. burgkeller@romantik.de b,l,d. **Rooms** 7. Few days in Feb (carnival). DC, MC, V. €€€

Trier

Hotel Petrisberg Large picture windows make the most of this hillside hotel's views over the old city. It's a modern building, yet rooms are anything but anonymous: some have murals and painted ceilings, some are in Scandinavian style, all are cosy. There are larger suites in the small annexe. Evening meals can be arranged. It's a hard 20-minute walk back from town. 54296 Trier, Sickingenstr. 11-13. **Map** p148 B2. (0651) 4640. FAX (0651) 46450. b. **Rooms** 35. Never. MC, V. €€

St Goar

Schlosshotel & Villa Rheinfels A comfortable, well-kept hotel with good food and wine. 56329 St Goar, Schlossberg 47. **Map** p148 B1. (06741) 8020. FAX (06741) 802802. info@burgrheinfels.de b,l,d. **Rooms** 54. €€€

Schmallenberg

Landhotel Gasthof Schutte A peaceful hotel with a wonderful swimming pool. Good food, smart rooms and sports facilities offered. 57392 Schmallenberg-Oberkirchen. **Map** p150 B5. (02975) 820. FAX (02975) 82522. landhotel@schuette.sou.de b,l,d. **Rooms** 64. €€€

Selm-Cappenberg

Hotel Kreutzkamp Traditional, brick-built country hotel with two lovely, old-fashioned dining rooms. Prior booking essential. 59379 Selm-Cappenberg, Cappenberger Damm 3. **Map** p150 A4. (02306) 750410. FAX (02306) 7504110. hotelkreutzkamp@t-online.de b,l,d. **Rooms** 15. €€

Trier

Villa Hügel Beautifully decorated early 1900s villa in a leafy residential area close to the centre of town. Rooftop terrace, indoor pool, solarium. 54295 Trier, Bernhardstr. 14. **Map** p148 B2. (0651) 937100 FAX (0651) 37958. info@hotel-villa-huegel.de b,d. **Rooms** 34. €€€

Wallerfangen

Villa Fayence For fine dining followed by a luxurious night, look no further than this elegant pink-washed villa. French-influenced food is served in style, accompanied by a formidable wine list. In the winter, guests consider the menu with a drink in the Baroque drawing room, in the summer, in the conservatory by the park.
66798 Wallerfangen, Haupstr. 12. **Map** p148 A2.
(06831) 96410. FAX (06831) 62068.
@ info@villafayence.de b,l,d. **Rooms** 4.
Occasionally. AE, DC, MC, V. €€€

Wesel

Waldhotel Tannenhäuschen Very plush, with good antique and reproduction furniture, deep carpets and spacious rooms, this comfortable hotel is set in large, pleasant grounds. The bedrooms are generous, some with four-posters. There is a pretty terrace, indoor swimming pool and cosy bars. Delicious breakfasts, lavish food.
46487 Wesel, Am Tannenhäuschen 7. **Map** p150 A4.
(0281) 96690. FAX (0281) 966999.
@ info@tannenhaeuschen.de b,l,d. **Rooms** 47.
24 Dec. AE, DC, MC, V. €€€

Werne

Hotel Baumhove The low, rough-beamed bar and dining room characterize this ancient house in the cobbled old town. The inn is divided into cosy sections, with a smarter gallery area reached by an open staircase. Dark corridors lead to rooms which are surprisingly modern; some overlook the marketplace. Good, hearty food.
59368 Werne, Markt 2. **Map** p150 B4. (02389) 989590. FAX (02389) 98959120.
@ hotelamkloster@baumhove.de b,l,d. **Rooms** 14.
Never. AE, DC, MC, V. €€

Wiedenbrück

Ratskeller Wiedenbrück Right in the centre of the historic town of Wiedenbruck is this prettily timbered and decorated town inn, dating from 1560. It has been run by five generations of the Surmann family, who have done a fine restoration job of the panelled bar and the beamed dining room. Unfussy bedrooms.
33378 Rheda-Wiedenbrück, Lange Strasse Markt 11. **Map** p150 B4. (05242) 9210. FAX (05242) 921100.
@ ratskeller@romantikhotels.com b,l,d. **Rooms** 33.
Christmas. AE, DC, MC, V. €€€

Wassenberg

Burg Wassenberg Ancient but sensitively modernized house with many original features.
41849 Wassenberg, Auf dem Burgberg 1. **Map** p150 A5. (02432) 9490. FAX (02432) 949100.
@ burgwassenberg@t-online.de b,l,d.
Rooms 31. €€€

Wasserliesch

Scheid Hubert Scheid's classical French cuisine (Michelin-starred) is the draw at this restaurant with rooms. Scheid's patisserie is in nearby Trier.
54332 Wasserliesch, Reinigerstr 48. **Map** p148 A2.
(06501) 13958. FAX (06501) 13959. b,l,d.
Rooms 13. €

Willingen

Stryckhaus The elegant country hotel in woodland setting is a wonderful place to relax by the pool. Good food and well-priced wines.
34508 Willingen. **Map** p150 B5. (05632) 9860.
FAX (05632) 69961. @ stryckhaus@t-online.de
b,l,d. **Rooms** 61. €€€

Winterberg

Berghotel Astenkrone A wonderfully plush country hotel. Superb swimming pool, golf.
59955 Winterberg-Altastenberg, Astenstr 24.
Map p150 B5. (02981) 8090. FAX (02981) 809198.
@ berghotel@astenkrone.de b,l,d. **Rooms** 43
€€€

NORTHERN GERMANY

LOWER SAXONY • THE NORTH COAST NORTHEAST GERMANY

NORTHERN GERMANY, which stretches from Lower Saxony on the Dutch frontier to Mecklenburg-West Pomerania bordering Poland, offers a wide variety of scenery, from the windswept landscapes of pancake-flat Schleswig-Holstein in the north to the densely forested Harz Mountains in the south. Most of our entries are located in and around the major seaport of Hamburg, such as in the historic towns of Bremen, Hannover and Lübeck, and in popular seaside resorts, ideal for family holidays. There are also a few off-the-beaten-track addresses on the North Frisian islands of Sylt and Föhr, off the mainland in the North Sea, where you can find some of Europe's finest beaches.

ALT DUVENSTEDT

Seehotel Töpferhaus Set in tranquil grounds close to the shores of the Bistensee, the Töpferhaus has wide views over the garden to the lake. The bedrooms are nicely furnished and modern, with marble-tiled bathrooms, and some have their own balcony or terrace. The whole hotel has been recently refurbished.
24791 Alt Duvenstedt, Am Bistensee. **Map** p150 C1. (04338) 99710. FAX (04338) 997171. @ info@toepferhaus.com b,l,d. **Rooms** 46. Never. AE, DC, MC, V. €€€

BAD DOBERAN

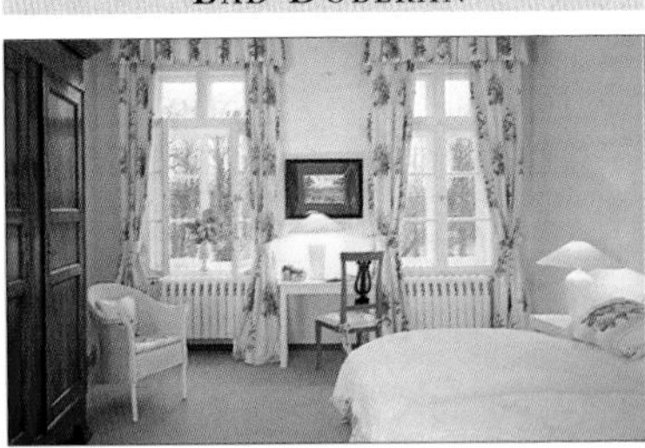

Friedrich Franz Palais This pleasant and stylish establishment, facing the shady park in the middle of town, was built in the late 18th century as a guesthouse for the local duke. Bedrooms are beautifully decorated in English country house style, while the public rooms are classical Biedemeier with historical prints on the walls.
18209 Bad Doberan, Am Kamp. **Map** p151 D2. (038203) 63036. FAX (038203) 62126. @ friedrich-franz-palais@t-online.de b,l,d.**Rooms** 45. In winter to Feb. AE, DC, MC, V. €€

AMRUM ISLAND

Ual Öömrang Wiartshüs A pretty, thatched hotel with a nautical flavour. It's not fancy, but is charmingly decorated and has a pretty garden.
25946 Nordseeheilbad Norddorf, Insel Amrum. **Map** p150 B1. (04682) 836. FAX (04682) 1432. b,l,d. **Rooms** 10. €€

BAD DOBERAN

Kurhotel Despite its drab exterior, the Kurhotel has something often lacking in the East – style. Warning: food is of the heavy regional variety.
18209 Bad Doberan, Am Kamp. **Map** p151 D2. (038203) 63036. FAX (038203) 62126. b,l,d. **Rooms** 60. €€€

FRAUENMARK

Schloss Frauenmark Large, lavishly decorated 19th-century country house. Competitive two-, three- and six-day packages are available.
19374 Frauenmark. **Map** p151 D2. (038723) 80171. FAX (038723 80172) @ info@schlossfrauenmark.de b,l,d. **Rooms** 9. €€

FRIEDRICHSTADT

Holländische Stube A charming set of terraced houses on the canal, pleasantly decorated.
25840 Friedrichstadt, Am Mittelburgwall 24-26. **Map** p150 C1. (04881) 93900. FAX (04881) 939022. @ klaus-peter-willhoeftt@t-online.de b,l,d. **Rooms** 10. €€

Bremen

Park Hotel Bremen Sheltered within a beautiful park, this sumptuous hotel provides the peace of the countryside combined with proximity to the town centre. The wonderful *trompe-l'oeil* ceiling in the hall and the Art Deco bar set the tone for the impeccable bedrooms. Breakfast by the lake. French cuisine. Health and fitness facilities.
28209 Bremen, Im Bürgerpark. **Map** p150 B3. (0421) 3408611. FAX (0421) 340 8602. @ reservierung@park-hotel-bremen.de b,l,d. **Rooms** 150. Never. AE, DC, MC, V. €€€€

Föhr Island

Landhause Altes Pastorat A perfect place for rest and recuperation: away from the bustle of the small island's port, a long brick building dating from the 17th and 18th centuries, filled with flowers, antiques and books. Upstairs, bedroom windows poke through the thatch to look out over the lush garden.
25938 Süderende, Haus Nr. 45. **Map** 150 B1. (04683) 226. FAX (04683) 250. @ altes.pastorat@inselfoehr.de b,d. **Rooms** 8. Nov. Not accepted. €€€

Celle

Utspann The former tannery makes a delightful little inn, tucked away by the north end of the city wall in the old part of the town, and is well located for sightseeing from the doorstep. The bedrooms have been imaginatively decorated in a lively rustic style, and all have baths. A cobbled courtyard and a wine cellar add to the charm.
29221 Celle, Im Kreise 13-14. **Map** p150 C3. (05141) 92720. FAX (05141) 927252. @ info@utspann.de b. **Rooms** 23. 22 Dec. to 5 Jan. AC, DC, V. €€€

Hamburg

Hanseatic The town villa feels more like a smart English club than a hotel. There is no sign outside; inside, each of the elegant and well-equipped bedrooms has a decanter of sherry. Home-made jams and a choice of 15 different teas, poured from silver teapots, are offered for breakfast. Close to the city centre.
22299 Hamburg, Sierichstr. 150. **Map** p150 C2. (040) 485772. FAX (040) 485773. @ service@hanseatic-hamburg.de b. **Rooms** 14. Never. DC, MC, V. €€€€

Hamburg

Raffles Vier Jahreszeiten Stylish and quiet yet central; luxurious bedrooms, three restaurants and coffee house.
20354 Hamburg, Neuer Jungfernstieg 9-14. **Map** p150 C2. (040) 34943151. FAX (040) 34942606. @ emailus.hvj@raffles.com b,l,d. **Rooms** 156. €€€€

Hamburg

Wedina A pretty group of buildings in a quiet street close to the station. It is wonderfully spacious and airy, with bold interior design.
20099 Hamburg, Gurlittstrasse 23. **Map** p150 C2. (040) 2808900. FAX (040) 2803894. @ info@wedina.de b. **Rooms** 95. €€€

Malente-Gremsmuhlen

Weisser Hof A lovely garden with ponds surrounds this black-and-white hotel. The bedrooms are large and comfortable.
23714 Malente-Gremsmuhlen, Vosstr. 45. **Map** p151 D1. (04523) 99250. FAX (04523) 6899. @ info@weisserhof.de. b,l,d. **Rooms** 18. €€€

Moraas

Heidehof The popular thatched hotel has a peaceful setting next to the village pond. Wood-panelled *stube* for informal dining and drinking.
19230 Moraas, Hauptstr. 15. **Map** p151 D2. (03883) 722140. FAX (03883) 729118. @ hotel-heiderhof@m-haupt.de b,l,d. **Rooms** 11. €€

For key to symbols see backflap. For price categories *see p147*

Hamburg

Strandhotel Blankenese The area is now a smart residential suburb, but when this delightful Art Nouveau hotel was built by the estuary of the Elbe in the early 1900s, the Blankensee area was a fishing village. The lovely bedrooms are furnished with antiques and modern art, and there is a beach terrace for peaceful drinks. Good food in the snug dining room.
22587 Hamburg, Strandweg 13. **Map** p150 C2.
(040) 862300. FAX (040) 864936. b,l,d. **Rooms** 15.
Never. AE, DC, MC, V. €€€

Hannover

Landhaus Ammann A combination of country-house atmosphere and city convenience, and, to top it all, a Michelin-starred kitchen and superlative cellar. The first-class food can be enjoyed either in the stylishly decorated dining room or on the terrace, which looks onto the garden and woods. Spacious, sleek bedrooms.
30173 Hannover, Hildesheimer Str. 185. **Map** 150 C3.
(0511) 830818. FAX (0511) 843 7749.
@ mail@landhaus-ammann.de b,l,d. **Rooms** 14.
1 week in Jan. AE, DC, MC, V. €€€€

Hannover

Georgenhof The heart of this wonderfully peaceful place, close to the Herrenhausen Gardens, is its much-acclaimed restaurant. Food here is modern, unfussy and expensive, served in a simple, almost austere beamed room. The bedrooms are similarly uncluttered, with little touches of ornamentation.
31067 Hannover 1, Herrenhäuser Kirchweg 20.
Map 150 C3. (0511) 702244. FAX (0511) 708559.
@ hotelgeorgenhof@gmx.de b,l,d. **Rooms** 14.
Never. AE, DC, MC, V. €€€

Lübeck

Kaiserhof Two period mansions were lovingly renovated to produce this smart hotel. The beautifully decorated public rooms invite guests to linger. Bedrooms are spacious and stylish; many have their own balcony. There is also an attractive terrace and superb swimming pool.
23560 Lübeck, Kronsforder Allee 11–13.
Map p151 D2. (0451) 703301.
FAX (0451) 795083. @ service@kaiserhof-luebeck.de
b,d. **Rooms** 59. Never.
AE, DC, MC, V. €€

Quickborn

Romantik Hotel Jagdhaus Waldfrieden Hunting-lodge style in an enchanting park. Enterprising food. Hamburg less than 30 minutes' drive away.
25451 Quickborn, Kieler Str. **Map** p150 C2.
(04106) 61020. FAX (04106) 69196. @ waldfrieden@romantikhotels.com b,l,d. **Rooms** 25. €€€

Rügen

Baumhaus The unassuming former woodcutter's lodge is situated on the edge of the Jasmund national park.
18546 Sassnet auf Rügen. **Map** p151 F1. (038392) 22310. FAX (038392) 66869. @ baumhaus.hagen@t-online.de b,l,d. **Rooms** 10. €

Salzhausen

Romantik Hotel Josthof A totally unmodernized farmhouse hotel: warm welcome, hearty meals. Some of the bedrooms are very large.
21376 Salzhausen, Am Lindenberg 1. **Map** p150 C2.
(04172) 90980. FAX (04172) 6225. @ josthof@romantikhotels.com b,l,d. **Rooms** 16. €€

Schwerin

Niederlandischerhof Elegant and sumptuous, with a lakeside setting. Excellent regional cuisine.
19055 Schwerin, Karl-Marx-Str. 12–13, Am Pfaffenteich. **Map** p151 D2. (0385) 591100. FAX (0385) 59110999. @ hotel@niederlandischer-hof.de b,l,d.
Rooms 33 plus 9 apartments in annexe. €€€

Nörten-Hardenberg

Burghotel Hardenberg For some 300 years this long timbered building, set in woods on the edge of the village, has offered refreshment and shelter to visitors. Modern standards of comfort do not spoil the traditional atmosphere. Two popular restaurants: the Novalis with enterprising modern food, and the more traditional Bürgmuhlen.

⊠ 37176 Nörten-Hardenberg, Hinterhaus 11a. **Map** p150 C4. (05503) 9810. FAX (05503) 981666. @ info@burghotel-hardenberg.de b,l,d. **Rooms** 44. 24 Dec. AE, DC, MC, V. €€€

Sylt Island

Hamburger Hof With a ravishing location right next to the sea, there is plenty for the energetic to do here but it's also a great place to get away from it all. The pretty little hotel is light and airy throughout. The bedrooms are unfussy and beautifully decorated, and have first-rate modern bathrooms. Evening bar.

⊠ 25999 Kampen/Sylt, Kurhausstr 3. **Map** p150 B1. (04651) 94600. FAX (04651) 43975. @ info@hamburger-hof-sylt.de b. **Rooms** 15. Never. Not accepted. €€€€

Sylt Island

Benen-Diken-Hof One of the smarter hotels on the island, this solid thatched house dates from 1841, with a very clever extension added in the 1980s. Inside, it is a plain but striking mix of antiques and modern furniture, with flower arrangements and paintings dotted about. Bedrooms are bright and uncluttered.

⊠ 25980 Keitum-Sylt, Süderstrasse 3. **Map** p150 B1. (04651) 93830. FAX (04651) 9383183. @ info@benen-diken-hof.de b, d. **Rooms** 40. Never. AE, DC, MC, V. €€€€

Walsrode

Landhaus Walsrode A tranquil stopover for travellers along the nearby motorways. Set in its own parkland, the 400-year-old farmhouse has been tastefully decorated to create an elegant guesthouse. In the evenings, drinks are served in the large drawing room or cosy reading room. A simple evening meal can be provided.

⊠ 29664 Walsrode, Oskar-Wolff-Str. 1. **Map** p150 C3. (05161) 98690. FAX (05161) 2352. @ landhauswa@aol.com b. **Rooms** 18. mid-Dec to mid-Jan. AE, MC, V. €€€

Sylt Island

Jörg Müller Pretty tiled gourmet restaurant attached to recently expanded hotel. Beautifully decorated rooms.

⊠ 25980 Westerland/Sylt, Süderstrasse 8. **Map** p150 B1. (04651) 27789. FAX (04651) 201471. @ hotel joergmueller@online.de b,l,d. **Rooms** 23. €€€€

Sylt Island

Seilerhof Tastefully furnished house in the pretty village of Keitum. Wholesome home cooking and a relaxed atmosphere. Book in advance!

⊠ 25980 Keitim-Sylt Ost, Gurstig 7. **Map** p150 B1. (04651) 93340. FAX (04651) 933444. @ info@seilerhofsylt.de b,d. **Rooms** 14. €€

Uslar

Menzhausen Attractive 16th-century building with modern annexe opposite. Lovely dining room. Under new management.

⊠ 37170 Uslar, Lange Str. 12. **Map** p150 C4. (05571) 92230. FAX (05571) 922330. @ hotel@menzhausen.de b,l,d. **Rooms** 74. €€

Worpswede

Eichenhof In the middle of the town but surprisingly rural, with ponds, fields and trees. Bright, pristine bedrooms and breakfast rooms.

⊠ 27726 Worpswede, Ostendorfer Str. 13. **Map** p150 B2. (04792) 2676. FAX (04792) 4427. @ eichenhof-hotel@t-online.de b,d. **Rooms** 20. €€€

For key to symbols see backflap. For price categories *see p147*

AUSTRIA

AUSTRIA

FOR VISITORS to Austria, one of the most striking things about the country is the sheer number of small hotels which have been run by the same family for generations: a fact reflected in the warm welcome and friendly atmosphere you encounter in so many of our entries. The hotels are as diverse as the countryside and you can find something to suit every taste; establishments range from simple mountain inns and smart winter sports hotels to lake-side hostelries, plush city-centre hotels and imposing castles. The heart of most Austrian lodgings is the *Stube*, a room which is usually wood-panelled, with huge tables and bench seats and warmed by a stove – an informal setting for a drink and a chat.

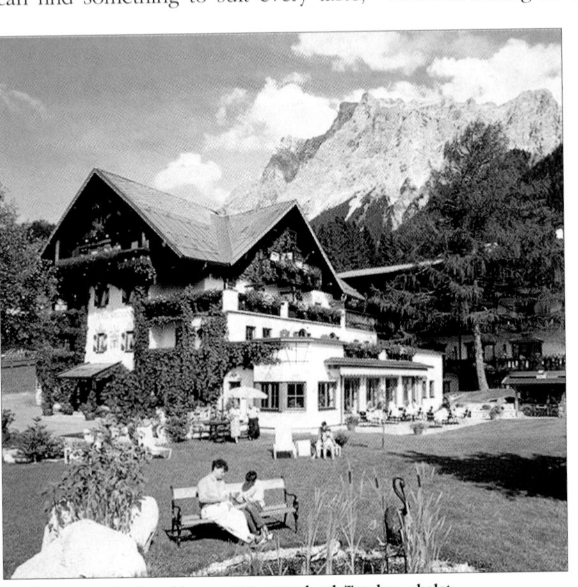

Spielmann Hotel, Ehrwald, page 191, a text-book Tyrolean chalet

AUSTRIA REGION BY REGION

AUSTRIA IS not a large country, but it divides neatly into five regions:

Western Austria
This comprises the states of Vorarlberg, Tyrol and Salzburgland. Vorarlberg is the classic Alpine province, practically cut off from the rest of the country by the Arlberg mountains. As you would expect, it has fine skiing hotels, but they brush shoulders with delightful family-run inns.

The Tyrol, with its dramatic mountains and picture-postcard villages, has many a country hotel set amidst breathtaking lake or mountain scenery. Some of the simpler hotels may strike you as surprisingly inexpensive for such a sought-after area.

Historic Salzburgland has some charming town hotels, with marvellous lakes and mountains within easy reach.

Northwestern Austria
Known as Oberösterreich, this is the home of the dumpling. It has a varied landscape, with mountains, lush valleys and lakes, and has some very attractive hotels in its medieval towns as well as some lovely country ones.

Northeastern Austria
Known as Niederösterreich, this includes Vienna, the capital of Austria. There are some lovely hotels in the famous Vienna woods – still popular with the Viennese for a day out – and a wide variety of inns and castle hotels. Vienna itself has plenty of smart hotels, but there is no shortage of less expensive *pensions*. As you would expect, any establishment outside the city centre (the area bounded by the Ringstrasse) will be cheaper.

Eastern Austria
Burgenland is the least typical state in the country – it was part of Hungary until 1921. It has a pleasantly mild climate, suitable for vines and fruit trees, which you will see in abundance.

Accommodation here is cheaper and simpler than in the rest of Austria. Goose with red cabbage is the ubiquitous (and filling) local dish.

Southern Austria
Kärnten is a popular tourist region and the hotels are of a particularly high standard. The Tauern mountains and clean, warm lowland lakes provide plenty of outdoor life.

Steiermark, the second largest state, has diverse country with fine skiing on the Dachstein range, gentle vine-covered hills in the south, and flat plains in the east. There are lakeside and castle hotels, and many attractive small inns.

IGHLIGHTS

HOTELS ILLUSTRATED on these introductory pages are by) means the only highlights. ther favourites include the ırkhotel Tristachersee, set ı a secluded lake (page)5); the Hotel König von ngarn, right in the centre Vienna (page 197); and eeuring Schlössle (page 191), a breathtaking 17th-century ıstle with fine views over ıke Constance.

OOD AND DRINK

AUSTRIA SHARES borders with six countries, so the ood has many interesting ıfluences and variations – ch pasta dishes from Italy, oulash from Hungary and ımplings from Bohemia – ıt, on the whole, it is ominated by meat. Don't verlook the renowned *'iener Schnitzel* (an escalope f veal in breadcrumbs) and, f course, the wonderful akes and pastries, many ›pped with cream.

Increasingly, however, ou'll find places to stay here there is an emphasis n healthy eating. '*Bio*' signs ıdicate the use of wholefood r organic products, while *3io* rooms' are furnished in atural materials.

Austrian-grown wine is ıainly white – there are pproximately 40,000 hectares)8,850 acres) of vineyards. here are some notable dry vhites. Try also the intense, uity Rieslings from the *'achau* region and the ıtractive sweet wine of the Ieusiedlersee region.

The beer is excellent, with ach region producing its wn brew. There are huge egional differences, and it is vise to go for the local peciality – Stiegl Bier in alzburg and Gösser Bier rom Steiermark, for instance.

The Austrians treat lunch, sually starting at about 2:30pm, as their main meal: hey'll eat their way through oup, a main course, and lessert. Supper or dinner is aten in the early evening, nd is usually cold meats, heese and bread. Mid-morning and mid-afternoon snacks are also common.

No stay in Austria is complete without a visit to one of the coffee houses. With wonderful rich smells of croissant, coffee and chocolate, they are great places to visit any time of the day.

Breakfast room, Landhaus Veronika, page 194

BEDROOMS AND BATHROOMS

IF YOU WANT twin beds, ask for them specifically when booking. A 'double' bed is usually two single mattresses in a 'two-mattress' frame, covered with two single duvets. It you require an en suite bathroom, be sure to specify this when you make your reservation.

OTHER PRACTICAL INFORMATION

BOOK AHEAD for hotels in Vienna, and for others in peak times, and state any special requirements. Confirm check-out times. Breakfast is typically a buffet of breads, cheese, fruit and cold meats. The standard of hotels and guesthouses is usually high.

Language German is spoken by 98 per cent of the population, but since most have good English it is easy to get by, especially in cities.

Currency From 1 January 2002, the European *euro* (written 'EUR'), made up of 100 *cents*.

Shops Generally open 8:30am–6pm Mon to Fri (many close for lunch), and until noon on Saturdays.

Tipping It is customary to round up the bill by around 10 per cent, even if the service charge is included. Don't leave it on the table: tell the waiter how much you are paying, including the tip.

Telephoning To phone within Austria, dial the full number, including the initial zero. To call Austria from the UK, dial 00 43, then the number, omitting the initial zero. From the US, 011 43.

Restaurants Note that you will be charged for each piece of bread you eat.

Public holidays 1 January; 6 January; Easter Monday; 1 May; Ascension Day; Whit Monday; Corpus Christi; 15 August; 26 October; 1 November; 8 December; 25 and 26 December.

USEFUL WORDS

Breakfast	*Frühstück*
Lunch	*Mittagessen*
Dinner	*Abendessen*
Free room?	*Zimmer frei?*
How much?	*Wieviel?*
Single room	*Einzelzimmer*
Double room	*Doppelzimmer*

AUSTRIA PRICE BANDS

AUSTRIAN HOTELS are officially classified by stars, from one to five, but don't be too swayed by this. Our price bands are much simpler to use, referring simply to the price of a standard double room in high season.

Breakfast is often, but not always, included in room prices quoted by hotels. In some areas you may be charged a local tax.

below 35 EUR
35–110 EUR
110–180 EUR
above 180 EUR

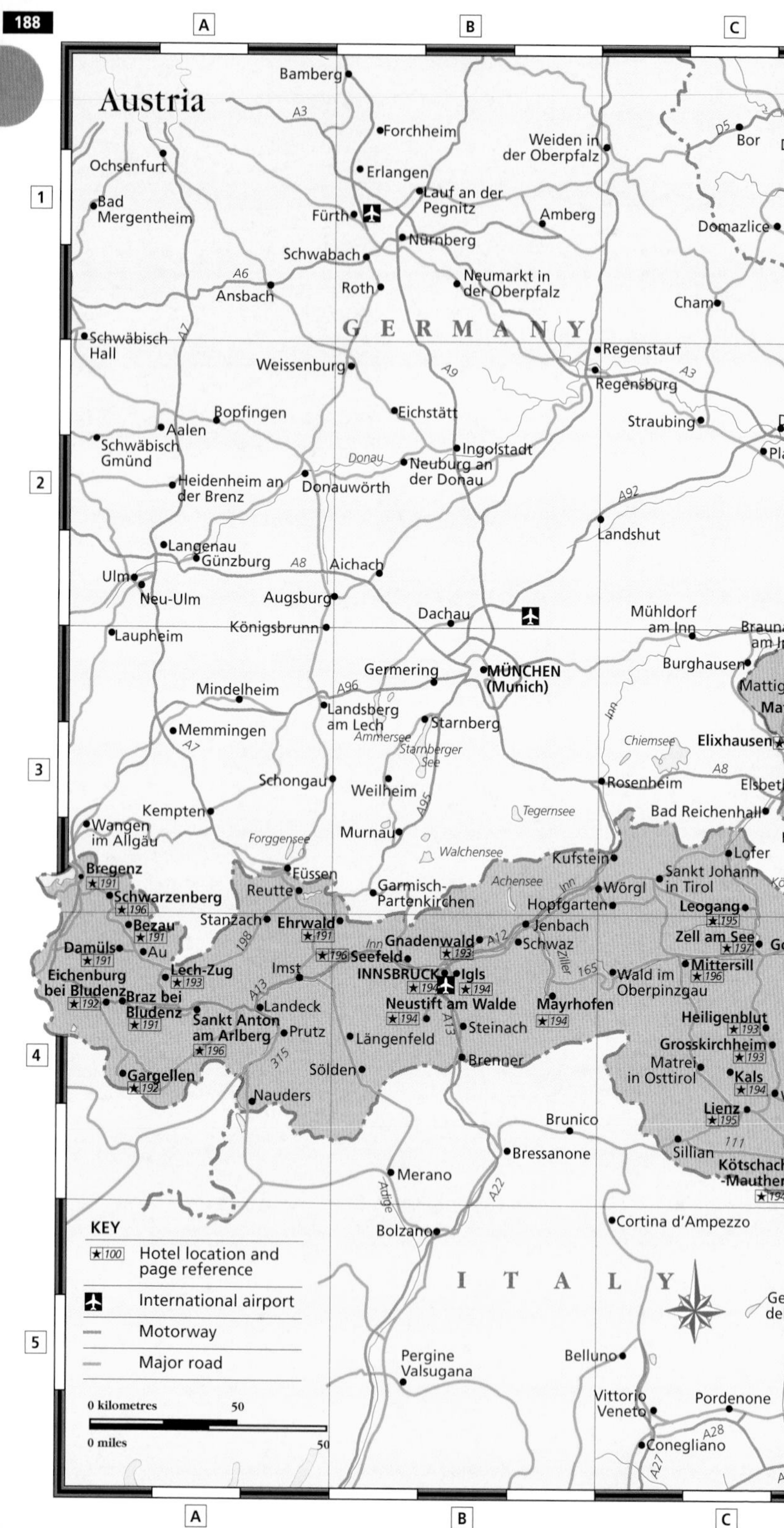
Austria
A
B
C
1
2
3
4
5
Bamberg
Forchheim
Erlangen
Ochsenfurt
Bad Mergentheim
Lauf an der Pegnitz
Fürth
Nürnberg
Weiden in der Oberpfalz
Bor
Amberg
Domazlice
Schwabach
Ansbach
Roth
Neumarkt in der Oberpfalz
Cham
GERMANY
Schwäbisch Hall
Weissenburg
Regenstauf
Regensburg
Bopfingen
Eichstätt
Straubing
Aalen
Schwäbisch Gmünd
Ingolstadt
Donau
Neuburg an der Donau
Heidenheim an der Brenz
Donauwörth
Landshut
Langenau
Günzburg
Aichach
Ulm
Neu-Ulm
Augsburg
Dachau
Mühldorf am Inn
Königsbrunn
Laupheim
Germering
MÜNCHEN (Munich)
Burghausen
Mindelheim
Landsberg am Lech
Ammersee
Starnberg
Starnberger See
Memmingen
Chiemsee
Elixhausen
Schongau
Weilheim
Rosenheim
Kempten
Tegernsee
Bad Reichenhall
Wangen im Allgäu
Forggensee
Murnau
Walchensee
Lofer
Kufstein
Bregenz ★191
Füssen
Achensee
Sankt Johann in Tirol
Schwarzenberg ★196
Reutte
Garmisch-Partenkirchen
Wörgl
Hopfgarten
Leogang ★195
Bezau ★191
Stanzach
Ehrwald ★191
Jenbach
Damüls ★191
Au
Gnadenwald ★193
Zell am See ★197
Seefeld ★196
Schwaz
Eichenburg bei Bludenz ★192
Lech-Zug ★193
Imst
INNSBRUCK ★194
Igls ★194
Wald im Oberpinzgau
Mittersill ★196
Braz bei Bludenz ★191
Landeck
Neustift am Walde ★194
Mayrhofen ★194
Sankt Anton am Arlberg ★196
Prutz
Steinach
Heiligenblut ★193
Längenfeld
Grosskirchheim ★193
Brenner
Matrei in Osttirol
Kals ★194
Gargellen ★192
Sölden
Nauders
Lienz ★195
Brunico
Sillian
Bressanone
Kötschach-Mauthen ★194
Merano
Cortina d'Ampezzo
Bolzano
ITALY
Pergine Valsugana
Belluno
Vittorio Veneto
Pordenone
Conegliano
KEY
★100 Hotel location and page reference
International airport
Motorway
Major road
0 kilometres 50
0 miles 50

D
E
F
1
2
3
4
5
CZECH REPUBLIC
AUSTRIA
SLOVENIA
CROATIA
Cercany
Hlinsko
Svitavy
Policka
Zdírec
Havlíkuv Brod
Sázava
Krelovice
Petrovice
Boskovice
Tábor
Jihlava
Velké Mezirící
Písek
Brno
Trebic
Zeletava
Jindrichuv Hradec
Ceské Budejovice
Trebon
Znojmo
Breclav
Volary
Cesky Krumlov
Heidenreichstein
Geras ★192
Gmünd
Haugsdorf
Weitra
Horn
Mistelbach an der Zaya
Zwettl
Hollabrunn
Berg bei Rohrbach
Freistadt ★192
Liebenau
Krems an der Donau
Kronberg am Russbach ★195
Stockerau
Mühldorf ★194
Weissenkirchen ★196
Klosterneuburg
WIEN (Vienna) ★197
Eferding
Linz ★194
Sankt Pölten
Purkersdorf
Enns
Melk
Wilhelmsburg
Dörfl ★192
Schwechat
Wels
Amstetten
Mödling
Bad Hall ★191
Steyr
Hainfeld
Baden
Ebreichsdorf
Vöcklabruck
Berndorf
Waidhofen an der Ybbs
Ternberg
Gmunden
Wiener Neustadt
Eisenstadt
Grünau im Almtal ★193
Mattersburg
Mariazell
Neunkirchen
Sopron
Traunsee
Grundlsee ★193
Mürzzuschlag
Aspang Markt
Deutschkreutz
Altasee ★190
Eisenerz
Langenwang
Liezen
Rottenmann
Trieben
Kapfenberg
Bernstein ★191
Trofaiach
Schladming
Sankt Johann am Tauern
Hartberg
Szombathely
Sebersdorf ★196
Weiz
Knittelfeld
Peggau
Judenburg
Gratwein
Scheifling
Gleisdorf
Fürstenfeld
Tamsweg
Neumarkt
Voitsberg
GRAZ ★193
Körmend
Predlitz
Obdach ★196
Feldbach
Jennersdorf
Lieboch
Wildon
Friesach
Mahldorf
Hüttenberg
Zalalövö
Althofen
Wolfsberg
Leibnitz
Bad Kleinkirchheim ★190
Diex ★191
Schwanberg
Afritz ★190
Rédics
Ossiacher See
Spielfeld
Völkermarkt
Muta
Treffen
Klagenfurt
Faakersee ★192
Wörthersee ★197
Maribor
Villach
Arnoldstein
Sittersdorf
Slovenska Bistrica
Cakovec
Eisenkappel
Ptuj
Varazdin
Bled
Kranj
Celje
Koprivnica
Tolmin
Trbovlje
LJUBLJANA
Zabok
Zabno
Gorizia
Trebnje
Potok
ZAGREB
Monfalcone
Postojna
Ribnica
Donau
Thaya
Traun
Enns
Mur
Raab
Drau
Drava
D1
D2
303
38
45
125
124
A8
A1
115
121
20
A4
A3
A9
25
71
A2
96
95
A23

Altaussee

Hubertushof Crammed with hunting trophies, this hilltop inn was built in 1894 for the present owner's grandparents and retains the atmosphere of a private house, with a grandfather clock and an open fire in the sitting room. The bedrooms are beautifully decorated and there are stunning views of lake and mountains from the terrace.
8992 Altausee, Puchen 86. **Map** p189 D3.
(03622) 71280. FAX (03622) 7221380. b.
Rooms 9. mid-Oct to 27 Dec; March; open at Easter. AE, DC, MC, V. €€

Attersee

Resident Häupl Run by the Häupl family for seven generations, now under new management, this large hotel with stunning views over the Attersee – the largest lake in the Austrian Alps – is noted for its first-rate restaurant. Interesting antiques are dotted about, and there are cosy places for reading or conversation.
4863 Seewalchen am Attersee, Haupstr 20-22.
Map p189 D3. (07662) 63630. FAX (07662) 636362.
@ info@resident-haeupl.at b,l,d. **Rooms** 33.
Never. AE, DC, MC, V. €€

Anif

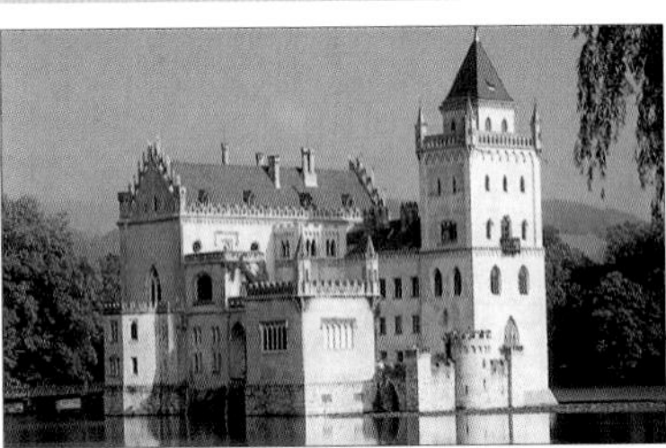

Schlosswirt Anif Originally the guesthouse to a nearby castle, this is now a lively inn, only 20 minutes' drive from Salzburg. There is a feeling of history about the place;
both food and ambience are traditional. Each bedroom is decorated in a different style. There is a 15th-century annexe opposite.
5081 Anif 22. **Map** p188 C3.
(06246) 72175. FAX (06246) 721758.
@ info@schlosswirt-anif.com b,l,d. **Rooms** 28.
3 weeks Nov. AE, DC, MC, V. €€€

Badgastein

Haus Hirt Here is a wonderful mixture of modern and traditional, with some split-level bedrooms and William Morris prints, and a fully equipped health farm. The delicious breakfast buffet features home-made jams, herbal teas and bread so popular that some guests go home with a loaf in their baggage.
5640 Badgastein, Kaiserpromenade 14. **Map** p188 C4.
(06434) 2797. FAX (06434) 279748. @ greatplaces@haus-hirt.com b,l,d. **Rooms** 30. 2 Nov to 15 Dec; 15 Apr to 15 May. AE, DC, V. €€€

Afritz

Hotel Lärchenhof Run by a sporting family, this mountain hotel caters for the same. There are three tennis courts and a pool; skiing in winter.
9542 Afritz-Verditz. **Map** p189 D4. (04247) 2134.
FAX (04247) 213411. @ heinz.tronigger@sunshine.at
b,d. **Rooms** 22. €€

Attersee

Villa Langer Quiet lakeside villa; informal, suitable for families. Each suite has a kitchenette, but dinner is available five nights a week.
4854 Weissenbach. **Map** p189 D3. (07663) 242.
FAX (07663) 24236. @ office@villalanger.at b,l,d.
Rooms 19. €€€

Badgastein

Villa Solitude Stuffed full of antiques and silks, this charming villa ten minutes' drive from the Gastein falls is peaceful and comfortable.
5640 Badgastein, Kaiser Franz Joseph Str 16.
Map p188 C4. (06434) 5101. FAX (06434) 2560.
b. **Rooms** 6. €€€€

Bad Kleinkirchheim

Hotel Römerbad Delicious wholefood cookery, many health treatments available, and skiing nearby. Most bedrooms have a balcony.
9546 Bad Kleinkirchheim. **Map** p189 D4.
(04240) 82340. FAX (04240) 823457.
@ office@roemerbadhotels.at b,d. **Rooms** 50. €€

BAD HALL

'hloss Feyregg As befits a castle (built 1720), is hotel is wonderfully quiet and secluded, and retains the feel of the private residence it was. ıch bedroom has its own small sitting room. ›oms look over the village church, or over the ›nderful gardens – which include an avenue ›ed with statues, a courtyard, and wild garden ›yond. There is an inn just below the castle, ıere guests can migrate for lunch or dinner.
] 4540 Bad Hall. **Map** p189 D3. (07258) 2591. b. **›oms** 12. 20–27 Dec. Not accepted. €€€

BREGENZ

Deuring Schlössle 'Breathtaking' is the word for this 17th-century castle overlooking Lake Constance. The reception rooms are huge; the bedrooms are large and furnished with antiques and silks. The hotel was taken over by chef Ernst Huber in 1989. The food he and his son prepare is light and fresh, using mainly local produce.
6900 Bregenz, Ehre-Guta-Platz 4. **Map** p188 A3.
(05574) 47800. FAX (05574) 4780080.
@ deuring@schloessle.vol.at b,l,d. **Rooms** 15.
2nd week in Feb. AE, DC, MC, V. €€€€

BERNSTEIN

rg Bernstein Everything you could wish for in ›astle: towers, fortifications, a dungeon, and a ›ights' Hall with a stuccoed ceiling which is ›w a restaurant. The staircase is thought to be Fischer von Erlach, the great Viennese ›oque architect. The bedrooms are vast, and ›h is furnished with antiques; no two are alike. telephones, televisions or minibars.
7434 Bernstein. **Map** p189 F3. (03354) 6382. (03354) 6520. @ burgbernstein@netway.at b,d. **›ms** 10. Never. AE, DC, MC, V. €€€

EHRWALD

Spielmann's Hotel Meadows surround this old Tyrolean chalet, and every bedroom has a balcony from which to admire the jagged mountain peaks. The food is cooked by the Spielmann father and son, both top-rated chefs and noted mountaineers. Near the Sonnenhang ski-lifts, and good hiking; facilities for children.
6632 Ehrwald. **Map** p188 B4. (05673) 22250.
FAX (05673) 22255. @ info@hotel-spielmann.com
b,l,d. **Rooms** 38. Mid-Oct to mid-Dec; after Easter to late May. MC, V. €€€

BEZAU

›sthof Sonne Geranium-filled window boxes ‹ painted shutters greet you at this edge-of-›ge inn. Cross-country skiing.
›870 Bezau. **Map** p188 A4. (05514) 2262. (05514) 2912. @ sonne-bezau@aon.at b,l,d. **ms** 30. €€

BRAZ BEI BLUDENZ

›thof Traube There is a permanent nanny ›, so it is popular with skiing families. Prior ›king essential.
›751 Braz bei Bludenz, Klostertalerstr 12. p188 A4. (05552) 281830. FAX (05552) 2810340. traube.braz@aon.at b,l,d. **Rooms** 19. €€

DAMÜLS

Berghotel Madlener The Madlener is a fine example of a chalet-style hotel, with open fires and bedrooms panelled in pale wood.
6884 Damüls, Schwende 22. **Map** p188 A4.
(05510) 2210. FAX (05510) 22115. @ berghotel.madlener@aon.at b,l,d. **Rooms** 24. €€€

DIEX

Gasthof Jesch A working farm with home-grown produce for the table. Simple and suitable for families; horse-riding available.
9103 Diex, Wandelitzen 10. **Map** p189 E4.
(04232) 7196. FAX (04232) 719690.
@ office@gasthof-jesch.at b,l,d. **Rooms** 22. €€

For key to symbols see backflap. For price categories *see p187*

Elixhausen

Romantik Hotel Gmachl In the family since 1538, and totally refurbished in 1987, the Gmachl is a profusion of old prints and dried flower decorations. The hotel's own butcher's shop sells its renowned Bratwurst to the locals as well as to guests. An annexe has 22 pleasantly done-out double bedrooms. Tennis and horse-riding.

5161 Salzburg-Elixhausen, Dorfstr. 14. **Map** p188 C3. (0662) 480212. FAX (0662) 48021272. romantikhotel@gmachl.com b,l,d. **Rooms** 34. late June to mid-July. AE, DC, MC, V. €€€

Gargellen

Alpenhotel Heimspitze This hotel feels remote, tucked away across the river from the small ski resort of Gargellen. It's a homely place, with woven rugs and painted furniture, and an adventure playground for children. The award-winning kitchen produces a daily-changing menu; home-made jams and cakes.

6787 Gargellen. **Map** p188 A4. (05557) 6319. FAX (05557) 631920. hotel@heimspitze.com b,l,d. **Rooms** 23. mid-Oct to mid-Dec; mid-Apr to June. AE, DC, MC, V. €€€

Faakersee

Gasthof Tschebull Hans and Willi Tschemernjak must be doing something right because their comfortable restaurant with rooms on the edge of the Faaker See is always busy. In the restaurant they serve up home-cured hams, home-made sausages, home-smoked fish and even home- distilled schnapps. Rooms range from simple to luxurious. Swimming lake, tennis courts, private beach.

9580 Egg am Faakersee, Egger Seuferstr. 26. **Map** p189 D4. (04254) 2191. FAX (04254) 219137. b,l,d. **Rooms** 13. Never. AE, DC, MC, V. €€

Geras

Alter Schüttkasten Geras The huge 17th-century building, once a granary belonging to a local monastery, has been perceptively and unfussily converted. The atmosphere is peaceful, the style simple. Two dining rooms offer local fish and game. There is good hiking in the woods of the Waldviertel. Under new management.

2093 Geras, Vorstadt 11. **Map** p189 E2. (02912) 332. FAX (02912) 33233. hotel.schuettkasten@ telecom.at b,l,d. **Rooms** 26. Never. DC, MC, V. €€

Dörfl

Pedro's Landhaus Extravagant and luxurious furnishings characterize Pedro's, a lavish joint venture by opera star Jose Carreras and Pedro Massana. Set in a park in the Vienna Woods.

3072 Dörfl 19, Kasten. **Map** p189 F3. (02744) 7387. FAX (02744) 7389. b,l,d. **Rooms** 14. €€€

Eichenberg bei Bregenz

Hotel Schönblick Dazzling views across Lake Constance lure both locals and visitors. There is a good restaurant and an indoor swimming pool.

6911 Eichenberg bei Bregenz. **Map** p188 A4. (05574) 45965. FAX (05574) 459657. hotel. schoenblick@schoenblick.at b,l,d. **Rooms** 25. €€

Faakersee

Inselhotel Informal hotel set on a small island; guests park by the shore and cross by private launch. Tennis, sailing; nanny in July, August.

9583 Faakersee, Faak am See. **Map** p189 D4. (04254) 2145. FAX (04254) 213677. info@inselhotel.at b,l,d. **Rooms** 32. €€

Freistadt

Gasthof Zum Goldenen Hirschen In the centre of this fine medieval town, a guesthouse with large bedrooms and imaginative cuisine.

4240 Freistadt, Böhmergasse 8-10. **Map** p189 D2. (07942) 722580. FAX (07942) 7225840. golden. hirsch@hotel-freistadt.at b,l,d. **Rooms** 32. €€

GNADENWALD

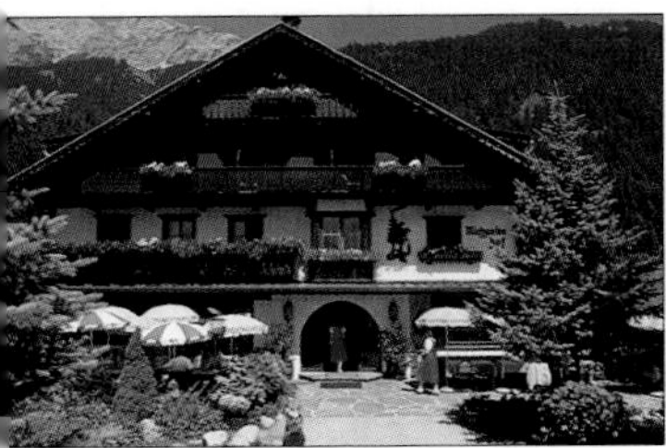

asthof Michaelerhof Louis Schiestl took over is former farmhouse more than 30 years ago, nd turned it first into a restaurant, then into an otel. His daughter Petra now runs the place, ffering the best in traditional cuisine as well as sian specialities. Bedrooms are pleasant. It has n internet room and a juice bar. Only 20 inutes' drive from central Innsbruck.
6060 Gnadenwald. **Map** p188 B4. (05223) 48128. X (05223) 481284. b,l,d. **Rooms** 20. 7–24 l and 11 Nov to 12 Dec. AE, DC, MC, V. €€

HEILIGENBLUT

Haus Senger This small hotel, owned by the former Olympic sportsman Hans Senger, was rebuilt in 1966, but beams, stone-flagged floors and open fires make for a perfect atmosphere. Some of the country-style bedrooms have a kitchenette. A separate wing houses a health and fitness area.
9844 Heiligenblut. **Map** p188 C4. (04824) 2215. FAX (04824) 22159. @ sengerja@magnet.at b,d,l. **Rooms** 15. Oct to mid-Dec; Easter to mid-June. AE, DC, MC, V. €€

GOLDEGG

otel der Seehof The village of Goldegg is eautifully preserved, with cobbled streets and ld houses. The Seehof, an inn since 1727, has een run by the Schellhorns for four generations. edrooms are cheerful, some featuring painted urniture. Lovely strudels by chef Sepp; skiing downhill and cross-country) with father, Franz. kate on the lake in winter, swim in summer.
5622 Goldegg am See. **Map** p188 C4. (06415) 1370. FAX (01645) 8276. @ seehof@saltzburg.co.at b, d. **Rooms** 30. Apr; Nov. DC, MC, V. €€€

LECH-ZUG

Gasthof Rote Wand This is a perfect place for health and fitness enthusiasts: as well as winter sports, there is a wide year-round choice of exercise programmes, including water gymnastics and weight training. The restaurant is very traditional, while the bedrooms are designer-fresh, with the beds up on split-level galleries.
6764 Lech-Zug am Arlberg. **Map** p188 A4. (05583) 34350. FAX (05583) 343540. @ gasthof@rotewand.com b,l,d. **Rooms** 38. May to Nov. MC, V. €€€€

GRAZ

chlossberg Hotel Stuffed full with lovely ntiques. Comfortable bedrooms and a roof arden with views over the town.
8010 Graz, Kaiser-Franz-Josef-Kai 30. **Map** p189 E4. (0316) 80700. FAX (0316) 807070. @ office@ chlossberg-hotel.at b. **Rooms** 54. €€€€

GROSSKIRCHHEIM

ationalparkhotel Schlosswirt Wildlife and owers abound around this inn. Good, raightforward food. Hiking and horseriding.
9843 Grosskirchheim-Döllach. **Map** p188 C4. (04825) 411. FAX (04825) 411165. schlosswirt@eunet.at b,l,d. **Rooms** 22. €€

GRÜNAU IM ALMTAL

Romantik Hotel Almtalhof Alpine air, a river, trees and flowers make this hotel special. Good food and fine wine list.
4645 Grünau im Almtal. **Map** p189 D3. (07616) 8204. FAX (07616) 820466. @ almtalhof@magnet.at b,l,d. **Rooms** 21. €€€

GRUNDLSEE

Gasthof zum Ladner A 255-year-old inn on the shore of the Grundlsee lake, close to the Totes Gebirge mountains. Private lakeside beach.
8993 Grundlsee, Gössl 1. **Map** p189 D3. (03622) 8211. FAX (03622) 82114. @ ladner@eunet.at b,l,d. **Rooms** 8, plus 2 apartments. €€

Linz

Wolfinger It may once have been a monastery, but little is spartan here. It's a tasteful city hotel, the walls covered in old mirrors and photographs, public rooms and bedrooms displaying much Biedermeier and Art Nouveau furniture. Most bedrooms overlook the quiet courtyard. Good views of the Hauptplatz from the breakfast room. ✉ 4020 Linz, Hauptplatz 19. **Map** p189 D2. ☎ (0732) 7732910. FAX (0732) 77329155. @ wolfinger@austria-classic-hotels.at 🍴 b. **Rooms** 46. ● Never. AE, DC, MC, V. €€€

Mühldorf

Burg Oberrana High up on a hill above the Danube valley, this white-walled castle has great views all around. More than 900 years old, it also has the oldest Romanesque chapel crypt in - Austria, some 200 years older than the castle itself. The well-restored bedrooms are furnished with antiques. Delicious home-made brandies. ✉ 3622 Mühldorg bei Spitz/Donau. **Map** p189 E2. ☎ (02713) 8221. FAX (02713) 8366. @ hotel-gutenbrunn@netway.at 🍴 b. **Rooms** 12. ● Nov to end Apr. AE, DC, V. €€€

Mayrhofen

Landhaus Veronika Set in meadows just five minutes' walk from the centre of the popular resort village of Mayrhofen, the Veronika is luxurious but cosy too. It has spacious aparments where guests can relax when bad weather makes outings difficult, and an indoor pool. There is no restaurant, but there are plenty in the village; guests can have breakfast brought to their rooms. ✉ 6290 Mayrhofen 250b. **Map** p188 B4. ☎ (05285) 63347. FAX (05825) 63819. @ bh13@netway.at 🍴 b. **Rooms** 10. ● Never. DC, MC, V. €€

Neustift am Walde

Landhaus Fuhrgassl-Huber Located in a wine-producing village and backing on to a vineyard, this homely *pension* has a fresh, spacious feel and big, comfortable bedrooms. You can taste the famous Fuhrgass-Huber from the nearby vineyard The area is peaceful and rural, yet Vienna is only half an hour's bus and tram ride away. ✉ 1190 Wien, Neustift am Walde, Rathstr 24. **Map** p188 B4. ☎ (01) 4403033. FAX (01) 4402714. @ landhaus@fuhrgassl-huber.at 🍴 b. **Rooms** 38. ● 1st week in Feb. AE, DC, MC, V. €€€

Igls

Schlosshotel Igls Small castle hotel with a luxurious indoor pool, a formal drawing room, and a cosy bar. Golf, ski areas nearby. ✉ 6080 Igls. **Map** p188 B4. ☎ (0512) 377217. FAX (0512) 378679. @ hotel@schlosshotel-igls.com 🍴 b,l,d. **Rooms** 18. €€€

Innsbruck

Weisses Rössl This establishment, set in a townhouse in central Innsbruck, is popular with the locals too for its well-priced restaurant. ✉ 6020 Innsbruck, Kiebachgasse 8 in der Altstadt. **Map** p188 B4. ☎ (0512) 583057. FAX (0512) 5830575. @ weissesl@roessl.at 🍴 b,l,d. **Rooms** 15. €€€

Kals

Hotel Taurerwirt Overlooking a beautiful valley, the homely Taurerwirt is perfect for open-air types: hiking, fishing and skiing close by. ✉ 9981 Kals am Grossglockner. **Map** p188 C4. ☎ (04876) 8226. FAX (04876) 822611. @ info@traurerwirt.at 🍴 b,l,d. **Rooms** 35. €€

Kötschach-Mauthen

Landhaus Kellerwand Owner Sissy Sonnleitner, a self-taught cook, was Austria's 'Chef of the Year in 1990. First-rate bedrooms. ✉ 9640 Kötschach-Mauthen. **Map** p188 C4. ☎ (04715) 2690. FAX (04715) 26916. @ sonnl@netway.at 🍴 b. **Rooms** 11. €€

SALZBURG

Hotel Schloss Mönchstein Sitting on the Mönchsberg crag above Salzburg, this elegant but friendly castle hotel is popular with both businesspeople and people on holiday. The rooms are well equipped; some have views of the city, and some of the gardens. New restaurant, terrace and bar.

5020 Salzburg, Mönchsberg Park 26. **Map** p188 C3. (0662) 8485550. FAX (0662) 848559. @ salzburg@monchstein.at b,l,d. **Rooms** 24. Never. AE, DC, MC, V. €€€€

ST GILGEN

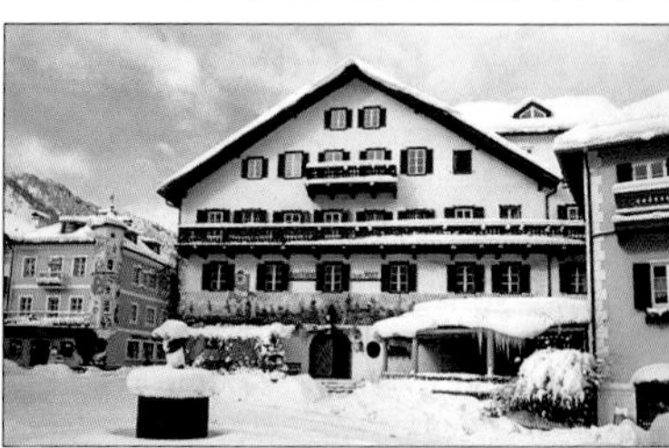

Gasthof Zur Post This charming inn was built in 1415, and its exterior is decorated with a fine painted frieze of a boar hunt. Oak beams and dark stone floors give it a wonderfully historic atmosphere. The comfortable bedrooms have views onto the streets. Mozart's mother was born in the village, and a fountain and statue in the square honours the composer.

5340 St Gilgen, Mozartplatz 8. **Map** p189 D3. (06227) 2157. FAX (06227) 2158600. b,l,d. **Rooms** 20. Never. AE, DC, MC, V. €€

SALZBURG

Stadtkrug Despite Salzburg's crowds of visitors, especially in the music season, this hotel retains a reputation for its serene atmosphere and unflustered, personal service. Smart but no-nonsense bedroom decoration and furnishings. The restaurant is one of the most popular in town; open late during the music festival.

5020 Salzburg, Linzer Gasse 20. **Map** p188 C3. (0662) 87 35 45. FAX (0662) 87 35 45 54. @ office@stadtkrug.at b,l,d. **Rooms** 35. 1 week in Mar. AE, DC, MC, V. €€€

ST WOLFGANG

Landhaus zu Appesbach A wonderful contrast to the busy lakeside resort of St Wolfgang, this elegant villa hotel has garden, lake and woods to keep it secluded. At first glance, the house has changed little since the Duke of Windsor stayed here in 1937, but it has been sympathetically modernized. Tennis courts and sauna.

5360 St Wolfgang am see. **Map** p189 D3. (06138) 2209. FAX (06138) 220914. @ landhaus@ping.at b,l,d. **Rooms** 26 , plus 9 suites. Nov to Easter. AE, DC, MC, V. €€€

KRONBERG AM RUSSBACH

Landhaus Kronberghof Ideal for horse-riding foodies: there are 70 horses, an indoor school and excellent food. Prior booking essential.

2123 Kronberg am Rossbach 3. **Map** p189 F2. (02245) 4304. FAX (02245) 43044. @ info@kronberghof.com b,l,d. **Rooms** 5. €€

LEOGANG

Landhotel Rupertus Jolly holiday hotel with supervised children's activities in summer. Adults appreciate the sauna, steam bath and gym.

5771 Leogang. **Map** p188 C3. (06583) 84660. FAX (06583) 846655. @ info@rupertus.net b,l,d. **Rooms** 27. €€

LIENZ (TRISTACHERSEE)

Parkhotel Tristachersee Wonderfully spacious, this retreat has a conservatory right on the lake. Luxurious rooms and award-winning restaurant.

9900 Lienz, Tristachersee. **Map** p188 C4. (04852) 67666. FAX (04852) 67699. @ tristachersee@oshirol.com b,l,d. **Rooms** 42. €€

MATTSEE

Iglhauser Bräu Ancient, comfortable family-run hostelry. Guests can windsurf in the nearby lake, sail in the hotel's dinghies, and row in their boats.

5163 Mattsee, Schlossbergweg 4. **Map** p188 C3. (06217) 5205. FAX (06217) 520533. b,l,d. **Rooms** 20. MC, V. €€

For key to symbols see backflap. For price categories *see p187*

Schwarzenberg

Gasthof Hirschen The distinctive 18th-century wooden-shingled inn, set in the centre of the village, has something for everyone. Families come for skiing, locals drop in for a drink, and in the summer it is popular with couples. The old house is traditional, but the annex very modern. The restaurant is popular with locals.
6867 Schwarzenberg. **Map** p188 A3.
(05512) 29440. FAX (05512) 294420.
@ info@hirschenschwarzenberg.at b,l,d. **Rooms** 32.
Never. AE, DC, MC, V. €€€

Seefeld

Viktoria Paul and Andrea Kirchmair run one of Austria's smallest 5-star hotels. Quality abounds, although the taste sometimes inclines to the kitsch, with extravagantly themed suites like the chocolate-boxy Montmartre, the Dolce Vita, with bold colours and Spanish avant-garde furniture, and the 5 Tibetans, with its Chinese screen, black lacquer furniture and bold red flower fabric.
6100 Seefeld, Geigenbühelweg 589. **Map** p188 B4.
(05212) 44410. FAX (05212) 4443. @ hotel@viktoria.at
b. **Rooms** 14 suites. Never. MC, V. €€€

Sebersdorf

Schlosshotel Obermayerhofen In the family of the Counts Kottulinksy since 1777, this fine castle has been a hotel only since the mid-1980s. Accommodation is wonderfully luxurious, with four-poster beds and lavish bathrooms. Chandeliers, a marvellous 18th-century jungle fresco and a private chapel add to the opulence.
8272 Sebersdorf. **Map** p189 F4. (03333) 2503.
FAX (03333) 250350. @ schlosshotel@obermayerhofen.at
b,l,d. **Rooms** 22. early Jan to end Feb.
DC, MC, V. €€€

Weissenkirchen

Raffelsbergerhof Smothered in wisteria and vines, this village inn used to be a ship-master's house, and the horses that pulled the barges up the Danube were stabled here. It is full of intriguing objects collected by the present owner's father; even the light-fittings are worth a second look. Charming bedrooms.
3610 Weissenkirchen. **Map** p189 E2.
(02715) 2201. FAX (02715) 220127.
@ raffelsberger@nextra.at b. **Rooms** 13.
Nov to early Apr. V. €€€

Mittersill

Nationalparkhotel Felben Children's activities, a profusion of farm animals, large bedrooms and heated pool make this perfect for families.
5730 Mittersill. **Map** p188 C4. (06562) 4407.
FAX (06562) 440772. @ info@felben.at
b,l,d. **Rooms** 25. €€

Obdach

Judenburger Hütte Sports lovers flock to this mountain haven near the small town of Obdach: tennis courts, swimming pools and skiing.
8742 St Wolfgang am Zirbitz. **Map** p189 E4.
(03578) 8202. FAX (03578) 820220. @ reception@judenburger-huette.at b,l,d. **Rooms** 13. €€

Salzburg

Hotel Zistelalm High on the Gaisberg crag and with walls covered in antlers, crackling log fires in winter and year-round views over the city.
5026 Saltzburg, Gaisberg 16. **Map** p188 C3.
(0662) 641067. FAX (0662) 642618.
@ zistelalm@ eunet.at b,l,d. **Rooms** 15. €€

St Anton am Arlberg

St Antoner Hof Four-poster beds, painted furniture, and an indoor pool cleverly mix the lavish with the traditional. New Austrian cuisine.
6580 St Anton am Arlberg. **Map** p188 A4.
(05446) 2910. FAX (05446) 3551.
@ hotel@antonerhof.at b,l,d. **Rooms** 37. €€€

WIEN (VIENNA)

Altstadt Vienna This spacious hotel in Josefstadt, an unspoilt baroque part of the city, is only ten minutes' walk from central Vienna. Owner Otto Ernst Wiesenthal, a seasoned traveller, has decorated the place according to his own definite tastes: a happy mix of antique and modern pieces. Friendly and helpful service; rooftop views over the city.
⊠ 1070 Wien, Kirchengasse 41. **Map** p189 F2.
(01) 5263399. FAX (01) 5234901. @ hotel@altstadt.at
b. **Rooms** 34. Never. AE, DC, MC, V. €€€

WIEN (VIENNA)

Hotel König von Ungarn Right in the centre of the old city, very close to St Stephen's Cathedral, and extremely popular. The building dates from the 18th century; inside, chandeliers, portraits and an enclosed courtyard all add to its charm. The bedrooms are comfortable but not over-grand. The restaurant serves traditional Austrian cuisine.
⊠ 1010 Wien, Schulerstr. 10. **Map** p189 F2.
(01) 515840. FAX (01) 515848. b,d. **Rooms** 33.
Never. AE, DC, MC, V. €€€€

WIEN (VIENNA)

Altwienerhof Although located in an unfashionable part of Vienna, the Altwienerhof is special. Its restaurant is visited by gourmets from all over the world (closed 1-21 Jan). The wine list is very good too. The rooms are sumptuous, and breakfast can be taken in the conservatory or the garden. Bargain prices with half-board.
⊠ 1150 Wien, Herklotzgasse 6. **Map** p189 F2.
(01) 8926000. FAX (01) 89260008.
@ office@altwienerhof.at b,l,d. **Rooms** 23.
2 weeks Jan. AE, DC, MC, V. €€

WIEN (VIENNA)

Römischer Kaiser Wien Here is authentic old-world flavour in a landmark Baroque building: there are chandeliers, arches, mouldings and giltwork in abundance. The hotel is centrally located in a narrow street just off the Kärntnerstrasse. If you are arriving by car, use the entrance on Krugerstrasse.
⊠ 1010 Wien, Annagasse 16. **Map** p189 F2.
(01) 512 77510. FAX (01) 512 775113.
@ info@rkhotel.bestwestern.at b. **Rooms** 24.
Never. AE, DC, MC, V. €€€€

SCHARDING

Förstingers Wirtshaus The 17th-century tavern retains old beams and vaulted ceilings.
⊠ 4780 Scharding am Inn, Unterer Stadtplatz 3.
Map p189 D2. (07712) 23020. FAX (07712) 23023.
@ romantikhotel-forstinger@magnet.at
b,l,d. **Rooms** 16. €€€

WIEN (VIENNA)

Hotel am Schubertring A central hotel, near the Staatsoper and Konzerthaus, this is a favourite of visiting artists and musicians. Quiet bedrooms.
⊠ 1010 Wien, Schubertring 11. **Map** p189 F2. (01) 717020. FAX (01) 7139966. @ hotel@schubertring.at b. **Rooms** 39. €€€

WÖRTHERSEE

Schloss Hallegg This 800-year-old castle offers wonderful views. Vast bedrooms. Summer only.
⊠ 9201 Krumpendorf am Wörthersee, Halleggerstr. 131.
Map p189 D4. (0463) 49311. FAX (0463) 493118.
@ reservations@schloss-hallegg.at b.
Rooms 10. €€€€

ZELL AM SEE

Hotel 'Der Metzgerwirt' The main building is more than 500 years old. Rooms in the new annexe look onto a courtyard and rose garden.
⊠ 5700 Zell am See, Saalfeldnerstr. 5. **Map** p188 C4.
(06542) 725200. FAX (06542) 7252034. @ info@romantik-hotel.at b,l,d. **Rooms** 40. €€

For key to symbols see backflap. For price categories *see p187*

SWITZERLAND

SWITZERLAND

THE MOUNTAINOUS GEOGRAPHY of Switzerland divides this small country into a number of self-contained localities. In the past, communication, even between neighbouring valleys, was minimal. Local differences are reinforced by the fact that four languages are spoken: French, German, Italian and Romansch, a Latinised form of Swiss German.

Switzerland has always been a highly popular European tourist destination, and, not surprisingly, its hoteliers are famous for their excellent and enthusiastic house-keeping. It is all too easy to think of Switzerland as mountains, lush valleys and chalet hotels. But it has some smart town hotels, too, and some beautiful lakeside ones.

The Walserhof, page 207, fine food in the seemingly ever-fashionable ski resort of Klosters

SWITZERLAND REGION BY REGION

WE DIVIDE Switzerland into five regions: Western, Northern, Central, Eastern and Southern. (In fact, the country is sub-divided into 26 cantons.)

Western Switzerland
This comprises Suisse Romande and Bern. Suisse Romande is the French-speaking area of the country and, in Geneva, which is culturally more French than the rest of the country, there are some very sophisticated hotels. But you can also find charming rural retreats and country house hotels nearby. Perhaps the best-known Alpine holiday region, the Bernese Alps, offers everyone's idea of mountain scenery and *chic* resorts.

Northern Switzerland
Separated from Germany and Austria by the Rhine and Lake Constance, this region encompasses Basel and the surrounding cantons. The main language is German, but there are French influences. Basel itself has its share of good hotels and there is no shortage of enchanting places to stay on beautiful Lake Constance.

Villa Principe Leopoldo, page 208

Central Switzerland
This is William Tell country. It takes in Lucerne, which is perhaps the country's most visited city. It has beautiful scenery and a wide choice of inns and hotels.

Eastern Switzerland
The least densely populated area of the country, Eastern Switzerland boasts some 360 sq km (140 sq miles) of glacier, and the fashionable ski resorts of Klosters and St Moritz. Apart from many charming winter sports hotels, there are some lovely country inns, too.

Southern Switzerland
This includes Valais and Ticino. Valais contains some

of the most dramatic and famous mountain scenery in the country: here, for example, is the village of Zermatta, dominated by the famous pyramid-shaped peak of the Matterhorn. It is also a very productive wine-growing region.

Magical Ticino, with its sunshine, lakes, mountains and flowers, has a number of beguiling lakeside inns.

Highlights

The hotels pictured on these introductory pages are by no means the only highlights. Other favourites include the welcoming chalet hotel of Aux Milles Etoiles (page 209), which is good for skiing and wonderfully peaceful; and the Chesa Salis at Bever (page 205), a charming village hotel with a warm welcome and first-rate food.

Food and Drink

Cheese and chocolate are synonymous with Switzerland, but each region has its own particular specialities. There are more than a hundred different varieties of cheese made in individual dairies, and the national dish is fondue. Lake fish are often on the menu; so also is *Rösti*, a delicious fried potato cake, and *raclette*, shavings of melted cheese. If you are feeling particularly hungry, try the *Berneplatte*, the classic dish of Bern which consists typically of a huge pile of *sauerkraut* (pickled cabbage) topped with sausages, ham and other ingredients. In the south, risotto and polenta are very popular. All over the country you will find delicious patisseries. The commonest delicacy is the cream-filled *gugelhopf*.

The first chocolate factory in Switzerland opened in 1819. Swiss chocolate is considered to be the best in the world and, perhaps not surprisingly, the Swiss eat and drink more chocolate per capita than any other nation. In 1875, milk chocolate was invented here, and in 1879 the first chocolate bar was made.

Most of the wine produced in the country is white, and is best drunk when young. There are more than 300 small wine-growing areas spread over the country. In the French-speaking part, try Fendant or Johannisberg. In the German-speaking there are some good dry reds. The beer is good, too. *Helles* is light, *Dunkles* dark.

Kirsch is the national 'hard' drink, made from cherry stones, with a variety of flavourings. In the Italian-speaking south of the country you will find Grappa.

Other Practical Information

Breakfast is usually a help-yourself buffet and consists of breads, cold meats, cereals, fruit and cheeses. In most hotels the 'double bed' is in fact two single beds pushed together with two single duvets.

In the German-speaking regions, the *stube*, or bar, is the focal point of many of the hotels and inns; in the Italian-speaking area, *grottos* are the equivalent.

Language English is spoken by most of the population as a second language.

Currency The Swiss *franc*, written 'F' or 'SF'.

Shops Normal shop hours are from 8am–12pm and 1:30–6:30pm. Saturday closing is at 11am except in the large cities.

Tipping A 15 per cent service charge is added to all hotel and restaurant bills. You only need leave more if you feel that the service has been unusually good.

Telephoning If you wish to make a phone call from Switzerland, dial the full area code. To call Switzerland from the UK, first dial the international code, 00 41 (from the US, 011 41), as usual omitting the first zero of the country area code.

Public holidays 1 January; Good Friday; Easter Monday; Ascension Day; Whit Monday; 1 August; 25 and 26 December.

Useful Words

French, German and Italian are spoken. See pages 217, 147 and 333.

Switzerland Price Bands

Swiss hotels are officially classified by stars, one to five. Our price bands are much simpler and, as elsewhere in the guide, refer to the cost of a standard double room in high season. Prices are normally quoted inclusive of breakfast and tax. However, in some places, a guest tax may be charged. In this event, a discount card is sometimes offered, giving reduced price entry to certain local attractions.

Ⓕ	Below 100 SF
ⒻⒻ	100–200 SF
ⒻⒻⒻ	200–300SF
ⒻⒻⒻⒻ	Over 300SF

Guarda Val, page 208, sits above Lenzerheide

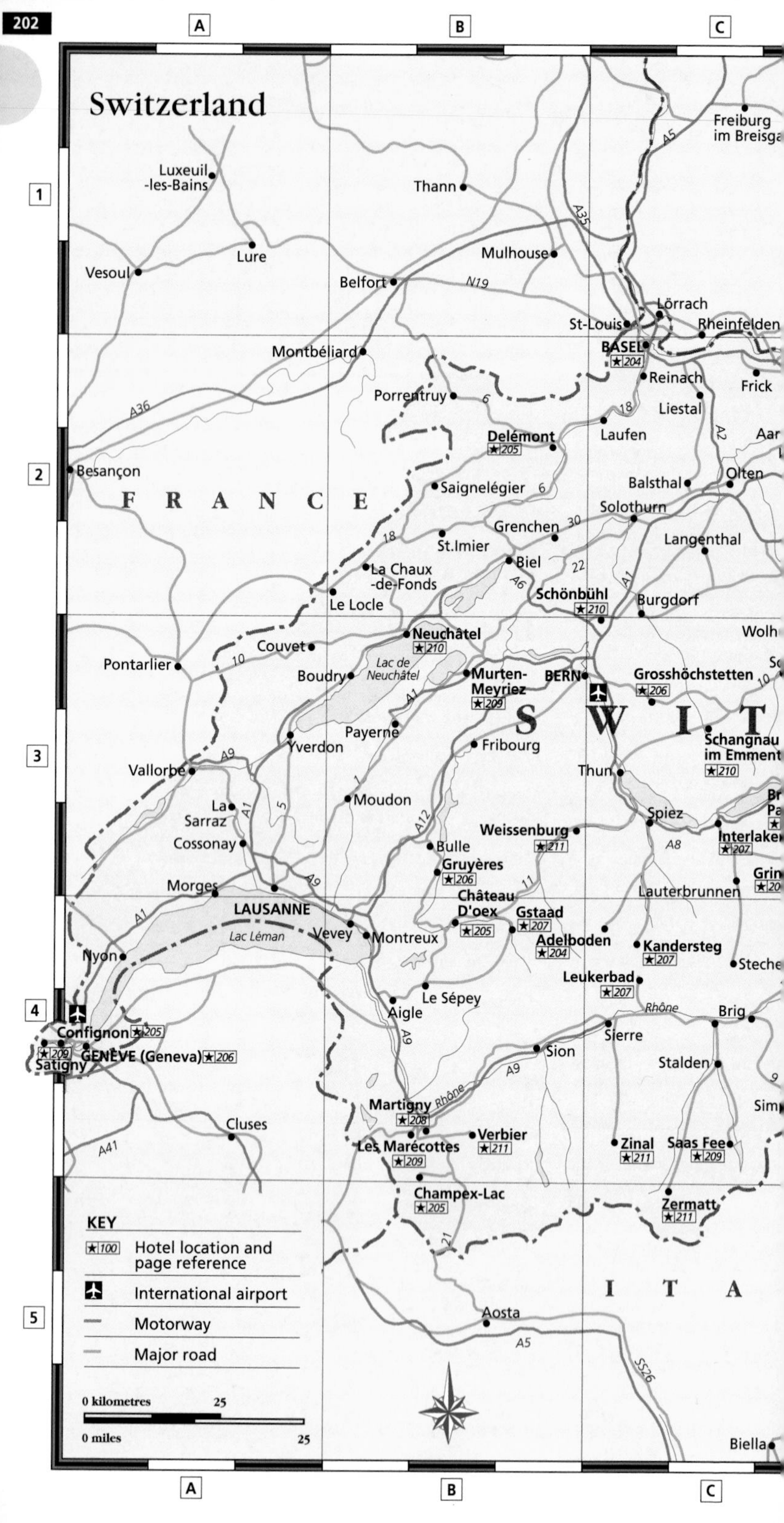

Switzerland
A
B
C
1
2
3
4
5
Freiburg im Breisga
Luxeuil -les-Bains
Thann
Lure
Mulhouse
Vesoul
Belfort
N19
Lörrach
St-Louis
Rheinfelden
Montbéliard
BASEL ★204
Reinach
Frick
Porrentruy
Liestal
A36
Delémont ★205
Laufen
Besançon
Balsthal
Olten
FRANCE
Saignelégier
Solothurn
Grenchen
Langenthal
St.Imier
Biel
La Chaux -de-Fonds
Schönbühl ★210
Burgdorf
Le Locle
Neuchâtel ★210
Couvet
Pontarlier
Boudry
Lac de Neuchâtel
Murten-Meyriez ★209
BERN
Grosshöchstetten ★206
SWIT
Payerne
Yverdon
Fribourg
Schangnau im Emment ★210
Vallorbe
Thun
Moudon
La Sarraz
Spiez
Weissenburg ★211
Interlaken ★207
Cossonay
Bulle
Gruyères ★206
Morges
Château D'oex ★205
Lauterbrunnen
LAUSANNE
Gstaad ★207
Lac Léman
Vevey
Montreux
Adelboden ★204
Kandersteg ★207
Nyon
Leukerbad ★207
Le Sépey
Aigle
Rhône
Brig
Confignon ★205
Sierre
Satigny ★209
GENÈVE (Geneva) ★206
Sion
Stalden
Martigny ★208
Rhône
Cluses
Verbier ★211
Les Marécottes ★209
Zinal ★211
Saas Fee ★209
Champex-Lac ★205
Zermatt ★211
ITA
Aosta
Biella
KEY
★100 Hotel location and page reference
International airport
Motorway
Major road
0 kilometres 25
0 miles 25

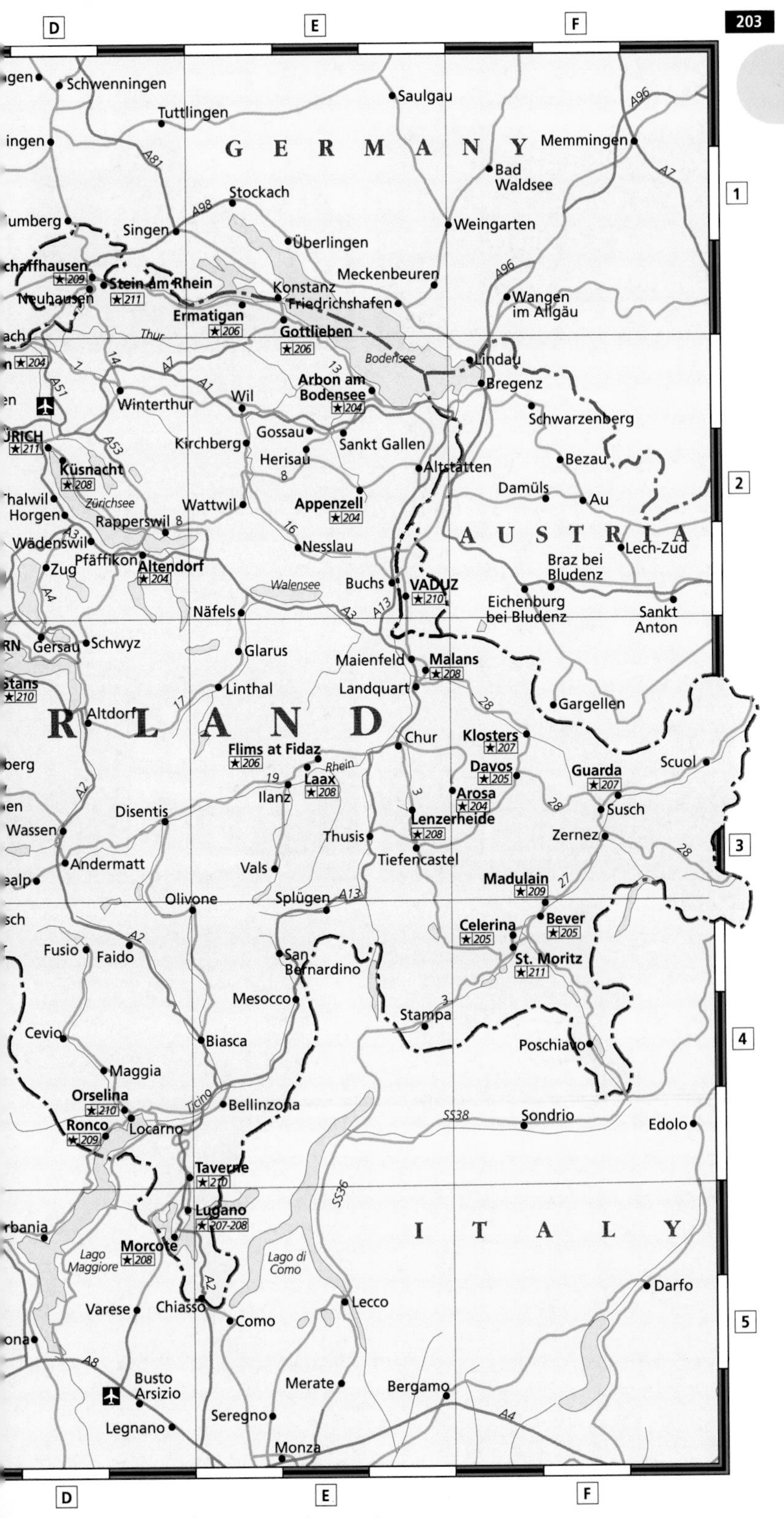

D
E
F
GERMANY
AUSTRIA
RLAND
ITALY
Schwenningen
Tuttlingen
Saulgau
Memmingen
Bad Waldsee
Stockach
Singen
Überlingen
Weingarten
Schaffhausen ★209
Stein am Rhein ★211
Neuhausen
Konstanz
Meckenbeuren
Friedrichshafen
Wangen im Allgäu
Ermatigan ★206
Gottlieben ★206
Bodensee
Lindau
Bregenz
Arbon am Bodensee ★204
Winterthur
Wil
Schwarzenberg
Zürich ★211
Gossau
Kirchberg
Herisau
Sankt Gallen
Altstätten
Bezau
Küsnacht ★208
Zürichsee
Thalwil
Horgen
Rapperswil
Wattwil
Appenzell ★204
Damüls
Au
Wädenswil
Pfäffikon
Altendorf ★204
Zug
Nesslau
Lech-Zud
Braz bei Bludenz
Walensee
Buchs
VADUZ ★210
Eichenburg bei Bludenz
Sankt Anton
Näfels
Gersau
Schwyz
Glarus
Maienfeld
Malans ★208
Stans ★210
Linthal
Landquart
Gargellen
Altdorf
Chur
Klosters ★207
Flims at Fidaz ★206
Rhein
Davos ★205
Guarda ★207
Scuol
Laax ★208
Ilanz
Arosa ★204
Susch
Disentis
Lenzerheide ★208
Wassen
Thusis
Zernez
Andermatt
Tiefencastel
Vals
Madulain ★209
Olivone
Splügen
Bever ★205
Celerina ★205
Fusio
Faido
San Bernardino
St. Moritz ★211
Mesocco
Stampa
Cevio
Biasca
Poschiavo
Maggia
Orselina ★210
Bellinzona
Ronco ★209
Locarno
Sondrio
Edolo
Taverne ★210
Lugano ★207-208
Morcote ★208
Lago Maggiore
Lago di Como
Darfo
Varese
Chiasso
Como
Lecco
Busto Arsizio
Merate
Bergamo
Legnano
Seregno
Monza
1
2
3
4
5

Adelboden

Bären The building dates from 1500, but it has been a hotel for only ten years. The proprietor, a local, has made it thoroughly comfortable, and it is especially popular with families. All the bedrooms are differently done out – one has a four-poster bed. Delicious *Rösti* and a range of French and German dishes in the restaurant.
3715 Adelboden BE. **Map** p202 C4. (033) 673 21 51. FAX (033) 673 21 90. @ hotel@baeren-adelboden.ch b,l,d. **Rooms** 14. mid-Nov to mid-Dec; May. AE, DC, MC, V. ⒻⒻⒻ

Appenzell

Romantik Hotel Säntis Colourful folk-art patterns adorn the outside of this lively inn. The restaurant serves local cheeses and wines, but the specialities are lake fish and sausages. Of the bedrooms, No.242 is very popular – it has a frilly four-poster.
am Landsgemeindeplatz, 9050 Appenzell AI. **Map** p203 E2. (071) 788 11 11. FAX (071) 788 11 10. @ romantikhotelsaentis@bluewin.ch b,l,d. **Rooms** 37. mid-Jan to mid-Feb. AE, DC, MC, V. ⒻⒻⒻ

Altendorf

Seehotel Hecht This popular place on the shores of Lake Zurich has been an inn since the 15th century. Today, the Hecht's seafood cuisine, served in a modern extension and outdoor terrace, draws people from all around – many come by boat. Accommodation is in the older part of the house. Simple, wood-panelled bedrooms; basic bathrooms.
8852 Altendorf SZ. **Map** p203 D2. (055) 451 01 00. FAX (055) 451 01 01. @ info@seehotel-hecht.ch b,l,d. **Rooms** 8. 2 weeks Jan. AE, DC, MC, V. ⒻⒻ

Arbon am Bodensee

Gastof Frohsinn A beer drinkers' paradise: the three-storied building is a brewery as well as an hotel. The basement is a beer cellar, with wooden benches and a vaulted ceiling. Some 500 litres (110 gal) of lager are produced twice a week, with a stronger brown beer in winter. Rooms are plain and neat; vegetarian dishes.
9320 Arbon, Romanshornerstr 15 TG. **Map** p203 E2. (071) 447 84 84. FAX (071) 446 41 42. @ frohsinn@tele-net.ch b,l,d. **Rooms** 13. Never. AE, DC, MC, V. ⒻⒻ

Arosa

Belri From this former finishing school at the top of Arosa, you can 'ski out, ski back'. The lifts to Weisshorn and Hornli are close.
7050 Innerarosa, Arosa GR. **Map** p203 F3. (081) 378 72 90. FAX (081) 378 72 90. @ belri@bluewin.ch b (summer); b,l,d (winter). **Rooms** 19. ⒻⒻ

Basel

Helvetia Known for its seafood and the Red Ox Bar. It's not overly pretty, but the bedrooms are sleek. It is close to the station and air terminal.
4051 Basel, Küchengasse 13 BS. **Map** p202 C2. (061) 272 06 88. FAX (061) 272 06 22. b,l,d. **Rooms** 17. ⒻⒻ

Basel

Teufelhof Run by theatre people. Each room is designed by the owner, who is an artist. Comfortable.
4051 Basel, Leonhardsgraben 47–49 BS. **Map** p202 C2. (061) 261 10 10. FAX (061) 261 10 04. @ info@teufelhof.com b,l,d. **Rooms** 33. ⒻⒻⒻ

Böttstein

Schloss Böttstein Built in 1250, this castle was refurbished in 1974. Comfortable bedrooms. The menu is international, with a French slant.
5315 Böttstein AG. **Map** p203 D2. (056) 269 16 16. FAX (056) 269 16 66. @ info@schloss-boettstein.ch b,l,d. **Rooms** 39. ⒻⒻ

Bever

Chesa Salis The fine 16th-century house was remodelled in the 1870s, and many rooms look like part of a giant doll's house. One room, for private parties, is completely wood-panelled, with tiny windows; one bedroom is painted like a music box, another has very low beams. Classic French and Italian cuisine, as well as local dishes.
☒ 7502 Bever GR. **Map** p203 F4. ☎ (081) 852 48 38. FAX (081) 852 47 06. @ reception@chesa-salis.ch 🍴 b,l,d. **Rooms** 17. ● mid-Oct to mid-Dec; after Easter to mid-June. AE, DC, MC, V. ⒻⒻⒻ

Champex-Lac

Hotel Belvédère Eccentric and informal, but comfortable, with a mish-mash of artifacts hanging from the ceilings and walls. The owner has several fighting cows, called Queens, to be found only in this area, and he has a video to tell you all about it. Fine country cooking and glorious views from the bar's stone terrace.
☒ 1938 Champex-Lac VS. **Map** p202 B4. ☎ (027) 783 11 14. FAX (027) 783 25 76. @ belvedere@dransnet.ch 🍴 b,l,d. **Rooms** 9. ● Never. MC, V. ⒻⒻ

Celerina

Stüvetta Veglia Choosing a room at this extraordinary hotel is an aesthetic challenge: each has been decorated by a different Swiss artist. Room 8 has Carigiet landscapes, and there are two Gimmi nudes in No.5. Bathrooms are luxurious. The gourmet restaurant is well known; people travel from St Moritz to sample specialities such as beef marinated in hay and herbs.
☒ 7505 Celerina GR. **Map** p203 F4. ☎ (081) 833 80 08. FAX (081) 833 45 42. @ info@stuvetta-veglia.ch 🍴 b,l,d. **Rooms** 18. ● Nov, Dec. AE, DC, MC, V. ⒻⒻⒻ

Confignon

Auberge de Confignon Combine rural peace with city sightseeing. The traffic-free village of Confignon is so close to Geneva that you can get into the city on the trolley-bus; there are views over the town and the Salève mountains. The simple inn is also an animated village bar. Italian-based food is cooked by the owner. All the bedrooms have been renovated.
☒1232 Confignon, Place de l'Eglise 6 GE. **Map** p202 A4. ☎ (022) 757 19 44. FAX (022) 757 18 89. 🍴 b,l,d. **Rooms** 14. ● Never. AE, DC, MC, V. ⒻⒻⒻ

Brünig Pass

Brünig Kulm At about 1,000m (3,330ft), the views from this simple chalet-style inn are fantastic. It is much favoured by skiers and walkers. Meals are substantial.
☒ 3860 Brunig BE. **Map** p202 C3. ☎ (033) 971 17 08. FAX (033) 971 17 49. 🍴 b,l,d. **Rooms** 6. ⒻⒻ

Château-d'Oex

Bon Accueil A typical Swiss chalet with open fires, good food and stunning views over the fields and mountains. Good for walking holidays.
☒ 1660 Château-d'Oex VD. **Map** p202 B4. ☎ (026) 924 63 20. FAX (026) 924 51 26. @ host-bon-accueil@bluewin.ch 🍴 b,l,d. **Rooms** 18. ⒻⒻ

Davos

Hotel Larix This peaceful chalet hotel is furnished with the owners' possessions. The location is convenient for the Jakobshorn ski lifts.
7270 Davos-Platz, Albertistr 9 GR. **Map** p203 F4. ☎ (081) 413 11 88. FAX (081) 413 33 49. @ hotel-larix@bluewin.ch 🍴 b,l,d. **Rooms** 20. ⒻⒻⒻ

Delémont

Du Midi This award-winning hotel provides excellent food in a brasserie, a restaurant and a gourmet dining room; Mediterranean influences. The bedrooms are pleasant.
☒ 2800 Delémont JU. **Map** p202 B2. ☎ (032) 422 17 77. FAX (032) 423 19 89. 🍴 b,l,d. **Rooms** 7. ⒻⒻ

For key to symbols see backflap. For price categories *see p201*

Gottlieben

Romantik Hotel Krone This restful hotel is set in the pretty village of Gottlieben, which dates from the 12th century; a short stroll along little lanes on the banks of the Rhine takes you past half-timbered houses and a monastery. Inside, there are some well-furnished bedrooms at the front with a view of the river streaming past outside; those in the back extension are plainer.
☒ 8274 Gottlieben TG. **Map** p203 E1. ☎ (071) 666 80 60. FAX (071) 666 80 69. @ krone@romantikhotel.ch 🍴 b,l,d. **Rooms** 25. ● 4 Jan to 6 Feb. 💳 AE, DC, MC, V. ⒻⒻ

Grosshöchstetten

Sternen This old farmhouse has been a village inn since the early 19th century, and it's still a classic, complete with a bowling alley. Its traditional decor make it a popular place with the diplomatic set from Bern, only 25km (19 miles) away. The new chef worked at London's Dorchester Hotel. Pleasant, simple bedrooms.
☒ 3506 Grosshöchstetten BE. **Map** p202 C3. ☎ (031) 710 24 24. FAX (031) 710 24 25. @ stegro@sternen-stegro.tr 🍴 b,l,d. **Rooms** 10. ● 1 week July, 1 week Aug. 💳 MC, V. ⒻⒻ

Grindelwald

Fiescherblick Grindelwald is the only one of this region's resorts accessible by car, so walkers and skiers flock to this hotel; many return regularly. Packed lunches are provided, and staff can advise on trails and mountain guides. In the lively restaurant, second helpings always offered. Most bedrooms are spacious.
☒ 3818 Grindelwald BE. **Map** p202 C3. ☎ (033) 854 53 53. FAX (033) 854 53 50. @ hotel@fiescherblick.ch 🍴 b,d. **Rooms** 25. ● mid-Nov to mid-Dec; after Easter to mid-May. 💳 AE, DC, MC, V. ⒻⒻⒻ

Gruyères

Hostellerie des Chevaliers Having been away for 20 years, the Corbot family took over their mountain inn again in 1998, but the management is now in the hands of Restaurant le Chalet Gruyères. The bedrooms have magnificent views of the meadows and mountains around this medieval town; bathrooms are functional.
☒ 1663 Gruyères FR. **Map** p202 B3. ☎ (026) 921 19 33. FAX (026) 921 25 52. @ hotel_chevaliers@bluewin.ch 🍴 b,l,d. **Rooms** 34. ● Jan, Feb. 💳 AE, DC, MC, V. ⒻⒻ

Ermatigen

Adler Dating from 1270, this tall, half-timbered building is the oldest inn in Thurgau. Try the fish dishes in the wood-panelled dining room.
☒ Dorfplatz, 8272 Ermatigen TG. **Map** p203 E1. ☎ (071) 664 11 33. FAX (071) 664 30 11. 🍴 b,l,d. **Rooms** 10. ⒻⒻ

Ermatigen

Hirschen A charming old lakeside inn where you can eat delicious fish and game while watching the boats on Lake Constance, shaded beneath white parasols and sycamore trees.
☒ 8272 Ermatigen TG. **Map** p203 E1. ☎ (071) 664 10 03. 🍴 b,l,d. **Rooms** 4. ⒻⒻ

Flims at Fidaz

Fidazerhof You can have a seriously healthy time in this ancient inn, with massage, reflexology, and vegetarian meals provided.
☒ 7019 Flims-Fidaz GR. **Map** p202 E3. ☎ (081) 911 53 03. FAX (081) 911 21 75. @ info@fidazerhof.ch 🍴 b,l,d. **Rooms** 10. ⒻⒻⒻ

Geneva

Tiffany This is a warm and well-liked hotel, close to the Stock Exchange. Decorations very Art Nouveau; the best bedrooms are at the top.
☒ 1 rue des Marbriers, 1204 Geneva GE. **Map** p202 A4. ☎ (022) 708 16 16. FAX (022) 708 16 17. @ info@hotel-tiffany.ch 🍴 b,l,d. **Rooms** 46. ⒻⒻⒻ

Guarda

Meisser Built in 1645 as a farmhouse, this was converted to an inn by the present owner's great-grandfather. Although tiny, Guarda is a popular tourist spot due to its decorated houses and local craftsmen. You can enjoy sweeping views while eating gastronomic food on the terrace, or simpler grills in the garden. All the rooms are different.
✉ 7545 Guarda GR. **Map** p203 F3. ☎ (081) 862 21 32. FAX (081) 862 24 80. @ info@hotel-meisser.ch 🍴 b,l,d. **Rooms** 22. ● Nov to mid-Dec (some apartments available). 💳 AE, DC, MC, V. ⒻⒻⒻ

Klosters

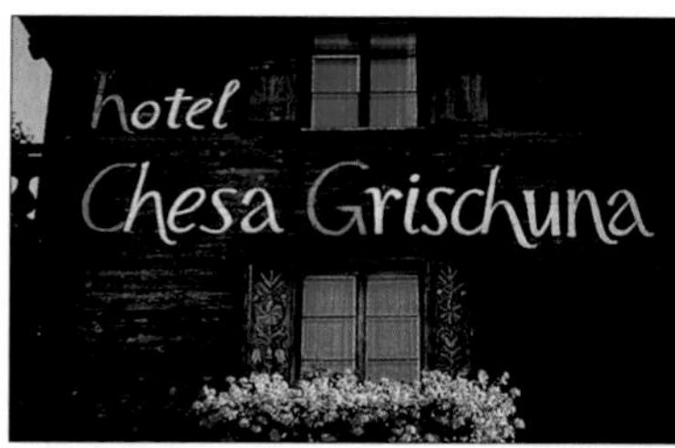

Chesa Grischuna Very close to the Gotschnagrat-Parsenn cable car, this was originally a railway hotel. Now it swarms with visitors. It is a natural *après-ski* meeting place, with a bar, a sitting room with games, and a restaurant serving local food as well as caviar. Range of summer activities added recently.
✉ 7250 Klosters Platz GR. **Map** p203 F3. ☎ (081) 422 22 22. FAX (081) 422 22 25. @ hotel@chesagrischuna.ch 🍴 b,l,d. **Rooms** 25. ● 19 Oct-12 Dec; 13 Apr-2 Jul. 💳 AE, DC, MC, V. ⒻⒻⒻⒻ

Interlaken

Hirschen Despite modern renovation, ancient timbers survive at this very welcoming, traditional inn, whose vast overhanging roof shelters a pavement terrace. Inside is a popular restaurant and a snug sitting room, and three upper stories of pleasantly decorated bedrooms. Some have balconies with views of the Jungfrau peak.
✉ 3800 Interlaken-Matten BE. **Map** p202 C3. ☎ (033) 822 15 45. FAX (033) 823 37 45. @ gasthofhirschen@bluewin.ch 🍴 b,l,d. **Rooms** 25. ● Nov. 💳 AE, DC, MC, V. ⒻⒻⒻ

Klosters

Walserhof Although the hotel is on the main road, all the bedrooms look out on to fields. Chef Beat Bolliger, one of Switzerland's best, provides a wide range of fine foods in the pretty restaurant, including his famous stuffed ravioli. Bedrooms are comfortable and bathrooms luxurious. Experience it while you can.
✉ 7250 Klosters Platz GR. **Map** p203 F3. ☎ (081) 410 29 29. FAX (081) 410 29 39. @ walsherhof@bluewin.ch 🍴 b,l,d. **Rooms** 14. ● late Oct to early Dec; mid-Apr to mid-June. 💳 AE, DC, MC, V. ⒻⒻⒻⒻ

Gstaad

Hotel Olden Farmers and jetsetters alike love this place. Local specialities as well as international dishes. Charming bedrooms. Large, quiet garden.
✉ 3780 Gstaad BE. **Map** p202 B4. ☎ (033) 744 34 44. FAX (033) 744 61 64. @ info@hotelolden.com 🍴 b,l,d. **Rooms** 16. ⒻⒻⒻⒻ

Kandersteg

Ruedihus Like a living museum, in the meadows beneath the mountains. Four-poster beds, 'Grandma's' jam, and no Coca-Cola – heavenly.
✉ 3718 Kandersteg BE. **Map** p202 C4. ☎ (033) 675 81 82. FAX (033) 675 81 85. @ voldenhorn@compuserve.com 🍴 b,l,d. **Rooms** 9. ⒻⒻⒻ

Leukerbad

Les Sources des Alpes A marvellously luxurious place: delicious unfattening food, thermal spring-water swimming pools and lots of spa treatments.
✉ 3954 Leukerbad VS. **Map** p202 C4. ☎ (027) 472 2000. FAX (027) 472 2001. @ sources@relaischateaux.ch 🍴 b,l,d. **Rooms** 30. ⒻⒻⒻⒻ

Lugano

Romantik Hotel Ticino 'Art and Gastronomy' is the motto at this 500-year-old palazzo.
✉ 6901 Lugano, Piazza Cioccaro 1 TI. **Map** p203 D5. ☎ (091) 922 77 72. FAX (091) 923 62 78. @ romantikhotelticino@ticino.com 🍴 b,l,d. **Rooms** 20. ⒻⒻⒻⒻ

Küsnacht

Hotel Ermitage am See You can hardly believe you are just seven minutes' drive from the centre of Zurich as you sit in the serene gardens of this 300-year-old lakeside house or wander through its spacious reception area, with antiques and paintings. Massive beds, white marble bathrooms. Michelin-starred restaurant, *Le Pavillon*.
8700 Küsnacht-Zurich, Seestr 80 ZH. **Map** p203 D2.
(01) 914 42 42. FAX (01) 914 42 43.
@ reservation@ermitage.ch b,l,d. **Rooms** 26.
Never. AE, DC, MC, V. ⒻⒻⒻⒻ

Lenzerheide

Romantik Maiensässhotel Guarda Val Standing in the middle of the pastures above Lenzerheide, this unique inn was created out of abandoned farmbuildings in the late 1960s. It now has many faithful regulars who return throughout the year and expect to stay in the same room. Bedrooms are stylish. Local dishes in the restaurant.
7078 Lenzerheide, Postfach 32. **Map** p203 E3.
(081) 385 85 85. FAX (081) 385 85 95.
@ hotel@guardaval.ch b,l,d. **Rooms** 34.
18 Apr to 1 Jun. MC, V. ⒻⒻⒻⒻ

Laax

Pöstli A charming stone building with green shutters in the delightful upper Rhine village of Laax. In 1978, marketing man Peter Panier came home and created this inn because he wanted 'the kind of hotel that I always wanted to stay in'. Now under new management. Food is traditional Swiss, and each bedroom is different – one of the singles has a sleigh bed.
7031 Laax GR. **Map** p203 E3. (081) 921 44 66.
FAX (081) 921 34 00. @ poestli@knf.ch b,l,d.
Rooms 7. May. AE, MC, V. ⒻⒻ

Lugano

Villa Principe Leopoldo & Residence This former holiday home of Leopold of Hapsburg has stunning views of Lugano, the mountains and the lake, and a scented, flower-covered terrace. It is well preserved, and decorated with portraits, busts and sporting prints. The bedrooms (all junior suites) are luxurious. Imaginative food.
6900 Lugano, Via Montalbano 5, TI.
Map p203 D5. (091) 985 88 55. FAX (091) 985 88 25.
@ info@leopoldohotel.ch b,l,d. **Rooms** 71.
Never. AE, DC, V. ⒻⒻⒻⒻ

Luzern (Lucerne)

Baslertor An unexpected bonus in this pleasant spot is the outdoor swimming pool. There is a cocktail bar and a cosy restaurant.
6003 Luzern, Pfistergasse 17 LU. **Map** p203 D3.
(041) 249 22 22. FAX (041) 249 22 33.
@ info@baslertor.ch b. **Rooms** 30. ⒻⒻⒻ

Malans

Weisskreuz The charming traditional inn is popular with locals and visitors. Good regional food. Modern bedrooms; excellent bathrooms.
7208 Malans GR. **Map** p203 E3. (081) 322 81 61.
FAX (081) 322 81 62. @ info@weisskreuz.com
b,l,d. **Rooms** 11. ⒻⒻⒻ

Martigny

Le Forum A popular stop-over from Italy to France. The food is first-rate and the welcome so warm you won't notice the uninspiring building.
1920 Martigny, Av du Grand-St-Bernard VS.
Map p202 B4. (027) 722 18 41. FAX (027) 722 79 25.
@ info@le-gourmet.ch b,l,d. **Rooms** 29. ⒻⒻ

Morcote

Carina Carlton In this charming location on the Lugano, you can have dinner sitting over the water. The terraced garden has a swimming pool. Church bells ring 66 times at 6am.
6922 Morcote TI. **Map** p203 D5. (091) 996 11 31.
FAX (091) 996 19 29. b,l,d. **Rooms** 22. ⒻⒻⒻ

LUZERN (LUCERNE)

Rebstock Each room is different in this 600-year-old hotel. Owner and art-collector Claudia Moser has covered the place in pictures. The three very different, but equally excellent restaurants serve local specialities. The breakfast buffet, featuring ten different kinds of bread and piles of fruit, is a dream.
⊠ 6006 Luzern, St Leodegarstr. 3. **Map** p203 D3. ☎ (041) 410 35 81. FAX (041) 410 39 17. @ rebstock@hereweare.ch 🍴 b,l,d. **Rooms** 30. ● Never. 💳 AE, DC, MC, V. ⒻⒻⒻ

LES MARÉCOTTES

Aux Mille Etoiles This is very much a family hotel – among the 25 rooms is a good selection of junior suites and family rooms. Ingrid Berner-Hol, one of the extended family who run the place, produces a newsletter every day with suggestions for ski trips, hikes and a weather report. Heated indoor swimming pool.
⊠ 1923 Les Marécottes VS. **Map** p202 B4. ☎ (027) 761 16 66. FAX (027) 761 16 00. @ mille.etoiles@omedia.ch 🍴 b,l,d. **Rooms** 25. ● Nov to mid-Dec; 4 weeks after Easter. 💳 DC, MC, V. ⒻⒻⒻ

MADULAIN

Stüva Colani Set in the middle of a village, this 200-year-old building has been opened up and beautifully modernised. The bright, airy Tavolini restaurant has a pasta menu perfect for children; for gastronomes, there is a separate gourmet restaurant. The hotel decoration blends old and new, with slate floors and pastel furnishings.
⊠ 7523 Madulain GR. **Map** p203 F3. ☎ (081) 854 17 71. FAX (081) 854 14 85. @ info@stueva-colani.ch 🍴 b,l,d. **Rooms** 17. ● Nov to mid Dec; after Easter to early June. 💳 AE, DC, MC, V. ⒻⒻ

MURTEN-MEYRIEZ

Le Vieux Manoir au Lac A French general built this lakeside manor house about a century ago. Each of the elegant bedrooms has a sitting area; two hexagonal suites in the old tower overlook the hotel's park and lake. There is a conservatory restaurant, and a beautiful breakfast room. The medieval town of Murten is a short drive away.
⊠ 3280 Murten-Meyriez FR. **Map** p202 B3. ☎ (026) 678 61 61. FAX (026) 678 61 62. @ welcome@vieuxmanoir.ch 🍴 b,l,d. **Rooms** 33. ● end Oct to Feb. 💳 AE, DC, MC, V. ⒻⒻⒻⒻ

RONCO

Albergo Ronco Fantastic views over Lake Maggiore. The home-made pasta is delicious; cakes can be eaten on the vine-covered terrace.
⊠ 6622 Ronco s/Ascona TI. **Map** p203 D4. ☎ (091) 791 52 65. FAX (091) 791 06 40. @ hotel-ronco@ticino.com 🍴 b,l,d. **Rooms** 20. ⒻⒻⒻ

SAAS FEE

Fletschhorn Waldhotel Stunning views (the hotel is located at around 1,800m/5,900ft) and splendid French cuisine. Delightful bedrooms.
⊠ 3906 Saas Fee VS. **Map** p202 C4. ☎ (027) 957 21 31. FAX (027) 957 21 87. @ info@fletschhorn.ch 🍴 b,l,d. **Rooms** 15. ⒻⒻⒻ

SATIGNY

Domaine de Châteauvieux Sample wonderful food and local wines in this popular old farmhouse. Plain bedrooms; generous breakfasts.
⊠ 1242 Satigny, Peney-Dessus GE. **Map** p202 A4. ☎ (022) 753 15 11. FAX (022) 753 19 24. @ reservation@chateauvieux.ch 🍴 b,l,d. Rooms 12. ⒻⒻⒻ

SCHAFFHAUSEN

Rheinhotel Fischerzunft Has one of the most acclaimed restaurants in the country, recently rebuilt. The bedrooms are chic.
⊠ 8200 Schaffhausen, Rheinquai 8 SH. **Map** p203 D1. ☎ (052) 632 05 05. FAX (052) 632 05 13. @ info@fischerzunft.ch 🍴 b,l,d. **Rooms** 10. ⒻⒻⒻ

For key to symbols see backflap. For price categories *see p201*

Neuchâtel

La Maison du Prussien The name of this hotel and restaurant, a converted brewery by a spectacular gorge, refers to the time when the region was part of Prussia. The 18th-century building has been sympathetically restored, with plain stone walls and exposed beams; romantic bedrooms with modern, luxurious bathrooms.

Au Gor du Vauseyon, 2006 Neuchâtel NE. **Map** p202 B3. (032) 730 54 54. FAX (032) 730 21 43. info@hotel-prussien.ch b,l,d. **Rooms** 10. 20 July to 7 Aug. AE, DC, MC, V. ⒻⒻ

Porto Ronco

La Rocca The Rocca's garden offer unbeatable views of Lake Maggiore from its hillside position by Porto Ronco, a writers' and artists' colony. The hotel is cosy, with a bar and terrace area, and holds occasional themed evenings with accordion music and barbecues. The refurbished bedrooms are bright and airy; all have balconies.

6613 Porto Ronco, Ascona TI. **Map** p203 D4. (091) 785 11 44. FAX (091) 791 40 64. hotel@la-rocca.ch b,l,d. **Rooms** 21. Nov to Mar. DC, MC, V. ⒻⒻⒻ

Orselina

Hotel Mirafiori It looks like many other holiday hotels in the popular Locarno area, high above Lake Maggiore. Yet the Mirafiori stands out for its warm welcome, its lush garden with swimming pool (superb views), and its excellent regional cooking. Some bedrooms are in hillside annexes; one is in its own, miniature cottage.

6644 Orselina, Via Al Parco TI. **Map** p203 D4. (091) 743 18 77. FAX (091) 743 77 39. info@mirafiori.ch b,l,d. **Rooms** 25. early Oct to mid-Mar. AE, DC, MC, V. ⒻⒻⒻ

Schangnau im Emmental

Kemmeriboden-Bad Set in a beautiful valley, this was originally built over a century ago for people coming to the sulphur springs. Now visitors come for much more, including fishing, walking, skiing and mountain climbing. The bedrooms are traditional, and some can sleep up to six. Lots of things for children to do.

6197 Schangnau im Emmental. **Map** p202 C3. (034) 493 77 77. FAX (034) 493 77 70. hotel@kemmeriboden.ch b,l,d. **Rooms** 29. 2 weeks Dec. AE, DC, MC, V. ⒻⒻ

Schönbühl bei Bern

Schönbühl A typical village hotel, with wood-panelled walls and a happy mix of antique and modern furniture.

3322 Schönbühl bei Bern BE. **Map** p203 C2. (031) 859 69 69. FAX (031) 859 69 05. info@gasthof-schoenbuehl.ch b,l,d. **Rooms** 12. ⒻⒻ

Stans

Engel This no-nonsense inn set between a lake and a mountain is under new management and has been rebuilt.

6370 Stans, am Dorfplatz NW. **Map** p203 D3. (041) 619 10 10. FAX (041) 619 10 11. info@engelstans.ch b,l,d. **Rooms** 18. ⒻⒻ

Taverne

Ristorante Motto del Gallo In an industrial area near a motorway, but stupendous food. Worth staying a night.

6807 Taverne-Lugano TI. **Map** p203 D4. (091) 945 28 71. FAX (091) 945 28 71. b,l,d. **Rooms** 3. ⒻⒻ

Vaduz

Gasthof Löwen See the 600-year-old fresco in this historic inn. Beautiful carpets, antiques and luxurious bathrooms.

Herrengasse 35, 9490 Vaduz FL. **Map** p203 E2. (0423) 238 11 44. FAX (0423) 238 11 45. office@hotel-loewen.li b,l,d. **Rooms** 8. ⒻⒻⒻ

ST MORITZ

Landhotel Meierei Surely the most romantic location in St Moritz for a hotel: it sits on the opposite shore of the lake from the town, but only a ten-minute walk away. Great views, especially at night, when the lights of St Moritz twinkle in the distance. The restaurant offers traditional Swiss food with modern twists.
7500 St Moritz GR. **Map** p203 F4. (081) 833 20 60. FAX (081) 833 88 38. @ info@hotel-meierei.ch b,l,d. **Rooms** 14 Apr, May, Oct, Nov. AE, DC, MC, V. ⒻⒻ

ZERMATT

Romantik Hotel Julen A proper family hotel, with resident children and a working sheepdog. The bedrooms are lavish; some at the top have their own sitting area. Don't miss the *Schaeferstube* (sheep room). The garden is large, and there are marvellous views of the Matterhorn. Adventure pool and many fitness facilities.
3920 Zermatt VS. **Map** p202 C5. (027) 966 76 00. FAX (027) 966 76 76. @ hotel.julen@zermatt.ch b,l,d. **Rooms** 34. Never. AE, DC, MC, V. ⒻⒻⒻⒻ

STEIN AM RHEIN

Rheinfels This ancient hostelry is by the river next to the bridge, with the terrace restaurant jutting out over the water. There is a medieval atmosphere: creaky wooden stairs, full-sized suits of armour, and old beams. Edi Schwegler's food is very popular, especially his fish and game in season. Bedrooms are functional.
8260 Stein am Rhein SH. **Map** p203 D1. (052) 741 21 44. FAX (052) 741 25 22. @ rheinfels@bluewin.ch b,l,d. **Rooms** 17. mid-Dec to mid-March. AE, MC, V. ⒻⒻ

ZURICH

Claridge Hotel Tiefenau Zurich is short on unusual hotels and sadly, this discreet 19th-century house near the university doesn't buck the trend. But it's got a homely feel, with plants and comfy sofas in the bar and library. Rooms are fully business-equipped; bathrooms small but luxurious. Local dishes feature in the restaurant.
8032 Zurich, Steinwiesstr 8-10 ZH. **Map** p203 D2. (01) 267 87 87. FAX (01) 251 24 76. @ info@claridge.ch b,l,d. **Rooms** 35. Christmas and New Year. AE, DC, MC, V. ⒻⒻⒻⒻ

VERBIER

Golf Hotel Unpretentious golfing hotel, friendly if a little old-fashioned. French cooking. Stunning views of Mont Blanc and the Trient.
1936 Verbier VS. **Map** p202 B4. (027) 771 65 15. FAX (027) 771 14 88. @ golfotel@axiom.ch b,l,d. **Rooms** 30. ⒻⒻⒻ

WEISSENBURG

Alte Post Set by the river, this characterful inn has open fires and wood-panelled bedrooms. Popular with skiers and canoeists. Good food.
3764 Weissenburg Dorf BE. **Map** p202 B3. (033) 783 15 15. FAX (033) 783 15 78. b,l,d. **Rooms** 10. ⒻⒻ

ZINAL

Le Besso Old inn at the top of the Val d'Anniviers. The proprietor likes taking guests out on hikes. Stunning views of the Matterhorn and glacier.
3961 Zinal VS. **Map** p202 C4. (027) 475 31 65. FAX (027) 475 49 82. @ besso@netplus.ch b,l,d. **Rooms** 10. ⒻⒻ

ZURICH

Helmhaus Family-run small hotel in peaceful position near business district. Friendly welcome, relaxed atmosphere, good breakfasts.
8001 Zurich, Schifflände 30 ZH. **Map** p203 D2. (01) 251 88 10. FAX (01) 251 04 30. @ hotel@helmhaus.ch b. **Rooms** 24. ⒻⒻⒻ

For key to symbols see backflap. For price categories *see p201*

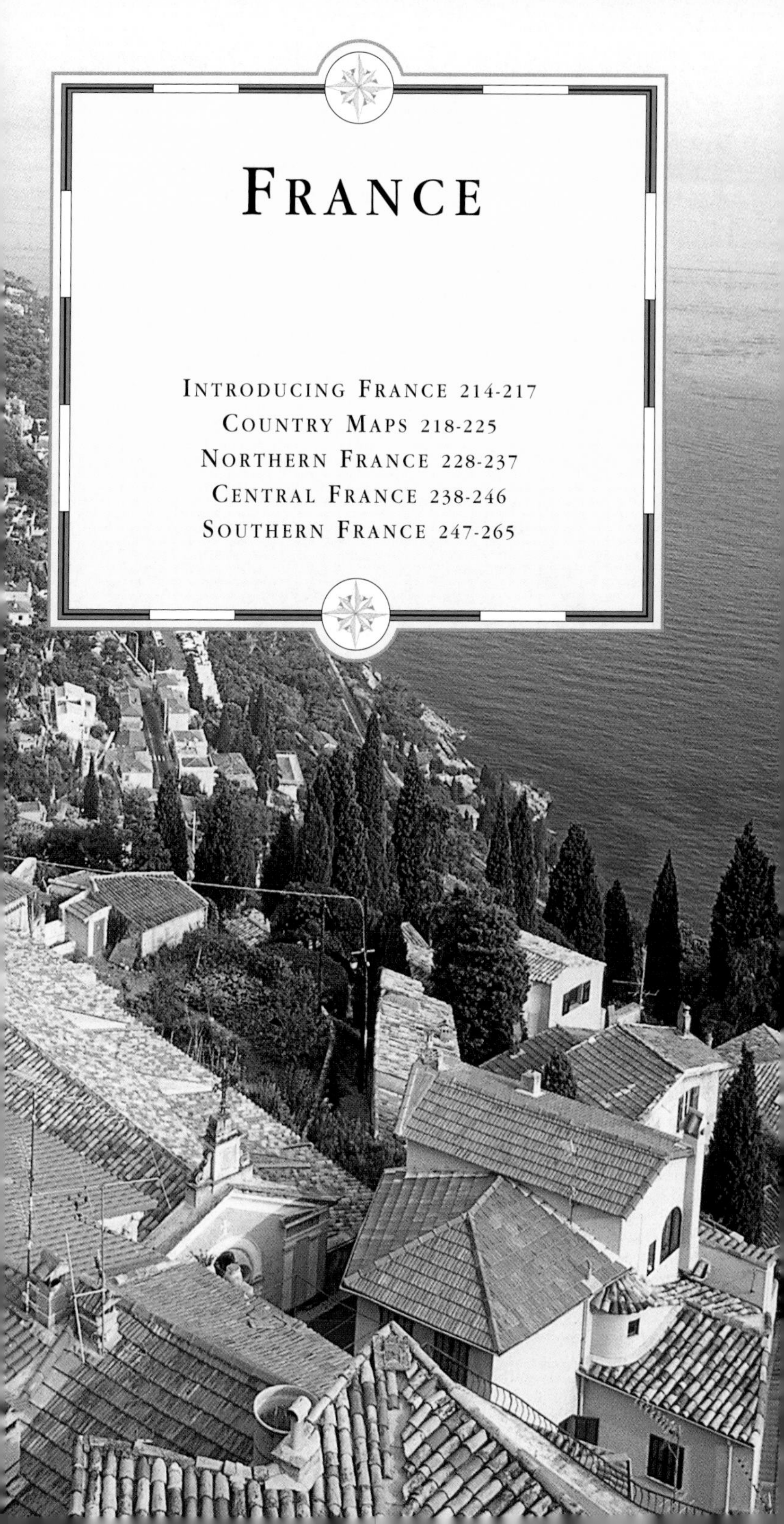

FRANCE

FRANCE

FRENCH HOTELS are beginning to enjoy a reputation as the point of your journey, rather than somewhere to be endured along the way. This is not a universal trend, but individual hoteliers have been adding personal attention, style and comfort to their existing culinary reputations. If you have a complaint or a compliment, this new breed of hands-on owner will be there to listen to you – with interest. Such hotels are typically family-run and housed in sympathetically-restored and furnished historic buildings – part of the landscape rather than modern intrusions. Often they are proud to proclaim their unique regional identity.

Château du Domaine St-Martin, at Vence, page 264, one of the most expensive hotels in France

FRANCE REGION BY REGION

IN THIS GUIDE the country has been divided into Northern France, Central France and Southern France.

Northern France

The plains of Picardy, with their traditional inns and converted châteaux, are bordered to the north by the Ardennes forests and to the east by the mountains and hills of Vosges. Paris and its surroundings dominate the centre of the region, its hotels ranging from chic townhouses to the grand buildings of the large hotels.

The Channel coast has its share of heavy industry and oil refineries, concentrated round Le Havre and Rouen, but close by lie the beautiful port of Honfleur, Bayeux with its memories of William the Conqueror's invasion of England (and the more recent D-Day landings), and the lush farmland of the Pays d'Auge and La Suisse Normande, with châteaux, mills and half-timbered inns. To the west of the Channel port of Cherbourg lies the monastery island of Le Mont-St-Michel; here begins the more rugged landscape of Celtic Brittany, with its manors and seaside hotels.

Central France

We define this region as beginning to the south of the Ile de France, and stretching from Nantes at the mouth of the Loire in the west, to the Jura mountains in the east. The great châteaux of the Loire Valley, many of which were remodelled during the Renaissance, are almost always breathtaking, and not all just for looking at: two exquisite examples of places to stay are the Château de Noirieux at Briollay, (page 239) and the Hostellerie du Château de Bellecroix at Chagny (page 239).

Burgundy stands out for the rustic buildings of the fragmented vineyards of the Côte d'Or; the religious showpieces at Vézelay, Fontenay and Cluny, and the splendid palaces of Dijon. Further east is Franche-Comté, with its alpine highlands, crystal rivers, and rolling farmland in the Saône valley.

Southern France

Poitou, to the north of the city of Bordeaux, and Aquitaine, stretching down to the western end of the

Pyrenees at Biarritz, make up the final section of France's Atlantic coastline. Mile upon mile of sandy beaches are backed by dunes and pine forests. The Romans left their imperial mark here – the great arch of Germanicus and the amphitheatre at Saintes are both worth a detour.

Medieval pilgrims travelling to the shrine of St James at Santiago de Compostela left a legacy of Romanesque churches such as those at Poitiers and Parthenay. The vineyards of Bordeaux have kept the city prosperous for centuries. A number of the château hotels in this region, (such as the one at Pauillac, page 258), run their own wine appreciation courses.

To the east lie the green, rolling hills, farms and manors of the Dordogne Valley and the caves and culinary delights of Périgord. The cave paintings at Lascaux are probably the most important in France – but if you prefer *foie gras*, walnuts and truffles, try Sarlat's fabulous Saturday market. In the far south-west, the French Pyrenees take you into Basque country, offering spectacular scenery – and mountain activities as tiring or thrilling as anybody could want. Returning to your Basque inn, or perhaps to the Hôtel de la Reine Sancie at Sauveterre-de-Béarn (page 263), with its spectacular position on medieval arches above the Gave d'Oloron river, will make you glad you survived the day intact.

Languedoc-Roussillon is squeezed in between the Mediterranean shore and the Massif Central range. Roussillon was Spanish until 1659, and the Fort de Salses still stands at the old border. Carcassonne is an amazingly well-restored medieval town and Nîmes still has much of the Roman about it.

The Massif Central is an enigmatic area, wild and hard on the Grands Causses, gentle in the Limousin and spectacular where the Lot, Aveyron and Tarn leave the Aubrac mountains through rugged gorges.

To the east lies the Rhône Valley and beyond are the French Alps with some traditional chalet hotels.

Provence is nowadays almost too familiar to need much description. The salt-marshes of the Camargue and the resorts of the Côte d'Azur have, as a back-drop, a highly-coloured and scented hinterland, where the Romans who built the theatre (still in use) at Vaison-la-Romaine may well have found Bronze Age remains. Hotels have found their way into *mas* – the Provençal farmhouses – and into villas originally built for private pleasure.

Highlights

The hotels illustrated on these introductory pages are just a taste of what you will find in the listings that follow. For peace, quiet and simple but delicious food, you could do far worse than the Auberge de l'Aiguebrun near Bonnieux (page 249). Champagne buffs will gravitate to the Château des Crayères in Reims (page 235), or to the Château de Courcelles (page 228), where the cellars house outstanding champagnes. Those who navigate principally by menu are unlikely to pass up a chance to stay at Jean-Marc Reynaud's eponymous restaurant at Tain l'Hermitage (page 246) or at Alain Ducasse's La Bastide de Moustiers (page 257). Those who crave a beach will take a close look at the well-priced and child-friendly Ti Al-Lannec at Trébeurden (page 237). Mountain air and a stunning view of Mont Blanc are both on offer at the Auberge du Bois Prin's classic chalet at Chamonix (page 240). Further south there are more panoramic views from the beautifully

The Paris Ritz, page 234, opulence on a lavish scale

Château de Brélidy at Brélidy in Brittany, page 227, a severe exterior, but relaxing inside

converted medieval Le Cagnard at Haut-de-Cagnes (page 254).

Food and Drink

French cooking is probably the subtlest, most varied and most imaginative in the world. It is not necessarily elaborate, but the care taken to choose, season and flavour the principal ingredients can lift dishes into the realms of the extraordinary.

In the late 1980s and early 1990s, some gastronomes felt that French food had lost its edge, at any rate compared with the new cuisines of Britain, Australia and the US Pacific Rim. Nowadays, our impression is that French food is re-inventing itself.

The range of styles is stupendous – in the north the coastal waters yield huge platters of *fruits de mer*, and travelling

Cuq-en-Terrasses, page 252

eastwards you find the ham, sausages, stout stews and tangy cheeses of Alsace. In the west the pork, cream and calvados of Normandy are neighbours to the Breton crêpes, seafood and lamb raised on the coastal salt marshes.

Moving southwest, the *foie gras*, truffles, *confits* and walnut oil of Périgord, the wine-based cookery of Bordeaux, and the shellfish and lobsters of Arcachon and Marennes eventually give way to the robust and often highly-spiced dishes of the Basque southwest.

Lyon can claim to be the gastronomic centre of France: in this fortunate city, Bresse chicken, Charolais beef, wild fowl from the Dombes, smoked sausage and freshwater fish from Franche-Comté and the Jura join forces with a host of local cheeses such as Vacherin, Cantal and Fourme d'Ambert.

The south of France has the brightest palette of colours: in the markets, aubergines, courgettes, asparagus, huge tomatoes, peppers, peaches and cherries contrast with black olives, walnuts, braids of garlic and wild mushrooms. The basis of many a dish is lamb from the Camargue, or red mullet and red snapper – combined with conger eel and monkfish to make *bouillabaisse*, the king of fish soups.

Entire books have been devoted to the wine of single French vineyards. All that can be said here is that prices range from the stratospheric to rock-bottom; and that it is a matter of pride for most restaurateurs to offer excellent value house wine (*vin du patron*) from the lower end of the scale. Do try them, if only to give your purse a rest.

France has been listing and classifying wine production areas for nearly 200 years. There are three principal classifications: *appellation contrôlée (AC)*, which guarantees origin and a certain standard, *vin délimité de qualité supérieure (VDQS)*, which distinguish good wines of local interest; and *vin de pays*, which is the humblest grade of all.

Virtually all the best wine-producing areas are dominated by their rivers. The Marne and the topmost reaches of the Seine flow through Champagne; the Loire through the vineyards producing the dry whites of Muscadet in the west, and of Pouilly and Sancerre in the east, and the sweeter wines of Touraine and Anjou at the centre. The Charente cuts Cognac in half; the Dordogne graces Bergerac and then, like the Garonne, empties into the Gironde estuary near Bordeaux, where the great wines of the Médoc, St Émilion, Pomerol and Graves are produced. From east of the Burgundian capital of Beaune, the Saône flows almost due south through the Mâconnais to join the Rhône, which itself continues south through the rich red wine-producing areas between the cities of Lyon and Avignon.

Bedrooms and Bathrooms

Unless otherwise specified, a double room has a double bed (*grand lit*). If you want twin beds (*deux lits*) be sure to ask for them – there may be an extra charge. Specify clearly if you want your own bathroom (*avec salle de bain en suite*).

Bathrooms may not have a bath (*une baignoire*). If a shower (*une douche*) will not do, be sure to say so when booking.

Other Practical Information

Weekend wedding parties can go on very noisily till dawn. It is worth asking if your booking will coincide with *un mariage* – and well worth revising your plans if it does.

The national summer holidays start around 14 July and end on 31 August; if possible, avoid travelling around these dates, for obvious reasons.

Language Most hotels have an English-speaker, or can find one at a pinch, but no matter how bad your French is, you will collect some goodwill by attempting to use it. If you are visiting Alsace-Lorraine, and you don't know the word in French, try German.

Currency Until recently, the French *franc*. From 1 January 2002, France switches over to the European *euro* (written 'EUR'), made up of 100 *cents*.

Château de Noirieux, page 239

Shops Food shops tend to open at about 7am, close around noon for lunch, and reopen in the late afternoon until 7pm. Food shops often open on Sunday mornings but stay closed on Monday mornings. Other shops usually open 9am–6pm Mon–Sat, and, except for the supermarkets and hyper-markets, take a lunch break.

Tipping A service charge is usually added in cafés and restaurants, but most French people leave a small tip at bars and 5 per cent at restaurants.

Telephoning Phoning abroad from hotels can be very expensive. Some public telephones take coins, others take *télécartes* (50 or 120 unit phonecards from post offices, *tabacs* and some cafés). Post offices have *cabines* – booths where you can call first and pay afterwards.

All French telephone numbers have ten digits: a two-figure area prefix, followed by an eight-digit number. If phoning from within France, always include the full area prefix. To phone France from the UK, dial 00 33, then the phone number, omitting the initial zero from the area prefix; from the US, 011 33.

Public holidays 1 January; Easter Sunday and Monday; Ascension Day (sixth Thursday after Easter); Whit Monday (second Monday after Ascension Day); 1 May; 8 May; 14 July; 1 November; 11 November; 25 December.

Useful Words

Breakfast	*Petit déjeuner*
Lunch	*Déjeuner*
Dinner	*Dîner*
Free room?	*Chambre libre?*
How much?	*Combien?*
A single	*Une chambre pour une personne*
A double	*Une chambre pour deux personnes*

France Price Bands

Our price bands refer to the price of a standard double room in high season *including* breakfast. (However, French hotels usually quote room prices excluding breakfast.)

€	under 75 EUR
€€	75–135 EUR
€€€	135–200 EUR
€€€€	over 200 EUR

Château de Nieuil, at Nieuil page 243, a former royal hunting lodge

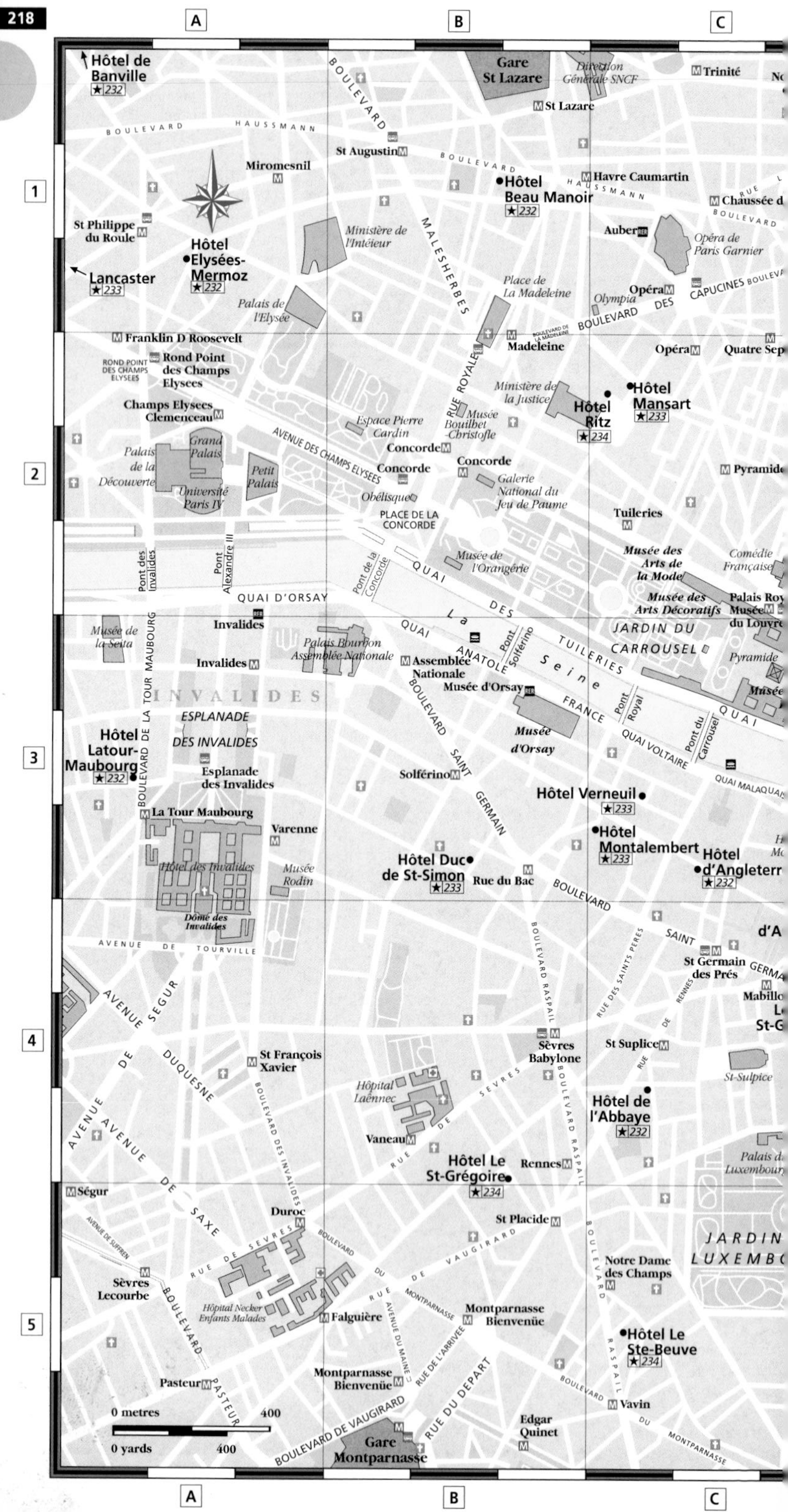

A
B
C
1
2
3
4
5
Hôtel de Banville ★232
Gare St Lazare
Direction Générale SNCF
Trinité
St Lazare
BOULEVARD HAUSSMANN
BOULEVARD
St Augustin
BOULEVARD HAUSSMANN
Miromesnil
Hôtel Beau Manoir ★232
Havre Caumartin
Chaussée d
St Philippe du Roule
Hôtel Elysées-Mermoz ★232
Ministère de l'Intéiur
MALESHERBES
Auber
Opéra de Paris Garnier
Lancaster ★233
Palais de l'Elysée
Place de La Madeleine
Opéra
Olympia
BOULEVARD DES CAPUCINES
BOULEVARD DE LA MADELEINE
Franklin D Roosevelt
Madeleine
Opéra
Quatre Sep
ROND POINT DES CHAMPS ELYSEES
Rond Point des Champs Elysees
RUE ROYALE
Ministère de la Justice
Hôtel Mansart ★233
Hôtel Ritz ★234
Champs Elysees Clemenceau
Espace Pierre Cardin
Musée Bouilhet Christofle
Grand Palais
AVENUE DES CHAMPS ELYSEES
Concorde
Palais de la Découverte
Petit Palais
Concorde
Concorde
Galerie National du Jeu de Paume
Pyramide
Université Paris IV
Obélisque
PLACE DE LA CONCORDE
Tuileries
Pont des Invalides
Pont Alexandre III
Pont de la Concorde
Musée de l'Orangerie
Musée des Arts de la Mode
Comédie Française
QUAI D'ORSAY
QUAI DES TUILERIES
La Seine
Musée des Arts Décoratifs
Palais Roy
Musée du Louvre
Musée de la Seita
Invalides
JARDIN DU CARROUSEL
Palais Bourbon Assemblée Nationale
Invalides
Assemblée Nationale
QUAI ANATOLE FRANCE
Pont Solférino
Pyramide
BOULEVARD DE LA TOUR MAUBOURG
INVALIDES
Musée d'Orsay
Musée
ESPLANADE DES INVALIDES
Pont Royal
Pont du Carrousel
QUAI
Hôtel Latour-Maubourg ★232
Musée d'Orsay
QUAI VOLTAIRE
Esplanade des Invalides
BOULEVARD SAINT GERMAIN
Solférino
QUAI MALAQUAIS
Hôtel Verneuil ★233
La Tour Maubourg
Varenne
Hôtel Montalembert ★233
Hôtel des Invalides
Hôtel Duc de St-Simon ★233
Hôtel d'Angleterr ★232
Musée Rodin
Rue du Bac
BOULEVARD SAINT
Dôme des Invalides
d'A
AVENUE DE TOURVILLE
BOULEVARD RASPAIL
RUE DES SAINTS PERES
St Germain des Prés
GERMA
Mabillo
RUE DE RENNES
AVENUE DE SEGUR
Sèvres Babylone
St Suplice
St Francois Xavier
AVENUE DE DUQUESNE
BOULEVARD DES INVALIDES
RUE DE SEVRES
St-Sulpice
Hôpital Laënnec
BOULEVARD RASPAIL
Hôtel de l'Abbaye ★232
AVENUE DE SAXE
Vaneau
Hôtel Le St-Grégoire ★234
Rennes
Palais du Luxembour
Ségur
AVENUE DE SUFFREN
Duroc
St Placide
JARDIN LUXEMBO
RUE DE SEVRES
BOULEVARD DU MONTPARNASSE
RUE DE VAUGIRARD
Notre Dame des Champs
Sèvres Lecourbe
BOULEVARD PASTEUR
Hôpital Necker Enfants Malades
Falguière
AVENUE DU MAINE
Montparnasse Bienvenüe
Hôtel Le Ste-Beuve ★234
RUE DE L'ARRIVEE
RUE DU DEPART
Montparnasse Bienvenüe
Pasteur
BOULEVARD RASPAIL
Vavin
0 metres 400
0 yards 400
BOULEVARD DE VAUGIRARD
Gare Montparnasse
Edgar Quinet
BOULEVARD DU MONTPARNASSE

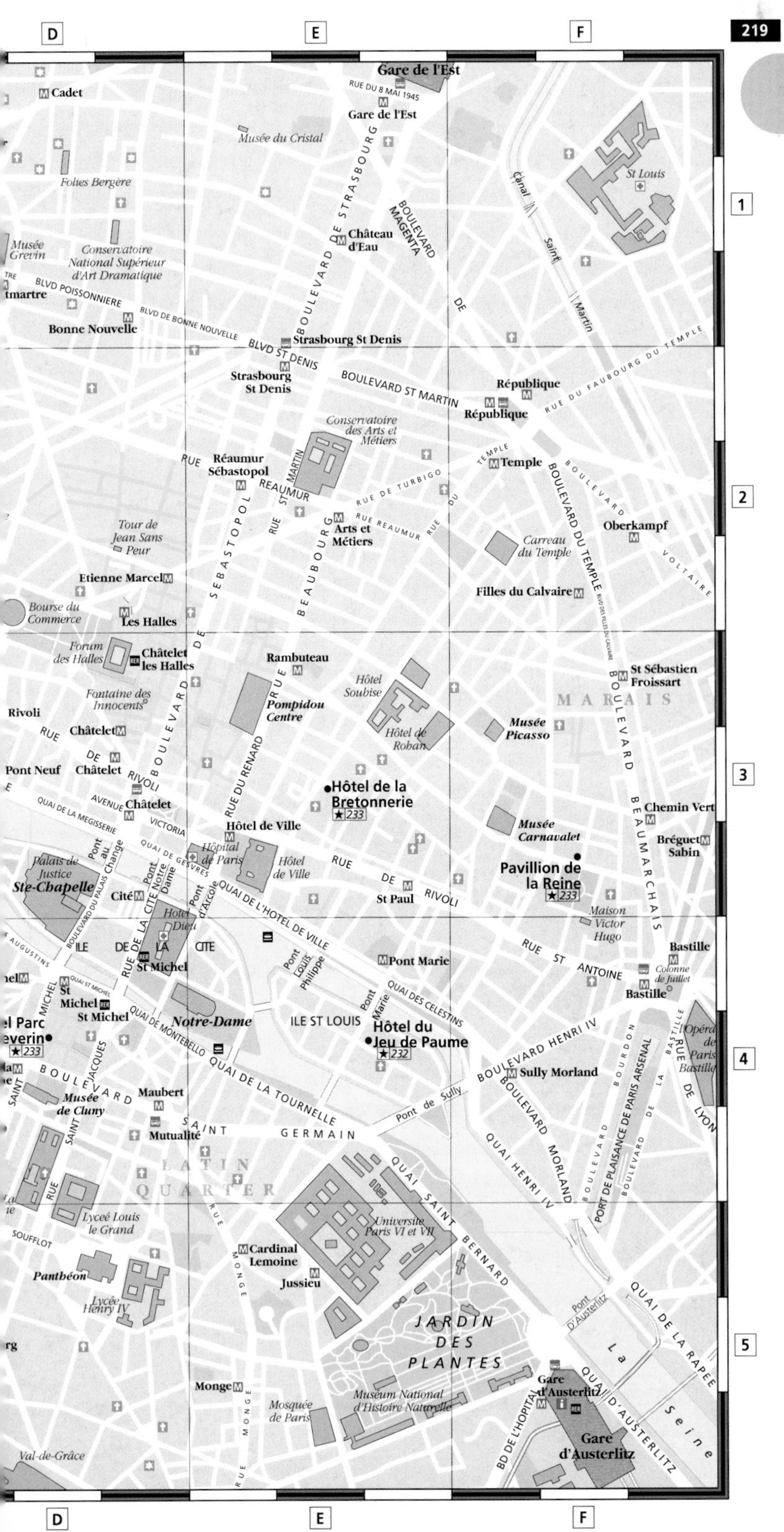
D
E
F
Gare de l'Est
Cadet
Gare de l'Est
Musée du Cristal
Folies Bergère
St Louis
Canal Saint Martin
Château d'Eau
Boulevard de Strasbourg
Boulevard Magenta
Musée Grevin
Conservatoire National Supérieur d'Art Dramatique
Blvd Poissonniere
Blvd de Bonne Nouvelle
Bonne Nouvelle
Strasbourg St Denis
Blvd St Denis
Strasbourg St Denis
Boulevard St Martin
République
République
Rue du Faubourg du Temple
Conservatoire des Arts et Métiers
Réaumur Sébastopol
Rue Reaumur
Rue St Martin
Rue de Turbigo
Temple
Boulevard du Temple
Boulevard Voltaire
Oberkampf
Arts et Métiers
Rue Reaumur
Tour de Jean Sans Peur
Boulevard de Sebastopol
Rue Beaubourg
Carreau du Temple
Filles du Calvaire
Etienne Marcel
Bourse du Commerce
Les Halles
Forum des Halles
Châtelet les Halles
Rambuteau
Hôtel Soubise
St Sébastien Froissart
Marais
Fontaine des Innocents
Pompidou Centre
Musée Picasso
Rivoli
Rue de Rivoli
Châtelet
Hôtel de Rohan
Boulevard Beaumarchais
Pont Neuf
Châtelet
Hôtel de la Bretonnerie
★233
Rue du Renard
Chemin Vert
Avenue Victoria
Châtelet
Quai de la Megisserie
Hôtel de Ville
Musée Carnavalet
Bréguet Sabin
Quai de Gesvres
Pont au Change
Hôpital de Paris
Hôtel de Ville
Pavillion de la Reine
★233
Palais de Justice
Ste-Chapelle
Pont Notre Dame
Rue de Rivoli
St Paul
Cité
Pont d'Arcole
Quai de l'Hotel de Ville
Maison Victor Hugo
Boulevard du Palais
Hotel Dieu
Ile de la Cité
Rue de la Cité
Rue St Antoine
Bastille
St Michel
Pont Louis Philippe
Pont Marie
Colonne de Juillet
Quai St Michel
St Michel
Pont Marie
Quai des Celestins
Bastille
Quai de Montebello
Notre-Dame
Ile St Louis
Hôtel du Jeu de Paume
★232
Boulevard Henri IV
Opéra de Paris Bastille
★233
Boulevard St Michel
Sully Morland
Boulevard Bourdon
Port de Plaisance de Paris Arsenal
Rue de Lyon
Rue Saint Jacques
Quai de la Tournelle
Musée de Cluny
Maubert
Boulevard Morland
Boulevard de la Bastille
Pont de Sully
Boulevard Saint Germain
Mutualité
Quai Henri IV
Latin Quarter
Quai Saint Bernard
Université Paris VI et VII
Rue Soufflot
Lycée Louis le Grand
Cardinal Lemoine
Panthéon
Rue Monge
Jussieu
Quai de la Rapée
Lycée Henry IV
Pont d'Austerlitz
Jardin des Plantes
La Seine
Monge
Gare d'Austerlitz
Muséum National d'Histoire Naturelle
Mosquée de Paris
Quai d'Austerlitz
Bd de l'Hopital
Gare d'Austerlitz
Val-de-Grâce
1
2
3
4
5

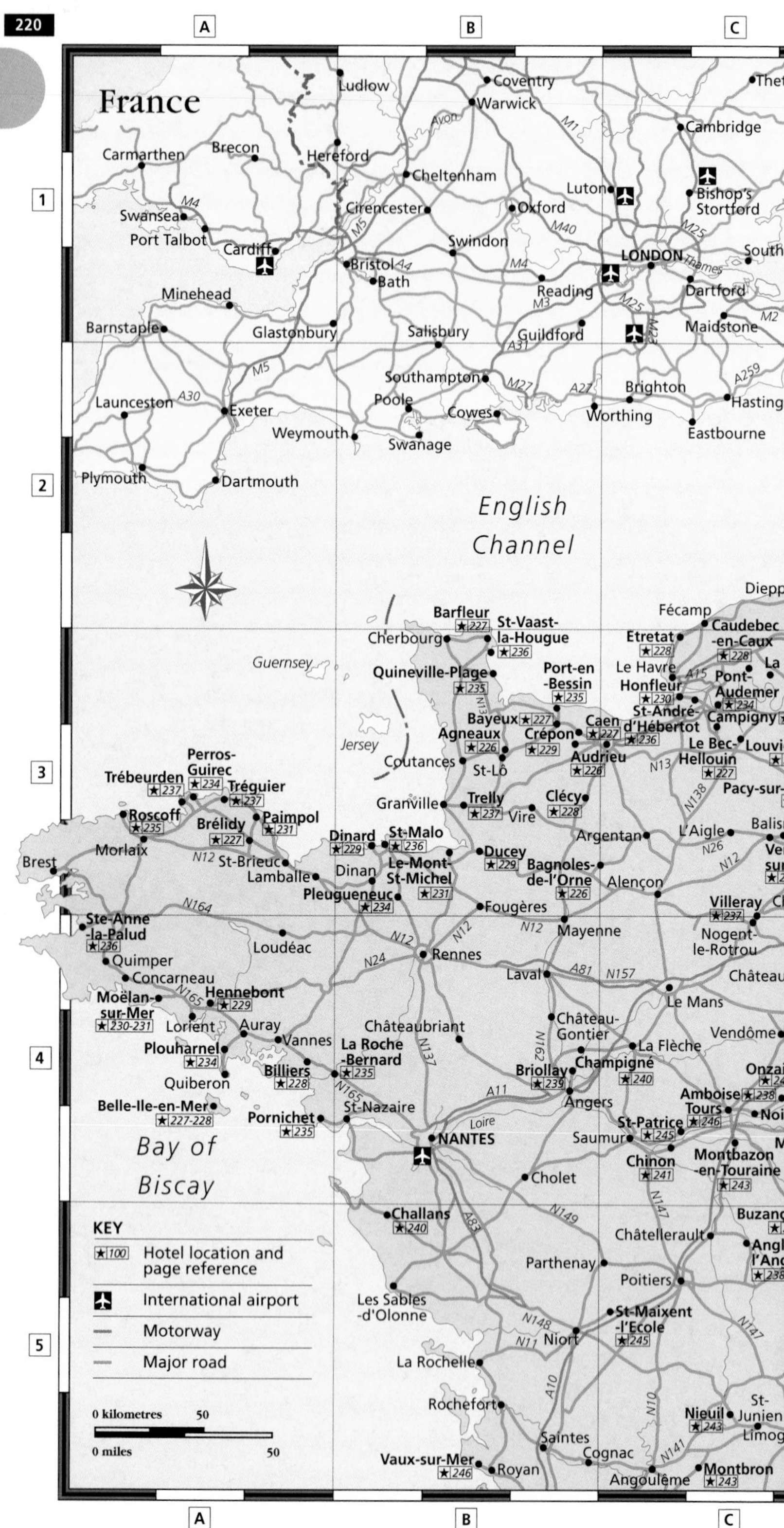
France
A
B
C
1
2
3
4
5
English Channel
Bay of Biscay
Ludlow
Coventry
Warwick
Cambridge
Carmarthen
Brecon
Hereford
Cheltenham
Luton
Bishop's Stortford
Swansea
Port Talbot
Cardiff
Cirencester
Oxford
Swindon
LONDON
Bristol
Bath
Reading
Dartford
Minehead
Barnstaple
Glastonbury
Salisbury
Guildford
Maidstone
Southampton
Brighton
Hastings
Launceston
Exeter
Poole
Cowes
Worthing
Eastbourne
Weymouth
Swanage
Plymouth
Dartmouth
Fécamp
Barfleur 227
St-Vaast-la-Hougue 236
Cherbourg
Etretat 228
Caudebec-en-Caux 228
Guernsey
Quineville-Plage 235
Port-en-Bessin 235
Le Havre
Honfleur 230
Pont-Audemer 234
St-André-d'Hébertot 236
Campigny
Bayeux 227
Agneaux 226
Crépon 229
Caen 227
Audrieu 226
Jersey
Coutances
St-Lô
Le Bec-Hellouin 227
Perros-Guirec 234
Trébeurden 237
Tréguier 237
Granville
Trelly 237
Vire
Clécy 228
Roscoff 235
Paimpol 231
Brélidy 227
Morlaix
Dinard 229
St-Malo 236
Argentan
L'Aigle
Brest
St-Brieuc
Lamballe
Dinan
Le-Mont-St-Michel 231
Ducey 229
Bagnoles-de-l'Orne 226
Alençon
Pleugueneuc 234
Fougères
Villeray 237
Ste-Anne-la-Palud 236
Mayenne
Nogent-le-Rotrou
Loudéac
Rennes
Quimper
Concarneau
Laval
Le Mans
Moëlan-sur-Mer 230-231
Hennebont 229
Lorient
Auray
Château-Gontier
Châteaubriant
Vendôme
Plouharnel 234
Vannes
La Roche-Bernard 235
La Flèche
Briollay 239
Champigné 240
Quiberon
Billiers 228
Angers
Amboise 238
Tours 246
Belle-Ile-en-Mer 227-228
St-Nazaire
St-Patrice 245
Pornichet 235
NANTES
Saumur
Chinon 241
Montbazon-en-Touraine 243
Cholet
Challans 240
Châtellerault
Parthenay
Poitiers
Les Sables-d'Olonne
St-Maixent-l'Ecole 245
Niort
La Rochelle
Rochefort
Nieuil 243
St-Junien
Saintes
Cognac
Vaux-sur-Mer 246
Royan
Angoulême
Montbron 243
KEY
100 Hotel location and page reference
International airport
Motorway
Major road
0 kilometres 50
0 miles 50

D
E
F
AMSTERDAM
Epe
A30
Katwijk aan Zee
Apeldoorn
Haaksbergen
DEN HAAG (The Hague)
Delft
Utrecht
Arnhem
Münster
Lek
ROTTERDAM
Waal
Nijmegen
Borken
Oss
Rhein
Recklinghausen
1
A57
DORTMUND
Roosendaal
Venray
Bochum
Vlissingen
Eindhoven
Venlo
Terneuzen
Antwerpen
Roermond
Oostende
N34
Brugge
A13
Maaseik
DÜSSELDORF
Leverkusen
A45
Dunkerque
Gent
Herselt
KÖLN (Cologne)
A4
A25
A2
Maastricht
Troisdorf
Kortrijk
A10
A4
BRUSSEL (Brussels)
A1
BONN
Bailleul
Tourcoing
N3
Rheinbach
Aire-sur-la-Lys
★226
LILLE
A8
N6
A4
A15
Liège
Mechernich
Tournai
Soignies
Meuse
A21
A1
Malmédy
Koblenz
A26
Lens
Péruwelz
A7
Charleroi
2
A23
Valenciennes
N4
Manhay
N39
Arras
A2
Maubeuge
A60
Cochem
Mosel
N25
Rochefort
Doullens
★228
Couvin
N5
Bastogne
Bitburg
A3
A26
N43
Hirson
N95
Albert
Etréaupont
★230
Revin
Charleville-Mézières
Bouillon
Birkenfeld
Amiens
N29
St-Quentin
A1
Vervins
★237
LUXEMBOURG
A1
Marle
Sedan
Mont-St-Martin
A62
Ste Preuve
★236
N43
Mettlach
Noyon
Laon
D964
Esch-sur-Alzette
N31
Compiègne
N44
Reims
★235
Thionville
Soissons
Courcelles-sur-Vesle
★228
Saarbrücken
Treil
Sept-Saulx
★236
Verdun
A4
A4
N3
Metz
Sarreguemines
Château-Thierry
A31
A4
N1
N3
Épernay
Châlons-sur-Marne
Pont-à-Mousson
Haguenau
Saverne
Meaux
Bar-le-Duc
PARIS
★232-234
Vitry-le-François
N4
Toul
Nancy
Marlenheim
★231
N4
Évry
N4
3
N19
Provins
Romilly-sur-Seine
St-Dizier
D964
Lunéville
★231
STRASBOURG
Barbizon
Seine
N77
A26
Fontainebleau
Ribeauvillé
★235
Nemours
Flagy
★229
A5
Troyes
★237
N19
Lapoutroie
★230
A5
N74
A31
Kaysersberg
★230
N7
A6
Sens
Chaumont
D164
Artzenheim
★226
N6
Joigny
★243
Châtillon-sur-Seine
Luxeuil-les-Bains
Illhaeusern
★230
N60
Langres
Rhine
Mulhouse
Auxerre
★238
N19
Lure
A35
N19
Chassignelles
★240
Vesoul
Belfort
St-Louis
BASEL
Gien
★242
A6
N71
N74
A31
4
Vézelay
★246
Avallon
★239
A36
Delémont
Varzy
Châteauneuf
★240
Dijon
Goumois
★242
St.Imier
N7
A38
★242
Besançon
Biel
Curtil-Vergy
★242
N5
A1
Beaune
★239
Gilly-les-Citeaux
Dôle
N83
Neuchâtel
Bourges
N6
Aloxe-Corton
★238
Nevers
D978
Meursault
★243-244
Chaublanc
★240
Pontarlier
BERN
Chagny
★239-240
Payerne
N5
Fribourg
Bannegon
★239
Mercurey
★242
Champagnole
Passenans
St-Amand-Montrond
N7
Lons-le-Saunier
LAUSANNE
Bulle
Coulandon
★251
Moulins
★245
A6
A1
Lac Léman
Digoin
Poisson
Cluny
★241
Nyon
Evian-les-Bains
★242
A71
Replonges
★244
Sion
5
Igé
★242
Mâcon
A40
Oyonnax
GENÈVE (Geneva)
Target
★263
N7
Bourg-en-Bresse
Echenevex
★241
Annemasse
Martigny
N6
A40
N144
Vichy
Roanne
★259
Villefranche-sur-Saône
N83
A42
Veyrier-du-Lac
★246
Talloires
★246
Chamonix
★240
Saône
N141
Riom
A72
Tarare
A46
Ambérieu-en-Bugey
Annecy le-Vieux
★238
Manigod
★242
Aosta
Megève
★243-244
A5
Clermont-Ferrand
Thiers
N82
LYON
★243
Bourgoin-Jallieu
Doussard
Le Tertenoz
★246
N89
Chambéry
D
E
F

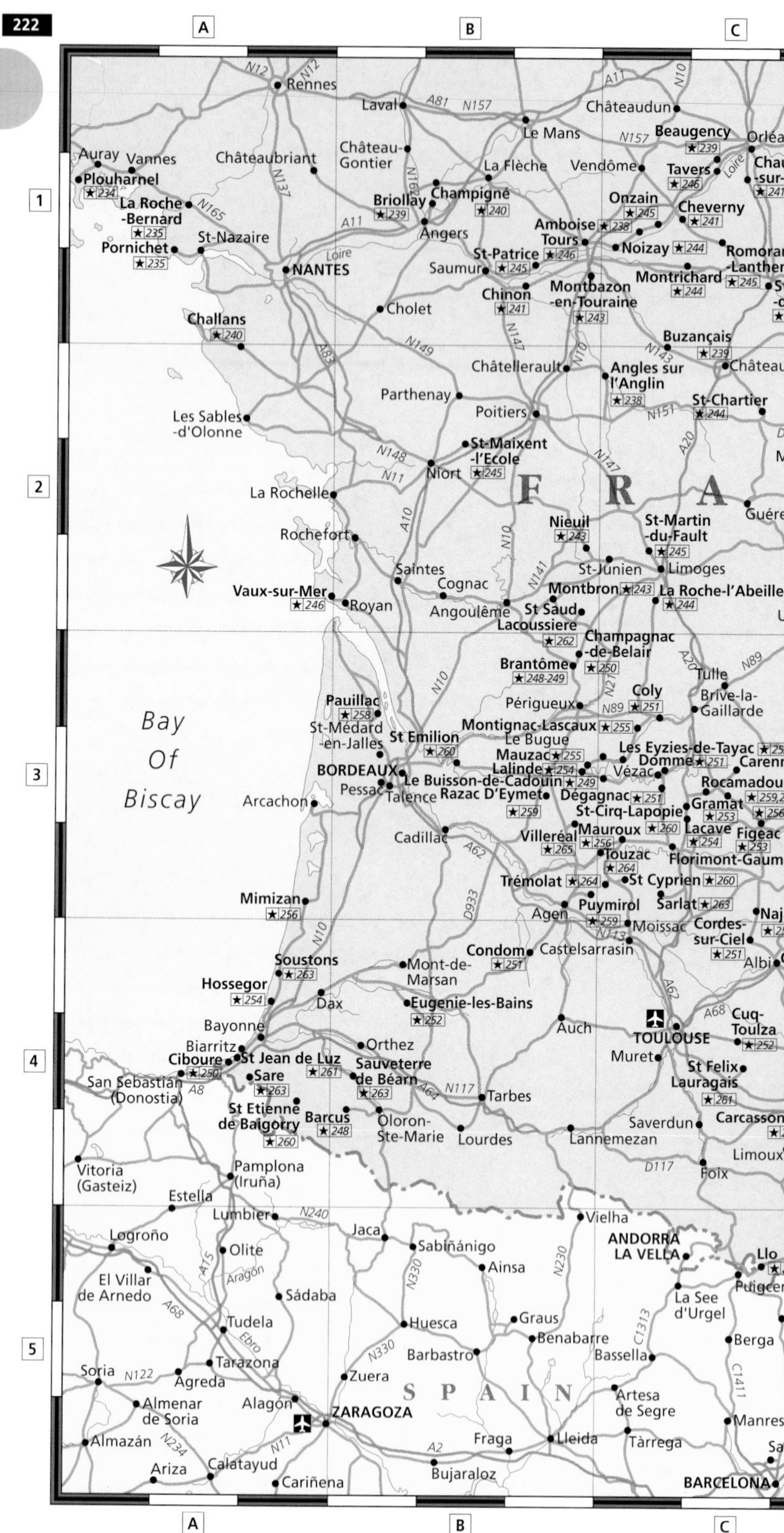
A
B
C
1
2
3
4
5
Rennes
Laval
Le Mans
Châteaudun
Beaugency ★239
Orléans
Auray
Vannes
Plouharnel ★234
Châteaubriant
Château-Gontier
La Flèche
Vendôme
Tavers ★246
Chaumont-sur-Loire ★241
La Roche-Bernard ★235
Briollay ★239
Champigné ★240
Onzain ★245
Cheverny ★241
Pornichet ★235
St-Nazaire
Angers
Amboise ★238
Tours
Noizay ★244
Romorantin-Lanthenay ★245
NANTES
Saumur
St-Patrice ★245
★246
Montbazon-en-Touraine ★243
Montrichard ★244
Chinon ★241
Cholet
Challans ★240
Buzançais ★239
Châtellerault
Angles sur l'Anglin ★238
Châteauroux
Parthenay
Poitiers
St-Chartier ★244
Les Sables-d'Olonne
St-Maixent-l'Ecole ★245
Niort
La Rochelle
FRANCE
Guéret
Nieuil ★243
St-Martin-du-Fault ★245
Rochefort
Saintes
St-Junien
Limoges
Cognac
Montbron ★243
La Roche-l'Abeille ★244
Vaux-sur-Mer ★246
Royan
Angoulême
St Saud Lacoussiere ★262
Champagnac-de-Belair ★250
Brantôme ★248-249
Tulle
Bay Of Biscay
Pauillac ★258
Périgueux
Coly ★251
Brive-la-Gaillarde
St-Médard-en-Jalles
St Emilion ★260
Montignac-Lascaux ★255
Le Bugue
Les Eyzies-de-Tayac ★252
Mauzac ★255
Domme ★251
BORDEAUX
Lalinde ★254
Vézac
Pessac
Talence
Le Buisson-de-Cadouin ★249
Rocamadour
Arcachon
Razac D'Eymet ★259
Dégagnac ★251
Gramat ★253
St-Cirq-Lapopie
Cadillac
Villeréal ★265
Mauroux ★260
Lacave ★254
Figeac ★253
★256
Touzac ★264
Florimont-Gaumier
Trémolat ★264
St Cyprien ★260
Mimizan ★256
Sarlat ★263
Agen
Puymirol ★259
Moissac
Cordes-sur-Ciel ★251
Najac
Condom ★251
Castelsarrasin
Albi
Soustons ★263
Mont-de-Marsan
Hossegor ★254
Dax
Eugenie-les-Bains ★252
Bayonne
Auch
TOULOUSE
Cuq-Toulza ★252
Biarritz
Orthez
Muret
Ciboure ★250
St Jean de Luz ★261
Sauveterre de Béarn ★263
St Felix Lauragais ★261
San Sebastian (Donostia)
Sare ★263
Tarbes
St Etienne de Baigorry ★260
Barcus ★248
Oloron-Ste-Marie
Lourdes
Lannemezan
Saverdun
Carcassonne
Limoux
Foix
Vitoria (Gasteiz)
Pamplona (Iruña)
Estella
Lumbier
Jaca
Vielha
Logroño
Olite
Sabiñánigo
Ainsa
ANDORRA LA VELLA
Llo
El Villar de Arnedo
Sádaba
Puigcerdà
La See d'Urgel
Tudela
Huesca
Graus
Benabarre
Berga
Barbastro
Bassella
Soria
Tarazona
Agreda
Zuera
SPAIN
Almenar de Soria
Alagón
ZARAGOZA
Artesa de Segre
Manresa
Almazán
Fraga
Lleida
Tàrrega
Ariza
Calatayud
Cariñena
Bujaraloz
BARCELONA
A11
A20
A62
A63
A64
A68
A81
A83
A10
A15
A2
A8
N10
N12
N89
N113
N117
N122
N137
N141
N143
N147
N148
N149
N151
N157
N162
N165
N21
N234
N240
N330
N230
N11
D933
D117
C1313
C1411
Loire
Ebro
Aragón

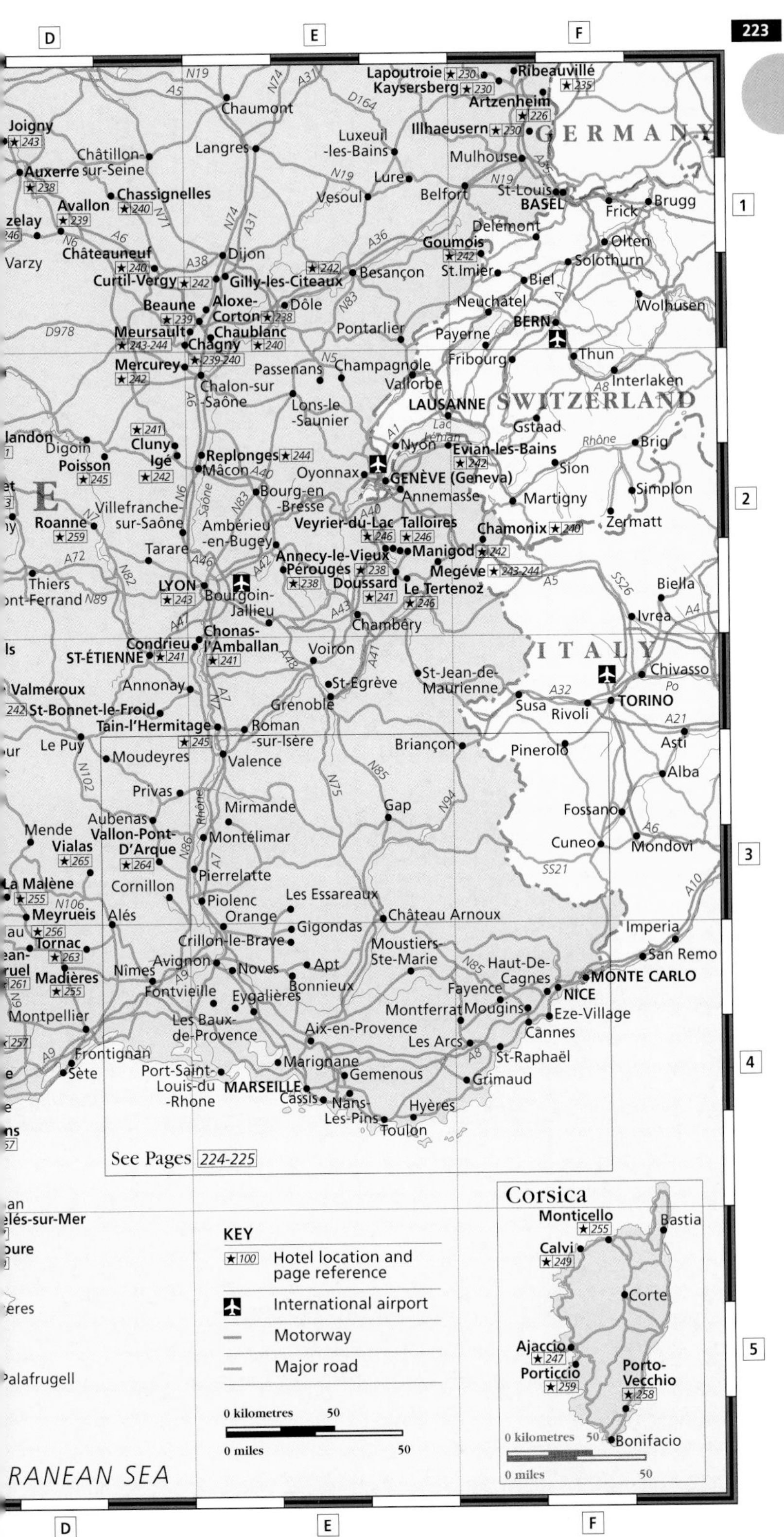
D
E
F
1
2
3
4
5
GERMANY
SWITZERLAND
ITALY
E
Joigny ★243
Auxerre ★238
Châtillon-sur-Seine
Chassignelles ★240
Avallon ★239
Vézelay ★246
Varzy
Châteauneuf ★240
Curtil-Vergy ★242
Gilly-les-Citeaux ★242
Chaumont
Langres
Dijon
Beaune ★239
Aloxe-Corton ★238
Dôle
Meursault ★243-244
Chaublanc ★240
Chagny ★239-240
Mercurey ★242
Chalon-sur-Saône
Passenans
Champagnole
Lons-le-Saunier
Luxeuil-les-Bains
Lure
Vesoul
Besançon
Pontarlier
Lapoutroie ★230
Kaysersberg ★230
Ribeauvillé ★235
Artzenheim ★226
Illhaeusern ★230
Mulhouse
Belfort
St-Louis
BASEL
Frick
Brugg
Delémont
Goumois ★242
St.Imier
Olten
Solothurn
Biel
Neuchâtel
Wolhusen
BERN
Payerne
Fribourg
Thun
Interlaken
Vallorbe
LAUSANNE
Lac Léman
Gstaad
Nyon
Evian-les-Bains ★242
Rhône
Brig
Sion
Oyonnax
GENÈVE (Geneva)
Annemasse
Martigny
Simplon
Zermatt
Chamonix ★240
Veyrier-du-Lac ★246
Talloires ★246
Manigod ★242
Annecy-le-Vieux
Pérouges ★238
Megéve ★243-244
Doussard ★241
Le Tertenoz ★246
Chambéry
Biella
Ivrea
Digoin
Cluny ★241
Igé ★242
Poisson ★245
Replonges ★244
Mâcon
Bourg-en-Bresse
Villefranche-sur-Saône
Roanne ★259
Ambérieu-en-Bugey
Tarare
Thiers
Clermont-Ferrand
LYON ★243
Bourgoin-Jallieu
Chonas-l'Amballan ★241
Condrieu
ST-ÉTIENNE ★241
Voiron
St-Egrève
Grenoble
St-Jean-de-Maurienne
Chivasso
Po
TORINO
Susa
Rivoli
Valmeroux
Annonay
St-Bonnet-le-Froid
Tain-l'Hermitage ★245
Roman-sur-Isère
Le Puy
Moudeyres
Valence
Briançon
Pinerolo
Asti
Alba
Privas
Mirmande
Gap
Fossano
Aubenas
Mende
Vallon-Pont-D'Arque ★264
Vialas ★265
Montélimar
Cuneo
Mondovi
Pierrelatte
La Malène ★255
Cornillon
Piolenc
Les Essareaux
Meyrueis ★256
Alés
Orange
Château Arnoux
Imperia
Gigondas
Crillon-le-Brave
Tornac ★263
Moustiers-Ste-Marie
San Remo
Nîmes
Avignon
Noves
Apt
Haut-De-Cagnes
MONTE CARLO
Madières ★255
Bonnieux
Fayence
NICE
Fontvieille
Eygalières
Montferrat
Mougins
Eze-Village
Montpellier
Les Baux-de-Provence
Aix-en-Provence
Cannes
Les Arcs
St-Raphaël
Frontignan
Sète
Port-Saint-Louis-du-Rhone
Marignane
Gemenous
MARSEILLE
Cassis
Nans-Les-Pins
Hyères
Grimaud
Toulon
See Pages 224-225
Corsica
Monticello ★255
Bastia
Calvi ★249
Corte
Ajaccio ★247
Porticcio ★259
Porto-Vecchio ★258
Bonifacio
0 kilometres 50
0 miles 50
KEY
★100 Hotel location and page reference
International airport
Motorway
Major road
0 kilometres 50
0 miles 50
MEDITERRANEAN SEA
Palafrugell

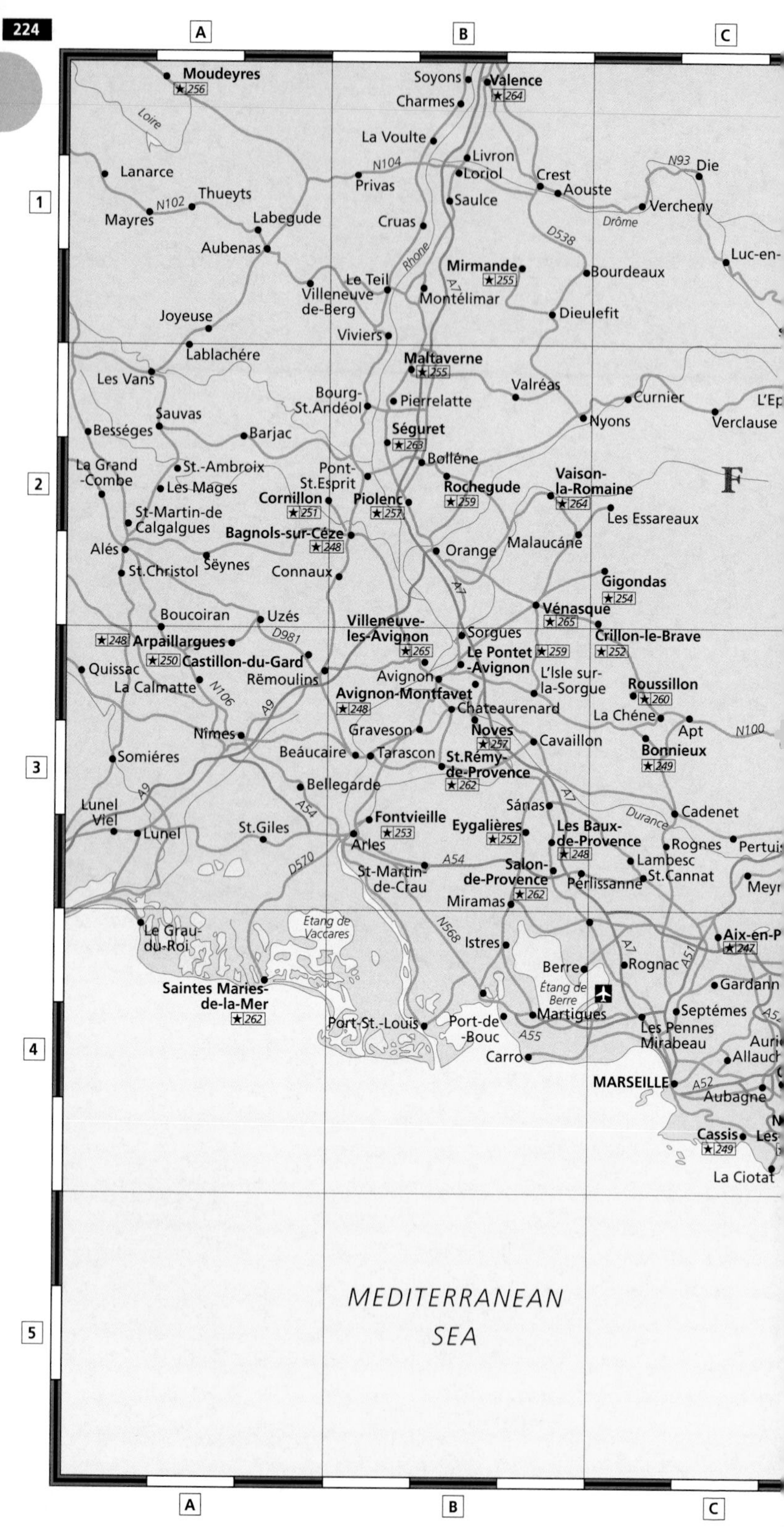
A
B
C
1
2
3
4
5
Moudeyres
256
Soyons
Valence
264
Charmes
Loire
La Voulte
Livron
Lanarce
N104
Loriol
Privas
N93
Die
Crest
Aouste
Thueyts
N102
Saulce
Vercheny
Mayres
Labegude
Cruas
Drôme
Aubenas
D538
Luc-en-
Rhone
Mirmande
255
Bourdeaux
Le Teil
Villeneuve-de-Berg
Montélimar
Dieulefit
Joyeuse
Viviers
Lablachére
Maltaverne
255
Les Vans
Bourg-St.Andéol
Valréas
Curnier
Pierrelatte
Nyons
Verclause
Sauvas
Séguret
263
Bességes
Barjac
Bolléne
La Grand-Combe
St.-Ambroix
Pont-St.Esprit
Vaison-la-Romaine
264
Les Mages
Rochegude
259
Cornillon
251
Piolenc
257
Les Essareaux
St-Martin-de Calgalgues
Bagnols-sur-Cèze
248
Malaucáne
Alés
Orange
Sëynes
St.Christol
Connaux
Gigondas
254
A7
Boucoiran
Uzés
Vénasque
265
Villeneuve-les-Avignon
265
248
Arpaillargues
D981
Sorgues
Crillon-le-Brave
252
250
Castillon-du-Gard
Le Pontet
259
Quissac
-Avignon
L'Isle sur-la-Sorgue
Rëmoulins
Avignon
La Calmatte
N106
Roussillon
260
Avignon-Montfavet
248
Chateaurenard
A9
La Chéne
Apt
N100
Graveson
Noves
257
Nîmes
Cavaillon
Beáucaire
Tarascon
Bonnieux
249
Somiéres
St.Remy-de-Provence
262
Bellegarde
A9
A54
Sánas
A7
Lunel Viel
Fontvieille
253
Cadenet
Durance
Lunel
St.Giles
Eygalières
252
Les Baux-de-Provence
248
Rognes
Arles
Pertuis
D570
A54
Lambesc
Salon-de-Provence
262
St-Martin-de-Crau
Perlissanne
St.Cannat
Meyr
Miramas
Etang de Vaccares
N568
Le Grau-du-Roi
A7
Aix-en-P
247
Istres
A51
Berre
Rognac
Saintes Maries-de-la-Mer
262
Étang de Berre
Gardann
Septémes
Martigues
Port-St.-Louis
Port-de-Bouc
A55
Les Pennes Mirabeau
Auri
Carro
Allauch
MARSEILLE
A52
Aubagne
Cassis
249
Les
La Ciotat
MEDITERRANEAN SEA
F

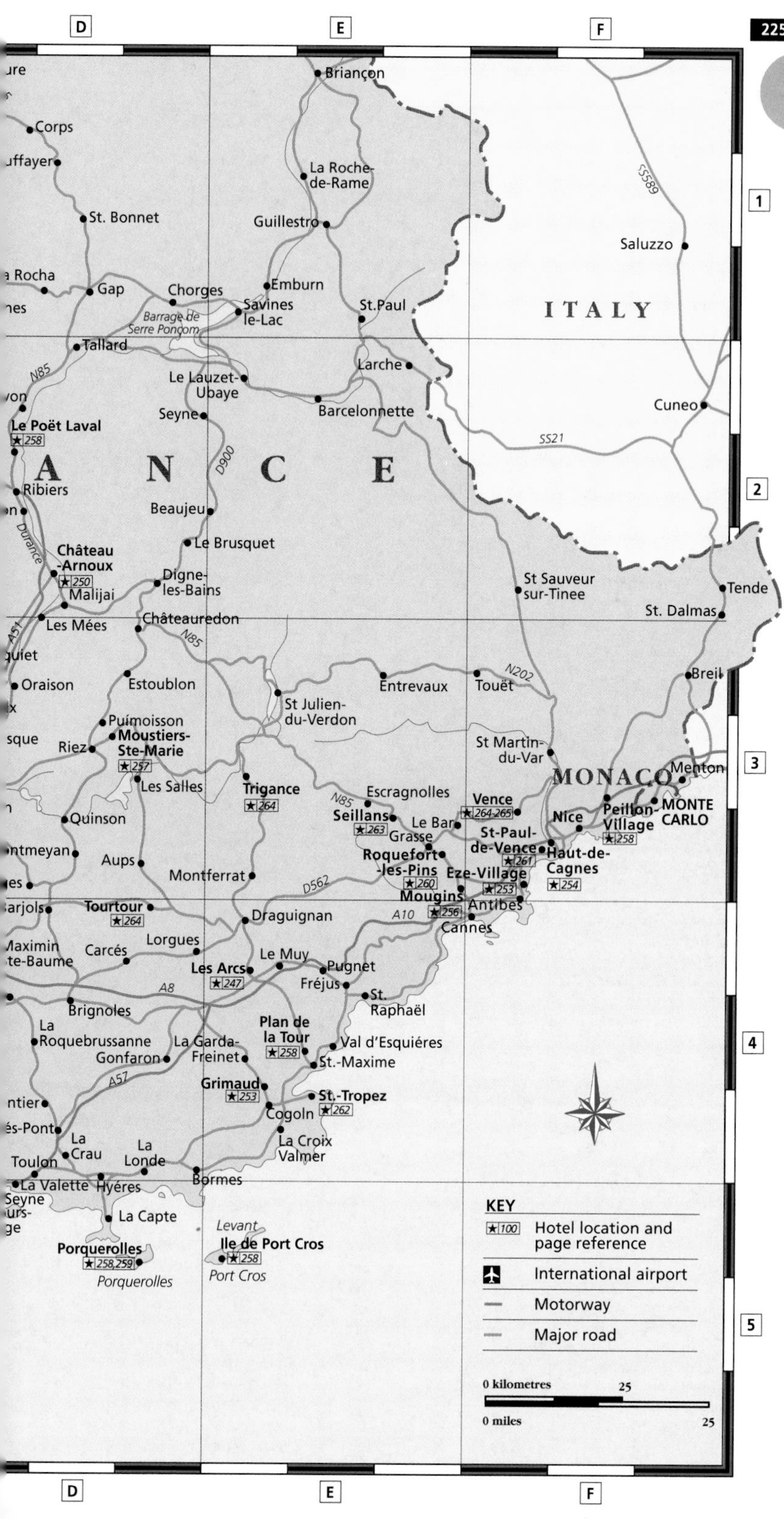
D
E
F
Briançon
Corps
La Roche-de-Rame
St. Bonnet
Guillestro
Saluzzo
Gap
Chorges
Emburn
Savines le-Lac
St.Paul
ITALY
Barrage de Serre Ponçom
Tallard
N85
Larche
Le Lauzet-Ubaye
Seyne
Barcelonnette
Cuneo
SS589
SS21
Le Poët Laval
★ 258
D900
ANCE
Ribiers
Beaujeu
Durance
Le Brusquet
Château-Arnoux
★ 250
Malijai
Digne-les-Bains
St Sauveur sur-Tinee
Tende
St. Dalmas
Les Mées
Châteauredon
A51
N85
Oraison
Estoublon
Entrevaux
Touët
N202
Breil
St Julien-du-Verdon
Puímoisson
Moustiers-Ste-Marie
★ 257
Riez
St Martin-du-Var
MONACO
Menton
Les Salles
Trigance
★ 264
Escragnolles
N85
Vence
★ 264-265
Peillon-Village
★ 258
MONTE CARLO
Nice
Quinson
Seillans
★ 263
Le Bar
Grasse
St-Paul-de-Vence
★ 261
Haut-de-Cagnes
★ 254
Roquefort-les-Pins
★ 260
Eze-Village
★ 253
Aups
Montferrat
D562
Mougins
★ 256
Antibes
Tourtour
★ 264
Draguignan
A10
Cannes
Carcés
Lorgues
Le Muy
Les Arcs
★ 247
Pugnet
Fréjus
St. Raphaël
A8
Brignoles
La Roquebrussanne
Plan de la Tour
★ 258
Val d'Esquiéres
Gonfaron
La Garda-Freinet
St.-Maxime
A57
Grimaud
★ 253
St.-Tropez
★ 262
Cogoln
La Crau
La Londe
La Croix Valmer
Toulon
Bormes
La Valette
Hyéres
La Capte
Levant
Ile de Port Cros
★ 258
Port Cros
Porquerolles
★ 258,259
Porquerolles
KEY
★ 100 Hotel location and page reference
International airport
Motorway
Major road
0 kilometres 25
0 miles 25
1
2
3
4
5

NORTHERN FRANCE

NORMANDY • BRITTANY • PICARDY AND PAS-DE-CALAIS
PARIS • CHAMPAGNE-ARDENNE • ALSACE-LORRAINE

NORTHERN FRANCE offers travellers an almost infinite array of choices in scenery and accommodation. The region stretches southwards from the plains of Picardy, through the apple orchards, lush countryside and converted mills of Normandy to rugged Brittany, with its austere granite chateaux and perfect seaside hotels for family holidays. Paris, at the heart of Northern France, is one of the most romantic cities in the world. It also boasts a large collection of very chic hotels. Pas-de-Calais, the rolling countryside behind the Channel ports of Calais and Boulogne, is ideal for weekend breaks from Britain. Wine lovers with more time to spare can go further east to Champagne.

AGNEAUX

Château d'Agneaux The rather austere exterior of this 13th-century château hides a comfortable hotel with attractive but not over-decorated rooms. Try for one in the turret. Though only just outside the town of Saint-Lô, this is a peaceful spot in hilly countryside. The restaurant serves fine food.
Avenue Ste-Marie, 50180 St-Lô-Agneaux, Manche. **Map** p220 B3. 02 33 57 65 88. FAX 02 33 56 59 21. @ chateau.agneaux@wanadoo.fr b,l,d. **Rooms** 14. Never. AE, DC, MC, V. €€

LES ANDELYS

La Chaîne d'Or An unrivalled position in the shadow of the ghostly ruins of 12th-century Château Gaillard gives this homely 18th-century inn a romantic flavour. Excellent Norman cuisine is served in the charming timbered dining room. Books, paintings, a pretty courtyard and airy elegant bedrooms add to its charms.
25-27 rue Grande, 27700 Les Andelys, Eure. **Map** p220 C3. 02 32 54 00 31. FAX 02 32 54 05 68. @ chaineor@wanadoo.fr b,l,d. **Rooms** 10. late Dec to late Jan. AE, MC, V. €€

AIRE-SUR-LA-LYS

Hostellerie des Trois Mousquetaires Grandly furnished family-run hotel in a mock Tudor house.
Château du Fort de la Redoute, 62120 Aire-sur-la-Lys, Pas-de-Calais. **Map** p221 D2. 03 21 39 01 11. FAX 03 21 39 50 10. @ phvenet@wanadoo.fr b,l,d. **Rooms** 33. €€€€

ARTZENHEIM

Auberge d'Artzenheim Brimming with rustic charm, an inn with a cosy beamed restaurant. Summer dining on the flower-filled terrace.
30 rue du Sponeck, 68320 Artzenheim, Haut-Rhin. **Map** p221 F4. 03 89 71 60 51. FAX 03 89 71 68 21. b,l,d. **Rooms** 10. €

AUDRIEU

Château d'Audrieu Ancestral pile of the Livry-Level family, transformed into a Relais et Château with huge rooms and an impressive wine list.
14250 Audrieu, Calvados. **Map** p220 B3. 02 31 80 21 52. FAX 02 31 80 24 73. @ audrieu@relaischateaux.com b,l,d. **Rooms** 29. €€€

BAGNOLES-DE-L'ORNE

Manoir du Lys A geranium-bedecked hunting lodge with pool and Michelin-starred cuisine.
La Croix Gauthier, Route de Juvigny, 61140 Bagnoles-de-l'Orne, Orne. **Map** p220 B3. 02 33 37 80 69. FAX 02 33 30 05 80. @ manoirdulys@lemel.fr b,l,d. **Rooms** 32. €€€

La Bouille

Le Saint Pierre An inviting stop in a picture-postcard village on the bank of the River Seine, an hour's drive from Paris. Three of the six stylishly modern bedrooms overlook the river. Close by, a small car ferry saves the long drive to the nearest bridge. Recent change of management; the new chef and owner is M. Dejoy.
4 place du Bateau, 76530 La Bouille, Seine-Maritime. **Map** p220 C3. 02 35 67 00 86. FAX 02 35 67 13 24. b,l,d. **Rooms** 7. Sun dinner, Mon. MC, V. €

Caen

Le Dauphin This lovingly restored former priory in the centre of Caen, a stone's throw from William the Conqueror's castle, has many fine features but one in particular that sets it apart: parking. Run by a lively husband-and-wife team, the atmosphere is welcoming, the rooms comfortable, and the (Norman) cuisine excellent.
29 rue Gémare, 14000 Caen, Calvados. **Map** 220 C3. 02 31 86 22 26. FAX 02 31 86 35 14. @ dauphin.caen@wanadoo.fr b,l,d. **Rooms** 37. 1 week Feb; late Oct to mid-Nov. AE, DC, MC, V. €€

Brélidy

Château de Brélidy Don't be put off by the severe granite walls, which are typical of 16th-century Breton architecture. Those who venture in will find a welcoming, family-run hotel, with relaxing bedrooms named after flowers. Added attractions are a billiard room, a Jacuzzi beneath an arbour in the garden, and an unspoilt setting.
Brélidy, 22140 Bégard, Côtes-d'Armor. **Map** p220 A3. 02 96 95 69 38. FAX 02 96 95 18 03. @ chateau.brelidy@worldonline.fr b,d. **Rooms** 15. Jan and Feb. AE, DC, MC, V. €€

Campigny

Le Petit Coq aux Champs The large thatched house – mostly 19th-century with a modern extension – blends the rustic, chic and eccentric. It is tucked away among the rolling meadows and forests of the Risle valley. All the rooms are differently done out; some have balconies over the garden. Impressive cooking.
La Pommeraie Sud, 27500 Campigny, Pont-Audemer, Eure. **Map** p220 C3. 02 32 41 04 19. FAX 02 32 56 06 25. @ le.petit.coq.aux.champs@wanadoo.fr b,l,d. **Rooms** 13. 3 weeks Jan. AE, DC, V. €€

Barfleur

Le Conquérant Abundant ivy softens the grey granite façade of this manor house with a walled garden, fresh new bedrooms and a *salon de thé*.
16-18 rue St-Thomas Becket, 50760 Barfleur, Manche. **Map** p220 B3. 02 33 54 00 82. FAX 02 33 54 65 25. b,d. **Rooms** 13. €

Bayeux

Hôtel d'Argouges Friendly, central yet quiet B&B in an 18th-century mansion with flower garden, dignified sitting room and a period feel.
21 rue St-Patrice, 14400 Bayeux, Calvados. **Map** p220 B3. 02 31 92 88 86. FAX 02 31 92 69 16. @ dargouges@aol.com b. **Rooms** 28. €€

Le Bec-Hellouin

Auberge de l'Abbaye Polished tiled floors and furniture, high-cholesterol cooking and heaps of atmosphere in a quintessential country inn.
Le Bec-Hellouin, 27800 Brionne, Eure. **Map** p220 C3. 02 32 44 86 02. FAX 02 32 46 32 23. b,l,d. **Rooms** 10. €€

Belle-Ile-en-Mer

Castel Clara Modern but tasteful retreat on this quiet island. Pricey but luxurious.
Goulphar, Belle-Ile-en-Mer, 56360 Bangor, Morbihan. **Map** p220 A4. 02 97 31 84 21. FAX 02 97 31 51 69. @ contact@castel-clara.com b,l,d. **Rooms** 39. €€€

For key to symbols see backflap. For price categories *see p217*

Clécy

Hostellerie du Moulin du Vey This creeper-clad former water mill is in a stunning part of the Orne Valley at the heart of La Suisse Normande, within a short drive of Caen. In summer, local dishes are served on a riverbank terrace among the willows; in winter, in a barn of a restaurant. The simple bedrooms are all differently done out. Le Vey, 14570 Clécy, Calvados. **Map** p220 B3. 02 31 69 71 08. FAX 02 31 69 14 14. reservations@moulinduvey.com b,l,d. **Rooms** 25. Dec, Jan. AE, DC, V. €

Doullens

Château de Remaisnil This lovely 18th-century house was once home to designer Laura Ashley, whose style still dominates the plush bedrooms. Now under new ownership, it reopens 1 July. Despite its vast grounds and rococo interior, it retains a homely feel. Nine cheaper rooms in the coach house will be ready in 2004. Remaisnil, 80600 Doullens, Picardie. **Map** p221 D2. 03 22 77 07 47. FAX 03 22 77 41 23. charles.carroll@wanadoo.fr b,d. **Rooms** 10. Dec, Jan, Feb. V. €€

Courcelles-sur-Vesle

Château de Courcelles A 17th-century château where Racine and Napoleon laid their heads. The landscaped garden setting is magical, and the hotel strikes all the right chords: huge bedrooms enlivened by colourful fabrics, friendly staff, *haute cuisine* presented in an airy dining room, and a cellar of phenomenal champagnes. 02220 Courcelles-sur-Vesle, Aisne. **Map** p221 D3. 03 23 74 13 53. FAX 03 23 74 06 41. reservation@chateau-de-courcelles.fr b,l,d. **Rooms** 18. Never. AE, DC, MC, V. €€€€€

Etretat

Domaine St Clair-Le Donjon Perched on a hill above the cliffs of Etretat, is this ancient castle with historical associations. It has been elegantly converted with ten highly original bedrooms, and ten additional rooms in the newly refurbished 19th-century villa. Views from the romantic mirrored dining room are spectacular. Chemin de St Clair, 76790 Etretat, Seine-Maritime. **Map** p220 C3. 02 35 27 08 23. FAX 02 35 29 92 24. info@hoteletretat.com b,l,d. **Rooms** 21. Never. AE, V. €€€

Belle-Ile-en-Mer

Le Clos Fleuri Near the picturesque island port of Le Palais, simple but chic, with lawns, fresh bedrooms and a delicious daily brunch. Bellevue, Route de Sauzon, Belle-Ile-en-Mer, 56360 Le Palais, Morbihan. **Map** p220 A4. 02 97 31 45 45. FAX 02 97 31 45 57. b,l,d. **Rooms** 20. €€

Billiers

Domaine de Rochevilaine Cluster of buildings on rocky headland, filled with Breton antiques. Pointe de Pen Lan-Sud, 56190 Billiers, Morbihan. **Map** p220 A4. 02 97 41 61 61. FAX 02 97 41 44 85. domaine@domainerochevilaine.com b,l,d. **Rooms** 37. €€€

Caudebec-en-Caux

Le Normandie A good position on the Seine marks out this friendly and well maintained hotel. 19 Quai Guilbaud, 76490 Caudebec-en-Caux, Seine-Maritime. **Map** p220 C3. 02 35 96 25 11. FAX 02 35 96 68 15. le-normandie@planete-b.fr b,l,d. **Rooms** 16. €

Connelles

Le Moulin de Connelles Mill enjoying perfect Seine-side setting, mature park and plush interior. 40 route d'Amfreville-sur-les-Monts, 27430 Connelles, Eure. **Map** p220 C3. 02 32 59 53 33. FAX 02 32 59 21 83. moulindeconnelles@moulindeconnelles.com b,l,d. **Rooms** 13. €€€

Flagy

Hostellerie du Moulin A half-timbered flour mill with cob walls and tremendous character, where the original workings are still operational and provide a focal point in the rustic sitting room. It enjoys a perfect setting too, beside the millstream set in fields. Pretty bedrooms with low rafters are tucked away in nooks and crannies.
2 rue du Moulin, 77940 Flagy, Seine-et-Marne. **Map** p221 D4. 01 60 96 67 89. FAX 01 60 96 69 51. b,l,d. **Rooms** 10. Dec to Jan. MC, V. €€

Hennebont

Château de Locguénolé A vast lawn extends from the château down to the Blavet estuary, popular for sailing, and the park hugs 2km (1 mile) of coast. Inside, wood-panelled rooms are filled with tapestries and antiques. Sweat off a fine seafood dinner in the Turkish bath.
Route de Port-Louis en Kervignac, 56700 Hennebont, Morbihan. **Map** p220 A4. 02 97 76 76 76. FAX 02 97 76 82 35. @ contact@chateau-de-locguenole.com b,l,d. **Rooms** 22. Jan. AE, DC, MC, V. €€€

Gisors

Château de la Râpée The decoration inside this 19th-century Gothic mansion is slightly eccentric (lots of antlers, carpets as wallcoverings), and public rooms can be a bit dark. But the location is tranquil, with fine country views, bedrooms are light and spacious and there are grounds to wander round. Serious classic regional cooking.
Bazincourt-sur-Epte, 27140 Gisors, Eure. **Map** p221 D3. 02 32 55 11 61. FAX 02 32 55 95 65. @ info@hotel-la-rapee.com b,l,d. **Rooms** 14. 16 Aug to 1 Sep; 20 Jan to 1 Mar. AE, MC, V. €€

Hesdin-l'Abbé

Hôtel Cléry The team at this small 18th-century chateau are dedicated, enthusiastic and welcoming. A tree-lined drive leads up to the elegant white façade but, despite the splendid Louis XV wrought-iron staircase, there is no formality in the pale, simply furnished interior. Some of the bedrooms are in annexes.
rue du Chateau, 62360 Hesdin-l'Abbé, Pas-de-Calais. **Map** p221 D2. 03 21 83 19 83. FAX 03 21 87 52 59. @ chateau.clery.hotel @najeti.com b,l,d. **Rooms** 22. Never. AE, DC, MC, V. €€

Crépon

Ferme de la Rançonnière Tapestries and fine furniture are scattered about this fortified old farmhouse. Huge breakfasts of eggs and cream.
Route d'Arromanches, 14480 Crépon, Calvados. **Map** p220 C3. 02 31 22 21 73. FAX 02 31 22 98 39. @ hotel@ranconniere.com b,l,d. **Rooms** 35. €

Dampierre

Auberge du Château Purpose-built in 1650 in rural surroundings just 30 minutes' drive from Paris. Low rafters and undulating floors.
1 Grande Rue, 78720 Dampierre, Yvelines. **Map** p221 D3. 01 30 47 56 56. FAX 01 30 47 51 75. b,l,d. **Rooms** 10. €€

Dinard

Hôtel Roche Corneille Faultless housekeeping and gastronomic menus at this seaside villa.
4 rue G Clémenceau, 35800 Dinard, Ille-et-Vilaine. **Map** p220 B3. 02 99 46 14 47. FAX 02 99 46 40 80. @ francois.garrigue@saint-malo.com b,l,d. **Rooms** 28. €€

Ducey

Auberge de la Sélune Crab pie is the most acclaimed dish in this modest inn. There is some unfortunate new decoration, but a pretty garden.
2 rue St-Germain, 50220 Ducey, Manche. **Map** p220 B3. 02 33 48 53 62. FAX 02 33 48 90 30. @ info@selune.com b,l,d. **Rooms** 20. €

For key to symbols see backflap. For price categories *see p217*

Honfleur

La Chaumière Just outside the colourful little port, this timbered farmhouse is typical of the region. Set amid orchards, it is now a Relais et Château hotel boasting sea views, a friendly staff, well-decorated bedrooms, and good honest Norman cooking. In the same ownership is the nearby La Ferme Saint-Siméon.
☒ Route du Littoral, Vasouy, 14600 Honfleur, Calvados. **Map** p220 C3. ☎ 02 31 81 63 20. FAX 02 31 89 59 23. @ chaumiere@relaischateaux.fr 🍴 b,l,d. **Rooms** 9. ● 5-31 Jan. 💳 AE, MC, V. €€€€

Illhaeusern

Hôtel des Berges One of the most highly regarded restaurants in the country, L'Auberge de l'Ill, has a number of select and beautifully furnished rooms, with a lush garden on the banks of the River Ill. It is run with verve by several generations of the Haeberlin family.
☒ 4 rue de Collonges, 68970 Illhaeusern, Haut-Rhin. **Map** p221 F4, p223 F1. ☎ 03 89 71 87 87. FAX 03 89 71 87 88. @ hotel-des-berges@wanadoo.fr 🍴 b,l,d. **Rooms** 11. ● last week Jan, Feb. 💳 AE, DC, MC, V. €€€€

Honfleur

Le Manoir du Butin This classic 18th-century half-timbered Norman manor is outside town, in shady grounds within spitting distance of the sea. The rustic, heavily beamed interior is warm and comfy, especially on chilly evenings when the fires are lit. Great regional cuisine and a large selection of *Calvados vieux*.
☒ Phare du Butin, 14600 Honfleur, Calvados. **Map** p220 C3. ☎ 02 31 81 63 00. FAX 02 31 89 53 20. @ accueil@hotel.lemanoir.fr 🍴 b,l,d. **Rooms** 10. ● mid-Nov to 5 Dec. 💳 AE, MC, V. €€€

Moëlan-sur-Mer

Manoir de Kertalg Forest walks, tennis, fly fishing, riding and sandy beaches are all within easy reach of this miniature chateau. It has all the qualifications: stone-built, with steep slate roofs and dormer windows, and set in a vast park. Decoration is refined, and, though it's officially a B&B, you can book a seafood supper.
☒ Route de Riec-sur-Belon, 29350 Moëlan-sur-Mer, Finistère. **Map** p220 A4. ☎ 02 98 39 77 77. FAX 02 98 39 72 07. @ kertalg@free.fr 🍴 b. **Rooms** 9. ● mid-Nov to Mar. 💳 MC, V. €€

Etréaupont

Le Clos du Montvinage Cheerful and spacious hotel located in the town, with pleasant, well-equipped bedrooms.
☒ 8 rue Albert Ledant, 02580 Etréaupont, Aisne. **Map** p221 E2. ☎ 03 23 97 91 10. FAX 03 23 97 48 92. 🍴 b,l,d. **Rooms** 19. €

Kaysersberg

Hôtel Résidence Chambard Ancient buildings with upmarket restaurant and pleasant rooms.
☒ 13 rue de Général de Gaulle, 68240 Kaysersberg, Haut-Rhin. **Map** p221 F4, p223 F1. ☎ 03 89 47 10 17. FAX 03 89 47 35 03. @ hotelrestaurantchambard @wanadoo.fr 🍴 b,l,d. **Rooms** 20. €€

Lapoutroie

Les Alisiers Great views from this modest farmhouse. Small but snug bedrooms. The kitchen specializes in Alsatian dishes.
☒ 5 Faudé, 68650 Lapoutroie, Haut-Rhin. **Map** p221 F4, p223 E1. ☎ 03 89 47 52 82. FAX 03 89 47 22 38. @ jacques.degouy@wanadoo.fr 🍴 b,l,d. **Rooms** 18. €€

Louviers

Hôtel La Haye-le-Comte Keep fit with tennis, *pétanque*, croquet, golf and mountain bikes.
☒ 4 route de La Haye-le-Comte, 27400 Louviers, Eure. **Map** p220 C3. ☎ 02 32 40 00 40. FAX 02 32 25 03 85. @ hotel-la-haye-le-comte@wanadoo. fr 🍴 b,l,d. **Rooms** 16. €€

Moëlan-sur-Mer

Les Moulins du Duc This converted mill is set in manicured gardens amongst the wooded hills of Finistère, just above the lowest tidal reaches of the Belon. The mill itself is a restaurant offering very serious food – particularly seafood, owing to the location near the coast. Accommodation is in comfortable cottages dotted around the grounds.
29350 Moëlan-sur-Mer, Finistère. **Map** p220 A4. 02 98 96 52 52. FAX 02 98 96 52 53. @ tqad29@aol.com b,l,d. **Rooms** 25. Dec to Feb. AE, DC, MC, V. €€

Montreuil-sur-Mer

Château de Montreuil The kind of luxury you would expect of a Relais et Châteaux is presented here with real flair, from captivating bedrooms – each one different – and elegant public rooms to the private English gardens. The cooking uses garden vegetables and herbs.
4 Chaussée des Capucins, 62170 Montreuil-sur-Mer, Pas-de-Calais. **Map** p221 D2. 03 21 81 53 04. FAX 03 21 81 36 43. @ chateau.de.montreuil@wanadoo.fr b,l,d. **Rooms** 18. mid-Dec to end Jan. AE, DC, MC, V. €€€

Montreuil-sur-Mer

Auberge de la Grenouillère Nicknamed 'the Froggery' by its fans (the walls are lined with froggy caricatures), a Michelin-starred riverside restaurant with rooms. The food, served on the outdoor terrace in good weather, is excellent and good value. Enchanting farmhouse rooms.
La Madelaine-sous-Montreuil, 62170 Montreuil-sur-Mer, Pas-de-Calais. **Map** p221 D2. 03 21 06 07 22. FAX 03 21 86 36 36. @ auberge.de.la.grenouillere@wanadoo.fr b,l,d. **Rooms** 4. Jan; Tue; Sep to June closed Tue and Wed. AE, DC, MC, V. €€

Paimpol

Le Repaire de Kerroc'h This quayside house built in 1793 has a romantic past, having once belonged to a pirate. Bedrooms differ in style. Old ones have a faded elegance, new ones are decorated in bright vivid colours. All are comfortable.
29 Quai Morand, Port de Plaisance, 22500 Paimpol, Côtes-d'Armor. **Map** p220 A3. 02 96 20 50 13. FAX 02 96 22 07 46. @ repaire2kerroch@wanadoo.fr b,l,d. **Rooms** 14. Never. MC, V. €€

Lunéville

Château d'Adoménil Moated château with turrets and hall, where a convivial air prevails.
Rehainvillier, 54300 Lunéville, Meurthe-et-Moselle. **Map** p221 F3. 03 83 74 04 81. FAX 03 83 74 21 78. @ adomenil@relaischateaux.com b,l,d. **Rooms** 14. €€€

Marlenheim

Le Cerf Picture-postcard-pretty inn, known for gastronomic Alsatian food. Modest rooms.
30 rue du Général-de-Gaulle, 67520 Marlenheim, Bas-Rhin. **Map** p221 F3. 03 88 87 73 73. FAX 03 88 87 68 08. @ info@lecerf.com b,l,d. **Rooms** 15. €€

Le Mont-St-Michel

Auberge St-Pierre On the mount's main street, you'll find home cooking and pleasing rooms.
BP 16, Grande Rue, 50170 Le Mont-St-Michel, Manche. **Map** p220 B3. 02 33 60 14 03. FAX 02 33 48 59 82. @ aubergesaintpierre@wanadoo.fr b,l,d. **Rooms** 20. €€

Pacy-sur-Eure

Château de Brécourt Splendid Louis XIII château, complete with moat and wooded park, boasting frescoed ceilings and fine furniture.
Douains, 27120 Pacy-sur-Eure, Eure. **Map** p220 C3. 02 32 52 40 50. FAX 02 32 52 69 65. @ brecourt@chateaucountry.com b,l,d. **Rooms** 30. €€€

For key to symbols see backflap. For price categories *see p217*

Paris

Hôtel de l'Abbaye St Germain This beautifully converted former abbey has quite a following for its faultless service, stylish rooms and calm ambience. Double rooms can be small; if you can afford it, go for a duplex. On fine days breakfast can be taken in a little paved courtyard bordered by flowering shrubs.
☒ 10 rue Cassette, 75006 Paris. **Map** p218 C4.
☎ 01 45 44 38 11. FAX 01 45 48 07 86.
@ hotel.abbaye@wanadoo.fr b. **Rooms** 44.
Never. AE, MC, V. €€€

Paris

Hôtel d'Aubusson The entrance to this fine hotel is through immense double doors, used for coaches in the 17th century when the honey-stone building was built. Inside are a lovely beamed *salon* and a breakfast room hung with tapestries. Restrained luxury defines the pale bedrooms.
☒ 33 rue Dauphine, 75006 Paris. **Map** p218 C4.
☎ 01 43 29 43 43. FAX 01 43 29 12 62.
@ reservationmichael@hoteldaubusson.com b. **Rooms** 50. Never. AE, DC, MC, V. €€€€

Paris

Hôtel d'Angleterre Some people say the elegance is a bit faded, but this former British embassy near the boulevard Saint-Germain is still a winner for its feeling of spacious calm. Echoes of former glories include fine mantelpieces and *trompe l'oeil* murals. All the rooms are differently done out and most are very roomy.
☒ 44 rue Jacob, 75006 Paris. **Map** p218 C3.
☎ 01 42 60 34 72. FAX 01 42 60 16 93.
@anglotel@ wanadoo.fr b. **Rooms** 27.
Never. AE, DC, MC, V. €€€

Paris

Hôtel de Banville The elegance doesn't stop at the furnishings in this 1930s town house north of Etoile. The hotel is strong on the personal touch: fresh flowers in the individually decorated bedrooms, beds turned down at night and ever-cheerful staff. A pianist is a regular feature in the comfortable bar/sitting area in the evenings.
☒ 166 bd Berthier, 75017 Paris. **Map** p218 A1.
☎ 01 42 67 70 16. FAX 01 44 40 42 77.
@ hotelbanville@wanadoo.fr b,l,d. **Rooms** 37, plus 1 suite. Never. AE, DC, MC, V. €€€

Paris

Hôtel Beau Manoir The clue is in the name: this hotel styles itself on a rural manor, with damask drapes and tapestries on wood-panelled walls.
☒ 6 rue de l'Arcade, 75008 Paris. **Map** p218 B1.
☎ 01 42 66 03 07. FAX 01 53 43 28 88. @ beau-manoir@ggwhotels.com b. **Rooms** 60. €€€€

Paris

Hôtel Elysées-Mermoz Attractive and fresh-looking, it has a conservatory-style foyer and well-designed bedrooms with Pierre Frey fabrics.
☒ 30 rue Jean-Mermoz, 75008 Paris. **Map** p218 A1.
☎ 01 42 25 75 30. FAX 01 45 62 87 10.
@ elymermoz@ worldnet.fr b. **Rooms** 27. €€€

Paris

Hôtel du Jeu de Paume Avant-garde conversion of a 17th-century tennis court by the architect owner, creating an atrium inside the old timbers.
☒ 54 rue St-Louis-en-l'Ile, 75004 Paris. **Map** p219 E4.
☎ 01 43 26 14 18. FAX 01 40 46 02 76. @ info@jeudepaumehotel.com b. **Rooms** 30. €€€€

Paris

Hôtel Latour-Maubourg The warmth of the owner/managers and the private-house feel make this a really special place to stay.
☒ 150 rue de Grenelle, 75007 Paris. **Map** p218 A3.
☎ 01 47 05 16 16. FAX 01 47 05 16 14.
@ info@latourmaubourg.com b. **Rooms** 10. 

Paris

Hôtel de la Bretonnerie The busy streets of the picturesque Marais and Pompidou Centre area surround this 17th-century townhouse, yet inside all is calm and comfort. Beams, tiled floors and hardwood furniture are offset by rich furnishings and wallcolourings. Bedrooms are surprisingly spacious; some have a mezzanine gallery.
22 rue Ste-Croix-de-la-Bretonnerie, 75004 Paris. **Map** p219 E3. 01 48 87 77 63. FAX 01 42 77 26 78. @ hotel@bretonnerie.com b. **Rooms** 29. Never. MC, V. €€

Paris

Lancaster Swiss hotelier Emile Wolf opened the Lancaster back in 1930, and it quickly attracted the glitterati of the day. The present owner has restored furniture and rooms to their former glory, incorporating into her elegant decorative scheme the hotel's collection of Boris Pastoukhoff paintings (he used them to pay his bills).
7 rue de Berri, 75008 Paris. **Map** p218 A1. 01 40 76 40 76. FAX 01 40 76 40 00. @ reservations@hotel-lancaster.fr b,l,d. **Rooms** 60. Never. AE, DC, MC, V. €€€€

Paris

Hôtel Duc de St-Simon From the elegant courtyard, the first glimpse of this gorgeous, if pricey, little hotel through two sets of French doors is pure magic. The *salon* is deliciously furnished with upholstered and antique pieces, pictures and ornaments, and has the private-house feel that the Swedish proprietor intended.
14 rue de St-Simon, 75007 Paris. **Map** p218 B3. 01 44 39 20 20. FAX 01 45 48 68 25. @ hotel.duc.de.saint.simon@wanadoo.fr b.**Rooms** 34. Never. AE, DC, MC, V. €€€€

Paris

Pavillon de la Reine Its location on the most harmonious square in the city is ideal and one of this handsome 17th-century mansion's main draws. Anne of Austria's home now has the air of a baronial hall, complete with huge hearth and wood panelling. You couldn't call it cosy, but it's precisely run and supremely comfortable.
28 place des Vosges, 75003 Paris. **Map** p219 F3. 01 40 29 19 19. FAX 01 40 29 19 20. @ contact@pavillon-de-la-reine.com b. **Rooms** 55. Never. AE, DC, MC, V. €€€€

Paris

Hôtel Mansart Beyond the modern lobby are immense, stately bedrooms with large mirrors and panelling picked out in gold.
5 rue des Capucines, 75001 Paris. **Map** p218 C2. 01 42 61 50 28. FAX 01 49 27 97 44. @ hotel.mansart@esprit-de-france.com b. **Rooms** 57. €€€

Paris

Hôtel Montalembert Choose between antique or high-tech furnishings in this sleek modern hotel.
3 rue Montalembert, 75007 Paris. **Map** p218 C3. 01 45 49 68 68. FAX 01 45 49 69 49. @ welcome@montalembert.com b,l,d. **Rooms** 56. €€€€

Paris

Hôtel Parc St-Severin This hotel is included for its penthouse suite: chic, bright and surrounded by a fabulous roof terrace with spectacular views.
22 rue de la Parcheminerie, 75005 Paris. **Map** p219 D4. 01 43 54 32 17. FAX 01 43 54 70 71. @ hotel-parc. severin@wanadoo.fr b. **Rooms** 27. €€

Paris

Hôtel Verneuil In a charming street, this recently refurbished hotel aims to provide the atmosphere of an elegant private house.
8 rue de Verneuil, 75007 Paris. **Map** p218 C3. 01 42 60 82 14. FAX 01 42 61 40 38. @ hotelverneuil@ wanadoo.fr b. **Rooms** 26. €€€

Paris

Le Relais St-Germain Cleverly mirrored and sleekly furnished as it is, the ground floor of this luxurious little hotel is cramped, so the spacious bedrooms come as an especially welcome surprise. These are offset by solid country antiques, deep sofas and rich fabrics. Breakfast is in a café that was a haunt of Hemingway and Picasso.
9 carrefour de l'Odéon, 75006 Paris. **Map** p218 C4. 01 43 29 12 05. FAX 01 46 33 45 30. b,l,d. **Rooms** 22. Never. AE, DC, MC V. €€€€

Paris

Hôtel Le St-Grégoire The interior of this tall townhouse has been designed with great flair, reflecting the passion of the owner's wife, who scoured antique shops and markets for *objets d'art*. These furnish the pretty sitting room, from where the restful colour scheme leads upstairs to comfortable bedrooms.
43 rue de l'Abbé-Grégoire, 75006 Paris. **Map** p218 C5. 01 45 48 23 23. FAX 01 45 48 33 95. hotel@saintgregoire.com b. **Rooms** 20. Never. AE, DC, MC, V. €€€€

Paris

Hôtel Ritz Since César Ritz opened his hotel in 1898, its sumptuous luxury has attracted devotees as diverse as Proust, Hemingway and royalty. The spirit of opulence lives on in each of the five magnificent *salons* and in the ornate bedrooms. A superb new health club and cookery school ensure that it's no anachronism.
15 place Vendôme, 75001 Paris. **Map** p219 F2. 01 43 16 30 30. FAX 01 43 16 36 68. resa@ritzparis.com b,l,d. **Rooms** 162. Never. AE, DC, MC, V. €€€€

Paris

Hôtel Le Ste-Beuve This friendly hotel is not luxurious, but likes to cosset its guests and has a policy of upgrading them to a better room if one is free. Another draw is the delicious breakfast; it is served at any time of the day or night in the refined, cream-painted *salon* where a fire blazes on wintry days.
9 rue Ste-Beuve, 75006 Paris. **Map** p218 B4. 01 45 48 20 07. FAX 01 45 48 67 52. saintebeuve @wanadoo.fr b. **Rooms** 22. Never. AE, DC, MC, V. €€€

Perros-Guirec

Le Manoir du Sphinx The cliffside garden of this lofty hotel leads down to the rocky shore.
67 chemin de la Messe, 22700 Perros-Guirec, Côtes d'Armor. **Map** p220 A3. 02 96 23 25 42. FAX 02 96 91 26 13. b,l,d. **Rooms** 20. €€

Pleugueneuc

Château de la Motte Beaumanoir It's only a B&B, but this 15th-century château with lake and landscaped garden is a great place for a break.
35720 Pleugueneuc, Ille-et-Vilaine. **Map** p220 B3. 02 99 69 46 01. FAX 02 99 69 42 49. la-motte-beaumanoir@wanadoo.fr b. **Rooms** 8. €€€€

Plouharnel

Les Ajoncs d'Or Cottagey, granite-built *logis* that seems frozen in time. Good Breton country fare.
Kerbachique, 56340 Plouharnel, Morbihan. **Map** p220 A4, p222 A1. 02 97 52 32 02. FAX 02 97 52 40 36. info@lesajoncsdor.com b,d. **Rooms** 17. €

Pont-Audemer

Belle-Isle-sur-Risle With a large island garden, it's hard to imagine a more romantic setting for this late 19th-century mansion.
112 route de Rouen, 27500 Pont-Audemer, Eure. **Map** p220 C3. 02 32 56 96 22. FAX 02 32 44 88 96. hotel@bellile.com b,l,d. **Rooms** 20. €€€

Port-en-Bessin

La Chenevière In summer the lawns are dotted with sun loungers, and tables and chairs, shaded by parasols, are set out on the terrace. But this refined Norman mansion will not only appeal to hedonists; the airy rooms are aesthetically pleasing too. Everywhere you look are paintings, architectural prints, ancient seals or *objets d'art*.
Escures-Commes, 14520 Port-en-Bessin, Calvados. **Map** p220 B3. 02 31 51 25 25. FAX 02 31 51 25 20. @ la.cheneviere@wanadoo.fr b,l,d. **Rooms** 22. Jan to mid-Feb. AE, DC, MC, V. €€€€

Reims

Château des Crayères A champagne buff's paradise: the park of this graceful Louis XVI mansion is bordered by the cellars of all the great vineyards. Decoration of the grand interior is skilfull and sympathetic, retaining a sweeping staircase, marble columns and wood panelling.
64 bd Henry-Vasnier, 51100 Reims, Marne. **Map** p221 E3. 03 26 82 80 80. FAX 03 26 82 65 52. @ crayeres@relaischateaux.fr b,l,d. **Rooms** 19. 3 weeks Christmas/New Year. AE, DC, MC, V. €€€€

Quineville-Plage

Château de Quineville The thought of an old-style French provincial hotel in a drab seaside resort at the northern end of Utah Beach may not set your pulse racing, but the Château de Quineville – a fine 18th-century building set in 12 hectares of land – is quaint and charming. Golf, riding, tennis and sailing are all nearby.
50310 Quineville-Plage, Manche. **Map** p220 B3. 02 33 21 42 67. FAX 02 33 21 05 79. @ chateau.quineville@wanadoo.fr b,l,d. **Rooms** 26. mid-Jan to mid-Mar. AE, DC MC, V. €€

La Roche-Bernard

Auberge Bretonne Home-grown fruit and vegetables feature large in Jacques Thorel's cooking, which has earned two Michelin stars for this Breton-style Relais et Chateaux inn. The cellar is equally impressive. Tasteful bedrooms. You must book months ahead.
2 place Duguesclin, 56130 La Roche-Bernard, Morbihan. **Map** p220 B4, p222 A1. 02 99 90 60 28. FAX 02 99 90 85 00. @ jacques.thorel@wanadoo.fr b,l,d. **Rooms** 8. mid-Nov to mid-Jan. AE, DC. €€€

Pornichet

Hôtel Sud Bretagne A family-run four-star with an eye-catching blue and white façade. Facilities include indoor pool, billiards and its own ketch.
42 bd de la République, 44380 Pornichet, Loire-Atlantique. **Map** p220 A4, p222 A1. 02 40 11 65 00. FAX 02 40 61 73 70. b,l,d. **Rooms** 30. €€€

Ribeauvillé

Le Clos Saint-Vincent An essential stopover on the Riesling wine route. Excellent cuisine.
Route de Bergheim, 68150 Ribeauvillé, Haut-Rhin. **Map** p221 F3, p223 F1. 03 89 73 67 65. FAX 03 89 73 32 20. @ closvincent@aol.com b,l,d. **Rooms** 24. €€€

La Roche-Bernard

Domaine de Bodeuc Welcoming touches await guests at this handsome house in large grounds, with recently enlarged restaurant.
56130 La Roche-Bernard, Morbihan. **Map** p220 B4. 02 99 90 89 63. FAX 02 99 90 90 32. b,l,d. **Rooms** 10. €€

Roscoff

Brittany From this well-furnished stone manor the next stop is Newfoundland. Huge bay windows take advantage of the light and views.
Bd Sainte-Barbe, 29680 Roscoff, Finistère. **Map** p220 A3. 02 98 69 70 78. FAX 02 98 61 13 29 @ hotel.brittany@wanadoo.fr b,d. **Rooms** 25. €€

For key to symbols see backflap. For price categories *see p217*

St-André-d'Hébertot

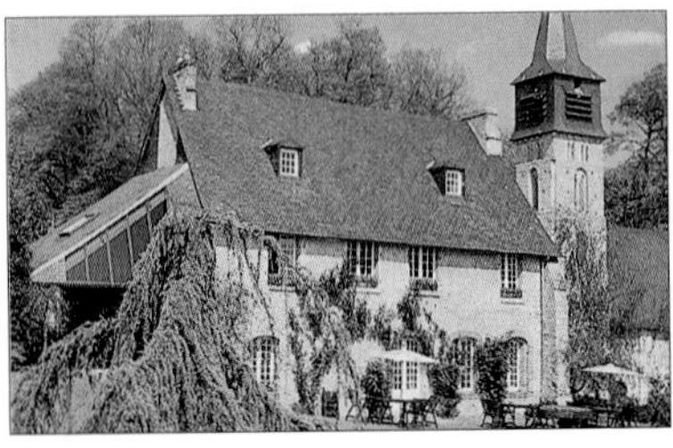

Auberge du Prieuré Be warned, dinner here is costly in comparison with the good-value rooms. These are split between a new but sympathetic annexe and the house, a 13th-century priory of honey stone, no less lovely inside than out, furnished with solid antiques and mellow fabrics. Beyond the leafy garden with a heated pool, lie orchards and fields.
St-André-d'Hébertot, 14130 Pont-l'Évêque, Calvados. **Map** p220 C3. 02 31 64 03 03. FAX 02 31 64 16 66. b,l,d. **Rooms** 12. Never. AE, MC, V. €€

St-Malo

La Korrigane Staying in this fine-looking town house near the harbour is like being a guest in an elegant home. The pale drawing room is furnished with books, photographs and ornaments, and in the bedrooms are easy chairs, antique mirrors and oil paintings. Too refined for children just back from the beach.
39 rue Le Pomellec, 35400 St-Malo, Ille-et-Vilaine. **Map** p220 B3. 02 99 81 65 85. FAX 02 99 82 23 89. @ lakorrigane.st.malo@wanadoo.fr b. **Rooms** 12. Never. AE, DC, MC, V. €€

Ste-Anne-la-Palud

Hôtel de la Plage With the sea and sandy beach on its doorstep, this hotel is ideal for families if a touch pricey. It combines chic with Breton simplicity; some bedrooms are all white with the odd antique. The dining room offers superb seafood and views from floor-to-ceiling windows.
Ste-Anne-la-Palud, 29550 Plonévez-Porzay, Finistère. **Map** p220 A4. 02 98 92 50 12. FAX 02 98 92 56 54. @ laplage@relaischateaux.fr b,l,d. **Rooms** 30. mid-Nov to Apr. AE, DC, MC, V. €€€€

Ste-Preuve

Le Domaine du Château de Barive A short drive from Reims, Laon and Liesse, this impressive 17th-century hunting lodge is the perfect place to stay for cathedral touring, as well as sampling first-class cuisine. Public rooms are gracious and formal, though you can dine in a more casual garden room. Vast estate to explore.
02350 Ste-Preuve, Aisne. **Map** p221 E3. 03 23 22 15 15. FAX 03 23 22 08 39. @ contact@lesepicuriens.com b,l,d. **Rooms** 14. Jan. AE, DC, MC, V. €€€

Rouen

Hôtel de la Cathédrale Off a quiet lane, a warren of rooms in faded yet elegant style. Some overlook a courtyard overflowing with flowers.
12 rue St-Romain, 76000 Rouen, Seine-Maritime. **Map** p220 C3. 02 35 71 57 95. FAX 02 35 70 15 54. @ arttra@wanadoo.fr b. **Rooms** 25. €

St-Malo

Le Valmarin Handsome grey-stone B&B in tree-filled grounds close to the harbour. Recent change of ownership.
7 rue Jean XXIII, 35400 St-Malo, Ille-et-Vilaine. **Map** p220 B3. 02 99 81 94 76. FAX 02 99 81 30 03. @ levalmarin@wanadoo.fr b. **Rooms** 12. €€

St-Vaast-la-Hougue

Hôtel de France et des Fuchsias The *raison d'être* of this congenial hotel is its restaurant.
20 rue Maréchal Foch, 50550 St-Vaast-la-Hougue, Manche. **Map** p220 B3. 02 33 54 42 26. FAX 02 33 43 46 79. @ france-fuchsias@wanadoo.fr b,l,d. **Rooms** 33. €

Sept-Saulx

Le Cheval Blanc Without spoiling this old *auberge*, the owners make more improvements inside and out every year. Outstanding food.
51400 Sept-Saulx, Marne. **Map** p221 E3. 03 26 03 90 27. FAX 03 26 03 97 09. @ cheval.blanc-sept-saulx@wanadoo.fr b,l,d. **Rooms** 24. €€

TRÉBEURDEN

Manoir de Lan-Kerellec A Relais et Château manor yet nonetheless unpretentious and intimate, standing on a grassy hillside above the rocky pink granite coast. Not surprisingly seafood is *de rigueur* in the nautical dining room. There are several beautiful bays a short walk away.
Allée Centrale, 22560 Trébeurden, Côtes d'Armor. **Map** p220 A3. 02 96 15 47 47. FAX 02 96 23 66 88. @ lankerellec@relaischateaux.fr b,l,d. **Rooms** 19. mid-Nov to 21 Dec, 5 Jan to mid-March. AE, DC, MC, V. €€€

VERNEUIL-SUR-AVRE

Hostellerie le Clos A jokey exterior of chequerboard and trellis-patterned brickwork, reminiscent of a Disneyland castle, masks a gorgeous little hotel. In the dining room, *trompe l'oeil* garden scenes divide windows looking out to the real thing. Half-board only at weekends.
98 rue de la Ferté-Vidame, 27130 Verneuil-sur-Avre, Eure. **Map** p220 C3. 02 32 32 21 81. FAX 02 32 32 21 36. @ hostellerie.leclos@wanadoo.fr b,l,d. **Rooms** 4, plus 6 suites. mid-Dec to mid-Jan. AE, DC, MC, V. €€€

TRÉBEURDEN

Ti Al-Lannec Child-friendly and good value, with steps down to the beach from its eyrie position, this is a hotel with a heart, run with loving care. Guests find books and fresh flowers placed in bedrooms, many of which have verandas. The sitting room is stunning, as are the garden and the views over the bay of Lannion.
Allée de Mézo-Guen, BP 3, 22560 Trébeurden, Côtes d'Armor. **Map** p220 A3. 02 96 15 01 01. FAX 02 96 23 62 14. @ resa@tiallannec.com b,l,d. **Rooms** 33. mid-Nov to mid-Mar. AE, DC, MC. €€

VILLERAY

Moulin de Villeray Formerly a derelict mill, now an idyllic rural retreat, with quiet bedrooms and a pleasant *salon* where pre-prandial drinks are served. The hub is the restaurant with its beams and massive fireplace. Half-board in high season. Further accommodation recently added at castle nearby.
Villeray, 6110 Condeau, Orne. **Map** p220 C3. 02 33 73 30 22. FAX 02 33 73 38 28. @ moulin.de.villeray@wanadoo.fr b,l,d. **Rooms** 40 Never. AE, DC, MC, V. €€

TRÉGUIER

Kastell Dinec'h An old stone farmhouse with a leafy garden shaded by conifers, a heated pool and small but appealing bedrooms.
Route de Lannion, 22220 Tréguier, Côtes-d'Armor. **Map** p220 A3. 02 96 92 49 39. FAX 02 96 92 34 02. @ kastell@club-internet.fr b,d. **Rooms** 15. €€€

TRELLY

La Verte Campagne Roses cover a farmhouse where bedrooms take second place to food; chef Pascal Bernou has won a Michelin star.
Hameau Chevalier, 50660 Trelly, Manche. **Map** p220 B3. 02 33 47 65 33. FAX 02 33 47 38 03. b,l,d. **Rooms** 7. €

TROYES

Le Champ des Oiseaux Fresh-looking bedrooms and bathrooms nestle beneath old timbers in this glorious 15th-century B&B in the town centre.
20 rue Linard Gonthier, 10000 Troyes, Aube. **Map** p221 E4. 03 25 80 58 50. FAX 03 25 80 98 34. @ message@champdesoiseaux.com b. **Rooms**12. €€

VERVINS

La Tour du Roy This atmospheric inn bristles with turrets outside and attractive features inside. Highly rated food.
Lieu-dit La Tour du Roy, 02140 Vervins, Aisne. **Map** p221 E2. 03 23 98 00 11. FAX 03 23 98 00 72. @ latourduroy@wanadoo.fr b,l,d. **Rooms** 22. €€

For key to symbols see backflap. For price categories *see p217*

Central France

Loire Valley • Poitou-Charentes • Limousin • Auvergne Bourgogne • Franche-Comté • Rhône-Alpes

The chateau-hotel comes into its own in the Loire Valley. Although it is possible to stay in castles all over Europe, there is a special charm about sleeping in a fairytale French Renaissance chateau with its turrets, steep roofs, dormer windows, formal garden and park. But there are chateau-hotels in other regions of Central France, such as the Limousin and Périgord. Many are old, solid bourgeois residences, flat-fronted, shuttered mansions with mansard roofs. There are also converted mills, and country and village inns full of character. To the east, in the upland regions of the Jura and Alp mountains, chalet-style hotels with steeply sloping roofs, shutters and wooden balconies, are prevalent.

Aloxe-Corton

Villa Louise On the edge of a village that is a Mecca for lovers of white wine, is this low 17th-century house. Inside, original timberwork and fireplaces are offset with an avant-garde interior and Art Deco furnishings. The tasteful bedrooms have swish bathrooms; breakfast is a feast of cheese, eggs and fruit.
✉ 9 rue Franche, 21420 Aloxe-Corton, Côte-d'Or. **Map** p221 E4, p223 E1. ☎ 03 80 26 46 70. FAX 03 80 26 47 16. @ hotel-villa-louise@wanadoo.fr 🍴 b. **Rooms** 12. mid-Jan to mid-Feb. AE, MC, V. €€

Auxerre

Parc des Maréchaux The best bedrooms are those looking on to the park from which the hotel takes its name, though all are spacious, in restful colours and furnished traditionally with wooden beds and antique chests. A large, dignified townhouse, it makes an exceedingly upmarket yet value-for-money B&B.
✉ 6 avenue Foch, 89000 Auxerre, Yonne. **Map** p221 D4, p223 D1. ☎ 03 86 51 47 77. FAX 03 86 51 31 72. @ contact@hotel-parcmarechaux.com 🍴 b. **Rooms** 25. Never. AE, DC, MC, V. €€

Amboise

Château de Pray The 13th-century fortress is well placed to visit some of the great chateaux. Splendid vantage point above the Loire.
✉ 37400 Amboise, Indre-et-Loire. **Map** p220 C4, p222 C1. ☎ 02 47 57 23 67. FAX 02 47 57 32 50. @ chateau.depray@wanadoo.fr 🍴 b,l,d. **Rooms** 19. €€

Annecy-le-Vieux

L'Abbaye Idiosyncratic abbey hotel in a suburb, with a stunning vaulted restaurant.
✉ 15 chemin de l'Abbaye, 74940 Annecy-le-Vieux, Haute-Savoie. **Map** p221 F5, p223 E2. ☎ 04 50 23 61 08. FAX 04 50 23 61 71. @ info@hotelabbaye-annecy.com 🍴 b,d. **Rooms** 18. €€€

Angles sur l'Anglin

Le Relais du Lyon d'Or In a contender for the prettiest village in France, a former royal tythe depot with terracotta floors and wooden beams.
✉ 4 rue d'Enfer, 86260 Angles sur l'Anglin, Vienne. **Map** p220 C5, p222 C2. ☎ 05 49 48 32 53. FAX 05 49 84 02 28. @ thoreau@lyondor.com 🍴 b,l,d. **Rooms** 10. €€

Bagnols

Château de Bagnols Restored medieval fortress with sumptuous, frescoed rooms. Devotées claim it's worth every *centime*. Outdoor pool.
✉ 69620 Bagnols, Rhône. **Map** p223 D3. ☎ 04 74 71 40 00. FAX 04 74 71 40 49. @ info@bagnols.com 🍴 b,l,d. **Rooms** 21. €€€€

Avallon

hâteau de Vault de Lugny From the moment ɔu arrive at the iron gates of this elegant home, ɔu feel like a guest at an exclusive house party. ɛacocks wander on the lawn along the drive, and the front door a butler relieves you of your bags. ıe decoration is tasteful and not too grand; ıests dine at one single long table.
11 rue du Château, 89200 Avallon, Yonne.
ap p221 E4, p223 D1. 03 86 34 07 86. FAX 03 86 34 5 36. @ hotel@lugny.com b,l,d. **Rooms** 12. mid-Nov to mid-Mar. AE, DC, MC, V. €€€€

Briollay

Château de Noirieux On the western reaches of the Loire château trail, this 17th-century manor house with 1920s additions eclipses all the local competition. Service is courteous with just the right amount of pampering. Rooms have stunning antiques, and the garden is shady and well-kept.
26 route du Moulin, 49125 Briollay, Maine et Loire.
Map p222 B1. 02 41 42 50 05. FAX 02 41 37 91 00.
@ noirieux@relaischateaux.com b,l,d.
Rooms 19. mid-Feb to mid-Mar.
AE, DC, MC, V. €€€€

Bannegon

uberge du Moulin de Chaméron A mixture of ater-mill museum and restaurant in deep country. summer, meals can be taken on the terrace by e mill stream. A swimming pool and wooded ardens amply make up for the comfortable but ɹll rooms in modern buildings across the garden.
Bannegon, 18210 Charenton-du-Cher, Cher.
ap p221 D5, p223 D2. 02 48 61 83 80. FAX 02 48 61 4 92. @ moulindechameron@wanadoo.fr
b,l,d. **Rooms** 14. mid-Nov to early March; on in low season. AE, MC, V. €€

Chagny

Hostellerie du Château de Bellecroix A former command post of the Knights of Malta, this turreted, creeper-clad castle was built in the 12th century with 18th-century additions. Annexe rooms are larger than those in the chateau, though the ones in the turrets are fun.
Route Nationale 6, 71150 Chagny, Saône-et-Loire.
Map p221 E5, p223 E1. 03 85 87 13 86.
FAX 03 85 91 28 62. @ info@chateau-bellecroix.com
b,l,d. **Rooms** 20. end Dec to mid-Feb.
AE, DC, MC, V. €€

Beaugency

'Abbaye The former Augustine convent, set by ı old bridge across the Loire, now makes a fine otel. Period rooms and fine cuisine.
2 quai de l'Abbaye, 45190 Beaugency, Loiret.
ap p220 C4, p222 C1. 02 38 44 67 35.
X 02 38 44 87 92. b,l,d. **Rooms** 17. €€

Beaune

hâteau de Challanges The setting for this late 3th-century mansion is a park of lawns and aths, minutes from the historic city.
Rue des Templiers, Challanges, 21200 Beaune, ôte-d'Or. **Map** p221 E4, p223 D1. 03 80 26 32 62.
X 03 80 26 32 52. b. **Rooms** 14. €€

Buzançais

L'Hermitage Owner-chef Claude Sureau runs a superior Logis de France, a small manor in a mature garden with a pavilion for summer dining.
36500 Buzançais, Indre. **Map** p222 C1. 02 54 84 03 90. FAX 02 54 02 13 19. @ csureau@aol.com
b,l,d. **Rooms** 14. €

Chagny

Hôtel Lameloise One of the great restaurants (three Michelin stars) in a calm, shuttered house.
36 place d'Armes, 71150 Chagny, Saône-et-Loire.
Map p221 E5, p223 E1. 03 85 87 65 65.
FAX 03 85 87 03 57. @ reception@lameloise.fr
b,l,d. **Rooms** 16. €€€

Chamonix

Le Hameau Albert 1er This refined reincarnation of the old Railway Hotel is now run by its founder's grandson. The most luxurious rooms are in Les Fermes, converted farm buildings with their own restaurant. Pierre Carrier's sublime cooking richly deserves its two Michelin stars.
BP 55-119 impasse du Montenvers, 74402 Chamonix, Haute Savoie. **Map** p221 F5, p223 F2. 04 50 53 05 09. FAX 04 50 55 95 48. @ infos@hameaualbert.fr
b,l,d. **Rooms** 27. Nov, restaurant closed 2 weeks May. AE, DC, MC, V. €€€

Champigné

Château des Briottières English parkland surrounds the de Valbray's gracious family seat. Th present young owners have opened their doors to guests, who find public rooms, furnished with family antiques and portraits, plus harmonious bedrooms. The de Valbrays join their guests for a pre-prandial drink. Mainly regional cuisine.
49330 Champigné, Maine-et-Loire. **Map** p220 B4, p222 B1. 02 41 42 00 02. FAX 02 41 42 01 55. @ briottieres@wanadoo.fr b,l,d. **Rooms** 15. Never. AE, DC, MC, V. €€€

Chamonix

Hôtel du Jeu de Paume Parisian style arrives in the Alps with the opening of the sister hotel of the Ile St-Louis Jeu de Paume. It follows the lines of a classic chalet, with wood dominating inside and out. In winter the hotel lays on a car to take guests to the ski lifts. Dinner on their return is superb.
705 route du Chapeau, Le Lavancher, 74400 Chamonix, Haute-Savoie. **Map** p221 F5, p223 F2. 04 50 54 03 76. FAX 04 50 54 10 75. @ jeu-de-paume-chamonix@wanadoo.fr b,l,d. **Rooms** 22. mid-May to mid-June; mid-Oct to mid-Dec. AE, DC, MC, V. €€€

Chaublanc

Moulin d'Hauterive Rustic chic, bright, romanti bedrooms and the inventive cooking of owner Mme Moille make a stay at this large converted mill an unusual blend of rural seclusion and goo living. In the large lawn behind are a little pool and tennis courts – and there's even a heliport.
Chaublanc, 71350 St-Gervais-en-Vallière, Saone et Loire. **Map** p221 E4, p223 E1. 03 85 91 55 56. FAX 03 85 91 89 65. @ info@moulinhauterive.com b,l,d. **Rooms** 20. Dec to mid-Feb. AE, DC, MC, V. €€

Challans

Château de la Vérie The beaches are just a short drive away from this lavishly furnished chateau.
Route de St-Gilles-Croix-de-Vie, 85300 Challans, Vendée. **Map** p220 B5, p222 A1. 02 51 35 33 44. FAX 02 51 35 14 84. @ verie@wanadoo.fr b,l,d. **Rooms** 21. €€

Chamonix

Auberge du Bois Prin Classic-style chalet, impeccably run. Great views and food.
69 chemin de l'Hermine, Les Moussoux, 74400 Chamonix, Haute-Savoie. **Map** p221 F5, p223 F2. 04 50 53 33 51. FAX 04 50 53 48 75. @ boisprin@relaischateaux.fr b;l,d. **Rooms** 11. €€€

Chassignelles

Hôtel de l'Ecluse A row of cottages on a canal – contains seven colourful, modestly priced bedrooms, a country-style dining room and bar.
2 Chemin de Ronde, 89160 Chassignelles, Yonne. **Map** p221 E4. 03 86 75 18 51. FAX 03 86 75 02 04. b,l,d. **Rooms** 9. €

Châteauneuf

Hostellerie du Château A 15th-century former presbytery in a medieval village. Quiet rooms.
Châteauneuf, 21320 Pouilly-en-Auxois, Côte-d'Or. **Map** p221 E4, p223 D1. 03 80 49 22 00. FAX 03 80 49 21 27. @ hdc@hostellerie-chateauneuf.com b,l,d. **Rooms** 17. €

Chaumont-sur-Tharonne

La Croix Blanche de Sologne The simple *logis* has a 200-year-old tradition of employing female chefs, and they have acquired a lofty reputation for their mainly Périgordian cuisine. The building dates back to 1424 and its rustic style is fitting: rooms are full of country antiques.
⊠ 5 place de l'Eglise, 41600 Chaumont-sur-Tharonne, Loir-et-Cher. **Map** p221 D4, p222 C1. ☎ 02 54 88 55 12. FAX 02 54 88 60 40. @ lacroixblanchesologne@wanadoo.fr b,l,d. **Rooms** 15. Never. AE, MC, V. €€

Cluny

Hôtel Restaurant de Bourgogne This 19th-century town hotel has a very French provincial air about it, and delightfully old-fashioned bedrooms are arranged around a calm courtyard garden. The restaurant specializes in Burgundian dishes. Recent change of ownership; now in the hands of the Colin family.
⊠ Place de l'Abbaye, 71250 Cluny, Saône-et-Loire. **Map** p221 E5, p223 D2. ☎ 03 85 59 00 58. FAX 03 85 59 03 73. @ contact@hotel-cluny.com b,l,d. **Rooms** 16. Dec to Jan. AE, MC, V. €€

Chinon

Hôtel Diderot This white-shuttered town house in a pleasant courtyard is run as a down-to-earth B&B. Some of the spotless, no-frills bedrooms have beams and fine views; some lead on to a terrace. Breakfasts are scrumptious, due to the hotel's wonderful supply of home-made jams. Now under new management.
⊠ 4 rue Buffon, 37500 Chinon, Indre-et-Loire. **Map** p220 C4, p222 B1. ☎ 02 47 93 18 87. FAX 02 47 93 37 10. @ hoteldiderot@hoteldiderot.com b. **Rooms** 28. mid-Jan to mid-Feb. AE, DC, MC, V. €

Echenevex

Auberge des Chasseurs This attractive converted farmhouse, situated at the foot of the Jura mountains, has been in the family of its owner, Dominique Lamy, since the mid-19th century. A Swedish decorator has freshened the interiors with a touch of Scandinavian paint magic. Satisfying food; pool; terrace; fine views over Lake Geneva to Mont Blanc.
⊠ Naz Dessus, 01170 Echenevex, Ain. **Map** p221 F5. ☎ 04 50 41 54 07. FAX 04 50 41 90 61. b,l,d. **Rooms** 15. Nov to Feb. AE, MC, V. €€

Cheverny

Château du Breuil Polished antiques in pale rooms and a sumptuous *salon* characterize this 18th-century chateau; vast parkland.
⊠ Route de Fougères-sur-Bièvre, 41700 Cheverny, Loir-et-Cher. **Map** p220 C4, p222 C1. ☎ 02 54 44 20 20. FAX 02 54 44 30 40. b,l,d. **Rooms** 18. €€€

Chonas-l'Amballan

Domaine de Clairefontaine Simple rooms and a Michelin star for Philippe Giradon's cuisine.
⊠ Chonas-l'Amballan, 38121 Reventin-Vaugris, Isère. **Map** p223 E3. ☎ 04 74 58 81 52. @ domaine.de.clairefontaine@gofornet.com FAX 04 74 58 80 93. b,l,d. **Rooms** 28. €€

Chonas-l'Amballan

Hostellerie Le Marais St-Jean The Giradons' farmhouse combines character with creature comforts; simple food and hordes of fans.
⊠ Chonas-l'Amballan, 38121 Reventin-Vaugris, Isère. **Map** p223 E3. ☎ 04 74 58 83 28. FAX 04 74 58 81 96. b. **Rooms** 10. €€

Condrieu

Hôtellerie Beau Rivage On the bank, or *rivage*, of the Rhône river; many rooms share the view. Friendly staff and Michelin-starred food.
⊠ 2 rue du Beau Rivage, 69420 Condrieu, Rhône. **Map** p223 D3. ☎ 04 74 56 82 82. @ hotel-beaurivage@wanadoo.fr FAX 04 74 59 59 36. b,l,d. **Rooms** 28. €€

Evian-les-Bains

La Verniaz et ses Chalets Nestled between Lake Geneva and the mountains in a mature tree- and flower-filled garden, an appealing hotel has been created from a clutch of old Alpine buildings. The dining room is dominated by a huge wood fire, over which meat and fish are cooked.
avenue D'Abondance, Neuvecelle-Eglise, 74500 Evian, Haute-Savoie. **Map** p223 E2. 04 50 75 04 90. FAX 04 50 70 78 92. verniaz@relaischateaux.com b,l,d. **Rooms** 35. mid-Nov to mid-Feb AE, DC, MC, V. €€€

Manigod

Chalets Hôtel de la Croix-Fry Enthusiasts return year after year, as a spell in this archetypal mountain chalet, built of dark wood, its terrace a sea of flowers, is a truly relaxing experience. The interior is simple and rustic, and it's no hardship that a minimum of three nights is required.
Route du Col de la Croix-Fry, 74230 Manigod, Thônes, Haute Savoie. **Map** p221 F5, p223 E2. 04 50 44 90 16. FAX 04 50 44 94 87. hotelcroixfry@wanadoo.fr b,l,d. **Rooms** 10. mid-Sep to mid-Dec; mid-Apr to mid-Jun. AE, MC, V. €€

Gilly-les-Cîteaux

Château de Gilly For Burgundy buffs, this stunning 14th-century Cistercian monastery in the heart of the Grands Crus will have irresistible appeal. Beautifully tended formal gardens set off the architecture, and the pale stone-vaulted dining room makes a magnificent setting for the gastronomic regional meals.
Gilly-les-Cîteaux, 21640 Vougeot, Côte d'Or. **Map** p223 E1. 03 80 62 89 98. FAX 03 80 62 82 34. contact@chateau-gilly.com b,l,d. **Rooms** 48. Never. AE, DC, MC, V. €€€

Mercurey

Hôtellerie du Val d'Or This early 19th-century coaching inn in the wine village of Mercurey makes a pleasant contrast with the many formal and extremely expensive establishments of the region. Devotees come here to savour Jean-Claude Cogny's Michelin-starred cooking; many return to stay in the neatly decorated bedrooms.
140 Grande Rue, 71640 Mercurey, Saône-et-Loire. **Map** p223 D2. 03 85 45 13 70. FAX 03 85 45 18 45. contact@le-valdor.com b,l,d. **Rooms** 12. mid-Dec to mid-Jan. V. €€

Curtil-Vergy

Hôtel Le Manassès Strictly for lovers of Burgundy: the hotel is in a vineyard and there's a wine museum in a barn. Bedrooms are modern, public rooms are furnished with antiques.
21220 Curtil-Vergy, Côte d'Or. **Map** p221 E4. 03 80 61 43 81. FAX 03 80 61 42 79. b. **Rooms** 12. €€

Gien

Hôtel du Rivage The hotel is contemporary and stylish, but the real draw is Christian Gaillard's cuisine. Rooms at the front have the view.
1 Quai de Nice, 45500 Gien, Loiret. **Map** p221 C1. 02 38 37 79 00. FAX 02 38 38 10 21. b. **Rooms** 19. €€€

Goumois

Hôtel Taillard This hotel in the Jura, close to the Swiss border, is efficiently run. Comfy rooms, pretty garden, breakfast terrace.
25470 Goumois, Doubs. **Map** p221 F4. 03 81 44 20 75. FAX 03 81 44 26 15. hotel.taillard@wanadoo.fr b,l,d. **Rooms** 22. €

Igé

Château d'Igé The medieval castle comes close to perfection, with ivy-clad turrets and a flower garden. A huge hearth warms diners.
71960 Igé, Saône-et-Loire. **Map** p221 E5. 03 85 33 33 99. FAX 03 85 33 41 41. ige@relaischateaux.fr b,l,d. **Rooms** 16. 

Meursault

Les Magnolias This old winegrower's house in peaceful surroundings has been converted into a B&B with great flair and is owned by a genial half-English man. Antiques pepper communal rooms and bedrooms; the ones in the eaves, with dormer windows, are most appealing. On fine days the substantial breakfasts can be eaten in a courtyard.
8 rue Pierre Joigneaux, 21190 Meursault, Côte-d'Or. **Map** p221 E4, p223 D1. 03 80 21 23 23. FAX 03 80 21 29 10. @ lesmagnolias@mageos.com b. **Rooms** 12. Dec to mid-Mar. AE, MC, V. €€

Montbron

Hostellerie Château Ste-Catherine At the end of a long drive through verdant gardens, stands a severe-looking stone manor house built around 1800 for the Empress Joséphine. First impressions are not reinforced by the warmth and charm of the interior, where walls are hung with tapestries and fires blaze in the hearths.
Route de Marthon, 16220 Montbron, Charente. **Map** p220 C5, p222 B2. 05 45 23 60 03. FAX 05 45 70 72 00. b,l,d. **Rooms** 18. Jan. AE, DC, MC, V. €€

Montbazon-en-Touraine

Domaine de la Tortinière Its hillside position in vast grounds lends this fairytale castle panoramas over the Indre valley. Built in 1861 in Renaissance style, it is smartly furnished, and offers an impressive array of activities including boating, tennis and mountain biking.
Route de Ballan-Miré - Les Gués de Veigné, 37250 Montbazon-en-Touraine, Indre-et-Loire. **Map** p220 C4, p222 B1. 02 47 34 35 00. FAX 02 47 65 95 70. @ contact@tortiniere.com b,l,d. **Rooms** 29. late Dec to Feb. MC, V. €€€

Nieuil

Château-Hôtel de Nieuil François I's former hunting lodge is a Renaissance castle with turrets, formal garden and magnificent rooms. But its charm lies in the warmth of the owners. The exuberant Monsieur Bodinaud manages a collection of fine cognacs. Madame used to be the chef, but has recently handed over that role.
Route de Fontafie, 16270 Nieuil, Charente. **Map** p220 C5. 05 45 71 36 38. FAX 05 45 71 46 45. @ chateaunieuilhotel@wanadoo.fr b,l,d. **Rooms** 14. early Nov to late Apr. AE, DC, MC, V. €€

Joigny

La Côte St-Jacques On the banks of the Yonne river avant-garde decor is coupled with tip-top cuisine – three Michelin stars.
14 fbg de Paris, 89304 Joigny, Yonne. **Map** p221 D4. 03 86 62 09 70. FAX 03 86 91 49 70. @ lorain@relaischateaux.com b,l,d. **Rooms** 32. €€€

Lyon

La Tour Rose In old Lyon, a restaurant with amazing rooms, each one reflecting a different period in the history of silk.
22 rue du Boeuf, 69005 Lyon, Rhône. **Map** p221 E5, p223 D2. 04 78 37 25 90. FAX 04 78 42 26 02. @ chavent@asi.fr b,l,d. **Rooms** 12. €€€€

Lyon

Villa Florentine A luxurious mix of Renaissance style with contemporary Italian design.
25 montée St-Barthélémy, 69005 Lyon, Rhône. **Map** p221 E5, p223 D2. 04 72 56 56 56. FAX 04 72 40 90 56. @ florentine@relaischateaux.fr b,l,d. **Rooms** 28. €€€€

Megève

Chalet du Mont d'Arbois Old pine furniture, log fires and fresh bedrooms in a traditional chalet.
447 chemin de la Rocaille, 74120 Megève, Haute-Savoie. **Map** p221 F5, p223 E2. 04 50 21 25 03. FAX 04 50 21 24 79. @ montarbois@relaischateaux.fr b,l,d. **Rooms** 29. €€€€

For key to symbols see backflap. For price categories *see p217*

Noizay

Château de Noizay Formal French gardens stretch away from this substantial 16th-century chateau. Inside, sturdy wooden stairs lead from the black and white tiled hall to the bedrooms, many of them furnished with four poster beds. The food and local Vouvray wines are excellent.
Route de Chançay, 37210 Noizay, Indre-et-Loire. **Map** p220 C4, p222 C1. 02 47 52 11 01. FAX 02 47 52 04 64. @ noizay@relaischateaux.com b,l,d. **Rooms** 19. mid-Jan to mid-March. AE, DC, MC, V. €€€

La Roche-l'Abeille

Moulin de la Gorce Two main reasons for a visit to this flour mill are the peace it enjoys and the food it produces. Built in the 1500s in an enviable position by a lake, it is now run by pastry chefs. Decoration varies: some country, some period, but the chintzy bedrooms look a touch out of place. Exceptional cuisine.
87800 La Roche-l'Abeille, Haute-Vienne. **Map** p220 C5. 05 55 00 70 66. FAX 05 55 00 76 57. @ moulindelagorce@wanadoo.fr b,l,d. **Rooms** 10. Dec to Mar. AE, DC, MC, V. €

Replonges

La Huchette The Gualdieri family have restored and enlarged this old inn and smartened it up considerably in the process. The bold decoration includes a colourful mural of country scenes in the beamed dining room, which specializes in regional dishes. The best and quietest bedrooms are those facing the large garden.
01750 Replonges, Ain. **Map** p221 E5, p223 E2. 03 85 31 03 55. FAX 03 85 31 10 24. @ lahuchette@wanadoo.fr b,l,d. **Rooms** 14. Never. AE, DC, MC, V. €€

St-Chartier

Château de la Vallée Bleue The Gasquets have owned and run this mini chateau since 1985, and more committed hoteliers would be hard to find. Flowers brighten the rooms; on chilly days a log fire blazes in the hall; service is caring; and an easy air pervades the hotel.
Route de Verneuil, St-Chartier, 36400 La Châtre, Indre. **Map** p221 D5, p222 C2. 02 54 31 01 91. FAX 02 54 31 04 48. @ valleebleue@aol.com b,d. **Rooms** 14, plus 1 suite. mid-Nov to mid-Mar. AE, MC, V. €€

Megève

Le Fer à Cheval Hansel and Gretel wood chalet with gleaming furniture and fresh fabrics.
36 route du Crêt-d'Arbois, 74120 Megève, Haute-Savoie. **Map** p221 F5, p223 F2. 04 50 21 30 39. FAX 04 50 93 07 60. @ feracheval@wanadoo.fr b,d. **Rooms** 47. €€€€

Meursault

Hôtel les Charmes Secluded grounds with tall trees surround this civilized 18th-century *maison bourgeoise*. The pool is a plus.
10 place du Murger, 21190 Meursault, Côte-d'Or. **Map** p221 E4, p223 D1. 03 80 21 63 53. FAX 03 80 21 62 89. b. **Rooms** 14. €€

Montrichard

Château de Chissay Plush fairytale-style castle. Great views and a pool.
Chissay-en-Touraine, 41400 Montrichard, Loir-et-Cher. **Map** p222 C1. 02 54 32 32 01. FAX 02 54 32 43 80. @ chissay@leshotelsparticuliers.com b,l,d. **Rooms** 32. €€€

Montrichard

Château de la Menaudière A small, beautifully furnished chateau with a snug bar, pretty courtyard and lawns, and a warm heart.
41401 Montrichard, Loir-et-Cher. **Map** p220 C4, p222 C1. 02 54 71 23 45. FAX 02 54 71 34 58. @ chat-menaudiere@wanadoo.fr b,l,d. **Rooms** 27. €€

St-Hilaire-de-Court

Château de la Beuvrière Dedicated château-hoppers can enjoy a night in the genuine medieval article without having to dip too far into their pockets. On a huge estate in the Cher valley, it has been carefully renovated, its lovely rooms full of family furniture. The pool is rather too close to the house – but that's just a quibble.
St-Hilaire-de-Court, 18100 Vierzon, Cher. **Map** p221 D4, p222 C1. 02 48 75 14 63. FAX 02 48 75 47 62. b. **Rooms** 13. mid-Nov to mid-Mar. AE, DC, MC, V. €

St-Martin-du-Fault

La Chapelle-St-Martin The trim and tidy manor house stands proud within its equally trim and tidy grounds with small lake and mature trees. Inside is decorated to the hilt, mixing antiques, modern conveniences and rich fabrics; bedrooms are equally impressive. Yet the ambience is relaxed. Fine swimming pool, tennis courts.
St-Martin-du-Fault, 87510 Nieul, Haute-Vienne. **Map** p220 C5, p222 C2. 05 55 75 80 17. FAX 05 55 75 89 50. chapelle@relaischateaux.fr b,l,d. **Rooms** 14. Never. AE, MC, V. €€€

St-Maixent-L'Ecole

Le Logis Saint-Martin Once you're ensconced in this pretty hotel, surrounded by woods, it seems impossible that the A10 motorway is so close. Built in the 17th century of pale stone, it has a tower converted into a smart split-level suite. Bertrand Heintz is a welcoming host, and the classic cuisine uses only organic produce.
Chemin de Pissot, 79400 St-Maixent-L'Ecole, Deux-Sèvres. **Map** p220 C5, p222 B2. 05 49 05 58 68. FAX 05 49 76 19 93. courrier@logis-saint-martin.com b,l,d. **Rooms** 11. Jan. AE, DC. €€

St-Patrice

Château de Rochecotte A vast park and formal garden enclose the grand family-run stately home; inside gorgeous furnishings enhance the classical rooms. Yet it retains the feel of a private home – the family could not be more welcoming nor the staff more attentive. Madame Pasquier serves consistently elegant cuisine.
St-Patrice, 37130 Langeais, Indre-et-Loire. **Map** p220 C4. 02 47 96 16 16. FAX 02 47 96 90 59. chateau.rochecotte@wanadoo.fr b,l,d. **Rooms** 35. Feb. AE, V. €€€

Onzain

Domaine des Hauts de Loire Characterful 19th-century hunting lodge. Michelin-starred cuisine.
Route de Herbault, 41150 Onzain, Loir-et-Cher. **Map** p220 C4, p222 C1. 02 54 20 72 57. FAX 02 54 20 77 32. hauts-loire@relaischateaux.fr b,l,d. **Rooms** 34. €€€

Pérouges

Ostellerie du Vieux Pérouges In the centre of the medieval town. Excellent traditional cooking; bedrooms are in four separate houses.
Place du Tilleul, 01800 Pérouges, Meximieux, Ain. **Map** p223 E2. 04 74 61 00 88. FAX 04 74 34 77 90. thibaut@ostellerie.com b,l,d. **Rooms** 28. €€

Poisson

La Reconce Handsome village hotel next door to La Poste restaurant, both admirably run by Denise and Jean-Noel Dauvergne.
Le Bourg, 71600 Poisson, Saône-et-Loire. **Map** p221 E5, p223 D2. 03 85 81 10 72. FAX 03 85 81 64 34. b,l,d. **Rooms** 7. €

Romorantin-Lanthenay

Grand Hôtel du Lion d'Or Gastronomic food in a flamboyant villa in this undiscovered town.
69 rue Georges Clémenceau, 41200 Romorantin-Lanthenay, Loir-et-Cher. **Map** p221 D4, p222 C1. 02 54 94 15 15. FAX 02 54 88 24 87. info@hotel-liondor.fr b,l,d. **Rooms** 16. €€€

Tavers

La Tonnellerie The internal garden of this 19th-century wine-merchant's house is glorious in summer, when tables are set out beneath the chestnuts. The modern regional cuisine is always a draw. The hotel is kept in pristine order by the delightful Marie-Christine Pouey; among the pretty floral bedrooms are four apartment suites.
12 rue des Eaux, Tavers, 45190 Beaugency, Loiret. **Map** p220 C4. 02 38 44 68 15. FAX 02 38 44 10 01. @ tonelri@club-internet.fr b,l,d. **Rooms** 20. Jan, Feb. AE, MC, V. €€€

Veyrier-du-Lac

La Demeure de Chavoire For total peace and tranquillity, look no further than this hotel on the shores of Lake Annecy. It forges a winning combination of classic elegance and modern luxury, with artistic decoration and romantic bedrooms named after local writers and beauty spots.
71 route d'Annecy-Chavoire, 74290 Veyrier-du-Lac, Haute-Savoie. **Map** p221 F5, p223 E2. 04 50 60 04 38. FAX 04 50 60 05 36. @ demeure.chavoire@wanadoo.fr b. **Rooms** 13. Nov. AE, DC, V. €€€

Tours

Château Belmont A refined 19th-cenury villa in Touraine stone. Sitting in a wicker chair inside the colonnade, sipping a cocktail and savouring the landscaped garden is just one of its treats. Luxurious bedrooms and delectable food at the Jean Bardet restaurant are others. The hotel is only 2km (about 1 mile) from the city centre.
57 rue Groison, 37100 Tours, Indre-et-Loire. **Map** p220 C4. 02 47 41 41 11. FAX 02 47 51 68 72. @ sophie@jeanbardet.com b,l,d. **Rooms** 21. Sun evening, Mon Nov to Mar. AE, DC, MC, V. €€€

Vézelay

Le Pontot The only hotel within the town walls of old Vézelay, this special B&B occupies an ancient, sprawling house, fortified and rebuilt over the centuries. Bedrooms range from ones with stone floors, rafters and rustic furniture to a suite in Louis XVI style. In autumn, breakfast is served in front of a splendid log fire; in summer, in the pretty walled garden.
Place du Pontot, 89450 Vézelay, Yonne. **Map** p221 D4, p223 D1. 03 86 33 24 40. FAX 03 86 33 30 05. b. **Rooms** 9. mid-Oct to Easter. DC, MC, V. €€€

Tain l'Hermitage

Reynaud Fine restaurant with rooms, the accent is on fish and home-grown vegetables. Glorious terrace beside the Rhône river.
82 avenue du President Roosevelt, 26600 Tain-l'Hermitage, Drôme. **Map** p223 D3. 04 75 07 22 10. FAX 04 75 08 03 53. b,l,d. **Rooms** 14. €

Talloires

Auberge du Père Bise Swanky inn on the lake, run by *mère et fille* Bise, exalted for their cuisine.
Route du Port, 74290 Talloires, Haute-Savoie. **Map** p221 F5, p223 E2. 04 50 60 72 01. FAX 04 50 60 73 05. @ reception@perebise.com b,l,d. **Rooms** 34. €€€€

Le Tertenoz

Au Gay Séjour A simple white and wood chalet with spectacular alpine views and hearty food.
Le Tertenoz de Seythenex, 74210 Faverges, Haute-Savoie. **Map** p221 F5. 04 50 44 52 52. FAX 04 50 44 49 52. @ hotel-gay-sejour@wanadoo.fr b,l,d. **Rooms** 11. €€

Vaux-sur-Mer

Résidence de Rohan Snug among the pines typical of this coast, a relaxed seaside B&B occupies a handsome white house. Outdoor pool.
Parc des Fées, 17640 Vaux-sur-Mer, Charente-Maritime. **Map** p222 B2, p220 B5. 05 46 39 00 75. FAX 05 46 38 29 99. @ info@residence-rohan.com b. **Rooms** 43. €€

SOUTHERN FRANCE

DORDOGNE AND AQUITAINE • MASSIF CENTRAL • PYRÉNÉES LANGUEDOC-ROUSSILLON • PROVENCE-CÔTE D'AZUR

THE DORDOGNE and the Lot, the fertile valleys in the southwest, are popular holiday spots. They offer a wealth of attractive small hotels and B&Bs in old mills, stables, manors and farmhouses. Further west is Bordeaux, with its incomparable vineyards, and the tree-bordered beaches of the Landes. The Massif Central, arguably the least spoilt part of France, has a range of hotels, from farmsteads and chalets to medieval stone-built inns and elegant restaurants with rooms. Many are very good value for money. To the southeast of the region, in Provence, whitewashed walls and tiled roofs, and shady courtyards with wrought-iron furniture, are typical.

AIX-EN-PROVENCE

Mas d'Entremont A cool courtyard lies at the heart of the hotel, a cluster of low, modern buildings. Their red roofs were constructed from old materials, giving them a softer, more rustic look. Wood pillars and beams abound in both the public rooms and the bedrooms, which are furnished with country pieces.

Montée d'Avignon, 13090 Aix-en-Provence. **Map** p224 C4. 04 42 17 42 42. FAX 04 42 21 15 83. entremont@wanadoo.fr b,l,d. **Rooms** 17. Nov to mid-Mar. MC, V. €€€

AIX-EN-PROVENCE

Villa Gallici From the terrace with its deep-cushioned seats shaded by plane trees, to the glamorous bedrooms with fabric-draped beds, the villa is perfect – interior-decorated to the last tie-back. Perhaps it's a little too perfect to put you completely at ease, but the restaurant excels.

Avenue de la Violette, 13100 Aix-en-Provence, Bouches-du-Rhône. **Map** p224 C4. 04 42 23 29 23. FAX 04 42 96 30 45. gallici@relaischateaux.com b,l,d. **Rooms** 22. Never. AE, DC, MC, V. €€€€

AIX-EN-PROVENCE

Hôtel des Quatre Dauphins Painted furniture graces the reception room and simple, tasteful bedrooms in this good-value *maison bourgeoise*.

54 rue Roux Alphéran, 13100 Aix-en-Provence, Bouches-du-Rhône. **Map** p224 C4. 04 42 38 16 39. FAX 04 42 38 60 19. b. **Rooms** 13. €€

AJACCIO, CORSICA

Hôtel Dolce Vita The glossy hotel has an acclaimed restaurant specializing in fish, and a glorious covered dining terrace.

Route des Sanguinaires, 20000 Ajaccio, Corse-du-Sud. **Map** p223 F5. 04 95 52 42 42. FAX 04 95 52 07 15. hotel@dolcevita.com b,l,d. **Rooms** 32. €€€€

LES ARCS

Le Logis du Guetteur From the outside the 11th-century fort has barely changed; inside, calm modern rooms enjoy incomparable views.

Place du Château, 83460 Les Arcs, Var. **Map** p225 E4. 04 94 99 51 10. FAX 04 94 99 51 29. le.logis.du.guetteur@wanadoo.fr b,l,d. **Rooms** 13. €€€

ARGELÈS-SUR-MER

Le Cottage Seaside hotel with pleasant garden and pool. Simple bedrooms, most with balconies.

21 rue Arthur Rimbaud, 66703 Argelès-sur-Mer, Pyrénées-Orientales. **Map** p223 D5. 04 68 81 07 33. FAX 04 68 81 59 69. info@hotel-lecottage.com b. **Rooms** 34. €€

Avignon-Montfavet

Les Frênes Comfort and good taste prevail at Les Frênes with its immaculate shuttered cream façade, tree-fringed pool and pastel-coloured bedrooms. Some are in outbuildings, scattered through the park in which the main house stands four-square. Provençal dishes crowd the menu.
645 avenue des Vertes-Rives, 84140 Avignon-Montfavet, Vaucluse. **Map** p224 B3. 04 90 31 17 93. FAX 04 90 23 95 03. @ contact@lesfrenes.com b,l,d. **Rooms** 18. Nov-Mar. AE, DC, MC, V. €€€€

Les Baux-de-Provence

L'Oustau de Baumanière The hotel makes the most of its splendid position high in the craggy Alpilles. You can swim with a view in the glorious pool, almost carved out of rock, and eat with one too on the panoramic terrace; the food is first-class. A few of the bedrooms are baronial, all are well-equipped.
13520 Les Baux-de-Provence, Bouches-du-Rhône. **Map** p224 B30. 04 90 54 33 07. FAX 04 90 54 40 46. @ oustau@relaischateaux.com b,l,d. **Rooms** 30. mid-Jan to Mar. AE, DC, MC, V. €€€€

Les Baux-de-Provence

Auberge de la Benvengudo With its shuttered façade almost hidden by creepers, the *auberge* gives the impression of being much older than its 20-odd years. A large garden and swimming pool, prepossessing bedrooms, and a snug *salon* make this a most inviting choice.
Vallon de l'Arcoule, 13520 Les Baux-de-Provence, Bouches-du-Rhône. **Map** p224 B3. 04 90 54 32 54. FAX 04 90 54 42 58. b,l,d. **Rooms** 24. Never. AE, V. €€€

Brantôme

Le Chatenet The Laxtons' dog may bound out to greet you at this friendly B&B. A fine, low stone manor tucked away from the hurly-burly down a country track off the main riverside road, its interior is graciously but comfortably furnished. In the garden, deckchairs are placed temptingly in shady spots.
24310 Brantôme, Dordogne. **Map** p222 B3. 05 53 05 81 08. FAX 05 53 05 85 52. @ chatenet.hotel@wanadoo.fr b. **Rooms** 10. occasionally, Nov to Apr. Not accepted. €€

Arpaillargues

Hôtel Marie d'Agoult Once home to Franz Liszt's mistress, now a civilized and secluded retreat.
Château d'Arpaillargues, Arpaillargues, 30700 Uzès, Gard. **Map** p224 A3. 04 66 22 14 48. @ savrychateau30@aol.com FAX 04 66 22 56 10. b,l,d. **Rooms** 30. €€

Bagnols-sur-Cèze

Château de Montcaud 19th-century house makes a sophisticated hotel. Superb restaurant.
Hameau de Combe-Sabran, 30200 Bagnols-sur-Cèze, Gard. **Map** p224 B2. 04 66 89 60 60. FAX 04 66 89 45 04. @ montcaud@relaischateaux.com b,l,d. **Rooms** 29. €€€€

Barcus

Hôtel Chilo A village hotel with views of the countryside that has been in the same family for three generations. Outstanding food; pool.
64130 Barcus, Pyrénées-Atlantiques. **Map** p222 A4. 05 59 28 90 79. FAX 05 59 28 93 10. @ martine.chilo@wanadoo.fr b,l,d. **Rooms** 11. €

Boissot

Auberge de Concasty Cheerful house and lawns on a family farm. Build up an appetite in the pool: Martine Causse's delicious local dishes are filling.
15600 Boissot, Cantal. **Map** p222 C3. 04 71 62 21 16. FAX 04 71 62 22 22. @ info@auberge-concasty.com b,d. **Rooms** 14. €€

Brantôme

Moulin de l'Abbaye Its riverside situation makes this delectable former mill a magical place. A superb outlook across the Dronne river to the old town is shared by the flowery terrace and some of the smart, variously styled bedrooms. Housekeeping is flawless, the Michelin-starred food imaginative and the staff courteous.
1 route de Bourdeilles, 24310 Brantôme, Dordogne. **Map** p222 B3. 05 53 05 80 22. FAX 05 53 05 75 27. moulin@relaischateaux.com b,l,d. **Rooms** 19. Nov to May. AE, DC, MC, V. €€€€

Calvi, Corsica

Auberge Relais de la Signoria Candlelit dinner on the palm-shaded terrace by the seductive pool is one of the joys of staying here, a simple but stylish 17th-century house with an exotic garden. If you can, opt for a room in the main house not the annexe.
Route de la Fôret de Bonifato, 20260 Calvi, Haute-Corse. **Map** p223 F5. 04 95 65 93 00. FAX 04 95 65 38 77. info@hotel-la-signoria.com b,l,d. **Rooms** 24. Nov to Mar. AE, MC, V. €€€€

Le Buisson-de-Cadouin

Manoir de Bellerive This calm, handsome manor overlooking the Dordogne was renovated by interior designers, who created some striking paint effects and stylish rooms. A magnificent colonnaded entrance has an elegant double staircase. Set in private parkland.
Route de Siorac, 24480 Le Buisson-de-Cadouin, Dordogne. **Map** p222 C3. 05 53 22 16 16. FAX 05 53 22 09 05. manoir.bellerive@wanadoo.fr b,l,d. **Rooms** 22. Jan, Feb. AE, DC, MC, V. €€

Carennac

Hostellerie Fénelon The little hotel, a cluster of red roofs and window boxes in a captivating village, represents excellent value for money. It's not fancy, but the welcoming hostess, Mme Raynal, offers a warm welcome, good honest cooking and a little swimming pool, at low cost. In good weather, meals can be taken on the dining terrace. Friendly, unobtrusive staff.
46110 Carennac, Lot. **Map** p222 C3. 05 65 10 96 46. FAX 05 65 10 94 86. b,l,d. **Rooms** 15. early Jan to mid-Mar. MC, V. €

Bonnieux

Auberge de l'Aiguebrun A beautiful, tranquil hotel, full of light and colour, in a green oasis by a waterfall in the river Aiguebrun. First-rate food.
Domaine de la Tour, RD 943, 84480 Bonnieux, Vaucluse. **Map** p224 C3. 04 90 04 47 00. FAX 04 90 04 47 01. sylvia.buzier@wanadoo.fr b,l,d. **Rooms** 11. €€€

Bonnieux

L'Hostellerie du Prieuré A chef from Maxim in Paris provides a fine Provençal table at this old *hôtel-Dieu* which retains all its original details.
84480 Bonnieux, Vaucluse. **Map** p224 C3. 04 90 75 80 78. FAX 04 90 75 96 00. hotelprieur@hotmail.com b,l,d. **Rooms** 10. €€

Carcassonne

Domaine d'Auriac Golf, tennis and swimming are a few attractions of this plush country house. Fine dining on a splendid terrace.
Route de St-Hilaire, 11009 Carcassonne, Aude. **Map** p224 C4. 04 68 25 72 22. FAX 04 68 47 35 54. auriac@relaischateaux.com b,l,d. **Rooms** 26. €€€

Cassis

Le Clos des Arômes A 50-year-old hotel jazzed up by the young, hospitable Bonnets. Bedrooms are small but pretty; not all have bathrooms.
10 rue Paul Mouton, 13260 Cassis, Bouches-du-Rhône. **Map** p222 C4. 04 42 01 71 84. FAX 04 42 01 31 76. b,l,d. **Rooms** 14. €

For key to symbols see backflap. For price categories *see p217*

Castelpers

Château de Castelpers The present owner's great-grandfather built the house in the 19th century on the ruins of an earlier mill. Visitors today find a reflective place, a rambling country house filled with old paintings, antiques and four-poster beds. Enveloping the building is a garden of rivers and tall trees. And all this at modest cost.
Castelpers, 12170 Lédergues, Aveyron. **Map** p222 C4. 05 65 69 22 61. FAX 05 65 69 25 31. b,d. **Rooms** 4. Oct to Mar. AE, DC, MC, V. €

Céret

La Terrasse au Soleil This luxurious ranch-like manor has an individual style and intimacy that is reflected in its warm colour schemes. The restaurant has a reputation for serious food, but serves brasserie-style lunches too. Bedrooms are in annexes, some with verandas.
Route de Fontfrède, 66400 Céret, Pyrénées-Orientales. **Map** p223 D5. 04 68 87 01 94. FAX 04 68 87 39 24. @ terrasse-au-soleil.hotel@wanadoo.fr b,l,d. **Rooms** 38. Never. AE, MC, V. €€€€

Castillon-du-Gard

Le Vieux Castillon Spectacular views across rolling, vineyard-dotted plains meet you at almost every turn in this pocket of mellow medieval houses at the heart of a pretty hill village. They have been ingeniously transformed to create a gem of a hotel. Standard rooms can be cramped; it's worth paying the extra to go upmarket.
30210 Castillon-du-Gard, Gard. **Map** p224 A3. 04 66 37 61 61. FAX 04 66 37 28 17. @ vieux.castillon@ wanadoo.fr b,l,d. **Rooms** 35. Jan to mid-Feb. AE, DC, MC, V. €€€

Champagnac-de-Belair

Le Moulin du Roc This former walnut mill has a heavenly setting on the banks of the Dronne river, encircled by a fertile garden. The interior is a delightful clutter of carved furniture, sumptuous fabrics, huge pictures and mill paraphernalia. The kitchen prepares delicate regional food.
24530 Champagnac-de-Belair, Dordogne. **Map** p222 C2. 05 53 02 86 00. FAX 05 53 54 21 31. @ moulinroc@aol.com b,l,d. **Rooms** 13. Jan to 7 Feb. AE, DC, MC, V. €€

Céret

Le Mas Trilles A delightful 17th-century former farmhouse with pool in a verdant landscape. Rooms are big and stylish but not elaborate.
Le Pont de Reynès, 66400 Céret, Pyrénées-Orientales. **Map** p223 D5. 04 68 87 38 37. FAX 04 68 87 42 62. b. **Rooms** 10. €€

Château-Arnoux

La Bonne Etape Imaginative cuisine in a hushed setting with a pool. The rooms are stunning.
Chemin du Lac, 04160 Château-Arnoux, Alpes-de-Haute-Provence. **Map** p225 D2. 04 92 64 00 09. FAX 04 92 64 36 37. @ bonneetape@realaischateaux.com b,l,d. **Rooms** 11. €€€€

Ciboure

Lehen Tokia 1920s Basque villa. Art Deco decor. Swimming pool, garden and fine sea view.
Chemin Achotarreta, 64500 Ciboure, St-Jean-de-Luz, Pyrénées-Atlantiques. **Map** p222 A4. 05 59 47 18 16. FAX 05 59 47 38 04. @ info@lehen-tokia.com b. **Rooms** 6, plus 1 suite. €€

Collioure

Hôtel Casa Païral An exotic enclosed garden lies at the heart of this alluring old Catalan-style B&B.
Empasse des Palmiers, 66190 Collioure, Pyrénées-Orientales. **Map** p223 D5. 04 68 82 05 81. FAX 04 68 82 52 10. @ roussellhotel@wanadoo. fr b. **Rooms** 28. €€

Coly

Manoir d'Hautegente This 13th-century manor has been through several incarnations: first it was a forge, then a mill, before becoming a private house. The hotel's charm is that it keeps the feel of home intact with fresh-coloured, antique-filled rooms. The menu features home-produced *foie gras*.
Coly, 24120 Terrasson, Dordogne. **Map** p223 C3.
05 53 51 68 03. FAX 05 53 50 38 52.
@ manoir.d.hautegente@wanadoo.fr b,d. **Rooms** 15.
Nov to Mar. AE, DC, MC, V. €€

Condom

Hôtel des Trois Lys The elegance of this white-shuttered honey-stone house extends from the outside in. An immense stone staircase leads to the bedrooms, some of which are huge and wood-panelled, with deep-pile carpet and pristine bathrooms. There is a pool at the back and a restaurant, Le Dauphin, next door.
38 rue Gambetta, 32100 Condom, Gers.
Map p222 B4. 05 62 28 33 33. FAX 05 62 28 41 85.
@ info@destroislys.com b,l,d. **Rooms** 10.
Feb. AE, DC, MC, V. €€

Coulandon

Le Chalet The chalet-style *logis*, deep in the Bourdonnais countryside, is an unsophisticated, traditional place: rooms are colourful and jolly rather than stylish. But for simple pleasures, the place is idyllic. In the wooded grounds are a pool and a large pond where guests can fish, and the little raised dining terrace has fine rural views.
03000 Coulandon, Allier. **Map** p221 D5, 223 D2.
04 70 46 00 66. FAX 04 70 44 07 09.
@ hotelchalet@cs3i.fr b,l,d. **Rooms** 28.
mid-Dec to end Jan. AE, DC, MC, V. €€

Cornillon

La Vieille Fontaine Built within the walls of a ruined castle in the medieval village of Cornillon, this hotel is the baby of the Audiberts. He is *patron* and talented chef; she is in charge of decoration. Her style is Provençal and unfussy, with touches of panache like the outside staircase encased in glass. Steep steps lead through terraced gardens to a hilltop pool.
30630 Cornillon, Gard. **Map** p224 A2. 04 66 82 20 56. FAX 04 66 82 33 64. @ vieillefontaine@libertysurf.fr
b,l,d.**Rooms** 8. Nov to Mar. AE, V. €€

Conques

Grand-Hôtel Sainte-Foy Partly timbered 17th-century inn. Large bedrooms, with views either over the abbey church, or the garden.
12320 St-Cyprien-sur-Dourdou, Conques, Aveyron. **Map** p222 C3. 05 65 69 84 03. FAX 05 65 72 81 04. @ hotelsaintefoy@hotelsaintefoy.fr b,l,d. **Rooms** 17. €€€

Cordes-sur-Ciel

Le Grand Ecuyer Michelin-starred cuisine, courtesy of pastry cook Yves Thuriès, in an old hunting lodge in this perfect medieval village.
79 Grand Rue Raimond VII, 81170 Cordes-sur-Ciel, Tarn. **Map** p222 C4. 05 63 53 79 50. FAX 05 63 53 79 51. @ grand.ecuyer@thuries.fr b,l,d. **Rooms** 13. €€

Dégagnac

Auberge sans Frontière The simple village inn in sleepy Dégagnac offers superb value for its hearty cuisine and trim bedrooms. The dining room also serves as a bar and sitting room.
Le Bourg, 46340 Dégagnac, Lot. **Map** p222 C3.
05 65 41 52 88. b,l,d. **Rooms** 4. €

Domme

Hôtel de l'Esplanade A breathtaking position on a cliff-edge above the Dordogne, superb food and pretty rooms.
24250 Domme, Dordogne. **Map** p222 C3. 05 53 28 31 41. FAX 05 53 28 49 92. @ esplanade.domme@wanadoo.fr b,l,d. **Rooms** 25. €€

Crillon-le-Brave

Hostellerie de Crillon-le-Brave A substantial former vicarage of ochre stone, set on a hilltop in Italianate gardens, houses a hotel that is luxurious and well run without losing its character. Inside, worn flagged floors, stone walls, rustic furniture, old books and comfy sofas.
Place de l'Eglise, 84410 Crillon-le-Brave, Vaucluse. **Map** p224 C2. 04 90 65 61 61. FAX 04 90 65 62 86. crillonbrave@relaischateaux.com b,d. **Rooms** 24, plus 8 suites. early Jan to early Mar. AE, DC, MC, V. €€€€

Eugénie-les-Bains

Les Prés d'Eugénie In a refined spa town, this B&B, part of a small empire owned by Michel Guérard, is run with warmth and flair by his wife Christine. Rooms in the 18th-century former nunnery are all beautifully furnished. Meals are taken across the garden in the renowned Les Prés d'Eugénie restaurant.
40320 Eugénie-les-Bains, Landes. **Map** p222 B4. 05 58 05 06 07. FAX 05 58 51 10 10. guerard@relaischateaux.com b,l,d. **Rooms** 45. part Dec. AE, DC, MC, V. €€€€€

Cuq-Toulza

Cuq-en-Terrasses This charming hotel, an abandoned presbytery until its conversion in 1990 by two London designers, is set in a fertile pocket of country known locally as Le Pays de Cocagne – the land of plenty – and its location offers stunning views of the surrounding countryside. Clean, fresh, colourful decor. Wonderful food.
Cuq Le Château, 81470 Cuq-Toulza, Tarn. **Map** p222 C4. 05 63 82 54 00. FAX 05 63 82 54 11. info@cuqenterrasses.com b,l,d. **Rooms** 8. mid-Nov to mid-Mar. AE, DC, MC, V. €€

Florimont-Gaumiers

La Daille British ex-pats Derek and Barbara Brown have been in charge this red-roofed farmhouse in rolling grounds for nearly 30 years. There used to be a restaurant here; now it's a congenial B&B, but their weekend afternoon teas have become a local institution. The bedrooms are in a separate, modern building; there is a minimum stay of three days.
24250 Florimont-Gaumiers, Dordogne. **Map** p222 C3. 05 53 28 40 71. b. **Rooms** 3. Oct to Apr. Not accepted. €€

Eygalières

Auberge Provençale Owner/chef Didier Pézeril creates culinary works of art in his characterful inn. The bedrooms are sweet and simple.
Place de la Mairie, 13810 Eygalières. **Map** p224 B3. 04 90 95 91 00. FAX 04 90 90 60 92. b,l,d. **Rooms** 4. €€

Eygalières

Hostellerie Mas dou Pastré Exquisite Provençal furnishings in a *mas* looking out to the Alpilles. Light lunches on a terrace; pool in the garden.
Route d'Organ, 13810 Eygalières, Bouches-du-Rhône. **Map** p224 B3. 04 90 95 92 61. FAX 04 90 90 61 75. b,d. **Rooms** 11. €€

Les Eyzies-de-Tayac

Le Centenaire Glossy Relais et Château with a lovely pool, a gym and surprisingly low prices.
2 av du Cingle, 24620 Les Eyzies-de-Tayac, Dordogne. **Map** p222 C3. 05 53 06 68 68. FAX 05 53 06 92 41. hotel.centenaire@wanadoo.fr b,l,d. **Rooms** 19. €€€

Les Eyzies-de-Tayac

Moulin de la Beune An oasis of calm at the heart of the tourist trail, with bright bedrooms and a Périgordian restaurant in the garden.
24620 Les Eyzies-de-Tayac, Dordogne. **Map** p222 C3. 05 53 06 94 33. FAX 05 53 06 98 06. b,l,d. **Rooms** 20. €

Fontvieille

Auberge La Régalido An idyllic garden and Jean-Pierre Michel's incomparable Provençal meals are two reasons to stay at this converted old mill. Friendly staff, individually decorated bedrooms with lots of extras, and an atmosphere of well-being complete the picture.
Rue Frédéric-Mistral, 13990 Fontvieille, Bouches-du-Rhône. **Map** p224 B3. 04 90 54 60 22. FAX 04 90 54 64 29. @ la-regalido@wanadoo.fr b,l,d. **Rooms** 15. Jan to 15 Feb. AE, DC, MC, V. €€€€

Gramat

Château de Roumégouse This castle hotel is a rarity: a flawless Relais et Châteaux establishment with prices that are not sky-high. The style changes from one bedroom to another, but fresh flowers appear in each, as well as in the airy reception rooms. In summer, meals are taken on the panoramic terrace.
Rignac, 46500 Gramat, Lot. **Map** p222 C3. 05 65 33 63 81. FAX 05 65 33 71 18. @ roumegouse@relaischateaux.fr b,l,d. **Rooms** 15. winter months. AE, DC, MC, V. €€€€

Gémenos

Relais de la Magdeleine This gem of a hotel, occupying a handsome 18th-century *bastide* (country house), has been run with warmth by the same family since 1932. All the bedrooms, even the cheapest, are prettily decorated, with fine furniture and paintings; bathrooms are spruce. You might come across a donkey in the garden.
13420 Gémenos, Bouches-du-Rhône. **Map** p224 C4. 04 42 32 20 16. FAX 04 42 32 02 26. @ contact@relaismagdeleine.com b,l,d. **Rooms** 24. Dec to mid-Mar. AE, MC, V. €€

Grimaud

Le Coteau Fleuri You don't have to meet the cheerful owner to feel positive about this hotel. It happens the moment you enter the spacious interior with its polished tile floors and white walls, and smell the fragrance of fresh flowers. Rooms and superb food have a Provençal flavour.
Place des Penitents, 83360 Grimaud, Var. **Map** p225 E4. 04 94 43 20 17. FAX 04 94 43 33 42. @ coteaufleuri@wanadoo.fr b,l,d. **Rooms** 14. Nov to mid-Jan. AE, DC, MC, V. €€

Eze-Village

Château de la Chèvre d'Or Smart hotel perched on a clifftop, where every bedroom has a view.
Rue du Barri, 06360 Eze-Village, Alpes-Maritimes. **Map** p225 F3. 04 92 10 66 66. FAX 04 93 41 06 72. @ reservation@chevredor.com b,l,d. **Rooms** 32, plus presidential suite. €€€€

Eze-Village

Château Eza Tapestries on stone walls and utter luxury, 400m (1,300ft) above the sea.
Rue de la Pise, 06360 Eze-Village, Alpes-Maritimes. **Map** p225 F3. 04 93 41 12 24. FAX 04 93 41 16 64. @ info@chateza.com b,l,d. **Rooms** 10. €€€€

Figeac

Château du Viguier du Roy Central, but with a peaceful cloister and interior garden. Warm sophistication in a setting of 12th-century origins.
rue Droite, 46100 Figeac, Lot. **Map** p222 C3. 05 65 50 05 05. FAX 05 65 50 06 06. @ hotel@chateau-viguier-figeac.com b,l,d. **Rooms** 21. €€€

Floure

Château de Floure Former Romanesque abbey with extensive grounds, a maze and a pool. Pleasing rooms and fine food add to its appeal.
1 allée Gaston Bonheur, 11800 Floure, Aude. **Map** p222 C4. 04 68 79 11 29. FAX 04 68 79 04 61. @ contact@chateau-de-floure.com b,l,d. **Rooms** 18. €€

Grimaud

Le Verger A low, pink house with white shutters, typical of the region, the Verger is decorated plainly but agreeably with country-style fabrics and furniture. A wisteria-covered terrace makes a perfect venue for summer dining. In the garden of lawns and hydrangeas, there are plenty of shady spots in which to escape the midday sun.
Route de Collobrières, 83360 Grimaud, Var. **Map** p225 E4. 04 94 55 57 80 FAX 04 94 43 33 92. b,l. **Rooms** 9. Never V. €€

Lacave

Château de la Treyne The origins of this near-perfect fortified manor date back to the 14th century. It is set in parkland, clinging to a cliff above the Dordogne river. Guests today find a harmonious blend of ornate and comfortable furniture in intimate rooms. Additional rooms have been added at another small chateau nearby.
Lacave, 46200 Souillac, Lot. **Map** p222 C3. 05 65 27 60 60. FAX 05 65 27 60 70. @ treyne@relaischateaux.com b,l,d. **Rooms** 24. mid-Nov to Easter. AE, DC, MC, V. €€€€

Lacabarède

Demeure de Flore Shielded from the road by a wooded garden, the 19th-century house may not be anything to write home about architecturally, but it certainly is once you look inside. Many of the bright rooms have floor-to-ceiling windows, and painstaking care has gone into their furnishing. Snack lunches by the pool are bliss.
106 Route Nationale, 81240 Lacabarède, Tarn. **Map** p223 D4. 05 63 98 32 32. FAX 05 63 98 47 56. @ demeure.de.flore@hotelrama.com b,l,d. **Rooms** 11. Jan. MC, V. €€

Lacave

Hôtel du Pont de l'Ouysse Tranquillity is guaranteed as the road leading to the hotel is a cul-de-sac. In warm weather, dining on the beautiful terrace that overlooks the river, sitting under a canopy of leafy trees and surrounded by shrubs, is magical. The seasonal menu features local produce.
Lacave, 46200 Souillac, Lot. **Map** p222 C3. 05 65 37 87 04. FAX 05 65 32 77 41. @ pont.ouysse@ wanadoo.fr b,l,d. **Rooms** 14. mid-Nov to March. AE, DC, MC, V. €€€

Gigondas

Les Florêts A tempting menu is accompanied by wine from the owner's vineyards in this family-run restaurant. Terrific terrace; plain rooms.
Route des Dentelles, 84190 Gigondas, Vaucluse. **Map** p224 C2. 04 90 65 85 01. FAX 04 90 65 83 80. b,l,d. **Rooms** 15. €€

Haut-de-Cagnes

Le Cagnard A restored medieval house with a panoramic position by the town ramparts.
Rue sous Barri, Haut-de-Cagnes, 06800 Cagnes-sur-Mer, Alpes-Maritimes. **Map** p225 F3. 04 93 20 73 21. FAX 04 93 22 06 39. @ cagnard@relaischateaux.com b,l,d. **Rooms** 24. €€€€

Hossegor

Les Huitrières du Lac The restaurant offers a lake view and suitably fishy menu. The view is shared by some of the large, simple rooms.
1187 av du Touring Club, 40150 Hossegor, Landes. **Map** p222 A4. 05 58 43 51 48. FAX 05 58 41 73 11. @ leshuitrieresdulac@wanadoo.fr b,l,d. **Rooms** 8. €€

Lalinde

Le Château Perched above the river, this mini chateau with a crop of turrets has comfy new rooms, a snug *salon* and established restaurant.
1 rue de la Tour, 24150 Lalinde, Dordogne. **Map** p222 B3. 05 53 61 01 82. FAX 05 53 24 74 60. b,l,d. **Rooms** 7. €€

Llo

L'Atalaya This rough-stone inn blends so well with the environment that it's hard to say where the craggy landscape stops and its walls begin. It has the double bonus of skiing on the doorstep in winter and hiking in summer. The rustic interior has polished wood and stone walls in the dining room; bedrooms are cosy.
Llo, 66800 Saillagouse, Pyrénées-Orientales.
Map p222 C5. 04 68 04 70 04. FAX 04 68 04 01 29.
@ atalaya@francimel.com b,l,d. **Rooms** 13.
Dec to Easter. MC, V. €€€

Malataverne

La Domaine du Colombier A watering place for pilgrims to Santiago de Compestela, this imaginatively converted stone house near the *autoroute* is an ideal stopover – indeed, so ideal that travellers may not want to leave. Now under the management of Anne and Thierry Chochois.
Route de Donzère, 26780 Malataverne, Drôme.
Map p224 B2. 04 75 90 86 86.
FAX 04 75 90 79 40. @ domainecolombier@voila.fr
b,l,d. **Rooms** 22, plus 3 suites. Never.
AE, DC, MC. €€

Madières

Château de Madières Spectacularly situated, teetering on the edge of a cliff above the Vis gorge, is this 14th-century fortress. Its rugged exterior masks a comfortable hotel, lovingly restored by the Brucys. It has an alluring galleried *salon*, and bedrooms where white walls are offset by strongly coloured furnishings.
Madières, 34190 Ganges, Hérault. **Map** p223 D4.
04 67 73 84 03. FAX 04 67 73 55 71. @ madieres@wanadoo.fr b,l,d. **Rooms** 9, plus 4 suites.
Nov to Easter. AE, MC, V. €€€

La Malène

Manoir de Montesquiou More like a castle than a manor and dating from the 15th century, this family-run establishment has a lurid history and a dramatic site between sheer rocks in the Gorges du Tarn. Inside, dark wood furniture and rich fabrics complete the picture. Some bedrooms are in the turrets, some have four-posters.
48210 La Malène, Lozère. **Map** p223 D3.
04 66 48 51 12. FAX 04 66 48 50 47.
@ montesquiou@demeurs-de-lozere.com b,l,d.
Rooms 12. Nov to Mar. DC, MC, V. €€

Mauzac

La Métairie Amid meadows and pine woods, is this tastefully done-up, creeper-clad farmhouse. Seductive pool and terrace; kind staff.
Millac, 24150 Mauzac, Dordogne. **Map** p222 B3.
05 53 22 50 47. FAX 05 53 22 52 93. @ metairie.la@wanadoo.fr b,l,d. **Rooms** 11, plus 1 suite. €€€

Mirmande

La Capitelle Old stone house with a great vista from the ramparts. Public rooms have vaulted ceilings, bedrooms are elegant and colourful.
Le Rempart, 26270 Mirmande, Drôme. **Map** p224 B1.
04 75 63 02 72. FAX 04 75 63 02 50.
@ capitelle@wanadoo.fr b,l,d. **Rooms** 11. €

Monticello, Corsica

A Pasturella Village life centres around the bar of this simple charming hostelry, where you will find delightful bedrooms and hearty food.
Monticello, 20220 l'Ile-Rousse, Haute-Corse.
Map p223 F5. 04 95 60 05 65. FAX 04 95 60 21 78.
b,l,d. **Rooms** 14. €

Montignac-Lascaux

Château de Puy Robert Plush furnishings and fine food at a neo-Renaissance Relais et Châteaux.
Route de Valojoulx, 24290 Montignac-Lascaux, Dordogne. **Map** p222 B3. 05 53 51 92 13.
FAX 05 53 51 80 11. @ chateau.puy.robert@wanadoo.fr
b,l,d. **Rooms** 38. €€€

For key to symbols see backflap. For price categories *see p217*

Mauroux

Hostellerie le Vert A side door leads into this 17th-century former farmhouse, now a compelling small hotel with exposed beams and stone walls. The bedrooms are attractive to return to at the end of a day out. The Philippes, a charming couple, work hard to ensure that guests have a perfect stay.
Mauroux, 46700 Puy-l'Evêque, Lot. **Map** p222 C3. 05 65 36 51 36. FAX 05 65 36 56 84. hotellevert@aol.com b,l,d. **Rooms** 7. mid-Nov to mid-Feb. AE, MC, V. €

Mimizan

Au Bon Coin du Lac The ever-cheerful and efficient Madame Caule warmly greets guests at her little stone-and-wood lakeside hotel. Monsieur Caule has gained a Michelin star and widespread renown for his gastronomic cooking. His speciality is seafood; it is served with due deference in the pretty, light dining room.
34 avenue du Lac, 40200 Mimizan, Landes. **Map** p222 A3. 05 58 09 01 55. FAX 05 58 09 40 84. b,l,d. **Rooms** 8. Feb. AE, DC, MC, V. €€

Meyrueis

Château d'Ayres Peace reigns in this handsome chateau set within the Cevennes national park. A splendid garden of mature cedars, oaks and sequoias is just one of its attributes. Others are wood-panelled rooms with superb antiques and paintings, and a menu of mouthwatering Languedoc specialities.
Route d'Ayres, 48150 Meyrueis, Lozère. **Map** p223 D3. 04 66 45 60 10. FAX 04 66 45 62 26. chateau-d-ayres@wanadoo.fr b,l,d. **Rooms** 27. mid-Dec to mid-Mar. AE, DC, MC, V. €€

Mougins

Les Muscadins The American owner has filled this appealing whitewashed hotel with antiques from the houses of *Muscadins* (18th-century fops) – hence the name. With a provençal garden and terrace with spectacular views, it is hard to resist. Bedrooms are sophisticated, and the Mediterranean cuisine is highly regarded.
18 blvd Courteline, 06250 Mougins, Alpes-Maritimes. **Map** p225 E3. 04 92 28 28 28. FAX 04 92 92 88 23. muscadins@alcyonis.fr b,d. **Rooms** 11. mid-Nov to mid-Dec. AE, DC, MC, V. €€€

Montsalvy

Auberge Fleurie At the core of this unpretentious inn are its two cheerful dining rooms, with red gingham tablecloths and gleaming wood dressers.
Place du Barry, 15120 Montsalvy, Cantal. **Map** p222 C3. 04 71 49 20 02. info@auberge-fleurie.com b,l,d. **Rooms** 7. €

Moudeyres

Le Pré Bossu This thatched stone cottage is set in fields and full of old-fashioned rural charm: wood floors, dressers, lace. Serious gourmet food.
43150 Moudeyres, Haute-Loire. **Map** p224 A1. 04 71 05 10 70. FAX 04 71 05 10 21. b,d. **Rooms** 6. €€

Mougins

Manoir de l'Etang This discreet and elegant 19th-century manor house offers a retreat from the bustle of fashionable Mougins – at a price.
allée du Manoir, 06250 Mougins, Alpes-Maritimes. **Map** 225 E3. 04 93 90 01 07. FAX 04 92 28 36 10. manoir.etang@wanadoo.fr b,l,d. **Rooms** 21. €€

Najac

L'Oustal del Barry A neat inn on the main square of a stunning village; a welcoming place which takes its cooking and wine very seriously.
Place du Bourg, 12270 Najac, Aveyron. **Map** p222 C3. 05 65 29 74 32. FAX 05 65 29 75 32. oustaldelbarry@caramail.com b,l,d. **Rooms** 22. €

Moustiers-Ste-Marie

La Bastide de Moustiers White-clad chefs collecting fresh vegetables and herbs from the garden are a common sight at Alain Ducasse's beautifully converted 17th-century *bastide*. With its exemplary cooking and its subtle decoration, the place is a celebration of Provence.
⊠ Chemin de Quinson, 04360 Moustiers-Ste-Marie, Alpes de Haute-Provence. **Map** p225 D3.
☎ 04 92 70 47 47. FAX 04 92 70 47 48.
@ contact@bastide-moustiers.com 🍴 b,l,d. **Rooms** 12.
● Never. AE, DC, MC, V. €€€€€

Noves

Auberge de Noves Not an auberge but a sumptuously fitted-out Provençal manor, owned and loved by three generations of the Lalleman family, and showing an inherited eye for detail. In a tranquil garden of olive, cypress and plane trees. Devotees can't stay away.
⊠ route de Châteaurenard, 13550 Noves, Bouches-du-Rhône. **Map** p224 B3. ☎ 04 90 24 28 28. FAX 04 90 24 28 00. @ noves@relaischateau.fr 🍴 b,l,d. **Rooms** 25.
● mid-Nov to Dec. AE, DC, MC, V.
€€€€

Najac

Hôtel Longcol A remote wooded valley of the Aveyron gorges shelters this ancient fortified farm. Owner Fabienne Luyckx is an accomplished hotelier, with a passion for Asian art, which is reflected in the bronzes, carvings and studded doors that fill the house. Prior booking essential.
⊠ 12270 La Fouillade, Najac, Aveyron. **Map** p222 C3.
☎ 05 65 29 63 36. FAX 05 65 29 64 28.
@ longcol@wanadoo.fr 🍴 b,l,d. **Rooms** 19.
● Never. MC, V. €€€

Olargues

Domaine de Rieumégé This is a hotel to suit every pocket, with accommodation ranging from simple, antique-filled bedrooms, to a luxury room and suite sharing a private pool. The stone house is set in the Haut Languedoc national park. The old barn makes a lovely dining room, and a fire warms the cosy *salon*.
⊠ Route de St-Pons, 34390 Olargues, Hérault.
Map p223 D4. ☎ 04 67 97 73 99. FAX 04 67 97 78 52.
@ rieumege@wanadoo.fr 🍴 b,l,d. **Rooms** 14.
● Oct to Mar. DC, MC, V. €€

Nans-les-Pins

Domaine de Châteauneuf Provençal-style 18th-century country house with lavish decoration.
⊠ Au Logis de Nans, 83860 Nans-les-Pins, Var.
Map p224 C4. ☎ 04 94 78 90 06. FAX 04 94 78 63 30.
@ chateauneuf@opengolfclub.com 🍴 b,l,d.
Rooms 30. €€€

Ornaisons

Relais du Val d'Orbieu The former mill has a large garden, pool and enviable wine cellar. Most of the airy bedrooms are in modern extensions.
⊠ 11200 Ornaisons, Aude. **Map** p223 D4. ☎ 04 68 27 10 27. FAX 04 68 27 52 44. 🍴 b,l,d. **Rooms** 20. €€

Piolenc

Auberge de l'Orangerie Entrance to the lively, distinctively decorated village inn is through an overgrown courtyard.
⊠ 4 rue de l'Ormeau, 84420 Piolenc, Vaucluse.
Map p224 B2. ☎ 04 90 29 59 88. FAX 04 90 29 67 74.
@ orangerie@orangerie.net 🍴 b,l,d. **Rooms** 5. €€

Pont-de-L'Arn

La Métairie Neuve The charming former farmhouse retains some of its original features: rafters, tiled floors and stone walls.
⊠ Bout Pont-de-L'Arn, 81660 Mazamet, Tarn.
Map p222 C4. ☎ 05 63 97 73 50. FAX 05 63 61 94 75.
@ lametairieneuve@wanadoo.fr 🍴 b,d. **Rooms** 14. €€

For key to symbols see backflap. For price categories *see p217*

Pauillac

Château Cordeillan-Bages Lovers of wine flock to this graceful *bordelais* château with its own vineyard; the wine list is extensive, of course, but it also hosts Ecole du Bordeaux wine courses. Public rooms have an English country house feel, while the bedrooms are the ultimate in designer chic.

Route des Châteaux, 33250 Pauillac, Gironde. **Map** p222 B3. 05 56 59 24 24. FAX 05 56 59 01 89. cordeillan@relaischateaux.com b,l,d. **Rooms** 25. mid-Dec to Jan. AE, DC, MC, V. €€€€

Plan-de-la-Tour

Mas des Brugassières Just 8km (5 miles) north of the resort of Ste-Maxime and set among vineyards, this comfortable *mas* has a friendly feel. Although it was built in the 1970s, the roof and floor tiles and the solid, wooden furniture are all traditional. The best bedrooms are those that have doors on to the garden.

Plan-de-la-Tour, 83120 Ste Maxime, Var. **Map** p225 E4. 04 94 55 50 55. FAX 04 94 55 50 51. mas.brugassieres@free.fr b. **Rooms** 14. 10 Oct to 20 Mar. MC, V. €€

Peillon-Village

Auberge de la Madone A twisting mountain road leads up to this appealing *logis*, where the Millo family welcome their guests with warmth and courtesy. Set just outside the village walls, the hotel offers a dining terrace, an organic Provençal restaurant and pleasant rooms (those in the annexe are cheapest).

06440 Peillon-Village, Alpes-Maritimes. **Map** p225 F3. 04 93 79 91 17. FAX 04 93 79 99 36. madone@chateauxhotels.com b,l,d. **Rooms** 15. 3 weeks Jan, mid-Oct to mid-Dec. MC, V. €€

Le Poët-Laval

Les Hospitaliers Owner Bernard Morin used to be an art dealer, which explains the many original pieces adorning this former stronghold. Spectacular views can be had from various vantage points; the best are the terrace, pool and top-floor *salon*. Service in the restaurant is superb.

26160 Le Poët-Laval, Drôme. **Map** p225 D2. 04 75 46 22 32. FAX 04 75 46 49 99. b,l,d. **Rooms** 22. mid-Nov to mid-Dec, Jan to mid-Mar. AE, DC, V. €€

Porquerolles

Auberge des Glycines This informal hotel in the port is brightly painted both inside and out, and set around a tree-filled courtyard.

Place d'Armes, 83400 Ile de Porquerolles, Var. **Map** p225 D5. 04 94 58 30 36. FAX 04 94 58 35 22. auberge.glycines@wanadoo.fr b,l,d. **Rooms** 11. €€€€

Ile de Port-Cros

Le Manoir Bedrooms in this handsome 19th-century manor have antiques and vistas over the fertile island. Good seafood.

Ile de Port-Cros, 83400 Hyères, Var. **Map** p225 E5. 04 94 05 90 52. FAX 04 94 05 90 89. lemanoir.portcros@wanadoo.fr b,l,d. **Rooms** 22. €€€

Porto-Vecchio, Corsica

Hôtel Belvédère Contemporary luxury, including a pool, private beach and rooms in the grounds.

Route de la Plage de Palombaggia, 20137 Porto-Vecchio, Corse-du-Sud. **Map** p223 F5. 04 95 70 54 13. FAX 04 95 70 42 63. info@nbcorsica.com b,l,d. **Rooms** 19. €€€€

Porto-Vecchio, Corsica

Grand Hôtel de Cala Rossa Glamorous modern hotel by the beach. Bedrooms are airy.

Cala Rossa, 20137 Porto-Vecchio, Corse-du-Sud. **Map** p223 F5. 04 95 71 61 51. FAX 04 95 71 60 11. patricia.biancarelli@wanadoo.fr b,l,d. **Rooms** 49. €€€€

Le Pontet-Avignon

Auberge de Cassagne Bungalow bedrooms in spruce grounds are done out in exuberant Provençal style. The *auberge* itself is a mellow old house and its location a leafy suburb. Chef Philippe Boucher is a protégé of the renowned Paul Bocuse, with his own reputation and Michelin star.

84130 Le Pontet-Avignon, Vaucluse. **Map** p224 B3.
04 90 31 04 18. FAX 04 90 32 25 09.
cassagne@wanadoo.fr b,l,d. **Rooms** 35.
Never. AE, DC, MC, V. €€€

Porticcio, Corsica

Le Maquis It started life some 50 years ago as a beach café; today it's a fashionable hotel with elegant rooms, its own beach, two swimming pools (one indoors, one out) and a tennis court which is floodlit at night. The rooms are luxurious and face the sea, and some have their own terraces.

20166 Porticcio, Corse-du-Sud. **Map** p223 F5.
04 95 25 05 55. FAX 04 95 25 11 70.
info@lemaquis. com b,l,d. **Rooms** 25.
Jan. AE, DC, MC, V. €€€€

Porquerolles

Mas du Langoustier Set on this unspoilt island, with no cars, the hotel is surrounded by its own extensive pine woods. Their scent wafts up to the original *mas* and modern building opposite, which houses the best of the bedrooms. There are two restaurants serving first-class food.

83400 Porquerolles, Var. **Map** p225 D5.
04 94 58 30 09. FAX 04 94 58 36 02.
langoustier@compuserve.com b,l,d. **Rooms** 52.
mid-Oct to Apr. AE, DC, MC, V. €€€€

Puymirol

Les Loges de l'Aubergade In a region not noted for its gastronomy, august cook Michel Trama offers outstanding food, wine and cigars in the ancient home of the Counts of Toulouse. Set around a patio, with a swimming pool at its centre, the modern rooms are done up with style.

52 rue Royale, 47270 Puymirol, Lot-et-Garonne.
Map p222 B3. 05 53 95 31 46. FAX 05 53 95 33 80.
trama@aubergade.com b,l,d. **Rooms** 10.
Feb. AE, DC, V. €€€€

Razac d'Eymet

La Petite Auberge A cosy farmhouse run by English in French style. Large grounds and swimming pool.

24500 Razac d'Eymet, Dordogne. **Map** p222 B3.
05 53 24 69 27. FAX 05 53 61 02 63.
lparazmet@aol.com b. **Rooms** 6. €

Roanne

Troisgros The legendary family-run restaurant has a suitably glossy dining room and high-tech bedrooms.

Place de la Gare, 42300 Roanne, Loire. **Map** p221 E5, p223 D2. 04 77 71 66 97. FAX 04 77 70 39 77.
troisgros@avo.fr b,l,d. **Rooms** 18. €€€€

Rocamadour

Les Vieilles Tours A medieval *gentilhommerie* with a snug *salon* in the turret and large, pleasing bedrooms. Lunch on request.

Lafage, 46500 Rocamadour, Lot. **Map** p222 C3.
05 65 33 68 01. FAX 05 65 33 68 59.
lesvieillestours@wanadoo.fr b,d. **Rooms** 17. €

Rochegude

Château de Rochegude A lavish Relais et Châteaux in a 12th-century fortress: palatial rooms, gourmet cuisine and fine wines.

26790 Rochegude, Drôme. **Map** p224 B2.
04 75 97 21 10. FAX 04 75 04 89 87. rochegude@relaischateaux.com b,l,d. **Rooms** 27. €€€€

Rocamadour

Domaine de la Rhue A skilful conversion of a 19th-century stable block has created a calm B&B with handsome evidence of its origins and flexible accommodation. Some of the country-style bedrooms have kitchenettes and their own garden entrances, making them ideal for families.

La Rhue, 46500 Rocamadour, Lot. **Map** p222 C3. 05 65 33 71 50. FAX 05 65 33 72 48. @ domainedelarhue@wanadoo.com b. **Rooms** 14. Oct to Easter. MC, V. €€

St-Cirq-Lapopie

La Pélissaria A 13th-century house clinging to a hillside in a captivating medieval village. The eccentric layout means that, from street-level, stairs lead down to the light bedrooms, many with terrific views over the Lot river. The hotel no longer has a restaurant, but there are several in the village.

St-Cirq-Lapopie, 46330 Cabrerets, Lot. **Map** p222 C3. 05 65 31 25 14. FAX 05 65 30 25 52. @ lapelissaria hotel@minitel.net b. **Rooms** 10. mid-Oct to mid-Apr. MC, V. €€

St-Bonnet-le-Froid

Auberge et Clos des Cimes The raison d'être of this unique hotel in an aptly named Auvergne village is its restaurant. Masterminded by talented chef Règis Marcon, it has won plaudits far and wide. His passion for mushrooms is evident in the names of the daringly decorated bedrooms, all boasting spectacular views.

43290 Le Village St-Bonnet-le-Froid, Haute-Loire. **Map** p223 D3. 04 71 59 93 72. FAX 04 71 59 93 40. @ contact@regismarcon.fr b,l,d. **Rooms** 12. Nov to Mar. AE, MC, V. €€€

St-Etienne-de-Baïgorry

Hôtel Arcé The Arcé family have been in charge here for five generations, and it is their hospitality that gives the hotel its special charm. In a pretty Basque village at the foot of the Pyrenees, it boasts a fabulous riverside location and a glorious dining terrace shaded by leafy chestnut trees.

64430 St-Etienne-de-Baïgorry, Pyrénées-Atlantiques. **Map** p222 A4. 05 59 37 40 14. FAX 05 59 37 40 27. @ reservation@hotel-arce.com b,l,d. **Rooms** 23. mid-Nov to mid-Mar. MC, V. €€€

Roquefort-les-Pins

Auberge du Colombier The charm of this low-built white *mas* lies in its heavenly large garden of tall trees and a pool.

06330 Roquefort-les-Pins, Alpes-Maritimes. **Map** p225 E3. 04 92 60 33 00. FAX 04 93 77 07 03. @ info@auberge-du-colombier.com b,l,d. **Rooms** 20. €€

Roussillon

Mas de Garrigon Modern hotel, built in Provençal style, run on house party lines.

Route de St-Saturnin d'Apt, Roussillon, 84220 Gordes, Vaucluse. **Map** p224 C3. 04 90 05 63 22. FAX 04 90 05 70 01. @ mas.de.garrigon@wanadoo.fr b,l,d. **Rooms** 9. €€€

St-Cyprien

L'Abbaye Walls and floors of delicate local stone throughout this enchanting hotel set in lush gardens, with a pool and tidy bedrooms.

24220 St-Cyprien, Dordogne. **Map** p222 C3. 05 53 29 20 48. FAX 05 53 29 15 85. @ hotel@abbaye-dordogne.com b. **Rooms** 23. €€

St-Emilion

Le Logis des Remparts Sit beneath a parasol or swim in the pool in the peaceful garden of this ancient stone-built house, now a cosy B&B.

18 rue Guadet, 33330 St-Emilion, Gironde. **Map** p222 B3. 05 57 24 70 43. FAX 05 57 74 47 44. @ logis-des-remparts@wanadoo.fr b. **Rooms** 17. €€

ST-JEAN-DU-BRUEL

Hôtel du Midi-Papillon Fans of this old rural posting inn have grown so numerous that bookings must be made months in advance. The welcoming Papillons continue a tradition of innkeeping of 150 years' standing. The food, all home-grown, home-reared or home-baked, is irresistible; prices are low.
12230 St-Jean-du-Bruel, Aveyron. **Map** p223 D4. 05 65 62 26 04. FAX 05 65 62 12 97. b,l,d. **Rooms** 18. mid-Nov to Easter. MC, V. €

ST-PAUL-DE-VENCE

La Grande Bastide The restoration of this country house combines new design with original materials such as local wood and stone. The 14 pastel-painted bedrooms are jazzed up with flamboyant Provençal prints. An alluring B&B where guests feel at home.
1350 route de la Colle, 06570 St-Paul-de-Vence, Alpes-Maritimes. **Map** p225 F3. 04 93 32 50 30. FAX 04 93 32 50 59. stpaullgb@voila.fr b,l. **Rooms** 14. end Nov to mid-Dec, early Jan to mid-Feb. AE, MC, V. €€€€

ST-MARTIN-VALMEROUX

Hostellerie de la Maronne Beyond a garden of lawns and trees lies the empty rolling countryside of the Auvergne, making this smartly decorated, grey-stone Relais du Silence a true haven. Madame De Cock's ambitious menu is accompanied by a tantalizing wine list.
Le Theil, 15140 St-Martin-Valmeroux, Cantal. **Map** p223 D3. 04 71 69 20 33. FAX 04 71 69 28 22. maronne@maronne.com b,d. **Rooms** 21. Nov to Mar. AE, DC, MC, V. €€

ST-PAUL-DE-VENCE

Le Hameau A path bordered by orange trees leads to this attractive white 1920s villa with red-tiled roofs. The scented garden of flowers and shrubs is the scene of unmissable breakfasts. Bedrooms are in rustic Provençal style; many have terraces or balconies. New owners have taken over from the Huvelins.
528 route de la Colle, 06570 St-Paul-de-Vence, Alpes-Maritimes. **Map** p225 F3. 04 93 32 80 24. FAX 04 93 32 55 75. lehameau@wanadoo.fr b. **Rooms** 17. mid-Nov to mid-Feb. MC, V. €€

ST-FÉLIX-LAURAGAIS

Auberge du Poids Public Michelin-starred restaurant in a village inn, with sublime food, rustic dining room and comfortable rooms.
31540 St-Félix-Lauragais, Haute-Garonne. **Map** p222 C4. 05 62 18 85 00. FAX 05 62 18 85 05. poidspublic@wanadoo.fr b,l,d. **Rooms** 10. €€

ST-JEAN-DE-LUZ

Le Parc Victoria The 19th-century villa is a model of style and correct housekeeping.
5 rue Cepé, 64500 St-Jean-de-Luz, Pyrénées-Atlantiques. **Map** p222 A4. 05 59 26 78 78. FAX 05 59 26 18 08. parcvictoria@wanadoo.fr b,l,d. **Rooms** 18. €€€€

ST-PAUL-DE-VENCE

La Colombe d'Or Elegantly rustic, with garden, pool and a marvellous art collection.
Place de Gaulle, 06570 St-Paul-de-Vence, Alpes-Maritimes. **Map** p225 F3. 04 93 32 80 02. FAX 04 93 32 77 78. contact@la-colombe-dor.com b,l,d. **Rooms** 26. €€€€

ST-PAUL-DE-VENCE

Les Orangers At the edge of the village, overlooking orange groves, is this chic, flower-filled Provençal farmhouse; impeccably kept.
Chemin des Fumerates, 06570 St-Paul-de-Vence, Alpes-Maritimes. **Map** p225 F3. 04 93 32 80 95. FAX 04 93 32 00 32. orangersauberge@aol.com b. **Rooms** 5. €€

St-Rémy-de-Provence

Château des Alpilles Nothing jars in this refined 19th-century manor house of pale stone, where bay trees flank the front door. The antique-laden *salons* feature moulded ceilings and mosaic floors; the Provençal bedrooms are spacious. Food can be eaten by the pool in summer.
Route Départmentale 31, 13210 St-Rémy-de-Provence, Bouches-du-Rhône. **Map** p224 B3. 04 90 92 03 33. FAX 04 90 92 45 17. @ chateau.alpilles@wanadoo.fr b,d. **Rooms** 15, plus 4 suites. mid-Nov to mid-Feb. DC, MC, V. €€€

Les Stes-Maries-de-la-Mer

Mas de la Fouque The exclusive Spanish-style ranch has an idyllic location beside a lagoon, where guests can glimpse flamingoes, egrets or the famous white horses of the Camargue. It's smart and luxurious yet family-run and friendly.
Route du Petit Rhône, 13460 Les Stes-Maries-de-la-Mer, Bouches-du-Rhône. **Map** p224 A4. 04 90 97 81 02. FAX 04 90 97 96 84. @ info@masdelafouque.com b,l,d. **Rooms** 19. mid-Nov to mid-Mar. AE, DC, MC, V. €€€€

St-Saud-Lacoussière

Hostellerie St-Jacques A cheerful ivy-clad village inn, whose exterior gives little hint of what lies beyond: beautiful gardens, sloping down to a pretty pool. The airy bedrooms and large summery bar/dining room have been decorated with care. The cooking doesn't disappoint. In summer, breakfast can be taken in the garden.
24470 St-Saud-Lacoussière, Dordogne. **Map** p222 B2. 05 53 56 97 21. FAX 05 53 56 91 33. @ hostellerie.st.jacques@wanadoo.fr b,l,d. **Rooms** 14, plus 2 suites. mid-Nov to Feb. AE, V. €€

Salon-de-Provence

L'Abbaye de Ste-Croix The highlight at this 12th-century former monastery is the Michelin-starred food, eaten in a charming, rustic dining room. The former cells house the bedrooms, but there's nothing Spartan about them now. A huge open fireplace warms the vaulted sitting room.
Route du Val-de-Cuech, 13300 Salon-de-Provence, Bouches-du-Rhône. **Map** p224 A4. 04 90 56 24 55. FAX 04 90 56 31 12. @ saintecroix@relaischateaux.com b,l,d. **Rooms** 25. Nov to mid-March. AE, DC, MC, V. €€€

St-Rémy-de-Provence

Domaine de Valmouriane A farmhouse and lovely garden, stylishly converted to plush hotel.
Petite Route des Baux, 13210 St-Rémy-de-Provence, Bouches-du-Rhône. **Map** p224 B3. 04 90 92 44 62. FAX 04 90 92 37 32. @ info@valmouriane.com b,l,d. **Rooms** 11. €€€€

St-Sernin-sur-Rance

Hôtel Carayon People flock from far and wide to sample Pierre Carayon's excellent cuisine. The riverside hotel offers great value for money.
Place du Fort, 12380 St-Sernin-sur-Rance, Aveyron. **Map** p222 C4. 05 65 98 19 19. FAX 05 65 99 69 26. @ carayon.hotel@wanadoo.fr b,l,d. **Rooms** 60. €

St-Tropez

La Ponche In the old town, an arty yet chic hotel in daring colours, where the seafood is superb. Overlooks a small fishing port and beach.
3 rue des Remparts, 83990 St-Tropez, Var. **Map** p225 E4. 04 94 97 02 53. FAX 04 94 97 78 61. @ hotel@laponche.com b,l,d. **Rooms** 18. €€€€

Salles-Curan

Hostellerie du Levezou A warm welcome and fine food await visitors to this 14th-century castle, set in a picturesque hill village.
Rue du Château, 12410 Salles-Curan, Aveyron. **Map** p223 D3. 05 65 46 34 16. FAX 05 65 46 01 19. @ info@hostelleriedulevezou.com b,l,d. **Rooms** 18. €

Sare

Hôtel Arraya Set on the main square of an archetypal Basque village, the 16th-century house was once a hostel for pilgrims to Santiago. It has an austere and off-putting façade, but inside lies an inn of great character and charm. Every corner and room is filled with polished pieces of fine local furniture. Adventurous cooking is a bonus.
⊠ 64310 Sare, Pyrénées-Atlantiques. **Map** p222 A4.
05 59 54 20 46. FAX 05 59 54 27 04.
@ hotel@arraya.com b,l,d. **Rooms** 20.
mid-Nov to late Mar. AE, MC, V. €€

Seillans

Hôtel des Deux Rocs A model hotel: an 18th-century house with blue shutters and a civilized air in a ravishing medieval village. The decor varies between the traditional in the public rooms and the dashing in the bedrooms. Breakfast in the cobbled square is a real treat. Recently taken over by French/English couple Bruno and Judy Germanaz.
⊠ Place Font d'Amont, 83440 Seillans, Var.
Map p225 E3. 04 94 76 87 32. FAX 04 94 76 88 68.
b,l,d. **Rooms** 14. Nov.to Feb. MC, V. €

Sauveterre-de-Béarn

Hôtel de la Reine Sancie A spectacular position on medieval arches above the Gave d'Oloron river makes this hotel exquisitely romantic. Rooms are pleasing and light, and a relaxed air prevails. To cap it all, the terrace is floodlit at night. The hotel is under the new ownership of two Irish brothers.
⊠ Rue du Pont de la Légende, 64390 Sauveterre-de-Béarn, Pyrénées-Atlantiques. **Map** p222 B4.
05 59 38 95 11. FAX 05 59 38 99 10.
b. **Rooms** 7. Never. AE, DC, MC, V. €

Target

Château de Boussac A chateau with all the accoutrements – moat, lake, park and magnificent rooms filled with Louis XV furniture – but none of the formality. Despite the grand setting, the charming Marquis and Marquise de Longueil welcome guests like old friends. The delectable dinners are eaten *en famille*.
⊠ Target, 03140 Chantelle, Allier. **Map** p223 D2.
04 70 40 63 20. FAX 04 70 40 60 03.
@ longueil@wanadoo.fr b,d. **Rooms** 5.
Dec to Mar. MC, V. €€

Sarlat

Hostellerie de Meysset Pine woods surround this long white house in the heart of Périgord Noir. Not surprisingly, the food is regional.
⊠ 62 Route Argentouleau, 24200 Sarlat, Dordogne.
Map p222 C3. 05 53 59 08 29. FAX 05 53 28 47 61.
b,l,d. **Rooms** 26. €€

Séguret

Auberge de Cabasse In rugged country, an appealing Swiss-run inn with its own vineyard.
⊠ Route de Sablet, 84110 Séguret, Vaucluse.
Map p224 B2. 04 90 46 91 12. FAX 04 90 46 94 01.
@ info@domaine-de-cabasse.fr b,l,d.
Rooms 14. €€€

Soustons

La Bergerie A pristine whitewashed house with trim grounds and a restful air; it's no hardship that the set dinner is obligatory.
⊠ Avenue du Lac, 40140 Soustons, Landes.
Map p222 A4. 05 58 41 11 43. FAX 05 58 41 21 61.
b,d. **Rooms** 12. €€

Tornac

Les Demeures du Ranquet The farmhouse restaurant, set in oak woods, is first class. The ten bedrooms are lush.
⊠ Route de St-Hippolyte, Tornac, 30140 Anduze, Gard.
Map p223 D4. 04 66 77 51 63. FAX 04 66 77 55 62.
@ ranquet@mnet.fr b,l,d. **Rooms** 10. €€€

Trémolat

Le Vieux Logis Wine and pigs once filled the dining room of this complex of farm buildings – a far cry from today's epitome of country chic, even though it has been home to the Giraudel-Destords for 400 years. Four-poster beds grace the rooms, antiques fill the *salon*'s every nook, and superb classic-modern cuisine is on offer.
24510 Trémolat, Dordogne. **Map** p222 C3.
05 53 22 80 06. FAX 05 53 22 84 89.
@ vieuxlogis@relaischateaux.com b,l,d. **Rooms** 26.
Never. AE, DC, MC, V. €€€€

Valence

Pic Despite the illustrious reputation of the restaurant, there isn't a hint of snobbery here. And though the great former owner Jacques Pic is dead, his daughter continues to create original dishes in their classic setting, as well as managing the more modest L'Auberge du Pin. Bedrooms are stunning.
285 avenue Victor-Hugo, 26001 Valence, Drôme.
Map p224 B1. 04 75 44 15 32. FAX 04 75 40 96 03.
@ pic@relaischateaux.com b,l,d. **Rooms** 15.
Never. AE, DC, MC, V. €€€€

Trigance

Château de Trigance You have to scale 100 rocky steps to gain access to this fabulous 11th-century castle, perched on a limestone peak. Owned by the Thomases for more than 30 years, it is a painstaking re-creation of the Middle Ages, with stone-vaulted dining room and canopied beds. Breakfast is taken on the battlements.
83840 Trigance, Var. **Map** p225 E3.
04 94 76 91 18. FAX 04 94 85 68 99.
@ trigance@relaischateaux.com b,l,d. **Rooms** 10.
Nov to late March. AE, DC, MC, V. €€€

Vence

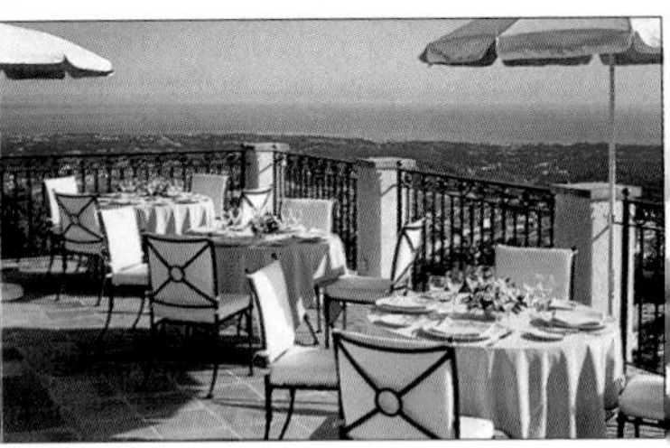

Château du Domaine St-Martin A stone's throw from the Matisse chapel, this former Templar stronghold is one of France's most expensive hotels. Bills will be extremely large, but devotees claim its sumptuous luxury and faultless service are worth it.
Avenue des Templiers, 06140 Vence, Alpes-Maritimes.
Map p225 F3. 04 93 58 02 02. FAX 04 93 24 08 91.
@ reservation@chateau-st-martin.com
b,l,d. **Rooms** 42. mid-Oct to mid-Feb.
AE, DC, MC, V. €€€€

Tourtour

L'Auberge St-Pierre The 16th-century building is a manor rather than an inn, with rooms that have a medieval flavour. Food is fresh from the farm.
Tourtour, 83690 Salernes, Var. **Map** p225 D4.
04 94 70 57 17. FAX 04 94 70 59 04. @ auberge stpierre@wanadoo.fr b,l,d. **Rooms** 16. €€

Touzac

La Source Bleue Cluster of old paper mills on the willow-fringed Lot makes a charming, restful, rustic retreat.
Moulin de Leygues, Touzac, 46700 Puy-l'Evêque, Lot. Map p222 C3. 05 65 36 52 01. FAX 05 65 24 65 69.
@ sourcebleue@wanadoo.fr b,l,d. **Rooms** 19. €€

Vaison-la-Romaine

Hostellerie Le Beffroi Old stone, beams and gleaming tiles abound in two hilltop houses.
Rue de l'Evêché Haute Ville, 84110 Vaison-la-Romaine, Vaucluse. **Map** p224 B2. 04 90 36 04 71.
FAX 04 90 36 24 78. @ lebeffroi@wanadoo.fr
b,l,d. **Rooms** 22. €€

Vallon-Pont-d'Arque

Le Manoir du Raveyron This rustic village inn offers simple accommodation, a warm welcome and excellent food at a very reasonable price.
rue Henri Barbuse, 07150 Vallon-Pont-d'Arc, Ardèche.
Map p223 D3. 04 75 88 03 59. FAX 04 75 37 11 12. @ le.manoir.du.raveyron@wanadoo.fr b,l,d. **Rooms** 14. €

Vence

La Roseraie A garden of palms, oleander and orange trees envelops this B&B, a *belle époque* villa of palest pink. Inside it has a lived-in feel, with walls covered in straw hats, dried flowers and old photos. One reader wrote to us of a disappointing experience here, but now under new management; further reports, please.
Avenue Henri Giraud, 06140 Vence, Alpes-Maritimes. **Map** p225 F3. 04 93 58 02 20. FAX 04 93 58 99 31. b. **Rooms** 14. mid-Nov to mid-Feb. AE, MC, V. €€

Villeréal

Château de Ricard An immaculate country house with manicured gardens, where even the ivy covering the façade looks perfect. Welcome extras include a library, billiard room and laundry. Interior decoration is the owners' forte, borne out by the chic rooms. A delicious dinner is served four nights a week.
Route de Beaumont, 47210 Villeréal, Lot-et-Garonne. **Map** p222 B3. 05 53 36 61 02. FAX 05 53 36 61 65. @ benjamin.deguilhem@wanadoo.fr b,d. **Rooms** 6. Oct to Apr. Not accepted. €€

Vialas

Hôtel Chantoiseau In the craggy landscape of the Cévennes, this 17th-century former post house boasts the most exciting restaurant for miles; here, mouthwatering Michelin-starred specialities are created by chef Patrick Pagès. Bedrooms are comfortable and well-kept if a trifle small, with splendid views.
48220 Vialas, Lozère. **Map** p223 D3. 04 66 41 00 02. FAX 04 66 41 04 34. b,l,d. **Rooms** 13. Nov to mid-Apr. AE, DC, MC, V. €€

Ydes

Château de Trancis The miniature Italianate chateau looks as if it has been transported from the banks of the Loire river, but in fact dates only from the 20th century. The interior has been fabulously furnished with antiques and rugs strewn on the polished floors. A charming Dutch couple run the place along house-party lines.
15210 Ydes, Cantal. **Map** p222 C3. 04 71 40 60 40. FAX 04 71 40 62 13. @ trancis@wanadoo.fr b,d. **Rooms** 7. 5 Jan to 5 Feb. AE, DC, MC, V. €€€

Vénasque

Auberge la Fontaine A classy restaurant with a bistro and five elegantly 'rustic' apartments.
Place de la Fontaine, Vénasque, 84210 Carpentras, Vaucluse. **Map** p224 B2. 04 90 66 02 96. FAX 04 90 66 13 14. @ fontvenasq@aol.com b,l,d. **Rooms** 5 apts. €€€

Villeneuve-les-Avignon

Hôtel de l'Atelier Built in the 16th century for a cardinal, a haven of calm with a delightful shady courtyard just outside the city centre.
5 rue de la Foire, 30400 Villeneuve-les-Avignon, Gard. **Map** p224 B3. 04 90 25 01 84. FAX 04 90 25 80 06. @ hotel-latelier@libertysurf.fr b. **Rooms** 23. €

Villeneuve-les-Avignon

La Magnaneraie Food is among the best of the region at this four star hotel with swimming pool.
37 rue Camp de Bataille, 30401 Villeneuve-les-Avignon, Gard. **Map** p224 B3. 04 90 25 11 11. FAX 04 90 25 46 37. @ magnaneraie.hotel@najeti.com b,l,d. **Rooms** 32, plus 4 apts. €€€

Vitrac

Auberge La Tomette A cheerful village inn among chestnut groves. Rustic panelled dining room, spotless bedrooms. Pool, garden.
15220 Vitrac, Cantal **Map** p222 C3. 04 71 64 70 94. FAX 04 71 64 77 11. @ latomette@wanadoo.fr b,l,d. **Rooms** 15. €

For key to symbols see backflap. For price categories *see p217*

FILHA
SB
NAUTILUS - SUB
NAUTILUS - SUB
SCOLA DE MERGULHO
TURBOLENTO
SESIMBRA

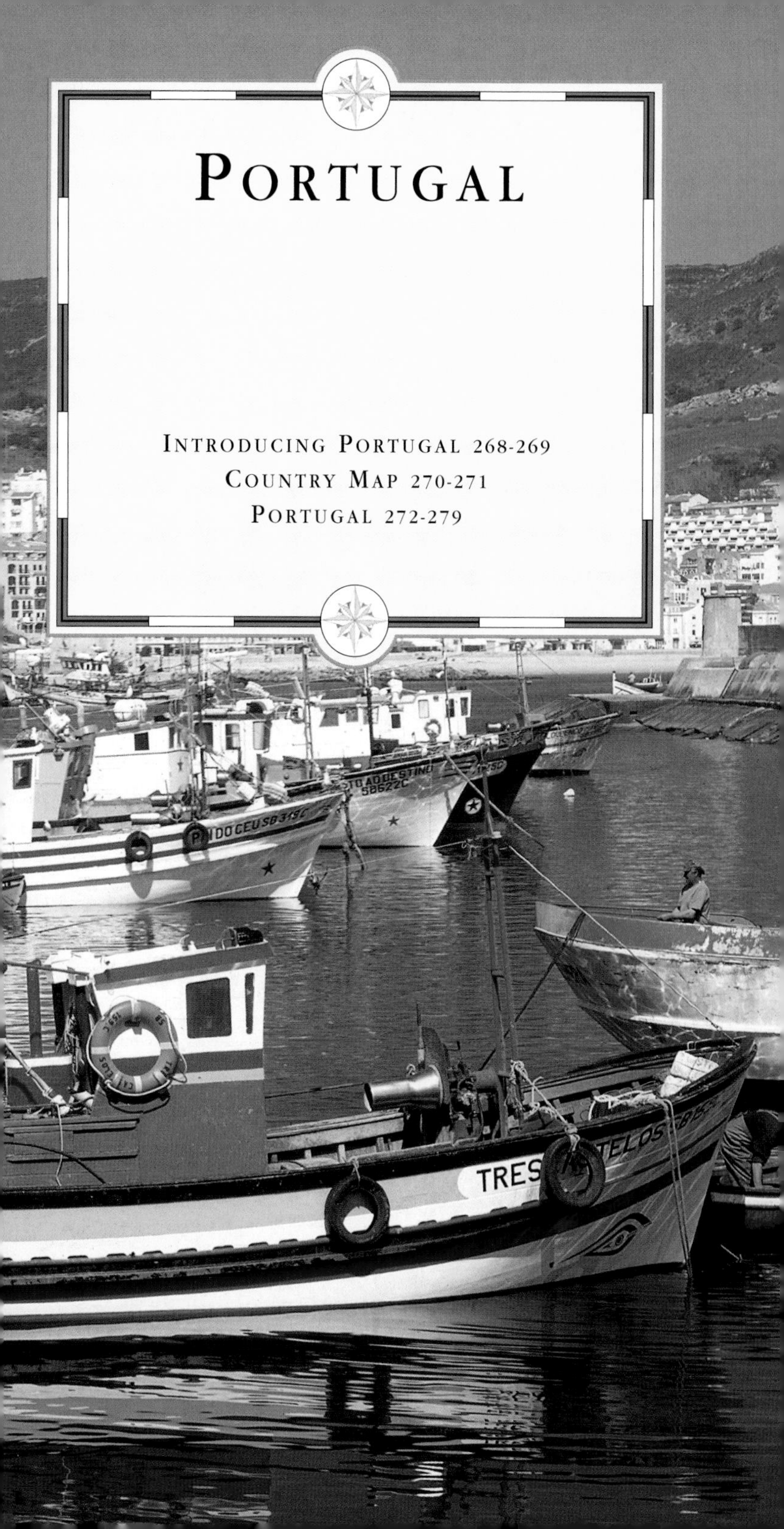

Portugal

PORTUGAL

SOME OF PORTUGAL'S most enticing places to stay are the grand but crumbling country houses which have opened their doors to paying guests as part of the *Turismo de Habitaçao* scheme. Choose between an apartment in a palace, a guest room in a *quinta* (manor house), or a *casa rustica* – a farm cottage converted into a self-catering apartment. There's also the government-run *pousada* network whose members offer a reliably high standard of accommodation, often in highly atmospheric or old historic buildings such as converted castles and monasteries. Many *pousadas* have the added advantage of being located in parts of the country otherwise lacking in interesting places to stay.

Castelo de Bom Jesus, a neo-Gothic 'castle' above Braga, page 272

PORTUGAL, REGION BY REGION

PORTUGAL CAN be divided into three regions: northern, central and southern.

Northern and Central Portugal
The granite-based Minho region is green from the masses of rain it receives. This is an agricultural area, and it's not at all unusual to see oxen pulling a cart, or women washing clothes in a water tank by the side of a country lane. There is plenty of accommodation in manor houses and farmhouses. The wild Atlantic coast at Viana do Castelo, and the fascinating historic towns of Barcelos and Guimarães, have a mix of *pousadas* and small, family-run guesthouses.

In the Douro valley, a steep gorge is flanked by terraced hillsides planted with vines which produce the region's port wine. Porto is the main city of the region. Places to stay include an Art Nouveau city-centre palace and a discreet, luxury 1940s hotel.

Inland, the old province of Trás-os-Montes is remote and mountainous, with the little-visited Beira Alta and Beira Baixa to the south. In the Beira Litoral, to the west, beautiful beaches of fine sand are pounded by Atlantic breakers; there are hotels in the resort of Póvoa de Varzim and near Aveiro.

The Ribatejo and the more interesting Estremadura which it flanks, encompass the coast all the way to Lisbon. There are attractive beach resort hotels, hill top castle *pousadas* (at Obidos and Setúbal), Coimbra with its ancient university, and the impressive palaces – and palace hotels – of Sintra and Estoril.

Southern Portugal
One of the most beautiful and little-known regions of Portugal is the Alentejo, an undulating landscape of grid-formation olive groves and cork oak forests. Here the *pousada* network comes into its own, with those at Evora and Vila Viçosa among the best. The Alentejo's Atlantic coast is a favourite among travelling surfers. There is a *pousada* with stunning panoramic views at Santa Clara-a-Velha.

The Algarve is now so built up that some travellers avoid it on principle. The exception is the area around Tavira, and the extreme west towards Sagres, where there are some excellent small guesthouses and villas.

Also included in this section are the islands of Madeira and the Azores. The latter may be difficult to reach (flights leave from Lisbon), but they are ideal places for getting away from it all, and for whale-watching. Accommodation is simple and atmospheric.

HIGHLIGHTS

HOTELS ILLUSTRATED on these introductory pages are by no means our only highlights. Unforgettable places also include Hotel Guincho at Cascais (page 273), a former sea fort; the Quinta da Alfarrobeira, a relaxed Algarve villa at Lagos (page 274); the Casa de Sezim, a relaxing and chic privately owned manor house with guest rooms in Guimarães (page 274); and the Convento de São Francisco, a cliff top monastery at São Miguel in the Azores (page 278).

Food and Drink

There are more than 365 recipes for *bacalhau* (salted codfish), the Portuguese national dish, so if you wish, you can eat it a different way every day of the year. People either love it or hate it, but it can be very good, especially cooked with chickpeas, olive oil and parsley. Other specialities are based on fish, often baked with potatoes and tomatoes in an earthenware dish. There are also simple meat dishes such as grilled rabbit, and more sophisticated ones such as steak in Madeira sauce. Often, people find that the simple country dishes are the most delicious.

Portuguese wines can be excellent, and their styles illustrate the country's wild variations in climate: acidic *vinho verde* and luscious ports, for instance, come from neighbouring regions. The deep reds of the Douro and Dão whites are also worth seeking out, along with the fruity southern reds.

Lunch runs from 1–3pm; dinner from 8pm to midnight, though all the *pousada* restaurants close promptly at 10pm. As part of the cover charge, you'll be brought a dish of savouries such as black pudding, grilled cheese and marinated olives.

Bedrooms and Bathrooms

If you want twin beds, ask for them specifically when booking. Unlike some other countries, double does mean a double – there's no sliding down the gap between two single mattresses pushed together. Most bathrooms are en suite and have a shower and bath combined. In some simple guesthouses, bathrooms are shared.

Other Practical Information

Some of the *pousadas* in historic buildings have just a few rooms which fill quickly; Lisbon's hotels and popular places on the coast are also often full at peak times.

Pousada de Santa Marinha, page 273

Breakfast is usually buffet-style, a spread of juices, breads and preserves, fruit, cheese, cold meats, cake and sometimes wine. Eggs, bacon and sausage are often provided in the *pousadas*.

Portuguese housekeeping standards mean that even the simplest place is usually spotlessly clean, and service extremely polite.

Note that signposting can be non-existent in rural areas, and in town centres there are complex one-way systems. Faxing ahead for a locator map is often worthwhile. But ask anyone the way, and they will invariably take great trouble to help you.

Language English is often not spoken – or understood.

Currency From 1 January 2002, the European *euro* (written 'EUR'), made up of 100 *cents*.

Shops Generally open 10am–7pm Mon–Fri, but many close for lunch or if business is slack, and, in Lisbon, for all of August. Some open 10am–1pm on Saturdays. Sunday opening is an alien concept. Banks are open 8:30am–3pm Mon–Fri.

Tipping A 10 per cent tip is the norm in restaurants; tipping taxi drivers is not obligatory, unless they have been particularly helpful.

Telephones Public call boxes are few. They take coins or phonecards. You can make use of the phone in almost any bar. It will be metered, and charged by the unit. For calls within Portugal, dial the entire nine-digit number including the first digit of the area code. To call Portugal from the UK (or the US), dial 00 351 (011 351).

Public holidays 1 January; Good Friday; 25 April (Anniversary of the Revolution); 1 May; 6 June (Corpus Christi); 10 June (Camões Day); 15 August; 5 October (Republic Day); 1 November; 1 December (Independence Day); 8 December (Feast of Immaculate Conception), 25 December.

Useful Words

Breakfast	*Pequeño-almoço*
Lunch	*Almoço*
Dinner	*Jantar*
Free room?	*Tem algum quarto livre?*
How much?	*Quanto?*
Single room	*Quarto individual*
Double room	*Quarto de casal*

Portugal Price Bands

Our price bands refer, as elsewhere in this guide, to the cost of a standard room in high season. Breakfast is usually included in the room price. Prices quoted tend to include all taxes, although this is not invariably the case.

€	under 75 EUR
€€	75–125 EUR
€€€	125–175 EUR
€€€€	over 175 EUR

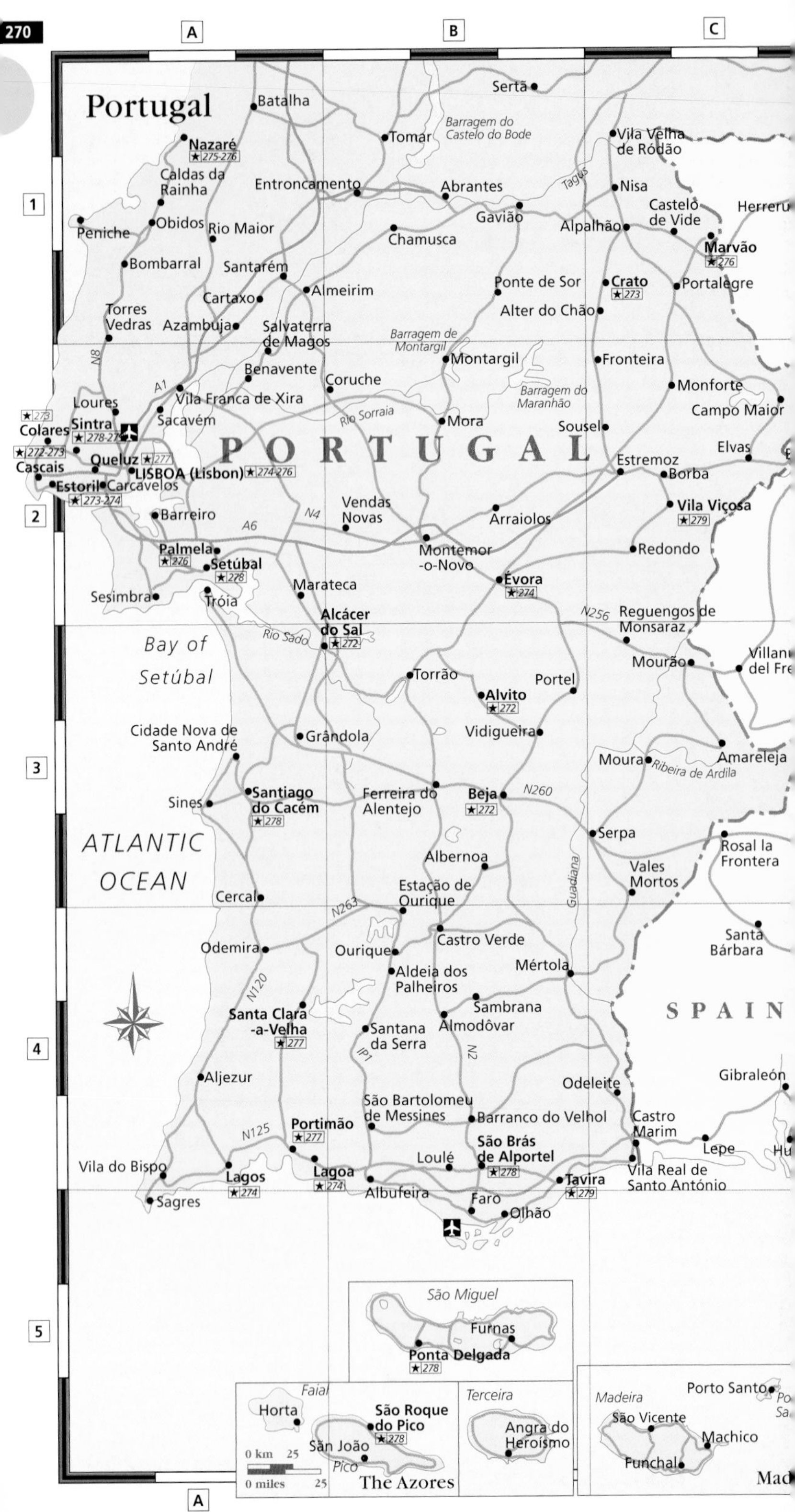

Portugal
PORTUGAL
SPAIN
ATLANTIC OCEAN
Bay of Setúbal
Batalha
Nazaré ★275-276
Caldas da Rainha
Peniche
Obidos
Rio Maior
Bombarral
Santarém
Cartaxo
Almeirim
Torres Vedras
Azambuja
Salvaterra de Magos
Benavente
Coruche
Tomar
Entroncamento
Abrantes
Chamusca
Sertã
Barragem do Castelo do Bode
Gavião
Tagus
Vila Velha de Ródão
Nisa
Alpalhão
Castelo de Vide
Marvão ★276
Herrera
Crato ★273
Portalegre
Ponte de Sor
Alter do Chão
Barragem de Montargil
Montargil
Fronteira
Monforte
Campo Maior
Barragem do Maranhão
Rio Sorraia
Mora
Sousel
Elvas
Estremoz
Borba
Vila Viçosa ★279
Redondo
Loures
Vila Franca de Xira
Sacavém
A1
N8
Colares ★273
Sintra ★278-277
Cascais ★272-273
Queluz ★277
LISBOA (Lisbon) ★274-276
Estoril ★273-274
Carcavelos
Barreiro
A6
N4
Vendas Novas
Arraiolos
Montemor -o-Novo
Évora ★274
Palmela ★276
Setúbal ★278
Sesimbra
Tróia
Marateca
Alcácer do Sal ★272
Rio Sado
N256
Reguengos de Monsaraz
Mourão
Torrão
Alvito ★272
Portel
Vidigueira
Grândola
Cidade Nova de Santo André
Sines
Santiago do Cacém ★278
Ferreira do Alentejo
Beja ★272
N260
Moura
Ribeira de Ardila
Amareleja
Serpa
Guadiana
Rosal la Frontera
Albernoa
Vales Mortos
Cercal
Estação de Ourique
N263
Castro Verde
Odemira
Ourique
Aldeia dos Palheiros
Mértola
Santa Bárbara
N120
Sambrana
Santa Clara -a-Velha ★277
Santana da Serra
Almodôvar
IP1
N2
Aljezur
Odeleite
Gibraleón
São Bartolomeu de Messines
Barranco do Velhol
Castro Marim
N125
Portimão ★277
São Brás de Alportel ★278
Lepe
Vila do Bispo
Lagos ★274
Lagoa ★274
Loulé
Tavira ★279
Vila Real de Santo António
Sagres
Albufeira
Faro
Olhão
São Miguel
Furnas
Ponta Delgada ★278
Faial
Horta
São Roque do Pico ★278
São João
Pico
Terceira
Angra do Heroísmo
0 km 25
0 miles 25
The Azores
Madeira
Porto Santo
São Vicente
Machico
Funchal
A
B
C
1
2
3
4
5

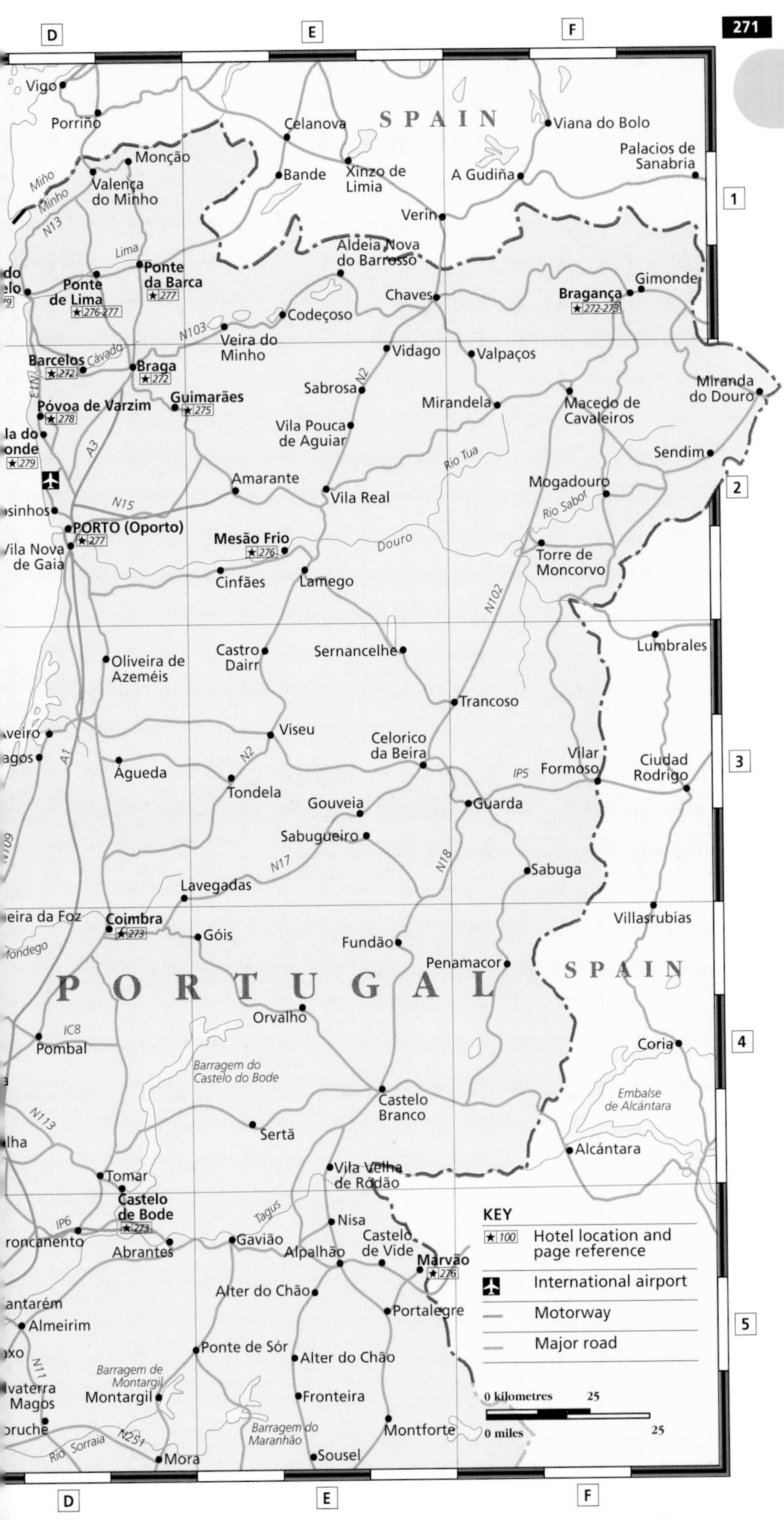

D
E
F
SPAIN
Vigo
Porriño
Celanova
Viana do Bolo
Palacios de Sanabria
Monção
Valença do Minho
Bande
Xinzo de Limia
A Gudiña
Verín
Miño
Minho
N13
Lima
Ponte da Barca
★277
Ponte de Lima
★276-277
Aldeia Nova do Barrosso
Chaves
Bragança
★272-273
Gimonde
Codeçoso
N103
Veira do Minho
Vidago
Valpaços
Barcelos
★272
Cávado
Braga
★272
Sabrosa
N2
Miranda do Douro
Mirandela
Macedo de Cavaleiros
Póvoa de Varzim
★278
Guimarães
★275
Vila Pouca de Aguiar
A3
Sendim
Rio Tua
Amarante
Mogadouro
N15
Vila Real
Rio Sabor
PORTO (Oporto)
★277
Mesão Frio
★276
Douro
Torre de Moncorvo
Vila Nova de Gaia
Cinfães
Lamego
N102
Oliveira de Azeméis
Castro Dairr
Sernancelhe
Lumbrales
Trancoso
Viseu
Celorico da Beira
A1
Águeda
N2
Tondela
Vilar Formoso
IP5
Ciudad Rodrigo
Gouveia
Guarda
Sabugueiro
N109
N17
N18
Sabuga
Lavegadas
Coimbra
★273
Villasrubias
Góis
Fundão
Penamacor
PORTUGAL
SPAIN
Orvalho
IC8
Pombal
Coria
Barragem do Castelo do Bode
Embalse de Alcántara
Castelo Branco
N113
Sertã
Alcántara
Vila Velha de Ródão
Tomar
Castelo de Bode
★273
IP6
Tagus
Nisa
Abrantes
Gavião
Alpalhão
Castelo de Vide
Marvão
★276
Alter do Chão
Almeirim
Portalegre
Ponte de Sór
Alter do Chão
N11
Barragem de Montargil
Montargil
Fronteira
Barragem do Maranhão
Montforte
Rio Sorraia
N251
Mora
Sousel
KEY
★100 Hotel location and page reference
International airport
Motorway
Major road
0 kilometres 25
0 miles 25
1
2
3
4
5
D
E
F

Alcácer do Sal

Dom Alfonso II Pousada In a stunning setting on the estuary of the river Sado, this pousada offers luxurious accommodation in the old castle of Alcácer do Sal. This is an area rich in history, natural history, long, sandy beaches and sporting pursuits ranging from golf to paint-ball. The restaurant specializes in local dishes.
7580 Alcácer do Sal. **Map** 270 A3. (26561) 3070. FAX (26561) 3074. guest@pousadas.pt b,l,d. **Rooms** 34. Never. AE, DC, MC, V. €€€

Alvito

Pousada Castelo de Alvito A life-sized knight in armour stands guard at reception – appropriate for this castle which looks as though it has come straight out of a picture book. The stylish rooms are large; some have original stone-arched and mullioned windows overlooking the village. Outside, peacocks stalk the grounds and pool.
7920 Alvito. **Map** p270 B3. (284) 48 07 00. FAX (284) 48 53 83. guest@pousadas.pt b,l,d. **Rooms** 20. Never. AE, DC, MC, V. €€€€

Barcelos

Quinta do Convento da Franqueira Englishma Piers Gallie produces some 30,000 bottles of vinho verde a year on this estate, owned by his family since 1965. The 16th-century building was once a monastery. Rooms are furnished with antique furniture in restful style; there's also a lounge with games, books and a bar. An ancient spring now feeds the swimming pool.
4755 Barcelos. **Map** p271 D2. (253) 83 16 06. FAX (253) 83 22 31. b. **Rooms** 5. 1 Nov–1 May. AE, V. €€

Cascais

Casa da Pergola There's something of the English manor house about this busy guesthouse in central Cascais, with its mantel clocks, wood-panelled sittingroom ceiling and tea and scones in the afternoon. The pretty front garden is not really for lounging, but rooms are comfortable and have a personal feel.
Avenida Valbom 13, 2750 Cascais. **Map** p270 A2. (21) 484 00 40. FAX (21) 483 47 91. pergolahouse@vizzavi.pt b. **Rooms** 10. 15 Dec–1 Feb. Not accepted. €€

Beja

Pousada de São Francisco Serene former convent which retains it Gothic chapel. The cloister has been glassed in.
7800 Beja. **Map** p270 B3. (284) 31 35 80. FAX (284) 32 91 43. info@pousadas.pt b,l,d. **Rooms** 34, plus 1 suite. €€€

Braga

Albergaria Senhora-a-Branca A city-centre hotel with large bedrooms and a roof terrace; good selection of restaurants in Braga's old town.
58 Largo da Senhora-a-Branca, 4710 Braga. **Map** p271 D2. (253) 26 99 38. FAX (253) 26 99 37. albergariasrabranca@oninet.pt b. **Rooms** 21. €

Braga

Castelo Bom Jesus Late-18th-cenutry Neo-Gothic 'castle' on a hill above Braga. An attractive place to stay.
Tenoes Bom Jesus, 4710 Braga. **Map** p271 D2. (253) 67 65 66. FAX (253) 67 76 91. b. **Rooms** 12. €€

Bragança

Moinho do Canico There is plenty of fishing to be had near this old watermill, now a guesthouse furnished in country style. Peaceful setting.
Av. Abade de Bacal, Ponte de Castrelos, 5300 Castrelos, Bragança. **Map** p271 F1. FAX (273) 32 35 77. moinho@bragancanet.pt b. **Rooms** 2. €

Cascais

Estalagem Villa Albatroz This small harbourfront hotel creates a cocoon of soft white carpets and soothing interiors that you won't want to leave. And you don't have to: the excellent restaurant has great views of the port, and the fashionably decorated bedrooms are inviting. Guests may use a neighbouring hotel's pool.
Rua Fernandes Tomás 1, 2750-342 Cascais. **Map** p270 A2. (21) 486 34 10. FAX (21) 484 46 80. villaalbatroz@albatrozhotels.com b,l,d. **Rooms** 10. Never. AE, DC, MC, V. €€€€

Estoril

Amazonia Lennox Each of the vast bedrooms are named after golf courses (St Andrews, Muirfield, and so on) and antique clubs and trophies decorate the walls; appropriate for a hotel near some great courses. The interiors are decorated with colours and furniture in keeping with the 1930s' architecture.
Rua Eng Álvaro Pedro de Sousa 5. **Map** p270 A2. (21) 468 04 24. FAX (21) 467 08 59. reservas@amazoniahotelis.com b,l,d. **Rooms** 34. Never. AE, DC, MC, V. €€

Coimbra

Hotel Quinta das Lágrimas The hotel is close to the centre of Coimbra in a 20-acre park with rare camphor tree, palms, figs and sequoias. The name means 'house of tears' after a 14th-century legend, but these days all is serene with a good quota of *luxe* all round. Among the attractions is a nine-hole pitch-and-putt golf course.
Apartado 5053, Santa Clara, 3041-901 Coimbra. **Map** p271 D4. (239) 802380. FAX (239) 441695. reservas@quintadaslagrimas.pt b,l,d. **Rooms** 39. Never. AE, DC, MC, V. €€€

Guimarães

Pousada Santa Marinha This former convent is now dedicated to earthly pleasures. The 12th-century building is monumental, but retains a human, homely scale. Due to reopen late 2003 after renovation work, with pool to follow in 2004. Try to book a cell-like room with four-poster bed in the old building.
Largo Domingos Leite Castro, 4810 Guimarães. **Map** p271 D2. (253) 51 12 49. FAX (253) 51 44 59. recepcao.stamarinha@pousadas.pt b,l,d. **Rooms** 51. Never. AE, DC, MC, V. €€€

Bragança

Pousada de São Bartolomeu A modern *pousada* with blonde-wood furnishings and views across the valley to Bragança castle and village.
5300 Bragança. **Map** p271 F1. (273) 33 14 93. FAX (273) 32 34 53. recepcao.sbartolomeu@pousadas.pt b,l,d. **Rooms** 28. €€€

Cascais

Hotel Fortaleza do Guincho This former sea-fort is virtually surrounded by ocean. Four-poster beds, open fires and a Michelin-starred restaurant.
Estrada do Guincho, 2750-642 Cascais. **Map** p270 A2. (21) 487 04 91. FAX (21) 487 04 31. reservations@guinchotel.pt b,l,d. **Rooms** 27. €€€€

Castelo de Bode

Pousada de São Pedro An homage to hydro-electric power, this relaxing *pousada* is close to a dam and large reservoir, good for windsurfing.
2300 Tomar. **Map** p271 D4. (249) 38 11 59. FAX (249) 38 11 76. info@pousadas.pt b,l,d. **Rooms** 25. €€€

Colares

Estalagem de Colares Dedicated owner Cristina de Sousa's country inn is surrounded by vineyards, and has a good regional restaurant.
Estrada Nacional 247, 2705-199 Colares. **Map** p270 A2. (21) 928 29 42. FAX (21) 928 29 83. b,l,d. **Rooms** 12. €€

Lagoa

Almansor A modern, upmarket hotel with some Moorish touches to the decoration, set next to a beautiful rocky cove. It's a busy place; facilities include indoor and outdoor pools and a beauty salon. There is live music and entertainment each night. Bedrooms are a gentler affair, with airy sea views and Portuguese print fabrics.
Praia do Carvoeiro, 8401-911 Carvoeiro, Lagoa.
Map p270 A4. (282) 35 11 00. FAX (282) 35 13 45.
@ almansor@mail.telepac.pt b,l,d. **Rooms** 293.
Never. AE, DC, MC, V. €€

Lagos

Quinta da Alfarrobeira A relaxed, environmentally conscious Dutch couple bought this farmhouse in 1996, and now rent out two self-contained cottages. Set back from the sea, with beautiful views, this is the perfect place to lounge by the pool, go for cycle rides, or read under the giant alfarrobeira tree.
Estrada do Palmares, 8600 Odeáxere, Lagos.
Map p270 A4. (282) 79 84 24. FAX (282) 79 96 30.
@ bakker@mail.telepac.pt None. **Rooms** 2 cottages.
Never. Not accepted. €€

Lisbon

As Janelas Verdes The small 18th-century palace hotel has the facilities of a much larger place. There's a beautiful courtyard garden and an antique-packed lounge to relax in, 24-hour room service and business facilities. Famous Portuguese novelist Eça de Queirós immortalized the house in his novel *Os Maias*. Recently extended.
Rua das Janelas Verdes 47, 1200-690 Lisbon.
Map p270 A2. (21) 396 81 43. FAX (21) 396 81 44.
@ jverdes@heritage.pt b. **Rooms** 29. Never.
AE, DC, MC, V. €€€€

Lisbon

Four Seasons Ritz With contemporary tapestries and assured decoration, this is one of Portugal's best and biggest hotels. Service is excellent, but despite the grandeur, there is no affectation. Renowned French chef Stéphane Hestin enhances the reputation of an already celebrated panoramic restaurant.
Rua Rodrigo da Fonseca 88, 1099-039 Lisbon.
Map p270 A2. (21) 381 14 23. FAX (21) 383 17 83.
@ reservations.lis@fourseasons.com b,l,d. **Rooms** 282.
Never. AE, DC, MC, V. €€€€

Crato

Flor da Rosa Pousada Once a monastery of the Order of the Knights of Malta, now a luxury hotel with swimming pool, gourmet restaurant and all mod cons.
7430-999 Crato. **Map** p270 C1. (245) 997210.
FAX (245) 997212. b,l,d. **Rooms** 24. €€€

Estoril

Hotel Palácio Once popular with deposed European royalty, the atmosphere is now relaxed. Great pool, lawn for sunbathing; golf nearby.
Rua do Parque, 2769 Estoril. **Map** p270 A2.
(21) 468 04 00. FAX (21) 468 48 67. @ palacioestoril@mail.telepac.pt b,l,d. **Rooms** 162. €€€€

Evora

Pousada de Evora–Lóios Evora is one of Portugal's highlights, and this *pousada* – a convent turned luxury hotel – is in the old town centre.
Largo Conde de Vila Flor, 7000-804 Evora.
Map p270 B2. (266) 73 00 70. FAX (266) 70 72 48.
@ guest@pousadas.pt b,l,d. **Rooms** 32. €€€€

Evora

Quinta da Espada Surrounded by cork oaks, this farm estate rents out several cottages. There is an honesty bar and a small pool.
Estrada de Arraiolos, 7002-501 Evora. **Map** p270 B2.
(266) 73 45 49. FAX (266) 73 64 64. @ quintadaespada@clix.pt b,d (by arrangement). **Rooms** 7. €

Lisbon

Palácio Belmonte Built as a palace in the 16th century, the hotel – a national monument – has wonderful views over Lisbon's Alfama quarter, and atmospheric interiors (in one suite, Wim Wenders filmed *Lisbon Story*). Guests have free range of salons, music room, library, café and art gallery.
✉ Páteo Dom Fradique 14, 1100-624 Lisbon. **Map** p270 A2. ☎ (21) 881 66 00. FAX (21) 881 66 09. @ office@palaciobelmonte.com 🍴 b (l,d on request). **Rooms** 8 suites plus 3 apts. Never. AE, MC, V. €€€€

Lisbon

Solar do Castelo Occupying a former 18th-century mansion built on the site of the kitchens of the even older Alcacova Palace, devastated by an earthquake in 1755, the Solar do Castelo has been transformed into an eclectic, design-conscious modern hotel by architect Vasco Massapina. The hotel has no restaurant.
✉ Rua das Cozinhas 2, 1100-181 Lisbon. **Map** p270 A2. ☎ (351) 218 870909. FAX (351)218 870907. @ solar.castelo@heritage.pt 🍴 b. **Rooms** 14. Never. AE, DC, MC, V. €€€€

Lisbon

Quinta Nova da Conceição Waking to the sound of cocks crowing in the morning, you could forget that this small guesthouse is only 12 minutes by metro from central Lisbon. Guests live with the family and their dogs in a house full of ancient objects and stained glass. Outside is a lush garden, pool and tennis court.
✉ Rua Cidade de Rabat 5–1, 1500 Lisbon. **Map** p270 A2. ☎ (21) 778 00 91. FAX (21) 772 47 65. @ qtnovaconceicao@netcabo.pt 🍴 b. **Rooms** 3. Never. AE, DC, MC, V. €€€

Nazaré

Quinta do Campo This very grand private home is still a working farm, and the garden can be a bit noisy, but the Quinta is a place well worth seeking out. Rooms vary: some have brass bedsteads and azulejos-tiled bathrooms, others floral fabrics and 1920s' baths; all have a special atmosphere, as do the sitting rooms and library.
✉ Valado dos Frades, 2450 Nazaré. **Map** p270 A1. ☎ (262) 57 71 35. FAX (262) 57 75 55. @ quintadocampo@mail.telepac.pt 🍴 b. **Rooms** 8, plus 7 apartments. Never. DC, MC, V. €€

Guimarães

Casa de Sezim A grand manor house; guest rooms are chic and full of character, with Murano glass chandeliers and dark wooden floors.
✉ Santo Amaro, 4800 Guimarães. **Map** p271 D2. ☎ (253) 52 30 00 FAX (253) 52 31 96. @ geral@sezim.pt 🍴 b (l,d on request). **Rooms** 9. €€

Guimarães

Paço São Cipriano Romantics will love the tower room with Sleeping Beauty bed; this palace has plenty else too, from topiary garden to pool.
✉ Tabuadelo, 4835-461 Guimarães. **Map** p271 D2. ☎ (253) 56 53 37. FAX (253) 56 58 89. @ info@pacoscipriano.com 🍴 b. **Rooms** 7. €€

Guimarães

Pousada Nossa Senhora da Oliveira
A popular historic-centre *pousada*, done out in Gothic style. Excellent food.
✉ Rua Santa Maria s/n, Apartado 101, 4801 Guimarães. **Map** p271 D2. ☎ (253) 51 41 57. FAX (253) 51 42 04. @ guest@pousadas.pt 🍴 b,l,d. **Rooms** 10. €€€

Lisbon

Britânia Restored in 1997 to its former glory from the Art Deco era, when it was built to Cassiano Branco's designs. No restaurant, but a clubby bar.
✉ Rua Rodrigues Sampaio 17, 1150–278 Lisbon. **Map** p270 A2. ☎ (21) 315 50 16. FAX (21) 315 50 21. @ britania.hotel@heritage.pt 🍴 b. **Rooms** 30. €€€€

Palmela

Castelo de Palmela Pousada Nestled within the hilltop castle of Palmela, this pousada offers panoramic views of the area, which includes the Costa Azul, the prehistoric caves at Quinta do Anjo and the Arrábida Natural Park, home to 450 species of beetle and much else besides. After a day's exploration, enjoy the impressive restaurant with fine local wines.
Castelo de Palmela, 2950-997 Palmela. **Map** p270 A2. (21) 235 1226. FAX (21) 233 0440. b,l,d. **Rooms** 28. Never. AE, DC, MC, V. €€€€

Ponte de Lima

Casa das Pereiras Large, ancient house in the old town. The dark landing – with its own altar – is lit by a stone window in the shape of a Maltese Cross. The hall and lounge – a mix of 1970s' sofas and suits of armour – can be chilly, but the bedrooms are well heated and atmospheric, with panelled ceilings and carved wooden beds; modern bathrooms.
Largo das Pereiras, 4990 Ponte de Lima. **Map** p271 D1. FAX (258) 94 29 39. b. **Rooms** 3. Never. Not accepted. €

Ponte de Lima

Casa de Outeiro With its oil paintings, Oriental rugs and ancient library and lounge smelling of woodsmoke and leather-bound books, Casa de Outeiro abounds in faded grandeur. It is owned by the same family as the nearby Quinta do Sanguerinho (see below). Rooms have ancient beds and terracotta- and black-tiled floors; there's also a self-contained apartment.
Arcozelo, 4990 Ponte de Lima. **Map** p271 D1. (258) 94 12 06. FAX (253) 60 26 01. b. **Rooms** 7. Never. AE. €€

Ponte de Lima

Casa de Pomarchão Choose between self-catering apartments or rustic cottages on this large but slightly crumbling estate. It has been in the same family for 500 years; the owners' apartments – which guests may get to see if they are invited in for an *aperitivo* – are crammed with family photos, armour and other heirlooms.
Arcozelo, 4990 Ponte de Lima. **Map** p271 D1. (258) 74 17 42. FAX (258) 74 27 42. b. **Rooms** 10 apts and cottages. mid-Dec to mid-Apr. Not accepted. €€

Lisbon

Lisboa Plaza This town-centre hotel has been owned by the same family since it was opened in 1953. Fine modern decor.
Tv. Salitre 7/Av. Liberdade, 1269–066 Lisbon. **Map** p270 A2. (21) 321 82 18. FAX (21) 347 16 30. plaza.hotels@heritage.pt b,l,d. **Rooms** 112. €€€€

Marvão

Pousada de Santa Maria A warm, friendly mountain-top *pousada* by the border with Spain. Restaurant has great views.
Rua 24 de Janeiro 7, 7330 Marvão. **Map** p270 C1, p271 E5. (245) 99 32 01. FAX (245) 99 34 40. enatur@mail.telepac.pt b,l,d. **Rooms** 29. €€€

Mesão Frio

Pousada Solar da Rêde This 18th-century manor house in the Douro wine region is now a beautifully restored *pousada*. Own vineyard.
Santa Cristina, 5040 Mesão Frio. **Map** p271 E2. (254) 89 01 30. FAX (254) 89 01 39. solar.da.rede@douroazul.com b,l,d. **Rooms** 29. €€€€

Nazaré

Hotel Praia This no-frills hotel is included for its central location in a lively resort. Bedrooms are modern and have balconies, some with sea views.
Av. Vieira Guimarães 39, 2450 Nazaré. **Map** p270 A1. (262) 56 14 23. FAX (262) 56 14 36. hotel.praia@clix.pt b,l,d. **Rooms** 40. €

Ponte de Lima

Quinta do Salguerinho At the end of a narrow granite lane and drive lined with acanthus plants and arum lilies, in a rambling garden, are these two cottages. The wood-built *alpendre* serves as a summer house and winter suntrap, and there are plenty of games and space for children. Rooms are traditionally furnished.
Lugar do Salguerinho, Arcozelo, 4990 Ponte de Lima. **Map** p271 D1. (258) 74 16 72. FAX (258) 93 13 20. @ info@center.pt b. **Rooms** 6, plus 1 suite. Never. AE, DC, MC, V. €

Queluz

Pousada Dona Maria I In 1995 this *pousada* opened in what were once the servants' quarters for the royal palace opposite; you may still get to witness the arrival of delegates on state occasions. Inside, the huge, high-ceilinged rooms are traditionally furnished with great flair. Makes a good base for Lisbon, 5km (3 miles) away.
2745 Queluz. **Map** p270 A2. (21) 435 61 58. FAX (21) 435 61 89. @ recepcao.dmaria@pousadas.pt b,l,d. **Rooms** 26. Never. AE, DC, MC, V. €€€

Portimão

Quinta Rosa de Lima This simple villa makes a pleasant change from the chain hotels of the Algarve, and is close to the beach, restaurants and nightlife of Praia da Rocha. The land by the villa – covered by vineyards and trees – belongs to the owners, so will never be built on. Inside, furniture is simple and rustic. Guests may use the pool at the nearby Penina hotel.
Estrada da Torre, 8500 Portimão. **Map** p270 A4. FAX (282) 41 10 97. b. **Rooms** 7. Dec. Not accepted. €

São Brás de Alportel

Pousada de São Brás Set back from the scrum of the Algarve's coastal strip, this *pousada* is a short drive from the port of Tavira with its restaurants and beaches. It's an unpretentious place, with bright and cheerful fabrics in the (small) rooms, a good pool and well-maintained tennis court and a pile of magazines in the bar.
8150-054 São Brás de Alportel. **Map** p270 B4. (289) 84 23 05. FAX (289) 84 17 26. @ info@pousadas.pt b,l,d. **Rooms** 31, plus 2 suites. Never. AE, DC, MC, V. €€€

Ponte da Barca

Torre de Quintela A friendly, family-owned farm estate with guest rooms, billiards table, vineyards and its own chapel. Closed Nov-March.
Nogueria, 4980 Ponte de Barca. **Map** p271 D1. (258) 45 22 38; mobile 0936 566 08 62. b; l,d on request. **Rooms** 3. €

Ponte de Lima

Casa das Torres This family-run 18th-century manor house has some guest rooms opening onto the terrace and swimming pool; there's also table tennis, billiards and a bar.
Lugar de Arribão, Facha, 4990 Ponte de Lima. **Map** p271 D1. FAX (258) 94 13 69. b. **Rooms** 3. €-€€

Porto (Oporto)

Hotel Castor A decent, central, inexpensive place to stay – rare for Porto – with a marble foyer, eclectic furnishings, and Italian restaurant.
Rua das Doze Casas 17, 4000-195 Porto. **Map** p271 D2. (22) 537 00 14. FAX (22) 536 60 76. b,l,d. **Rooms** 63. €

Porto (Oporto)

Hotel Infante de Sagres In central Porto, an Art Nouveau feast for the eyes, with stained-glass stairwell and lounges filled with *chinoiserie*.
Praça D. Filipa de Lencastre 62, 4050-259 Porto. **Map** p271 D2. (223) 398 500. FAX (223) 398 599. @ his.sales@mail.telepac.pt b,l,d. **Rooms** 72. €€€€

Santa Clara-a-Velha

Pousada Santa Clara-a-Velha Balconies and terraces make the most of the hilltop location, which gives a 360-degree view of forests, hills and lake. The main attraction is the setting, but the standard of the accommodation is high. Don't miss the chance to eat here: the chef has won an award for her regionally inspired dishes.
7665 Santa Clara-a-Velha. **Map** p270 A4. (283) 88 22 50. FAX (283) 88 24 02. @ info@pousadas.pt b,l,d. **Rooms** 19. Never. AE, DC, MC, V. €€€

Sintra

Casa Miradouro The Swiss owner of this red-and-yellow striped house just outside the centre of Sintra has lavished care and attention on each of the light, airy rooms; many have great views in different directions, to the Pena Palace on the hill and towards the sea. There's also a large, comfortably furnished sitting room.
Rua Sotto Mayor 55, Apartado 1027, 2710 Sintra. **Map** p270 A2. (21) 910 71 00. FAX (21) 924 18 36. @ mail@casa-miradouro.com b. **Rooms** 6. early Jan to mid-Feb. AE, MC, V. €€

Setúbal

Pousada de São Filipe Bedrooms are in the former dungeons, but there are no ghosts here – or so they say. This is one of the nicest *pousadas* close to Lisbon. In summer there are *fado* nights (*fado* is a mix of blues and flamenco). The restaurant is a good place to start the evening before going on to the packed bars of Setúbal.
2900 Setúbal. **Map** p270 A2. (265) 55 00 70. FAX (265) 53 92 40. @ recepcao.sfilipe@pousadas.pt b,l,d. **Rooms** 16. Never. AE, DC, MC, V. €€€

Sintra

Tivoli Palácio Seteais Escapists will love this 18th-century pleasure palace on a hill above Sintra; it's now a five-star hotel exuding contentment. There are plenty of tapestries and plush fabrics but the pastoral wall-paintings and pale wood floors keep everything light. Terraces make the most of the splendid views.
Av. Barbosa do Bocage 10, Seteais, 2710-517 Sintra. **Map** p270 A2. (21) 923 32 00. FAX (21) 923 42 77. @ reservas.seteais@tivoli.pt b,l,d. **Rooms** 30. Never. AE, DC, MC, V. €€€€€

Póvoa de Varzim

Luso-Brasileiro An unpretentious hotel built in 1910 in the middle of the action in one of northern Portugal's popular beach resorts.
Rua dos Cafés 16, 4490 Póvoa de Varzim. **Map** p271 D2. (252) 69 07 10. FAX (252) 69 07 19. b. **Rooms** 62. €

Pico

Casa das Barcas A black-and-white house with traditional rooms; fishing and diving nearby.
Cais Velho, 9940 São Roque do Pico, Azores. **Map** p270 B5. (292) 64 28 47. FAX (292) 64 26 61. @ info@cazasdopico.com b (l,d by arrangement). **Rooms** 4. €€

Santiago do Cacém

Quinta da Ortiga Pousada Restful pousada in a typical Alentejo farm estate, a few minutes from Santiago do Cacém and the beaches of the San Vicente Coast. Terraced gardens, swimming pool.
7540 Santiago do Cacém. **Map** p270 A3. (269) 82 2871. FAX (269) 82 2073. b,l,d. **Rooms** 40. €€

São Miguel

Convento de São Francisco Sleep in an antique bed in front of an open fire in this 17th-century island monastery.
9680 Vila Franca do Campo, São Miguel, Azores. **Map** p270 B5. (296) 58 35 32. FAX (296) 58 35 34. b. **Rooms** 10. €€

Tavira

Quinta do Caracol A collection of whitewashed buildings, this quinta has the look of a small village. The accommodation consists of two-bedroomed apartments with brick floors, a small kitchen and sitting area; outside, an old water tank has been turned into a pool. Dinner is based on the best produce at market that day.
Rua São Pedro, 8800 Tavira. **Map** p270 B4. (281) 32 24 75. FAX (281) 32 31 75. quintadocaracol@netc.pt b (l,d by arrangement). **Rooms** 7 apartments. Never. AE. €€

Vila do Conde

Quinta São Miguel de Àrcos The hunting rifle over the fireplace, the antique beds and bright spreads, and the homely sitting room set the rustic style at this old farmhouse. There's a good restaurant in the village nearby. Not much English is spoken, except by the owners' son Antonio who lives in the house.
Rua da Igreja 209, 4480-018 Arcos, Vila do Conde. **Map** p271 D2. (919) 37 22 02. FAX (252) 65 20 94. ajr@vodafone.pt b. **Rooms** 5. Never. AE. €

Viana do Castelo

Casa de Santa Ana The spotless rooms with antique beds, wood floors and drawn-threadwork curtains each have a private terrace or balcony, the latter with views of the sea. In the garden you can sit out under a pergola and catch the scent of orange blossom and the gentle sound of a trickling fountain.
Lugar da Armada, 4900-012 Afife. **Map** p271 D1. (217) 78 31 33. FAX (258) 98 17 74. stana@netcabo.pt **Rooms** 6. b,d (by arrangement). 1 Jan to end Feb. Not accepted. €

Vila Viçosa

Pousada Dom João IV The lavishly restored hotel was originally a convent for the ladies of the noble Bragança family. It has kept the best of the old – including frescoed side chapels – and merged them with a contemporary take on cloisters and kitchen garden. The whole place is stylish but very relaxing; the food is excellent.
7160 Vila Viçosa. **Map** p270 C2. (268) 98 07 42. FAX (268) 98 07 47. recepcao.djoao@pousadas.pt b,l,d. **Rooms** 36. Never. AE, DC, MC, V. €€€

Sintra

Quinta da Capela This elegant 16th-century farmhouse has antique-filled rooms, polished terracotta floors, and a sauna and small gym.
Estrada Velha de Colares, 2710 Sintra. **Map** p270 A2. (21) 929 01 70. FAX (21) 929 34 25. quintadacapela@hotmail.com b. **Rooms** 8. €€€

Tavira

Convento de Santo António Formerly home to Capuchin monks, this 17th-century monastery maintains its aura of calm. Cloisters, garden, swimming pool.
Atalaia 56, 8800 Tavira. **Map** p270 B4. FAX (281) 32 56 32. b. **Rooms** 6. €€

Viana do Castelo

Pousada do Monte Santa Luzia A grand hotel built in 1903 on a hill above town, where the air is scented by pine needles. Bedrooms are large.
4900 Viana do Castelo. **Map** p271 D1. (258) 80 03 70. FAX (258) 82 88 92. fernandofernandes@pousadas.pt b,l,d. **Rooms** 48. €€€

Vila Viçosa

Casa de Peixinhos A manor house guesthouse with antiques, leather armchairs and the Passanha family's coat of arms over the fireplace. Dinner by arrangement (book 24 hours ahead).
7160 Vila Viçosa. **Map** p270 C2. (268) 98 04 72. FAX (268) 88 13 48. b,l,d. **Rooms** 9. €€

Spain

Spain

It is said that Spain is not one country, but several. It has by far the greatest range of landscapes in Europe, four distinct languages, many cultures, and, in Madrid and Barcelona, two of Europe's most dynamic cities. The country which was once known for its high-rise package ghettoes today offers a broad and eclectic choice of characterful accommodation; from former monastic cells to dream-like Gaudíesque hotels, and from converted castles to farmsteads. Even Tenerife, that temple of 'pile-it-high and sell-it-cheap' tourism, also offers the traveller a stunningly-sited *parador* and numerous rural hideaways.

Hotel San Gil, page 325, one of Seville's most striking buildings

Spain Region by Region

Spain divides roughly into six regions and two major cities.

Northwest Spain
The long beaches and green, rural landscapes of Galicia, Asturias and Cantabria are a world away from package-holiday Spain. The region varies enormously in its landscapes, from the mountains and valleys of the Picos de Europa, to Spain's little-known fjord country, the Rias Baixas. Here, *casas rurales*, or country holiday homes (page 284), are very popular. The city of Santiago de Compostela, its great cathedral for centuries the goal of pilgrims, has both luxurious and spartan accommodation for its many thousands of visitors.

Northeast Spain
From the Atlantic and Bilbao in the west, Northeast Spain runs through the Basque country, Navarra, La Rioja, Aragon, the Pyrenees and northern Catalonia to reach the Mediterranean.

By contrast to Bilbao's exuberantly new-wave Guggenheim Museum, San Sebastian is long-established as the most elegant and fashionable of all the Spanish seaside resorts. It offers an interesting, wide range of accommodation and some very fine luxury hotels. Walkers in the the Pyrenees are less pampered, with *refugios*, basic mountain huts, and more comfortable *residencias-casa de payés*, as *casas rurales* are called in these parts.

Eastern Spain
Spain's eastern coastline is the land of the Costas, from Brava in the north to Blanca in the south. Long stretches (though by no means the whole coastline) are marred by fast-buck holiday developments, but step just a little way back from the beach bars and discos and normal service is quickly resumed.

Barcelona
Rivalling or surpassing Madrid in many aspects, Barcelona may officially be number two in Spain, but it is *numero uno* as far as most visitors are concerned. Its Old Town oozes an ancient and salty atmosphere but the city is probably best know for its Modernist architecture, some of the most original of which comes from the stable of the hugely talented Antoni Gaudí. Barcelona has some superb

The Real at Santander, page 304, built for a king's entourage

visitor attractions, great bars and a buzzing nightlife. The city's most characterful hotels are on or just off Spain's most famous street, Las Ramblas.

Central Spain

Taking in the provinces of Castilla Y León, Castilla-La Mancha and Extremadura, the sun-scorched central plateau (*meseta*) surrounding Madrid is the Spain of Cervantes' Don Quixote and El Cid: epic landscapes dotted with picturesque windmills and imposing castles. A deep sense of history permeates the region, captured in the awe-inspiring Gothic cathedrals of Burgos and León, the stunningly-preserved medieval capital of Toledo, the perfect Renaissance architecture of Salamanca and the fairy-tale towers of Segovia's castle.

To the west is wild and parched Extremadura, Spain's most remote area. It receives relatively few foreign visitors, but Cuenca, with its famous hanging houses, the marvellous Roman city of Mérida and the Gothic-Renaissance buildings of Cáceres make the trip well worthwhile. Government-run hotels, or *paradores* (page 284), offer some of the best places to stay in the Central region.

Madrid

Not nearly as attractive nor as visitor-friendly as Barcelona, Madrid is a large modern capital, chiefly visited for its world-class museums and art galleries. However, it also has Spain's best shopping, excellent bars, and the country's most frenetic nightlife. In Madrid, accommodation is largely functional, with location rating higher than character.

Andalucia

This is the Southern Spain of popular imagination – flamenco, bullfighting, sherry, white cubist villages (*pueblos blancos*) and fields of sunflowers. It is also an enormously varied region, from desert in the east to the vast watery Doñana National Park in the west, with the snow-topped Sierra Nevada mountains, the historic city of Granada and long golden beaches nearby. In the historic Moorish-influenced cities of Granada, Seville and Córdoba, Andalusia boasts three of Spain's most beautiful and popular tourist destinations. Literally all kinds of accommodation are found in Andalucia, with the emphasis switching in recent years from coastal to rural.

The Islands

The Canaries and the Balearics have long been a byword for cheap, packaged tourism. There are exceptions however, the most striking being the northwest coast of Mallorca, which now features some of Spain's finest country house properties. Peace and quiet and individual rural accommodation can also be found in the beautiful, lesser-known Canary Islands of La Palma and La Gomera.

Highlights

Hotels illustrated on these introductory pages are by no means our only highlights. Other high points include the splendid Ritz in Madrid, page 311; the charming Castillo el Collado, page 300; Almud, page 303, a stable block converted into a B&B with exquisite taste; and luxurious Finca Buenvino, page 320.

Rural Tourism

A policy of *Agroturismo* or *turismo rural* (rural tourism) has been embraced by the Spanish government to help convert *fincas* (farms or estates) into country holiday homes known as *casas rurales*. Properties vary in size and may be in the wilds or just a mile or two from a busy resort. Owners usually accept just a few visitors at one time. Facilities and atmosphere vary greatly. Most allow for self-catering. What all *casas*

Hotel El Montiboli, La Vila Joiosa, page 327

Canoeing, organized by the Posada de Sigueruelo, page 313

rurales should have in common is that they offer peaceful surroundings, an insight into local culture and some degree of personal service. They are most numerous in Northern and Central Spain, and in Catalonia, where they are called *casa de pagès* or *casa de payés*. They are also becoming common in Galicia and Cantabria (*casas de labranza*) and in Andalucia.

Monastic Cells

Spain has a long tradition of offering rooms to pilgrims and travellers. See, for example, page 299. Nowadays this form of hospitality is extended to tourists in some 150 monasteries and convents. A cell can consist of anything from a room almost as spartan as it sounds, deep in the heart of a monastery, to a charming converted apartment with its own garden.

Cells are most often found in Benedictine and Cistercian monasteries and convents in rural towns and villages, or around such cities as Burgos, León, Madrid and Segovia. Some of these stipulate married couples only, others have single-sex restrictions, and in others you will be expected to help with the washing up and to tidy your room.

Parador de Hondarribia, page 299

Paradores

Spain's most notable hotel grouping is the state-run chain of *paradores* (*parador* means inn or stopping place). The most famous are housed in stunning historic buildings: former palaces, castles, royal hunting lodges, monasteries and so on. All are furnished and decorated in strictly vernacular style and should offer local cuisine of a high standard. But there are also modern, functional *paradores*, deliberately sited where there is (or was) a dearth of other satisfactory accommodation. The advantages of this type of *parador* are usually a splendid location and views worth travelling miles to enjoy.

Paradores started as a cheap form of lodging, but they are now expensive and many have been overtaken by converted properties offering similar, but better-value accommodation. Moreover, as government-run hotels, they can lack the personal touch and warmth of welcome.

Food and Drink

Spanish cuisine is as varied as its many regions. In the north is abundant fish and seafood from the Atlantic; the mountains and hills provide hams, sausages and game, which are often combined with beans to form hearty stews (a recurring theme throughout the country). The Basque Country, with its orientation towards the sea, is recognised as the gastronomic centre of all Spain.

In Madrid and the central region, game is plentiful and one-pot meat-and-pulse stews are generally the order of the day. Suckling pig and lamb, sausages and other pork dishes are common. *Cocido madrileno*, a slow-simmered stew of beef, chicken, ham, pork belly, chickpeas plus various other items, is the regional favourite.

The cuisine of both south and east coasts is mainly Mediterranean, but influenced by the Moors who introduced olives, oranges, almonds, saffron and rice. The last of these two are in Spain's most famous dish, *paella*, which has many ingredients, including seafood, chicken, rabbit and pork.

Catalonia's sophisticated and inventive combinations include fish and seafood stews and classic *romesco* sauce (red peppers, tomatoes and chillies).

Fried fish is the food of the south, with *fritura de pescados* (deep-fried squid and fish) a favourite with both visitors and locals. By contrast, some of Spain's best *jamón serrano* (cured ham) comes from the mountains of Andalucia.

Gazpacho, a chilled raw soup based on tomatoes, cucumber and peppers, is a Spanish culinary classic, as are *tapas*. Originating in Andalucia, but served all over Spain, *tapas* are snacks whose name stems from the traditional bartender's practice of covering a glass with a saucer or *tapa* (cover) on which was placed a bite-sized morsel. *Tapas* are nowadays eaten as snacks or combined to make up a full meal. Classic *tapas* include *tortilla* (potato omelette), *albondigas* (meatballs), cured ham, cheese, olives and many types of fish and seafood

La Rioja is the country's most prestigious wine-producing region, while the Pinedès region of Catalonia is the home of sparkling wine, or *cava*, as well as producing high-quality still wines. Sherry is Spain's great vinous invention, named after Jerez de la Frontera in Andalucia, where it is still made.

The lavish Bobadilla at Loja, page 321, makes a Moorish 'village'

Bedrooms and Bathrooms

Double beds are sometimes provided as conventional doubles as in Britain and the USA; sometimes as two singles pushed together. If you want a double, ask for a *cama de matrimonio*.

Other Practical Information

Book well in advance for hotels in Madrid, Barcelona and in any resort in high season. During Spain's festivities (including Easter Week) rooms are impossible to get, or charged at outrageously inflated prices.

Spanish breakfasts tend to be simple – coffee, rolls and fruit juice. *Paradores*, however, increasingly offer wide-choice buffet breakfasts. Lunch is traditionally the main meal of the day, starting around 1pm. Dinner is served late in the evening, around 9pm (earlier in tourist resorts); in summer, restaurants may open past midnight as people eat dinner later and later. At weekends, restaurants tend to be filled at lunchtime by large and boisterous family groups.

Language Spanish (Castillian) is the national language; you may also come across Catalan, Gallego (in Galicia) and Euskera (in the Basque Country). English is spoken widely in tourist centres and most, but not all, large towns.

Currency From 1 January 2002, the European *euro* (written 'EUR'), made up of 100 *cents*.

Shops Traditionally open 10–2pm and 5–8pm, Mon–Fri, and on Saturday morning. In resorts they may open all day and at weekends.

Tipping The Spanish rarely tip waiters more than 5 per cent. It is usual to tip tour guides and taxi drivers 10 per cent, and to leave a small amount for chambermaids.

The Maria Cristina, page 303

Telephoning Spanish phone numbers have no zero in front of the area code. To call Spain from the UK dial 00 34; from the US, 011 34, then the full number.

Public holidays 1 January; 6 January; Maundy Thursday, Good Friday and Easter Sunday; 1 May; 15 August; 12 October; 1 November; 6 December; 25 December.

Useful Words

Breakfast	*Desayuno*
Lunch	*Comida*
Supper	*Cena*
Free room?	*¿Habitación libre?*
How much?	*¿Cuánto?*
Single	*Habitación individual*
Double	*Un habitación doble*

Spain Price Bands

Spanish hotels are officially classified by stars, from one to five. Don't be distracted: our price bands are simpler and refer to the price of a standard double room in high season, almost always excluding breakfast. Hotels rarely quote prices exclusive of VAT; other unexpected extras are rare.

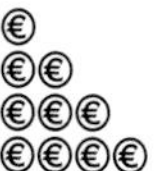

€	up to 70 EUR
€€	70–120 EUR
€€€	120–170 EUR
€€€€	over 170 EUR

A
B
C
1
2
3
4
5
Spain
ATLANTIC OCEAN
PORTUGAL
Ortigueira
Cervo
Viveiro
Figueras del Mar
★298
Ferrol
Neda
★301
Fene
Ribadeo
★300
N634
Villalonga
★306
A CORUÑA
Betanzos
Villalba
N634
Taramundi
★303
Carballo
N550
A9
N640
Figueras
★298
A Toxa (Toja)
★306
C552
Rábade
Santiago de Compostela
★304
N547
Melide
LUGO
Muros
Cornide
★296
Ulla
A6
Embalse de Belesar
La Estrada
Lalín
Ribeira
Chantada
Escairón
★296
Villafranca del Bierzo
Cambados
★295
Monforte
PONTEVEDRA
★300
Carballiño
A52
OURENSE
VIGO
Ponteareas
Puebla de Trives
★299
N550
N540
Bayona
★293-294
Xinzo de Limia
Monção
A Gudiña
A52
Valença do Minho
Miño
Minho
A Guarda (La Guardia)
★299
A52
Verín
★305
Viana do Castelo
Lima
N101
N212
Chaves
Bragança
N2
Braga
Guimarães
N15
Rio Tua
Rio Sabor
Vila Real
Matosinhos
PORTO (Oporto)
Douro
Vila Nova de Gaia
Lamego
Torre de Moncorvo
A1
Oliveira de Azeméis
Aveiro
Viseu
Celorico da Beira
Vagos
IP5
Vilar Formoso
Guarda
★308
Figueira da Foz
Mondego
Coimbra
Pombal
Barragem do Castelo do Bode
Leiria
Castelo Branco
Coria
Embalse de Alcántara

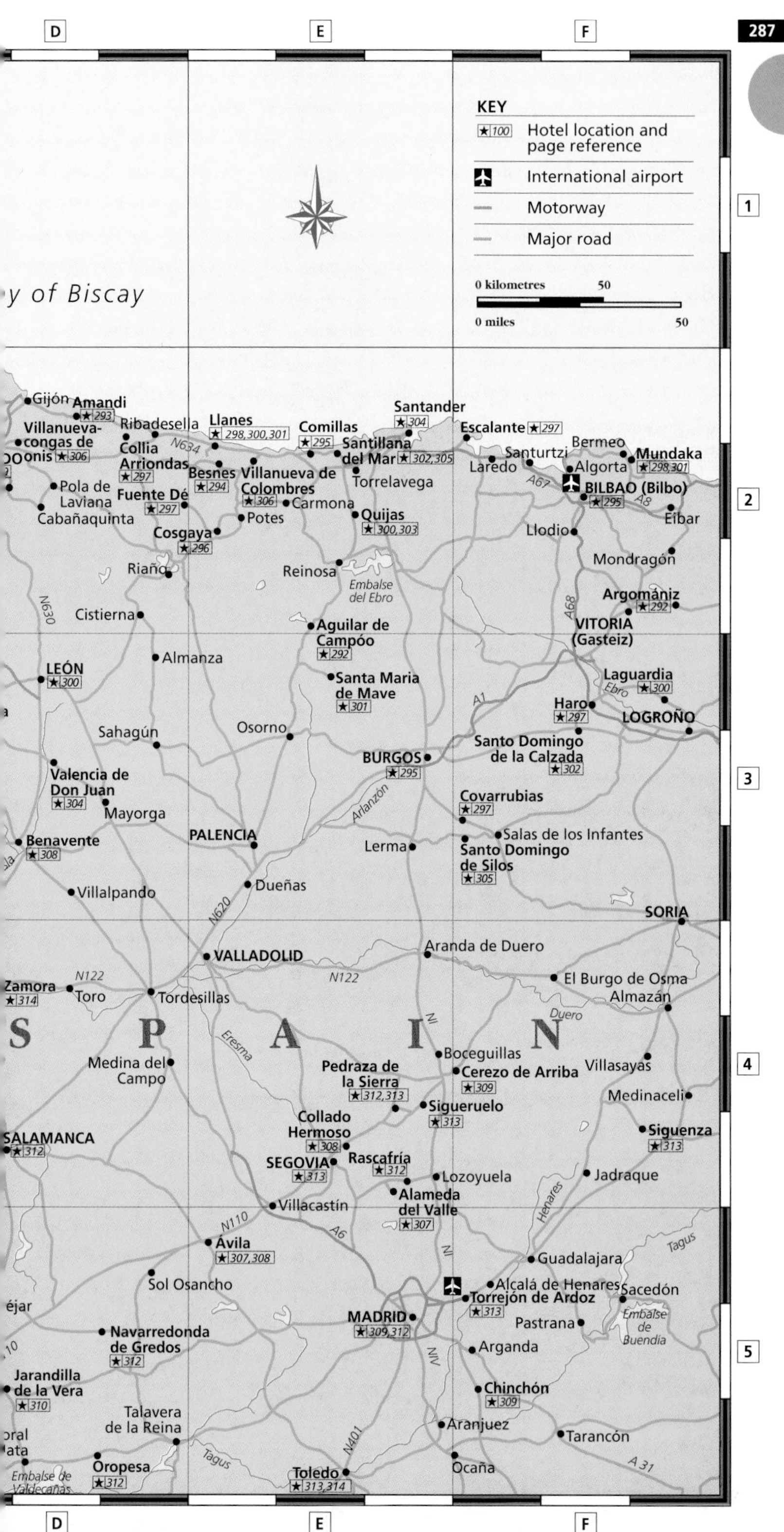
KEY
100 Hotel location and page reference
International airport
Motorway
Major road
0 kilometres 50
0 miles 50
y of Biscay
Gijón
Amandi 293
Villanueva-congas de onis 306
Ribadesella
Llanes 298,300,301
Comillas 295
Santander 304
Santillana del Mar 302,305
Escalante 297
Bermeo
Mundaka 298,301
Santurtzi
Laredo
Algorta
BILBAO (Bilbo) 295
Collia Arriondas 297
Besnes 294
Villanueva de Colombres 306
Torrelavega
Pola de Laviana
Cabañaquinta
Fuente Dé 297
Carmona
Potes
Quijas 300,303
Eibar
Llodio
Cosgaya 296
Riaño
Reinosa
Embalse del Ebro
Mondragón
Argomániz 292
Cistierna
Aguilar de Campóo 292
VITORIA (Gasteiz)
Almanza
LEÓN 300
Santa Maria de Mave 301
Laguardia 300
Ebro
Haro 297
LOGROÑO
Sahagún
Osorno
Santo Domingo de la Calzada 302
BURGOS 295
Valencia de Don Juan 304
Mayorga
Arlanzón
Covarrubias 297
Benavente 308
PALENCIA
Lerma
Salas de los Infantes
Santo Domingo de Silos 305
Dueñas
Villalpando
SORIA
VALLADOLID
Aranda de Duero
Zamora 314
Toro
Tordesillas
N122
El Burgo de Osma
Almazán
Duero
S P A I N
Eresma
Boceguillas
Medina del Campo
Pedraza de la Sierra 312,313
Cerezo de Arriba 309
Villasayas
Medinaceli
Sigueruelo 313
Collado Hermoso 308
SALAMANCA 312
Siguenza 313
SEGOVIA 313
Rascafría 312
Lozoyuela
Jadraque
Alameda del Valle 307
Villacastín
Henares
Ávila 307,308
Tagus
Guadalajara
Sol Osancho
Alcalá de Henares
Torrejón de Ardoz 313
Sacedón
MADRID 309,312
Pastrana
Embalse de Buendía
Navarredonda de Gredos 312
Arganda
Jarandilla de la Vera 310
Chinchón 309
Talavera de la Reina
Aranjuez
Tarancón
Oropesa 312
Toledo 313,314
Ocaña
Embalse de Valdecañas
N634
N630
A67
A8
A68
A1
N620
NI
N110
A6
NIV
N401
A 31
D
E
F
1
2
3
4
5

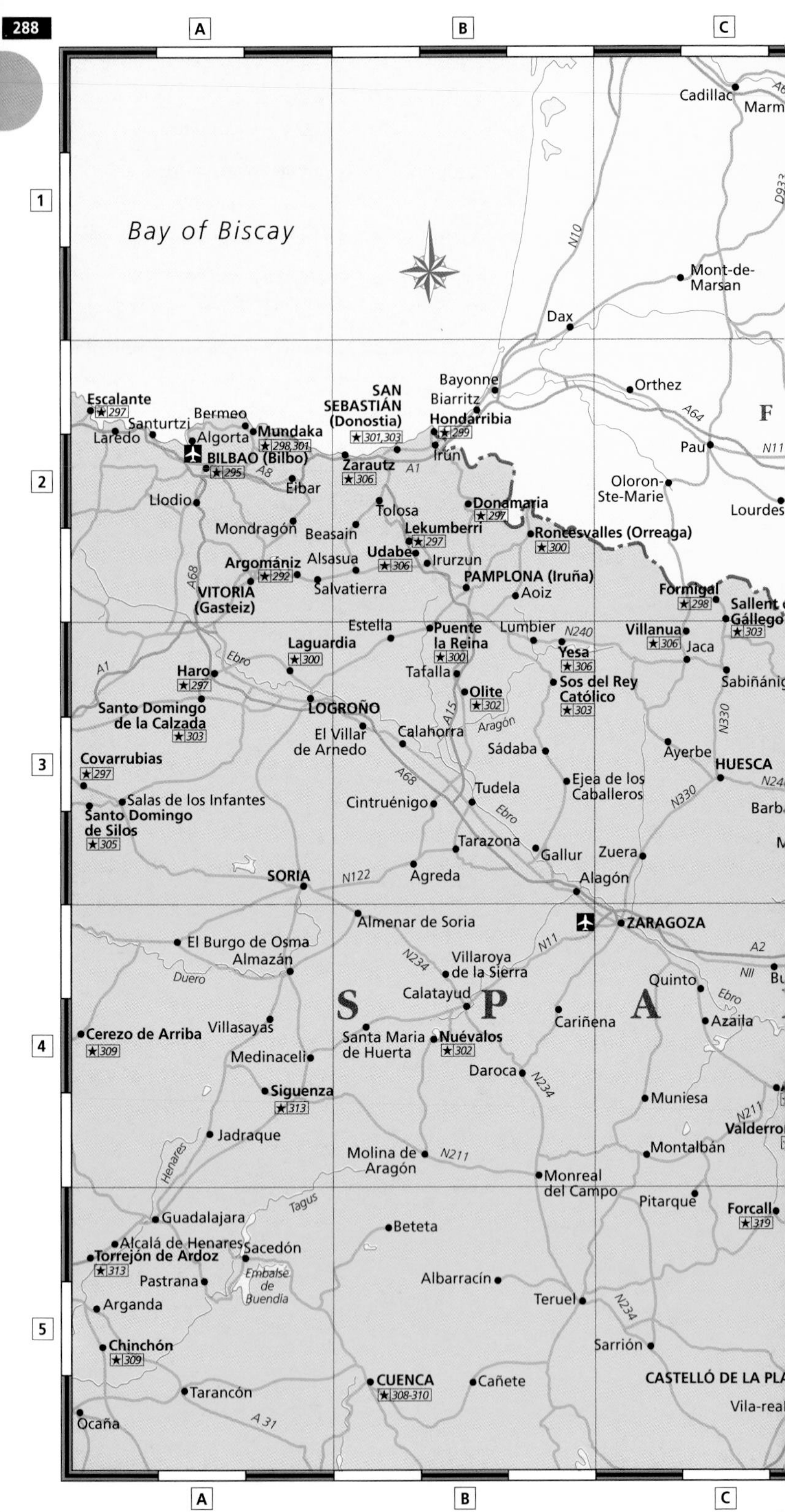
A
B
C
1
2
3
4
5
Bay of Biscay
Cadillac
Marm
Mont-de-Marsan
Dax
N10
Bayonne
Biarritz
Orthez
A64
F
Pau
N11
Oloron-Ste-Marie
Lourdes
Escalante
297
Santurtzi
Laredo
Bermeo
Algorta
Mundaka
298,301
BILBAO (Bilbo)
295
A8
Eibar
SAN SEBASTIÁN (Donostia)
301,303
Zarautz
306
A1
Hondarribia
299
Irún
Llodio
Mondragón
Beasain
Tolosa
Lekumberri
297
Donamaria
297
Roncesvalles (Orreaga)
300
Argomániz
292
Alsasua
Udabe
306
Irurzun
PAMPLONA (Iruña)
Aoiz
VITORIA (Gasteiz)
Salvatierra
A68
Formigal
298
Sallent de Gállego
303
Estella
Laguardia
300
Puente la Reina
300
Lumbier
N240
Yesa
306
Villanua
306
Jaca
A1
Haro
297
Ebro
Tafalla
Olite
302
Sos del Rey Católico
303
Sabiñánigo
Santo Domingo de la Calzada
303
LOGROÑO
El Villar de Arnedo
Calahorra
A15
Aragón
Sádaba
Ayerbe
N330
HUESCA
Covarrubias
297
A68
Tudela
Ejea de los Caballeros
N330
Salas de los Infantes
Santo Domingo de Silos
305
Cintruénigo
Ebro
Tarazona
Gallur
Zuera
SORIA
N122
Agreda
Alagón
Almenar de Soria
ZARAGOZA
El Burgo de Osma
Almazán
N234
Villaroya de la Sierra
N11
A2
NII
Duero
Calatayud
Quinto
Ebro
S
P
A
Cariñena
Azaila
Cerezo de Arriba
309
Villasayas
Santa Maria de Huerta
Nuévalos
302
Medinaceli
Daroca
N234
Siguenza
313
Muniesa
N211
Valderrobres
Jadraque
Molina de Aragón
N211
Montalbán
Henares
Monreal del Campo
Tagus
Pitarque
Forcall
319
Guadalajara
Beteta
Alcalá de Henares
Sacedón
Torrejón de Ardoz
313
Embalse de Buendia
Pastrana
Albarracín
Teruel
N234
Arganda
Chinchón
309
Sarrión
CUENCA
308-310
Cañete
CASTELLÓ DE LA PLA
Tarancón
Vila-real
A 31
Ocaña

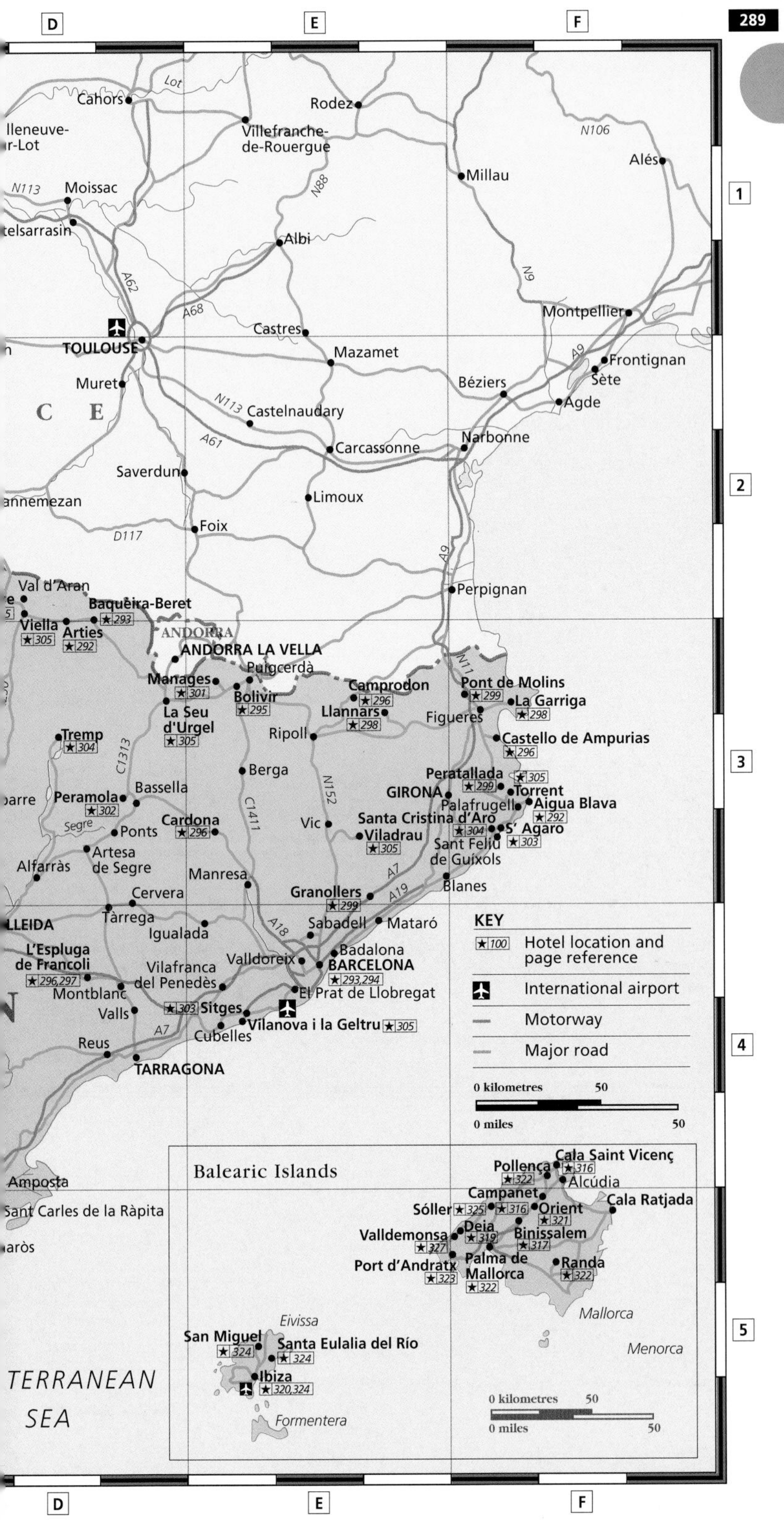

D
E
F
1
2
3
4
5
Cahors
Lot
Rodez
Villefranche-de-Rouergue
N106
Alés
Millau
N113
Moissac
N88
Albi
N9
A62
A68
Montpellier
Castres
TOULOUSE
Mazamet
A9
Frontignan
Sète
Béziers
Agde
Muret
N113
Castelnaudary
A61
Carcassonne
Narbonne
Saverdun
Limoux
Foix
D117
A9
Perpignan
Val d'Aran
Baqueira-Beret
293
Viella
305
Arties
292
ANDORRA
ANDORRA LA VELLA
Puigcerdà
Manages
301
Bolivir
295
Camprodon
296
Pont de Molins
299
La Garriga
298
N11
La Seu d'Urgel
305
Llannars
298
Figueres
Tremp
304
Ripoll
Castello de Ampurias
296
C1313
Berga
Peratallada
299
305
Torrent
GIRONA
N152
Palafrugell
Aigua Blava
292
Peramola
302
Bassella
C1411
Segre
Ponts
Cardona
296
Vic
Santa Cristina d'Aro
304
S' Agaro
303
Viladrau
305
Sant Feliu de Guíxols
Artesa de Segre
Alfarràs
Manresa
A7
Blanes
Cervera
Granollers
299
A19
Tàrrega
LLEIDA
Igualada
A18
Sabadell
Mataró
L'Espluga de Francoli
296,297
Badalona
Valldoreix
BARCELONA
293,294
Vilafranca del Penedès
Montblanc
El Prat de Llobregat
303
Sitges
Valls
A7
Vilanova i la Geltru
305
Cubelles
Reus
TARRAGONA
KEY
100
Hotel location and page reference
International airport
Motorway
Major road
0 kilometres 50
0 miles 50
Balearic Islands
Amposta
Sant Carles de la Ràpita
Pollença
322
Cala Saint Vicenç
316
Alcúdia
Campanet
Sóller
325
316
Orient
321
Cala Ratjada
Valldemonsa
327
Deia
319
Binissalem
317
Port d'Andratx
323
Palma de Mallorca
322
Randa
322
Mallorca
Eivissa
San Miguel
324
Santa Eulalia del Río
324
Menorca
Ibiza
320,324
TERRANEAN SEA
Formentera
0 kilometres 50
0 miles 50

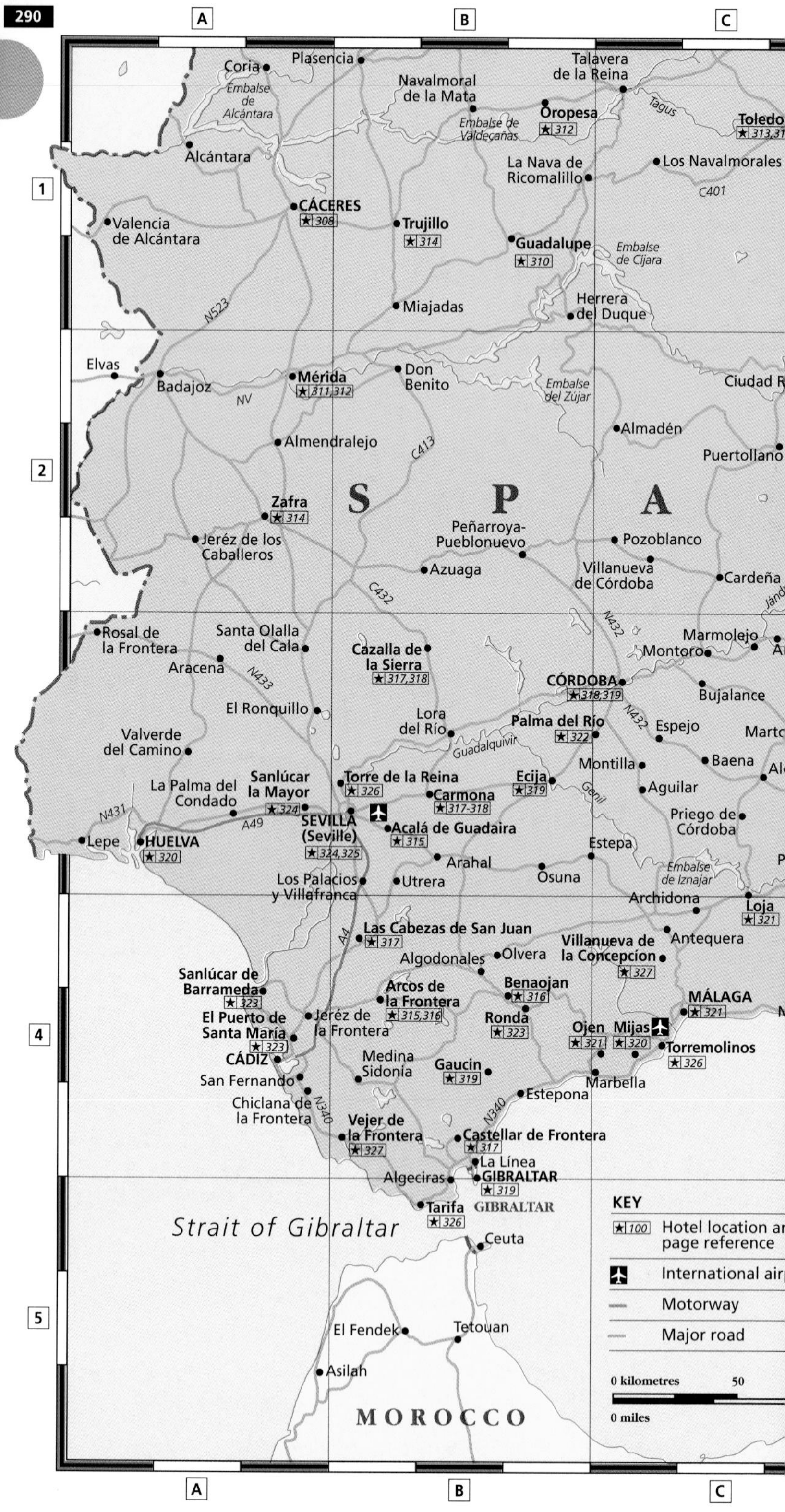
A
B
C
1
2
4
5
Coria
Plasencia
Talavera de la Reina
Navalmoral de la Mata
Oropesa
312
Toledo
Tagus
Embalse de Alcántara
Embalse de Valdecañas
Alcántara
La Nava de Ricomalillo
Los Navalmorales
C401
CÁCERES
308
Valencia de Alcántara
Trujillo
314
Guadalupe
310
Embalse de Cíjara
N523
Miajadas
Herrera del Duque
Elvas
Badajoz
NV
Mérida
311,312
Don Benito
Embalse del Zújar
Ciudad R
Almadén
Almendralejo
C413
Puertollano
S P A
Zafra
314
Peñarroya-Pueblonuevo
Pozoblanco
Jeréz de los Caballeros
Azuaga
Villanueva de Córdoba
Cardeña
C432
N432
Rosal de la Frontera
Santa Olalla del Cala
Cazalla de la Sierra
317,318
Marmolejo
Montoro
Aracena
N433
CÓRDOBA
318,319
Bujalance
El Ronquillo
Lora del Río
Palma del Río
322
Espejo
Valverde del Camino
Guadalquivir
Montilla
Baena
Sanlúcar la Mayor
324
Torre de la Reina
326
Carmona
317-318
Ecija
319
Aguilar
La Palma del Condado
Genil
Priego de Córdoba
N431
A49
SEVILLA (Seville)
324,325
Acalá de Guadaira
315
Lepe
HUELVA
320
Estepa
Arahal
Osuna
Embalse de Iznajar
Los Palacios y Villafranca
Utrera
Archidona
Loja
321
Las Cabezas de San Juan
317
A4
Villanueva de la Concepcíon
327
Antequera
Algodonales
Olvera
Sanlúcar de Barrameda
323
Arcos de la Frontera
315,316
Benaojan
316
MÁLAGA
321
El Puerto de Santa María
323
Jeréz de la Frontera
Ronda
323
Ojen
321
Mijas
320
Torremolinos
326
CÁDIZ
Medina Sidonia
Gaucin
319
San Fernando
Marbella
Estepona
Chiclana de la Frontera
N340
Vejer de la Frontera
327
Castellar de Frontera
317
La Línea
Algeciras
GIBRALTAR
319
Tarifa
326
GIBRALTAR
Strait of Gibraltar
Ceuta
El Fendek
Tetouan
Asilah
MOROCCO
KEY
100
Hotel location ar
page reference
International air
Motorway
Major road
0 kilometres
50
0 miles

D
E
F
CUENCA
★ 308-310
Cañete
CASTELLÓ DE LA PLANA
Vila-real
Tarancón
A 31
N330
Embalse de Alarcón
Sagvnt
Lliria
A7
Alarcón
★ 307
VALENCIA
★ 327
A-111
Torrente
El Toboso
Mota del Cuervo
Pedro Muñoz
Alcázar de San Juan
Villarrobledo
L'Alcúdia
Tomelloso
La Roda
Júcar
Alzira
Manzanares
Albacete
Gandía
La Solana
Xátiva
★ 327
N430
Almansa
N322
N301
Denia
★ 318
Castell de Castells
★ 317
Moraira
★ 320
Valdepeñas
Villanueva de los Infantes
Alcoy
Villena
Penaguila
★ 323
Yecla
Benidorm
N340
A7
Elda
La Villa Joiosa
★ 327
Hellín
Jumilla
San Juan de Alicante
ALICANTE (Alacant)
Embalse del Cenajo
Segura
Elche
★ 319
Los Marines
Cieza
N322
Moratalla
Tabarca
★ 326
Archena
★ 315
Villacarrillo
Caravaca de la Cruz
Orihuela
Mula
Ubeda
★ 326,327
Cazorla
★ 318
Torrevieja
MURCIA
★ 321
Alcantarilla
N332
Jódar
Quesada
Alhama de Murcia
Huéscar
Totana
Lorca
Mazarrón
Cartagena
A92
Baeza
Aguilas
N334
Albox
Guadix
MEDITERRANEAN SEA
N340
Sierra Nevada
Turre
★ 326
Mojacar
★ 320
Bubión
★ 317
Orgiva
★ 321
Pechina
★ 322
Berja
ALMERÍA
San Jose
N340
Adra
The Canary Islands
0 kilometres 50
0 miles 50
Barlovento
★ 316
Santa Cruz de la Palma
Los Llanos de Aridane
Brena Baja
La Palma
Fuencalience
San Cristobal de la Laguna
Puerto de la Cruz
Santa Cruz de Tenerife
La Gomera
Las Palmas de Gran Canaria
San Sebastián de l Gomera
★ 324
Santa Maria de Gufa
Tafira Alta
Telde
Tenerife
El Hierro
San Nicolas de Tolentino
Valverde
Frontera
Gran Canaria
Melilla
1
2
3
4
5
D

NORTHERN SPAIN

GALICIA • ASTURIAS • CANTABRIA • BASQUE COUNTRY NAVARRA • ARAGON • LA RIOJA • CATALONIA

With its Atlantic climate, the north coast is surprisingly green. The Pyrenees make a wonderful setting for rustic retreats, and, to the east, there are a few still unspoilt fishing villages on the Costa Brava. Northern Spain offers a vast choice of accommodation, from mountain hideaways, village inns and country mansions to palaces and converted monasteries, seaside villas and resort hotels. The great selection from the state-run parador network ranges from crenellated hilltop castles with vaulted rooms to handsome modern buildings. In Barcelona, the principal city of the north, are many large hotels, some ultra-modern, others with simpler old-world charm.

AGUILAR DE CAMPÓO

Posada Santa María la Real Typical of the region's Romanesque architecture, this timbered Cistercian monastery has been thoughtfully converted. Much of the original craftsmanship has been preserved, with duplex bedrooms in the old dormitories and a barn of a restaurant.
Avenida Cervera s/n, 38400 Aguilar de Campóo, Palencia. **Map** p287 E2. (979) 122000. FAX (979) 122552. posada.romanico@telefonica.net b,l,d. **Rooms** 18. Christmas, second half Jan. Not accepted. €

ALCAÑIZ

Parador de Alcañiz Also called Parador de la Concordia, this 12th-century hill castle combines the romance of the past – Gothic walls, cloisters, medieval murals - with the comforts of the present – white-walled bedrooms with carved furniture and tiled floors. Generous meals are served in a massive beamed dining hall.
Castillo Calatravos s/n, 44600 Alcañiz, Teruel. **Map** p288 C4. (978) 830400. FAX (978) 830366. alcaniz@parador.es b,l,d. **Rooms** 37. Never. AE, DC, MC, V. €€

ARGÓMANIZ

Parador de Argómaniz An ideal stopover, a handsome old building with a cavernous dining hall and sober, well-equipped bedrooms.
Carretera N1, 01192 Argómaniz, Alava. **Map** p287 F2, p288 A2. (945) 293200. FAX (945) 293287. argomaniz@parador.es b,l,d. **Rooms** 53. €€

ARTIES

Besiberri Modern variation on the Swiss chalet theme. Cosy, and family-run, it provides all comforts after a hard day on the ski slopes.
El Fuerte 4, 25599 Arties, Lérida. **Map** p289 D2. (973) 640829. FAX (973) 642696. b. **Rooms** 17. €€€

ARTIES

Parador Don Gaspar de Portolá By the smart ski resort of Baqueira-Beret, a parador littered with hunting trophies and comfy chairs.
Carretera de Baqueira, 25599 Arties, Lérida. **Map** p289 D2. (973) 640801. FAX (973) 641001. arties@parador.es b,l,d. **Rooms** 57. €€

ASTORGA

Gaudí Excellent *tapas* are served in the bar of this elegant modern hotel (marble floors, chandeliers) on the main square.
Plaza Eduardo de Castro 6, 24700 Astorga, León. **Map** p286 D3. (987) 615654. FAX (987) 615040. b,l,d. **Rooms** 35. €

Amandi

La Casona de Amandi At the foot of the Asturias, yet only ten miles from the beaches, La Casona has the look and feel of a much-loved home. Surrounded by a huge flower-packed garden, it has several small sitting rooms inside, with good antique furniture, where you can always find a corner to yourself. At the time of going to press the hotel is for sale.
Amandi, 33300 Villaviciosa, Asturias. **Map** p286 D2.
(98) 5890130. FAX (98) 5890129. b. **Rooms** 9.
Oct to June. MC, V. €€

Barcelona

Arts Stylish contemporary hotel with a waterfront location. Sophisticates flock to the minimalist 44-storey building, its grounds dwarfed by a gigantic gold whale sculpture. There are splendid vistas of city and sea from the bedrooms, suites and duplex apartments which top the luxury scale.
Carrer de la Marina 19-21, 08005 Barcelona. **Map** p289 E4. (93) 221 1000. FAX (93) 221 1070.
@ reservas@rcspain.com.com b,l,d. **Rooms** 483.
Never. AE, DC, MC, V. €€€€

Barcelona

Claris A Neo-Classical façade masks a dazzling interior of pillars and sweeping marble floors, and at the top is a rooftop pool. It is not all uncompromising modernity though: Roman mosaics decorate walls and some bedrooms have Chesterfields and antiques. There is also a small museum of Egyptian treasures.
Pau Claris 150, 08007 Barcelona. **Map** p289 E4.
(93) 487 6262. FAX (93) 215 7970.
@ claris@derbyhotels.es b,l,d. **Rooms** 124.
Never. AE, MC, V. €€€€

Barcelona

Condes de Barcelona In the heart of the 'Modernisma' or Art Nouveau area, this sleek, glossy hotel attracts an equally slick and glossy clientele. It occupies two 19th-century former palaces, facing each other across a quiet side street. A roof terrace, plunge pool and tempting restaurant are bonuses.
Paseo de Gracia 73–75, 08008 Barcelona. **Map** p289 E4. (93) 467 4786. FAX (93) 467 4785. @ reservas@condesdebarcelona.com b,l,d. **Rooms** 183.
Never. AE, DC, MC, V. €€€€

Baqueira-Beret

Gran Melia Royal Tanau At Spain's most elegant ski resort, a swanky five-star hotel with luxurious bedrooms.
Carretera de Beret s/n, Naut Aran, 25598 Baqueira-Beret, Lérida. **Map** p289 D2. (973) 644446. FAX (973) 644344.
b,l,d. **Rooms** 30. €€€€

Barcelona

Le Méridien The curved lines of the 1930s recur throughout this lavish five-star hotel. Despite its size, it is warm and welcoming.
Ramblas 111, 08002 Barcelona. **Map** p289 E4.
(93) 3184432. FAX (93) 3017776. @ reservas.barcelona@lemeridien.com b,l,d. **Rooms** 212. €€€€

Barcelona

Rivoli Ramblas Art Deco building and avant-garde design are combined in a great location. Spectacular views from the roof terrace.
Ramblas 128, 08002 Barcelona. **Map** p289 E4.
(93) 4817676. FAX (93) 3175053. @ reservas@rivolihotels.com b,l,d. **Rooms** 130. €€€€

Bayona

Parador de Turismo de Bayona Huge, with impressive amenities and a terrific site within a pre-Roman wall on the Monte Real peninsula.
36300 Bayona, Pontevedra. **Map** p286 A3.
(986) 355000. FAX (986) 355076.
@ baiona@parador.es b,l,d. **Rooms** 122. €€€

Barcelona

Duques de Bergara The airy foyer of this ornate Art Nouveau building has a distinctly Edwardian feel, with its imposing marble staircase, smart tiled floor and potted plants. Renovated in 1998, the decoration and furnishings are appealing thoughout. Suites have private terraces. The restaurant is Catalan.
Bergara 11, 08002 Barcelona. **Map** p289 E4. (93) 301 5151. FAX (93) 317 3442. @ duques@hoteles-catalonia.es b,l,d. **Rooms** 149. Never. AE, DC, MC, V. €€€€

Barcelona

Ritz The name alone conjures up an image of luxury and elegance, realized in each imposing salon and restaurant. Though splendid, it is not intimidating, largely due to the professional yet friendly staff. The Barcelona Ritz opened in 1919; both public rooms and bedrooms blend original fittings with modern facilities.
Gran Via de les Corts Catalanes 668, 08010 Barcelona. **Map** p289 E4. (93) 510 1161. FAX (93) 317 3640. @ reservas@ritzbcn.com b,l,d. **Rooms** 121. Never. AE, DC, MC, V. €€€€

Barcelona

Gran Hotel Havana The 19th-century façade belies the avant-garde design inside. The Havana has a great central location and a lively atmosphere. Live music is played each evening in the bar-lounge built around an atrium. Meticulous attention to detail is evident in the elegant bedrooms. Pool currently being built.
Gran Via de les Corts Catalanes 647, 08010 Barcelona. **Map** p289 E4. (93) 4121115. FAX (93) 4122611. @ reservas@hoteles-silken.com b,l,d. **Rooms** 145. Never. AE, DC, MC, V. €€€€

Begur

Aigua Blava A hotel that puts a tasteful slant on the idea of the holiday village. It is located over pine-covered cliffs and flower-filled gardens, at the head of a picturesque creek, and its group of pristine whitewashed buildings contain everything you could possibly need.
Platja de Fornells, 17255 Begur, Gerona. **Map** p289 F3. (972) 622058. FAX (972) 622112. @ hotelaiguablava@aiguablava.com b,l,d. **Rooms** 85. early Nov to late Feb. AE, DC, MC, V. €€€€

Bayona

Villa Sol Antiques, pictures and books fill the tall rooms of this grand villa in a lush garden, home to the hospitable Rodríguez family.
Palos de la Frontera 12, 36300 Bayona, Pontevedra. **Map** p286 A3. (986) 355691. FAX (986) 355691. b. **Rooms** 8. €€

Benasque

Aragüells In winter the lively bar is packed with locals and visiting skiers. Attic rooms are prettiest, but all have great views.
Avenida los Tilos s/n, 22440 Benasque, Huesca. **Map** p289 D3. (974) 551619. FAX (974) 551664. @ info@hotelaraguells.com b. **Rooms** 19. €

Besnes

La Tahona A cobbled track ends at this hotel with mountain views. Inside it has Spanish flair: beams, whitewashed walls and red tiles.
33578 Alles-Besnes, Peñamellera Alta, Asturias. **Map** p287 E2. FAX (98) 5415749. @ latahona@ctv.es b,l,d. **Rooms** 25. €€

Bielsa

Parador del Monte Perdido In a remote valley of streams and stunning scenery is this modern parador with rustic rooms.
22350 Bielsa, Huesca. **Map** p288 C2. (974) 501011. FAX (974) 501188. @ parador@bielsa.es b,l,d. **Rooms** 39. €€

BENASQUE

Hotel Ciria This central family-run hotel is one of the best in the popular skiing area of the Benasque valley. It has excellent facilities, and a warm, welcoming atmosphere. Local lamb and game dishes are the specialities at the splendid restaurant, El Fogaril. The most attractive bedrooms are the ones in the eaves.
✉ Avenida de los Tilos s/n, 22440 Benasque, Huesca. **Map** p289 D3. ☎ (974) 551612. FAX (974) 551686. @ hotelciria@hotelciria.com 🍴 b,l,d. **Rooms** 44. ● Never. 💳 MC, DC, V. €€

BOLVIR DE CERDANYA

Torre del Remei Up in the Pyrenean forest, Josep María and Loles Boix have created a five-star winner in their stylish Belle Epoque summer palace. Exquisitely decorated with Grecian marble, Italian furniture and Tibetan carpets, it also boasts an exceptional restaurant. Golf, riding and mountain-climbing nearby.
✉ Camí Reial s/n, 17539 Bolvir de Cerdanya, Gerona. **Map** p289 E3. ☎ (972) 140182. FAX (972) 140449. @ info@torredelrmei.com 🍴 b,l,d. **Rooms** 21. ● Never. 💳 AE, MC, V. €€€€

BILBAO

López de Haro Don't be put off by the somewhat severe architecture; inside the old HQ of the republican newspaper *El Liberal* lies a hotel that is both luxurious and vibrant. It is also handy for the Guggenheim Museum. Guests can choose from a clubby English-style bar, a *salón de té* with live music and the trendy Club Náutico restaurant.
✉ Obispo Orueta 2, 48009 Bilbao, Vizcaya. **Map** p287 F2. ☎ (94) 4235500. FAX (94) 4234500. @ lh@hotellopezdeharo.com 🍴 b,l,d. **Rooms** 53. ● Never. 💳 AE, DC, MC, V. €€€€

BURGOS

Landa Palace The 1960s realization of a Gothic fantasy, described variously as charming and pretentious. Its origins lie in a 14th-century tower, bought by a restaurateur, who had it dismantled and rebuilt on the Madrid road. Around it, he built the rest: vaulted pool and dining room, spiral stairs and sumptuous suites.
✉ Carretera Madrid km235, 09001 Burgos. **Map** p287 E3. ☎ (947) 257777. FAX (947) 264676. @ landapal@teleline.es 🍴 b,l,d. **Rooms** 36. ● Never. 💳 MC, V. €€€€

BOLVIR DE CERDANYA

Chalet del Golf On a golf course and popular with enthusiasts, this newish chalet has an abundance of wood in snug rooms.
✉ Devesa del Golf, 17539 Bolvir de Cerdanya, Gerona. **Map** p289 E3. ☎ (972) 884320. FAX (972) 884321. @ golf@chaletdelgolf.net 🍴 b,l,d. **Rooms** 33. €€€€

BURGOS

Méson del Cid On a square opposite the cathedral, this literary-themed hotel has been decorated with great style and sensitivity.
✉ Plaza Santa Maria 8, 09003, Burgos. **Map** p287 E3. ☎ (947) 208715. FAX (947) 269460. 🍴 b,l,d. **Rooms** 28. €€€

CAMBADOS

PT del Albariño Built around a courtyard garden with palm trees and a fountain, the parador offers cool and relaxed accommodation. Swimming pool.
✉ Paseo de Cervantes s/n, 36630, Cambados, Pontevedra. **Map** p286 A3. ☎ (986) 542250. FAX (986) 542068. 🍴 b,l,d. **Rooms** 58. €€€

COMILLAS

Casal del Castro Grand drawing rooms reflect the past of this 17th-century house in a beach resort popularized by King Alfonso XII.
✉ San Jerónimo, 39520 Comillas, Cantabria. **Map** p287 E2. ☎ (942) 720036. FAX (942) 720061. @ hccastro@infonegocio.com 🍴 b,l,d. **Rooms** 42. €€

For key to symbols see backflap. For price categories *see p285*

Camprodon

Edelweiss Standing in the heart of a pretty Pyrenean town, with hills rising behind it, is this four-star hotel with a pleasing brick façade and balconied, white-shuttered windows. Inside are public rooms with panelled walls and ceilings, dotted with tasteful reproduction furniture. Swimming nearby, and shiatsu by arrangement.
☒ Carretera de Sant Joan 28, 17867 Camprodon, Gerona. **Map** p289 E3. (972) 740614. FAX (972) 740605. @ info@edelweisshotel.net b,d (weekends and holidays). **Rooms** 21. Christmas. MC, V. €€

Castello de Ampurias

Allioli The charm of this 200-year-old Catalan farmhouse eclipses its less-than-ideal location in a dip below a main road. Inside, its character is enhanced with well-placed lamps, antiques and flowers, and huge hams hanging to dry over the snug bar. The beamed, whitewashed bedrooms have a country elegance; spotless bathrooms.
☒ 17486 Castelló de Ampurias, Gerona. **Map** p289 F3. (972) 250320. FAX (972) 250300. @ h.r.allioli@turinet.net b,l,d. **Rooms** 42. mid-Dec to mid-Feb. AE, MC, V. €€

Cardona

Parador de Turismo de Cardona Commanding panoramic views in every direction, this mellow medieval fortress seems to grow out of the rocky hilltop. The interior is equally impressive, with a sense of period evoked through the solid oak furniture and rich fabrics. Imaginative regional cuisine is served in the fine dining room.
☒ Castell de Cardona s/n, 08261 Cardona, Barcelona. **Map** p289 E3. (93) 8691275. FAX (93) 8691636. @ cardona@parador.es b,l,d. **Rooms** 54. Never. AE, DC, MC, V. €€

Castrillo de los Polvazares

Hostería Cuca la Vaina In this tranquil spot, only birdsong or the morning rooster are likely to disturb your peace. A new hotel in a medieval town, it was purpose-built to reproduce the local architecture. The result is harmonious and stylish. All the rooms are decorated differently; even corridors are brightened with plants or flowers.
☒ Jardín s/n, 24718 Castrillo de los Polvazares, León. **Map** p286 C3. FAX (987) 691078. b,l,d (weekends and Aug). **Rooms** 7. Jan and Mondays (except Aug). V. €

Cornide-Calo

Casa Grande de Cornide A pretty garden, with pool, encircles this antique-filled house, with fine paintings and a library.
☒ Cornide-Calo 15886, Teo, A Coruña. **Map** p286 B2. (981) 805599. FAX (981) 805751. @ infor@casagrandedecornide.com b,l. **Rooms** 10. €€

Cosgaya

Hotel del Oso A traditional-style house, with flowered balconies and arched veranda. Tennis court and pool, cosy rooms.
☒ 39582 Cosgaya, Cantabria. **Map** p287 E2. (942) 733018. FAX (942) 733036. @ recepcion@hoteldeloso.com b,l,d. **Rooms** 34. €€

Escairón

Torre de Vilariño A 17th-century rustic stone house in an off-the-beaten-track village. Antonio García Beltrán is a genial host.
☒ Fión 47, 27548 Escairón, Lugo. **Map** p286 B3. (982) 452260. FAX (982) 452260. b,l,d. **Rooms** 9. €

L'Espluga de Francolí

Hostal del Senglar Simple, whitewashed hotel in a pretty garden. Food is hearty.
☒ Plaza Montserrat Canals 1, 43440 L'Espluga de Francolí, Tarragona. **Map** p289 D4. (977) 870121. FAX (977) 870127. @ recepcion@hostaldelsenglar.com b,l,d. **Rooms** 40. €

Collia Arriondas

Posada del Valle Nigel and Joanne Burch have transformed a late-19th-century 'priest's farmhouse' on a rock outcrop with stunning views over the Picos into a cosy, friendly family hotel. There's a garden for guests, set in an organic farm with wildflower meadows, cider apples and sheep. Walk, surf, fish and canoe to your heart's content. ☒ 33549 Collia Arriondas, Asturias. **Map** p287 D2. (985) 841 157. FAX (985) 841 559. @ hotel@posadadelvalle.com b,d. **Rooms** 12. mid-Oct to late Mar. MC, V. €€

Donamaría

Donamariako Benta In one of the least spoilt parts of the Pyrenees, on a secondary pilgrim route to Santiago, this rough-stone inn is a perfect retreat for jaded town dwellers in search of a rural idyll. It is a hospitable place, too. There are two sitting rooms, furnished with originality, and modest bedrooms in an annexe. ☒ Barrio de la Venta 4, 31750 Donamaría, Navarra. **Map** p288 B2. FAX (948) 450708. @ donamariako@jet.es b,l,d. **Rooms** 5. Christmas; Sun night, Mon. MC, V. €

Covarrubias

Arlanza Ask for a room on the cobbled square and watch village life go by. An old nobleman's house, the Arlanza's dark, beamed interior is done out in rustic style, with a fine tiled staircase and modestly furnished bedrooms. Meals are the highlight: soup so hot that it has to be eaten with a wooden spoon, and local wild boar. ☒ Plaza Mayor 11, 09346 Covarrubias, Burgos. **Map** p287 F3. (947) 406441. FAX (947) 400502. @ reservas@hotelarlanza.com b,l,d. **Rooms** 38. mid-Dec to mid-March. AE, DC, MC, V. €

Escalante

San Román de Escalante A refined 17th-century house is the setting for this restaurant with rooms, plenty of class and a Michelin star. Guests who stroll in the lovely garden will encounter modern sculptures, while the period-style rooms are filled with paintings, old and new. ☒ Carretera de Escalante-Castillo km2, 39795 Escalante, Cantabria. **Map** p287 F2, p288 A2. (942) 677745. FAX (942) 677643. @ sanromanescalante@mundivia.es b,l,d. **Rooms** 16. late Dec to late Jan. AE, DC, MC, V. €€€

Fuente Dé

Parador Río Deva The stupendous panoramic setting, high in the Picos de Europa, makes up for the dull rooms at this modern parador. ☒ 39588 Fuente Dé, Cantabria. **Map** p287 D2. (942) 736651. FAX (942) 736654. @ fuentede@parador.es b,l,d. **Rooms** 78. €€

Haro

Los Agustinos Old monastery with vast beamed sitting room. Plain bedrooms. ☒ San Agustín 2, 26200 Haro, La Rioja. **Map** p287 F3, p288 A3. (941) 311308. FAX (941) 303148. @ losagustinos@aranzazu-hotels.com b,l,d. **Rooms** 62. €€

Lecumberri

Ayestaran This friendly hotel, with tennis court, is split between summer and winter buildings. Both are simple but with welcoming rooms. ☒ Aralar 22–27, 31870 Lecumberri, Navarra. **Map** p288 B3. FAX (948) 504127. @ hotelayestaran@terra.es b,l,d. **Rooms** 76. €

Lena

Hostería del Huerna Modest mountain hotel, a favourite with *Madrileños* seeking a cheap weekend break. In winter, the snug salon has an open fire. Rather small bedrooms. ☒ Riopaso, 33628 Lena, Asturias. **Map** p287 D2. (98) 5496414. FAX (98) 5496431. b,l,d. **Rooms** 30. €

Figueras

Mas Pau Just outside Figueras, home to the Dalí museum, stands this 17th-century farmhouse in mature grounds. The public rooms are done out in *modernista* style (Spanish Art Nouveau), with mirrors, wicker chairs and ferns; old photographs jostle for space on stone walls. The seven suites are restful in pale shades.
Carretera de Besalú, Avinyonet de Puigventós, 17742 Figueras, Gerona. **Map** p286 C2. (972) 546154. FAX (972) 546326. @ info@maspau.com b,l,d. **Rooms** 20. 6 Jan to 15 Mar. AE, DC, MC, V. €€

Formigal

Villa de Sallent There is no off-season for this hotel at the foot of a Pyrenean ski resort: in summer, it's a base for walkers. A modern building of stone and slate, it has a wood-panelled interior full of pine furniture that lends it a Scandinavian feel. The owners are restaurateurs so satisfying meals are guaranteed. Three- and four-star rooms.
Urbanización Formigal, 22640 Sallent de Gállego, Huesca. **Map** p288 C2. (974) 490223. FAX (974) 490150. @ hotelvillasallent@lospirineos.com b,l,d. **Rooms** 40. Never. AE, DC, MC, V. €€

Figueras del Mar

Palacete de Peñalba This confection of a house, built in 1912 by a follower of Gaudí, is now a national monument. Signs of its eccentric Art Nouveau style are much in evidence: the curved double stairs to the entrance, the glazed and tiled atrium, and the original furniture that has been preserved. Meals can be taken in the owners' waterfront restaurant. Nearby golf club.
El Cotarelo s/n, 33794 Figueras del Mar, Asturias. **Map** p286 C2. (98) 5636125. FAX (98) 5636247. b. **Rooms** 12. Never. MC, V. €€

La Garriga

Termes La Garriga In a spa town 35km (22 miles) north of Barcelona, this is ideal for the energetic or those keen to get into shape: there's a health centre, a pool, bikes for guests' use and golf nearby. Even if keeping fit leaves you cold, the yellow-painted hotel with light, elegantly decorated rooms is a comfortable base.
Banys 23, 08530 La Garriga, Barcelona. **Map** p289 F3. (93) 8717086. FAX (93) 8717887. @ termes@termes.com b,l,d. **Rooms** 22. Never. AE, MC, V. €€€€

Llanars

Grèvol A well-equipped Pyrenean base, which reinvents the classic Swiss chalet. Pool and sauna.
Carretera de Camprodon a Setcases s/n, 17869 Llanars, Gerona. **Map** p289 E3. (972) 741013. FAX (972) 741087. @ info@hotelgrevol.com b,l,d. **Rooms** 36. €€€

Llanes

La Arquera Modern B&B with bright, cheerful exterior and mountain views, handy for the pretty port of Llanes and its beaches.
La Arquera s/n, 33500 Llanes, Asturias. **Map** p287 E2. (98) 5402424. FAX (98) 5400175. @ arquera@infonegocio.com b. **Rooms** 13. €€

Llanes

Gran Hotel Paraíso In the lively main street close to the seafront, this contemporary hotel has standard rooms and small apartments.
Pidal 2, 33500 Llanes, Asturias. **Map** p287 E2. (98) 5401971. FAX (98) 5402590. @ ampudia@jazzfree.com b. **Rooms** 22. €€

Mundaka

El Puerto A simple, traditional house with shady garden, much-loved by surfers who flock to this part of the Basque coast.
Portu Kalea 1, 48360 Mundaka, Vizcaya. **Map** p287 F2, p288 A2. (94) 6876725. FAX (94) 6876726. @ hotelelpuerto@euskalnet.net b. **Rooms** 11. €€

Granollers

Fonda Europa In a pleasant market town, behind a distinctive orange façade with blue and white panels, is this delightfully traditional Catalan hotel. It has been in the capable hands of the Parellada family since 1714. They have furnished the hotel with taste and refinement, and provide unfailingly courteous service.

Anselm Clavé 1, 08400 Granollers, Barcelona. **Map** p289 E3. (93) 8700312. FAX (93) 8707901. b,l,d. **Rooms** 7. Never. AE, DC, MC, V. €€

Hondarribia (Fuenterrabia)

Obispo This elegant Renaissance house has been converted with restraint. The traditional stone and wood interior, set about with period furniture, has been softened by light, floral fabrics and each bedroom designed with style. There is a terrace with views over the bay, two sitting rooms and a cafeteria.

Plaza del Obispo, 20280 Hondarribia, Guipúzcoa. **Map** p288 B2. (943) 645400. FAX (943) 642386. @ reception@hotelobispo.com b. **Rooms** 17. late Dec to mid-Jan. AE, MC, V. €€

A Guarda

Convento de San Benito Behind its simple exterior, the interior of this 16th-century convent has been restored with sympathy and flair. Reception is in the old portico, where ornate detailing has been preserved. Also intact are the cloister, fountain and turnstiles, which gave the nuns access to the outside world. The converted cells make charming bedrooms.

Plaza de San Benito s/n, 36780 A Guarda, Pontevedra. **Map** p286 A3. (986) 611166. FAX (986) 611517. b. **Rooms** 24. 2 weeks in Jan. AE, MC, V. €

Hondarribia (Fuenterrabia)

Parador de Hondarribia Everything about this 12th-century castle is simply stunning. Friendly staff, modern comforts and medieval architecture combine to produce a warmth and elegance with instant appeal. Each antique-filled room has its own character; a lovely courtyard invites relaxation. Excellent local restaurants.

Plaza de Armas 14, 20280 Hondarribia, Guipúzcoa. **Map** p288 B2. (943) 645500. FAX (943) 642153. @ hondarribia@parador.es b. **Rooms** 36. Never. AE, DC, MC, V. €€€

Oviedo

Hotel de la Reconquista Sumptuous salons and bedrooms behind an impressive façade.

Gil de Jaz 16, 33004 Oviedo, Asturias. **Map** p287 D2. (98) 239529. FAX (98) 246011. @ reservas@hoteldelareconquista.com b,l,d. **Rooms** 142. €€€€

Peratallada

Castell de Peratallada Medieval castle with splendid vaulted dining room and tented beds.

Plaça del Castell, 17113 Peratallada, Baix Empordà, Gerona. **Map** p289 F3. (972) 634021. FAX (972) 634011. @ casteperat@aplitec.com b,l (winter), d (summer). **Rooms** 8. €€

Puebla de Trives

Casa Grande de Trives This distinguished 18th-century house has an elegant interior.

Marqués de Trives 17, 32780 Puebla de Trives, Orense. **Map** p286 B3. FAX (988) 332066. @ informacion@casagrandedetrives.com b, d (by arrangement, low season). **Rooms** 9. €

Pont de Molins

Molipark This old mill, furnished with antique-shop bargains, has a fine restaurant and a few modestly priced bedrooms.

Carretera Les Escaules, 17706 Pont de Molins, Gerona. **Map** p289 F3. (972) 529271. FAX (972) 529101. @ molipark@intercom.es b,l,d. **Rooms** 7. €€

For key to symbols see backflap. For price categories *see p285*

Laguardia

Castillo El Collado This unusual hotel represents one man's dream of a lifetime. Señor Javier spent ten years converting the *castillo* (fortified manor) and has furnished it with flair. All the bedrooms are differently done out with an appealing hint of decadence. There is a bar, smart restaurant and fine selection of Riojas in the cellar.
Paseo El Collado 1, 01300 Laguardia, Alava. **Map** p287 F3. (945) 621200. FAX (945) 600878. @ hcastillocollado@euskalnet.net b,l,d. **Rooms** 8. Never. AE, DC, MC, V. €€

León

Parador Hotel de San Marcos This 16th-century former monastery has a monumental Renaissance façade, a superb cloister and epic public rooms. Good pictures (ancient and modern), tapestries and excellent furniture dress the interior. Most bedrooms are in a modern annexe. Some refurbishment planned for early 2004.
Plaza San Marcos 7, 24001 León. **Map** p287 D30. (987) 237300. FAX (987) 233458. @ leon@parador.es b,l,d. **Rooms** 225. Never. AE, DC, MC, V. €€€

Laguardia

Posada Mayor de Migueloa Great sensitivity shows in the conversion of this 17th-century stone mansion, which contains the smallest of the Rioja wineries. Historically everything is of a piece, and takes you back to Spain's Golden Century. The owners, experts on Rioja, also produce delicious food.
Mayor 20, 01300 Laguardia, Alava. **Map** p287 F3. (945) 621175. FAX (945) 621022. @ reservas@mayordemigueloa.com b,l,d. **Rooms** 8. 22 Dec to 22 Jan. AE, DC, MC, V. €€

Llanes

El Habana This peaceful country hotel at the foot of the Sierra de Cuera range simply bursts with character. Bedrooms are spacious. Some face the mountains; all have heated brick floors, antique furniture and modern bathrooms. Wander in the vast gardens, swim in the pool, or visit one of 30 local beaches.
La Pereda s/n, 33509 Llanes, Asturias. **Map** p287 E2. (98) 5402526. FAX (98) 5402075. @ hotel@elhabana.net b,l,d. **Rooms** 10. Dec to Feb. AE, MC, V. €€

Pontevedra

Parador Casa del Barón A refined yet welcoming parador, with air conditioning, in the old town.
Barón 19, 36002 Pontevedra. **Map** p286 A3. (986) 855800. FAX (986) 852195. @ pontevedra@parador.es b,l,d.**Rooms** 47. €€

Puente La Reina

Hotel del Peregrino Once a staging post for pilgrims to Santiago, now a stylish restaurant with rooms and a fine gastronomic reputation.
Carretera de Pamplona 11, 31100 Puente La Reina, Navarra. **Map** p288 B3. (948) 340075. FAX (948) 341 190. @ delperegrino@teleline.es b,l,d. **Rooms** 13. €€€

Quijas

Casona Torre de Quijas Antique-filled but child-friendly stone mansion.
Barrio Vinueva 76, 39590 Quijas, Cantabria. **Map** p287 E2. (942) 820645. FAX (942) 838255. @ informacion@torredequijas.com b,d (by arrangement, high season). **Rooms** 22. €€

Ribadeo

PT de Ribadeo Relaxed, friendly parador in a quiet backwater of town overlooking the harbour. Interesting selection of fish on the menu.
Amador Fernández s/n, 27700, Ribadeo, Lugo. **Map** p286 C2. (982) 128825. FAX (982) 128346. @ ribadeo@parador.es b,l,d. **Rooms** 47. €€

LLANES

La Posada de Babel Camelias and fruit trees flourish in the seclusion of the small park that surrounds this alluring hotel. It is housed in a striking modern building, the back of which is entirely glazed. Inside, the style is generally traditional, with period furniture. One of the bedrooms is in a separate little cottage.
☒ La Pereda, 33509 Llanes, Asturias. **Map** p287 E2. (98) 5402525. FAX (98) 5402622. @ laposadadebabel@retemail.es b,d. **Rooms** 11. 1 Nov to 28 Feb. AE, DC, MC, V. €€

MUNDAKA

Atalaya Close to the fishing port of Mundaka, the Atalaya is the best hotel on this stretch of coast, and as tranquil as the church and shoreline it overlooks. It is scrupulously maintained; rooms are rather small, but they are attractively done out and the beds are large. The aroma of fresh bread and coffee is an irresistible call to breakfast.
☒ Itxaropen Kalea 1, 48360 Mundaka, Vizcaya. **Map** p287 F2, p288 A2. (94) 6177000. FAX (94) 6876899. b,d. **Rooms** 11. Never. AE, DC, MC, V. €€

MERANGES

Can Borrell At the head of a valley near Andorra, in a picture-postcard mountain village nearly 1,500m (5,000ft) above sea-level, is this family-run farmhouse. Rooms have wonderful wood ceilings and beams; one has a breathtaking view. Service is friendly and personal, and the restaurant deserves its high local reputation.
☒ Retorn 3, 17539 Meranges, Gerona. **Map** p289 E3. (972) 880033. FAX (972) 880144. @ info@canborell.com b,l,d. **Rooms** 9. Mon–Thu early Jan to end Apr (except Easter). MC, V. €€

NEDA

Pazo da Merced On the grassy bank of the Ría del Ferrol a handsome 17th-century house of dressed stone has been transformed by its architect owner into a stunning, homely B&B. Walls of ancient stone and glass abut, and antiques sit happily beside contemporary furniture. Comfortable bedrooms. Library.
☒ 15510 Neda, La Coruña. **Map** p286 B2. (981) 382200. FAX (981) 380104. @ reservas@pazodamerced.com b, d. **Rooms** 8. mid-Dec to mid-Jan. AE, DC, MC, V. €€

RONCESVALLES (ORREAGA)

La Posada Views are of forests and mountains from this simple inn. Bedrooms have pretty floor tiles from Valencia. Food is robust
☒ Carretera de Francia s/n, 31650 Roncesvalles, Navarra. **Map** p288 B2. (948) 760225. FAX (948) 760266 b,l,d. **Rooms** 17. €

SAN SEBASTIÁN (DONOSTIA)

Hotel de Londres y de Inglaterra The grandeur of a bygone era is maintained in this white-stuccoed seafront hotel.
☒ Zubieta 2, 20007 San Sebastián, Guipúzcoa. **Map** p288 B2. (943) 440770. FAX (943) 440491. @ reservas@hlondres.com b,l,d. **Rooms** 148. €€€€

SALAS

Castillo de Valdés Salas Atmospheric castle redolent of the 16th century, with thick stone walls and cloisters around a paved courtyard.
☒ Plaza de la Campa s/n, 33860 Salas, Asturias. **Map** p286 C2. (98) 5830173. FAX (98) 5830183. @ hotel@castillovaldesalas.com b,l,d. **Rooms** 12. €€

SANTA MARÍA DE MAVE

Hostería El Convento A handsome medieval convent in orchards, abutting a lovely church. Accommodation is plain but comfortable.
☒ 34492 Santa María de Mave, Palencia. **Map** p287 E3. (979) 123611. FAX (979) 125492. @ hosteria@hosteriaelconvento.com b,l,d. **Rooms** 25. €

For key to symbols see backflap. For price categories *see p285*

Nuévalos

Monasterio de Piedra The centuries drop away as you walk the long, echoing corridors or climb the massive vaulted stairs of this 12th-century Cistercian monastery. Much of the original building is intact: cloisters, frescoes and alabaster windows that cast a dreamy opaque light. The former cells are now modern bedrooms. Free entry to the National Park is included.
50210 Nuévalos, Zaragoza. **Map** p288 B4. (976) 849011. FAX (976) 849054. b,l,d. **Rooms** 61. Never. AE, DC, MC, V. €€

Peramola

Can Boix Far from the crowds, a modern hotel with large, well-equipped rooms, by the foot of the Roca del Corb and overlooking the green valley of the Río Segre. Joan Pallarès, the owner/chef, is a cheerfully visible presence who has a deft touch in his kitchen.
Can Boix s/n, 25790 Peramola, Lleida. **Map** p289 D3. (973) 470266. FAX (973) 470281. hotel@canboix.com b,l,d. **Rooms** 41. mid-Jan to mid-Feb. AE, DC, MC, V. €€

Olite

Parador del Príncipe de Viana Occupying part of an ancient castle, the former residence of the kings of Navarre, this parador has all the usual attributes: huge rooms, heavy furniture, tapestries and a baronial air. It also has a good kitchen. The bedrooms, in a rebuilt wing, are mundane compared to the rest of the building.
Plaza de los Teobaldos 2, 31390 Olite, Navarra. **Map** p288 B3. (948) 740000. FAX (948) 740201. olite@parador.es b,l,d. **Rooms** 43. Never. AE, DC, MC, V. €€

Pravia

Casona del Busto From the outside, there is little suggestion of the building's 16th-century origins as a minor palace. Inside, however, there is an abundance of handsome dark wood and stone, two inner tile-floored courtyards and a tangible sense of history. The bedrooms, beamed and furnished in regional style, are attractive and relaxing at modest prices.
Plaza Rey Silo 1, 33120 Pravia, Asturias. **Map** p287 D2. (98) 5822771. FAX (98) 5822772. b,l,d. **Rooms** 26. Never. AE, V. €€

Santillana del Mar

Complejo Los Infantes Stone floors and vast carved chests, beamed ceilings and chandeliers in this characterful 18th-century house.
Avenida L'Dorat 1, 39330 Santillana del Mar, Cantabria. **Map** p287 E2. (942) 818100. FAX (942) 840103. hinfantes@mundivia.es b,l,d. **Rooms** 28. €€€

Santillana del Mar

Posada Santa Juliana Beamed bedrooms share the town's medieval flavour. No public rooms, meals are served in the bar opposite.
Carrera 19, 39330 Santillana del Mar, Cantabria. **Map** p287 E2. (942) 840106. FAX (942) 840170. santajuliana@santillanadelmar.com b,l,d. **Rooms** 6. €

Santillana del Mar

Siglo XVIII This manor outside the medieval town has been revamped in traditional Cantabrian style. Pool and gardens.
Revolgo 38, 39330 Santillana del Mar, Cantabria. **Map** p287 E2. (942) 840210. FAX (942) 840211. sigloxviii@arrakis.es b. **Rooms** 16. €€

Santo Domingo de la Calzada

Parador de Santo Domingo de la Calzada Modern feel despite the stone vaulting.
Plaza del Santo 3, 26250 Santo Domingo de la Calzada, La Rioja. **Map** p287 F3. (941) 340300. FAX (941) 340325. sto.domingo@parador.es b,l,d. **Rooms** 61. €€

QUIJAS

Hostería de Quijas The garden in which this 17th- to 18th-century former palace is set has been well cared for over the past two centuries. Inside are antiques and uncovered stonework, with wooden beams and pillars in the dining room. The whole place is a haven of peace and quiet – especially if you have a room on the garden side. Barrio Binueva s/n, 39590 Quijas, Cantabria. **Map** p287 E2. (942) 820833. FAX (942) 838050. quijas@terra.es b,l,d. **Rooms** 19. 15 Dec to 24 Jan. AE, DC, MC, V. €€

SALLENT DE GÁLLEGO

Almud Mariano Martín de Cáceres and his wife, María José, have converted an old stable block into a village B&B with exquisite taste. He is an architect and she has a passion for antiques. Her finds and family heirlooms fill the beautifully decorated yet homely rooms. A night here feels more like staying with friends than in a hotel. Espadilla 3, 22640 Sallent de Gállego, Huesca. **Map** p288 C2. FAX (974) 488540. hotel_almud@ctv.es b,d. **Rooms** 10. Never. AE, DC, MC, V. €€

S'AGARÓ

Hostal de la Gavina With two fine Costa Brava beaches on view from its perch on a promontory, this private palace has gradually become a public one. Wall-to-wall antiques include exquisite tapestries, and each room has a different style. The cuisine skilfully marries seafood with the best of local produce. New health spa. Plaza de la Rosaleda, 17248 S'Agaró, Gerona. **Map** p289 F3. (972) 321100. FAX (972) 321573. gavina@lagavina.com b,l,d. **Rooms** 74. mid-Oct to Easter. AE, DC, MC, V. €€€€

SAN SEBASTIÁN (DONOSTIA)

Maria Cristina This grand hotel is a picture of elegance with its Louis XV and *belle époque* public rooms, yet the Maria Cristina is bang up to date behind the scenes. Bedrooms are light, fresh and meticulously kept. The stone-columned 'Easo' restaurant serves excellent Basque specialities. Pool under construction. Oquendo 1, 20004 San Sebastián, Guipúzcoa. **Map** p288 B2. (943) 437600. FAX (943) 437676. hmc@westin.com b,l,d. **Rooms** 136. Never. AE, DC, MC, V. €€€€

SITGES

Capri Pictures and antiques fill this cheerful family-run hotel, 500m from beach. Pool. Slightly cheaper sister hotel (Veracruz) over the road. 13–15 Avenida Sofia, 08870 Sitges, Barcelona. **Map** p289 E4. (93) 8110267. FAX (93) 8945188. info@grup-carbonell.com b. **Rooms** 30. €€€

SITGES

La Santa Maria Refreshingly unpretentious hotel with two seafront restaurants, invariably packed. Accommodation is clean, pleasant and simple. Pg. de la Ribera 52, 08870 Sitges. **Map** p289 E4. (93) 8940999. FAX (93) 8947871. info@lasantamaria.com b,l,d. **Rooms** 63. €€

SOS DEL REY CATÓLICO

Parador Turístico Sos del Rey Católico Modern, rustic style in a captivating hill village. Arquitecto Sainz de Vicuña 1, 50680 Sos del Rey Católico, Zaragoza. **Map** p288 B3. (948) 888011. FAX (948) 888100. sos@parador.es b,l,d. **Rooms** 66. €€

TARAMUNDI

La Rectoral In remote, spectacular country, this attractive 18th-century stone house adheres to regional traditions in decoration and cooking. 33775 Taramundi, Asturias. **Map** p286 C2. (98) 5646767. FAX (98) 5646777. larectoral@infonegocio.com b,l,d. **Rooms** 18. €€€

For key to symbols see backflap. For price categories *see p285*

SANTA CRISTINA DE ARO

Mas Torrellas This restored country house is a triumph of personality and keen pricing over pampering. Catalan vaultings support almost every ceiling. Bedrooms are neat and clean; try for one with a view. The cellar bar has wine barrels from every Spanish region. Tennis court
☒ Carretera Santa Cristina a Castillo de Aro km1,713, 17246 Santa Cristina de Aro, Gerona. **Map** p289 F3.
(972) 837526. FAX (972) 837527. b,l,d.
Rooms 18. mid-Oct to mid-Mar.
AE, DC, MC, V. €€

SANTANDER

Real King Alfonso XIII used to summer in Santander and the Real was built in 1917 for his entourage. Today, its five stars should stand for location (it's on a spectacular site overlooking the bay), amenities, staff, atmosphere and an unstuffy elegance. You probably have to leave Cantabria to do better.
☒ Paseo Pérez Galdós 28, 39005 Santander, Cantabria.
Map p287 E2. (942) 272550. FAX (942) 274573.
@ reservas@hotelreal.es b,l,d. **Rooms** 123.
Never. AE, DC, MC, V. €€€€

SANTANDER

Las Brisas If you are looking for an elegant villa at very reasonable prices, you need look no further than this yellow-and-white affair in a quiet area of Santander by the Sandinero beach. Jesús García, an English speaker, owns and runs this friendly hotel of 13 smallish but stylish bedrooms and smart bathrooms. There is a pleasant garden.
☒ La Braña 14, 39005 Santander, Cantabria.
Map p287 E2. (942) 275011. FAX (942) 281173.
@ abrisas@cantabria.org b. **Rooms** 13. Jan.
AE, DC, MC, V. €€

SANTIAGO DE COMPOSTELA

Parador de Santiago de Compostela Stroll in the cloisters of one of the four magical courtyards, as travellers have for 500 years, and you will feel a palpable sense of history. Europe's oldest hotel was opened in 1499 as a pilgrims' hostel. The façade is breathtaking, and salons and bedrooms rich and grand.
☒ Plaza do Obradoiro 1, 15705 Santiago de Compostela, La Coruña. **Map** p286 B2. (981) 582200. FAX (981) 563094. @ santiago@parador.es b,l,d. **Rooms** 129.
Never. AE, DC, MC, V. €€€€

TORTOSA

Parador Tortosa There are views from many vantages in this ancient Moorish castle; the best are from the pool on the ramparts.
☒ Castillo de la Zuda s/n, 43500 Tortosa, Tarragona.
Map p289 D4. (977) 444450. FAX (977) 444458.
@ tortosa@parador.es b,l,d. **Rooms** 72. €€

TREDÒS

Hotel de Tredòs A new stone and slate hotel, popular with skiers and mountaineers for its well-equipped bedrooms and friendly staff.
☒ Carretera a Baqueira-Beret km 177.5, 25598 Viella, Lérida. **Map** p289 D3. (973) 644014. FAX (973) 644300. b,d. **Rooms** 43. €€

TREMP

Casa Guilla Rambling farmhouse run by Brits as a guesthouse: bedrooms in the old animal pens, bar in the stables and lounge in hayloft.
☒ Santa Engràcia, 25636 Tremp, Lérida. **Map** p289 D3.
FAX (973) 252080. @ info@casagvilla.com b,l,d.
Rooms 4. €

VALENCIA DE DON JUAN

Villegas With only five bedrooms, the Villegas looks and feels like a private house. The fresh bedrooms all open out onto the shady garden with pool.
☒ Palacio 10, 24200 Valencia de Don Juan, León.
Map p287 D3. (987) 750161. b,l,d. **Rooms** 6. €

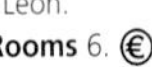

Santillana del Mar

Parador de Turismo Gil Blas This glorious manor of worn stone, with tiled roof and courtyard garden, is in perfect harmony with the medieval square in which it stands. It was built some 500 years ago as the Barreda Bracho family's country retreat, and the old house has great charm. Some rooms are in a new annexe. ✉ Plaza Ramón Pelayo 11, 39330 Santillana del Mar, Cantabria. **Map** p287 E2. ☎ (942) 818000. FAX (942) 818391. @ santillanagb@parador.es 🍴 b,l,d. **Rooms** 28. ● Never. AE, DC, MC, V. €€€

La Seu d'Urgell

El Castell de Ciutat Modern and luxurious, this 'Relais et Châteaux' hotel is refreshingly unaffected. Jaume and Ludi Tàpies have instilled their mountain retreat with a truly welcoming atmosphere, and have won plaudits for their Catalan and French regional dishes. ✉ Carretera de Lérida a Puigcerdà km 129, 25700 La Seu d'Urgell, Lérida. **Map** p289 D3. ☎ (973) 350000. FAX (973) 351574. @ elcastell@relaischateaux.com 🍴 b,l,d. **Rooms** 38. ● Never. AE, DC, MC, V. €€€

Santo Domingo de Silos

Tres Coronas de Silos Santo Domingo is a classic Castillian village, renowned for its 900-year-old convent where Gregorian chants are still sung daily. This cosy family hotel, on the main village square, is in a large 18th-century house faithfully restored by local craftsmen, with snug rooms and a pleasing dining room. ✉ Plaza Mayor 6, 09610 Santo Domingo de Silos, Burgos. **Map** p287 F3. ☎ (947) 390047. FAX (947) 390065. 🍴 b,l,d. **Rooms** 16. ● Christmas and New Year. AE, DC, MC, V. €€

Torrent

Mas de Torrent This inland island of serenity is only 8km (5 miles) from the smartest beaches of the Costa Brava. The Mas de Torrent is a hotel of taste, housed in a restored 18th-century farm with 20 family bungalows, and run by courteous, gentle people. Rooms are individually and exquisitely decorated. The restaurant is a gem. ✉ Afors s/n, 17123 Torrent, Gerona. **Map** p289 F3. ☎ (972) 303292. FAX (972) 303293. @ reservas@mastorrent.com 🍴 b,l,d. **Rooms** 39. ● Never. AE, DC, V. €€€€

Verín

Parador de Verín Situated opposite the fortress of Monterrel, this modern parador has a leafy setting on its own hilltop plus a pool. ✉ Subida al Castillo, 32600 Verín, Ourense. **Map** p286 B3. ☎ (988) 410075. FAX (988) 412017. @ verin@parador.es 🍴 b,l,d. **Rooms** 23. €€

Viella

Parador de Viella New parador where a picture window in the semi-circular lounge frames dramatic mountain scenery. Health spa. ✉ Carretera del Túnel, 25530 Viella, Lérida. **Map** p289 D2. ☎ (973) 640100. FAX (973) 641100. @ viella@parador.es 🍴 b,l,d. **Rooms** 118. €€

Viladrau

Hostal de la Glòria The Formatjes family have created a homely hotel in their classic Catalan house, decked out with copper pots and plates. ✉ Torreventosa 12, 17406 Viladrau, Gerona. **Map** p289 E3. ☎ (93) 8849034. FAX (93) 8849465. @ informacio@hostaldelagloria.com 🍴 b,l,d. **Rooms** 22. €

Vilanova i la Geltrú

César A pair of sisters are in charge of this highly regarded restaurant with rooms. ✉ Carrer Isaac Peral 4–8, 08800 Vilanova i la Geltrú, Barcelona. **Map** p289 E4. ☎ (93) 8151125. FAX (93) 8156719. @ vilanova@hotelcesar.net 🍴 b,l,d. **Rooms** 36. €€€

For key to symbols see backflap. For price categories *see p285*

A Toxa

Gran Hotel de La Toja Islands make a special setting, and this hotel, sheltered off the Arosa estuary, is one of the nicest. It has magnificent views, gardens and pinewoods and excellent facilities. The old half of the hotel is genuine Art Nouveau with a stunning staircase and stained glass windows. Staff are very welcoming.
36991 A Toxa, Pontevedra. **Map** p286 A2. (986) 730025. FAX (986) 730026. @ info@latojagran hotel.com b,l,d. **Rooms** 197. Never. AE, DC, MC, V. €€€

Villanueva-Cangas de Onís

Parador de Cangas de Onís Close to Covadonga, the site of the Christians' first victory over the Moors, and beside the River Sella, this welcoming gem of a hotel used to be the monastery of San Pedro de Villanueva. It has a magnificent courtyard, cloister and small church. The restaurant and rooms are in a new building.
Villanueva s/n, 33550 Cangas de Onís, Asturias. **Map** p289 D2. (98) 5849402. FAX (98) 5849520. @ cangas@parador.es b,l,d. **Rooms** 64. Never. AE, DC, MC, V. €€€

Udabe

Venta Udabe When Javier Hernández Goñi and Laura Ganuza Tudela bought this inn, it was a ruin and they have worked extremely hard to restore it. In the garden of the traditional rustic building, they have added a pool. Dining is on the terrace in summer, and in winter there's a roaring fire. Superb food.
Valle de Basaburúa, 31869 Udabe, Navarra. **Map** p288 B2. (948) 503105. FAX (948) 503400. @ info@hotelventaudabe.com b,l,d. **Rooms** 8. late Dec to late Jan. AE, DC, MC, V. €€

Villanueva de Colombres

La Casona de Villanueva In a quiet hamlet in magnificent countryside between the eastern end of Los Picos and the sea, is this 18th-century farmhouse. Inside are oak beams, comfy beds, furniture from past and present and practical bathrooms. Top-notch home cooking can be praised with the help of the resident dictionary.
33590 Villanueva de Colombres, Asturias. **Map** p287 E2. (98) 5412590. FAX (98) 5412514. @ info@lacasonadevillanueva.com b,d. **Rooms** 8. Jan and Feb. MC, V. €€

Villalonga

Pazo El Revel The lush garden (with a pool) almost encroaches on the covered terrace of this old Galician *pazo* with plain tiled rooms.
Camino de la Iglesia s/n, 36990 Villalonga, Pontevedra. **Map** p286 C2. (986) 743000. FAX (986) 743390. @ hotelocapazorevel@ocahotels.com b. **Rooms** 22. €€

Villanúa

La Casa Visitors to this Alpine-style hotel – under new management – are greeted by the glow of wood on floors and panelled walls.
Carretera de Francia km 658.5, 22870 Villanúa, Huesca. **Map** p288 C3. (974) 378136. FAX (974) 378198. b,l,d. **Rooms** 16. €€

Yesa

Hospedería de Leyre A simple, peaceful hotel in beautiful country, set in an outbuilding of an active 11th-century Benedictine monastery.
Monasterio de Leyre, 31410 Yesa, Navarra. **Map** p288 B3. (948) 884100. FAX (948) 884137. @ hotel@monasteriodeleyre.com b,l,d. **Rooms** 33. €€

Zarautz

Karlos Arguiñano Seafood is the speciality at this chic, castellated beachfront restaurant with pretty rooms.
Mendilauta 13, 20800 Zarautz, Guipúzcoa. **Map** p288 B2. (943) 130000. FAX (943) 133450. @ kahotel@karlosnet.com b,l,d. **Rooms** 12. €€€€

Central Spain

Castilla y Leon • Castilla-La Mancha
Extremadura • Madrid

Towns and sleepy villages dot Central Spain's unspoilt landscape of mountains, lakes, olive trees, orchards and almond groves. As in the North, old buildings such as mills and castles, townhouses and country posadas, have been skilfully converted to hotels and paradors. For sheer size, there is little that can equal the monumental castle parador at Sigüenza. But for romance, few places can compare with the former monastery at Chichón with its beautiful courtyard – a feature of so many Spanish buildings. The capital, Madrid, is set at the heart of the country. The city's hotels range from the gloriously restored Ritz to a peaceful 1930s villa with a pretty garden setting.

Alameda del Valle

La Posada de Alameda A popular refuge for the city-weary, this new *posada* has an incomparable setting in the Lozoya Valley, 90km (55 miles) north of Madrid. The large bedrooms have views over a varied, unspoilt landscape, encompassing mountains, lakes and almond groves. The walls are adorned with interesting modern pictures.
Grande 34, 28749 Alameda del Valle, Madrid. **Map** p287 E4. (91) 8691337. FAX (91) 8690163. @ laposada@laposadadealameda.com b,l,d. **Rooms** 22. Never. MC, V. €€

Alarcón

Parador Marqués de Villena One half expects to see Don Quixote's horse Rocinante tethered by the courtyard well of this hilltop Moorish fortress. Behind the thick walls lie a vaulted dining chamber, a great hall which now doubles as sitting room and cafeteria, and bedrooms which echo the medieval theme.
Avenida Amigos del Castillo, 16213 Alarcón, Cuenca. **Map** p291 E1. (969) 330315. FAX (969) 330303. @ alarcon@parador.es b,l,d. **Rooms** 14. Never. AE, DC, MC, V. €€€

La Alberca

Las Batuecas The chestnut and cherry trees of the Sierra de Francia surround this impressive stone house. Covered terrace and grassy garden.
Avda Las Batuecas 6, 37624 La Alberca, Salamanca. **Map** p286 C5. (923) 415188. FAX (923) 415055. @ lasbatuecas@teleline.es b,l,d. **Rooms** 38. €

Avila

Gran Hotel Palacio Valderrábanos Through the important entrance, every beam and arch reeks of the past. Try for a room with a cathedral view.
Plaza Catedral 9, 05001 Avila. **Map** p287 E5. (920) 211023. FAX (920) 251691. @ reservas@palaciovalderrabanoshotel.com b,l,d. **Rooms** 73. €€

Avila

Hostería de Bracamonte The walls of the cheerful bar are lined with photographs of the glitterati fans of this typical Castillian hotel, with its natural stonework and tapestry wallhangings.
Bracamonte 6, 05001 Avila. **Map** p287 E5. (920) 251280. FAX (920) 253838. b,l,d. **Rooms** 24. €

Avila

Sancho de Estrada A medieval castle with thick stone walls, towers, coats of arms and an interior to match. Simple bedrooms but fabulous views.
Castillo de Villaviciosa, 05130 Avila. **Map** p287 E5. (920) 291082. FAX (920) 293460. @ hotelesmajora@hotelesmajora.com b,l,d. **Rooms** 14. €€

For key to symbols see backflap. For price categories *see p285*

Almagro

Parador de Almagro Hand-painted signs ensure that guests don't get lost in this rambling modern building on the site of an old convent. Its rooms are arranged around 14 small quads. Painted ceilings, vivid tapestries and pottery add colour to the public rooms; bedrooms are simpler. There are flowers everywhere and a friendly ambience.
Ronda de San Francisco, 13270 Almagro, Ciudad Real. **Map** p291 D2. (926) 860100. FAX (926) 860150. almagro@parador.es b,l,d. **Rooms** 54. Never. AE, DC, MC, V. €€

Cáceres

Meliá Cáceres The old town within the ramparts contains a host of fine mansions, built for generations of aristocrats. This serene hotel is in one of these mansions, a solid wooden door leading into a well-preserved, stylish interior, arranged around a courtyard. Vaulted stables make a wonderfully atmospheric bar.
Plaza de San Juan 11, 10003 Cáceres, Extremadura. **Map** p290 A1. (927) 215800. FAX (927) 214070. melia.caceres@solmelia.es b,l,d. **Rooms** 86. Never. AE, DC, MC, V. €€€

Avila

Parador de Turismo de Avila All that remains of the original 16th-century building is the tower, housing some small bedrooms, and the courtyard, shaded by a great pine. Bedrooms in the new part are larger and airier; some have four-poster beds, some fine views. The sun-trap terrace is an appealing place to relax.
Marqués de Canales de Chozas 2, 05001 Avila. **Map** p287 E5. (920) 211340. FAX (920) 226166. avila@parador.es b,l,d. **Rooms** 61. Never. AE, MC, DC, V. €€

Cáceres

Parador de Cáceres A splendid 14th-century palace with a slender tower houses this elegant parador, its façade almost untouched since its foundation. Unlike many in the chain, the snug public rooms don't have massive proportions, and bedrooms are simply attractive. Delightful inner courtyard. Classic regional cuisine.
Ancha 6, 10003 Cáceres, Extremadura. **Map** p290 A1. (927) 211759. FAX (927) 211729. caceres@parador.es b,l,d. **Rooms** 33. Never. AE, DC, MC, V. €€€

Benavente

Parador Rey Fernando II de León The 12th-century castle keep survives as a drawing room. New swimming pool.
Paseo de Ramón y Cajal s/n, 49600 Benavente, Zamora. **Map** p287 D3. (980) 630304. FAX (980) 630303. benavente@parador.es b,l,d. **Rooms** 38. €€

Ciudad Rodrigo

Conde Rodrigo Handsome 16th-century exterior, rather bland interior. Good-value restaurant.
Plaza de San Salvador 9, 37500 Ciudad Rodrigo, Salamanca. **Map** p286 C5. (923) 461404. FAX (923) 461408. info@conderodrigo.com b,l,d. **Rooms** 34. €

Collado Hermoso

El Molino del Río Viejo Gorgeous old mill which stands amid poplars; the cosiest bedrooms are the ones in the eaves. Book well ahead.
Carretera N110 km 172, 40170 Collado Hermoso, Segovia. **Map** p287 E4. (921) 403063. FAX (921) 403051. molinorioviejo@telefonica.net b,l,d. **Rooms** 9. €€

Cuenca

Leonor de Aquitania An honest inn in the heart of the old town. The ground floor is flagstoned, walls bear tapestries or hunting trophies.
San Pedro 60, 16001 Cuenca. **Map** p288 B5. (969) 231000. FAX (969) 231004. reservas@hotelleonordeaquitania.com b,l,d. **Rooms** 46. €€

Cerezo de Arriba

Casón de la Pinilla Ranch-style hotel on the outskirts of a sleepy village, minutes from the ski slopes of La Pinilla. In the restaurant the accent is on local specialities. In summer, breakfast and drinks are served on the long, balconied porch. With a playroom and activities ranging from riding to canoeing, the Casón caters to all ages.
40592 Cerezo de Arriba, Segovia. **Map** p287 F4, p288 A4. (921) 557201. FAX (921) 557209. casonpinilla@teleline.es b,l,d. **Rooms** 12. Never. AE, DC, MC, V. €

Ciudad Rodrigo

Parador de Ciudad Rodrigo Enrique II The whole of the 12th-century fortified town of Ciudad Rodrigo is a historical monument. This castle stands at the centre of the old town. Most of the rooms look inward towards the lovely enclosed gardens. Try for one of the bedrooms overlooking the Agueda river and the town.
Plaza del Castillo 1, 37500 Ciudad Rodrigo, Salamanca. **Map** p286 C5. (923) 460150. FAX (923) 460404. ciudadrodrigo@parador.es b,l,d. **Rooms** 35. Never. AE, DC, MC, V. €€€

Chinchón

Parador de Chinchón Soothe body and mind at this 15th-century former convent. Simple but elegant decoration includes the original frescoes on the main staircase; the internal courtyard is glorious. Outside are trees and flowers, bamboos and fountains, and a spectacular colonnaded swimming pool.
Avenida del Generalísimo 1, 28370 Chinchón, Madrid. **Map** p287 F5, p288 A5. (91) 8940836. FAX (91) 8940908. chinchon@parador.es b,l,d. **Rooms** 38.

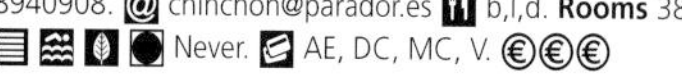

Never. AE, DC, MC, V. €€€

Cuenca

Parador de Cuenca This 16th-century former convent is perched dramatically above a gorge in the upper town, with rooms ranged around a calm courtyard. Staff are friendly and capable. Nearby is the Museum of Spanish Abstract Art, in one of the 'Casas Colgadas' which literally hang over the gorge.
Subida San Pablo s/n, 16001 Cuenca. **Map** p288 B5, p291 E1. (969) 232320. FAX (969) 232534. cuenca@parador.es b,l,d. **Rooms** 63. Never. AE, DC, MC, V. €€€

Madrid

Best Western Hotel Carlos V It looks like any other slick city hotel but, family-run, this one has a heart, as well as a beautifully furnished lounge.
Maestro Victoria 5, 28013 Madrid. **Map** p287 E5. (91) 5314100. FAX (91) 5313761. recepcion@hotelcarlosv.com b. **Rooms** 67. €€€

Madrid

Conde de Orgaz A modern hotel with well-appointed bedrooms, handy for the airport and the Campo de las Naciones Exhibition Centre.
Avenida Moscatelar 24, 28043 Madrid. **Map** p287 E5. (91) 7489760. FAX (91) 3880009. reservasconde@zenithoteles.com b,l,d. **Rooms** 91. €€€

Madrid

Emperatriz This large hotel with pale decoration and upholstered furniture manages to create an oasis of calm in the city centre.
López de Hoyos 4, 28006 Madrid. **Map** p287 E5. (91) 5638088. FAX (91) 5639804. comercial@hotel-emperatriz.com b,l,d. **Rooms** 158. €€€€

Madrid

Gran Hotel Tryp Reina Victoria Ernest Hemingway stayed in this grand hotel, which has a plush modern interior and marble hall.
Plaza de Santa Ana 14, 28012 Madrid. **Map** p287 E5. (91) 5314500. FAX (91) 5220307. recvic@trypnet.com b,l,d. **Rooms** 201. €€€€

Cuenca

Posada de San José Formerly the home of the painter Martinez del Mazo, this simple, charming hotel looks out over allotments and the cliffs of the Júcar gorge. For a view, book a room with a bathroom. Polished floors and furniture reassure you that this is a well-run house. The welcome is friendly, and so are the prices.
Julián Romero 4, 16001 Cuenca. **Map** p288 B5, p291 E1. (969) 211300. FAX (969) 230365. @ info@posadasanjose.com b,d. **Rooms** 31. Never. AE, DC, MC, V. €

Guadalupe

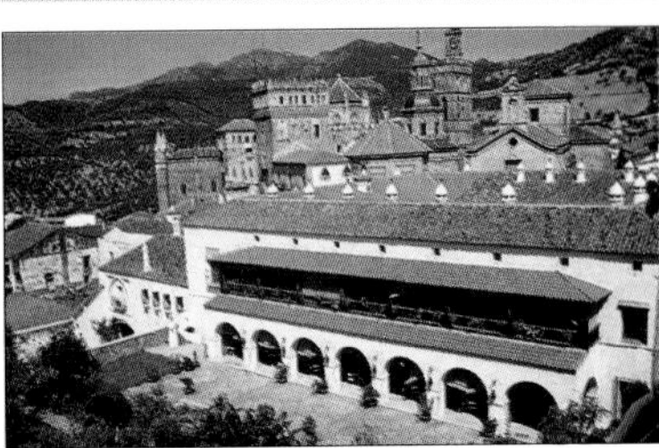

Parador Zurbarán Pilgrims used to shelter in this 18th-century hospital, and it still accommodates weary travellers. Orange trees shade an inner court where arcades lead to the salons and dining room. Bedrooms are attractively decorated; those in the modern building have outstanding views over monastery, village and mountains.
Marqués de la Romana 12, 10140 Guadalupe, Cáceres. **Map** p290 B1. (927) 367075. FAX (927) 367076. @ guadalupe@parador.es b,l,d. **Rooms** 41. Never. AE, DC, MC, V. €€

Guadalupe

Hospedería del Real Monasterio This is part fortress and part monastery. The Franciscans (still in residence) have created a hotel within their own walls. Gathered round a Gothic cloister are sitting rooms, a dining room and large bedrooms. The church has a splendid collection of paintings, including some by Zurbarán.
Plaza de Juan Carlos I, 10140 Guadalupe, Cáceres. **Map** p290 B1. (927) 367000. FAX (927) 367177. b,l,d. **Rooms** 47. mid-Jan to mid-Feb. MC, V. €

Jarandilla de la Vera

Parador Carlos V It was at this remote fortified manor that Holy Roman Emperor Charles V spent his last nights before retiring to the monastery at Yuste in 1556. It is complete down to the towers and a drawbridge. The cool arcade, upper veranda and vast, comfortable rooms make you realize why the emperor chose this spot.
Avenida de García Prieto 1, 10450 Jarandilla de la Vera, Cáceres. **Map** p287 D5. (927) 560117. FAX (927) 560088. @ jarandilla@parador.es b,l,d. **Rooms** 53. Never. AE, DC, MC, V. €€

Madrid

Husa Princesa This modern five-star hotel has terrific amenities, from piano bar to aerobics room, and a great location for sightseeing.
Princesa 40, 28008 Madrid. **Map** p287 E5. (91) 5547229. FAX (91) 5427328. @ hhpreservas@husa.es b,l,d. **Rooms** 275. €€€€

Madrid

Melia Barajas Well outside the city centre, but conveniently near the airport, Barajas is a useful stopover hotel with a pool, gym and golf course.
Avenida de Logroño 305, 28042 Madrid. **Map** p287 E5. (91) 7477700. FAX (91) 7478717. @ tryp.barajas@solmelia.com b,l,d. **Rooms** 229. €€€€

Madrid

Mónaco Famous for putting up King Alfonso XIII in the early 1900s and for a stint as the city's most upmarket brothel.
Barbieri 5, 28004 Madrid. **Map** p287 E5. (91) 5224630. FAX (91) 5211601. @ hotelmonaco2000@yahoo.es b. **Rooms** 34. €€

Madrid

Santo Domingo A step from Plaza de España, a hotel of pastel tones, marble floors, deep carpets and trendy furnishings in differently styled rooms.
Plaza de Santo Domingo 13, 28013 Madrid. **Map** p287 E5. (91) 5479800. FAX (91) 5475995. @ reserva@hotelsantodomingo.com b,l,d. **Rooms** 120. €€€

MADRID

Palace Haunt of the famous – from matadors to politicians – and the infamous (Mata Hari allegedly stayed here). The Palace matches the Ritz (see right) in grandeur; perhaps because it's much larger, service is not as personal. But it's worth a visit just to see the magnificent Art Nouveau rotunda with its Neo-Classical columns.
Plaza de las Cortes 7, 28014 Madrid.
Map p287 E5. (91) 3607777. FAX (91) 3607778.
@ reservations.palacemadrid@westin.com b,l,d. **Rooms** 465. Never. AE, DC, MC, V. €€€€

MADRID

Ritz The Madrid Ritz has been tending to the whims of the wealthy since 1910, when it was built at the instigation of King Alfonso XIII. Public rooms are furnished with priceless carpets and tapestries, the spacious bedrooms with antiques. All this and faultless service make this Ritz one of Spain's top hotels.
Plaza de la Lealtad 5, 28014 Madrid. **Map** p287 E5.
(91) 5212857. FAX (91) 7016776. @ reservas@ritz.es
b,l,d. **Rooms** 167. Never.
AE, DC, MC, V. €€€€

MADRID

La Residencia de El Viso If Madrid's large hotels leave you cold, try this delightful 1930s villa with a quiet garden. Once inside, you can hardly believe that the location is so central. The bedrooms have co-ordinating fabrics; public rooms have high-backed chairs upholstered in red. Classic local dishes feature on the menu.
Nervión 8, 28002 Madrid. **Map** p287 E5.
(91) 5640370. FAX (91) 5641965.
@ reservas@residenciadelviso.com b,l,d. **Rooms** 12.
Never. AE, DC, V. €€€

MADRID

AC Santo Mauro Behind wrought-iron gates, an impressive, French-designed late 19th-century palace houses this luxurious hotel, with new annexe. With its stucco and original features intact, sophisticated modern furniture and decoration have been introduced to great effect, using marble, stained oak, wild silk and velvet.
Zurbano 36, 28010 Madrid. **Map** p287 E5.
(91) 3196900. FAX (91) 3085477. @ santo-mauro@ac-hotels.com b,l,d. **Rooms** 51.
Never. AE, DC, MC, V. €€€€

MADRID

Serrano A brutally modern façade masks a bright, exclusive hotel with period furniture and welcome personal touches.
Marqués de Villamejor 8, 28006 Madrid.
Map p287 E5. (91) 5769626. FAX (91) 5753307.
@ serranoroyal@husa.es b. **Rooms** 34. €€€

MADRID

Suite Prado Specialist hotel with glossy modern apartments and room service. Baby-blue carpets and pastel armchairs are typical of the style.
Manuel Fernández y González 10, 28014 Madrid.
Map p287 E5. (91) 4202318. FAX (91) 4200559.
@ hotel@suiteprado.com b,l,d. **Rooms** 18. €€€€

MADRID

Wellington The bullfighting fraternity has long been associated with this genteel 1950s hotel. Top-floor bedrooms have private terraces.
Velásquez 8, 28001 Madrid. **Map** p287 E5.
(91) 5754400. FAX (91) 5764164. @ wellington@hotel-wellington.com b,l,d. **Rooms** 276. €€€€

MÉRIDA

Tryp Medea Indoor and outdoor pools, squash courts, sauna and gym are among the amenities at this pampering, amphitheatre-style hotel.
Avenida de Portugal, 06800 Mérida, Badajoz.
Map p290 A2. (924) 372400. FAX (924) 373020.
@ tryp.medea@solmelia.com b,l,d. **Rooms** 126. €€

MADRID

Villa Real In a building dating from 1900, the Villa Real is in the grand tradition of its neighbour the Palace (see p311) but is slightly kinder on the pocket – weekend rates are particularly reasonable. As well as more formal salons, there is an intimate bar. Service is carried out impeccably by a polite staff.
Plaza de las Cortes 10, 28014 Madrid. **Map** p287 E5. (91) 4203767. FAX (91) 4202547. @ villareal@derbyhotels.es b,l,d. **Rooms** 115. Never. AE, DC, MC, V. €€€€€

OROPESA

Parador de Oropesa Built of sand-coloured stone in 1402, this was the first castle to be converted into a parador in 1930. The interior as impressive as the exterior, preserving origi floors and vaulting. Breathtaking views of the Sierra de Gredos and Tajo valley from the tow and terraces.
Plaza del Palacio 1, 45560 Oropesa, Toledo. **Map** p287 D5, p290 B1. (925) 430000. FAX (925) 430777. @ oropesa@parador.es b,l,d. **Rooms** 48. Never. AE, DC, MC, V. €

MÉRIDA

Parador Vía de la Plata Though much of the building is modern, this parador's historical association is evident in many touches. It is full of Roman artefacts, its 16th-century chapel is now a sitting room and past the reception area is a cloistered courtyard. Upstairs, most of the large bedrooms overlook the Moorish gardens.
Plaza de la Constitución 3, 06800 Mérida, Badajoz. **Map** p290 A2. (924) 313800. FAX (924) 319208. @ merida@parador.es b,l,d. **Rooms** 82. Never. AE, DC, MC, V. €€

PEDRAZA DE LA SIERRA

El Hotel de la Villa The walled medieval hillt town, dominated by its castle, is a maze of higgledy-piggledy streets lined with beautifull preserved houses. In one of these is this stylis hotel, a stunning mix of the traditional and the contemporary. Its comfortable bedrooms are a different, with glossy well-equipped bathroom
Calzada 5, 40172 Pedraza de la Sierra, Segovia. **Map** p287 E4. (921) 508651. FAX (921) 508653. @ info@hoteldelavilla.com b,l,d. **Rooms** 38. N AE, DC, MC, V. €€

NAVARREDONDA DE GREDOS

Parador de Gredos The exterior of this 1920s parador is stone, its interior wood. Massive rooms boast beams and hunting trophies.
Carretera Barraco–Béjar km42, 05635 Navarredonda de Gredos, Avila. **Map** p287 D5. (920) 348048. FAX (920) 348205. @ gredos@parador.es b,l,d. **Rooms** 74. €€

RASCAFRÍA

Santa María de El Paular Guests share this tasteful 14th-century monastery at the foot of the Sierra de Guadarrama with Benedictine monks.
Carretera M-604 km 26,500, 28741 Rascafría, Madrid. **Map** p287 E4. (91) 8691011. FAX (91) 8691006. @ reservas@paular.com b,l,d.**Rooms** 44. €€€

SALAMANCA

NH Palacio de Castellanos Swish hotel in a 15th-century monastery, with a vaulted glass r
San Pablo 58, 37008 Salamanca. **Map** p287 D4. (923) 261818. FAX (923) 261819. @ nhpalaciodecastellanos@nh-hotels.com b,l,d. **Rooms** 62. €€€€

SALAMANCA

Hotel Residencia Rector An abundance of marble and stained glass, and a warm ambien behind a Renaissance-style façade.
Paseo Rector Esperabe 10, 37008 Salamanca. **Map** p287 D40. (923) 218482. FAX (923) 214008. @ hotelrector@telefonica.net b. **Rooms** 13. €€

Pedraza de la Sierra

La Posada de Don Mariano Televisions are only provided on request, as they would look too brash in the exquisitely decorated bedrooms. Each has its own character and is furnished using carefully chosen antiques. Avoid the rooms above the lively bar, whose ceiling does not provide solid enough protection against the noise.
Mayor 14, 40172 Pedraza de la Sierra, Segovia. **Map** p287 E40. (921) 509886. FAX (921) 509887. b,l,d. **Rooms** 18. Never. AE, DC, MC, V. €€

Toledo

Hostal del Cardenal This beautiful house in central Toledo was a cardinal's summer home. Birds sing and fountains play in the Moorish garden, where dinner can be taken in the summer. Inside are handsome antiques and an elegant staircase. Room sizes vary; there is one small suite. The restaurant is next door.
Paseo de Recaredo 24, 45004 Toledo. **Map** p287 E5, p290 C1. (925) 224900. FAX (925) 222991. @ cardenal@hostaldelcardenal.com b,l,d. **Rooms** 27. Never. AE, MC, V. €€

Sigueruelo

Posada de Sigueruelo A visit to this quiet village inn is to sample rural life at its best. In the rugged country that surrounds Sigueruelo, you can go hiking, cycling, riding or canoeing. The friendly staff at the Posada will organize it for you. On your return, the hotel's shady terrace and a drink will beckon. Rooms are small but have stone walls, beams, antiques and plenty of atmosphere.
Badén 40,40590 Sigueruelo, Segovia. **Map** p287 E4. FAX (921) 508135. @ posada@sigural.com b,d. **Rooms** 6. Never. MC, V. €€

Torrejón de Ardoz

La Casa Grande A farm founded in the 18th century by Empress Maria of Austria to supply the Imperial College makes a stunning hotel. Massive beamed rooms are decorated with antiques that once belonged to the Russian royal family. In the principal suite is a Baroque bed where Catherine the Great is alleged to have slept.
Madrid 2, 28850 Torrejón de Ardoz, Madrid. **Map** p287 F5. (91) 6753900. FAX (91) 6750691. @ lcg@lacasagrande.es b,l,d. **Rooms** 8. Aug. AE, DC, MC, V. €€€

Segovia

Infanta Isabel A handsome 19th-century townhouse opposite the cathedral, this hotel is furnished classically with flair.
Plaza Mayor 12, 40001 Segovia. **Map** p287 E4. (921) 461300. FAX (921) 462217. @ admin@hotelinfantaisabel.com b,l,d. **Rooms** 37. €€

Segovia

Los Linajes Tiled floors, beams and carved furniture produce a charming effect in this hotel nestling below the cathedral but with country views.
Dr Velasco 9, 40003 Segovia. **Map** p287 E4. (921) 460475. FAX (921) 460479. @ hotelloslinajes@terra.es b,l,d. **Rooms** 53. €€

Sigüenza

Parador de Turismo de Sigüenza Perched above the town, this huge medieval castle has a vast sitting room, snug bar and panoramic views.
Plaza del Castillo, 19250 Sigüenza, Guadalajara. **Map** p287 F4, p288 A4. (949) 390100. FAX (949) 391 364. @ siguenza@parador.es b,l,d. **Rooms** 81. €€

Toledo

María Cristina An old orphanage that preserves its heritage, this hotel and its dining room are especially popular at weekends and *fiestas*.
Marqués de Mendigorria 1, 45003 Toledo. **Map** p287 E5, p290 C1. (925) 213202. FAX (925) 212650. @ reservas@hotelmariacristina.com b,l,d. **Rooms** 74. €€

Trujillo

Finca de Santa Marta This country manor house, where oil and wine used to be produced, has been converted into a perfect rural getaway. Modern facilities blend sympathetically with the fabric of the building and with the regional furniture, yielding bright, comfortable and attractive rooms.
Pago San Clemente s/n, 10200 Trujillo, Cáceres. **Map** p290 B1. (927) 319203. FAX (927) 334115. henri@facilnet.es b, d. **Rooms** 16. Never. MC, V. €€

Zafra

Parador de Zafra A 15th-century fortress with round towers conjures images from the days of the Conquistadors. Highlights are the stunning white marble patio, over which most bedrooms look, and the magnificent staircase leading to them. The swimming pool in the walled garden is a delight.
Plaza del Corazón de María 7, 06300 Zafra, Badajoz. **Map** p290 A2. (924) 554540. FAX (924) 551018. zafra@parador.es b,l,d. **Rooms** 45. Never. AE, MC, DC, V. €€

Trujillo

Parador de Trujillo Partly housed within the 16th-century convent of Santa Clara, and partly in a modern building, this parador has proved immensely popular. It's set in a maze of quiet streets yet has with views over the Extremadura countryside. Rebuilding programme undertaken in 2003.
Plaza Santa Beatriz de Silva 1, 10200 Trujillo, Cáceres. **Map** p290 B1. (927) 321350. FAX (927) 321366. trujillo@parador.es b,l,d. **Rooms** 46. Never. AE, DC, MC, V. €€

Zamora

Parador Condes de Alba y Aliste If you need a reason to go to Zamora, this is it. A glorious Renaissance courtyard, with cloister below and enclosed galleries above, masks an interior perfectly in keeping with its 18th-century restoration. Half the rooms are in a new wing over a public pool. Friendly, efficient service.
Plaza de Viriato 5, 49001 Zamora. **Map** p287 D4. (980) 514497. FAX (980) 530063. zamora@parador.es b,l,d. **Rooms** 52. Never. AE, DC, MC, V. €€

Toledo

Parador de Turismo de Toledo Contemporary hilltop parador, built sympathetically in local style, with a pool and great views over the city.
Cerro del Emperador, 45002 Toledo. **Map** p290 C1. (925) 221850. FAX (925) 225166. toledo@parador.es b,l,d. **Rooms** 76. €€€

Toledo

Pintor El Greco This 17th-century house in the Jewish quarter, with colourful furnishings and modern comforts, makes an excellent base.
Alamillos del Tránsito 13, 45002 Toledo. **Map** p290 C1. (925) 285191. FAX (925) 215819. info@hotelpintorelgreco.com b. **Rooms** 33. €€

Zafra

Huerta Honda Window boxes overflowing with geraniums enliven this white villa with calm bedrooms, amusing decor and excellent food.
López Asme 30, 06300, Zafra, Badajoz. **Map** p290 A2. (924) 554100. FAX (924) 552504. reservas@hotelhuertahonda.com b,l,d. **Rooms** 45. €€

Zamora

Hostería Real de Zamora Housed in a 16th-century palace of the Inquisition. Comfortable tile-floored rooms. Excellent Basque cuisine.
Cuesta de Pizarro 7, 49001 Zamora. **Map** p287 D4. FAX (980) 534545. hostzamora@hosteriasreales.com b,l,d. **Rooms** 23. €€

SOUTHERN SPAIN

ANDALUCIA • MURCIA • VALENCIA
CANARY ISLANDS • BALEARIC ISLANDS

JUST A FEW KILOMETRES from the busy coast of Southern Spain and into the hills of Andalucia, is some of the country's most beautiful scenery – rolling hills, chestnut forests, olive and citrus groves. In this region, there are a number of handpicked hotels, some occupying historic buildings such as converted convents, others in airy modern houses. The fine cities of the South – Granada, Córdoba and Seville – all have small gems of hotels. Further north, in Alicante, hard by the concrete blocks of the Costa Blanca, is a hotel in Europe's largest palm grove. In the Balearic and Canary Islands, away from the tourist track, are some of the least spoilt settings for some of the most desirable hotels.

ANTEQUERA

Parador de Antequera A hotel that provides pampering for lovers of modern design, with lush gardens that soften the severe lines of the white-painted building. The spacious, light interior is decorated in pale shades with a predominance of wood and a welcome scattering of comfy leather chairs. The restaurant offers traditional dishes.
✉ 29200 Antequera, Málaga. **Map** p290 C4. ☎ (95) 2840261. FAX (95) 2841312. @ antequera@parador.es 🍴 b,l,d. **Rooms** 55. Never. AE, DC, MC, V. €€

ARCOS DE LA FRONTERA

Cortijo Faín Near Arcos de Frontera, a clifftop White Town teetering over the Guadalete valley, this delightful Andalusian manor is set with its gardens in the centre of a huge olive grove. The warmly furnished rooms of varying sizes have iron or brass bedsteads, and the calm public areas and library are dotted with paintings and antiques.
✉ Carretera de Algar km 3, 11630 Arcos de la Frontera, Cádiz. **Map** p290 B4. ☎ (956) 231396. FAX (956) 231961. @ cortijofain@eresmas.com 🍴 b,l,d. **Rooms** 11. Never. AE, MC, V. €€

ALCALÁ DE GUADAIRA

Oromana This fine white house on the outskirts of Seville contains lofty communal rooms, a cosy bar and cool, pale bedrooms. Friendly staff.
✉ Avenida Portugal s/n, 41500 Alcalá de Guadaira, Seville. **Map** p290 B3. ☎ (95) 5686400. FAX (95) 5686424. @ reservas@ hoteloromana.com 🍴 b,l,d. **Rooms** 30. €€

ARCHENA

Termas Flamboyant plasterwork, domes and arches decorate this comfortable spa hotel.
✉ Balneario de Archena, 30600 Archena, Murcia. **Map** p291 F3. ☎ (968) 670100. FAX (968) 671002. @ reservas@balneariodearchena.com 🍴 b,l,d. **Rooms** 70. €€

ARCOS DE LA FRONTERA

El Convento Former convent in the heart of historic Arcos. Good regional cooking, fine views of the Guadalete valley.
✉ Maldonado 2, 11630 Arcos de la Frontera, Cádiz. **Map** p290 B4. ☎ (956) 702333. FAX (956) 704128. @ hotelelconvento@terra.es 🍴 b,l,d. **Rooms** 11. €

ARCOS DE LA FRONTERA

Parador Casa del Corregidor An old magistrate's house with a spectacular clifftop setting and two terraces that take advantage of the vista.
✉ Plaza de España or del Cabildo, 11630 Cádiz. **Map** p290 B4. ☎ (956) 700500. FAX (956) 701116. @ arcos@parador.es 🍴 b,l,d. **Rooms** 24. €€

Arcos de la Frontera

Hacienda El Santiscal This delightful restored 15th-century manor house is within sight of the white city of Arcos and has sweeping views out over the Arcos lake and the Santiscal mountains. The impressive list of local outings, activities and expeditions on offer ranges from horse-riding to sherry tasting.

Avenida El Santiscal 129, 11630 Arcos de la Frontera, Cádiz. **Map** p290 B4. (956) 708313. FAX (956) 708268. reservas@santiscal.com b,l,d. **Rooms** 12. Never. AE, DC, MC, V. €€€

Barlovento, La Palma

La Palma Romántica For keen stargazers, there's an observatory at this well-equipped Canary Island hotel, set between mountains and sea. It's worth negotiating the twisting road to this side of La Palma for the glorious scenery, wildlife and silence. Rooms are large; all have a balcony, and some suites have a jacuzzi. A welcoming place.

Las Llanadas s/n, 38726 Barlovento, La Palma. **Map** p291 E4. (922) 186221. FAX (922) 186400. reservas@hotellapalmaromantica.com b,l,d. **Rooms** 44. Never. MC, V. €€

Baeza

Hospedería Fuentenueva The building's colourful history includes years as a women's prison, then as home to a judge. Now a lively, unconventional hotel, it is managed by a co-operative of five enthusiastic young people. The pleasing rooms retain their Moorish heritage; the public ones are often used for art exhibitions.

Paseo Arca del Agua s/n, 23440 Baeza, Jaén. **Map** p291 D3. (953) 743100. FAX (953) 743200. fuentenueva@fuentenueva.com b,l,d. **Rooms** 12. Never. AE, DC, MC, V. €€

Benaoján

Molino del Santo Not far from Ronda, where you can watch kestrels soaring below you, is a delightful mill on a scented mountainside. Converted by the English owner-managers, it makes a glorious hideaway. The rooms are simply and comfortably furnished; most have terraces overlooking the beautiful pool.

Barriada Estación s/n, 29370 Benaoján, Málaga. **Map** p290 B4. (95) 2167151. FAX (95) 2167327. molino@logiccontrol.es b,l,d. **Rooms** 18. mid-Nov to mid-Feb. DC, MC, V. €€€€

Cala Ratjada, Mallorca

Ses Rotges This captivating pink house is French-run and boasts one of the island's most highly regarded restaurants.

Rafael Blanes 21, 07590 Cala Ratjada, Mallorca. **Map** p289 F5. (971) 563108. FAX (971) 564345. hotel@sesrotges.com b,l,d. **Rooms** 24. €€

Cala Sant Vicenç, Mallorca

Cala Sant Vicenç A handsome, well-run hotel on the north coast, with two restaurants.

Maressers 2, 07469 Cala Sant Vicenç, Mallorca. **Map** p289 F5. (971) 530250. FAX (971) 532084. info@hotelcala.com b,l,d. **Rooms** 38. €€€€

Campanet, Mallorca

Hotel Rural Monnaber Nou This country hotel looks out over hillsides. Facilities are first-rate.

Possessió Monnaber Nou, 07310 Campanet, Mallorca. **Map** p291 F3. (971) 877176. FAX (971) 877127. info@monnaber.com b,l,d. **Rooms** 25. €€€

La Carolina

Hotel de la Perdiz This beamed hotel has the air of a hunting lodge: hunting trophies, huge hearths and solid furniture. Pretty garden.

Carretera N IV, 23200 La Carolina, Jaén. **Map** p291 D2. (953) 660300. FAX (953) 681362. nhperdiz@nh_hoteles.es b,l,d. **Rooms** 85. €€

BINISSALEM, MALLORCA

Scott's The discreet plaque outside this elegant English-owned merchant's house on the main square only hints at the unobtrusive luxury inside. It's meticulously decorated and furnished, the flowers are fresh, the beds a dream, and you can always find a quiet corner to yourself. Breakfast is to die for. Children over 12 only.
Plaza de la Iglesia 12, 07350 Binissalem, Mallorca. **Map** p289 F5. (971) 870100. FAX (971) 870267. @ reserve@scottshotel.com b. **Rooms** 17. Never. AE, MC, V. €€€€

LAS CABEZAS DE SAN JUAN

Hacienda de San Rafael A very special hotel in an old olive mill amid sunflower fields, its white walls clad in bougainvillea. The charming Anglo-Spanish owners have revamped the interior in stunning traditional style. Pool, riding, golf. Some rooms are air-conditioned.
Apartado 28, Carretera Nacional IV, 41730 Las Cabezas de San Juan, Seville. **Map** p290 B4. (44 20) 8563 2100. FAX (44 20) 8563 2300. @ trihotelmktg@dial.pipex.com b,l,d. **Rooms** 11, plus 3 apts. Nov to Mar. None. €€€€

BUBIÓN

Villa Turística de Bubión Not a hotel but a complex of apartments, the Villa Turística consists of a cluster of low-rise houses built along traditional designs. Apartments are decorated with local textiles and ceramics, and each has a fireplace for chilly evenings. There is also a dining room/bar.
Barrio Alto s/n, 18412Bubión, Granada. **Map** p291 D4. (958) 763909. FAX (958) 763905. @ bubion@villabubion.com b,l,d. **Rooms** 40 apartments. Never. AE, MC, V. €€

CARMONA

Casa de Carmona A 16th-century palace in the heart of town, stylishly and faithfully restored, with opulent public rooms, a porticoed central patio and a delightful enclosed garden. The fabrics in the individual and well-equipped rooms set off the antiques. Outside, a shaded terrace gives a distant view of Seville. Top-class.
Plaza de Lasso 1, 41410 Carmona, Seville. **Map** p290 B3. (95) 4191000. FAX (95) 4190189. @ reserve@cascadecarmona.com b,l,d. **Rooms** 34. Never. AE, DC, MC, V. €€€€

CASTELL DE CASTELLS

Pensión Castells Friendly *pension* in a quiet mountain village. Guided walks, satisfying evening meals.
San Vicente 18, 03793 Castell de Castells, Alicante. **Map** p291 F5. FAX (96) 5518254. @ darburn@wanadoo.es b,l,d (for groups). **Rooms** 4. €

CASTELLAR DE LA FRONTERA

Casa Convento La Almoraima A 17th-century hunting lodge built by the dukes of Medinaceli, this country house hotel has a fine rural setting.
Finca La Almoraima, 11350 Castellar de la Frontera, Cádiz. **Map** p290 B4. (956) 693002. FAX (956) 693214. @ rleon1@traesa.es b,l,d. **Rooms** 24. €€

CAZALLA DE LA SIERRA

Hospedería La Cartuja A haven of peace for artists who not only stay in this unusual, restored monastery, but also exhibit their work here.
Carretera A-455 km 2.5, 41370 Cazalla de la Sierra, Seville. **Map** p290 B3. (95) 4884516. FAX (95) 4884707. @ cartujsv@teleline.es b,l,d. **Rooms** 12. €€

CAZALLA DE LA SIERRA

Posada del Moro Julia Piñero has lavished love and attention on her appealing hotel, furnishing rooms with carefully chosen pieces and pictures.
Paseo del Moro s/n, 41370 Cazalla de la Sierra, Seville. **Map** p290 C3. FAX (95) 4884858. @ sangoy2001@hotmail.com b,l,d. **Rooms** 15. €

Carmona

Parador Alcazár del Rey Don Pedro The original hilltop Moorish fortress was made into a palace for Don Pedro the Cruel. It is now an unashamedly efficient commercial hotel, making the most of the stupendous view. The large public rooms are decorated with suits of armour and tapestry wallhangings.
Alcázar, 41410 Carmona, Seville. **Map** p290 B3.
(95) 4141010. FAX (95) 4141712.
@ carmona@parador.es b,l,d. **Rooms** 63.
Never. AE, DC, MC, V. €€€

Cazalla de la Sierra

Las Navezuelas In a broad valley in the hills north of Seville is this converted old olive mill, set on a large farm in a UNESCO biosphere reserve. It's a simple place, with a warm welcome, excellent home cooking and spotless rooms. There are cattle, sheep and goats on the farm, deer and wild boar in the woods and fish in the river.
Apartado 14, 41370 Cazalla de la Sierra, Seville.
Map p290 B3. FAX (95) 4884764. @ navezuela@arrakis.es b,d. **Rooms** 9. 2 Jan to 25 Feb.
MC, V. €

Córdoba

Alfaros Córdoba was the Moorish capital and this large, well-appointed hotel reflects its mixed heritage in an otherwise modern décor. All its rooms are light and airy, the services are up-to-date and efficient, and the swimming pool is wonderful. Don't miss seeing the Mezquita, the mosque-cathedral, which is simply stunning.
Alfaros 18, 14001 Córdoba. **Map** p290 C3.
(957) 491920. FAX (957) 492210.
@ alfaros@maciahoteles.com b,l,d. **Rooms** 133.
Never. AE, DC, MC, V. €€€

Córdoba

Amistad Córdoba In the Barrio de la Judería, the old Jewish quarter with a synagogue to rival Toledo's, an opening in a Moorish wall reveals an excellent modern hotel. The public rooms are deliberately simple, with flashes of local colour. The sizeable bedrooms are more richly furnished and equipped. The service is impeccable.
Plaza de Maimónides 3, 14004 Córdoba.
Map p290 C3. (957) 420335. FAX (957) 420365.
@ nhamistadcordoba@nh-hotels.com b,l,d. **Rooms** 84. Never. AE, DC, MC, V. €€€

Cazorla

Parador de Cazorla This modern parador in the beautiful wooded landscape of the Sierra de Cazorla is based on a typical Andalusian *cortijo*.
Sierra de Cazorla s/n, 23470 Cazorla, Jaén. **Map** p291 D3. (953) 727075. FAX (953) 727077.
@ cazorla@parador.es b,l,d. **Rooms** 34. €€

Córdoba

El Conquistador A modern building designed in Moorish style. Bedrooms are elegant; those at the front have views of the Mezquita. Quiet patio.
Magistral González Francés 15-17, 14003 Córdoba.
Map p290 C3. (957) 481102. FAX (957) 474677.
@ conquist@teleline.es b,l,d. **Rooms** 128. €€€

Córdoba

González In one of the Jewish quarter's narrow streets, this hotel has a cool marble interior and Moorish arches leading to a pretty flowery patio.
Manríquez 3, 14003 Córdoba. **Map** p290 C3.
(957) 479819. FAX (957) 486187. @ hotelgonzalez@wanadoo.es b. **Rooms** 17. €€

Denia

Rosa Parisian Michel Kessous has converted his modest *pension* into a fine villa with Florentine balconies. Some self-catering bungalows.
Congre 3, Las Marinas, 03700 Denia, Alicante.
Map p291 F2. (96) 5781573. FAX (96) 6424774.
b,l,d. **Rooms** 40. €€

Córdoba

Parador de Córdoba High above the heat of the city is this parador, built from the ruins of the summer palace built for Abderramán I. This is where Europe's first palm trees were grown. The building and decor are a fusion of Arabic and Andalusian, the rooms large and airy. The dining room is a showcase for regional dishes and wines. ✉ Avenida de la Arruzafa s/n, 14012 Córdoba. **Map** p290 C3. ☎ (957) 275900. FAX (957) 280409. @ cordoba@parador.es b,l,d. **Rooms** 94. Never. AE, DC, MC, V. €€

Gaucín

Cortijo Puerto del Negro In the beautiful hills behind the Costa del Sol, this well-run country-house hotel provides an oasis away from the bustle. Rooms with terracotta floors and wood-panelled ceilings have appropriately rustic furnishings and restful colour schemes. Meals – Anglo-French affairs – are often served on the creeper-covered terrace. ✉ Apartado 25, 29480 Gaucín, Málaga. **Map** p290 B4. ☎ FAX (952) 151239. @ puertodelnegro@mercuryin.es b,l,d. **Rooms** 4. Nov-Jan. MC, V. €€€€

Deiá, Mallorca

La Residencia This creeper-clad 16th-century manor house, set by the unspoilt northwestern coast, is a delight. It's surrounded by tiered gardens and woodland, and filled with antiques, bright rugs and modern art. The restaurant is one of the island's best. Rooms vary in size. Own art gallery. Tennis coaching available. ✉ Son Canals s/n, 07179 Deiá, Mallorca. **Map** p289 F5. ☎ (971) 636046. FAX (971) 639270. @ reservas@hotel-laresidencia.com b,l,d. **Rooms** 63. Never. AE, MC, V. €€€€

Granada

Carmen de Santa Inés A beautiful old Arab house with a lovely patio is the setting for this small but perfectly formed bed and breakfast hotel, in the same ownership as the Palacio de Santa Inés (see page 320). Bedrooms are cool and airy. Those rooms that don't have views of the Alhambra overlook a varied garden. ✉ Placeta de Porras 7, 18010 Granada. **Map** p291 D3. ☎ (958) 226380. FAX (958) 224404. @ sinescal@teleline.es b. **Rooms** 9. Never. AE, DC, MC, V. €€

Forcall

Palau dels Osset y Miró In the remote El Maestrat area, this 17th-century house on the porticoed main square is an oasis of rural comfort. ✉ Plaza Mayor 16, 12310 Forcall, Castellón. **Map** p289 C5. ☎ (964) 177524. FAX (964) 177556. @ hotel@hotelpalau.com b,l,d. **Rooms** 20. €€

Gibraltar

Rock Favoured by glitterati, this colonial-style hotel prides itself on its service. Stupendous views from its perch above the bay. ✉ 3 Europa Road, Gibraltar. **Map** p290 B4. ☎ (350) 73000. FAX (350) 73513. @ rockhotel@gibnynex.gi b,l,d. **Rooms** 100. €€€€

Granada

América Home from home with cheerful rooms done out in colourful fabrics. Some overlook the Alhambra gardens, others a pretty patio. ✉ Real de la Alhambra 53, 18009 Granada. **Map** p291 D3. ☎ (958) 227471. FAX (958) 227470. @ reservas@hotelamericagranada.com b,l. **Rooms** 17. €€

Granada

Reina Cristina Poet and playwright García Lorca stayed in this refined 19th-century house with a glazed courtyard. Small but relaxing rooms. ✉ Tablas 4, 18002 Granada. **Map** p291 D3. ☎ (958) 253211. FAX (958) 255728. @ clientes@hotelreinacristina.com b,l,d. **Rooms** 43. €€

Granada

Palacio de Santa Inés It is as elegant as its smaller sister, the Carmen de Santa Inés (see page 319), but the 'palace' has dark *caisson* ceilings, a picture-lined gallery and a slightly grander air. There are also some amazing fresco fragments attributed to Alejandro Mayner, a disciple of Rafael. Substantial annexe recently added.
Cuesta de Santa Inés 9, 18010 Granada. **Map** p291 D3. (958) 222362. FAX (958) 222465. @ sinespal@teleline.es b. **Rooms** 36. Never. AE, DC, MC, V. €€

Huelva

Finca Buenvino Many people are drawn back to this family home in the Sierra de Aracena. Here, the air is pervaded with the scent of jasmin in summer and woodsmoke in winter. Rooms are very pretty and individual, there's crystal and linen at dinner, and a pool with a seemingly endless view. Cottages with pools also available.
Los Marines, 21208 Huelva. **Map** p290 A3. (959) 124034. FAX (959) 501029. @ sam@buenvino.com b,l (by request),d. **Rooms** 4. Aug; Christmas to New Year. MC, V. €€€

Granada

Parador San Francisco This immensely popular 14th-century former convent in the Alhambra's gardens is still a place of tranquillity. This is partly thanks to the superb views over the Generalife, the Albaicín and the snowy peaks of the Sierra Nevada. Inside, wooden saints stand in alcoves between finely furnished galleries. Book early.
Real de la Alhambra, 18009 Granada. **Map** p291 D3. (958) 221440. FAX (958) 222264. @ granada@parador.es b,l,d. **Rooms** 36. Never. AE, DC, MC, V. €€€€

Ibiza Town, Ibiza

El Palacio At the top of a maze of steep streets lined with bougainvillea-clad houses, this classic mansion with an enclosed courtyard garden has been transformed into a paradise for film buffs. The bar has posters and other movie memorabilia, and every gorgeous room or suite is dedicated to a star – Garbo, Bogart, Monroe, James Dean.
Calle de la Conquista 2, 07800 Ibiza. **Map** p289 E5. (971) 301478. FAX (971) 391581. @ etienne@ctv.es b. **Rooms** 8. Nov to Mar. MC, V. €€€€

La Herradura

Los Fenicios In one of the Costa del Sol's least built-up resorts, this hotel stands out from the crowd for its unusual architecture and unique lift.
Paseo Andrés Segovia, 18697 La Herradura, Granada. **Map** p290 C4. (958) 827900. FAX (958) 827910. @ sol.los.fenicios@solmelia.com b,l,d. **Rooms** 42. €€€

Mijas

Club Puerta del Sol Sporty types will enjoy the tennis, pool and gym; others will love the views and garden of this chic horseshoe-shaped hotel.
Carretera Fuengirola-Mijas, 29650 Mijas, Málaga. **Map** p290 C4. (95) 2486400. FAX (95) 2485462. @ reservas@hotelclubpuertadelsol.com b,d. **Rooms** 130. €€

Mojácar

Mamabel's Lovingly run by Isabel Aznar and Jean Marie Rath, both lovers of art and antiquities. Sea views from terraces; delicious food.
Embajadores 5, 04638Mojácar, Almería. **Map** p291 E4. FAX (9504) 72448. @ mamabel2@indalmedia.com b,d. **Rooms** 9. €€

Moraira

Swiss Hotel Moraira Exclusivity is the byword at this estate of smart villas set back from the sea. Lavish rooms, large pool.
Urbanización Club Moraira, 03724, Alicante. **Map** p291 F2. (96) 5747104. FAX (96) 5747074. @ brapahotel@telefonica.net b. **Rooms** 25. €€€

Jaén

Parador Castillo de Santa Catalina This impressive hill-top fortress, of the same vintage and style as the Alhambra, now looks benignly over a pretty valley filled with olive trees. Most rooms share the view. Some furniture will excite 1960s fans, but there are also paintings and tapestries borrowed from the national collection.
Castillo de Santa Catalina, 23001 Jaén. **Map** p290 C3. (953) 230000. FAX (953) 230930. jaen@parador.es b,l,d. **Rooms** 45. Never. AE, DC, MC, V. €€

Loja

La Bobadilla Set like an Andalusian village in its own huge grove of olive trees and Spanish oak, this is a gem that sets the standards by which other hotels are measured. Rooms are large, lavish, and rich in marble, silk and wood. Extras include two pools, a Turkish bath, and two fine restaurants supplied from the organic farm.
Finca La Bobadilla, 18300 Loja, Granada. **Map** p290 C3. (958) 321861. FAX (958) 321810. info@la-bobadilla.com b,l,d. **Rooms** 62. Occasionally in Jan. AE, DC, MC, V. €€€€

Málaga

Parador de Málaga-Gibralfaro The views are the prime asset of this parador, set in the peaceful gardens of the Gibralfaro far above the bustling port and summer heat of the city. Rooms are large and comfortable, with their own balconies. Summer dining is on a terrace and the bar, often busy with locals, serves excellent snacks.
Monte de Gibralfaro, 29016 Málaga. **Map** p290 C4. (952) 221902. FAX (952) 221904. gibralfaro@parador.es b,l,d. **Rooms** 38. Never. AE, DC, MC, V. €€€

Orient, Mallorca

L'Hermitage In the mountainous interior of the island a 17th-century manor, cloister and new annexe cluster together amid citrus groves to form an appealing hotel. Rooms in the house have bags of character, those in the annexe have modern comforts. There are two snug lounges, a cosy bar, dining room and lovely terrace.
Carretera Alaro–Bunyola, 07349 Orient, Mallorca. **Map** p289 F5. (971) 180303. FAX (971) 180411. info@hermitage-hotel.com b,l,d. **Rooms** 24. early Nov to early Feb. AE, DC, MC, V. €€€€

Morella

Cardenal Ram Heavy furniture highlights the character of this 16th-century mansion with its gleaming wood floors, beams and stone arches.
Cuesta Suñer 1, 12300 Morella, Castellón. **Map** p289 C5. (964) 173085. FAX (964) 173218. hotelcardenalram@ctv.es b,l,d. **Rooms** 19. €

Murcia

Arco de San Juan The award-winning bold interior is tempered by fine antique furniture and a traditional façade. Near the cathedral.
Plaza de Ceballos 10, 30003 Murcia. **Map** p291 F3. (968) 210455. FAX (968) 220809. info@arcosanjuan.com b,l,d. **Rooms** 100. €€€

Ojén

Refugio de Juanar A comfortable rustic refuge in Marbella's wild hinterland, this hunting lodge offers snug rooms and robust regional cooking.
Sierra Blanca, 29610 Ojén, Málaga. **Map** p290 C4. (95) 2881000. FAX (95) 2881001. juanar@sopde.es b,l,d. **Rooms** 26. €€

Orgiva

Taray Bedrooms here are huge and modestly priced. Lovely garden of olives and orange trees, ideal walking and riding countryside beyond.
Carretera Tablate-Albuñol, 18400 Orgiva, Granada. **Map** p291 D4. (958) 784525. FAX (958) 784531. tarayalp@teleline.es b,l,d. **Rooms** 15. €

PALMA DE MALLORCA

Palacio Ca Sa Galesa This small, central 16th-century *palacio* offers stylish comfort with 20th-century amenities, and views of the bay and cathedral from its terrace. Oriental rugs dress wood floors and the comfy public rooms are set about with antiques. Indoor spa. Free tea is served every afternoon, sherry in the evening. ✉ Miramar 8, 07001 Palma de Mallorca. **Map** p289 F5. ☎ (971) 715400. FAX (971) 721579. @ reservas@palaciocasagalesa.com 🍴 b (l, d via room service). **Rooms** 12. Never. AE, DC, MC, V. €€€€

PALMA DE MALLORCA

Son Vida Ever since this 13th-century castle was turned into a luxury hotel in 1961, it has attracted the rich and famous, from Haile Selassie and Zsa Zsa Gabor to the Spanish royal family. Within the splendid building are all the facilities you would expect and more; outside is a glorious subtropical park and two golf courses. ✉ Raixa 2, 07013 Palma de Mallorca. **Map** p289 F5. ☎ (971) 606029. @ reservas@hotelsonvida.com 🍴 b,l,d. **Rooms** 167. Never. AE, DC, MC, V. €€€€

PALMA DE MALLORCA

San Lorenzo Pass through a wrought-iron gate on an old town street and, with the discovery of this hidden place, leave the cares of the world behind. The rooms are large, light and elegant with stylish bathrooms to match; two have their own roof terrace. A French Art Deco bar and a bougainvillea-hung garden complete the escape. ✉ San Lorenzo 14, 07012 Palma de Mallorca. **Map** p289 F5. ☎ (971) 728200. FAX (971) 711901. @ info@hotelsanlorenzo.com 🍴 b. **Rooms** 6. Never. AE, DC, MC, V. €€€

PALMA DEL RÍO

Hospedería de San Francisco Bedrooms in this converted 15th-century Franciscan monastery are the former cells. They have few luxuries but plenty of character, bedspreads woven by nuns and hand-painted basins. There is a comfy sitting room, beamed bar and huge dining hall, though the summer venue for meals is the lovely cloister. ✉ Avenida Pío XII 35, 14700 Palma del Río, Córdoba. **Map** p290 B3. ☎ (957) 710183. FAX (957) 710236. @ hospederia@casasypalacios.com 🍴 b,l,d. **Rooms** 35. Never. AE, MC, V. €€

PALMA DE MALLORCA

Born This old mansion was originally the Marquis of Ferrandell's town base. Magnificent staircase and chandeliers, palm-planted courtyard. ✉ Sant Jaume 3, 07012 Palma de Mallorca. **Map** p289 F5. ☎ (971) 712942. FAX (971) 718618. @ hotel-born@hotmail.com 🍴 b. **Rooms** 30. €€

PECHINA

Balneario Sierra Alhamilla Roman baths survive at this 18th-century spa hotel. Bedrooms are traditional, with arched ceilings and double doors. The tiled dining room is barrel-vaulted. ✉ 04259 Pechina, Almería. **Map** p291 E4. ☎ (950) 317413. FAX (950) 160257. 🍴 b,l,d. **Rooms** 20. €

POLLENÇA, MALLORCA

Formentor This ritzy hotel is set on a stunning promontory. Own beach and famous buffet lunch. ✉ Playas de Formentor, 07470 Port de Pollença, Mallorca. **Map** p289 F5. ☎ (971) 899101. FAX (971) 865155. @ reservas@hotelformentor.net 🍴 b,l,d. **Rooms** 127. €€€€

RANDA, MALLORCA

Es Recó de Randa Old stone house in a peaceful village, now a restaurant with rooms. Ask for a bedroom with a view of the mountains. ✉ Font 13, 07629 Randa, Mallorca. **Map** p289 F5. ☎ (971) 660997. FAX (971) 662558. @ esreco@fehm.es 🍴 b,l,d. **Rooms** 14. €€€

Penáguila

Mas de Pau A valley of olives and almonds in the Sierra de Aitana is the setting for this rural house. Part of its appeal is a gorgeous pool with glazed roof and wrap-around windows, that allows you to swim and admire the view all year. Staff are attentive and polite, but bedrooms are cramped – especially those on the second floor.

Carretera Alcoi-Penáguila km 9, 03815 Penáguila, Alicante. **Map** p291 F2. (96) 5513111. FAX (96) 5513109. b,l,d. **Rooms** 12. Never. AE, DC, MC, V. €

El Puerto de Santa María

Monasterio San Miguel This large Baroque building was built in the 18th century by the Duke of Medinaceli to house the Clarisas Capuchinas order of nuns. It is now a smart, busy hotel with antique art and modern facilities. It is a popular venue for concerts and conferences – the former chapel can seat 600.

Virgen de los Milagros 27, 11500 El Puerto de Santa María, Cádiz. **Map** p290 A4. (956) 540440. FAX (956) 542525. monasterio@jale.com b,l,d. **Rooms** 165. Never. AE, DC, V. €€€€

Port d'Andratx, Mallorca

Villa Italia Built in the 1920s by an eccentric Italian for his lover, Villa Italia is now patronized by a steady stream of glitterati. Marble floors, linen sheets, stucco ceilings, round baths, Roman capitals, personal service and a host of other hand-made details keep them coming. If it's all too much, retreat to the beautiful garden.

Camino Sant Carles 13, 07157 Port d'Andratx, Mallorca. **Map** p289 F5. (971) 674011. FAX (971) 673350. info@hotelvillaitalia.com b,l,d. **Rooms** 16. Never. AE, MC, V. €€€€

Ronda

Parador de Ronda Ronda is one of Spain's most spectacularly situated cities and this purpose-built parador has an incomparable spot, teetering precipitously above the Tajo gorge. If you can, book a top-floor suite – they have balconies and spectacular views – and watch the birds at close range. The dining room has a solid reputation.

Plaza de España s/n, 29400 Ronda, Málaga. **Map** p290 B4. (95) 2877500. FAX (95) 2878188. ronda@parador.es b,l,d. **Rooms** 78. Never. AE, DC, MC, V. €€€

Ronda

Husa Reina Victoria The Reina Victoria enjoys a clifftop setting with matchless views.

Jerez 25, 29400 Ronda, Málaga. **Map** p290 B4. (95) 2871240. FAX (95) 2871075. reinavictoriaronda@husa.es b,l,d. **Rooms** 89. €€€

Sanlúcar de Barrameda

Los Helechos This early 20th-century Andalusian building has quiet rooms that provide a refuge in a central location. Pool under construction.

Plaza Madre de Dios 9, 11540 Sanlúcar de Barrameda, Cádiz. **Map** p290 A4. (956) 361349. FAX (956) 369650. b. **Rooms** 56. €

Sanlúcar de Barrameda

Posada de Palacio This unconventional, homely B&B occupies a fine house near the sherry *bodegas* in the old town. Stone-tiled courtyard.

Caballeros 11, 11540 Sanlúcar de Barrameda, Cádiz. **Map** p290 A4. (956) 364840. FAX (956) 365060. posadadepalacio@terra.es b,l,d. **Rooms** 27. €

Sanlúcar de Barrameda

Tartaneros An inviting cafeteria in Art Nouveau style occupies most of the ground floor, while antiques and curiosities furnish the other rooms.

Tartaneros 8, 11540 Sanlúcar de Barrameda, Cádiz. **Map** p290 A4. (956) 385393. FAX (956) 385394. hoteltartaneros@telefonica.net b. **Rooms** 22. €€

For key to symbols see backflap. For price categories *see p285*

San Miguel, Ibiza

Hacienda Na Xamena The focal point of this glamorous clifftop *hacienda* is its terrace and pool overlooking sea and pine-wooded hills. Inside, dazzling white curved walls are offset with touches of vivid blue, terracotta, stone and wood to create a haven of understated luxury.
Na Xamena, 07815 San Miguel, Ibiza. **Map** p289 E5. (971) 334500. FAX (971) 334514. hotelhacienda@retemail.es b,l,d. **Rooms** 63. Nov to Apr. AE, DC, V. €€€€

Sanlúcar La Mayor

Hacienda Benazuza El Bullihotel Unlike many other large hotels, this *hacienda* has not sacrificed its soul. The buildings span diverse cultures and centuries, from the thousand-year-old Arabic enclosing wall to a 16th-century Spanish coat of arms. Public rooms have Moorish ceilings. Three-star Michelin chef in residence.
Virgen de las Nieves s/n, 41800 Sanlúcar La Mayor, Seville. **Map** p290 A3. (95) 5703344. FAX (95) 5703410. hbenazuza@elbullihotel.com b,l,d. **Rooms** 44. mid-Jan. AE, DC, MC, V. €€€€

San Sebastián, Gomera

Parador de La Gomera High above the main town of this volcanic island, where Columbus made his last stop before America, the parador is full of maritime mementoes. The decoration is exemplary: polished wood floors, rugs, potted plants, pitched beamed roofs, and furniture that gleams in the spacious bedrooms.
38800 San Sebastián de La Gomera, Santa Cruz de Tenerife. **Map** p291 E5. (922) 871100. FAX (922) 871116. gomera@parador.es b,l,d. **Rooms** 60. Never. AE, DC, MC, V. €€€

Santa Eulalia del Río, Ibiza

Les Terrasses A traditional Ibizan house, done out with panache by a Frenchwoman, Françoise Pialoux. The house, bedrooms (in a converted farm building), two pools and gardens are on different levels. Peaceful nooks and crannies give it the intimacy of a private villa.
Apartado 1235, Carretera de Santa Eulalia, 07800 Santa Eulalia del Río, Ibiza. **Map** p289 E5. (971) 332643. FAX (971) 338978. lesterrasses@interbook.net b,l,d. **Rooms** 7. Occasionally in Jan. MC, V. €€€

St Antonio de Portmany, Ibiza

Pikes Ibiza Its setting amid pine woods draws a smart crowd to this stylish *finca*. Five-star amenities are combined with informality.
Aptdo 104, 07820 Sant Antonio de Portmany, Ibiza. **Map** p289 E5. (971) 342222. FAX (971) 342312. reservas@pikeshotel.com b,l,d. **Rooms** 27. €€€€

Seville

Alfonso XIII Sumptuous mock Moorish palace. Exotic gardens without, grand rooms and formal service within.
San Fernando 2, 41004 Seville. **Map** p290 B3. (95) 4917000. FAX (95) 4917099. maria.yerga@westin.com b,l,d. **Rooms** 147. €€€€

Seville

Casa Imperial Arranged around four peaceful courtyards, Seville's most palatial mansion hotel has comfortable suites with their own kitchens.
Imperial 29, 41003 Seville. **Map** p290 B3. (95) 4500300. FAX (95) 4500330. info@casaimperial.com b,l,d. **Rooms** 26. €€€€

Seville

Casas de la Judería Suites (some self-catering), separated by courtyards. Pool due in 2004.
Callejón Dos Hermanas 7, Plaza de Santa María la Blanca, 41004 Seville. **Map** p290 B3. (95) 4415150. FAX (95) 4422170. juderia@casasypalacios.com b,d. **Rooms** 97. €€€€

SEVILLE

Patio de la Alameda For people who relish their independence, this handsome building has been converted into 22 pleasant one-bedroom apartments. Each has a sitting room and kitchen and can accommodate up to four people. There's a daily maid service; if you don't feel like cooking, there are plenty of local restaurants and bars.
Alameda de Hércules 56, 41002 Seville.
Map p290 B3. (95) 4904999. FAX (95) 4900226.
@ informacionalcliente@patiosdesevilla.com b.
Rooms 22. Never. AE, DC, MC, V. €€

SEVILLE

San Gil Classified as one of the hundred most interesting buildings in the city, the San Gil marks the careful restoration of an early 1900s mansion. A wealth of original detail remains, including a striking tiled entrance and enclosed garden with fountains, palms, an ancient cypress and original mosaics. The cool bedrooms have crisp lines.
Parras 28, 41002 Seville. **Map** p290 B3.
(95) 4906811. FAX (95) 4906939. @ sangil.reservas@fp-hoteles.com b. **Rooms** 61. Never.
AE, DC, MC, V. €€€

SEVILLE

Patio de la Cartuja The residential hotel version of Patio de la Alameda (see above) is similar in almost every respect, even down to the furnishings. The two are run under the combined name 'Patios de Sevilla'. The Cartuja has a long terrace, dotted with tables, chairs and parasols, and balconies decorated with geraniums.
Lumbreras 8-10, 41002 Seville.
Map p290 B3. (95) 4900200. FAX (95) 4902056.
@ informacionalcliente@patiosdesevilla.com b.
Rooms 34. Never. AE, DC, MC, V. €€

SEVILLE

Taberna del Alabardero The poet José Antonio Cavestany once lived in this 19th-century mansion in the heart of the city. Now it's a restaurant with rooms, elegantly decorated and specializing in a hybrid Basque-Andalusian cuisine. Breakfast, tea or drinks can be taken in the romantic central court with a stained-glass roof.
Zaragoza 20, 41001 Seville. **Map** p290 B3. (954) 502721. FAX (954) 563666. @ hotel.alabardero@esh.es
b,l,d. **Rooms** 7. Aug. AE, DC, MC, V.
€€€€

SEVILLE

Doña María A brand new hotel behind an old façade, with Andalusian decoration, a glorious patio overflowing with plants and a rooftop pool.
Don Remondo 19, 41004 Seville. **Map** p290 B3.
(90) 2500524. FAX (95) 4219546.
@ reservas@hdmaria.com b. **Rooms** 64. €€€€

SEVILLE

Murillo A treasure trove of antiques, from ornate screens to a sedan chair, in a handsome town house at the heart of the Barrio de Santa Cruz.
Lope de Rueda 7 & 9, 41004 Seville.
Map p290 B3. (95) 4216095. FAX (95) 4219616.
@ reservas@hotelmurillo.com b. **Rooms** 57. €

SEVILLE

Los Seises Art Deco motifs inject style into elegant pastel rooms in this 16th-century palace which preserves a Roman mosaic and Arab well.
Segovias 6, 41004 Seville. **Map** p290 B3. (95) 4229495. FAX (95) 4224334. @ info@hotellosseises.com
b,l,d. **Rooms** 42. €€€€

SÓLLER, MALLORCA

Finca Ca N'aí Captivating old Mallorcan house, nestling in a valley scented with the fragrance of oranges. Popular for its first-rate restaurant.
Camí Son Sales 50, 07100 Sóller, Mallorca.
Map p289 F50. (971) 632494. FAX (971) 631899.
@ finca-canai@terra.es b,l,d. **Rooms** 13. €€€€

Sierra Nevada

El Lodge After a long day on the piste, you can ski to the door of this modern chalet and relax in a Jacuzzi bath with a view of the surrounding peaks. It is one of Spain's premier ski hotels, built of Finnish pine, warm and soundproofed, with a comfy sitting room, a bar flaunting ski mementoes and snug log-cabin-style bedrooms.
Maribel 8, 18196 Sierra Nevada, Granada. **Map** p291 D4. (958) 480600. FAX (958) 481314. b,l,d. **Rooms** 19. 27 Apr to 28 Nov. AE, DC, MC, V. €€€€

Turre

Finca Listonero Restaurateurs Graeme Gibson and David Rice run this farmhouse in the hills above the unspoilt Almería coast. It has been stylishly converted and seamlessly extended, and functions along house-party lines. The setting is peaceful but sandy beaches, golf, tennis, riding and walking are all within easy reach. Daily menu of international dishes.
Cortijo Grande, 04630 Turre, Almería. **Map** p291 E4. FAX (950) 479094. listonero@wanadoo.es b,l,d. **Rooms** 6. Never. MC, V. €€

Tarifa

Hurricane Winds from the Straits of Gibraltar make Tarifa a great spot for windsurfing, the main attraction of this hip, casual place. Enclosed by a wild palm-filled garden, it has a romantic terrace, where dinner is served under Moorish arches. Ask for one of the simple, tasteful rooms on the garden side.
Carretera Málaga–Cádiz, 11380 Tarifa, Cádiz. **Map** p290 B5. (956) 684919. FAX (956) 680329. info@hotelhurricane.com b,l,d. **Rooms** 33. Never. AE, DC, MC, V. €€€

Úbeda

Palacio de la Rambla This 16th-century mansion in the centre of town, ancestral home of the Marquesa de la Rambla, makes a unique, historic B&B. At its heart is a beautiful ivy-clad Renaissance patio, around which are the four most interesting bedrooms, furnished with antiques and engravings.
Plaza del Marqués 1, 23400 Úbeda, Jaén. **Map** p291 D3. (953) 750196. FAX (953) 750267. palaciorambla@terra.es b. **Rooms** 8. mid-July to mid-Aug. AE, V. €€

Illa de Tabarca

Casa del Gobernador This 18th-century colonial mansion, once the governor's house, wouldn't look out of place in the pirate haven of Tortuga.
Arzola s/n, 03138 Illa de Tabarca, Alicante. **Map** p291 F2. FAX (965) 961272. b. **Rooms** 14. €

Torre de la Reina

Cortijo Torre de la Reina National Monument filled with books, knick-knacks, rugs and heavy furniture. New Arabic-style garden.
Paseo de la Alameda, 41209 Torre de la Reina, Seville. **Map** p290 B3. (95) 5780136. FAX (95) 5780122. info@torredelareina.com b,l,d. **Rooms** 12. €€€

Torremolinos

Hotel Miami Palms, banana trees, a lagoon-like swimming pool – in its walled enclosure, the Miami has an exotic, almost Caribbean feel.
Calle Aladino 14, 29620, Torremolinos, Málaga. **Map** p290 C4. (952) 385255. FAX (952) 053447. jmdejens@teleline.es b. **Rooms** 26. €€

Turre

Cortijo El Nacimiento Off the tourist track, this farmhouse has been turned into a guesthouse (with pool) by its genial organic farmer owners. You can taste the fruit of their labours at meals.
Cortijo El Nacimiento, 04639 Turre, Almería. **Map** p291 E4. (950) 528090. b,d. **Rooms** 5. €

Úbeda

Parador de Úbeda Eyecatching blue-and-white tiles on the façade announce this refined parador. Its glorious courtyard is set with tables and chairs and bursting with greenery. This is a friendly place, particularly evident in the tile-floored public rooms; bedrooms, some of which lead off a glazed gallery, do not disappoint.
Plaza de Vázquez Molina s/n, 23400 Úbeda, Jaén. **Map** p291 D3. (953) 750345. FAX (953) 751259. @ ubeda@parador.es b,l,d. **Rooms** 36. Never. AE, DC, MC, V. €€€

La Vila Joiosa (Villajoyosa)

Hotel El Montíboli This brightly luxurious hotel has carefully not grown past its ability to deliver a warm welcome to every guest. It is set on its own little headland. Below the hotel is a pool with a view, and down by the beach is another pool with a little lunch-time restaurant. Choose between a room with terrace and a bungalow.
03570 La Vila Joiosa, Alicante. **Map** p291 F2. (96) 5890250. FAX (96) 5893857. @ montiboli@servigroup.es b,l,d. **Rooms** 55. Never. AE, DC, MC, V. €€€€

Valldemossa, Mallorca

Vistamar de Valldemosa On cliffs near the pretty port of Valldemossa is this lovely old villa, now a comfortable country hotel with a penchant for modern art. The beamed rooms are cool and attractive. The sea, though close, is unreachable on foot, but the pool is panoramic.
Carretera Andraitx km 2, 07170 Valldemossa, Mallorca. **Map** p289 F50. (971) 612300. FAX (971) 612583. @ info@vistamarhotel.es b,l,d. **Rooms** 19. Nov to Jan. AE, DC, MC, V. €€€€

Xátiva

Hostería Mont-Sant The small Mont-Sant is superbly located above the town and below the castle, and has spectacular views of both from each of the attractive rooms. Its grounds are surrounded by architectural remains dating back to the 12th century. The restaurant's regional dishes can be eaten inside or *al fresco*.
Castillo s/n, 46800 Xátiva, Valencia. **Map** p291 F2. (62) 275081. FAX (62) 281905. @ montsant@servidex.com b,l,d. **Rooms** 15. mid-Jan. AE, DC, MC, V. €€€

Valderrobres

Torre del Visco Relais & Châteaux hotel overlooking the Tastavins valley. Stylish bedrooms, four sitting rooms. Mountain bikes available.
44587 Fuentespalda, Teruel. **Map** p288 C4. (978) 769015. FAX (978) 769016. @ torredelvisco@torredelvisco.com b,l,d (obligatory). **Rooms** 14. €€€€

Valencia

Ad Hoc Brickwork and beams are incorporated into the modern interior of this 19th-century old-quarter building with maximum effect.
Boix 4, 46003 Valencia. **Map** p291 F1. (96) 3919140. FAX (96) 3913667. @ adhoc@adhochoteles.com b,l,d. **Rooms** 28. €€€€

Vejer de la Frontera

Convento de San Francisco Remnants from its days as a convent are preserved in this friendly hotel, as well as Roman and medieval finds.
La Plazuela s/n, 11150 Vejer de la Frontera, Cádiz. **Map** p290 B4. (956) 451001. FAX (956) 451004. @ convento-san-francisco@tugasa.com b,l,d. **Rooms** 25. €€

Villanueva de la Concepción

Posada del Torcal In glorious country, a typical *cortijo*, with sunny colours and unusual furniture.
Partido de Jeva, 29230 Villanueva de la Concepción, Málaga. **Map** p290 C4. (95) 2031177. FAX (95) 203 1006. @ laposada@mercuryin.es b,l,d. **Rooms** 10, plus 22 villas. €€€

ITALY

Italy

ITALY'S BEST places to stay are often at the very cheap or the very expensive end of the spectrum. Many cities offer little in between, but away from urban centres the choice is wider. Often old farm estates in beautiful countryside have been restored to incorporate guest accommodation. Some of the two-star *pensioni* are truly excellent, run by hardworking owners: their hospitality and cooking can be unique. For glamour, head for a top hotel in a historic building – even if your budget restricts your stay to one night. Whether it's in the centre of Milan, deep in the countryside, surrounded by vineyards or on a fortified hill top, chances are it will be unforgettable.

Villa d'Este, Lake Como, page 343, a beautiful hotel with romantic grounds and a glittering interior

Italy Region by Region

IN THIS GUIDE, Italy has been divided into three areas: Northern Italy, Central Italy and Southern Italy.

Northern Italy

This is the wealthiest part of the country. The business lunch and the corporate weekend keep some very good hotels and restaurants in business, from Milan – centre of the textile and fashion trade – to Bologna, the medieval city at the heart of Italy's version of silicon valley. Venice, sinking under the weight of its visitors, has a few good-value places to stay, but only if you know the score; and, of course, it has its famous, luxury canalside *palazzi* – at a price.

Perhaps the most interesting experiences are provided by the small historic towns such as Ravenna, Bergamo and Parma, with their artistic and architectural treasures, and hotels that exude ***bonhomie*** and serve up classic North Italian cooking. But don't overlook the Italian lakes of Como, Orta and Maggiore: they have a wistful, old-fashioned appeal with one or two absolutely glorious *grande dame* hotels.

The mountainous northern-most parts of Italy were acquired at the beginning of the 20th century, from what used to be southern Austria, Slovenia and parts of France. Alpine-style chalet guest-houses with balconies full of geraniums, and dumplings on the menu, are an incongruous feature in these parts.

The Adriatic coastline is flat, with grill-pan sunbathing and genuinely warm hospitality. On the opposite side of the country is the Ligurian Riviera. Here is the smart resort of Portofino; the former fishing village with its mini-scule harbour is for many travellers a must-see-and-be-seen-at stopover. Its hotel prices are off the top end of the scale, but you can always visit for the day and then stay in nearby Santa Margherita or Rapallo, which offer much better value.

Central Italy

Florence is one the highlights of many a modern grand tour. Its outstanding places to stay include a palace in the hills outside town. For fewer crowds, head for the walled towns such as Lucca, or go east towards Umbria or even little-visited Le Marche (The Marches'), where there are some fine country hotels near the medieval cities of Arezzo and Sansepolcro.

The island of Sardinia is said to have the clearest water for snorkelling and scuba diving. Choose between the glitzy Costa Smeralda or quieter, and more beautiful backwaters.

Rome and its province of Lazio could keep you busy for weeks, and there are plenty of choices of lodgings, with a mix of one-stars and classic grand Italian hotels in the centre and more spacious places with gardens in the outer districts.

On the other side of the country, the Abruzzo and Molise are empty, mountainous quarters from which thousands have emigrated over the past 200 years. Hotels are sparse and itineraries need planning.

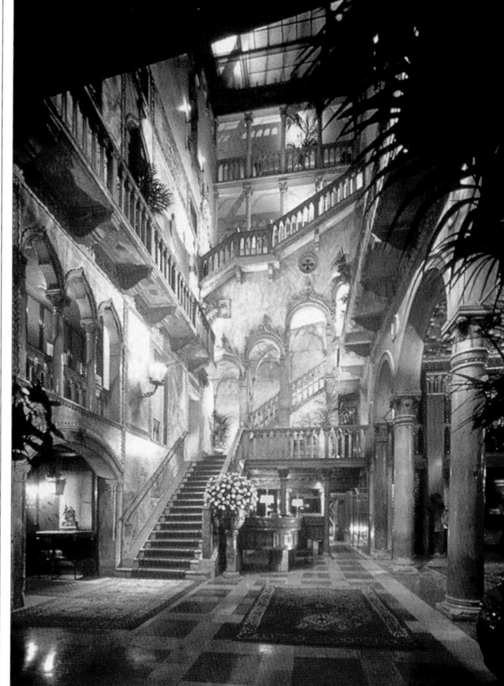

Venice's Danieli, page 356 – in a famed location overlooking the lagoon

Southern Italy

The landscape becomes dramatically rugged on the Amalfi peninsula south of Naples. Here there's a choice between excellent family-run *pensioni* or luxury *palazzi* in villages such as Ravello. The islands of Ischia and Capri in the Bay of Naples have accommodation in every price band, and are at their best in early spring before the holiday crowds arrive.

Puglia, in the 'heel' of Italy, has become fashionable among Italians, as have the Aeolian islands and Pantelleria. There are many villas for rent here, but few recommendable hotels. Sicily is a different world, with palm trees, citrus groves and volcanic beaches. There are some great places to stay here, though, again, not in large numbers. We believe we have featured the most captivating, from the fashionable resort of Taormina to the capital, Palermo.

The remarkable La Posta Vecchia, Palo Laziale, page 365

Highlights

HOTELS ILLUSTRATED on these pages are by no means the only highlights. Other favourites include the Baia d'Oro in Gargnano (page 345), for its fabulous setting on Lake Garda; the Salivolpi farmhouse hotel in Castellina in Chianti (page 360), perfect for family holidays; Rome's Hassler (page 367), a luxurious experience in old-world living; and the charming Bellevue Syrene in Sorrento (page 379), for its stunning clifftop setting.

Food and Drink

EATING OUT is one of the obvious pleasures of a holiday in Italy, and the regional differences add to the experience. Indeed, there is such a variety of regional cuisine that it is impossible to do it justice here.

Villa Franca, Positano, page 378 with great views of the plunging Amalfi coastline

Northern dishes tend to be pork, veal and dairy based, with creamy sauces. In the south, vegetables and fish predominate, and many pasta dishes are accompanied by 'raw' sauces in which tomatoes, for example, are sweated with garlic and oil for just a few moments so that the freshness of the ingredients comes through. Among the many highlights of Italian cooking are Milanese risotto, coloured by saffron and flavoured with rosemary and the juices from a veal roast; and fresh mozzarella from around Naples, which spills cream from its centre when you cut into it.

For some of the best places for local delicacies, look out for the '*Agriturismo*' signs, usually a crossed knife and fork. Cheese, salami, homemade pasta, honey and other farm produce can be enjoyed in delightful, simple surroundings.

Villa Franca, Positano, page 378

A *ristorante* is usually quite a formal place, with ranks of knives and forks and often a business clientele. The more informal *osteria* serves regional specialities, though the term is being highjacked by smarter establishments. The *birreria* (pubs) and *vineria* (wine bars) often offer meat and local cheese-based snacks (a snack is a *merenda*). The most enjoyable *trattorie* are the local, family-run places where the absence of a written menu, or a set menu with no choices, is usually a sign that the food will be simple, but unpretentious and delicious.

Space doesn't permit more than a brief sketch of Italian wine. Among the oustanding regions are Tuscany (for Brunello di Montalcino and Vino Nobile di Montepulciano); Friuli; and Le Langhe, a little-known region of Piemonte in Northern Italy (for the weighty Barolos and the earthy Barberas).

When eating out, most Italians order a bottle with a label only on special occasions. The norm is to have a carafe of house wine (usually local and perfectly quaffable). Ask for *un quarto* (quarter) or *un mezzo* (half) litre.

Lunch is generally from 12:30–3pm; dinner from 8–11pm or midnight, often followed by a stroll around the piazza, a coffee or a visit to a *gelateria* (ice-cream parlour).

Dinner starts with *antipasto* (seafood salad, or a selection of salami), followed by *il primo* (pasta or a soup) and on to the main business of *il secondo* (the meat or fish course). Vegetables (*contorni*) are ordered separately. Dessert (*dolci*) usually comes from the trolley. Most places make a cover charge (*pane e coperto*) and may also add a 10 per cent service charge. Take your receipt (*ricevuta fiscale*) when you leave the restaurant, or you can be subject to an on-the-spot fine; this strange law was introduced as an attempt to cut down on tax evasion.

Bedrooms and Bathrooms

The (potentially embarrassing) Italian word for a double bed is a *matrimoniale*. If you don't specify this, twin beds are automatically allocated. However, you can ask for these to be made up as a double if all the *matrimoniales* are taken. Make it clear if you want a room with en suite bathroom (*con bagno*); there are different

Stately Principe di Savoia in Milan, page 348

price tariffs for rooms with shared facilities. A shower is a *doccia*. Most places have showers and baths combined.

Other Practical Information

You'll often find air-conditioning in hotels, but heating in anything but the depths of winter should not be taken for granted.

Language Italians are good linguists. English, French and German are widely spoken, especially in tourist areas.

Currency From 1 January 2002, the European *euro* (written 'EUR'), made up of 100 *cents*.

Shops Open 8 or 9am–12:30 or 1pm Mon–Sat, and then from 3:30–7 or 8pm. Museum times tend to follow the same pattern. In northern cities, businesses and some shops are open through the day. Shops are closed on Sunday except in tourist resorts, but usually you'll find a *pasticceria* (essentially, a delicatessen) open first thing in the day for essentials.

Tipping Waiters don't rely on tips in the same way as in other European countries (if lucky, they will get a share of the profits), but Italians usually round up the bill.

Telephoning Many hotels, especially the unassuming kind, make no profit from phone calls their guests make – a pleasant change from other European countries.

As well as public call boxes (which take coins and phone-cards – called a *scheda telefonica*), in most big towns there are Telecom Italia offices with private phone booths – handy for long-distance calls.

To make a phone call within Italy, always dial the full prefix, even for a local number. To call Italy from the UK, dial 00, then the international dialling code 39; then the number, including the initial zero; from the US, 001 39.

Public holidays 1 January; 6 January; Easter Monday; 25 April (Liberation Day); 1 May; 15 August (Ferragosto, or Assumption); 1 November (All Saints); 8 December (Immaculate Conception); 25 and 26 December.

Useful Words

Breakfast	*Prima colazione*
Lunch	*Pranzo*
Dinner	*Cena*
Free rooms?	*Camere libere?*
How much?	*Quant'è?*
A single	*Una camera singola*
A double	*Una camera doppia*

Italy Price Bands

Most hotel prices vary according to whether it's low or high season. The maximum price is displayed (by law) on the back of the room's door.

Our price bands refer as usual to the price of a standard double room with bathroom in high season.

Breakfast is usually included in the price quoted; local taxes can creep in as an extra at any time, especially in the historic or 'art' cities.

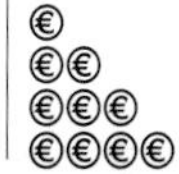

€	under 105 EUR
€€	105–170 EUR
€€€	170–230 EUR
€€€€	above 230 EUR

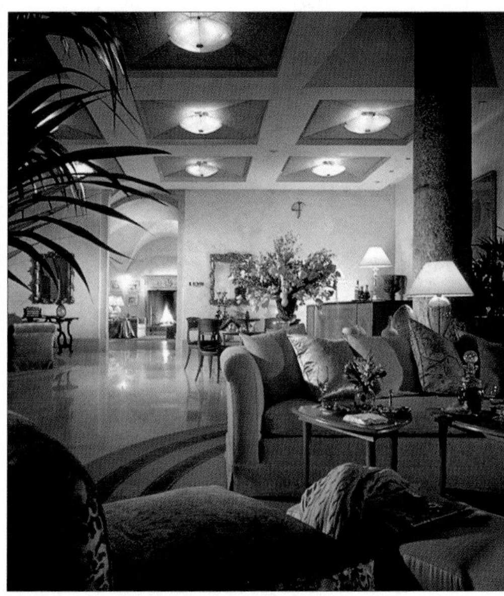

The lobby of the Four Seasons, Milan, page 348

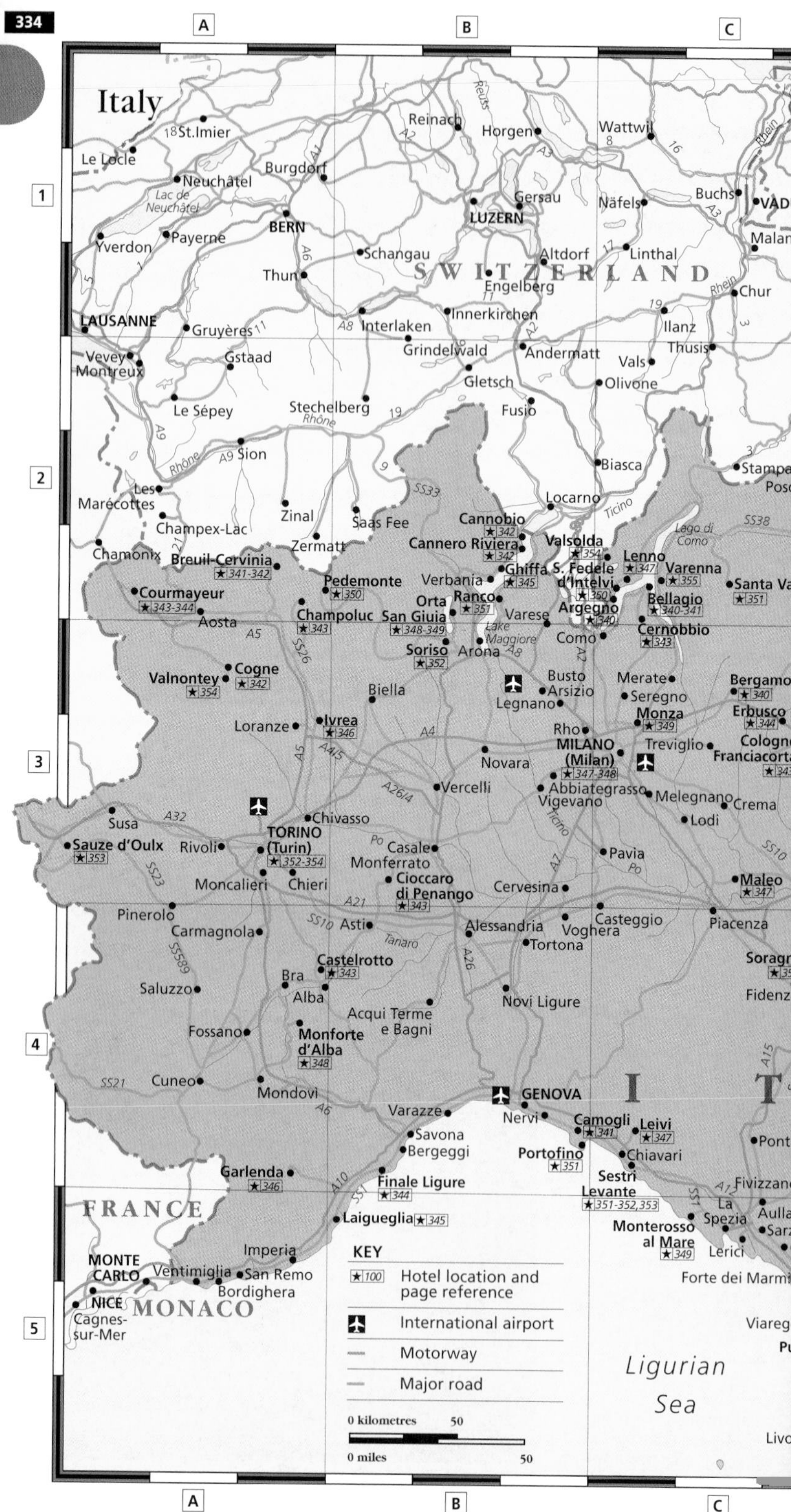
Italy
SWITZERLAND
FRANCE
MONACO
Ligurian Sea
LAUSANNE
BERN
LUZERN
MILANO (Milan)
TORINO (Turin)
GENOVA
Courmayeur 343-344
Breuil-Cervinia 341-342
Cogne 342
Valnontey 354
Pedemonte 350
Champoluc 343
San Giuia 348-349
Orta
Ranco 351
Soriso 352
Cannobio 342
Cannero Riviera 342
Ghiffa 345
Valsolda 354
S. Fedele d'Intelvi 350
Argegno 340
Lenno 347
Varenna 355
Bellagio 340-341
Cernobbio 343
Santa Va 351
Bergamo 340
Erbusco 344
Monza 349
Cologne Franciacorta 343
Ivrea 346
Sauze d'Oulx 353
Cioccaro di Penango 343
Castelrotto 343
Monforte d'Alba 348
Maleo 347
Soragn 35
Camogli 341
Leivi 347
Portofino 351
Sestri Levante 351-352,353
Monterosso al Mare 349
Finale Ligure 344
Laigueglia 345
Garlenda 346
KEY
★100 Hotel location and page reference
International airport
Motorway
Major road
0 kilometres 50
0 miles 50

D
E
F
1
2
3
4
5
Füssen
Kufstein
Lofer
Hallein
Salzach
Ehrwald
Inn
Hopfgarten
Leogang
Radstadt
198
Schwaz
Zell am See
311
INNSBRUCK
Igls
Ziller
165
A13
Landeck
AUSTRIA
167
A10
315
Heiligenblut
Rennweg
Sölden
Brenner
Nauders
Matrei
in Osttirol
Mallnitz
Brunico
(Bruneck)
Lienz
Lagundo
(Algund)
★345
Merano
(Meran)
★348
Bressanone (Brixen)
★341
100
Spittal
Sillian
111
San Vigilio
★352
Marlengo
★346
Siusi Allo
★353 Sciliar
Villandro
★357
Mauthen
Paternion
Ortisei (St Ulrich) ★349
Bolzano
(Bozen)
Fie Allo Sciliar
(Vols am Schlern)
★344
Cortina
d'Ampezzo
★343-344
Ravascletto
Caldaro
★342
Tarvisio
SS42
A22
San Osvaldo
★352
Sauris
SS51
SS12
Redagno
di Sopra
★351
Gemona
del Friuli
Mantua
★346
Pieve d'Alpago
★350
Belluno
A23
TRENTO
★353
Pergine
★350
Adige
UDINE
Feltre
SS13
San Floriano
del Collio
★352
Pordenone
A27
Vittorio
Arco
Follina
★345
Fiume
Veneto
★345
Rovereto
Conegliano
A28
San Floriano
★352
Cavaso del Tomba
★342
Solighetto
Cervignano
del Friuli
Lago di
Garda
A22
Gorizia
SS12
Bassano del
Grappa
Asolo
★340
Portobuffole
★349
Gardone Riviera
★344-345
A4
Monfalcone
Thiene
Latisana
Treviso
★354
A31
Cittadella
Rivarotta
★352
Torri del Benaco
★353-354
Brenta
Trieste
★354
Levada
★347
Gargagnago
★344
Vicenza
Zerman di Mogliano
Veneto ★357
Múggia
Sirmione
★352-353
Trissino
★354
Mestre
VENEZIA
(Venice)
★355-357
Verona
★357
A4
Padova
(Padua)
Mira
★349
Gulf of
Venice
Villafranca
di Verona
San Bonifacio
★350
Laguna
Veneta
Finale
Montagnana
Monselice
SS10
Este
Mantova
Legnago
Vescovana
★357
Chioggia
Adige
Ostiglia
Cavarzare
A22
A13
Rovigo
Adria
Pomponesco
Po
Mirandola
Bondeno
Panaro
Ferrara
★344
Codigoro
Carpi
Reggio nell'
Emilia
★350
Modena
★348
Comacchio
Castelfranco
Emilia
★342
Y
Argenta
L
Adriatic
Sea
Reno
Portonovo
★367
BOLOGNA
★341
A14
Castel Guelfo
★342
Ravenna
Pavullo nel
Frignano
Castel
San Pietro
Lugo
Imola
Bagnacavallo
Faenza
A1
Brisighella
★341
Forlì
SS9
Cervia
Cesenatico
SS325
Portico
di Romagna
★350
Cesena
Borgo San
Lorenzo
Rimini
Pistoia
★366
Vicchio di Mugello
★371
SAN MARINO
Sesto
★351
SAN MARINO
A11
Pesaro
★366
Artimino
★358
Fiesole ★361
A14
Fano
Arno
Montegridolfo
Mercatale
Val di Pesa
★364
FIRENZE
(Florence)
★360-363
Pontassieve
SS16
Regello
★368
SS3bis
Urbino
SS3
Senigallia
Falconara
Marittima
Greve in Chianti
Fossombrone
Certaldo ★359
★359
Panzano in Chianti
★365
Sansepolcro
ANCONA
Chiaravalle
Radda in Chianti ★366,368
Jesi
Castellina in Chianti ★359-360
Panicale
★363
Osimo
Volterra
★371
Monteriggioni ★362
Città di Castello

A
B
C
1
2
3
4
5
Livorno
Barberino Val d'Elsa ★359
Greve in Chianti
Certaldo ★359
Panzano in Chianti ★365
San Gimignano ★368-369
Poggibonsi
Radda in Chianti ★366,368
Rosignano Solvay
Volterra ★371
Lecchi in Chianti ★363
Castellina in Chianti ★359-360
Arezzo
Cecina
Monteriggioni ★362
Monte San Savino ★364
Morra ★364
Pievescola ★366
Siena ★370
Castelnuovo Berardenga ★359
Sovicille ★370 371
Pomarance
Cortona ★361
San Benedetto ★368
San Gimignano ★368-369
Sinalunga ★370
A1
Lago Trasimeno
San Vincenzo
Massa Marittima
Montefollonico ★362
Pienza ★364
Castiglione del Lago
Castel del Piano Umbro ★358
Monticchiello ★363
Fontignano ★363
Piombino
Follonica
Roccastrada
Ombrone
Bagno Vignoni ★359
SS2
Sarteano ★370
Elba
Cetona ★361
Portoferraio ★360
Capolivieri
Lacona ★360
Punta Ala ★366
Monte Castello di Vibio ★362
Grosseto
Scansano ★370
Prato ★367
San Lorenzo Nuovo
Orvieto
Lago di Bolsena
Manciano
Montefiascone
Orbetello
SS3
Giglio ★361
Porto Ercole ★367
Giglio
Montalto di Castro
Viterbo
Vetrella
Giannutri
Tarquinia
Civita Castellana
Civitavecchia
Lago di Bracciano
A12
Cerveteri
Palo Laziale ★365
Tevere
Tyrrhenian Sea
KEY
★100 Hotel location and page reference
International airport
Motorway
Major road
0 kilometres 25
0 miles 25

D
E
F
1
2
3
Adriatic Sea
Falconara Marittima
Chiaravalle
ANCONA
Jesi
Osimo
Loreto
Recanati
Cingoli
Fabriano
Macerata
Civitanova Marche
Tolentino
Fermo
Porto San Giorgio
Muccia
Amandola
A14
San Benedetto del Tronto
Ascoli Piceno
Triponzo
Bovara di Trevi ★360
Arquola del Tronto
Giulianova
Teramo
Roseto degli Abruzzi
Pineto
Atri
Posta
A24
Montesilvano Marina
Pescara
A L Y
Antrodoco
Francavilla al Mare
L'Aquila
Chieti
Ortona
A25
Fiamignamo
Pescara
SS5
Lanciano
SS16
Popoli
A14
A24
Celano
Casoli
Vasto ★371
SS5
Avezzano
Sulmona
Scanno ★378
SS17
Villa Santa Maria
Palestrina
Pescasserol
Roccaraso
Anagni
Alatri
Sora
Castel di Sangro
Lucito
Ferentino
Frosinone
Ceccano
Isernia
Campobasso
SS88
Sezze
A1
Cassino
Latina
Priverno
Venafro
Bojano
Pratella
Piedimonte Matese
Sabaudia
Terracina
Formia
Dragoni ★374
San Feice Circeo ★368
Gaeta
Minturno
Telese Terme
Baia Domizia ★373
Mondragone
Capua
Caserta
Benevento
Maddaloni
Zannone
Aversa
A1
Acerra
A16
Ponza ★364
NAPOLI (Naples) ★375-376
Avellino
A30
Pozzuoli
Portici
Resina
Ischia
D
E

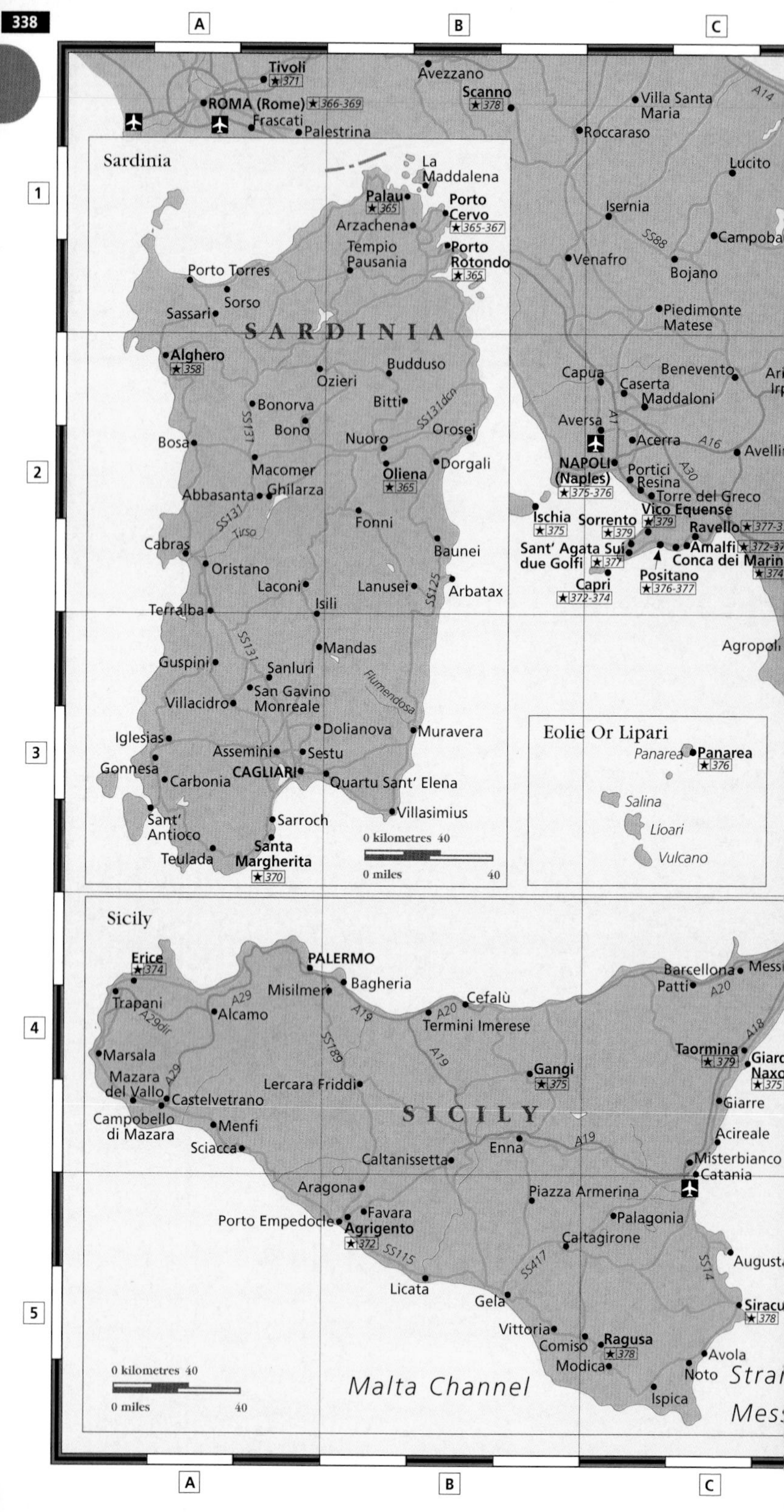
A
B
C
1
2
3
4
5
Tivoli ★371
ROMA (Rome) ★366-369
Frascati
Palestrina
Avezzano
Scanno ★378
Villa Santa Maria
Roccaraso
A14
Lucito
Isernia
SS88
Campoba
Venafro
Bojano
Piedimonte Matese
Sardinia
La Maddalena
Palau ★365
Porto Cervo ★365-367
Arzachena
Tempio Pausania
Porto Rotondo ★365
Porto Torres
Sorso
Sassari
SARDINIA
Alghero ★358
Ozieri
Budduso
Bonorva
Bitti
SS131dcn
Bono
SS131
Orosei
Nuoro
Bosa
Dorgali
Macomer
Oliena ★365
Abbasanta
Ghilarza
Tirso
Fonni
Cabras
Baunei
Oristano
Laconi
Lanusei
SS125
Arbatax
Isili
Terralba
Mandas
Guspini
Sanluri
Flumendosa
San Gavino Monreale
Villacidro
Dolianova
Muravera
Iglesias
Assemini
Sestu
Gonnesa
CAGLIARI
Carbonia
Quartu Sant' Elena
Villasimius
Sarroch
Sant' Antioco
Santa Margherita ★370
Teulada
0 kilometres 40
0 miles 40
Capua
Benevento
Caserta
Maddaloni
Aversa
A1
Acerra
A16
Avelli
A30
NAPOLI (Naples) ★375-376
Portici
Resina
Torre del Greco
Ischia ★375
Sorrento ★379
Vico Equense ★379
Ravello ★377-3
Sant' Agata Sui due Golfi ★377
Amalfi ★372-37
Conca dei Marin ★374
Positano ★376-377
Capri ★372-374
Agropoli
Eolie Or Lipari
Panarea
Panarea ★376
Salina
Líoari
Vulcano
Sicily
Erice ★374
PALERMO
Trapani
Misilmeri
Bagheria
A29
Cefalù
Barcellona
Messi
Patti
A20
Alcamo
A19
Termini Imerese
A29dir
SS189
A18
Marsala
Taormina ★379
Giarc Naxo ★375
Gangi ★375
Mazara del Vallo
Castelvetrano
Lercara Friddi
Giarre
Campobello di Mazara
Menfi
SICILY
Acireale
Sciacca
Enna
Caltanissetta
Misterbianco
Catania
Aragona
Piazza Armerina
Favara
Porto Empedocle
Agrigento ★372
Palagonia
SS115
Caltagirone
SS417
SS14
Augusta
Licata
Gela
Siracu ★378
Vittoria
Comiso
Ragusa ★378
Avola
Modica
Noto
Malta Channel
Ispica
Strai
Mess
0 kilometres 40
0 miles 40

D
E
F
1
2
3
4
5
Rodi Garánico
Vieste
Sannicandro Garganico
San Giovanni Rotondo
Mattinata
Manfredonia
A14
Margherita di Savoia
Trinitapoli
Barletta
Cerignola
Ofanto
Trani
Bisceglie
Canosa di Puglia
Andria
Molfetta
Corato
A14
Giovinazzo
BARI
Minervino Murge
Bitonto
Lavello
Mola di Bari
Melfi
SS93
Adelfia
Polignano a Mare
Venosa
Monópoli ★375
Savelletri di Fasano ★378
Strait of Otranto
Altamura
Putignano
Gravina di Puglia
Santeramo in Colle
Selva di Fasano ★378
Fasano ★374
ALY
Gióia del Colle
Cisternino ★374
Ostuni
Irsina
Alberobello ★372
Brindisi
E847
Matera ★375
Mottola
Potenza
SS407
Castellaneta
Francavilla Fontana
SS7
Mesagne
Massafra
Squinzano
Taranto
Grottaglie
San Cataldo
Sala Consilina
Pisticci
Manduria
Campi Salentina
Lecce
Agri
A3
Copertino
Nardò
SS106
Otranto ★376
Galatone
Maglie
Sapri
Lauria
Gallipoli
Maratea ★375-376
Ionian Sea
Casarano
Tricase
Ugento
Gagliano del Capo
Castrovillari
Cassano allo Ionio
Altomonte ★372
Corigliano Calabro
Rossano
Certraro ★373
Acri
SS106
Paola
Rende
Cosenza
San Giovanni in Fiore
Cirò Marina
Petilia Policastro
Amantea
A3
Crotone
Nicastro
Cutro
Sambiase
San Eufemia Lamezia
CATANZARO
Parghelia ★377
Vibo Valentia
KEY
★100 Hotel location and page reference
International airport
Motorway
Major road
Rosarno
Stilo ★379
Taurianova
Polistena
Palmi
Cittanova
Siderno
Locri
0 kilometres 50
0 miles 50
Reggio di Calabria
SS106

Northern Italy

Piedmont • Valle d'Aosta
Liguria • Lombardia • Venetia • Emilia-Romagna

The Northern third of Italy encompasses a rich diversity of landscapes, from the high jagged peaks of the Alps and the Dolomites, through the lakes of Lombardy, to two strips of Mediterranean coast and the great Veneto plain. There is a similarly wide choice of types of hotel. In the mountains are traditional Alpine and Tyrolean chalets, simple and homely; lakes such as Como, Maggiore and Garda are the setting for some of the most romantic hotels, both luxury and budget, in Italy; and the Veneto plain has its share of Palladian villas and other aristocratic houses turned into hotels. Also well served are the great cities of the north, most notably Milan and the incomparable Venice.

Argegno

Belvedere Simple and good value, in a dreamy position on the shores of Lake Como. Although rooms are small, they all have private shower or bath and the best have wonderful lake views. The lady of the house is Scottish – hence the tartan bar. Her Italian husband is an accomplished cook, and eating on the terrace is a special pleasure.
Via Milano 8, 22010 Argegno, Como. **Map** p334 C2. 031 82 11 16. FAX 031 82 15 71. @ capp.belvedere@libero.it b. **Rooms** 17. Nov to March. MC, V. €€

Asolo

Villa Cipriani In a beautiful medieval hilltop village this former home of poet Robert Browning is a sophisticated hotel with a heart, a jewel of the ITT Sheraton group. Bedrooms are gracious (try for an 'exclusive' or terrace room) and there is a charming garden with commanding views. The hotel is popular with wedding parties.
Via Canova 298, 31011 Asolo, Treviso. **Map** p335 E3. 0423 52 34 11. FAX 0423 95 20 95. @ villacipriani@sheraton.com b,l,d. **Rooms** 31. Never. AE, DC, MC, V. €€€€

Asolo

Albergo Al Sole In a superb position, perched above Piazza Maggiore, a cool, sophisticated hotel with plenty of luxurious touches.
Via Collegio 33, 31011 Asolo, Treviso. **Map** p335 E3. 0423 52 81 11. FAX 0423 52 83 99. @ info@albergoalsole.com b,l,d. **Rooms** 23. €€€

Bellagio

La Pergola Tucked away in tiny Pescallo, just to the south of Bellagio, is this rustic, old-fashioned, family-run hotel with a splendid view.
Piazza del Porto 4, Pescallo, 22021 Bellagio, Como. **Map** p334 C2. 031 95 02 63. FAX 031 95 02 53. @ lapergola@tin.it b,l,d. **Rooms** 11. €€

Bergamo

Agnello d'Oro Tall, narrow inn on a tiny square in the city's medieval core. Cosy restaurant; the bright bedrooms verge on the basic.
Via Gombito 22, 24129 Bergamo. **Map** p334 C3. 035 24 98 83. FAX 035 23 56 12. b,l,d. **Rooms** 20. €

Bergamo

Gourmet Eating on the shady terrace is a main attraction at this *città alta* restaurant-with-rooms. Bedrooms are large and light. Good bathrooms.
Via San Vigilio 1, 24129 Bergamo. **Map** p334 C3. FAX 035 437 30 04. @ il.gourmet@tiscali.it b,l,d. **Rooms** 11. €

BELLAGIO

Florence The handsome 18th-century building occupies a prime position in Bellagio, pearl of Lake Como. An arcaded terrace makes a welcoming entry to the attractive foyer, with its beamed and vaulted ceiling and stone fireplace. Bedrooms have a similar rustic charm, with antiques and pretty fabrics. Excellent value.
Piazza Mazzini 46, 22021 Bellagio, Como.
Map p334 C2. 031 95 03 42. FAX 031 95 17 22.
@ hotflore@tin.it. b,l,d. **Rooms** 38.
late Oct to mid-April. AE, MC, V. €€

BELLAGIO

Hotel du Lac A stone's throw from the Florence (see above) this is another popular Bellagio hotel, with a delightful setting on the piazza, a welcoming atmosphere and high standards of housekeeping and cooking. At breakfast you will find real marmalade and real orange juice; lunch or dinner on the lakeside terrace is a delight.
Piazza Mazzini 32, 22021 Bellagio, Como.
Map p334 C2. 031 95 03 20. FAX 031 95 16 24.
@ hoteldulac@tin.it b,l,d. **Rooms** 47.
Nov to end Mar. MC, V. €€

BRESSANONE (BRIXEN)

Elephant In a pretty town, Tyrolean in character, an old inn named after a beast which stabled here during a journey over the Alps for the amusement of Emperor Ferdinand of Austria. Old-fashioned comfort, impressive public rooms. Bedrooms are less characterful. Excellent food.
Via Rio Bianco 4, 39042 Bressanone, Bolzano.
Map p335 E2. 0472 83 27 50. FAX 0472 83 65 79.
@ info@hotelelephant.com b,l,d. **Rooms** 44.
Nov to early Dec; Jan to mid-Mar.
AE, DC, MC, V. €€€

BREUIL-CERVINIA

Hermitage Here Alpine charm comes with a sophisticated veneer, as befits a luxury hotel. A real haven. Bedrooms are spacious; the cosiest are the top-floor rooms with beamed ceilings. The Matterhorn is ever-present, both in paintings and, in all its glory, through the windows.
Via Piolet 1, 11021 Breuil-Cervinia, Aosta.
Map p334 A2. 0166 94 89 98. FAX 0166 94 90 32.
@ info@hotel hermitage.com b,l,d. **Rooms** 40.
end April to early Jul; end Aug to end Nov.
AE, DC, MC, V. €€€€

BOLOGNA

Orologio Above-average breakfasts and views over Piazza Maggiore are the plus points, along with well-equipped, well-lit bedrooms.
Via 1V Novembre 10, 40123 Bologna. **Map** p335 D4.
051 23 12 53. FAX 051 26 05 52. @ orologio@inbo.it
b. **Rooms** 34. €€€€

BRESSANONE (BRIXEN)

Dominik Ideal for the fitness-conscious, with pool, sauna, solarium and skiing nearby. Light, airy, set amid lawns and terraces.
Unterdrittelgasse 13, 39042 Bressanone. **Map** p335 E2.
0472 83 01 44. FAX 0472 83 65 54. @ dominik@relaischateaux.com b,l,d. **Rooms** 36. €€€

BRISIGHELLA

Relais Torre Pratesi Massive, sturdy early 16th-century tower and adjoining farmhouse. Carefully restored and elegantly furnished.
Via Cavina 11, Cavina, 48013 Brisighella, Ravenna.
Map p335 E5. 0546 845 45. FAX 0546 845 58.
@ info@torrepratesi.it b,l,d. **Rooms** 9. €€€

CAMOGLI

Cenobio dei Dogi In a beautiful park overlooking the bay, a sober luxury hotel, formerly a summer palace of Genoa's *doges*.
Via Cuneo 34, 16032 Camogli, Genova.
Map p334 B4. 0185 72 41. FAX 0185 77 27 96.
@ cenobio@cenobio.it b,l,d. **Rooms** 106. €€€

For key to symbols see backflap. For price categories *see p333*

Breuil-Cervinia

Les Neiges d'Antan This welcoming mountain hotel in the shadow of the Matterhorn was previously the family home of its hands-on owners, the Biches. Excellent local cuisine and wines are served in the comfortable, beamed dining room. Home-made jams are a highlight of breakfast.
Frazione Crêt de Perrères, 11021 Breuil-Cervinia, Aosta. **Map** p334 A2. 0166 94 87 75. FAX 0166 94 88 52. @ info@lesneigesdantan.it b,l,d. **Rooms** 24. May, June, mid-Sept to mid-Oct. MC, V. €€€

Cannero Riviera

Cannero This friendly hotel has been run by the same capable family since the early 1900s. Downstairs, terraces and big windows make the most of the setting. A 15-room extension has recently been added in an adjoining 18th-century house and there are four rooms for disabled use.
Via Lungo Lago 2, 28821 Cannero Riviera, Lago Maggiore. **Map** p334 B2. 0323 78 80 46. FAX 0323 78 80 48. @ info@hotelcannero.com b,l,d. **Rooms** 55, plus 10 self-catering apartments. Nov to early Mar. AE, DC, MC, V. €€

Caldaro

Leuchtenburg Swim, fish and sail on Lake Caldaro (or Kalterer See) from this homely, unpretentious *pensione* beneath the ruins of Leuchtenburg castle. In the white-painted, low-arched tavern, guests take hearty breakfasts and three-course dinners of regional dishes. Bedrooms have painted furniture and tiled floors.
Klughammer 100, 39052 Caldaro, Bolzano. **Map** p335 D2. 0471 96 00 93. FAX 0471 96 01 55. @ pensionleuchtenburg@iol.it b,l,d. **Rooms** 19. Nov to Mar. V. €

Castel Guelfo

Locanda Solarola The innovative and much-praised cuisine (Michelin star) is the main draw to this very individual establishment, the creation of Antonella Scardovi and Valentino Parmiani. Meals are served in an attractive beamed dining room, with the homely kitchen open to view. Bedrooms are lacey and Edwardian.
Via Santa Croce 5, 40023 Castel Guelfo, Bologna. **Map** p335 E4. 0542 67 01 02. FAX 0542 67 02 22. @ solarola@imola.queen.it b,l,d. **Rooms** 15. 3 weeks Jan. AE, DC, MC, V. €€€

Cannobio

Pironi At the heart of this unspoilt lakeside village, an arcaded medieval building, beautifully preserved yet with all modern comforts.
Via Marconi 35, Cannobio, Verbania. **Map** p334 B2. 0323 706 24. FAX 0323 721 84. @ info@pironihotel.it b. **Rooms** 12. €€

Castelfranco Emilia

Villa Gaidello Just nine pleasantly furnished rooms (seven suites) at a lovely 18th-century farmhouse amid peaceful grounds.
Via Gaidello 18, 41013 Castelfranco Emilia, Modena. **Map** p335 D4. 059 92 68 06. FAX 059 92 66 20. @ gaidello@tin.it b,l,d. **Rooms** 9. €€

Cavaso del Tomba

Locanda Alla Posta Handsome inn with an unfussy restaurant serving inventive dishes, and large, plain, light bedrooms. Very good value.
Piazza XIII Martiri 13, 31034 Cavaso del Tomba, Treviso. **Map** p335 E3. FAX 0423 54 31 12. b,l,d. **Rooms** 7. €

Cogne

Bellevue The Bellevue is situated in a picturesque French-speaking valley; much Alpine decoration, but very comfortable and with spa facilities.
Rue Grand Paradis 22, 11012 Cogne, Aosta. **Map** p334 A3. 0165 748 25. FAX 0165 74 91 92. @ bellevue@relaischateaux.com b,l,d. **Rooms** 38; 3 chalets. €€€

Castelrotto

Cavallino d'Oro This hostelry on the central square dates back to 1393. It is full of character; its two panelled *Stube* make charming dining rooms, serving excellent local cuisine, while public rooms are distinguished by finely carved furniture. Pretty painted furniture in some bedrooms, splendid four-poster beds in others.
Piazza Kraus 1, 39040 Castelrotto, Bolzano. **Map** p334 A4. 0471 70 63 37. FAX 0471 70 71 72. cavallino@cavallino.it b,l,d. **Rooms** 21. early Nov to mid-Dec. AE, DC, MC, V. €€

Champoluc

Villa Anna Maria The village of Champoluc is the main community of a steep-sided valley beneath the mighty Monte Rosa. This 1920s chalet-style villa on a wooded hill is a quiet, charming place: wood panelling, simple but cosy furnishings and country decorations. Not all the bedrooms have a private bathroom.
Via Croues 5, 11020 Champoluc, Aosta. **Map** p334 A2. 0125 30 71 28. FAX 0125 30 79 84. hotelannamaria@tiscali.it b,l,d. **Rooms** 20. Never. MC, V. €

Cernobbio

Villa d'Este When the flash and the famous come to Lake Como, they usually head for historic Villa d'Este. Built in 1568 by Cardinal Tolomeo Gallio, it saw many illustrious visitors before becoming a hotel in 1873. Its glittering interior and romantic grounds are the setting for many sporting and leisure activities. The food is suitably sumptuous.
Via Regina 40, 22012 Cernobbio, Como. **Map** p334 C2. 031 34 81 44. FAX 031 34 88 44. info@villadeste.it b,l,d. **Rooms** 164. Oct to Feb. AE, DC, MC, V. €€€€€

Cioccaro di Penango

Locanda del Sant' Uffizio Its position in the Monferrato hills and the willing but informal service make this converted 15th-century monastery a truly relaxing place. Some of the bedrooms have terraces opening onto the garden, a quiet oasis. Get in training for the multi-course *menu degustazione*.
14030 Cioccaro di Penango, Asti. **Map** p334 B3. 0141 91 62 92. FAX 0141 91 60 68. santuffizio@thi.it b,l,d. **Rooms** 33. 3 weeks Jan, 3 weeks Aug. AE, DC, MC, V. €€€

Cologne Franciacorta

Cappuccini Former hilltop monastery, decorated with a fitting simplicity and restrained elegance.
Via Cappuccini 54, 25033 Cologne Franciacorta, Brescia. **Map** p334 C3. 0307 15 72 54. FAX 0307 15 72 57. info@cappuccini.it b,l,d. **Rooms** 7. €€€

Cortina d'Ampezzo

Ancora Stylish and sophisticated, with a large, popular terrace for drinks and tea. Personable, energetic owner, Flavia Sartor. Good food.
Corso Italia 62, 32043 Cortina d'Ampezzo, Belluno. **Map** p335 E2. 0436 32 61. FAX 0436 32 65. info@hotelancoracortina.com b,l,d. **Rooms** 49. €€

Cortina d'Ampezzo

Franceschi Park Twin-turretted hotel with a comfortable interior. A good choice for families.
Via Cesare Battisti 86, 32043 Cortina d'Ampezzo, Belluno. **Map** p335 E2. 0436 86 70 41. FAX 0436 29 09. franceschi@hotel.franceschi.it b,l,d. **Rooms** 40. €€

Courmayeur

Meuble La Grange Good-value B&B in a renovated old barn; bright, cosy interior and warm atmosphere. Sauna and gym.
Strada La Brenva, Entrèves, 11013 Courmayeur, Aosta. **Map** p334 A2. 0165 86 97 33. FAX 0165 86 97 44. lagrange@mbtlc.it b. **Rooms** 23. €€

Cortina d'Ampezzo

Menardi The Menardi family opened their hotel in 1836. Since then, it has gained balconies adorned with cheerful window-boxes, an extra line of rooms sprouting from the roof, and an annexe. Furnishings are somewhat dated, but the standard of food, service and welcome is high.
Via Majon 110, 32043 Cortina d'Ampezzo, Belluno. **Map** p335 E2. 0436 24 00. FAX 0436 86 21 83. @ info@hotelmenardi.it b,l,d. **Rooms** 49. Apr to May, Oct to Dec. DC, MC, V. €€€

Fie allo Sciliar (Vols/Schlern)

Romantik Hotel Turm A solid former courthouse with typical, yet stylish, Tyrolean hospitality. Bedrooms vary in size, but are all different, with regional furniture and somewhere cosy to sit. You might find a ceramic stove in one, naive paintings in another. The apartments are good value, as is the elegantly presented food.
Piazza dell Chiesa 9, 39050 Fie Allo Sciliar, Bolzano. **Map** p335 E2. 0471 72 50 14. FAX 0471 72 54 74. @ info@hotelturm.it b,l,d. **Rooms** 40. mid-Nov to mid-Dec. MC, V. €€€

Erbusco

L'Albereta The soft hills and vineyards of around Erbusco offer an ample supply of ingredients for an indulgent break, especially if you prefer your comforts with a contemporary, suave touch. Rooms in the 19th-century villa are chic and comfortable. The cuisine, by Gualtiero Marchesi, has gained him two Michelin stars.
Via Vittorio Emanuele 11, 25030 Erbusco, Brescia. **Map** p334 C3. 030 776 05 50. FAX 030 776 05 73. @ info@albereta.it b,l,d. **Rooms** 52. Never. AE, DC, MC, V. €€€€

Finale Ligure

Punta Est Finale Ligure is one of the pleasanter resorts along this stretch of Italian Riviera, and the Punta Est is its most notable hotel. It comprises an old villa standing high above the coastal road on a rocky promontory, augmented by a modern annexe. Breakfast, served on bone china, is taken in a bright, canopied room.
Via Aurelia 1, 17024 Finale Ligure, Savona. **Map** p334 B4. FAX (019) 60 06 11. @ info@puntaest.it b,l,d. **Rooms** 40. Oct to March. AE, MC, V. €€€

Courmayeur

Palace Bron A tall, smartly furnished hotel (Oriental rugs, chandeliers) set above the town in a grassy garden. Great views of Mont Blanc.
Via Plan Gorret 41, 11013 Courmayeur, Aosta. **Map** p334 A2. 0165 84 67 42. FAX 0165 84 40 15. @ hotelpb@tin.it b,l,d. **Rooms** 26. €€€

Ferrara

Locanda Borgonuovo In the heart of this old city, a friendly, personally-run guesthouse. Simple rooms, generous breakfasts. Bicycles available.
Via Cairoli 29, 44100 Ferrara. **Map** p335 E4. 0532 21 11 00. FAX 0532 24 83 28. @ info@borgonuovo.com b. **Rooms** 4. €

Gardone Riviera

Villa del Sogno Luxurious villa, exotic gardens, breathtaking views over Lake Garda. Spacious, light bedrooms and swimming pool.
Via Zanardelli 107, 25083 Gardone Riviera, Brescia. **Map** p335 D3. 0365 29 01 81. FAX 0365 29 02 30. @ info@villadelsogno.it b,l,d. **Rooms** 30. €€€€

Gargagnago

Foresteria Serego Alghieri On the vast Casal dei Ronchi estate, superb self-catering apartments.
Via Stazione 2, 37020 Gargagnago, Verona. **Map** p335 D3. (045) 770 36 22. FAX (045) 770 35 23. @ serego@easyasp.it b. **Rooms** 8 apartments for 2,3 or 4 people. €€€

Fiume Veneto

L'Ultimo Molino The 17th-century building is one of the last working mills in the area; though not used since the 1970s, the three wooden wheels are set in motion each evening. Inside, original character is preserved, and pretty fabrics are teemed with rustic furniture and elegant lighting. Bathrooms are sparkling and well-equipped.
Via Molino 45/A, 33080 Bannia di Fiume Veneto, Pordenone. **Map** p335 F3. 0434 95 79 11. FAX 0434 95 84 83. @ ultimo.mulino@adriacom.it b,l,d. **Rooms** 8. 10 days Jan. AE, DC, MC, V. €€

Gardone Riviera

Villa Fiordaliso Built in 1902 and once home to Gabriele d'Annunzio and later to Mussolini's mistress Claretta Petacci, the lakeside villa is sumptuously decorated. The huge Claretta suite has a magnificent marble bathroom. The restaurant, which spills out into the garden, serves superb food; good wine list.
Corso Zanardelli 132, 25083 Gardone Riviera, Brescia. **Map** p335 D3. 0365 20 158. FAX 0365 29 00 11. @ info@villafiordaliso.it b,l,d. **Rooms** 7. Nov to early Feb. AE, DC, MC, V. €€€€

Follina

Villa Abbazia This special hotel, in a village graced by an enchanting Cistertian abbey, consists of two buildings: a 17th-century *palazzo* and a charming little Art Nouveau villa. Rooms in both are decorated with great flair. Eat in the hotel's romantic restaurant, La Corte. Free admission to Asolo golf club.
Piazza IV Novembre 3, 31051 Follina, Treviso. **Map** p335 E3. 0438 97 12 77. FAX 0438 97 00 01. @ info@ hotelabbazia.it b,l,d. **Rooms** 18. Jan. AE, DC, MC, V. €€€

Gargnano

Baia d'Oro To appreciate the fabulous setting of this gaily painted hotel, arrive by boat. From the romantic terrace, you can almost dip your hand into Lake Garda and enjoy simply cooked fresh fish. The bedrooms are not to everyone's taste, with shiny fabrics and mirrored glass bedheads, but they are comfortable, with new bathrooms.
Via Gamberera 13, 25084 Gargnano, Brescia. **Map** p335 D3. 0365 71 171. FAX 0365 72 568. @ info.hotelbaiadoro@libero.it b,d. **Rooms** 13. mid-Nov to mid-March. Not accepted. €€

Ghiffa

Park Hotel Paradiso Atmospheric early 1900s villa in a pretty Lake Maggiore village. Ask for a lakeside room with balcony or garden.
Via Guglielmo Marconi 20, 28823 Ghiffa, Novara. **Map** p334 B2. 0323 595 48. FAX 0323 598 78. b,l,d. **Rooms** 20. €€

Iseo

I Due Roccoli Beautifully situated in wooded grounds above Lake Iseo, with very comfortable rooms and suites. Relais du Silence.
Via Silvio Bonomelli, 25049 Iseo, Brescia. **Map** p334 C3. 030 982 29 77. FAX 030 982 29 80. @ relais@idueroccoli.com b,l,d. **Rooms** 19. €€

Lagundo (Algund)

Der Pünthof A medieval farmhouse is at the core of this hotel, encircled by orchards and vines. The most appealing rooms are in the square tower.
Via Steinach 25, 39022 Laguno, Bolzano. **Map** p335 D2. 0473 44 85 53. FAX 0473 44 99 19. @ info@puenthof.com b. **Rooms** 12. €

Laigueglia

Splendid Mare Vaulted ceilings and a well testify to the monastic origins of this neat hotel. Small garden, with pool, where drinks are served.
Piazza Bardaro 3, 17020 Laigueglia, Savona. **Map** p334 B5. 0182 69 03 25. FAX 0182 69 08 94. @ info@splendidmare.it b,l,d. **Rooms** 45. €€

Gargnano

Villa Giulia The Bombardelli family gradually upgraded their late 19th-century villa from humble *pensione* to three-star hotel, but managed to retain the feel of a private guesthouse. The airy public rooms include an elegant dining room with Murano chandeliers and gold walls. Favourite bedrooms are those in the eaves.
Viale Rimembranza 20, 25084 Gargnano, Brescia. **Map** p335 D3. 0365 710 22. FAX 0365 727 74. info@villagiulia.it b,l,d. **Rooms** 23. mid-Oct to week before Easter. AE, MC, V. €€€

Isola dei Pescatori

Verbano Lacking the grandeur of adjacent Isola Bella, this tiny fishing island on Lake Maggiore nevertheless has plenty of local colour, as does the large villa occupying one end. Its restaurant is the *raison d'être* – home-made pastas are a speciality. But there are also simple, old-fashioned bedrooms with balconies and beautiful views.
Via Ugo Ara 2, 28049 Isola dei Pescatori, Stresa, Novara. **Map** p334 B3. (0323) 30 408. FAX (0323) 33 129. hotelverbano@tin.it b,l,d. **Rooms** 12. Jan, Feb. AE, DC, MC, V. €€

Garlenda

La Meridiana This smart country house hotel is inland from the Riviera, in attractive grounds opening onto countryside, with a large pool. Most of the accommodation is in air-conditioned suites, airy and bright with modern fabrics; less expensive double rooms too. Noted restaurant.
Via Ai Castelli 11, 17033 Garlenda, Savona. **Map** p334 A4. 0182 58 02 71. FAX 0182 58 01 50. meridiana@relaischateuax.fr b,l,d. **Rooms** 30. Nov to mid-March. AE, DC, MC, V. €€€€€

Ivrea

Castello San Giuseppe On an isolated hill with commanding views, this *castello* was originally a monastery before becoming a Napoleonic fort. Its atmosphere remains far more reflective than military. The hotel is centred round a peaceful inner garden with ornamental pond and shady trees. Bedrooms are rustically stylish.
10010 Chiaverano d'Ivrea, Torino. **Map** p334 A3. 0125 42 43 70. FAX 0125 64 12 78. info@castello.sangiuseppe.it b,d. **Rooms** 21. early Jan to early Feb. AE, DC, MC, V. €€

Manerba del Garda

Villa Schindler Set among olive trees and cypresses, a late 18th-century villa with a romantic atmosphere. Art courses and pool.
Via Bresciana 68, 25080 Manerba del Garda, Brescia. **Map** p335 D3. 0365 65 10 46. FAX 0365 55 48 77. info@villaschindler.it b. **Rooms** 13. €

Mantua

Broletto Neat, straightforward accommodation in a renovated 16th-century townhouse. Unbeatable location at the heart of the city.
Via Accademia 1, 46100 Mantova. **Map** p335 D2. 0376 22 36 78. FAX 0376 22 12 97. hotel.broletto@libero.it b. **Rooms** 16. €

Mantua

San Lorenzo Marvellous views of aristocratic Mantua from the terrace of this plush, ornately furnished hotel, opened in 1967.
Piazza Concordia 14, 46100 Mantova. **Map** p335 D2. 0376 22 05 00. FAX 0376 32 71 94. hotel@hotelsanlorenzo.it b. **Rooms** 32. €€

Marlengo

Romantik Hotel Oberwirt Public rooms are typically Tyrolean, with carved furniture and nick-nacks. Great food, two pools and a spa.
Via San Felice 2, Marlengo, 39020 Merano, Bolzano. **Map** p335 D2. 0473 22 20 20. FAX 0473 44 71 30. info@oberwirt.com b,l,d. **Rooms** 51. €€

LEIVI

Ca'Peo Generous seasonal menus and wines chosen from 350 vintages have ensured a wide reputation for Franco and Melly Solari's rambling farmhouse restaurant. The attractive bay-windowed dining room enjoys magnificent views over the bay and hills east of Portofino. An annexe houses modern, airy apartments.
Via dei Caduti 80, 16040 Leivi, Genova. **Map** p334 C4. 0185 31 96 96. FAX 0185 31 96 71. nicosol@libero.it b,l,d. **Rooms** 3 suites, 2 apartments. Nov. AE, DC, MC, V. €

LEVADA

Gargan Excellent dinners (home-made pasta and bread) are one of the attractions of this charming farm guesthouse. On the ground floor, a series of interconnecting dining rooms are elegantly furnished with antiques, lace curtains and pictures on white walls. Bedrooms have pretty wrought-iron bedsteads and floors strewn with rugs.
Via Marco Polo 2, 35017 Levada di Piombino Dese, Padova. **Map** p335 E3. 049 935 03 08. FAX 049 935 00 16. gargan@gargan.it b,d. **Rooms** 6. Jan, Aug. Not accepted. €

LENNO

San Giorgio A path lined with potted plants leads through lawns to the lakeside terrace of this large, atmospheric 1920s villa on the shores of Lake Como. Inside, spacious public rooms are filled with flowers, antiques and ornate mirrors. Bedrooms have a pleasantly dated feel but are very comfortable, with heavenly views.
Via Regina 81, Tremezzo, 22016 Lenno, Como. **Map** p334 C2. 0344 40 415. FAX 0344 41 591. sangiorgio.hotel@libero.it b,l,d. **Rooms** 26. mid-Oct to early Apr. AE, DC, MC, V. €€

MALEO

Albergo del Sole This fine inn, noted for its simple but delicious regional dishes, is now run by the son and daughter of Franco Colombani who created it. The building displays the same robust restraint as the cooking. The three bedrooms are above the dining room. They have individual high points and good bathrooms and are traditionally furnished.
Via Trabattoni 22, 26847 Maleo, Milano. **Map** p334 C3. 0377 58 142. FAX 0377 45 80 58. b,l,d. **Rooms** 3. Jan, Aug. AE, DC, MC,V. €€

MILAN

Antica Locanda Leonardo The trendy interior is a cross between Philippe Starck and a teenager's bedroom. Friendly service. Rare city garden.
Corso Magenta 78, 20121 Milano. **Map** p334 C3. 02 46 33 17. FAX 02 4801 9012. desk@leoloc.com b. **Rooms** 23. €€

MILAN

Antica Locanda Solferino In arty Brera district, an eccentric great aunty's country house. Paisleys, huge wardrobes, Jacuzzis in some rooms.
Via Castelfidardo 2, 20121 Milano. **Map** p334 C3. 02 657 01 29. FAX 02 657 13 61. info@anticalocandasolferino.it b. **Rooms** 11. €€

MILAN

Pierre Milano Smoothly run hotel, stylish and calm. Recently renovated rooms mix the occasional antique into contemporary design.
Via de Amicis 32, 20123 Milano. **Map** p334 C3. 02 7200 0581. FAX 02 805 21 57. info@hotelpierremilano.it b,d. **Rooms** 51. €€€€

MILAN

Spadari Al Duomo Contemporary, very central boutique hotel. Deluxe doubles have lovely balconies; standard rooms are small.
Via Spadari 11, 20123 Milano. **Map** p334 C3. 02 7200 2371. FAX 02 861 184. reservation@spadarihotel.com b. **Rooms** 40. €€€

For key to symbols see backflap. For price categories *see p333*

Merano (Meran)

Castel Fragsburg The setting's the thing at this 300-year-old former hunting lodge with commanding views of the Texel massif. The long, wisteria-covered terrace, seemingly suspended over the mountainside, is a lovely place on which to eat or drink. Bedrooms all have carved pine furniture, pretty country fabrics and balconies.
Via Fragsburg 3, 39012 Merano, Bolzano. **Map** p335 D2. 0473 24 40 71. FAX 0473 24 44 93. info@fragsburg.com b,l,d. **Rooms** 18. Nov to Easter. MC, V. €€€

Milan

Four Seasons Hotel Milano This serene former monastery is only a few steps from Milan's main shopping street. It exudes confidence, *joie de vivre*, the smell of a business deal. Everything is of the highest quality, from the Frette bedlinen and underfloor heating in the marble bathrooms to the 220 staff who cater to every whim.
Via Gesù 8, 20121 Milano. **Map** p334 C3. 02 77088. FAX 02 77 08 50 04. mil.reservations@fourseasons.com b,l,d. **Rooms** 118. Never. AE, DC, MC, V. €€€€

Merano (Meran)

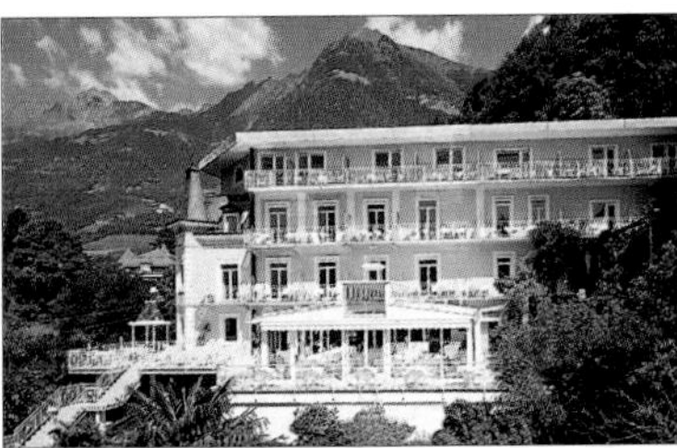

Villa Tivoli It's almost in countryside, surrounded by a terraced garden filled with more than 2,000 plant varieties. The interior is cool and chic, spacious and light; bedrooms all have south-facing balconies. The mountainous breakfast buffet could probably see you through to the excellent dinner.
Via Verdi 72, 39012 Merano, Bolzano. **Map** p335 D2. 0473 44 62 82. FAX 0473 44 68 49. info@villativoli.it b,l,d. **Rooms** 20. mid-Dec to mid-Mar. AE, MC, V. €€

Milan

Principe di Savoia A colourful stained-glass ceiling in the winter garden is one of the period features of this stately evocation of the late 1890s/early 1900s. Bedrooms are superbly elegant and there is a breathtaking new Presidential Suite. The downmarket location is a drawback.
Piazza della Repubblica 17, 20124 Milano. **Map** p334 C3. 02 62 30 55 55. FAX 02 65 37 99. res047principedisavoia@luxurycollection.com b,l,d. **Rooms** 404. Never. AE, DC, MC, V. €€€€

Modena

Canalgrande Stylish, peaceful villa set in lovely gardens in the city centre. Neoclassical, stuccoed reception rooms; vaulted cellar restaurant.
Corso Canalgrande 6, 41100 Modena. **Map** p335 D4. 059 21 71 60. FAX 059 22 16 74. info@canalgrandehotel.it b,l,d. **Rooms** 70. €€

Monforte d'Alba

Giardino da Felicin Standing among hills and vineyards, a family-run restaurant-with-rooms. Good food, fine wines, light, spacious bedrooms.
Via Vallada 18, 12065 Monforte d'Alba, Cuneo. **Map** p334 A4. 0173 782 25. FAX 0173 78 73 77. albrist@felicin.it b,l (Sun only),d. **Rooms** 13. €€

Montagnana

Aldo Moro Useful address within this handsome town's superb rectangle of medieval walls: a smart restaurant with modern, efficient rooms.
Via G. Marconi 27, 35044 Montagnana, Padova. **Map** p335 D3. 0429 813 51. FAX 0429 828 42. info@hotelaldomoro.com b,l,d. **Rooms** 34. €

Orta San Giulio

Orta Pleasantly old-fashioned, spacious central hotel with an endearingly shabby façade. Around the corner, its terrace overhangs Lake Orta.
28016 Orta San Giulio, Novara. **Map** p334 B2. 0322 902 53. FAX 0322 90 56 46. info@hotelorta.it b,l,d. **Rooms** 35. €€

MIRA

Romantik Hotel Villa Margherita Less than a half-hour drive from Venice, this polished hotel is also well-placed for visits to the stately villas of the Brenta Canal. Nowadays the flat landscape is more industrial than rural, but this former country villa is all sophistication, with attractive public rooms and a well-regarded restaurant.
Via Nazionale 416, 30030 Mira, Venezia. **Map** p335 E3. 041 426 58 00. FAX 041 426 58 38. @ hvillam@tin.it b,l,d. **Rooms** 19. Never. AE, DC, MC, V. €€€

MONZA

Hotel de la Ville Monza is synonymous with fast cars, but it also has a Neoclassical Villa Reale, surrounded by a lovely park. This fine hotel overlooks it. Owned for three generation by the Nardi family, it is dignified and traditional. Its Derby Grill restaurant is renowned.
Viale Regina Margherita 15, 20052 Monza, Milano. **Map** p334 C3. 039 38 25 81. FAX 039 36 76 47. @ reservation@ hoteldelaville.com b,l,d. **Rooms** 62. 3 weeks Aug; Christmas and New Year. AE, DC, MC, V. €€€€

MONTEROSSO AL MARE

Porto Roca Along a beautiful, almost inaccessible strip of coastline, Monterosso (which can be reached by car) is the largest of the stunning Cinque Terre perched villages, and Porto Roca is by far the best hotel. Sitting on a headland, it's chief assets are the wonderul views (make sure your room has one) and a glorious terrace.
Via Corone 1, 19016 Monterosso al Mare, La Spezia. **Map** p334 C5. 0187 81 75 02. FAX 0187 81 76 92. @ portoroca@portoroca.it b,l,d. **Rooms** 43. early Nov to mid-Mar. AE, DC, MC, V. €€€€

ORTISEI (ST ULRICH)

Uhrerhof Deur The peace is broken only by the sound of ticking clocks (the name means 'House of the Clocks'). This traditional chalet is set in a tucked-away hamlet. Outside, a grassy garden with wonderful views; inside, bright, simple, immaculate rooms with plenty of homely details. Also two apartments and health complex.
Bulla, 39046 Ortisei, Bolzano. **Map** p335 E2. 0471 79 73 35. FAX 0471 79 74 57. @ info@uhrerhof.com b,d. **Rooms** 12. Nov to late Dec. MC, V.. €

ORTA SAN GIULIO

Piccolo Hotel Olina A highly enjoyable restaurant. Warm-toned, comfortable bedrooms (some with tiled floors and wooden ceilings).
Via Olina 40, 28016 Orta San Giulio, Novara. **Map** p334 B2. 0322 90 56 56. FAX 0322 90377. @ 010101@europe.com b,l,d. **Rooms** 16. €

PARMA

Torino Quiet yet in the heart of the city, close to all the main sights, and with the bonus of a private garage. Rooms are clean, small and plain.
Via Mazza 7, 43100 Parma. **Map** p334 C4. 0521 28 10 46. FAX 0521 23 07 25. @ info@hotel-torino.it b. **Rooms** 39. €€

PARMA

Villa Ducale A Neoclassical mansion house approached through a flower-filled garden. Several bedrooms have small terraces.
Via Moletolo 53A, 43100 Parma. **Map** p334 C4. 0521 27 27 27. FAX 0521 78 07 56. @ info@villaducalehotel.com b,l,d. **Rooms** 47. €€

PORTOBUFFOLE

Villa Giustinian Unstuffy, but not cosy: rooms are of awesome dimensions. Elaborate suites in the main house, simpler rooms in the old stables.
Via Giustiniani 11, 31019 Portobuffole, Treviso. **Map** p335 F3. 0422 85 02 44. FAX 0422 85 02 60. @ villagiustinian@libero.it b,l,d. **Rooms** 43. €€

For key to symbols see backflap. For price categories *see p333*

PEDEMONTE

Villa del Quar The owner lives in the fine main villa, her luxury hotel occupies the east wing. Public rooms are memorable: a galleried sitting room, and two dining rooms resplendent in silk, gilt and Murano glass. Bedrooms are more restrained, with opulent bathrooms. The lovely pool sparkles invitingly in the garden.
Via Quar 12, 37020 Pedemonte, Verona. **Map** p334 A2. 045 680 06 81. FAX 045 680 06 04. @ villadelquar@c-point.it b,l,d. **Rooms** 22. Jan to mid-Mar. AE, DC, MC, V. €€€€€

PIEVE D'ALPAGO

Dolada A Michelin-starred restaurant with rooms, a warm welcome from the De Pra family, and stunning views of snow-capped mountains and the Santa Croce lake and valley far below are your rewards for negotiating the narrow, winding roads that lead here. Cookery courses are also available.
Via Dolada 21, Plois, 32010 Pieve d'Alpago, Belluno. **Map** p335 E2. 043 747 91 41. FAX 043 747 80 68. @ dolada@tin.it b,l (not Mon, Tue except Jul & Aug),d. **Rooms** 7. Never. AE, DC, MC, V. €

PERGINE

Castel Pergine For novelty, good value and fun this medieval hilltop fortress is hard to beat. Past and present co-exist in a friendly, mildly offbeat atmosphere. Age-worn steps and vaulted chambers lead to the airy lobby. Bedrooms, while not luxurious, are furnished with simple good taste. Strolls round the ramparts are a highlight.
Via al Castello 10, 38057 Pergine, Valsugana, Trento. **Map** p335 D2. 0461 531158. FAX 0461 531329. @ verena@castelpergine.it b,l,d. **Rooms** 21. Nov to Apr. AE, MC, V. €

PORTICO DI ROMAGNA

Al Vecchio Convento The stylishly rustic dining room, at the back of the house, is the main focus; here Signor Cameli cooks traditional dishes with flair. A stone staircase leads to the bedrooms, also traditional and decorated with classy simplicity. Handsome antiques include some particularly splendid bedsteads.
Via Roma 7,47010 Portico di Romagna, Forlì. **Map** p335 E5. 0543 96 70 53. FAX 0543 96 71 57. @ info@vecchioconvento.it b,l,d. **Rooms** 15. early Jan to early Feb. AE, MC, V. €

REGGIO NELL'EMILIA

Albergo delle Notarie In the centre of town, a calm, elegant hotel with mainly spacious rooms and suites. Acclaimed restaurant.
Via Palazzolo 5, 42100 Reggio nell'Emilia. **Map** p335 D4. 0522 45 35 00. FAX 0522 45 37 37. b,l,d. **Rooms** 51. €€

REGGIO NELL'EMILIA

Posta The austere façade of this comfortable hotel in the historic centre hides an embellished rococo interior. Full of charming flourishes.
Piazza del Monte 2, 42100 Reggio nell'Emilia. **Map** p335 D4. 0522 43 29 44. FAX 0522 45 26 02. @ booking@hotelposta.re.it b. **Rooms** 42. €€€

SAN BONIFACIO

Relais Villabella The core of this former rice mill is a smart, well-regarded restaurant. Elegant public rooms and bedrooms. Pool.
Via Villabella 72, 37047 San Bonifacio, Verona. **Map** p335 D3. 045 610 17 77. FAX 045 610 17 99. @ relaisvilla@libero.it b,l,d. **Rooms** 10. €€€

SAN FEDELE D'INTELVI

Villa Simplicitas A saffron-coloured 19th-century villa high above the lakes and their bustle. Old-fashioned in a charming, tasteful way.
22028 San Fedele Intelvi, Como. **Map** p334 C2. 031 83 1132 FAX 031 83 0455. @info@villasimplicitas.it b,l,d. **Rooms** 10. 

Portofino

Eden In chic, crowded Portofino, hotel rooms are at a premium, and the Eden is one waterfront, whose shaded garden makes a quiet enclave. Bedrooms and bathrooms are small but spotless. There is no sitting room, but a trattoria-style dining room and a terrace overlooking the garden.

Vico Dritto 20, 16034 Portofino, Genova. **Map** p334 B4. 0185 26 90 91. FAX 0185 26 90 47. @ eden@ifree.it b,l,d. **Rooms** 12. Never. AE, DC, MC, V. €€€

Ranco

Il Sole di Ranco The Brovelli family opened their inn on the shores of Lake Maggiore in 1850; today it is a smart restaurant (two Michelin stars) with rooms. Carlo Brovelli cooks, aided by his son. Dining on the vine-covered terrace is a delight. Bedooms are mainly contemporary suites, ranging in size and price.

Piazza Venezia 5, 21020 Ranco, Varese. **Map** p334 B2. 0331 97 65 07. FAX 0331 97 66 20. @ ivanett@tin.it b,l,d. **Rooms** 14. Dec to mid-Feb. AE, DC, MC, V. €€€

Portofino

Splendido One of Italy's most famous hotels, dripping in chic, where languid elegance is the order of the day – as well as a deep pocket for paying the bill. It is set on the hillside over the harbour, with a wonderfully sited swimming pool and a glitzy terrace on which to see and be seen.

Salita Baratta 16, 16034 Portofino, Genova. **Map** p335 B4. 0185 26 95 51. FAX 0185 26 96 14. @ reservations @splendido.net b,l,d. **Rooms** 66. mid-Nov to March. AE, DC, MC, V. €€€€€

Redagno di Sopra

Zirmerhof The dimly lit hall with intricate wood carving, old fireplace and ticking grandfather clock, sets the tone at this mountain hotel. The place has a cosy, homely atmosphere. Rooms vary in size, but are all attractive, with traditional furniture. Good local cooking and wine list.

39040 Redagno di Sopra, Bolzano. **Map** p335 E2. 0471 88 72 15. FAX 0471 88 72 25. @ info@zirmerhof.com b,l,d. **Rooms** 32. early Nov to Christmas; end Feb to mid-May. MC, V. €

San Floriano

Obereggen Modest chalet, just yards from ski lifts, with a cosy bar and good food. Plump duvets add a touch of comfort to the simple rooms.

Via Obereggen 8, San Floriano, 39050 Nova Ponente, Bolzano. **Map** p335 F3. 0471 61 57 22. FAX 0471 61 58 89. @ info@hotelobereggen.it b,d. **Rooms** 24. €

Santa Valburga

Gasthof Eggwirt The traditional *Stube* is the heart of this excellent value, family-oriented *gasthof*. Less personal bedrooms; superb views.

39016 San Valburga d'Ultimo, Bolzano. **Map** p334 C2. 0473 79 53 19. FAX 0473 79 54 71. @ eggwirt@rolmail.net b,l,d. **Rooms** 21. €

Sesto

Berghotel Tirol A modern chalet in a very pretty town, overlooking classic Alpine scenery. Pine-furnished, new pool, hospitable.

Via Monte Elmo 10, Moso, 39030 Sexten, Bolzano. **Map** p335 D5. 0474 71 03 86. FAX 0474 71 04 55. @ info@berghotel.com b,d. **Rooms** 36. €€€€

Sestri Levante

Grand Hotel Villa Balbi Swanky pink palace with spacious bedrooms (the best are in the 18th-century core). Heated pool in garden.

Viale Rimembranza 1, 16039 Sestri Levante, Genova. **Map** p334 C4. 0185 429 41. FAX 0185 48 24 59. @ villabalbi@tigullio.it b,l,d. **Rooms** 99. €€€

Rivarotta

Villa Luppis A rambling building, in the Luppis family since the 1800s. Rooms include a long, dreamy dining room, all pale pink and white, with antique furniture, silver and fresh flowers. Long corridors lead to well-furnished bedrooms with king-size beds. The fine old park contains a pool and fitness centre. Daily minibus to Venice. Via San Martino 18, 33080 Rivarotta, Pordenone. **Map** p335 F3. 0434 62 69 69. FAX 0434 62 62 28. hotel@villaluppis.it b,l,d. **Rooms** 39. Never. AE, DC, MC, V. €€€

San Osvaldo

Gasthof Tschötscherhof The narrow road from Siusi leads through meadows, orchards and vineyards to this idyllic chalet farmhouse. Its white painted façade is almost obscured by clambering vines and tumbling geraniums. Inside, an old *Stube*, with gently ticking clock, rough wood floor and neat bedrooms. San Osvaldo 19, 39040 Siuisi, Bolzano. **Map** p335 E2. 0471 70 60 13. FAX 0471 70 48 01 info@tschoetscherhof.com b,l,d. **Rooms** 8. Dec to end Feb V. €

San Floriano del Collio

Golf Hotel Castello Formentini This hotel, with nine-hole golf course, forms part of ancient Castello Formentini. The interior is tastefully decorated with family furniture and pictures and the Formentini family's restaurant is close by. An excellent address in an area with few fine hotels. Via Oslavia 2, 34070 San Floriano del Collio, Gorizia. **Map** p335 F3. 0481 88 40 51. FAX 0481 88 40 52. isabellaformentini@tiscalinet.it b. **Rooms** 16. mid-Nov to end Feb. AE, DC, MC, V. €€€

San Vigilio

Locanda San Vigilio An air of exclusivity pervades this hotel, set idyllically on its own lush Lake Garda headland. Right on the lake is the elegant dining room, with ceramic stove and sideboards displaying plates and bottles. You can also eat on a flowery arched veranda. Bedrooms in the main house are particularly lovely. San Vigilio, 37016 Garda, Verona. **Map** p335 E2. 045 7256688. FAX 045 627 81 82. info@punta-sanvigilio.it b,l,d. **Rooms** 14. Nov to Easter. AE, DC, MC, V. €€€€

Sestri Levante

Miramare Huge arched windows make the most of the view at this pink, shuttered house on Baia del Silenzio. Cool and contemporary. Via Cappellini 9, 16039 Sestri Levante, Genova. **Map** p334 C4. 0185 48 08 55. FAX 0185 410 55. miramare @miramaresestrilevante.com b,l,d. **Rooms** 43. €€€

Sirmione

Villa Cortine Palace Luxury headland hotel with fabulous exotic gardens, dotted with fountains and statuary. The 1950s extension is unfortunate. Via Grotte 6, 25019 Sirmione, Brescia. **Map** p335 D3. 030 990 58 90. FAX 030 91 63 90. info@hotel villacortine.com b,l,d. **Rooms** 54. €€€€

Soriso

Al Sorriso Michelin two-star restaurant whose dining room is a picture of elegance. Rooms more ordinary (and affordable) than you might expect. Via Roma 18, 28018 Soriso, Novara. **Map** p334 B3. 0322 98 32 28. FAX 0322 98 33 28. sorriso@alsorriso.com b,l,d. **Rooms** 8. €€€

Torino (Turin)

Conte Biancamano Central hotel whose public rooms are decorated, with a touch of faded grandeur, with chandeliers and paintings. Corso Vittorio Emanuele II 73, 10128 Torino. **Map** p334 A3. 011 562 32 81. FAX 011 562 37 89. cbhtl.to@iol.it b. **Rooms** 24. €€

SAUZE D'OULX

Il Capricorno The busy ski resort of Sauze d'Oulx attracts a fairly smart Italian clientele, winter and summer, as well as foreign skiers. This chalet hotel makes a good base, being cosily traditional, with rough beams and hand-made furniture, and set in an isolated position on the wooded slopes above the village. Good cooking.
Case Sparse 21, Le Clotes, 10050 Sauze d'Oulx, Torino. **Map** p334 A3. 0122 85 02 73. FAX 0122 85 00 55. b,l,d. **Rooms** 7. mid-Apr to mid-June, mid-Sept to Nov. MC, V. €€

SIRMIONE

Grifone Very good value. The Grifone restaurant serves excellent fresh fish and a mouthwatering selection of *antipasti*. Its terrace overlooks both Lake Garda and the ramparts of Sirmione's *castello*, as well as a scrap of sandy beach. And it has simple, inexpensive rooms that although basic are very clean. Those on the top floor have the best views.
Vicolo Bisse (Via Bocchio) 5, 25019 Sirmione, Brescia. **Map** p335 D3. (030) 91 60 14. FAX (030) 91 65 48. b,l,d. **Rooms** 16. Nov to Mar. Not accepted. €

SESTRI LEVANTE

Helvetia This charming hotel with a warm, personal atmosphere is distinguished by its pristine white façade and pretty yellow awnings. Signor Pernigotti devotes himself wholeheartedly to his hotel and its guests, and provides all sorts of unexpected extras (including bicycles). Excellent buffet breakfast served on the terrace.
Via Cappuccini 43, 16039 Sestri Levante, Genova. **Map** p334 C4. 0185 41 175. FAX 0185 45 72 16. @ helvetia@hotelhelvetia.it b. **Rooms** 21. Nov to Feb. MC, V. €€

SIUSI ALLO SCILIAR

Bad Ratzes Set in a clearing surrounded by dense forest, this family-orientated hotel at first looks disconcertingly modern and anonymous. But the warmth of its owners, the Scherlins, gives it heart. The decor is conventional and a bit dated, but there are extensive public rooms, including a playroom, and bedrooms are comfortable.
Via Ratzes 29, 39040 Siusi allo Sciliar, Bolzano. **Map** p335 E2. 0471 70 61 31. FAX 0471 70 71 99. @ info@badratzes.it b,l,d. **Rooms** 45. Apr to May, Oct to Nov. MC, V. €€

TORINO (TURIN)

Turin Palace Dating from 1872, the city's most impressive hotel, with sumptuous, modernized rooms decorated with antiques.
Via Sacchi 8, 10128 Torino. **Map** p334 A3. 011 562 55 11. FAX 011 561 21 87. @ palace@thi.it b,l,d. **Rooms** 122. €€€

TORINO (TURIN)

Villa Sassi In the hills just outside the city, a beautiful and luxurious 17th-century villa with many original features. Individual bedrooms.
Strada al Traforo di Pino 47, 10132 Torino. **Map** p334 A3. 011 898 05 56. FAX 011 898 00 95. @ info@villasassi.com b,l,d. **Rooms** 16. €€€

TORRI DEL BENACO

Europa Happy, welcoming and good value 1950s villa decorated in the style of the period. Pleasant setting, and shady terrace for dining.
Via Gabriele d'Annunzio 13-15, 37010 Torri del Benaco, Verona. **Map** p335 D3. & FAX 045 725 5206. @ info@europa.net b,l,d. **Rooms** 18. €€

TRENTO

Accademia Sophisticated town hotel in an attractive medieval house. Clean white lines are enlivened by vibrant rugs and antique pieces.
Vicolo Colico 4-6, 38100 Trento. **Map** p335 D2. 0461 23 36 00. FAX 0461 23 01 74. @ info@accademiahotel.it b,l,d. **Rooms** 42. €€

Soragna

Locanda del Lupo An extremely comfortable place to stay, in an area without many good addresses. This rather grand 18th-century coaching inn, in a small town near Cremona, was originally noted as a restaurant. It still serves interesting dishes, and has spacious bedrooms simply yet harmoniously furnished with antiques.
Via Garibaldi 64, 43019 Soragna, Parma. **Map** p334 C4. 0524 59 71 00. FAX 0524 59 70 66. info@locandadellupo.com b,l,d. **Rooms** 46. Christmas. AE, DC, MC, V. €€

Torri del Benaco

Gardesana Dining off the freshest of fish on the first-floor terrace of this comfortable hotel is a delight: it makes the perfect vantage point for watching harbour life in the pretty Lake Garda fishing village. The building itself has a long history, though the interior is modernized. The spruce bedrooms are thoughtfully equipped.
Piazza Calderini 20, 37010 Torri del Benaco, Verona. **Map** p335 D3. 045 72 25 411. FAX 045 72 25 771. info@hotel-gardesana.com b,d. **Rooms** 34. early Nov to end Feb. AE, DC, MC, V. €€

Torino (Turin)

Victoria This modern, practical hotel in the heart of the shopping district is lifted far from the rut by its imaginative interior, the warmth of its welcome, and its excellent value for money. Quietly situated, public rooms and some bedrooms overlook a verdant garden. Each bedroom is differently done out; public rooms are equally attractive.
Via Nino Costa 4, 10123 Torino. **Map** p334 A3. 011 561 19 09. FAX 011 561 18 06. reservation@hotelvictoria-torino.com b. **Rooms** 106. Never. AE, DC, MC, V. €€

Trissino

Relais Ca' Masieri The restaurant is set in a fine old shuttered mansion, with a shady terrace on which to dine in fine weather. It's no penance to eat indoors, however: the dining room is charming, decorated with delicate 18th-century frescoes. The food is delightful too. The bedrooms are in an adjacent old building.
Via Masieri 16, 36070 Trissino, Vicenza. **Map** p335 E3. 0445 49 01 22. FAX 0445 49 04 55. info@camasieri.com b,l,d. **Rooms** 12. late Jan to mid-Feb. AE, DC, MC, V. €€

Treviso

Albergo Campeol Across the street from the owners' atmospheric restaurant, Beccherie. There are plain, spacious rooms with excellent views of old Treviso. &
Piazza Ancillotto 4, 31100 Treviso. **Map** p335 E3. & FAX 0422 566 01. b. **Rooms** 14. €

Trieste

Duchi d'Aosta On the city's main square, a neo-Renaissance palace whose interior exudes the dignity and grandeur of a bygone age.
Piazza Unità d'Italia 2, 34121 Trieste. **Map** p335 F3. 040 760 00 11. FAX 040 36 60 92. info@grandhotelduchidaosta.com b,l,d. **Rooms** 55. €€€€

Valnontey

Petit Dahu In a little hamlet near Cogne, in the Gran Paradiso National Park, a tiny, homely hotel made up of two old stone-built houses. The owner can act as hiking guide; his wife cooks.
Valnontey 27, 11012 Aosta. **Map** p334 A3. 0165 74 146. FAX 0165 74 95 64. b,d. **Rooms** 8. €

Valsolda

Stella d'Italia The delightful shaded terrace juts right out onto Lake Lugano, offering lovely views. Ask for a room in the old wing of the hotel.
Piazza Roma 1, San Mamete, 22010 Valsolda, Como. **Map** p334 C2. 0344 68 139. FAX 0344 68 729. info@stelladitalia.com b,l,d. **Rooms** 34. €€

VENICE

Pensione Accademia A longtime favourite Venice *pensione*, the Accademia is loved for its rare garden setting (roses and fruit trees, canalside patio). Inside the shuttered 17th-century mansion, bedrooms have been renovated to a good standard with inlaid wood floors and antiqued mirrors. The public rooms are plainer.
Fondamenta Bollani, Dorsoduro 1058, 30123 Venezia. **Map** p335 E3. 041 521 01 88. FAX 041 523 91 52. @ info@pensioneaccademia.it b. **Rooms** 30. Never. AE, DC. MC, V. €€

VENICE

Bucintoro This simple, old-fashioned, family-run *pensione* has fabulous views from every room. Some, such as Nos 1 and 11, have windows overlooking both San Giorgio Maggiore and San Marco, and are much in demand by artists. No 4 has a large bed, airy curtains, and the lagoon waters gently lapping below. All rooms are plain, clean and light. Basic breakfasts.
Riva San Biagio 2135, 30122 Venezia. **Map** p335 E3. 041 522 32 40. FAX 041 523 52 24. b. **Rooms** 28. Dec, Jan. MC, V. €€

VENICE

Bisanzio For those who value uncomplicated comfort and convenience rather than character, this is a pleasant, quiet hotel set back from the Riva degli Schiavoni. The reception area is spacious and streamlined, with sitting areas and a bar. Best of the bedrooms are those with private terraces and rooftop views, and the family rooms.
Calle della Pieta, Castello 3651, 30122 Venezia. **Map** p335 E3. 041 520 31 00. FAX 041 520 41 14. @ e-mail@bisanzio.com b. **Rooms** 50. Never. AE, DC, MC, V. €€€€

VENICE

Gritti Palace As Somerset Maugham wrote, there are few greater pleasures than taking a drink on the Gritti's terrace at sunset, watching Salute church bathed in colour. Before bed, he advised, glance at the portrait of Doge Andrea Gritti, who, after a tumultuous life, spent his last years here in peace.
Campo Santa Maria del Giglio, San Marco 2467, 30124 Venezia. **Map** p335 E3. 041 296 12 22. FAX 041 296 11 00. @ grittipalace@luxurycollection.com b,l,d. **Rooms** 91. Never. AE, DC, MC, V. €€€€€

VARENNA

Hotel du Lac The bedrooms are small, but the terrace of this friendly hotel, by the side of Lake Como, is memorable.
Via del Prestino 4, 23829 Varenna, Lecco. **Map** p334 C2. 0341 83 02 38. FAX 0341 83 10 81. @ albergodulac@tin.it b,l. **Rooms** 17. €€

VENICE

Agli Alboretti Simple, spotless bedrooms with tiny bathrooms near the Accademia. Breakfast in summer under a pergola on the rear terrace.
Rio Terra Foscarini, Dorsoduro 884, 30123 Venezia. **Map** p335 E3. 041 523 00 58. FAX 041 521 01 58. @ alboretti@gpnet.it b,d. **Rooms** 20. €€€

VENICE

Locanda Ai Santi Apostoli Lovely third-floor *palazzo* apartment transformed into an elegant B&B. Stylish sitting room and spacious bedrooms.
Strada Nuova, Cannaregio 4391, 30131 Venezia. **Map** p335 E3. 041 521 26 12. FAX 041 521 26 11. @ aisantia@tin.it b. **Rooms** 10. €€€

VENICE

Hotel des Bains The setting for *Death in Venice*, still evocative of that *belle époque* period.
Lungomare Marconi 17, Lido, 30126 Venezia. **Map** p335 E3. 041 526 59 21. FAX 526 01 13. @ desbains@sheraton.com b,l,d. **Rooms** 191. €€€€

For key to symbols see backflap. For price categories *see p333*

Venice

Londra Palace This venerable hotel can claim to be in the top league. Public rooms are cool and elegant, with good food served in the romantic dining room. Front bedrooms (the hotel boasts 100 windows onto the lagoon) have matchless views, and the quality of furniture and original paintings is impressive.

Riva degli Schiavoni 4171, 30122 Venezia. **Map** p335 E3. 041 520 05 33. FAX 041 522 50 32. @ info@hotelondra.it b,l,d. **Rooms** 53. Never. AE, DC, MC, V. €€€€

Venice

Quattro Fontane A wide, shady terrace encircles this 150-year-old mock-Tyrolean building. It has lots of character, with charmingly decorated reception rooms filled with mementos of the owners' travels. Bedrooms in the main house are individual; those in the annexe are more streamlined, with gaily painted bathrooms.

Via Quattro Fontane 16, 30126 Lido, Venezia. **Map** p335 E3. 041 526 02 27. FAX 041 526 07 26. @ info@quattrofontane.com b,l,d. **Rooms** 58. mid-Nov to Mar. AE, DC, MC, V. €€€€

Venice

Piccola Fenice Right by La Fenice theatre and sister hotel to the well-known Fenice et des Artistes. The spacious suites for up to six people are perfect for families. Bathrooms are prettily tiled with generous basins; furniture is attractive; and there are facilities for making breakfast. The topmost apartment has a little terrace.

Calle della Madonna, San Marco 3614, 30124 Venezia. **Map** p335 E3. FAX 041 520 49 09. @ piccolafenice@fenicehotel.it **Rooms** 7 suites. two weeks Jan. AE, MC, V. €€€

Venice

La Residenza This grand Gothic *palazzo* overlooking Campo Bandiera e Moro appeals to true lovers of Venice. For a modest two-star, it has a deliciously immodest setting, with a vast, lavishly stuccoed Baroque hall. Some of the rooms are quaintly old-fashioned, but taking breakfast here in the early morning light is a treat.

Campo Bandiera e Moro, Castello 3608, 30122 Venezia. **Map** p335 E3. 041 528 5315. FAX 041 523 8859. @ info@venicelaresidenza.com b. **Rooms** 15. Never. MC, V. €€

Venice

Danieli This palace became a hotel in 1822, thereafter housing a raft of famous figures.

Riva degli Schiavoni, Castello 4196, 30122 Venezia. **Map** p335 E3. 041 522 64 80. FAX 041 520 02 08. @ res072.danieli@starwoodhotels.com b,l,d. **Rooms** 234. €€€€

Venice

Locanda Ca' Foscari Budget one-star hotel, a cut above the norm. Modest but pristine bedrooms; some have their own bathroom.

Calle della Frescada, Dorsoduro 3887B, 30123 Venezia. **Map** p335 E3. 041 71 04 01. FAX 041 71 08 17. @ info@locandacafoscari.com b. **Rooms** 11. €

Venice

Locanda Sturion If you can conquer the steep stairs, you will find plush, handsomely decorated bedrooms, two of which overlook Grand Canal.

Calle del Sturion, San Polo 679, 30125 Venezia. **Map** p335 E3. 041 523 62 43. FAX 041 522 83 78. @ info@locandasturion.com b. **Rooms** 11. €€€

Venice

Raspo da Ua For local colour and little money, plus the chance to enjoy Burano at night minus the crowds, a restaurant with simple rooms.

Via Galuppi 560, 30012 Burano, Venezia. **Map** p335 E3. 041 527 20 14. FAX 041 73 03 97. b,l,d. **Rooms** 6. €

Venice

Venice Rentals London-based specialists offering a wide selection of apartments from cosy studios to luxurious *palazzos*. In a city where hotels are booked months in advance, this is a delightful and cost-effective way to become part of its fabric. Enjoy, if only for a short time, the domestic pleasures of being *un veneziano*.

Various apartments throughout Venice.
FAX 041 276 9798. @ mail@venicerentals.com
None. **Rooms** apartments sleeping from 1 to 12.
Never. AE, DC, MC, V. €–€€€

Verona

Torcolo This B&B is an inexpensive option at the heart of lively Verona. Owner Silvia Pommari extends a warm welcome and her staff are helpful. Bedrooms vary, displaying several styles – 18th-century, Art Nouveau, modern. Most have somewhat cramped bathrooms; the best have separate shower cubicles.

Vicolo Listone 3, 37121 Verona. **Map** p335 D3.
045 800 75 12. FAX 045 800 40 58.
@ hoteltorcolo@virgilo.it b. **Rooms** 19.
early Jan to early Feb. AE, DC, MC, V. €€

Verona

Gabbia d'Oro In this stylish hotel you will find an attention to detail rarely encountered. The decorative flair and individuality of the owner is evident from the moment you enter. Public rooms include a vibrant orangery, complete with Romeo and Juliet, a pair of parrots. The bedrooms are suitably romantic.

Corso Portoni Borsari 4a, 37121 Verona.
Map p335 D3. 045 800 30 60. FAX 045 59 02 93.
@ gabbiadoro@easyasp.it b. **Rooms** 27.
Never. AE, DC, MC, V. €€€€

Vescovana

Villa Pisani A rare opportunity to stay in a magnificent, little-changed country *palazzo*, built in the 16th century for Cardinal Pisani, with gardens created in the 19th century by Evalina van Millingen, Countess Pisani. A nobleman's life at affordable prices. Lunch and dinner on request. Swimming pool.

Via Roma 19, 35040 Vescovana, Padua.
Map p335 E3. FAX 0425 92 00 16.
@ info@villapisani.it b. **Rooms** 8. Never.
AE, DC, MC, V. €€

Venice

Serenissima A stone's throw from St Mark's, with simple but pretty bedrooms and many attractive modern paintings on white walls.

Calle Goldoni, San Marco 4486, 30124 Venezia.
Map p335 E3. 041 520 00 11. FAX 041 522 32 92.
@ info@hotelserenissima.it b. **Rooms** 37. €€€

Verona

Colomba d'Oro Slick central hotel where a muralled foyer evokes Renaissance Verona. Some bedrooms are traditional in style, others modern.

Via Carlo Cattaneo 10, 37121 Verona. **Map** p335 D3.
045 59 53 00. FAX 045 59 49 74.
@ info@colombahotel.com b. **Rooms** 51. €€€

Villandro

Steinbock Bedrooms are beamed, with new pine beds and plump white duvets. The restaurant is noted for its regional Tyrolean dishes.

Santo Stefano 38, 39043 Villandro, Bolzano.
Map p335 E2. 0472 84 31 11. FAX 0472 84 34 68.
@ ansit.steinbock@yahoo.it b,l,d. **Rooms** 15. €

Zerman di Mogliano Veneto

Villa Condulmer For the price of a three-star hotel in Venice you can stay in this impressive 18th-century villa only 20 minutes' drive away.

Via Preganziol 1, 31021 Mogliano Veneto, Treviso.
Map p335 E3. 041 59 72 700. FAX 041 59 72 777. @ info@hvc.ve.it b,l,d. **Rooms** 45. €€€

For key to symbols see backflap. For price categories *see p333*

CENTRAL ITALY

TUSCANY • UMBRIA
LE MARCHE • ABRUZZO • LAZIO • SARDINIA

With the capital, Rome, at its core, Central Italy contains a range of beautiful landscapes and towns rich in culture and history, including ancient palaces, churches and towers. Tuscany in particular offers a wealth of memorable hotels, ranging from hilltop hamlets converted for the purposes, to atmospheric pensioni *in Florence and Siena. Umbria and the Marche offer some wonderful rural retreats in their gentle, pastoral countryside. The glossy island of Sardinia, included in this section, has plenty of luxury seaside haunts, plus a few simpler alternatives. If Rome is your destination, then the very best of hotels, from inexpensive to top-of-the-range, are described here.*

ALGHERO, SARDINIA

Villa Las Tronas Aloof on its rocky promontory, this castellated 19th-century folly has a grand interior and businesslike staff. Request a sea view (which costs extra) to avoid looking out onto Alghero's apartment blocks. Alghero's old town is nearby, and handy for morning espresso or cappuccino; breakfast here is not a strong point.
Lungomare Valencia 1, 07041 Alghero, Sardinia. **Map** p338 A2. 079 98 18 18. FAX 079 98 10 44. @ info@hvlt.com b,l,d. **Rooms** 26. Never. AE, DC, MC, V. €€€€

ARTIMINO

Paggeria Medicea Terracotta pantiles, cool arcades and a formal garden characterize this hotel in a village near Florence. Created from the servant's wing of a 16th-century Medici villa, it is imbued with an understated elegance. Dinner is served on a terrace overlooking vineyards; food is Tuscan with a Renaissance flavour.
Viale Papa Giovanni XXIII, 59015 Artimino, Firenze. **Map** p335 D5. 055 87 51 41. FAX 055 875 14 70. @ hotel@artimino.com b,l,d. **Rooms** 37. mid-Dec to early Jan. AE, DC, MC, V. €€

ASSISI

Santa Maria degli Ancillotti Hilltop retreat set in olive groves and vineyards. Excellent two-room suites with mini kitchens and terraces.
Sterpeto 42, 06086 Assisi, Perugia. **Map** p337 D1. FAX 075 803 97 64. @ info@santamariadegliancillotti.com b,d. **Rooms** 8. €€

ASSISI

Subasio Assisi's grand hotel, somewhat elderly, but splendidly sited near the Basilica.
Via Frate Elia 2, 06082 Assisi, Perugia. **Map** p337 D1. 075 81 22 06. FAX 075 81 66 91. @ s.elisei.hotelsubasio@interbusiness.it b,l,d. **Rooms** 62. €€€

BEVAGNA

L'Orto degli Angeli Romantic hotel in a fine frescoed nobleman's town house with a hanging garden at its core. A gem.
06031 Bevagna, Perugia. **Map** p337 D2. 0742 36 01 30. FAX 0742 36 17 56 @ ortoangeli@ortoangeli.it b,l,d. **Rooms** 9. €€

CASTEL DEL PIANO UMBRO

Villa Aureli Two self-catering apartments for 4-6 people in the magical home of Count Serego Alighieri, little altered since the 1700s. Pool.
Via Cirenei 70, 06071 Castel del Piano Umbro, Perugia. **Map** p336 C1. 075 514 04 44. FAX 075 514 94 08. @ villa.aureli@libero.it **Rooms** 2 apartments. €€

Asproli

Poggio d'Asproli This elegant stonebuilt farmhouse is the home of hotelier and artist Bruno Pagliari. Some of his work, mixed in with antiques, decorates the house. The sitting room has a huge fireplace and inviting sofas, and along one side of the room is a terrace for eating out on or just absorbing the peace.
Frazione, Asproli 7, 06059 Todi, Perugia. **Map** p336 C2. FAX 075 885 33 85. @ poggiodasproli@email.it b,d. **Rooms** 8. early Jan to Feb. AE, MC, V. €€

Bagno Vignoni

Posta Marcucci If you're exploring the countryside around Siena, this hotel in a small spa town is worth seeking out for its service (friendly and solicitous) and its cuisine. Breakfast on the terrace is particularly good. Another treat is the open-air thermal pool in a quiet corner of the garden.
Via Ara Urcea 43, Bagno Vignoni, 53027 San Quirico d'Orcia, Siena. **Map** p336 B2. 0577 88 71 12. FAX 0577 88 71 19. @ info@postamarcucci.it b,l,d. **Rooms** 35. 3 weeks Jan. AE, DC, MC, V. €

Assisi

Umbra Just off Assisi's main square a row of old houses, some dating back to medieval times, have been connected to create a hotel with the feeling of a private home. There's a terrace, covered by a pergola, for dining out on. The public rooms are elegant; bedrooms are simpler, and some have lovely countryside views.
Via degli Archi 6, 06081 Assisi, Perugia. **Map** p337 D1. 075 81 22 40. FAX 075 81 36 53. @ humbra@mail.caribusiness.it b,d. **Rooms** 25. early Jan to mid-Mar. AE, DC, MC, V. €

Barberino Val d'Elsa

Il Paretaio Country estate with a simple but stylish 17th-century farmhouse at its heart. Many guests come for the horse riding. Inside, bedrooms are rustic, with equestrian prints, worn terracotta floors and whitewashed walls; one of the nicest is in the old dovecot. Meals are communal, eaten round a long larchwood table.
San Filippo, 50021 Barberino Val d'Elsa, Firenze. **Map** p335 D5, p336 B1. (055) 805 92 18. FAX (055) 805 92 31. @ ilparetaio@tin.it b,l,d. **Rooms** 6, plus 2 apartments. Never. Not accepted. €

Castellina in Chianti

Belvedere di San Leonino 15th-century house. Well-equipped rooms, garden, terrace, pool.
Loc. San Leonino 23, 53011 Castellina in Chianti, Siena. **Map** p336 B1. 0577 74 08 87. FAX 0577 74 09 24. @ info@hotelsanleonino.com b,l,d. **Rooms** 28. €€

Castelnuovo Berardenga

Relais Borgo San Felice A hamlet on the wine estate has become a luxurious hotel.
San Felice, 53019 Castelnuovo Berardenga, Siena. **Map** p336 B1. 0577 35 92 60. FAX 0577 35 90 89. @ info@borgosanfelice.it b,l,d. **Rooms** 43. €€€€

Cenerente

Castello dell'Oscano Historic castle in an ancient steep pine forest. Some rooms are in the less atmospheric Villa Ada next door.
Strada della Frocella 37, 06070 Cenerente, Perugia. **Map** p336 C1. 075 58 43 71. FAX 075 69 06 66. @ info@oscano.com b,d. **Rooms** 34. €€€

Certaldo

Osteria del Vicario The approach through modern Certaldo is discouraging, but press on to the old town and this simple, well-priced inn.
Via Rivellino 3, 50052 Certaldo Alto, Firenze. **Map** p335 D5, p336 B1. FAX 0571 66 82 28. @ info@osteriadelvicario.it b,l,d. **Rooms** 11. €

For key to symbols see backflap. For price categories *see p333*

Bovara di Trevi

Casa Giulia There's a three-day minimum stay at this red-brick country villa, but that's no hardship as it's a good base for Assisi, Perugia, Spoleto and Todi. The owners are welcoming, and their private collection of antique cameras, old toys and *objets d'art* give a personal touch. Bedrooms are plain but comfortable.
Via Corciano 1, 06039 Bovara di Trevi, Perugia. **Map** p337 D2. 0742 782 57. FAX 0742 38 16 32. 53027 @ info@casagiulia.com b. **Rooms** 7. Never. MC, V. €

Castellina in Chianti

Salivolpi For a farmhouse holiday in Chianti country at a much lower price that many of the nearby 'hamlet' hotels, Salivolpi is a sound choice. The guesthouse comprises two low old stone farmhouses and a new bungalow in a large garden on the edge of the village. The neat bedrooms contain huge old carved beds.
Via Fiorentina 89, 53011 Castellina in Chianti, Siena. **Map** p336 B1. 0577 74 04 84. FAX 0577 74 09 98. @ info@hotelsalivolpi.com. b. **Rooms** 19. Never. AE, MC, V. €

Canalicchio di Collazzone

Relais il Canalicchio In the countryside 35km (20 miles) south of Perugia, a hilltop village has been turned into a stylish hotel complete with gym, sauna and billiard room. Grinding stones and local ceramics are much in evidence, and there are antiques too in the public rooms. Some bedrooms have private terrace gardens.
Via della Piazza 4, 06050 Canalicchio, Perugia. **Map** p336 C2. 075 8707325. FAX 075 8707296. @ relais@relaisilcanalicchio.it b,l,d. **Rooms** 51. Never. AE, DC, MC, V. €€€

Castellina in Chianti

Tenuta di Ricavo A whole hamlet abandoned in the 1950s has now been converted into a hotel that's owned and run by the Scotoni and Lobrano families. It's very well done out, with large, whitewashed vaulted rooms and a jumble of old rather than antique furniture. The 'Black Sheep' restaurant is popular with non-residents.
Località Ricavo, Castellina in Chianti 53011, Siena. **Map** p336 B1. 0577 74 02 21. FAX 0577 74 11 14. @ ricavo@ricavo.com b,l,d. **Rooms** 22. mid-Nov to Easter. MC, V. €€€

Isola d'Elba

Capo Sud Island complex of little villas in a quiet spot with fine bay views. Rooms are modern and simple, scattered around the grounds.
Lacona Elba I, 57031 Capoliveri. **Map** p336 A2. 0565 96 40 21. FAX 0565 96 42 63. @ info@hotelcaposud.it b,l,d. **Rooms** 40. €€

Isola d'Elba

Villa Ottone Across the bay from Portoferraio, in leafy grounds close to the sea, is this polished hotel whose main building is an 18th-century villa.
Ottone, 57037 Portoferraio, Elba, Livorno. **Map** p336 A2. 0565 93 30 42. FAX 0565 93 32 57. @ hotel@villaottone.com b,l,d. **Rooms** 80. €€€€

Firenze (Florence)

Annalena A traditional *pensione* with solid comforts and a huge drawing room. Bedrooms vary in size; acceptable bathrooms.
Via Romana 34, 50125 Firenze. **Map** p335 D5. 055 22 24 02. FAX 055 22 24 03. @ annalena@hotelannalena.it. b. **Rooms** 20. €€

Firenze (Florence)

Grand Early 1900s *palazzo* whose winter garden lobby is especially evocative. Bedrooms, frescoed with Renaissance scenes, have all modern luxury.
Piazza Ognissanti 1, 50123 Firenze. **Map** p335 D5. 055 28 87 81. FAX 055 21 74 00. @ grandflorence@luxurycollection.com b,l,d. **Rooms** 107. €€€€

CETONA

La Frateria di Padre Eligio Film-maker Anthony Minghella stayed here to revise a script; others come here on retreat (there are no TVs, radios or newspapers) or simply on honeymoon or holiday. A community of young people runs the place; expect wonderful food and beautifully furnished, candlelit rooms.
Convento di San Francesco, 53040 Cetona, Siena. **Map** p336 C2. 0578 23 82 61. FAX 0578 23 92 20. @ frateria@ftbcc.it b,l,d. **Rooms** 7. early Jan to mid-Feb. AE, MC, V. €€€

FIESOLE

Bencistà The Bencistà was built as a monastery in the 14th century and has polished tile floors, tall windows, gleaming furniture and an air of serenity, yet bills itself modestly as a *pensione*. Bedrooms have whitewashed walls and solid old furniture; some have glorious views over Florence and the Tuscan hills. A set menu is offered for dinner, which starts promptly at 7.30pm.
Via B da Maiano 4, 50014 Fiesole. **Map** p335 D5. FAX 055 591 63. @ pensionebencista@iol.it b,l,d. **Rooms** 42. Never. Not accepted. €€

CORTONA

Relais Il Falconiere Owner Riccardo Baracchi was born in this small villa. His wife, Silvia, is also from the area and is the chef. Their excellent restaurant attracts diners from a wide area – the food really is special. Vaulted bedrooms are traditionally furnished. The pool overlooks a hillside of cypress trees and olives.
Località San Martino 370, 52044 Cortona, Arezzo. **Map** p336 C1. 0575 61 26 79. FAX 0575 61 29 27. @ info@ilfalconiere.com b,l,d. Rooms 19. Never. AE, MC, V. €€€€

FIESOLE

Villa San Michele This villa was designed by Michelangelo, and if the antiques look as though they are from the 17th century that's because they probably are. Grandeur and authenticity is San Michele's hallmark. One of the many pleasures is taking breakfast in the *loggia*, looking across green hillsides to Florence below.
Via Doccia 4, 50014 Fiesole. **Map** p335 D5. 055 567 82 00. FAX 055 567 82 50. @ reservations@villasanmichele.net b,l,d. **Rooms** 45. Dec to mid-Mar. AE, DC. €€€€

FIRENZE (FLORENCE)

Royal This B&B hotel is cool and elegant, and its large, peaceful garden and parking spaces are a huge plus. Bedrooms are functional; some are small. Good value for money.
Via delle Ruote 52, 50123 Firenze. **Map** p335 D5. 055 48 32 87. FAX 055 49 09 76. b. **Rooms** 33. €€€

FIRENZE (FLORENCE)

Tornabuoni Beacci On the elegant prime shopping street, a long-established *pensione* with old-world atmosphere. Rooftop terrace.
Via de Tornabuoni 3, 50123 Firenze. **Map** p335 D5. 055 21 26 45. FAX 055 28 35 94. @ info@bthotel.it b,d. **Rooms** 28. €€€

ISOLA DEL GIGLIO

Pardini's Hermitage Smartly modern island villa with balconied bedrooms, reached from Giglio Porto by boat, car, donkey or an hour's walk.
Cala degli Alberi, 58013 Giglio Porto, Grosseto. **Map** p336 A3. 0564 80 90 34. FAX 0564 80 91 77. @ hermitage@hfs.it b,l,d. **Rooms** 15. €€

GUBBIO

Villa Montegranelli A severe exterior contrasts with the light 18th-century style of the spacious public rooms. The villa is popular for functions.
Monteluiano, 06024 Gubbio, Perugia. **Map** p337 D1. 075 922 01 85. FAX 075 927 33 72. @ villa.montegranelli@tin.it b,l,d. **Rooms** 21. €€

Firenze (Florence)

Excelsior Florence's grandest hotel is made from two 19th-century houses that stand next to the River Arno. Its fabulous interiors abound in oil paintings, marble staircases, statues and stained glass windows. The rooms are spacious and old-fashioned in style; many have good views over the river. Close to the train station.
Piazza d'Ognissanti 1, 50123 Firenze. **Map** p335 D5. 055 28 87 81. FAX 055 21 74 00. @ grandflorence@luxurycollection.com b,l,d. **Rooms** 107. Never. AE, DC, MC, V. €€€€

Firenze (Florence)

Morandi alla Crocetta This house just behind the archaeological museum was a brothel in Medici times, and subsequently a convent. The Antuono family has lived here since the 1920s, and now runs the first-rate hotel. There are many special touches, from frescoed rooms to phones in the bathrooms.
Via Laura 50, 50121 Firenze. **Map** p335 D5. 055 234 47 47. FAX 055 248 09 54. @ welcome@hotelmorandi.it b. **Rooms** 10. Never. AE, DC, MC, V. €€€

Firenze (Florence)

Loggiato dei Serviti This vaulted hotel is airy and calm, and is set in a traffic-free square by the Ospedale degli Innocenti. The decoration is spare and elegant, with carved wooden bedheads and a few well-chosen pieces of furniture. The place is popular with visiting art historians so book well in advance. Breakfast is very good.
Piazza della SS Annunziata 3, 50122 Firenze. **Map** p335 D5. 055 28 95 92. FAX 055 28 95 95. @ info@loggiatodeiservitihotel.it b. **Rooms** 29. Never. AE, DC, MC, V. €€€

Firenze (Florence)

Porta Rossa Italy's second oldest hotel, dating from 1386, is a purposeful, bustling and civilized place. Leather couches and stained glass decorate the vaulted reception area. Bedrooms are comparatively plain but are large; it's worth asking for the tower suite with its views over town. Best of all is the hotel's central location, close to Piazza della Signoria.
Via Porta Rossa 19, 50123 Firenze. **Map** p335 D5. 055 28 75 51. FAX 055 28 21 79. b. **Rooms** 78. Never. AE, DC, MC, V. €€

Massa e Cozzile

Villa Pasquini Once the retreat of an aristocratic family, little has changed since the 19th-century.
Via Vacchereccia 56, Margine Coperta, 51010 Massa e Cozzile, Pistoia. **Map** p335 D5. 0572 722 05. FAX 0572 91 08 88. @ info@villapasquini.com b,d. **Rooms** 12. €

Monte Castello di Vibio

Fattoria di Vibio All is effortless simplicity and relaxed elegance at this 18th-century farmhouse.
Località Buchella-Doglio 9, 06057 Monte Castello di Vibio, Perugia. **Map** p336 C2. 075 874 96 07. FAX 075 878 0014. @ info@fattoriadivibio.com b,l,d. **Rooms** 14. €€

Montefollonico

La Chiusa The restaurant, an old olive oil mill, is the centrepiece, but great care has been given to the bedrooms and suites. Superb bathrooms.
Via della Madonnina 88, 53040 Montefollonico, Siena. **Map** p336 B1. 0577 66 96 68. FAX 0577 66 95 93. @ info@ristorantelachiusa.it b,l,d. **Rooms** 15. €€€

Monteriggioni

Borgo San Luigi Farmhouse country hotel in vast, lush grounds. Copious buffets, pool, tennis.
Località Strove, Via della Cerreta 7, 53035 Monterriggioni, Siena. **Map** p335 D5, p336 B1. 0577 30 10 55. FAX 0577 30 11 67. @ info@relais-borgo sanluigi.it b,l,d. **Rooms** 73. €€€

Firenze (Florence)

Torre di Bellosguardo This 16th-century villa with tower rests on a hill overlooking the city, just south of the Porta Romana. It aims to be a home from home and what makes the place special is the affable owner Giovanni Franchetti. Bedrooms are large and solidly furnished. There is a minimum two-night stay at weekends.
Via Roti Michelozzi 2, 50124 Firenze. **Map** p335 D5. 055 229 81 45. FAX 055 22 90 08. b,l. info@torrebellosguardo.com b,l. **Rooms** 16. Never. AE, DC, MC, V. €€€€

Fontignano

Villa di Monte Solare The Iannarones run this 18th-century villa hotel along houseparty lines, offering regional cuisine using fresh ingredients. They have restored the formal garden, and another 'secret' garden behind it. Some rooms are in the converted farmhouse with its own pool down the hill. Minimum stay three days.
Località Fontignano, 06070 Fontignano, Perugia. **Map** p336 C2. 075 83 23 76. FAX 075 83 55 462. info@villamontesolare.it b,l,d. **Rooms** 28. Never. AE, DC, MC, V. €€

Firenze (Florence)

Villa Cora A pleasure palace on the outskirts of Florence, this Renaissance-style 19th-century mansion was once the home of Baron Oppenheim and later Napoleon's wife Empress Eugenia. The formal interior includes ceilings encrusted with stucco, Murano glass chandeliers and regally draped beds.
Viale Niccolò Machiavelli 18, 50125 Firenze. **Map** p335 D5. 055 229 84 51. FAX 055 22 90 86. reservations@villacora.it b,l,d. **Rooms** 48. Never. AE, DC, MC, V. €€€€

Lecchi in Chianti

San Sano The village's old watchtower forms the core of this hotel, with bedrooms in the former village houses, each connected by courtyards, passageways and stone steps. The dining room is in the former stables. Guest rooms are rustic in style, but stay the right side of overly countrified, and have modern bathrooms.
San Sano, 53010 Lecchi in Chianti, Siena. **Map** p336 B1. 0577 74 61 30. FAX 0577 74 61 56. info@sansanohotel.it b,d. **Rooms** 14. Jan to Feb. AE, DC, MC, V. €

Montevettolini

Villa Lucia Informal yet elegant farmhouse B&B run by Italian-American Lucia Vallera. Shady garden and terrace; small pool.
Via dei Bronzoli 1443, 51015 Montevettolini, Pistoia. **Map** p335 D5. 0572 61 77 90. FAX 0572 62 88 17. villalucia@yahoo.com b; d on request. **Rooms** 7. €€

Monticchiello di Pienza

L'Olmo Old farmhouse with double room, suites and apartment. Delicious breakfasts.
Podere Ommio 27, 53020 Monticchiello di Pienza, Siena. **Map** p336 B1. 0578 75 51 33. FAX 0578 75 51 24. info@olmopienza.it b,d. **Rooms** 7. €€

Panicale

Le Grotte di Boldrino This former *palazzo* hewn into Panicale's walls is small and intimate. The decor juxtaposes new with old.
Via Virgilio Ceppari, 06064 Panicale, Perugia. **Map** p335 E5, p336 C1. 075 83 71 61. FAX 075 83 71 66. b,l,d. **Rooms** 11. €

Perugia

Brufani The Brufani has recently undergone a serious expansion, including 55 new rooms, sauna, pool and gym. Stunning views as before.
Piazza Italia 12, 06121 Perugia. **Map** p336 C1. 075 573 25 41. FAX 075 572 02 10. brufani@tin.it b,l,d. **Rooms** 63, plus 31 suites. €€€€

For key to symbols see backflap. For price categories *see p333*

Mercatale Val di Pesa

Salvadonica Olive oil and wine are still produced on this large farm estate. The guest rooms are in a couple of huge farmhouses; there are also ten apartments in the grounds. It's an easy drive into Florence; there are many alternative distractions on site, including horseriding, billiards, tennis and football.
Via Grevigiana 82, 50024 Mercatale Val di Pesa, Firenze. **Map** p335 D5. 055 821 80 39. FAX 055 821 80 43. @ info@salvadonica.com b. **Rooms** 5. Nov to Feb. AE, DC, MC, V. €

Montefalco

Villa Pambuffetti A rose-pink brick villa located between Assisi and Perugia, with views of the Umbrian hills. Owners Alessandra and Mauro Angelucci have preserved the original 1920s' interiors, decorated with Tiffany lamps and cane chairs; the bathrooms are in authentic period style but with modern plumbing and fittings.
Via della Vittoria 20, 06036 Montefalco, Perugia. **Map** p337 D2. 0742 37 94 17. FAX 0742 37 92 45. @ villabianca@interbusiness.it b,d. **Rooms** 15. Never. AE, DC, MC, V. €€€

Monte San Savino

Castello di Gargonza The village, abandoned earlier this century, has now been turned into a place to stay. It's not strictly a hotel (most accommodation is in the village houses let by the week), but the place is informal and good value. There are basic rooms for a one-night stop, with breakfast in the old oil-pressing house.
Gargonza, 52048 Monte San Savino, Arezzo. **Map** p336 B1. 0575 84 70 21. FAX 0575 84 70 54. @ gargonza@gargonzo.it b,l,d. **Rooms** 8; 24 houses. 3 weeks Nov, 3 weeks Jan. AE, DC, MC, V. €€

Morra

Palazzo Terranova An imposing, classically proportioned country house commanding wide views over the Umbrian countryside. Lavishly restored by its English owners, Sarah and Johnny Townsend, with bedrooms named after Verdi operas. The whole house can be taken by one party. Attentive, professional service.
Loc Ronti, 06010 Morra, Perugia. **Map** p336 C1. 075 857 00 83. FAX 075 857 00 14. @ booking@palazzoterranova.com b,l,d. **Rooms** 10. Never. AE, DC, MC, V. €€€€

Pienza

Il Chiostro di Pienza Half the rooms in this stylishly converted monastery overlook the cloister, the rest have serene hill views.
Corso Rosellino 26, 53026 Pienza, Siena. **Map** p336 B1. 0578 74 84 00. FAX 0578 74 84 40. @ ilchiostro@jumpy.it b,l,d. **Rooms** 29. €€€

Pisa

Royal Victoria Original features at this dignified 1840s hotel include exquisite *trompe l'oeil* drapery. Rooms vary in size and style; all are fairly basic.
Lungarno Pacinotti 12, 56126 Pisa. **Map** p334 C5. 050 94 01 11. FAX 050 94 01 80. @ mail@royalvictoria.it b. **Rooms** 48. €€

Poggio Mirteto Scalo

Borgo Paraelios Immaculately executed country club-style hotel. Individually furnished rooms and suites are spread around gardens and courtyards.
02040 Poggio Catino, Rieti. **Map** p337 D3. 0765 262 67. FAX 0765 262 68. @ info@borgoparaelios.it b,l,d. **Rooms** 15. €€€€

Isola di Ponza

Santa Domitilla On this alluring island, close to Chiaia di Luna beach and the pretty port.
Via Panoramica, 04027 Isola di Ponza, Latina. **Map** p337 D5. 0771 80 99 51. FAX 0771 80 99 55. @ info@santadomitilla.com b,l,d. **Rooms** 50. €€€€

Oliena, Sardinia

Su Gologone This low white villa in the wooded foothills of the Supramonte mountains has guest rooms with whitewashed walls and tiled floors. Despite the large number of rooms, it feels small and personal, and the area is extremely peaceful. Excellent food, such as spit-roasted suckling pig.
Oliena, 08025 Nuoro, Sardinia. **Map** p338 B2.
0784 28 75 12. FAX 0784 28 76 68.
@ gologone@tin.it b,l,d. **Rooms** 77.
mid-Nov to mid-Mar, except Christmas.
AE, DC, MC, V. €€€

Palo Laziale

La Posta Vecchia The artworks and antiques in this seaside mansion, lapped by the Tyrrhenian sea, were chosen by former owner John Paul Getty. It is probably Italy's most remarkable hotel. During building work, the foundations of a Roman villa were discovered; they can now be viewed through glass panels in the floor.
00055 Palo Laziale, Ladispoli. **Map** p336 C3.
06 994 95 01. FAX 06 994 95 07. @ info@lapostavechhia.com b,l,d. **Rooms** 19.
mid-Nov to end Mar. AE, DC, MC, V. €€€€

Palau, Sardinia

Capo d'Orso This relaxed hotel is only a short boat ride away from the busy Costa Smeralda, but miles away in spirit. The life of the place revolves around two white slivers of beach, the pool and a series of shaded terraces. Rooms are in a low-rise block unremarkable in style, but each has a balcony or terrace facing the sea.
Località Cala Capra, 07020 Palau, Sardinia.
Map p338 B1. 0789 70 20 00. FAX 0789 70 20 09.
@ capo.orso@libero.it b,l,d. **Rooms** 75.
mid-Oct to mid-May. AE, DC, MC, V. €€€€

Panzano in Chianti

Villa le Barone This 16th-century villa in the countryside south of Florence is run along the lines of a house party, with honesty bar and a 'reception' in the form of a visitor's book. Rooms have the feeling of a private home furnished with personal effects. There are two sitting rooms and a pool with a view to lounge by.
Via San Leolino 19, 50020 Panzano in Chianti, Firenze.
Map p335 D5, p336 B1. 055 85 26 21. FAX 055 85 22 77. @ info@villalebarone.it b,l,d. **Rooms** 30.
Nov to Mar. AE, MC, V. €€€€

Porto Cervo, Sardinia

Balocco A stylishly rustic modern hotel in lush gardens, close to the chic harbour of Porto Cervo.
Via Liscia di Vacca, 07020 Porto Cervo, Sassari, Sardinia. **Map** p338 B1. 0789 915 55.
FAX 0789 915 10. @ hotelbalocco@tiscalinet.it b.
Rooms 34. €€€€

Porto Cervo, Sardinia

Capriccioli An affordable villa-type hotel close to a pretty beach. Half-board in high season.
Capriccioli, 07020 Porto Cervo, Sassari, Sardinia.
Map p338 B1. 0789 960 04 (summer), 0789 82321 (winter). FAX 0789 964 22. @ hotelcapriccioli@tiscalinet.it
b,l,d. **Rooms** 45. €€€€

Porto Cervo, Sardinia

Le Ginestre Little luxury villas among trees and flowering shrubs. Most of the rooms have balconies with sea views.
07020 Porto Cervo, Sassari, Sardinia. **Map** p338 B1.
0789 92 030. FAX 0789 940 87. @ info@leginestrehotel.com b,l,d. **Rooms** 80. €€€€

Porto Rotondo, Sardinia

Sporting An oasis of luxury in tastefully simple neo-rustic buildings scattered around a promontory. Strong yachting contingent.
Olbia, 07020 Porto Rotondo, Sassari, Sardinia.
Map p338 B1. 0789 340 05. FAX 0789 343 83.
@ sportreserv@tin.it b,l,d. **Rooms** 27. €€€€

Pesaro

Villa Serena There's no haughtiness at the villa of the Pinto family – or to give them their full title, the counts Pinto de Franca y Vergaes. The polished interior with its old master paintings exudes simplicity and calm, and good food is served in a down-to-earth atmosphere. Bedrooms range from antique-packed to faded gentility.
Via San Nicola 6/3, 61100 Pesaro. **Map** p335 F5.
0721 552 11. FAX 0721 559 27. @ info@villa-serena.it
b,l,d. **Rooms** 9. first 3 weeks Jan.
AE, DC, V. €€

Pistoia

Villa Vannini This part of Tuscany has relatively few great places to stay, so this attractive villa is particularly welcome. It is managed by the welcoming Bordonaro family. The excellent cuisine is based on Tuscan specialities; pre-dinner drinks are served on the terrace under cedar trees. Bedrooms are furnished in floral fabrics and with good furniture.
Villa di Piteccio 6, 51030 Pistoia. **Map** p335 D5.
0573 420 31. FAX 0573 425 51. @ info@villavannini.it
b,l,d. **Rooms** 8. Never. AE, DC, MC, V. €

Pievescola

Relais La Suvera This 16th-century fortified villa once belonged to film-maker Luchino Visconti. Although he may not have had anything to do with the canopied beds and elaborate decorative style worthy of a film set, you feel he would have approved. The place is fun, sybaritic, romantic – and expensive.
Pievescola, 53030 Siena. **Map** p336 B1.
0577 96 03 00. FAX 0577 96 02 20.
@ lasuvera@lasuvera.it b,l,d. **Rooms** 31.
Nov to mid-April. AE, DC, MC, V. €€€€

Porto Cervo, Sardinia

Pitrizza On a headland surrounded by sapphire water, Pitrizza is a collection of villas, scattered through a garden leading to a small beach and seawater pool. Its strong point is the way it has combined peace and sociability – it's quiet but there's also a clubhouse with lively bar/restaurant.
Porto Cervo, 07020 Sardinia. **Map** p338 B1.
0789 93 01 11. FAX 0789 93 06 11.
@ pitrizza@luxurycollection.com b,l,d.
Rooms 55. Sep to Apr.
AE, DC, MC, V. €€€€

Pugnano

Casetta delle Selve Nicla Menchi, the characterful owner of this elevated farmhouse B&B, has created an interior stunningly different from the norm. Great breakfasts.
56010 Pugnano, San Giuliano Terme, Pisa.
Map p334 C5. FAX 050 85 03 59. b. **Rooms** 6. €

Punta Ala

Alleluja The most inviting of the exclusive hotels in this chic yachting-and-boutique town.
Via del Porto, 58040 Punta Ala, Grosseto.
Map p336 A2. 0564 92 20 50. FAX 0564 92 07 34.
@ alleluja.puntaala@baglionehotels.com b,l,d.
Rooms 38. €€€€

Radda in Chianti

Podere Terreno Old farmhouse guesthouse. Vines, olive groves, great home cooking. Half board.
Via Terreno 21, Volpaia, 53017 Radda in Chianti, Siena. **Map** p335 D5, p336 B1. 0577 73 83 12.
FAX 0577 73 84 00. @ podereterreno@chiantinet.it b,d.
Rooms 7. €€€

Rome

Condotti The comfy sofas in the glossy foyer are the only place to lounge. There is a frescoed breakfast room. Bedrooms are harmonious.
Via Mario De'Fiori 37, 00187 Roma. **Map** p336 C4, p338 A1. 06 679 46 61. FAX 06 679 04 57.
@ info@hotelcondotti.com b. **Rooms** 17. €€€€

Porto Cervo, Sardinia

Romazzino One of Europe's grandest beach hotels, the Romazzino has exclusive use of a white-sand bay. The hotel is on the large side but has the feel of a smaller place; families will feel comfortable. There are Moorish touches to the decoration, and service and food are top class.
07020 Porto Cervo, Costa Smeralda, Sardinia. **Map** p338 B1. 0789 97 71 11. FAX 0789 977 618. @ res067_romazzino@sheraton.com b,l,d. **Rooms** 94. mid-Oct to late Apr. AE, DC, MC, V. €€€€€

Portonovo

Emilia At this modest clifftop villa a short drive from the small resort of Portonovo, rooms are angled so that most have a sea view. Inside are some stupendous wall coverings – an illustrious band of 20th-century artists have paid for a stay here by donating a work. The food is very good, with fish a speciality.
Via Poggio 149a, 60020 Portonovo, Ancona. **Map** p335 E4. 071 80 11 45. FAX 071 80 13 30. @ info@hotelemilia.com b,l,d. **Rooms** 29. end Dec to end Feb. AE, DC, MC, V. €€€€

Porto Ercole

Il Pellicano This terracotta villa by the sea combines the best of a luxury hotel (great service and fine seafood cuisine) with an easygoing atmosphere and contemporary decoration. There's swimming off the flat rocks, and you don't have to move from the poolside to choose from a huge array of antipasti.
Cala dei Santi, 58, 58018 Porto Ercole, Grosseto. **Map** p336 B3. 0564 85 81 11. FAX 0564 83 34 18. @ info@pellicanohotel.com b,l,d. **Rooms** 50. Nov to Mar. AE, DC, V. €€€€

Prato

Villa Rucellai Potted lemon trees and clipped topiary characterize this country villa on the outskirts of industrial Prato. It has been in the Rucellai Piqué family since 1740 and is evidently a family home, but guests are free to use the grand hall and sitting room. Breakfast is taken at a communal table. Bedrooms are simple.
Via di Canneto 16, 59100 Prato. **Map** p336 C2. FAX 0574 46 03 92. @ canneto@masternet.it b. **Rooms** 11. Never. Not accepted. €

Rome

De Consoli A slick city hotel, perfectly placed for visiting the Vatican or for shopping in Via Cola di Rienzo. Whirlpool baths help restore tired bones.
Via Varrone 2/d, 00193 Rome. **Map** p336 C4. 06 68 89 29 72. FAX 06 68 21 22 74. @ info@hoteldeiconsoli.com b. **Rooms** 28. €€€€

Rome

Hassler Above the Spanish Steps, with fabulous views from the rooftop, restaurant and gym. Host to Europe's glitterati in its *dolce vita* days.
Piazza Trinità dei Monti 6, 00187 Roma. **Map** p336 C4. 06 69 93 40. FAX 06 67 89 991. @ hasslerroma@mclink.it b,l,d. **Rooms** 100. €€€€

Rome

Lord Byron Originally a monastery, now a small, lavishly furnished hotel in the residential district of Parioli with an acclaimed restaurant.
Via de Notaris 5, 00197, Roma. **Map** p336 C4. 06 322 04 04. FAX 06 322 04 05. @ info@lordbyronhotel.com b,l,d. **Rooms** 36. €€€€

Rome

Raphael Cloaked in ivy, and set back from Piazza Navona, with a startlingly theatrical foyer behind its discreet façade. Lovely roof terrace.
Largo Febo 2, 00186 Roma. **Map** p336 C4. 06 68 28 31. FAX 06 687 89 93. @ info@raphaelhotel.com b,l,d. **Rooms** 60. €€€€

For key to symbols see backflap. For price categories *see p333*

Radda in Chianti

Relais Fattoria Vignale This hotel has an appealingly domestic feel, decorated with muted colours, fresh flowers, oil paintings and standard lamps. Breakfast is served on the terrace or in the vaulted breakfast room. The 'taverna' on-site does snacks, and there's a very good restaurant – also called the Vignale – a short walk away.
Via Pianigiani 8, 53017 Raddi in Chianti, Siena. **Map** p336 B1. 0577 73 83 00. FAX 0577 73 85 92. vignale@vignale.it b,l,d. **Rooms** 40. early Jan to mid-Mar. AE, DC, MC, V. €€€

Rome

Eden Extensively refurbished in1994, Eden is unashamedly status-conscious, flaunting its designer labels and its famous guests – among them have been actors Tom Cruise and Nicole Kidman. Decoration is a mix of neutral shades, oil paintings and openfires. The Michelin-starred terrace restaurant looks out over Rome's rooftops.
Via Ludovisi 49, 00187 Roma. **Map** p336 C4. 06 47 81 21. FAX 06 482 15 84. reservations@hotel-eden.it b,l,d. **Rooms** 121. Never. AE, DC, MC, V. €€€€

Reggello

Villa Rigacci A 15th-century hilltop farmhouse with ivy-covered façade, open fires in winter, and tiled, stone-flagged and archwayed interiors. It makes a great bolthole close to Florence (30km/23 miles away). Furniture is highly polished and antique; bedrooms are mostly spacious; and food is a mix of international and Italian cuisine.
Vággio 76, 50066 Reggello. **Map** p335 E5. 055 865 67 18. FAX 055 865 65 37. hotel@villarigacci.it b,l,d. **Rooms** 28. Never. AE, MC, V. €€

Rome

Empire Palace Smart new executive hotel, opened in September 1999 in a 19th-century palace which was built as the Roman residence of the aristocratic Venetian Mocenigo family. The contemporary decoration combines Venetian elements with an astral theme, such as a night sky painted on the lobby ceiling.
Via Aureliana 39, 00187 Roma. **Map** p336 C4. 06 42 12 81. FAX 06 42 12 84 00. gold@ empirepalacehotel.com b,l,d. **Rooms** 113. Never. AE, DC, MC, V. €€€€

Rome

Villa del Parco In a peaceful area a 20-minute bus ride from the centre of Rome. Inside, all is elegant and tranquil. Bedrooms vary in size.
Via Nomentana 110, 00161 Roma. **Map** p336 C4. 06 4423 77 73. FAX 06 4423 75 72. info@hotelvilladelparco.it b. **Rooms** 29. €€

San Benedetto

Il Rosolaccio A hilltop farmhouse well restored by an English couple, Steven and Natalie Music. Also self-catering apartments. Pool.
San Benedetto 34, 53037 San Gimignano, Siena. **Map** p336 B1. 0577 94 44 65. FAX 0577 94 44 67. music@rosolaccio.com b,d. **Rooms** 6. €

San Felice Circeo

Punta Rossa Secluded setting above a rocky shore. Pleasant holiday hotel. Very large suites.
Via delle Batterie 37, Quarto Caldo, 04017 San Felice Circeo, Latina. **Map** p337 D5. 0773 54 80 85. FAX 0773 54 80 75. punta_rossa@iol.it b,l,d. **Rooms** 33. €€€€

San Gimignano

L'Antico Pozzo A 15th-century house in the middle of town, beautifully restored in 1990 and furnished with fine, simple taste.
Via San Matteo 85, 53037 San Gimignano, Siena. **Map** p336 B1. 0577 94 20 14. FAX 0577 94 21 17. info@anticopozzo.com b. **Rooms** 18. 

ROME

D'Inghilterra This used to be the guest accommodation for the Torlonia palace and a regal air survives, with antique mirrors and classically decorated rooms. It's in a great spot close to the Spanish Steps and Trevi fountain. Some of the more expensive rooms have their own terrace. Rates do not include breakfast.
Via Bocca di Leone 14, 00187 Roma. **Map** p336 C4. 06 69 92 22 43. FAX 06 679 86 01. @ reservation.hir@royaldemeure.com b,l,d. **Rooms** 98. Never. AE, DC, MC, V. €€€€

ROME

Sole al Pantheon In an unbeatable location opposite the Pantheon, this ancient building has been a hotel since 1467. It is distinctively and imaginatively decorated, with white leather seating and tiled floors lending a glamorous tone to the public areas. The bedrooms are all different. Bar and a leafy enclosed terrace.
Piazza della Rotonda 63, 00186 Roma. **Map** p336 C4. 06 678 04 41. FAX 06 69 94 06 89. @ hotsole@flashnet.it b. **Rooms** 25. Never. AE, DC, MC, V. €€€€

ROME

Majestic A beautiful wrought iron 'cage' lift and many mirrors and fittings survive from the 1880s when this classic, old-world hotel was built. There are bougainvillaea and olive trees in pots on the terraces, eight sizes of bed, a formal restaurant and a late-night brasserie with live jazz. Double-glazing keeps traffic noise to a minimum.
Via Veneto 50, 00187 Roma. **Map** p336 C4. 06 42 14 41. FAX 06 488 09 84. @ hotelmajestic@flashnet.it b,l,d. **Rooms** 96. Never. AE, DC, MC, V. €€€€

SAN GIMIGNANO

Casale del Cotone A former hunting lodge 2km (1 mile) north of San Gimignano, this is now a classy farmhouse-style B&B. Bedrooms are airy and refined, furnished with just one or two interesting pieces; the sitting areas and breakfast room are done out in the same mix of rustic and antique style.
Loc. Il Cotone 59 'Cellole', 53037 San Gimignano, Siena.**Map** p336 B1. FAX 0577 94 32 36. @ info@ casaledelcotone.com b,d. **Rooms** 11, plus 3 apts. Never. AE, MC, V. €

SAN GIMIGNANO

Il Casolare di Libbiano Country seclusion combined with proximity to San Gimignano and Siena at this tastefully furnished old farmhouse.
Libbiano 3, 53037 San Gimignano, Siena. **Map** p336 B1. FAX 0577 94 60 02. @ info@casolarelibbiano.it b,l,d. **Rooms** 8. €€

SAN GIMIGNANO

Relais Santa Chiara Just outside the town gates, an elegant, traditional hotel offering comfort and convenience. Pool; garden; private parking.
Via Matteotti 15, 53037 San Gimignano, Siena. **Map** p336 B1. 0577 94 07 01. FAX 0577 94 20 96. @ rsc@rsc.it b,l. **Rooms** 41. €€€

SAN GIMIGNANO

Le Renaie Modest sister hotel to the nearby Villa San Paolo, with lower prices. Peaceful location, pool and access to San Paolo's tennis courts.
Pancole, 53037 San Gimignano, Siena. **Map** p336 B1. 0577 95 50 44. FAX 0577 95 51 26. @ lerenaie@iol.it b,l,d. **Rooms** 25. €€

SAN GIMIGNANO

Villa San Paolo A hillside villa with terraced gardens, tennis courts, pool and intimate lounges.
Strada per Certaldo, 53037 San Gimignano, Siena. **Map** p336 B1. 0577 95 51 00. FAX 0577 95 51 13. @ info@hotelvillasanpaolo.com b. **Rooms** 18. €€€

For key to symbols see backflap. For price categories *see p333*

Santa Margherita, Sardinia

Is Morus Relais This Mediterranean take on a country-house hotel is in a blissfully quiet corner of the island, far from any resorts. Bedrooms are white and uncluttered; some in the main building have sea views. There are also villas in the wooded garden. The private beach is a few steps away, with crystal-clear water.
Santa Margherita di Pula, 09010 Pula, Sardinia. **Map** p338 A3. 070 92 11 71. FAX 070 92 15 96. ismorusrelais@tin.it b,l,d. **Rooms** 85. Nov to Easter. AE, DC, MC, V. €€€€

Siena

Villa Scacciapensieri This villa lies just north of the city, close enough to hear church bells tolling. The bedrooms are a mix of styles: some suites are full of antiques, others have painted country furniture. Breakfast and dinner are served outdoors. The Nardi family are very helpful hosts.
Via di Scacciapensieri 10, 53100 Siena. **Map** p336 B1. 0577 414 41. FAX 0577 27 08 54. villa.scacciapensieri@tin.it b,l,d. **Rooms** 31. Christmas to mid-Mar. AE,DC,MC,V. €€€€

Siena

Certosa di Maggiano A former Carthusian monastery on the outskirts of Siena now makes a restfully pampering hotel. The elegant cloisters date from the 14th century. Excellent modern cuisine is served in vaulted arcades round the central courtyard, in a ceramic-packed room inside, or next to the swimming pool.
Strada di Certosa 82, 53100 Siena. **Map** p336 B1. 0577 28 81 80. FAX 0577 28 81 89. info@certosadimaggiano.it b,l,d. **Rooms** 17. Never. AE, MC, V. €€€€€

Sinalunga

Locanda dell'Amorosa A working farm is the setting for this upmarket inn. Bedrooms, in the main house and in stone outbuildings on the estate, are simple, with whitewashed walls, tiled floors, and gleaming bathrooms. Dinner is served in the old stable block and food is a modern rendition of traditional Tuscan specialities.
53048 Sinalunga, Siena. **Map** p336 B1. 0577 67 72 11. FAX 0577 63 20 01. locanda@amorosa.it b,l,d. **Rooms** 21. early Jan to early Mar. AE, DC, MC, V. €€€€€

Sarteano

Relais Club Le Anfore Tastefully decorated old farmhouse guesthouse in unspoilt countryside. Spacious bedrooms; pool, tennis, riding.
Via di Chiusi 30, 53047 Sarteano, Siena. **Map** p336 C2. & FAX 0578 26 55 21. leanfore@priminet.com b,d. **Rooms** 10. €€

Scansano

Antico Casale Captivating hotel in the coastal Maremma. Pretty bedrooms, terrace with views over a green, unspoilt valley. Riding offered.
Castagneta, 58054 Scansano, Grosseto. **Map** p336 B2. 0564 50 72 19. FAX 0564 50 78 05. info@anticocasalediscausano.com b,l,d. **Rooms** 32. €€

Siena

Palazzo Ravizza A charming family run *pensione* in the best tradition. Rooms have lovely views over the Tuscan landscape. Pretty dining room.
Pian dei Mantellini 34, 53100 Siena. **Map** p336 B1. 0577 28 04 62. FAX 0577 22 15 97. bureau@palazzoravizza.it b,l,d. **Rooms** 36. €€

Sovicille

Borgo Pretale A group of grey stone houses clustered round a massive watchtower, artfully transformed into a stylish hotel.
Pretale, 53018 Sovicille, Siena. **Map** p336 B1. 0577 34 54 01. FAX 0577 34 56 25. info@borgopretale.it b,l,d. **Rooms** 35. €€€

Spoleto

Gattapone Built in the 1960s by the present owner's father, this hotel is a mix of knowingly retro pieces and high-tech extras. Regular guests include musicians at the local jazz festival and creative companies running seminars, but the architecture and stunning clifftop location above the village have a wide appeal.
Via del Ponte 6, 06049 Spoleto, Perugia. **Map** p337 D2. 0743 22 34 47. FAX 0743 22 34 48. hgattapone@tin.it b. **Rooms** 15. Never. AE, DC, MC, V. €€€

Vasto

Villa Vignola A small seaside hotel in a resort on the Abruzzo coast, with a big commitment to service. The decoration of the white clifftop villa has some Moorish influences though the style of bedrooms is a hybrid of Mediterranean and English country-house styles. The restaurant is strong on fish specialities.
Vignola, 66054 Vasto Marina, Chieti. **Map** p337 F3. 0873 31 00 50. FAX 0873 31 00 60. villavignola@interfree.it b,l,d. **Rooms** 5. Christmas. AE, DC, MC, V. €€

Torgiano

Le Tre Vaselle Wonderful village hotel owned by the winemaking Lungarotti family – sampling their wine at dinner is a must. The sitting rooms are marked by huge fireplaces, stripy furniture, card tables and a grand piano. Rooms are in annexes next to the main building. Breakfast is lavish. Recent addition: an olive oil museum.
Via Garibaldi 48, 06089 Torgiano, Perugia. **Map** p336 C2. 075 988 04 47. FAX 075 988 02 14. 3vaselle@3vaselle.it b,l,d. **Rooms** 60. Never. AE, DC, MC, V. €€€

Vicchio di Mugello

Villa Campestri This square Renaissance villa on a hillside south of Vicchio is one of the area's few good places to stay. Bedrooms are grand; some are in the main house, others in a farmhouse next door. Public rooms mix tapestries with Art Nouveau stained glass.
Via di Campestri 19, 50039 Vicchio di Mugello, Firenze. **Map** p335 D5. 055 849 01 07. FAX 055 849 01 08. villa.campestri@villacampestri.it b,l,d. **Rooms** 22. mid-Nov to mid-Mar. AE, MC, V. €€€

Sovicille

Relais Borgo di Toiano Hamlet-turned-hotel, its terraces dotted with roses. Restful and uncluttered interiors; some rooms with view; pool.
Toiano, 53018 Sovicille, Siena. **Map** p336 B1. 0577 31 46 39. FAX 0577 31 46 41. toiano@sienanet.it b. **Rooms** 10. €€

Spello

La Bastiglia Smartly restored old mill-house with panoramic views from nearly all its rooms. Some are suites with private terraces.
Piazza Valle Gloria 7, 06038 Spello, Perugia. **Map** p337 D2. 0742 65 12 77. FAX 0742 30 11 59. fancelli@labastiglia.com b,l,d. **Rooms** 33. €€

Tivoli

Adriano Restaurant-with-rooms next to Hadrian's Villa. Elegant dining room; swanky bedrooms. Pretty garden and lovely adjacent park.
Villa Adriana 194, 00010 Tivoli, Roma. **Map** p337 D4, p338 A1. 0774 38 22 35. FAX 0774 53 51 22. adriano@libero.it b,l,d. **Rooms** 9. €€

Volterra

Villa Nencini Old-fashioned stone country hotel on the edge of town. Some rooms are cramped.
Borgo Santo Stefano 55, 56048 Volterra, Pisa. **Map** p335 D5, 336 A1. 0588 863 86. FAX 0588 806 01. villanencini@interfree.it b,d. **Rooms** 35. €

For key to symbols see backflap. For price categories *see p333*

Southern Italy

Campania • Calabria
Basilicata • Puglia • Sicily

There is almost no end of opportunities for outdoor activities in the magnificent landscapes of southern Italy. The region as a whole is liberally endowed with wildlife and a rich array of ancient archaeological remains, not least those of the Romans at Pompei and the Greeks in Sicily. The cuisine, too, with its eclectic heritage and diversity of tastes, provides the excuse to dawdle on the coast or in the rustic mountain villages. Though good hotels are not so thick on the ground as in the rest of the country, the choice includes some of the very best, particularly along the stunning Amalfi coast. In contrast is the south's capital, the anarchic metropolis of Naples, which should not be missed.

Agrigento, Sicily

Foresteria Baglio della Luna A sturdy medieval tower is at the core of this peaceful country hotel, which offers superb views of Agrigento's Valley of the Temples. The building has been sympathetically restored to retain much of the original structure; ancient walls surround the garden. Fine food, home-produced wine.
Contrada Maddalusa, 92100 Agrigento, Sicilia. **Map** p338 B5. 0922 51 10 61. FAX 0922 59 88 02. bagliodellaluna@tin.it b,l,d. **Rooms** 24. Never. AE, DC, MC, V. €€€€

Amalfi

Luna-Torre Saracena In the 13th century, St Francis of Assisi chose this glorious spot on the cliff above a Saracen tower for a monastery. His cloister remains, together with some of the medieval buildings, but even the modern additions are charming at this luxurious historic hotel, owned by the same family since 1822.
Via P Comite 33, 84011 Amalfi, Salerno. **Map** p338 C2. 089 87 10 02. FAX 089 87 13 33. info@lunahotel.it b,l,d. **Rooms** 43. Never. AE, MC, V. €€€€

Alberobello

Dei Trulli In pleasant pine-shaded grounds, several conical-roofed *trulli* are joined to form freestanding apartments with small veranda.
Via Cadore 32, 70011 Alberobello, Bari. **Map** p339 E2. 080 432 35 55. FAX 080 432 35 60. info@hoteldeitrulli.it b,l,d. **Rooms** 27. €€€

Altomonte

Barbieri Modern lakeshore hotel with great views of Altomonte, a superb restaurant, new gym and modest but comfortable rooms.
Via Italo Barbieri 30, 87042 Altomonte, Cosenza. **Map** p339 D3. 0981 94 80 72. FAX 0981 94 80 73. casabarbieri@casabarbieri.it b,l,d. **Rooms** 50. €

Amalfi

Lidomare Small B&B hotel on Amalfi's Piazza del Duomo. Some of the arched, whitewalled bedrooms have views over the sea and Jacuzzis.
Largo Ducci Piccolomini 9, 84011 Amalfi, Salerno. **Map** p338 C2. 089 87 13 32. FAX 089 87 13 94. lidomare@amalficoast.it b. **Rooms** 15. €€

Capri

Punta Tragara Smart, cubelike Le Corbusier building hanging dramatically over the cliff.
Via Tragara 57, 80073 Capri, Napoli. **Map** p338 C2. 081 837 08 44. FAX 081 837 77 90. hotel.tragara@capri.it b,l,d. **Rooms** 27, plus 8 suites. €€€€

Amalfi

Santa Caterina Built in 1902, this sumptuous hotel on the coast road just outside Amalfi combines attractive décor with superb views, fine dining and impeccable service. Ask for one of the freestanding villas in the surrounding lemon groves. A private lift leads down the cliff to the pool and beach.
Strada Statale Amalfitana 9, 84011 Amalfi, Salerno. **Map** p338 C2. 089 87 10 12. FAX 089 87 13 51. @ info@hotelsantacaterina.it b,l,d (not Jan, Feb). **Rooms** 66. Never. AE, DC, MC, V. €€€€

Capri

Luna This old-fashioned seaside hotel's many pluses more than make up for the slightly overblown décor. The Luna has what must be one of the best locations on the island, perched on the cliffs of the south coast. Views from the spacious rooms are exhilarating. The pool is large by local standards.
Viale Matteotti 3, 80073 Capri, Napoli. **Map** p338 C2. 081 837 04 33. FAX 081 837 74 59. @ luna@capri.it b,l,d. **Rooms** 54. Nov to Easter. AE, MC, V. €€€€

Baia Domizia

Della Baia Antiques and modern furniture are blended with books, plants and flowers to create a homely atmosphere at this modern seafront hotel, run by three sisters. The bedrooms all have balconies and there are lounge chairs on the veranda and lawn for sun worshippers. The home-cooked food is good.
Via dell'Erica, 81030 Baia Domizia, Caserta. **Map** p337 E5. 0823 72 13 44. FAX 0823 72 15 56. @ info@hoteldellabaia.it b,l,d. **Rooms** 56. Oct to mid-May. AE, DC, MC, V. €€

Capri

Pensione Quattro Stagione This flower-filled village house near the Marina Piccola is the closest thing in Capri to a traditional *pensione.* The rooms are comfortable, the views from the bougainvillea-shaded terrace lovely, and dinner (on request) a lively taste of Italy. Rates are extremely reasonable, so book well ahead.
Via Marina Piccola 1, 80073 Capri, Napoli. **Map** p338 C2. 081 837 00 41. FAX 081 837 79 09. @ quattro.stagioni@libero.it b. **Rooms** 13. Nov to end Mar. MC, V. €€

Capri

Scalinatella A profusion of arches and oriental ornamentation gives a Moorish feel to this spotless white hotel where no expense has been spared.
Via Tragara 10, 80073 Capri, Napoli. **Map** p338 C2. 081 837 0633. FAX 081 837 8291. b,l. **Rooms** 30. €€€€

Capri

Villa Krupp Lenin and Gorky once lived in this serene clifftop villa, which is now a simple, popular, family-run hotel. Bright, spacious rooms.
Viale Matteotti 12, 80073 Capri, Napoli. **Map** p338 C20. 081 837 03 62. FAX 081 837 64 89. b. **Rooms** 12. €€

Capri

Villa Sarah Small modern hotel, set in its own vineyards and orchard, with well-kept rooms and delightful terraced gardens. Very reasonable prices.
Via Tiberio 3/A, 80073 Capri, Napoli. **Map** p338 C2. 081 837 78 17. FAX 081 837 72 15. @ info@villasarah.it b. **Rooms** 20. €€

Cetraro

Grand Hotel San Michele An imposing villa with huge grounds and several small houses. Kitchen gardens supply the excellent restaurant.
Loc. Bosco 8/9, 87022 Cetraro, Cosenza. **Map** p339 D4. 0982 910 12. FAX 0982 914 30. @ sanmichele@sanmichele.it b,l,d. **Rooms** 59. €€€

For key to symbols see backflap. For price categories *see p333*

CAPRI

Villa Brunella The setting's the thing here: this attractive modern hotel is built on steep terraced slopes among lemon groves, with fabulous sea views and large grounds. The spacious rooms make the most of the light and views, as do the large dining terrace and the pool. Lots of steps to and from the bedrooms.
Via Tragara 24A, 80073 Capri, Napoli. **Map** p338 C2. 081 837 01 22. FAX 081 837 04 30. @ villabrunella@capri.it b,l,d. **Rooms** 20. AE, DC, MC, V €€€€

ERICE, SICILY

Moderno Modernity is relative in ancient Erice, but this charming hotel has skillfully blended a 19th-century building with contemporary design and traditional Sicilian crafts. The bedrooms are spacious, the restaurant serves an excellent, wide-ranging menu and the view from the roof terrace over the tiles is delightful.
Via Vittorio Emanuele 63, 91016 Erice, Trapani, Sicilia. **Map** p338 A4. 0923 86 93 00. FAX 0923 86 91 39. @ modernoh@tin.it b,l,d. **Rooms** 41. Never AE, DC, MC, V. €€

ERICE, SICILY

Elimo In the centre of the old hill village of Erice, in the same street as the Moderno (see above right), is this picturesque medieval house. It has been brought up to modern standards, with attractive public rooms and individually designed bedrooms, but retains much of its character. Courtyard and roof terrace for idle hours.
Via Vittorio Emanuele 75, 91016 Erice, Trapani, Sicilia. **Map** p338 A4. 0923 86 93 77. FAX 0923 86 92 52. @ elimoh@comeg.it b,l,d. **Rooms** 21. Never. AE, DC, V. €€€

FASANO

La Silvana Fasano is a good place from which to explore *trulli* country, with many examples of the conical-roofed stone houses in the area, and this modern, family-run hotel makes a good base. Many of the spacious, plainly furnished rooms have views; most have a private bathroom. Popular local restaurant.
Viale de Pini 87, 72010 Selva di Fasano, Brindisi. **Map** p339 F2. 080 433 11 61. FAX 080 433 19 80. @ hotellasilvana@libero.it b,l,d. **Rooms** 18. mid-Jan to mid-Feb. AE, DC, MC, V. €

CISTERNINO

Villa Cenci Choose between rooms in the cool white villa or those in the traditional *trulli*. Home-grown vegetables and wine.
Via per Ceglie Messapica, 72014 Cisternino, Brindisi. **Map** p339 F2. 080 444 82 08. FAX 080 444 33 29. b. **Rooms** 59. €

CONCA DEI MARINI

Belvedere Fabulous views of the Amalfi Coast, and a lift to the seawater pool and beach.
Via Smeraldo 19, 84010 Conca dei Marini, Salerno. **Map** p338 C2. 089 83 12 82. FAX 089 83 14 39. @ belvedere@belvederehotel.it b,l,d. **Rooms** 35. €€€

DRAGONI

Villa de Pertis Plain, comfortable and very reasonably priced. Excellent regional food. Walk, cycle, read, think, wind down.
Via Ponti 30, 81010 Dragoni, Caserta. **Map** p337 F5. 082 386 66 19. @ info@villadepertis.it b,l,d. **Rooms** 7. €

FASANO

Masseria Marzalossa Fortified 17th-century farmhouse in olive and citrus groves. Pool, shady courtyards, excellent regional cuisine.
Contrada Pezze Vicine 65, 72015 Fasano, Brindisi. **Map** p339 F2. FAX 080 441 37 80. b,d. **Rooms** 9. €€€

Gangi, Sicily

Tenuta Gangivecchio Paolo Tornabene has made a peaceful, secluded retreat of this converted 13th-century monastery, now run as a restaurant-with-rooms. Inside are tiled floors, whitewashed walls and beamed ceilings. The classic Sicilian food, using homegrown almonds, vegetables and herbs, is mouthwatering.
C da Gangivecchio, 90024 Gangi, Sicilia.
Map p338 B4. 0921 68 91 91. FAX 0921 68 91 91.
@ paolotornabene@interfree.it b,l,d. **Rooms** 10.
July. MC, V. €€

Isola d'Ischia

La Villarosa In the centre of the little island town of Ischia, a few steps from the harbour and lido, a jungle of a garden surrounds this low-key spa hotel. Inside, a traditional country house atmosphere prevails, with elegant bedrooms (many with balconies) and antique-furnished salons. Dining terrace with fine rooftop views.
Via Giacinto Gigante 5, 80077 Porto d'Ischia, Napoli.
Map p338 B2. 081 99 13 16. FAX 081 99 24 25.
@ hotel@lavillarosa.it. b,l,d. **Rooms** 50.
Nov to Mar. AE, DC, MC, V. €€€

Giardini-Naxos, Sicily

Arathena Rocks Away from the crowds by the sands of the busy resort but right on the rocky seafront, is this friendly family-run hotel. It's a delightful place, with seafront gardens and large pool with bar, cheerful balconied bedrooms (many with views of Mount Etna) and public rooms bright with ceramics.
Via Calcide Eubea 55, 98035 Giardini-Naxos, Sicilia.
Map p338 C4. 0942 513 49. FAX 0942 516 90.
@ arathena@taormina-ol.it b,l,d. **Rooms** 49.
Nov to Mar. AE, DC, MC, V. €

Maratea

La Locanda delle Donne Monache This restored monastery in the centre of the seaside village offers many pleasures, including a charming garden, pool, private beach and a boat. Inside, the foyer's flamboyance gives way to modern chic in the bedrooms. The restaurant specializes in regional Italian cuisine.
Via Carllo Mazzei 4, 85046 Maratea, Potenza.
Map p339 D3. 0973 87 74 87. FAX 0973 87 76 87.
@ locanda@mondomaratea.it b,l,d. **Rooms** 29.
Never. AE, DC, MC, V. €€€€

Isola d'Ischia

Il Monastero Charming *pensione* built into the walls of the 14th-century islet castle. Good food, reasonable prices and superb views.
Castello Aragonese 3, 80070 Ischia, Napoli.
Map p338 B2. FAX 081 99 24 35. @ ilmonastero@castelloaragonese.it b,d. **Rooms** 21. €

Matera

Italia In the heart of the lively old city, a homely, yet immaculate hotel with a delightful garden. Superb value for money.
Via Ridola 5, 75100 Matera. **Map** p339 E2.
0835 33 35 61. FAX 0835 33 00 87.
@ albergoitalia@tin.it b,l,d. **Rooms** 46. €

Monópoli

Il Melograno Coolly sophisticated farmhouse hotel, set among olive and lemon groves.
Contrada Torricella 345, 70043 Monópoli, Bari.
Map p339 E2. 080 690 90 30. FAX 080 74 79 08.
@ melograno@melograno.com b,l,d. **Rooms** 37.
€€€€

Naples

Grande Albergo Vesuvio Elegant 1880s hotel with one of Naple's finest restaurants and wonderful views of the Castel dell'Oro.
Via Partenope 45, 80121 Napoli. **Map** p337 F5, p338 C2. 081 764 00 44. FAX 081 764 44 83.
@ info@vesuvio.it b,l,d. **Rooms** 163. €€€€

Maratea

Santavenere Splendidly set amid lawns and trees which sweep down to the rocky shore on the edge of Maratea, the low, arcaded Santa Venere exudes an air of quiet sophistication. The spacious, tastefully furnished rooms all have a terrace or balcony with views of this startlingly beautiful, wild stretch of coast.
Via Fiumicello di Santa Venere, 85046 Maratea. **Map** p339 D3. 0973 87 69 10. FAX 0973 87 76 54. @ santavenere@mondomaratea.it b,l,d. **Rooms** 38. Oct to Apr. AE, DC, MC, V. €€€

Naples

Santa Lucia The impeccably upmarket Santa Lucia, set overlooking the bay and the Castel dell'Ovo, is one of the best-known hotels in southern Italy. The public rooms are opulently decorated with frescoes, marble, stucco and antiques; the bedrooms are only marginally less elaborate. The service and cuisine are flawless.
Via Partenope 46, 80121 Napoli. **Map** p337 F5, p338 C2. 081 764 06 66. FAX 081 764 85 80. @ reservations@santalucia.it b,l,d. **Rooms** 96. Never. AE, DC, MC, V. €€€€

Maratea

Romantik Hotel Villa Cheta Elite This lavish Art Nouveau confection of ochre and cream stucco is perched high on the clifftop, with dizzying views over one of Italy's most spectacular stretches of coast. Excellent cuisine and carefully chosen antiques and paintings reflect the best of life during the heyday of the Grand Tour.
Via Timponi 46, 85041 Acquafredda di Maratea, Potenza. **Map** p339 D3. 0973 87 81 34. FAX 0973 87 81 35. @ villacheta@tin.it b,l,d. **Rooms** 23. Nov to Mar. AE, DC, MC, V. €€€

Panarea

Raya Modern and stylish, this eye-catching cascade of pink and white bungalows stretches down from the island village to the sea. Inside, ethnic art from Polynesia, Africa and Asia abounds. All rooms have sea views and terraces; the open-air restaurant overlooks the port. No young children.
Via San Pietro, 98050 Panarea, Messina. **Map** p338 C3. 090 98 30 13. FAX 090 98 31 03. @ info@hotelraya.it b,l,d. **Rooms** 30. mid-Oct to Easter. AE, DC, MC, V. €€

Naples

Miramare In an Art Nouveau villa, a charming seafront hotel offering small but well-furnished rooms, a roof garden and bar.
Via Nazario Sauro 24, 80132 Napoli. **Map** p337 F5, p338 C2. 081 764 75 89. FAX 081 764 07 75. @ info@hotelmiramare.com b. **Rooms** 30. €€€€

Naples

Paradiso Good rooms, excellent food, and a stunning location in peaceful Posillipo area, with the whole bay and city spread out at your feet.
Via Catullo 11, Posillipo, 80122 Napoli. **Map** p338 C2. 081 761 41 61. FAX 081 761 34 49. @ paradiso.na@bestwestern.it b,l,d. **Rooms** 72. €€€

Otranto

Albania Stylish modern hotel, ultra-efficient and spotlessly clean, with light and airy rooms and a seafood restaurant.
Via S Francesco di Paola 10, 73028 Otranto, Lecce. **Map** p339 F3. 08 36 80 18 77. FAX 08 36 80 11 83. @ mtenore@libero.it b,l,d. **Rooms** 26. €€

Positano

Casa Albertina A popular town-centre hotel, imaginatively decorated with local crafts. Bedrooms have sea views. Half-board in high season.
Via della Tavolozza 3, 84017 Positano, Salerno. **Map** p338 C2. 089 87 51 43. FAX 089 81 15 40. @ info@casalbertina.it b,l,d. **Rooms** 20. €€€

Parghelia

Baia Paraelios Holiday-camp style, but without the razzmatazz. This attractive, child-friendly hotel on the far southern toe of Italy consists of 72 small bungalows, sprawled across a wooded hill by a picture-postcard bay of white sand and dazzling blue sea. There are three pools, an open-air bar and a seaside terrace dining room. Fornaci, 89861 Parghelia, Catanzaro. **Map** p339 D5. 0963 60 00 04. FAX 0963 60 00 74. @ bbaiaparaelios@parmatour.com b,l,d. **Rooms** 72 bungalows. Oct to May. AE, DC, MC, V. €€€€

Positano

Il San Pietro Unabashedly catering for the jetset, the San Pietro is an architectural masterpiece, merging imperceptibly into the cliff face east of Positano. Each individually designed room has a flower-laden terrace, and even the bathrooms have magnificent views. Superb gourmet cuisine completes a sumptuous package. Private beach. Via Laurito 2, 84017 Positano, Salerno. **Map** p338 C2. 089 87 54 55. FAX 089 81 14 49. @ reservations@ilsanpietro.it b,l,d. **Rooms** 61. Nov to Mar. AE, DC, MC, V. €€€€

Positano

Miramare Set on a steep hill just west of the main beach, a series of old fishermen's houses now make up this delightful small hotel. All the bedrooms have private, sea-facing terraces and spacious bathrooms. Another terrace has been glassed in, with bougainvillaea hanging from the ceiling, to form a splending breakfast room. Via Trara Genoino 25-27, 84017 Positano, Salerno. **Map** p338 C2. 089 87 50 02. FAX 089 87 52 19. @ miramare@starnet.it b. **Rooms** 15. Nov to Mar. AE, DC, MC, V. €€€

Positano

Le Sirenuse An 18th-century *palazzo* still run by its aristocratic owners, the Sirenuse has expanded to include more rooms and a web of private and public terraces, but still manages to retain house-party charm and exclusivity. Delightful Venetian and Neapolitan furniture complements original ceramics. First-class gourmet cuisine. Via Colombo 30, 84017 Positano, Salerno. **Map** p338 C2. 089 87 50 66. FAX 089 81 17 98. @ info@sirenuse.it b,l,d. **Rooms** 62. Never. AE, DC, MC, V. €€€€

Positano

Palazzo Murat This haven of tranquillity in the town centre boasts 17th-century decoration and antique furnishings, and a profusion of flowers. Via dei Mulini 23, 84017 Positano, Salerno. **Map** p338 C2. 089 87 51 77. FAX 089 81 14 19. @ info@palazzomurat.it b,d. **Rooms** 31. €€€€

Ravello

Palumbo A lovingly restored 12th-century *palazzo*, with lavish décor and superb food. Past guests include Wagner, DH Lawrence and JFK. Via San Giovanni del Toro 16, 84010 Ravello. **Map** p338 C2. 089 85 72 44. FAX 089 85 81 33. @ reception@hotelpalumbo.it b,l,d. **Rooms** 18. €€€€

Ravello

Villa Maria A charmingly restored villa with terrace views and shady gardens. Some facilities shared with modern Hotel Giordano next door. Via Santa Chiara 2, 84010 Ravello, Salerno. **Map** p338 C2. 089 85 72 55. FAX 089 85 70 71. @ villamaria@villamaria.it b,l,d. **Rooms** 23. €€

Sant'Agata Sui Due Golfi

Don Alfonso The only Michelin three-star in southern Italy, with a few rooms attached. Corso Sant'Agata 11, 80064 Sant'Agata Sui Due Golfi, Napoli. **Map** p338 C2. 081 878 00 26. FAX 081 533 02 26. @ donalfonso@syrene.it b,l,d. **Rooms** 5. €€

For key to symbols see backflap. For price categories *see p333*

Positano

Villa Franca It's a long, hard climb from the beach back up to the Villa Franca, but it is worth it. Its position gives it stunning views over the town and along the Amalfi Coast. The bedrooms are charming, using traditional painted ceramics alongside crisp blue and white to mirror the sun and Mediterranean beyond. Roof terrace.
Via Pasitea 318, 84017 Positano, Salerno. **Map** p338 C2. 089 87 56 55. FAX 089 87 57 35. info@villafrancahotel.it b,d. **Rooms** 38. Nov-Mar. AE, DC, MC, V. €€€€

Ravello

Villa Cimbrone In a romantic setting, this enchanting 12th-century villa has splendid stone fireplaces and stone floors, and is crammed with knick-knacks, books, oil paintings and antiques. White Gothic doors lead to comfortable, exquisitely decorated bedrooms with the feel of a private house.
Via Santa Chiara 26, 84010 Ravello, Salerno. **Map** p338 C2. 089 85 74 59/85 80 72. FAX 089 85 77 77. info@villacimbrone.it b,d. **Rooms** 19. Nov to Mar. AE, MC, V. €€€€

Ragusa, Sicily

Eremo della Giubliana In tranquil rolling farmland, this 15th-century fortified convent now makes a glamorous hideaway hotel. It has been beautifully modernized yet retains much of its original structure, with splendid archways and pitch and limestone floors. Local produce and wines make up the bulk of the fine menu.
km 9, Contrada Giubiliana SP per Marina di Ragusa, 97100 Ragusa, Sicilia. **Map** p338 C5. 0932 66 91 19. FAX 0932 66 91 29. info@eremodellagiubliana.it b,l,d. **Rooms** 15. Never. AE, MC, V. €€€€

Siracusa, Sicily

Grand Hotel This is a truly grand hotel, with an imposing circular marble staircase, gracious Art Deco rooms filled with fine art, Murano glass chandeliers and antique furnishings. There is a luxuriant indoor garden, and a roof garden restaurant with fine views of the harbour and the old town. Some bedrooms have sea views.
Viale Mazzini 12, 96100 Siracusa, Sicilia. **Map** p338 C5. 0931 46 46 00. FAX 0931 46 46 11. b,l,d. **Rooms** 58. Never. AE, DC, MC, V. €€€

Savelletri

Masseria San Domenico A fortified refuge-turned-country house, now a hotel with spa.
Litoranea 379, 72010 Savelletri di Fasano, Brindisi. **Map** p339 F2. 080 482 77 69. FAX 080 482 79 78. info@masseriasandomenico.com b,l,d. **Rooms** 50. €€€€

Scanno

Mille Pini This neat, simple, friendly chalet sits at the foot of the chairlift up to Monte Rotondo, the highest point in the Apennines.
Via Pescara 2, 67038 Scanno, L'Aquila. **Map** p337 E4, p338 B1. 0864 74 72 64. FAX 0864 74 98 18. b,l,d. **Rooms** 23. €

Selva di Fasano

Sierra Silvana Comfortable country hotel consisting of a cluster of modern buildings around an imposing four-room *trulli*.
Via D Bartolo Boggia 5, 72010 Selva di Fasano, Brindisi. **Map** p339 E2. 080 433 13 22. FAX 080 433 12 07. sierrasilvana@tin.it b,l,d. **Rooms** 120. €€

Siracusa, Sicily

Domus Mariae A former convent in a quiet quarter, still run by Ursuline nuns, with an ornate chapel, modern furnishings and air of calm.
Via Vittorio Veneto 76, 96100 Siracusa, Sicilia. **Map** p338 C5. 0931 248 54. FAX 0931 248 58. htldomus@sistemia.it b,l,d. **Rooms** 12. €€

Sorrento

Bellevue Syrene The Syrene opened in 1824 and was a favourite stop of Empress Eugénie of France. It has fabulous views of the bay from its clifftop position, and its many charms include a salon devoted to original Dali paintings, a Pompeii-style dining room, a wisteria arcade, peaceful courtyards, local ceramics and frescoes.
Piazza della Vittoria 5, 80067 Sorrento, Napoli. **Map** p338 C20. 081 878 10 24. FAX 081 878 39 63. info@bellevue.it b,l,d. **Rooms** 76. Never. AE, DC, MC, V. €€€

Taormina, Sicily

Villa Belvedere The simple but stylish Belle Epoque hotel has commanding views of town, sea and mountain. Other pluses are pretty flower gardens, attractive public rooms and a tantalising pool deck surrounded by giant palms. The rooms are clean and bright; some have private terraces.
Via Bagnoli Croci 79, 98039 Taormina, Messina, Sicilia. **Map** p338 C4. 0942 237 91. FAX 0942 62 58 30. info@villabelvedere.it b,l. **Rooms** 49. mid-Nov to mid-Mar. AE, DC, MC, V. €€

Taormina, Sicily

San Domenico Palace In the heart of historic Taormina is this supremely luxurious former monastery. It caters unashamedly to the international jetset, and its beautiful cloisters and rooms are filled with art pieces. Other attractions are and enchanting garden, excellent sea views, and a wonderful restaurant.
Piazza San Domenico 5, 98039 Taormina, Sicilia. **Map** p338 C4. 0942 61 31 11. FAX 0942 62 55 06. reservations-san-domenico@thi.it b,l,d. **Rooms** 108. Never. AE, DC, MC, V. €€€€

Taormina, Sicily

Romantik Hotel Villa Ducale A ten-minute walk from Taormina leads to this hotel with panoramic views from all rooms. Built by the grandparents of the current owners, it is interestingly furnished, with no two rooms alike. There is even a library for those who want to while away lazy hours on the flower-bedecked terrace.
Via Leonardo da Vinci 60, 98039 Taormina, Messina, Sicilia. **Map** p338 C4. 0942 281 53. FAX 0942 287 10. villaducale@tao.it b. **Rooms** 15. Dec to Feb. AE, DC, MC, V. €€€

Sorrento

La Badia A friendly family hotel with great charm and views over town, in a converted monastery set among olive and citrus groves.
Via Nastro Verde 8, 80067 Sorrento, Napoli. **Map** p338 C2. 081 878 11 54. FAX 081 807 41 59. info@hotellabadia.it b,l,d. **Rooms** 14. €

Sorrento

Grand Hotel Excelsior Vittoria Two elegantly furnished 19th-century villas and a 1920s Swiss chalet. Stunning clifftop terrace and lush gardens.
Piazza Tasso 34, 80067 Sorrento, Napoli. **Map** p338 C2. 081 807 10 44. FAX 081 877 12 06 exvitt@exvitt.it b,l,d. **Rooms** 98. €€€€

Stilo

San Giorgio A handsome 17th-century cardinal's palace, now a family-run village hotel, with fine views and a lively atmosphere.
Via Citarelli 8, 89049 Stilo, Reggio di Calabria. **Map** p339 E5. & FAX 0964 77 50 47. b,l,d. **Rooms** 14. €

Vico Equense

Capo la Gala Almost invisible modern hotel, carved from a series of terraces in the cliff-face, with bland rooms but a homely atmosphere.
Via Luigi Serio 8, Capo la Gala, 80069 Vico Equense, Napoli. **Map** p338 C2. 081 801 57 58. FAX 081 879 87 47. info@capogala.com b,l,d. **Rooms** 18. €€€

For key to symbols see backflap. For price categories *see p333*

GREECE

GREECE

SMALL HOTELS of character are quite a new phenomenon in Greece: most have been in operation for little more than ten years, and many are in traditional buildings which have been in the same family for generations and have been lovingly restored. Greece has a very rich vernacular architecture – among the many choices we list are a cave-like island cliff dwelling, an 18th-century bandit chieftain's tower, a Venetian townhouse and a mountain mansion. Most Greek hotels are family-run, friendly and informal, but with little emphasis on luxuries such as room service and ambitious food.

Oía Mare Villas, page 390, fabulously sited on the island of Santorini

GREECE, REGION BY REGION

GREECE CAN be divided into two obvious parts: mainland and the islands.

Mainland Greece

The Gulf of Corinth and the Corinth Canal slice Greece into two. The southern Peloponnese offers a wide range of landscapes, from rugged, treeless mountains to gentle farmland, lush valleys and sandy beaches. There are lovely small hotels in historic buildings in towns such as Yíthion and Návplion, in medieval fortresses like Monemvasiá, and in the tiny castles of the Máni region and the stone villages of Arkadia.

Central and northern Greece are equally varied. The capital, Athens, a huge urban sprawl, is short of hotels of distinction, as are other main towns, but there are unique places to stay throughout the mainland. Among them are the rugged, dry-stone-walled homes of the Zagoria villages and restored neo-classical mansions in small ports such as Galaxídi, near Delphi.

The Islands

Of the thousands of Greek islands, only some hundred are inhabited. These are divided into six groups, plus Crete, largest of all the islands and an administrative region in its own right. Closest to Athens are the tiny Argo-Saronic islands, popular with foreign visitors and Athenians escaping from the city. The group includes car-free Ydra, and Spétses with its choice of excellent small resort hotels.

The white villages, blue-domed churches and mountainous, arid landscapes of the Cyclades islands are among the best-known images of Greece. Despite the popularity of Mykonos, Páros and Santoríni, there are a number of charmingly simple places to stay, ideal for peace and quiet.

Tourism is still relatively new to the large, widely spaced islands of the North-east Aegean group, where most beds are in small, simple *pensions* and larger holiday hotels.

The Dodecanese group, close to the Turkish coast, includes tiny isles such as Sými along with larger neighbours such as Rhodes, which receives hundreds of thousands of visitors annually. Many of the most charming hotels are in impressively restored neo-classical houses.

The Sporades and Ionian islands are dominated by the package holiday market, with few hotels of real character. Kýthira, in the Ionian group, is the exception, with some attractive small hotels in its white-washed village capital.

Crete, Greece's largest island and most southerly, is almost a country in its own right. Many of its most interesting and attractive places to stay are in old Venetian-Turkish townhouses.

Highlights

The hotels illustrated on these introductory pages are by no means the only highlights. Some of the most memorable places to stay in Greece include La Moara, in Nymfaía (page 391), run by one of the country's leading winemaking dynasties; Hotel Malvásia, within the fortress walls of Monemvasía (page 389); and the charmingly quirky Xenonas Karamarli in Makrinítsa (page 388).

Food and Drink

The best Greek food is the simplest: fish straight from the net; fresh vegetables served as salad with wild thyme and oregano. Restaurants in tourist areas have multilingual menus but the food in places off the beaten track is often better. In smaller villages you will be invited into the kitchen to see what's simmering on the stove or waiting to be grilled.

Méze, a selection of dishes served simultaneously, is a Greek mainstay. As well as olives and strong-flavoured feta cheese made from goat's or sheep's milk, *méze* might include roasted peppers, grilled cheese, humous (a purée of chickpeas and sesame seeds), taramasalata (a dip made of cod roe), and little sausages.

Greek seafood – especially *astakós* (lobster), *garídhes* (shrimp) and *barboúnia* (red mullet) – is expensive and is usually priced according to weight. Meat is usually veal, lamb or chicken, sometimes game; goat meat is regarded as a delicacy to be reserved for special occasions. The traditional Greek salad, with tomatoes, onion, cucumber, olives, peppers and feta cheese, is a meal in itself. Dinner, usually eaten late, is the main meal of the day.

Greek wine has improved in recent years. Good-quality red, white and rosé wines are now available throughout Greece, in addition to the traditional retsina, a white wine flavoured with pine resin, not to everyone's taste.

Best Western Hotel Europa, near the ruins at Ancient Olympia, page 390

Bedrooms and Bathrooms

If you want a double bed, ask for it specifically when booking, as most rooms are twin bedded. Most hotels offer en suite WC and shower as standard.

Water is usually heated by solar power and electric water heaters; at the end of a long summer day, water may be scaldingly hot.

Other Practical Information

Book ahead from June to September, when Greeks as well as foreign visitors take their holidays. Tourism is highly seasonal, and many hotels on the islands close from October until April. In small hotels, breakfast is often the only meal served.

Language English is very widely spoken, especially in the resort areas.

Currency From 1 January 2002, the European *euro* (written 'EUR'), made up of 100 *cents*.

Shops Most open 8am–1pm, and from 5–8pm Mon–Sat.

Tipping Formal tipping is not customary, but it is not unusual to round up the bill.

Telephoning To phone within Greece, dial the full number. To phone Greece from Britain, dial the country code 00 30, then the number, omitting the initial zero; from the US, 011 30.

Public holidays 1 January; 6 January; Shrove Monday; 25 March; Good Friday, Easter Sunday and Easter Monday; 1 May; Whit Monday; 15 August; 28 October; 25 and 26 December.

Useful Words

The system of transliteration used here to represent Greek is the one used by the Greek government.

Breakfast	*Topro-ee-no*
Lunch	*Tome-see-mer-ya-no*
Dinner	*Totheep-no*
How much?	*Posokanee?*
Free room?	*E-che-teh tho-ma-tee-a?*
Single (room)	*Mo-na krevat-ya*
Double (with a double bed)	*Thee-klee-no meh thee-plo dre-va-tee*

Greece Price Bands

Maximum room rates are displayed on each bedroom door. Discounts may be offered for longer stays. Greek hotels are classified in five categories, but don't be swayed by this. Our price bands, which refer to the price of a double room in high season, are simpler to use.

€	below 45 EUR
€€	45–65 EUR
€€€	65–90 EUR
€€€€	above 90 EUR

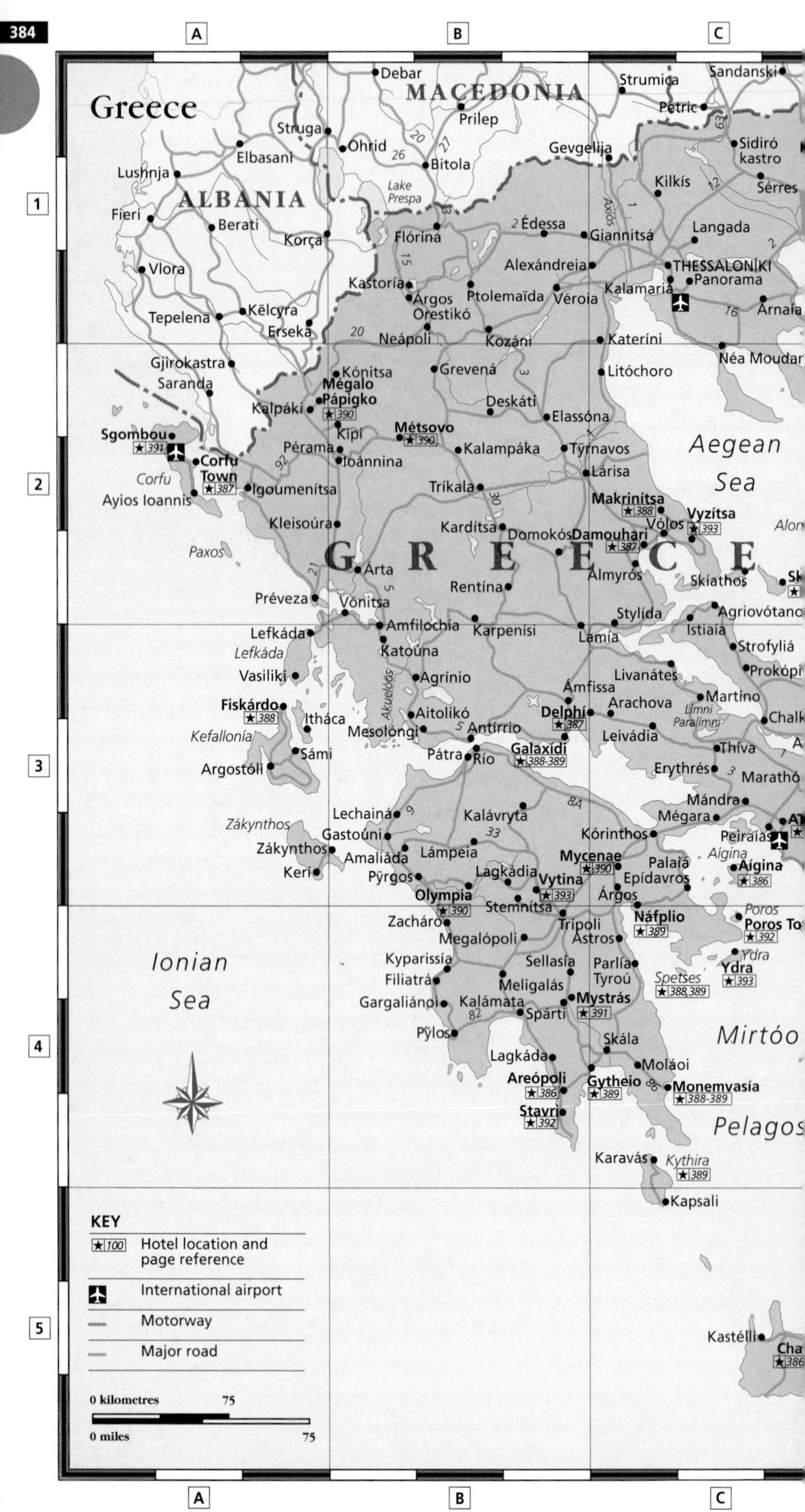
Greece
A
B
C
1
2
3
4
5
MACEDONIA
ALBANIA
GREECE
Debar
Prilep
Strumica
Sandanski
Petric
Struga
Ohrid
Bitola
Elbasani
Lushnja
Fieri
Berati
Korça
Lake Prespa
Gevgelija
Sidiró kastro
Kilkís
Sérres
Langada
Édessa
Giannitsá
Axiós
Flórina
Alexándreia
THESSALONÍKI
Panorama
Kalamariá
Kastoriá
Árgos Orestikó
Ptolemaïda
Véroia
Árnaia
Vlora
Tepelena
Këlcyra
Erseka
Neápoli
Kozáni
Kateríni
Néa Moudar
Gjirokastra
Saranda
Kónitsa
Mégalo Pápigko
390
Grevená
Litóchoro
Kalpáki
Deskáti
Elassóna
Sgombou
391
Kipi
Métsovo
390
Pérama
Ioánnina
Kalampáka
Týrnavos
Aegean
Sea
Corfu Town
387
Corfu
Ayios Ioannis
Igoumenítsa
Tríkala
Lárisa
Makrinítsa
388
Vyzítsa
393
Vólos
Kleisoúra
Kardítsa
Domokós
Damouhari
387
Paxos
Árta
Almyrós
Skiáthos
Rentína
Préveza
Vónitsa
Stylída
Agriovótano
Amfilochía
Karpenísi
Lamía
Istiaia
Lefkáda
Lefkáda
Katoúna
Strofyliá
Vasilikí
Agrínio
Livanátes
Prokópi
Ámfissa
Fiskárdo
388
Arachova
Martino
Itháca
Aitolikó
Delphi
387
Límni
Paralímni
Chalk
Akuelóös
Kefallonía
Mesolóngi
Antírrio
Leivádia
Sámi
Pátra
Río
Galaxídi
388-389
Thíva
Argostóli
Erythrés
Marathó
Mándra
Lechainá
Kalávryta
Mégara
Zákynthos
Gastoúni
Kórinthos
Peiraías
Zákynthos
Lámpeia
Mycenae
390
Aígina
Amaliáda
Palaiá
Aígina
386
Kerí
Pýrgos
Lagkádia
Epídavros
Vytina
393
Olympia
390
Árgos
Stemnítsa
Náfplio
389
Poros
Poros To
392
Zacháro
Trípoli
Ástros
Megalópoli
Ionian
Sea
Kyparissía
Sellasía
Parlía
Ydra
Ydra
393
Filiatrá
Meligalás
Tyroú
Spetses
388,389
Gargaliánoi
Kalámata
Mystrás
391
Spárti
Pýlos
Mirtóo
Skála
Lagkáda
Moláoi
Areópoli
386
Gytheio
389
Monemvasía
388-389
Stavri
392
Pelagos
Karavás
Kythira
389
Kapsali
Kastélli
Cha
386
KEY
100
Hotel location and page reference
International airport
Motorway
Major road
0 kilometres
75
0 miles
75

D
E
F
1
2
3
4
5
Kûrdzhali
Madan
Orestiáda
Didymóteicho
Stavroúpoli
Nymfaía
★391
Xánthi
Komotiní
Souflí
Alexandroúpoli
Enez
Thásos
Samothráki
Samothráki
Thracian
Sea
Imroz
Abide
Mýrina
Limnos
Babaeski
Lüleburgaz
Uzunköprü
Hayrabolu
TURKEY
Ispala
Keşan
Ballı
Ilarköy
Gelibolu
Saray
Àerkezköy
Àorlu
Tekirdaê
Silivri
Durusu Gölü
Sarıyer
ISTANBUL
Küçük Çekmece
Alibey Barajı
Sea of Marmara
Yalova
Bandirma
Gönen
Çan
Must. Kempalpasa
Ezine
Edremit
Balikesir
Baba Burun
Behramkale
Awalik
Sindirgi
Soma
Ágios Efstrátios
Lesvos
Mytilíni
Skýros
Skýros
Borlu
Manísa
Salihli
Karaburun
IZMIR
Chíos
Volissós
★393
Psará
★392
Vessa
Vrontádos
Chíos
Çesmie
Pyrgí
TURKEY
Aydin
Nazilli
Denizli
Söke
Sámos
Sámos
Çine
Kemel
Ándros
Armenistis
Ikaría
★389
Tínos
Ornos
★392
Mykonos
Delos
Mýkonos Town
★391
Ermoúpoli
★381
Syros
Psarou
★393
Selimiye
Mugla
Náxos
Náxos
Páros
Léfkes
★390
Kástro
Aigíali
★386
Amorgós
Kálymnos
Bodrum
Kos
Kos
Mílos
Íos
Íos
★387
Oía
★390-392
Firá
★388
Santoríni
Astipálaia
Sými
Sými Town
★392
Ródos
Rhodes Old Town
★391
Salakos
Líndos
Rhodes
Kattavía
MEDITERRANEAN SEA
Kárpathos
Kásos
Sea of Crete
Réthymno
★390-391, 393
Irákleio
Crete
Elounda
Ágios Nikólaos
★386
Zarós
Mártha
Ierápetra
100
11c
2
51
200
210
550
230
240
300

Agios Nikolaos, Crete

Hotel St Nicolas Bay Village-style arrangement of simply furnished bungalows and suites, among lush gardens on a private headland 2km west of Agios Nikolaos. Three pools, five restaurants, four bars, private beach, antique shop, art gallery and boutique, billiards room, health centre and watersports centre.
PO Box 47, GR-72100 Agios Nikolaos, Crete.
Map p385 E5. (28410) 25041. FAX (28410) 24556.
@ stnicolas@otenet.gr b,l,d. **Rooms** 107.
Nov to Mar. AE, MC, DC, V. €€€€

Athens

John's Hotel Among the star features of the modern, medium-rise hotel are: its attractive Art Nouveau-style bar and foyer; a palm tree-studded garden and terrace; and a 15m (50ft) pool with waterfall. It is set in a residential suburb, close to the airport and some 30 minutes' drive to the city centre. Service is cool yet professional.
Pandoras 3 & Lazaraki, 16674 Glyfada, Athens.
Map p384 C3. (210) 894 6837/9. FAX (210) 898 0210.
b,l,d. **Rooms** 68. Never.
AE, MC, DC, V. €€€€

Athens

Andromeda Hotel A real find: a small boutique hotel, on a quiet side street 20-30 minutes' walk from Syntagma Square and the historic city centre. It is dotted with designer objects and antique carpets; its many amenities include laundry service and 24-hour room service. The restaurant serves Oriental and Polynesian specialities.
Timoleontos Vassou 22, 11521 Athens.
Map p384 C3. (210) 641 5000. FAX (210) 646 6361.
@ reservations@andromedaathens.gr b,l,d. **Rooms** 42.
Never. AE, MC, DC, V. €€€€

Chaniá, Crete

Casa Delfino Suites This sensitively restored Venetian mansion is close to the bustling harbourside, yet its elegant studios are quiet and private. Rooms are extremely well-furnished, combining all mod cons (Jacuzzi, minibar) with classic style; rooftop views over the castle, out to sea, and inland. Shady pebble-mosaic courtyard.
Theofanous 9, 73100 Chaniá, Crete.
Map p384 C5. (28210) 87400. FAX (28210) 96500.
@ casadel@cha.forthnet.gr b. **Rooms** 22 studios.
Never. AE, MC, V. €€€€

Aigíali, Amorgós

Hotel Egialis Small family-run hotel perched on a hillside. Excellent sandy beach 10 minutes' walk away. Open-air terrace bar, pool, restaurant.
84008 Aigíali, Amorgós. **Map** p385 E4. (22850) 73393. FAX (22850) 73395. @ info@aegialis.com
b,l,d. **Rooms** 30. €€€€

Aigíali, Amorgós

Lakki Village The ferocious but amiable Nikki Gavalas queens it over this family-owned pension right on a long, shallow sandy bay.
84008 Aigíali, Amorgós. **Map** p385 E4. (22850) 73505. FAX (22850) 73244. @ lakkivillage@hotmail.com
b,l,d. **Rooms** 30. €€

Aígina

Aiginitiko Arhontiko Early-19th century mansion close to the harbour. Creatively decorated rooms. Roof garden.
18010 Aígina. **Map** p384 C3. (22970) 24968. FAX (22970) 24156. @ fotisvoulgarakis@aig.forthnet.gr
b. **Rooms** 12. €€

Areópoli

Pirgos Kapetanakou Rooms in this unusual miniature 18th-century castle are comfortable but very plain, with polished wood floors, stone walls and minimal furniture.
23062 Areópoli, Máni, Peloponnese. **Map** p384 B4. (27330) 51233. FAX (27330) 51401. b. **Rooms** 7. €€

Chaniá, Crete

Hotel Nostos Archetypal picture-postcard Greece: down a charming narrow pedestrian street in the heart of the old town, is this café/bar/hotel, painted in bright blue, yellow and pink. Small round café tables, rush chairs and pots of flowers complete the picture. The studio rooms have gallery beds and balconies with great views of the castle and the mountains.
Zambeliou 42-46, 73131 Chaniá, Crete. **Map** p384 C5. (28210) 94743. FAX (28210) 94740. b. **Rooms** 12. Never. MC, V. €€€

Damouchari

Hotel Damouchari This eclectically stylish rustic hotel, set close to a white pebble beach in a tiny fishing hamlet, is one of the nicest places to stay in all Greece. Rooms are colourfully painted and inventively furnished with antiques and curios from all over the Pilion region. Owned and run by a very friendly husband-and-wife team. Prior booking essential.
Damouchari, Pilio. **Map** p384 C2. FAX (24260) 49840. b. **Rooms** 14. Oct to May. MC, V. €€€

Chaniá, Crete

Suites Pandora A peaceful location on a quiet street is one of the attractions of this small collection of suites in a 19th-century mansion. Others are the views of the old town and boats in the harbour, the attractive courtyard and balconies, and the rooftop café terrace. Rooms are furnished in simple traditional style, with double brass beds and stone-flagged floors.
Lithinon 29, 73100 Chania, Crete. **Map** p384 C5. (28210) 43588. FAX (28210) 57864. b. **Rooms** 10 suites. Nov to Mar. DC, MC, V. €€€€

Folégandros

Hotel Cástro The Cástro has been run by the same family for five generations. It's set on a quiet lane among traditional whitewashed cottages and enjoys breathtaking clifftop sea views. It's a long hike to the nearest swimming place, but the hotel is excellent value for money; it was fully refurbished in 1993. There's a roof terrace and a very attractive breakfast room.
Despo Danassi-Kallianta, 84011 Folégandros Town, Folégandros. **Map** p385 D4. FAX (22860) 41230. b. **Rooms** 12. Sep to May. AE, MC, V. €€€

Athens

Marble House This friendly, efficient family-run hotel is at the end of a quiet cul-de-sac, within an easy walk of the Plaka. Excellent value.
Zinni Anastasiou 35, 11741-Koykaki, Athens. **Map** p384 C3. (210) 923 4058. FAX (210) 922 6461. b. **Rooms** 16. €€

Corfu town, Corfu

Hotel Bella Venezia Central, Neo-Classical building, originally a bank, with tasteful high-ceilinged rooms. Secluded inner courtyard.
Zampeli 4, 49100 Corfu Town, Corfu. **Map** p384 A2. (26610) 46500. FAX (26610) 20708. @ belvenht@hol.gr b. **Rooms** 32. €€€

Delphi

Hotel Acropole A modern, family-run hotel with plain décor but good facilities, friendly management and balconies with superb views.
Filellinon 13, 33054 Delphi. **Map** p384 B3. (22650) 82675. FAX (22650) 83171. @ delphi@delphi.com.gr b. **Rooms** 42. €€

Ermoúpoli, Syros

Esperance Rooms and Studios Elegant town house hotel; air-conditioned rooms furnished with simple elegance. Friendly manager.
Akti Papagou & Floegandrou 1, 84100 Ermoúpoli, Syros. **Map** p385 D4. (22810) 81671. FAX (22810) 85707. @ espernik@otenet.gr b. **Rooms** 35. €€€

For key to symbols see backflap. For price categories *see p383*

Galaxídi

Ganimede Hotel This charming *pension*, run by the friendly Italian owner, occupies a traditional 19th-century sea captain's house. Some rooms have elaborate painted, coffered wooden ceilings, others are plain and simple. The courtyard with fountain, vines and flowers is a delightful place to enjoy Brunello's excellent breakfasts and evening aperitifs.

Gurguris St 16, 33052 Galaxídi. **Map** p384 B3. (22650) 41328. FAX (22650) 42160. @ bruno@gsp.gr b,l,d. **Rooms** 8. Nov to Christmas. V. €€

Makrinítsa

Xenonas Karamarli Each room in this lovingly restored 18th-century mansion is different and imbued with style. The delightful decor includes mock-Byzantine frescoes, carved wooden furniture and old rugs. All rooms are en suite. Admire the panoramic view over the town of Volos and the Gulf of Volos from the terrace café, where breakfast, drinks and *meze* are served.

36511 Makrinítsa, Pílio. **Map** p384 C2. (24280) 99570. FAX (24280) 99779. b. **Rooms** 10. Never. DC, MC, V. €€€€

Kounoupsa, Spetses

Hotel Nissia The Nissia features a palatial collection of villas designed in traditional local style, laid out around a splendid pool. The core of the hotel is a restored 19th-century building. Rooms are large and luxurious, with polished wooden floors and modern replicas of traditional furniture, and include a full kitchen.

18050 Kounoupitsa, Spetses. **Map** p384 C4. Athens office (210) 346 2879. FAX (210) 346 5313. @ nissia@otenet.gr b,l,d. **Rooms** 31 apartments. end Oct to end Feb. AE, DC, MC, V. €€€€

Monemvasía

Kellia Inn The Kellia was once a monks' dormitory and its rooms are appropriately plainly furnished. The monastery church is still outside, and both are overshadowed by the towering cliffs of Monemvasía. There's plenty of open space here with a big café terrace outside and a courtyard behind. The tourist office runs the inn in friendly but minimalist fashion.

Kástro, 23070 Monemvasía, Laconia. **Map** p384 C4. (27320) 61520. FAX (27320) 61767. @ kellia@yahoo.com b. **Rooms** 11. Never. V. €€€

Firá, Santorini

Athina These simple, almost Spartan suites, built on three levels, overlook the caldera and feature a wonderful cliffside swimming pool.

Kato Firá, 84700 Firá, Santorini. **Map** p385 D4. (22860) 24910. FAX (22860) 24913. b. **Rooms** 9 suites. €€€€

Firá, Santorini

Enigma Apartments A simple yet elegant and quiet complex of small apartments built into the cliff face, with superb views out over the caldera.

Enigma Apartments, 84700 Firá, Santorini. **Map** p385 D4. (22860) 24024. FAX (22860) 24023. b. **Rooms** 8. €€€€

Firá, Santorini

Homeric Poems Stylish suites partly built into the cliffside, each with its own terrace.

Firostefani, 84700 Firá, Santorini. **Map** p385 D4. (22860) 24661. FAX (22860) 24660. @ x-ray-kilo@otenet.gr b. **Rooms** 16 €€€€

Fiskárdo, Kefalloniá

Erissos This pretty two-storey village house has been attractively restored to offer simple rooms with balconies (nice harbour views) and kitchen facilities. Service is minimal.

28084 Fiskárdo, Kefalloniá. **Map** p384 A3. (26740) 41327. FAX (26740) 41342. b. **Rooms** 4. €

MONEMVASÍA

Lazareto Despite its rustic, traditional exterior the Lazareto is a modern hotel, set in grassy gardens. It is dramatically overlooked by the cliffs of Monemvasía and faces across the bay to Gefyra village and the mainland mountains; its attractive bar-terrace offers a fine place from which to admire the sunset. Rooms are well equipped.
☒ 23070 Monemvasía, Laconia. **Map** p384 C4. (27320) 61991. FAX (27320) 61992. @ lazaretohotel@yahoo.com b,l,d. **Rooms** 14. Never. DC, MC, V. €€€€

NÁFPLIO

Hotel Byron A delightful owner-managed hotel in traditional buildings next to the 11th-century Venetian fortress, in the heart of the port. Rooms are simple but pretty, with polished wooden floors and some antique furniture. Most have fine views over the bay and across stone churches and tiled roofs; some have private terraces. There's also a very attractive café terrace.
☒ Platonos 2, 21100 Náfplio. **Map** p384 C4. (27520) 22351. FAX (27520) 26338. @ byronhotel@otenet.gr b. **Rooms** 18. Never. MC, V. €€

MONEMVASÍA

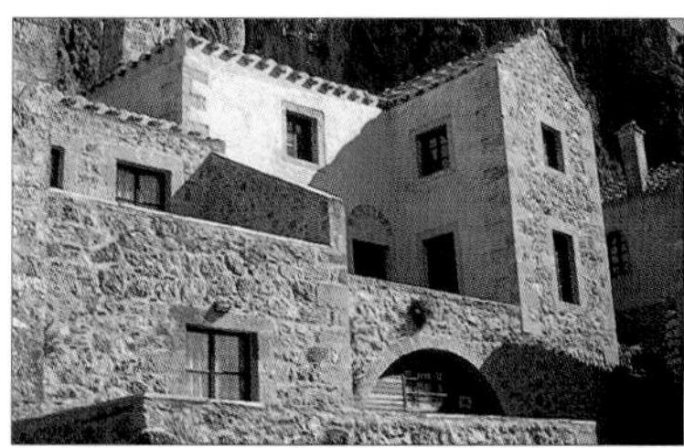

Hotel Malvásia This unusual hotel is spread over three medieval Venetian buildings around the deserted ruined fortress town of Monemvasía. Each room is decorated in individual style, but all have polished wood or flagstone floors, traditional textiles and antique furniture. The best are in the original Malvásia Hotel building, where there is a bar/café.
☒ Kástro, 23070 Monemvasía, Laconia. **Map** p384 C4. (27320) 61323. FAX (27320) 61722. b,l,d. **Rooms** 30. Never. MC, V. €€

NTÁPIA, SPETSES

Zoë's Club A good choice for families: this attractive self-catering complex is on the outskirts of Ntápia and is very private and secluded. Its design – modern but influenced by the traditional architecture of the island – incorporates luxurious living rooms and full kitchens, terraces and balconies, flower-filled garden and a huge pool.
☒ Ntápia, Spetses. **Map** p384 C4. (22980) 74447/8. FAX (22980) 72841. @ zoesclub@aig.forthnet.gr b. **Rooms** 22, 6 suites, 2 maisonettes. Nov to Feb. AE, DC, MC, V. €€€€

GALAXÍDI

Hotel Galaxa Delightful rooms in a traditional sea captain's house with great views of the harbour. Very friendly management.
☒ Eleftherias & Kennedy, Chirolakas, 33052 Galaxídi. **Map** p384 B3. (22650) 41620. FAX (22650) 42053. b. **Rooms** 10. €€€

GYTHEIO

Hotel Aktaion Neo-Classical style building right on the harbour; rooms are plain but comfortable, with high ceilings and modern furniture.
☒ Vas. Pavlou 39, 23200 Gytheio. **Map** p384 B4. (27330) 23500. FAX (27330) 22294. b. **Rooms** 22. €€€

IKARÍA

Cavos Bay Hotel Modern but sensitively designed hotel on the edge of a pretty village with an excellent sandy beach. Fine views.
☒ 83301 Armenistis, Ikaría. **Map** p385 E4. (22750) 71381. FAX (22750) 71380. @ cavos@ika.forthnet.gr b. **Rooms** 63. €€€

KYTHIRA

Hotel Margarita This grand 19th-century mansion in one of Greece's prettiest villages is the island's finest hotel. Superb sea views.
☒ 80100 Chora, Kythira. **Map** p384 C40. (27360) 31711. FAX (27360) 31325. @ margarita@hotel-margarita.com b. **Rooms** 12. €€€€

For key to symbols see backflap. For price categories *see p383*

Oía, Santorini

Caldera Villas This collection of cliff-edge cave-villas extends down several levels from the main street, close to the centre of Oía village and its many restaurants. There are fantastic views from the pool and terraces, where there is also a café and breakfast area. Rooms are in traditional dazzling white-and-blue décor.
84702 Oía, Santorini. **Map** p385 D4.
(22860) 71285. FAX (22860) 71425. @ caldera-villas@san.forthnet.gr b. **Rooms** 12.
Nov to Mar. AE, MC. €€€€

Olympia

Best Western Hotel Europa Don't worry, it doesn't feel like a chain hotel and is easily the best in Olympia. It is set just outside both the modern town and the ancient ruins, on a hillside above farmland. There's an attractive pool and gardens with a taverna and a tennis court. The modern rooms have fine views. Good service.
27065 Ancient Olympia. **Map** p384 B3.
(26240) 23850. FAX (26240) 23166. @ hoteleuropa@hellasnet.gr b,l,d. **Rooms** 80.
Never. AE, MC, V. €€€€

Oía, Santorini

Oía Mare Villas Balanced on the edge of cliffs overlooking the caldera of Santorini this is one of the most magnificently sited accommodations in all Greece. The suites are in beautiful traditional-style buildings painted dazzling white, and simply but elegantly furnished, and there's a fabulous small pool with bar and terrace. Book well ahead (up to a year in advance).
84702 Oía, Santorini. **Map** p385 D4.
FAX (0286) 71070. b. **Rooms** 13 suites.
Nov to March. AE, MC, V. €€€€

Réthymno, Crete

Mythos Suites Hotel This 16th-century Venetian mansion is set on a quiet street in the picturesque old quarter of town, and is within easy walking distance of sights and beaches. It was tastefully restored in 1994, and great attention to detail has been paid in the lighting and decoration. Bright bar and breakfast area and sunny terraces.
12 Karaoli Square, 74100 Réthymno, Crete.
Map p385 D5. (28310) 53917. FAX (28310) 51036.
@ mythoscr@ otenet.gr b,l,d. **Rooms** 15.
Feb to Mar. Not accepted. €€€€

Léfkes, Páros

Lefkes Village Set in 5 acres of grounds, the 'village' comprises 20 attractive, Neo-classical and Cycladic-style rooms round a pool with a taverna.
84400 Léfkes, Páros. **Map** p385 D4. (22840) 41827. FAX (22840) 42398. @ lefkesvl@otenet.gr
b,l,d. **Rooms** 20. €€€€

Megálo Pápigko

Saxónis Houses Highly rated, fashionable getaway comprising a small complex of restored 18th-century stone houses with pretty gardens.
Megálo Pápigko, 44004 Ioannina. **Map** p384 A2.
(26530) 41615. FAX (26530) 41891. b.
Rooms 8. €€€

Métsovo

Apollon Stone-built with a polished wood interior, this sturdy hotel offers great views of the Pindhos mountains in all directions.
Tositsa 19, 44200 Métsovo. **Map** p384 B2.
(26560) 41844. FAX (26560) 42110. b,l,d.
Rooms 42. €€€

Mycenae

Hotel Belle Hélène This simple guesthouse hosted 19th-century archaeologists and still provides comfortable, peaceful lodgings.
Christous Iouda, 21200 Mykínai. **Map** p384 C3.
(27510) 76225. FAX (27510) 76179. b,l,d.
Rooms 8. €

Réthymno, Crete

Vecchio Hotel Apartments These attractive apartments provide excellent value. They are set in a quiet street in the heart of the old quarter; the building is new but decorated in pale blue and terracotta to fit the style of its medieval surroundings. The super pool is a real bonus. Rooms are simple and modern, well appointed and elegantly painted.
Daliani 4, 74100 Réthymno, Crete. **Map** p385 D5. (28310) 54985. FAX (28310) 54986. b. **Rooms** 27. (extra charge). Nov to Mar. V. €€

Rhodes Old Town, Rhodes

S. Nikolis' Hotel The main building of this pretty bougainvillea-draped hotel oozes history and features two medieval arched rooms. Set on a cobbled street below the walls built by the Knights of St John, it overlooks the ruins of the Roman market. Rooms have all mod cons; some have a veranda, patio or balcony.
Hippodamou 61, 85100 Rhodes. **Map** p385 F4. (22410) 34561. FAX (22410) 32034. nikolis@hol.gr b,l,d. **Rooms** 20. Dec to Jan. AE, MC, V. €€

Rhodes Old Town, Rhodes

Cava D'Oro Built into the ancient city walls, this was the residence of the Italian garrison commander during Italy's occupation of Rhodes (1912–45); it became a small hotel in 1987. It is a short walk to both the centre of the old town and the ferry harbour. Rooms are simply decorated but quiet and comfortable. There is a small courtyard for breakfast and drinks.
Kisthinou 15, 85100 Rhodes. **Map** p385 F4. (22410) 36980. FAX (22410) 77332. b. **Rooms** 13. Nov-Mar. Not accepted. €€€

Sgombou, Corfu

Casa Lucia Casa Lucia – a collection of colourful cottages in a lush garden with immaculate lawns, bougainvillea and flowers – is the perfect family holiday-spot. It's hard to believe that the raucous nightlife and mass-market resorts of the Corfu coast are just a few minutes' drive away. Each cottage is individually decorated.
49083 Sgombou, Corfu. **Map** p384 A2. 2661 091419. FAX 2661 091732. caslucia@otenet.gr self-catering. **Rooms** 8 cottages and 2 studios. Never. Not accepted. €€€

Mýkonos Town, Mýkonos

Belvedere Right in the heart of the Old Town, this luxury hotel features 40 rooms with all mod cons; there's even a gym and Jacuzzi.
Rohari, 84600 Mýkonos. **Map** p385 D4. (22890) 25122. FAX (22890) 25126. contact@belvederehotel.com b,l,d. **Rooms** 47. €€€€

Mystrás

Hotel Byzantion Location makes this hotel: all rooms have a view of the castle. Comfortable and modern with good facilities, if a bit sterile.
23100 Neos Mystrás. **Map** p384 B4. (27310) 83309. FAX (27310) 20019. b. **Rooms** 26. €€

Nymfaía

La Moara Owned by the Boutari winemaking family, this former watermill is now a luxury hotel with a superb wine bar and restaurant.
3 Victor Hugo St, 54625 Thessaloniki. **Map** p385 D1. (22310) 552320. FAX (22310) 524430. yboutaris@kiryianni.gr b,d. **Rooms** 8. €€€€

Oía, Santorini

Hotel Aethrio A beautiful complex of suites and rooms which has been decorated with art, antiques and curios.
84702 Oía, Santorini. **Map** p385 D4. (22860) 71040. FAX (22860) 71930. info@aethrio.com b, l. **Rooms** 20. €€€€

For key to symbols see backflap. For price categories *see p383*

Stavri

Pirgos Tsitsiri Located in an ancient village and built around the old stronghold of one of the region's clan chieftains, this feels like a real bandit's hideout. The views over the mountains and across the Messinian Gulf are awesome. Rooms are pleasant though simple and traditional, with wooden floors and striped wool rugs and cushions.
23071 Stavri, Máni. **Map** p384 B4.
(27330) 56297. FAX (27330) 56296. b,l,d.
Rooms 20. Oct-Apr. MC, V. €€€

Sými Town, Sými

Les Catherinettes This is one of the prettiest small hotels in all Greece, with polished wood floors, elaborately painted ceilings and dadoes, and tall windows overlooking the charming harbour. It is efficiently run by the friendly owner Julie and her daughter Marina. There is a good traditional taverna downstairs on the quayside, and beaches are close by.
85600 Sými. **Map** p385 F4. (22460) 72698.
FAX (22460) 72698. marine-epe@rho.forthnet.gr b,l,d.
Rooms 6, 4 studios. Never. Not accepted. €€

Sými Town, Sými

Hotel Aliki Two steps from the sea, in a peaceful location a few minutes from the Gialós harbour area, this pretty 19th-century sea captain's mansion is now a well-run A-Class hotel. Rooms are en suite, simply and comfortably furnished; ask for a balcony and sea view. There are café tables on the quay and a comfortable bar and lobby area.
Akti G Gennimata, 85600 Sými. **Map** p385 F4.
(22460) 71665. FAX (22460) 71655.
info@simi-hotelaliki.gr b. **Rooms** 15.
Oct to Apr. MC, V. €€€€

Sými Town, Sými

Opera House A collection of blue-and-white Neo-Classical-style buildings house these cool, airy studios. Each has a large kitchen; all are traditionally furnished with wooden couches and colourful rugs. Bathrooms are functional. It's very quiet here, with tree-filled gardens and an attractive outdoor café-bar, though it's just a five-minute stroll to the harbour tavernas.
85600 Sými. **Map** p385 F4. (22460) 72034.
FAX (22460) 72035. operasym@otenet.gr b. **Rooms** 19 studios. Never. MC, V. €€

Oía, Santorini

Museum Hotel This historic mansion on the main street of this cliff-side village has panoramic views. Rooms are artistically decorated.
Oía, 84702 Santorini. **Map** p385 D4. (2286) 71515.
FAX (2286) 71516. museumhotel@msn.com b.
Rooms 9 suites. €€€€

Ornos, Mýkonos

Kivotos Clubhotel Art and artefacts abound in this luxury resort built in Cycladic village-style around a gorgeous saltwater pool. Private beach.
84600 Ornos, Mýkonos. **Map** p385 D4.
(22890) 24094. FAX (22980) 22844.
kivotos1@hol.gr b,l,d. **Rooms** 40. €€€€

Poros Town, Poros

Sto Roloi Three comfortable self-contained apartments in a 200-year-old stone-built island house. Tastefully decorated. A real find.
18020 Poros. **Map** p384 C4. 2298 025808.
FAX 2109 633705. sto_roloi@hotmail.com
not served. **Rooms** 3 apartments. €€

Psará (Chíos)

Psará Apartments For would-be castaways, 15 fully equipped apartments near the sandy beach of Psará, a tiny Aegean island near Chios.
Psará Island, Chios. **Map** p385 D3.
(22740) 61180 FAX (22740) 61195. b.
Rooms 15. €€

VYTINA

Art Hotel Mainalon The exterior features an imaginative and stylish use of decorative brickwork and lovely wooden balconies. Inside is a harmonious blend of traditional and modern; the walls are hung with paintings from the owner's collection of modern Greek painters. There is also an attractive courtyard. Service can be patchy however.
22010 Vytina, Arcadia. **Map** p384 B3. (27950) 22217. FAX (27950) 22200. b. **Rooms** 51. Never. Not accepted. €€€€

YDRA

Hotel Bratsera Built in the 19th century as a sponge warehouse, the Bratsera is nowadays by far the best hotel on this fashionable artistic island and provides surprisingly good value. Rooms are a mix of traditional and modern, with built-in beds or antique brass-and-iron bedsteads, fridge and TV. It has a lovely pool and restaurant.
18040 Ydra. **Map** p384 C4. (22980) 53971. FAX (22980) 53626. @ bratsera@yahoo.com b,l,d. **Rooms** 23. Nov to Feb. AE, DC, MC, V. €€€€

VYZÍTSA

Archontiko Blana A stone's throw from the main square of the peaceful village and shaded by giant plane trees, the mansion enjoys stupendous views west across the Gulf of Volos. Polished woodwork, shuttered windows and carved wooden doors impart local flavour; minibar fridges add a touch of luxury. Penthouse suite with a tiny sauna and whirlpool bath.
37010 Vyzítsa, Pilío. **Map** p384 C2. (24230) 86840. FAX (24230) 22164. @ archontiko-blana@mailbox.gr b. **Rooms** 4. Never. MC, V. €€€€

YDRA

Ippokampos Hotel A friendly and unpretentious hotel, two steps from the harbourfront in the centre of traffic-free Ydra town. It is decorated in traditional white-and-blue painted woodwork; the flagstoned courtyard is a mass of potted greenery and brilliant bougainvillea. The simply furnished rooms are bright and airy. There is a café-bar downstairs (music in the evenings).
18040 Ydra. **Map** p384 C4. (22980) 53453. FAX (22980) 52501. @ ippokamp@hol.gr b. **Rooms** 16. Nov to Feb. MC, V. €€€€

PSAROU, MÝKONOS

Grecotel Mýkonos Blu This luxury complex boasts unbeatable facilities, including two superb restaurants and range of watersports.
84600 Psarou, Platys Gialos, Mýkonos. **Map** p385 D4. (0289) 27780. FAX (0289) 27783. @ sales-mb@grecotel.gr b,l,d. **Rooms** 102 bungalows. €€€€

RÉTHYMNO, CRETE

Hotel Fortezza This modern, family-run hotel may be short on charm but it's long on facilities and has an excellent central location.
Melissinou 16, 74100 Réthymno, Crete. **Map** p385 D5. (28310) 55551. FAX (28310) 54073. @ mliodak@ret.forthnet.gr b. **Rooms** 54. €€€

SKÓPELOS

Archontiko Inn This traditional mansion with shutters, painted ceilings & balconies is built round two shady flagstoned courtyards where you can eat breakfast or have evening drinks.
3703 Hora Skópelou. **Map** p384 C2. (2424) 022765. FAX (2424) 022049. b,l,d. **Rooms** 10 €€

VOLISSÓS, CHÍOS

Volissós Houses A cluster of traditional stone houses, renovated by Athenian sculptor Stella Tsakiri, and converted into comfortable suites.
Pirgos, Volissós 82103, Chíos. **Map** p385 E3. (2274) 21413. FAX (2274) 21521. @ info@volissostravel.gr **Rooms** 9. €€

For key to symbols see backflap. For price categories *see p383*

Indexes

Each country featured in the guide has two indexes, one of hotel names, the other of hotel locations.

Hotel Names
In this index, hotels are arranged in order of the most distinctive part of their name; very common prefixes such as 'Albergaria' 'Albergo' 'Auberge', 'Gasthof', 'Gjestehus', 'Hostal', 'Hospedería' 'Hostellerie' 'Hostería', 'Hotel', 'Hôtellerie' 'Ostellerie', 'Pension' and 'Pensjonat', as well as definite and indefinite articles and common prepositions, such as 'à', 'de', 'de la', 'del', 'die', 'du','t', 'zum' and 'zur' are omitted or ignored in the alpha order.

Hotel Locations
In this index, hotels are listed by the name of the city, town or village they are in or near. Common prefixes, articles and prepositions are again ignored in the alpha order.

Austria

Hotel Names

Hotel Locations

Belgium and Luxembourg

Hotel Names

Hotel Locations

Denmark

Hotel Names

Hotel Locations

France

Hotel Names

Hotel Locations

Germany

Hotel Names

Landhotel, Der, Hotel, Gasthaus, Gasthof etc omitted

Hotel Locations

Great Britain

Hotel Names

Hotel Locations

Greece

Hotel Names

Hotel Locations

Ireland

Hotel Names

Hotel Locations

Italy

Hotel Names

Hotel Locations

The Netherlands

Hotel Names

Hotel Locations

Norway

Hotel Names

Hotel Locations

Portugal

Hotel Names

Hotel Locations

Spain

Hotel Names

El, La, Las omitted

Hotel Locations

Sweden

Hotel Names

Hotel Locations

Switzerland

Hotel Names

Hotel Locations